Feminism and Psychoanalysis

A Critical Dictionary

Edited by

Elizabeth Wright

Advisory editors
Dianne Chisholm
Juliet Flower MacCannell
Margaret Whitford

BLACKWELL
Reference

Copyright © Basil Blackwell Ltd 1992
Editorial organization © Elizabeth Wright 1992

First published 1992
First published in USA 1992

Blackwell Publishers
108 Cowley Road
Oxford OX4 1JF
UK

Three Cambridge Center
Cambridge, Massachusetts 02142
USA

British Library Cataloguing in Publication Data
A CIP catalogue record for this book is available from the British Library.

Library of Congress Cataloging-in-Publication Data
Feminism and psychoanalysis: a critical dictionary / edited by
Elizabeth Wright.
    p.   cm. – (Blackwell reference)
Includes bibliographical references and index.
ISBN 0-631-17312-9 (hb); ISBN 0-631-18347-7 (pb)
1. Psychoanalysis and feminism – Dictionaries.
I. Wright, Elizabeth (Eva Elizabeth)
BF175.4.F45F462   1992   92–6812
   150.19'5'082—dc20   CIP

Typeset in 10 on 12pt Sabon by Hope Services (Abingdon) Ltd.

Contents

Acknowledgements

A dictionary is a collective venture. My first debt is to the advisory editors, Dianne Chisholm, Juliet Flower MacCannell and Margaret Whitford, who have given most generously of their time at every point. They have provided invaluable assistance with the compilation of entries, essential practical support in securing contributors, and expert criticism on the manuscript in its final stages. Secondly, I want to thank the contributors for their commitment, friendliness, patience and staying power. I also want to thank the following for aid and advice: Parveen Adams, Jessica Benjamin, Elizabeth Bronfen, Claire Kahane, Marianne Hirsch, Nancy Miller, Dianne Hunter, Naomi Segal, Bob Walding, Anna Wright and Margot Zutshi. This was a project calling for much collaboration between author and publisher. My thanks therefore go to my editor Alyn Shipton and to his colleagues at Blackwells for help and encouragement at various stages. In particular, Richard Beatty, Stephan Chambers, Ruth Savage, and Jason Pearce, and to the copy-editor Gillian Bromley. Finally I would like to thank Edmond Wright for his unfailing intellectual, moral and clerical support throughout the work.

E.E.W.
Girton College
Cambridge

Contributors

Sally Alexander
History Workshop Journal,
Polytechnic of East London

Emily Apter
Department of French and Italian,
University of California at Davis

Alison Assiter
Enterprise in Higher Education,
Polytechnic of North London

Mieke Bal
University of Amsterdam

Danielle Bergeron
Groupe Interdisciplinaire Freudien
de Recherches et d'Interventions
Cliniques et Culturelles (GIFRIC)
Québec

Teresa Bernardez
The Michigan Psychoanalytic
Council

Phillipa Berry
King's College, Cambridge

Marie-Claire Boons-Grafé
Department of Philosophy,
University of Paris VIII

Malcolm Bowie
Institute of Romance Studies,
University of London

Rosi Braidotti
Department of Women's Studies,
University of Utrecht

Teresa Brennan
Social and Political Sciences,
Universities of Amsterdam and
Cambridge

Harry Brod
Women's and Gender Studies
Program, and Philosophy
Department, Kenyon College,
USA

Elisabeth Bronfen
Department of English, University
of Munich

Marie-Hélène Brousse
École de la Cause Freudienne,
Paris

Beverley Brown
Centre for Criminology and the
Social and Philosophical Study of
Law, University of Edinburgh

Victor Burgin
Board of Studies in Art History,
University of California at Santa
Cruz

Judith Butler
Humanities Center, Johns
Hopkins University

Dianne Chisholm
Department of English, University
of Alberta

Rey Chow
Department of Comparative Literature, University of Minnesota, Minneapolis

Karin M. Cope
Humanities Center, Johns Hopkins University

Joan Copjec
Center for the Study of Psychoanalysis and Culture, State University of New York at Buffalo

Nicola Diamond
Department of Sociology, University of Exeter

Sheila Ernst
The Women's Therapy Centre, London

Caroline Evans
Central St Martin's College of Art and Design, London, and Goldsmiths' College, University of London

Mary Evans
University of Kent at Canterbury

Jane Flax
Department of Political Science, Howard University, Washington DC

John Forrester
Department of History and Philosophy of Science, University of Cambridge

Carla Freccero
Department of Literature, University of California at Santa Cruz

Carol Gilligan
Graduate School of Education, Harvard University

Beverly Greene
Department of Psychology, St John's University, Queens, New York

Jean Grimshaw
Department of Humanities, Bristol Polytechnic

Elizabeth Grosz
Department of Critical Theory, Philosophy and Women's Studies, Monash University

Elizabeth Guild
Robinson College, Cambridge

Sandra Harding
Department of Philosophy, University of Delaware

Marianne Hirsch
Department of Comparative Literature, Dartmouth College, Hanover, New Hampshire

Dianne Hunter
Department of English, Trinity College, Connecticut

Biodun Iginla
University of Minnesota Press

Claire Kahane
Department of English, State University of New York at Buffalo

Debra Keates
Johns Hopkins University

Evelyne Keitel
John F. Kennedy-Institute for North American Studies, The Free University of Berlin

Julia Lupton
Program in Comparative Literature, University of California at Irvine

ix

CONTRIBUTORS

Juliet Flower MacCannell
*Department of English and
Comparative Literature,
University of California at Irvine*

David Macey
*Killingworth Village, Newcastle
upon Tyne*

Maureen Mahoney
*School of Social Science,
Hampshire College, Amherst,
Massachusetts*

Nancy K. Miller
*English Department, City
University of New York Graduate
Center*

Toril Moi
*Graduate Program in Literature,
Duke University*

Henrietta Moore
*Department of Anthropology,
London School of Economics and
Political Science*

Michael Moriarty
*Gonville and Caius College,
Cambridge*

Irene Philipson
*Beatrice M. Bain Research Group,
University of California,
Berkeley*

Griselda Pollock
*Department of Fine Art,
University of Leeds*

Ellie Ragland-Sullivan
*Department of English, University
of Missouri at Columbia*

Estelle Roith
*Writer and Psychoanalytic
Therapist, London*

Joanna Ryan
*Writer and Psychoanalytic
Therapist, London*

Janet Sayers
*Faculty of Social Sciences,
University of Kent at Canterbury*

Naomi Schor
*Department of Romance Studies,
Duke University*

Naomi Segal
St John's College, Cambridge

Paul Julian Smith
*Department of Spanish and
Portuguese, University of
Cambridge*

Abigail Solomon-Godeau
*Department of Art History,
University of California at Santa
Barbara*

Martin Stanton
*Centre for Psychoanalytic Studies,
University of Kent at Canterbury*

Judith Still
*Department of French, University
of Nottingham*

Susan Rubin Suleiman
*Department of Romance
Languages and Literatures,
Harvard University*

Jo-Ann Wallace
*Department of English, University
of Alberta*

Simon Watney
London

Patricia Waugh
*School of English, University of
Durham*

Valerie Wayne
Department of English, University of Hawaii at Manoa

Jeffrey Weeks
Department of Economics and Social Science, Bristol Polytechnic

Demaris Wehr
Episcopal Divinity School, Cambridge, Massachusetts

Margaret Whitford
Department of French, Queen Mary and Westfield College, University of London

Linda Williams
Program in Film Studies, University of California at Irvine

Kathleen Woodward
Center for Twentieth Century Studies, University of Wisconsin at Milwaukee

Elizabeth Wright
Girton College, Cambridge

Elisabeth Young-Bruehl
Haverford College, Pennsylvania

Mechthild Zeul
Psychoanalyst, Madrid

Slavoj Žižek
Institute of Sociology, University of Ljubljana

Editorial Note

Freud bibliographical entries: All references are to the *Standard Edition of the Complete Psychological Works of Sigmund Freud*, (abbreviated as *SE*) 24 vols., trans. and ed. by James Strachey, in collaboration with Anna Freud, assisted by Alix Strachey and Alan Tyson. London: The Hogarth Press and the Institute of Psycho-Analysis, 1953–73. Works that take up less than a whole volume are referred to by page numbers.

Lacan bibliographical entries: Wherever possible translations are cited. In the case of British and American editions of the same work the page numbers correspond.

Throughout the dictionary the convention '1987 [1977]' indicates an earlier edition in the original language.

Cross-references to other entries are given in SMALL CAPITALS; the index may be used to facilitate further reference. Each entry has its own bibliography, the authors of all items of which are listed in the index.

Introduction

This is not a dictionary in a conventional sense, for it does not merely define terms, but explores, historizes and politicizes them; nor does it pretend to present them objectively, but rather places them in the context of a dialogue between two discourses. Its purpose is not only to conceptualize the field of feminist psychoanalytic practice but to generate critical inter-implications between feminism and psychoanalysis. Between these two fields there is a space for transformations.

Of what, then, does this dictionary consist if it is not a lexicon? Entries are listed in the form of an alphabetized compilation of concepts and themes, applications and disciplines, theorists and practitioners. Most of the entries deal with major psychoanalytical concepts that appear repeatedly in contemporary feminist studies, sometimes extensively borrowed from psychoanalysis and sometimes merely alluding to it. The explication of these concepts in the dictionary necessarily involves a short history of psychoanalytic usage, the feminist adaptation of that usage, and the consequences of introducing re-utilized concepts into psychoanalytic theory and practice (e.g. CASTRATION COMPLEX; PERVERSION; PRE-OEDIPAL). Conversely, we have chosen some feminist concepts that could be imported into psychoanalysis for re-utilization (e.g. GENDER; RADICAL LESBIANISM; WOMAN-IDENTIFIED WOMAN). There is a greater number of psychoanalytic than feminist concepts, since it is feminism that is re-explicating psychoanalysis rather than vice versa. Feminism is making a political move in appropriating psychoanalysis for its project, as well as pushing psychoanalysis to its theoretical and clinical limits.

We do not want to give the impression that this inter-implication occurs only at the conceptual level, for we are aware that there are established applications and disciplines where feminism and psychoanalysis converge and re-constitute themselves both theoretically (e.g. ART; LITERATURE; LITERARY AND TEXTUAL CRITICISM) and practically (e.g. CLINICAL PERSPECTIVES; MICHIGAN PSYCHOANALYTIC COUNCIL; WOMEN'S THERAPY CENTRE). Among significant names we take theorists and practitioners in psychoanalysis who initiated the engagement with feminism, as well as ones who are continuing to re-appropriate psychoanalysis for feminism. On the other hand, feminist theorists who are not analysts but who use psychoanalysis are not listed by name but have been absorbed into the entries on practices and disciplines: it would have been difficult to distinguish among the large number of feminists who extrapolate creatively a *bricolage* of applications from psychoanalytic theory.

There is a reason for giving feminism priority in the title. Most of the entries are written by feminists or by other writers participating in the debate between the two fields, the emphasis being on an extended field of feminism rather than merely on the genesis of a feminist psychoanalysis. Thus there are inevitably a number of entries where psychoanalysis is peripheral, often because it has not been regarded as sufficiently relevant to the discourse (*see* ANTHROPOLOGY AND CROSS-CULTURAL ANALYSIS; MATERIALIST FEMINIST CRITICISM; RACE/IMPERIALISM; SCIENCE).

In terms of procedure the editors have solicited entries from international scholars currently working in the two fields. These contributors have documented not only the history of a concept and other interrelated concepts, but also the debate and controversy surrounding it, its political importance for feminism, and the theorists and practitioners who have coined or used it.

The dictionary has been planned to extend in three directions in order that the impact of psychoanalysis on feminism may be adequately assessed.

First, there is a distinct historical dimension. Wherever possible, entries include a concept's history, the debates and controversies surrounding the concept, and its political importance. The emphasis is on providing a record of continuing theoretical explorations that tends towards conceptual mobility rather than fixity. Hence the evolution of a concept is more important for its contribution to the two fields than for any inherent historical interest. The historical dimension also comes into force for the entries on those psychoanalysts after Freud who have passed into history and whose theories engaged and are still engaging feminists (e.g., ANNA FREUD, DEUTSCH, HORNEY, JONES, JUNG, KLEIN, LACAN).

The history of the women's movement has gone through a number of phases or 'waves'. Some entries (e.g. FEMINIST HISTORY; FEMINISM BEFORE PSYCHOANALYSIS), sketch out the movement's earliest moments. Although feminism has grappled with a concept of sexuality and desire from Mary Wollstonecraft's *A Vindication of the Rights of Woman* (1792) onwards, critical dialogue between feminism and psychoanalysis begins with Simone de Beauvoir's *La deuxième sexe* (1949) and continues after an interval with Betty Friedan's *The Feminine Mystique* (1963). Each protests that in psychoanalytic discourse woman is defined as inferior and only with reference to man. This phase is followed by a second, which intensifies the protest against the social stereotyping of women within patriarchy and produces classic feminist positions such as those of Kate Millett's *Sexual Politics* (1970), Shulamith Firestone's *The Dialectic of Sex: The Case for Feminist Revolution* (1970), and Germaine Greer's *The Female Eunuch* (1970). All these continued to signal rebellion against difference as inequality, seeing femininity as socially constructed and calling for radical changes in society which would eliminate sexual difference. Juliet Mitchell's critique in *Psychoanalysis and Feminism* (1974) forcefully intersected with this second phase, challenging these assumptions with a sustained and closely argued case for psychoanalysis as a theory able to explain the process whereby women and men came to internalize an oppressive ideology. Psychoanalysis could not be held responsible for this process; on the contrary, it could have the political effect of raising consciousness and instigating social change. Out of this focus of women on themselves as a collective consciousness emerged a third phase which changed the terms of the debate after the mid-1970s: now women's difference from men was no longer seen as a disadvantage, but as a source of pride and occasion for confidence. Adrienne Rich's *Of Woman Born: Motherhood as Experience and Institution* (1976) theorized and lyricized lesbianism as a radical movement, opposed to the compulsory heterosexuality of patriarchal society. An alternative model of female identity was proposed by a New York group calling itself 'Radicalesbians', which tried to get away from the idea of lesbianism as an exclusively sexual identity. These separatist approaches may be contrasted with some of the French feminist theories discussed below, which never quite abandon the feminine position; in articulating the position as psychic rather than social, they leave space for the subversion of binary divisions (*see* FEMINISM OF DIFFERENCE).

The second dimension of the dictionary is the psychoanalytical, centring on Freud and Lacan, beginning with Freud's 'discovery' of the unconscious in the course of his researches into the bodily symptoms of hysteria. His several attempts to construct a narrative adequate to female sexuality all end up with the same bleak theme: the girl is a little man until the castration complex. She starts out by desiring her mother as actively as does the boy, but while in the throes of the oedipus complex she sees that she 'lacks' a penis. The girl turns away from her equally lacking mother in the direction of her father, in the ultimate hope that a child from him will fill the lack. In this scenario both boy and girl are subject to castration, give up the parent of the opposite sex and identify with the sex that matches their biology. Early feminists objected to the notion of femininity as an inferior version, a 'second sex' (de Beauvoir).

INTRODUCTION

But Freud has been used by other feminists who, in the wake of Mitchell, continue to assert, to a world that still largely finds it inconceivable, that gender is psychically constructed, not biologically given: both boy and girl are bisexual until the vicissitudes of the oedipus and castration complex. This further points to the fragility of the gender definition, always slipping and never finally secure for either sex (*see* BIOLOGY; BISEXUALITY; SEXUAL DIFFERENCE).

Feminist psychoanalysis, however, evolved into two conflicting narratives, two re-readings, one made by OBJECT-RELATIONS THEORY in Britain and North America, the other by Lacanian theory in France. British and North American feminists would like to challenge patriarchal power within the social structure and change family and labour relations; French feminists want to challenge patriarchal power as it functions on a symbolic level and clear a space for women in discourse.

Object-relations theory concentrates on the pre-oedipal relation between mother and child as a moment before the realization of the father's place in the social order disrupts the symbiotic relation between mother and child. In Britain and America this has led to a normative emphasis on motherhood, with the mother's subjectivity seen as secondary to that of the child. Among feminists in America there has at least been an attempt to foreground the mother as an independent social being with desires of her own (*see* CHODOROW). In both countries the attempt to focus upon the mother/child relation has tended to ignore the question of sexual difference: whereas in Britain the emphasis seems to be on the relation between a mother and a sexually undifferentiated child, in America Chodorow's revision of this state of affairs places the gender role of the child in the foreground of the debate (boys are treated differently from girls from a very early age), but the actual acquisition of gender is seen as unproblematic.

In France the pre-oedipal relation is likewise at the centre of feminist psychoanalysis, but there it has led to a more subversive account of gender acquisition. Curiously enough, this was only achieved by both ambivalently accepting and rigorously opposing the revisionary reading of Freud made by Lacan. Whereas the ego in object-relations theory was regarded as rudimentarily present from the beginning and grew in strength via the interaction with a 'good enough mother' (Winnicott's term), for Lacan the subject constitutes itself via an illusory mirror image of wholeness, which remains a fiction throughout life. The mirror stage inaugurates the subject's alienation, an Imaginary moment which already borders on the Symbolic through the mother's desire, structured as it is by the Father's law and language. Though the child tries to identify with the mother's desire, the Father as the figure of law (unlike Freud's natural father) insists that the child take its place in the order of language as 'he' or 'she'. The possessing or not possessing of the phallus (not the biological organ) determines the way both sexes assume their lack: both have to give up being the phallus for the mother (*see* PHALLUS: DEFINITIONS). According to this theory, then, castration is a symbolic event suffered by both sexes, irrespective of their biological sex.

While some feminists accept Lacan's 'phallocentrism', arguing that he develops Freud's non-biologist thinking to its logical conclusion by showing how men and women are constructed in a patriarchal system, others take the argument further by maintaining that Lacan does not merely lay down the phallic law, but reveals the frailty of psychic identity and the mobility of desire, both of which point to the fictionality of gender definitions (*see* IMAGINARY; PHALLOGOCENTRISM; PHALLUS: FEMINIST IMPLICATIONS). This particularly applies when it is a question of the existence of Woman, who according to Lacan is nothing but an effect of phallic fantasy. The woman is under erasure, because she represents lack within the phallocentric order of language. Of her essence she is 'not all': there is no positive term for her in the Symbolic. Precisely because of this, however, she has access to something that goes beyond the phallic economy. It is because Woman is not adequately defined within the patriarchal order that Real effects make themselves felt in relation to her (*see* JOUISSANCE; REAL; SYMPTOM).

Many French and French-inspired feminists vigorously object to this marginalizing of the feminine. In a variety of ways they have attempted to read Freud and Lacan so as either to turn marginality into an advantage or to re-conceptualize the feminine. In either case they have, like the object-relations theorists, returned to the pre-oedipal relation between child and mother, more especially between daughter and mother; but, unlike the object-relations theorists, they have constructed a less repressive narrative of the relation of the infant to the mother's body, though the various positions they adopt do owe something to the way they have read, or re-read, Klein and Winnicott. Kristeva associates psychic repression with the actual structures of language and sees the pre-oedipal as a play of bodily rhythms and pre-linguistic exchanges between infant and mother. Her displacement of the Lacanian Imaginary by the semiotic, a pre-symbolic process of resistance producing effects throughout life (and thus not confined to the pre-oedipal moment), has been hailed by feminists who are looking for a way of undermining patriarchy without subscribing to a feminine essence. But despite the considerable following she has acquired, there is also a feeling that she is at a distance from feminism because of her refusal of the category of woman (*see* KRISTEVA). A number of French theorists and/or analysts have gone in a different direction altogether. Cixous, for instance, tries to ground a new, specifically feminine language and feminine writing in the child's – and woman's – pleasurable relation to the mother's body, a pleasure denied to them by the fathers of psychoanalysis. She has developed a particular practice of writing in order to launch a critique of phallocentric language and to render specific the materiality of women's sexuality, which she sees as a source of fluidity, multiple productivity and diffuse energy (*see* ÉCRITURE FÉMININE; FEMININE ECONOMY). Like Cixous, Irigaray wants to clear a space for women within the Symbolic which allows for a subjectivity that is not defined by the patriarchal order. Her concept of a Symbolic Mother and her stress on the necessity for a maternal genealogy are a direct challenge to the hegemony of Lacan's Phallus (*see* IRIGARAY; MOTHER–DAUGHTER RELATIONSHIP; PATRIARCHY).

Many feminists hold the view that, while psychoanalysis may have enabled women to understand how they internalize 'femininity' in a patriarchal society, it has not given them any clues as to how to liberate themselves from its oppressiveness, in that it does not suggest any forms of political struggle. Others argue that psychoanalysis does not need politicizing because its central discovery, the unconscious, returns the subjective element to politics: the unconscious reveals the precariousness of identity and therefore psychoanalysis is already of political use to feminism. This suggests, then, that the political dimension of psychoanalysis is implied in the challenge to supposed objectivities (*see* REPRESENTATION). The dilemma for feminists is that so far there has been no way of reconciling the notion of the feminine as a general problem for both sexes (a challenge to binary divisions) with the historical need for women to find a collective voice in an oppressive phallocentric reality.

The third, political, dimension focuses on the possible re-utilization of psychoanalytic theory and practice so as to facilitate social change. If we have to accept that the unconscious is not merely the effect of the repressive social world, if we have to live with the notion of subjectivity as caught up in fantasy and the compulsion to repeat, how do we reconcile these factors with the legitimacy of political protest? The only way forward seems to be to face up to the fact that, even if there is a structuring psychical process, a collective illusion of totalization and fixity which cannot be reduced either to biology or to social history, it is nevertheless not beyond emancipatory revision. Even if we always have to refer to the Other, the pre-existent law of language and social order, the form of our reference can be modified and a different way of producing the social bond could result (*see* UNCONSCIOUS). That is to say, the text (whether the subject as text, the literary text or the text of history) is constituted by certain relations which depend on how certain places are occupied: a politicized cultural practice will show how knowledge is produced by a reader him/herself, determined by whoever is in the place of power (*see* LITERARY AND TEXTUAL CRITICISM; READING AS/LIKE A WOMAN). This makes cultural practice an essential field of struggle in exploring the relation between the psychic and the social. The psyche resists its total social determination via the subject's relation to fantasy, that excess of desire which gives a subject the capacity to confer meaning, to intervene in the world and make a difference. What disrupts the Symbolic is precisely the force of desire and fantasy, variable though it be according to the contingencies of the social–historical. Psychoanalysis provides a theory of how fantasies originate and how they are projected out (*see* FANTASY; PSYCHICAL REALITY; UNCANNY). If psychoanalysis can help to identify certain insistent transgenerational primal fantasies, the collusion of culture with these fantasies might be more easily exposed. The concerted opposition of women to being relegated to the twin poles of idealization and denigration is an obvious example of refusing powerful patriarchal fantasies. Feminism is therefore right to see the personal as the political (*see* PERSONAL/AUTOBIOGRAPHICAL CRITICISM). The question, then, is what forms of deconstructive practice would be most conducive to revealing the psychic disempowering of women via concrete social relations (*see* MATERIALIST FEMINIST CRITICISM; M/F; PATRIARCHY).

This dictionary therefore spells out a cultural politics through a living dialogue between theory and practice, feminist theorists and psychoanalytic theorists, feminists and feminists. It is a cultural politics which widens the scope of sexual politics by covering a range of aesthetic and literary studies and which clarifies new developments in cultural feminism and psychoanalysis (e.g. ART; FEMINIST CINEMA; LITERATURE; REPRESENTATION). It accounts for the diverse ways in which feminists have taken up the struggle over the production, distribution and transformation of meaning in a number of specific cultural practices in order to challenge the forms of representation which constrain and oppress them. Moreover, the dictionary is topically responsive to fields that have been marginalized (POSTMODERNISM; RACE/IMPERIALISM; feminist PHILOSOPHY; feminist SCIENCE), thus extending the concept of culture rather than incorporating the margins into what classical psychoanalysis takes 'culture' or 'civilization' to be.

Hence this dictionary is not only a device for learning, but is also an experiment in cartography, mapping conceptual and political intersections in order to extend a vital and critical engagement. We hope that it will be looked upon as an intervention in its own right, enabling those who consult it to take a panoramic view of struggles past, present and future, and to see a range of strategies in action, where part of the fascination is in seeing where there is alliance, where there is conflict, and where these two might yet lead.

ELIZABETH WRIGHT

A

androgyny Androgyny is an archetypal image of the union of masculine and feminine natures in one being. The word is from the Greek *andro* (male) and *gyn* (female), and it 'defines a condition under which the characteristics of the sexes, and the human impulses expressed by men and women, are not rigidly assigned' (Heilbrun, 1964, p. x). It is a concept central to Jungian psychology, since individuation requires coming to know (integrate, or 'befriend') unconscious aspects of one's psyche. For a woman, this means, among other things, integrating her masculine side (animus), and for a man, his feminine side (anima). The Self (the central, governing archetypal image behind the individuation process) combines both masculine and feminine elements, and is the centre and totality of the psyche. Among Jungian analysts, June Singer (1976) is perhaps best known for her treatment of androgyny.

The androgyne (a being of both sexes, also called hermaphrodite) is central to many creation myths, including Plato's and Genesis 1. Many Native American shamans, called *berdaches*, manifested androgyny (sex-reversal or bisexuality) during trances. Christianity seems largely lacking in androgynous imagery, since the Godhead is usually referred to as 'Father' and conceived of as male or pure Spirit, and since Jesus the Christ is male. However, Jung discerned an androgyny in Christ. In like manner, some feminist theologians have searched for, and found, images of the Divine Feminine, to complement the mostly masculine nature of the Godhead in Christianity (Mollenkott, 1988).

In the 1970s androgyny became popular as an ideal among feminists in the United States. Psychologist Sandra Bem (1987) became one of the best known feminist theorists for her empirical testing for androgyny among boys and girls and men and women; Carolyn Heilbrun (1964) was one of the best known from a literary point of view. Both Bem's and Heilbrun's concerns were political: to free the human personality from the restricting prison of sex-role stereotyping. In the late 1970s and 1980s, Bem's and other feminist psychologists' concern with androgyny received sharp feminist criticism. Certain feminist theologians

1

ANDROGYNY

(Goldenberg, 1979; Daly, 1978) were especially critical of the apolitical nature of androgyny. By the mid-1980s, Bem was convinced that, although androgyny had seemed a desirable goal, it was problematical theoretically because it failed to examine the degree to which our perceptions and our social world are governed by gender (Bem, 1987, p. 245). She therefore proposed a 'gender schema theory', in which each sex can perform the functions stereotypically attributed to the other one, and in which 'masculine' and 'feminine' are no longer uncritically accepted as givens but seen as ideals of human functioning.

Feminist controversy over the concept of androgyny is not resolved. 'Essentialist feminists' who believe that there are basic female and male 'natures' (Jungians tend to be among them) are more likely to embrace the concept than 'social constructivists', who believe that what is seen as 'female' and 'male' natures is culturally specific. The controversy is *not* about whether or not it is desirable for both sexes to be home-makers *and* politicians, etc., a view which essentialist feminists and social constructive feminists both embrace. Rather, it is about an issue with far deeper consequences for our understanding of human beings: whether or not there is anything 'feminine' and 'masculine' that is *natural*, biological, psychological, spiritual to be 'integrated' by the opposite sex or not. Most feminists in the United States today believe that there are differences between the sexes, and that these differences are socially constructed. In addition, a more finely tuned feminist awareness of the differences between women is emerging. These shifts in perspective tend to make androgyny an outgrown ideal, although one that surely served a purpose along the way.

See also ESSENTIALISM; JUNG; SEXUAL DIFFERENCE.

BIBLIOGRAPHY

Bem, Sandra, 1987: 'Gender schema theory and child development', *The Psychology of Women: Ongoing Debates*, ed. Mary Roth Walsh. London: Thames and Hudson, pp. 226–45.

Daly, Mary, 1978: *Gyn/Ecology: The Metaethics of Radical Feminism*. Boston: Beacon Press.

Goldenberg, Naomi, 1979: *Changing of the Gods: Feminism and the End of Traditional Religions*. Boston: Beacon Press.

Heilbrun, Carolyn, 1964: *Toward a Recognition of Androgyny*. New York and London: Norton.

Jung, C. G., 1953–68: *Collected Works*, ed. Sir Herbert Read, Michael Fordham, and Gerhard Adler, trans. R. F. C. Hull. Princeton: Princeton University Press, especially vol. 12, *Psychology and Alchemy*, vol. 14, *Mysterium Coniunctionis* and essay, 'Psychology of the transference', in vol. 16, *The Practice of Psychotherapy*.

Mollenkott, Virginia Ramey, 1988: *The Divine Feminine: The Biblical Imagery of God as Female*. New York: Crossroad.

ANTHROPOLOGY AND CROSS-CULTURAL ANALYSIS

Singer, June, 1976: *Androgyny: Toward a New Theory of Sexuality*. New York: Doubleday.

DEMARIS S. WEHR

anthropology and cross-cultural analysis The relationship between anthropology and psychoanalysis, inaugurated by the publication of 'Totem and taboo' (Freud, 1913) has often been an uneasy one. The crux of the issue is what analytical weight and status should be given to cross-cultural variation. The terms of the debate on this point were set in Europe in the 1920s by the disagreement which emerged between the anthropologist Bronislaw Malinowski and the psychoanalyst Ernest JONES Malinowski, 1927) over whether or not the OEDIPUS COMPLEX was universal. Malinowski asserted that in the matrilineal society of the Trobriand Islands, the oedipus complex could be observed, but the conflict was not between father and son, but between the boy and his mother's brother; as a consequence, cultural variation in family forms gives rise to variation in psychic structures and in developmental processes. Jones countered with the claim that psychoanalysis was a universal theory about complexes and developmental processes which could not be seen as sociologically or culturally determined (see Coward, 1980). The result of this disagreement was a split between anthropology and psychoanalysis which had a profound effect on subsequent developments in the former. Social anthropology asserted its primary interest in groups and social organization rather than in individuals, and was remarkably devoid – in mainstream writings – of any theory of the person, until the 1970s.

The situation in the United States was somewhat different, because of the successful development in the 1920s – and continuing influence – of what came to be known as the 'culture and personality' school. This fruitful, but contentious, collaboration between psychology and anthropology was exemplified by the work of Margaret Mead and others (Stocking, 1986). Hence, American socio-cultural anthropology retained an interest in collective symbols, processes of socialization, fantasy, dreams and ethnopsychiatry, and this interest has recently given rise to a renaissance in psychoanalytic and psychological anthropology. However, this work, like its European counterpart, failed to develop a theory of the person, which is curious given that, since the 1930s, a certain amount of work has been done in European and American anthropology on the variability in cultural concepts of the person. However, there is now a growing body of work on concepts of the person, although much of it not from a psychoanalytic or psychodynamic perspective; in the context of this work, there has been a renewed interest in questions of gender identity, but with the exception of the examples discussed below, most of this work is not psychoanalytically oriented. The question of self and self-identity, and the cross-cultural variations in the concept and constitution of self have proved to be a fruitful area of new research; nevertheless, this work rarely takes the question of GENDER seriously and there has been no consideration of the question of subjectivity (Heelas and Lock, 1981; Shweder and Levine, 1984; White and Kirkpatrick, 1985).

In recent years, there have been a number of examples of the application of psychoanalytic theories and therapeutic techniques to anthropological work, mainly emerging from the American tradition. The theoretical basis of this work is varied, much of it focusing either on the oedipal conflict or on the PRE-OEDIPAL period and the nature of mother–child relations. Many authors also draw on ego psychology, self-psychology and the object-relations school, rather than Lacanian theory, the impact of which upon psychoanalytic anthropology has been minimal (*see* OBJECT-RELATIONS THEORY). Overall, the influence of the feminist critique of psychoanalysis and of feminist theory in general has been almost negligible, with the exception of some new work on maternal attachment (discussed below). A number of anthropologists have noted the similarities between the ethnographic interview and both the analytic session and the diagnostic interview. Transference and countertransference are thought by many anthropologists to be a necessary feature of anthropological fieldwork, and several authors have used these concepts in the description and analysis of the dialogue between self and other established in the ethnographic encounter, forming the basis for much anthropological interpretation (e.g. Riesman, 1977; *and see* TRANSFERENCE/COUNTERTRANSFERENCE).

The recording and analysis of dreams has produced a large literature (see Tedlock, 1987). A whole variety of conventional anthropological areas of enquiry or types of data, including free association, symbolic exegesis, possession, healing and religious experience, have been analysed using psychoanalytic approaches (see Obeyesekere, 1981; Crapanzano, 1980). Authors writing on these topics sometimes fit their findings into an explicit theoretical framework, but more frequently they utilize general psychoanalytic, psychodynamic or psychological ideas to highlight the relationship between the personal and the social, the conscious and the UNCONSCIOUS, the culturally specific and the universal. Thus, in the case of dream analysis, some anthropologists use dreams to elicit clues about informants' psychodynamics; some study indigenous uses of dreams and dream interpretations; some examine the extent to which dreams are 'coded' and contain unresolved conflicts or childhood fantasies; while yet others link dream thought to the process of myth-making and dominant cultural symbols (see Kracke, 1987; Herdt, 1987a; Kilborne, 1981). Though the degree to which individual authors stress or explicitly examine the relationship between cultural specificity and universality varies greatly, most authors who utilize these approaches in their work seem to favour a position which stresses the unity of human psychic structure and the universality of human emotions (fear, anxiety, jealousy, aggression) and human psycho-social experience (attachment, loss, grief, oedipal conflict).

This does not mean, however, that the Malinowski/Jones debate has been completely resolved, because the question of cultural variation remains problematic, for two reasons. First, how are emotions, psycho-social experience and developmental processes affected by culture? Anthropological work spends a great deal of time mapping out examples of cultural specificity, yet there is a residual unease which is reflected in the use of words like 'filtered', 'masked', 'channelled', 'distorted' to describe the effects of cultural models/meanings/experience on universal processes and structures. Second, some anthropologists – many of whom do not use psychoanalytic approaches or theories in their work – are unconvinced by arguments which posit the unity of human psychic structures, emotions and psycho-social experience. They argue that there is insufficient evidence and that the clear existence of cultural variation, rather than providing examples of how universal structures and processes work out in culturally specific circumstances, actually throws doubt on the *a priori* assumption of the existence of such universals. Cultural variation thus remains a problem both for those who posit universals and for those who do not.

Anthropologists who are concerned to describe and analyse the culturally specific nature of human emotions and psycho-social experience usually attempt to do so by examining the relationships between individual experience and cultural forms. This is because, assuming that there are universal psychic structures and processes, variations in cultural systems are assumed to give rise to variations in individual experience. Thus it is the interrelationship between culture and individual, the social and the personal, that is the crucial one.

Obeyesekere developed the term 'personal symbols' to show how cult devotees in Sri Lanka used symbols drawn from the public realm of culture to express personal conflicts and fantasies. Personal fantasies and life narratives help, in turn, to re-vitalize and re-work public (that is cultural) symbolism (Obeyesekere, 1981). Several researchers have discussed the ways in which the psychodynamics of particular individuals lead them to participate in particular, culturally defined, roles as healers or cult followers or shamans. Early work of this kind tended to empha-

5

size the way in which cultural institutions or symbol systems could be seen as having a particular emotional function – as, for example, in the work of Melford Spiro, who argued that cultural institutions and symbols provide 'culturally constituted defence mechanisms' on which individuals draw in their attempts to manage personal conflicts (Spiro, 1987). More recent work, like that of Obeyesekere, emphasizes instead the specific meanings attached to experience and emotions. However, most psychoanalytic anthropology sees cultural symbolism – including myth and ritual – as being the expression, in some way or other, of unconscious FANTASY. Some writers still view culture as the collective fantasy of humankind, betraying, through specific cultural patterns, universal conflicts and anxieties; others are more concerned to stress the fact that symbol systems not only reflect unconscious fantasies – usually thought to be the response to pre-oedipal and oedipal conflicts – but also provide interactive models through which individuals can organize their own fantasies (Obeyesekere, 1981; *and see* JUNG).

The question of the possible universality of infantile anxieties and therefore of the typical fantasies associated with them stimulated a series of studies in psychoanalytic anthropology on the cross-cultural variation in child care and socialization. The pioneering work in this field was done by the Whitings, who were interested in investigating the contention that fantasies and thus developmental processes might vary across cultures depending on the nature of childcare and socialization (Whiting and Whiting, 1975). Debates in this area mirror the Malinowski/Jones controversy regarding the oedipus complex. Recent work in psychoanalytic anthropology tends to emphasize that all children, whatever the culturally specific nature of their experience, family structures and symbol systems, experience anxieties associated with breaking out of the mother–child dyad, and with finding some sort of resolution to the conflicts produced by jealousy, rivalry, love and DESIRE in the oedipal phase. Current re-thinking of the oedipus complex stresses that it does not have an invariant form, but that it is a complex fantasy which results from cognitive, developmental and physiological events which children experience during maturation and which are connected with the development of a symbolic capacity (Lidz and Lidz, 1989; Pollock and Ross, 1988).

The one area in psychoanalytic anthropology where gender is treated seriously and where the feminist critique has had some influence, albeit an indirect one, is in the discussion of pre-oedipal dynamics. Much new research focuses on how boys must repudiate an initial maternal attachment and identification with the mother. The context for this work in anthropology has been the longstanding interest in the discipline in initiation rites. Some writers argue that while these rites serve oedipal functions, they also serve to undo the feminine identification of the initiates, often making explicit reference to the separation of boys from mothers and to the substitution of feminine aspects of self or attributes for male ones. Gilbert Herdt's work on the Sambia of Melanesia stresses the symbolic substitution of the penis for the breast. This substitution takes place in the context of lengthy rites of initiation which involve the initiands in ritual fellation (Herdt, 1987b). There are many other examples from Melanesia of the ritualization of indigenous concerns about boys' primary identification with the mother (Herdt, 1982, 1984; Lidz and Lidz, 1986). However, this work on pre-oedipal dynamics, while interesting, focuses almost entirely on males, and very little cross-cultural work has been done on female children and pre-oedipal dynamics.

Ultimately, it may be that the contribution of psychoanalytic anthropology to the cross-cultural study of psychic structures and processes is limited by its adherence to major psychoanalytic models and theories. There is much evidence in anthropological writings that the concept of the person based on the humanist notion of the SUBJECT is not universal: concepts of the person and the acting, knowing subject vary enormously cross-culturally. What is more, the culturally specific persons who are conceived of and conceptualized in ways which are quite distinct from that of the Western person are also constituted differently. For example, in many African societies, persons are not thought of as being radically distinct or separate from other persons, and in some cases they are believed to contain within them parts of other persons and of the natural world (see Fortes,1981; Dieterlen, 1941). Even so, this lack of separation does not affect the ability of such persons to achieve emotional maturity or to act as autonomous individuals. It is evidence of this kind that could be used to produce a radical critique of certain psychoanalytic theories and to question assumptions about the universality of developmental processes; but anthropology has yet to produce such a critique, and seems to prefer instead to demonstrate cultural variations in what are assumed to be universals.

This provides a particularly crucial problem when it comes to a consideration of gender identity. It seems likely that the binary model of gender which underlies Western psychoanalytic theories – including those of the French feminist psychoanalysts (*see* IRIGARAY) – is an inappropriate one for understanding notions of gender and gender identity in all the societies of the world. It seems probable that anthropologists have been hampered in their attempts to utilize cross-cultural data to interrogate dominant psychoanalytic theories of gender acquisition by their reluctance to consider Lacan's re-reading of Freud. Anthropology has a concept of the person and of the self, but it has yet to develop a notion of the subject and of subjectivity. The notion of subjectivity and of the constitution of the subject in LANGUAGE would be of particular value to anthropologists, who are used to dealing with cultural variation in meanings and symbol systems. It would also move psychoanalytic anthropology away from an almost exclusive concern with cultural variation towards a theory of the constitution of the subject, which would leave room for the mutually determining effects of culture, race, gender, class, sexuality and history – as well as possibly other forms of difference – on the constitution of the subject.

Anthropology has yet to come to terms with the fact that it is not enough to recognize the differences between cultures, or even the differences between subjects or individuals in the same culture, but that it is also necessary to recognize the differences within each subject. One cannot help remarking that if psychoanalytic anthropology were more attuned to contemporary developments in feminist theory, then this task would be a great deal easier.

See also FEMINISM OF DIFFERENCE; RACE/IMPERIALISM.

BIBLIOGRAPHY

Coward, Rosalind, 1980: 'On the universality of the oedipus complex: debates on sexual divisions in psychoanalysis and anthropology', *Critique of Anthropology*, 15/4, pp. 5–28.

Crapanzano, Vincent, 1980: *Tuhami: Portrait of a Moroccan*. Chicago: Chicago University Press.

Dieterlen, Germain, 1941: *Les Ames de Dogon*. Paris: Institut d'Ethnologie.

Fortes, Meyer, 1987: *Religion, Morality and the Person*. Cambridge: Cambridge University Press.

Freud, Sigmund, 1913: *Totem and Taboo*, SE, 13, pp. ix–164.

Heelas, Paul, and Lock, Andrew, 1981: *Indigenous Psychologies: The Anthropology of the Self*. London: Academic Press.

Herdt, Gilbert, 1987a: 'Selfhood and discourse in Sambia dream sharing', Tedlock, 1987, pp. 55–85.

Herdt, Gilbert, 1987b: 'Transitional objects in Sambia initiation rites', *Ethos*, 15, pp. 40–57.

Herdt, Gilbert, ed. 1982: *Rituals of Manhood: Male Initiation in New Guinea*. Berkeley: University of California Press.

Herdt, Gilbert, ed. 1984: *Ritualized Homosexuality in Melanesia*. Berkeley: University of California Press.

Kilborne, Benjamin, 1981: 'Dream interpretation and culturally constituted defense mechanisms', *Ethos*, 9, pp. 294–312.

Kracke, Waud H., 1987: 'Myth in dreams, thought in images: an Amazonian contribution to the psychoanalytic theory of the primary process', Tedlock, 1987, pp. 31–54.

Lidz, Theodore, and Lidz, Ruth W., 1986: 'Turning woman things into men: masculinisation in Papua New Guinea', *Psychoanalytic Review*, 73, pp. 118–35.

Lidz, Theodore, and Lidz, Ruth W., 1989: *Oedipus in the Stone Age*. New York: International University Press.

Malinowski, Bronislaw, 1927: *Sex and Repression in Savage Society*. London: Routledge.

Obeyesekere, Gannanath, 1981: *Medusa's Hair: An Essay on Personal Symbols and Religious Experience*. Chicago: Chicago University Press.

Pollock, Geoffrey H., and Ross, Jeffrey M., 1988: *The Oedipus Papers*. Madison, Conn.: International University Press.

Riesman, Paul, 1977: *Freedom in Fulani Social Life: An Introspective Ethnography*. Chicago: Chicago University Press.

Shweder, Richard, and Levine, Robert, 1984: *Culture Theory: Essays on Mind, Self and Emotion*. Cambridge: Cambridge University Press.

Spiro, Melford, 1987: *Culture and Human Nature: Theoretical Papers of Melford Spiro*, ed. B. Kilborne and L. L. Langness. Chicago: Chicago University Press.

Stocking, George, ed. 1986: *Malinowski, Benedict, Mead and Others*. Madison, Wis.: Wisconsin University Press.

Tedlock, Barbara, ed. 1987: *Dreaming: Anthropological and Psychological Interpretations*. Cambridge: Cambridge University Press.

White, Geoffrey, and Kirkpatrick, John, 1985: *Person, Self and Experience: Exploring Pacific Ethnopsychologies*. Berkeley: University of California Press.

Whiting, Beatrice, and Whiting, John, 1975: *Children of Six Cultures: A Psycho-Cultural Analysis*. Cambridge, Mass.: Harvard University Press.

HENRIETTA L. MOORE

art Historically psychoanalysis demonstrated an interest in art and artists. Freud's case study of Leonardo da Vinci (1910) established a model for psychobiographical analysis of the relations between the lives and works of artists. Subsequently Ernst Kris published *Psychoanalytical Explorations in Art* (1952) which concentrated rather upon the dynamics of creativity. More recently Julia Kristeva's 'Motherhood according to Giovanni Bellini' (in Kristeva, 1980) also used biographical material to develop a reading of a particular artist's *oeuvre* in order to propose a theory about the significance of the maternal body. Significantly, the subject of analysis was a masculine artist.

Feminist use of psychoanalytic theory in the production and analysis of art is distant from psychobiography, which has so much in common with the traditional artist-focused emphasis of art history. Feminist applications of the insights of psychoanalysis have developed a systemic critique of the function of the image, the gaze, the spectator and IDENTIFICATION, with the emphasis on the process of subjectivity at a general rather than an individual level. Furthermore, in the light of Lacanian revisions of Freudian theory, it is argued that subjectivity itself is coincident with the acquisition of both LANGUAGE and a sexual identity. Thus psychoanalytic theory is used as a means both to identify and to disrupt the production of the current forms of SEXUAL DIFFERENCE. Sexuality and sexual difference are defined as REPRESENTATION, and hence the process of visual representation is analysed in terms of the function of representation in the formation of the sexed subject – primal sights – and in terms of its continuing necessity as a site for the perpetual cultural process of shaping and working the subject, conceptualized as precarious and unfixed. Psychoanalytic theory is deployed to identify both the necessary content of representation – the psychic dramas perpetually re-enacted – and the means by which we are captured by representation, drawn into its field and effect by means of its management of both dread and PLEASURE, anxiety and DESIRE.

In relation to FEMININITY, visual representation becomes a critical site for two main reasons. On the one hand, it has been shown how as an image, 'woman' is recruited to service in a phallocentric regime of sexual difference at the level of icon offered to and mastered by a gaze which is appropriated as masculine and phallic. On the other, the specificity of femininity appears unrepresented, indeed unrepresentable within a phallic order; and thus feminist interventions at the level of artistic practice adumbrate critical readings of, and disruptive positions *vis-à-vis*, prevailing culture in order to re-negotiate a means of representing femininity in terms other than its current function as negative. The major influences have come from film theory, particularly Laura Mulvey's 'Visual pleasure and the narrative cinema' (in Mulvey, 1988) which initiated a shift in feminist cultural analysis from ideology critique to cultural forms and institutions as apparatuses of pleasure working upon the viewer through management of FANTASY and desire. This has led to feminist analysis of what has been comprehensively defined as 'sexuality in the field of vision' (Rose, 1986). Rose emphasizes the metaphorical and political significance of vision in the scenarios hypothesized by Freud to explain the realization of anatomical difference between the sexes and the onset of castration anxiety. This in turn has shaped dominant ways of representing the female form in art as deficient, lacking the necessary organ. It has also produced the demand for aesthetic perfection as a defence against the anxiety aroused by the sight of female difference. In the painting of the female nude, for instance, the body is idealized by being without blemish, without reference to the genital specificity which according to Freud, registers as mutilated or lacking *vis-à-vis* a male form. This artistically fashioned ideal is then further 'beautified' by formal means in the painterly skill by which it is manufactured for a viewer, which Freud called the surplus of aesthetic pleasure (Freud, 1908). Idealization works both at the level of what is represented iconically in an image, and in the pleasures that images and their formal qualities, particularly their harmony or seeming perfection, provide in the unconscious.

In 1973 Laura Mulvey's case study of pop artist Allen Jones, 'You don't know what is happening, do you, Mr. Jones?' utilized Freudian theories of castration and FETISHISM to analyse the systematic conversion in erotic and pornographic imagery of the female form into a fetish for the missing phallus. 'The true exhibit is always the phallus. Women are simply the scenery onto which men project their narcissistic fantasies' (Mulvey, 1987; see also Silverman, 1988; also art historical studies by Simons, 1988; Pollock, 1988; Pointon, 1990; Nochlin, 1986; Bernheimer, 1987). She concluded that women must begin to develop imageries to explore their own fantasies and desires. In 1974 two events offered new theorizations of the formation of femininity under a phallocentric order: the publication of Juliet Mitchell's *Psychoanalysis and Feminism* and the *Patriarchy* conference (May 1974). Artists and filmmakers became engaged in a parallel examination of feminine subjectivity by means of counter-narrative, text and image, installation and discourse. Mary Kelly's multi-part installation *Post Partum Document* (1983) was conceived as a continuing documentation and critical theorization of the reciprocal process of socialization of mother and child during the first five years of life. It contradicted the dominant representations of woman as 'naturally' nurturing through a series of key artistic strategies. First, it refused to produce icons, since any image of the female form was thought to be inevitably subject to fetishistic and voyeuristic readings of the body of woman as the object of a possessive or sadistic gaze. Second, the *Document* inscribed a feminine subjectivity, specifically discovering the formation of a maternal one across the items it displayed – nappy liners, vests, plaster casts, found objects, the child's drawings and first written words – which constituted a symptomatic narrative of the intersubjective relations between mother and child, signifying specifically feminine modes of NARCISSISM and FETISHISM. The token objects, freighted with memory traces, carried inscriptions, written in both diaristic and analytically intellectual modes. This dual discourse, in line with feminist critiques of LACAN, resisted the silencing of woman in the construction of her as mute icon. The discourse was symptomatic, speaking the anxiety and fantasies of the mother as a subject produced in a psychic interchange with the child, within the current social division of labour making women the primary childcarers. But this text, shaped within the unconscious processes of the maternal subject, was subjected to a critical revision, informed by feminist political theory and its critical reading of psychoanalysis which was perceived as a paradoxical instrument for feminist practice. As a result of Kelly's work, innovative theorizations have emerged about the formation of the 'maternal feminine' and the significance of the maternal body as the repressed but necessary support for subjectivity and language. There is now a body of feminist work which has the maternal dyad as a key axis, for instance in works by Kati Campbell such as *Dyad* (1989) and *Père-version* (1990), while the questions of femininity and language problematized by paternal readings of Lacanian theories have been creatively explored in ways both parallel to, and influenced by, the writings of Luce IRIGARAY and Hélène Cixous, for instance in the paintings by Mary Scott in the *Imago* series.

The closest correspondences with Kelly's project lay not in the visual arts, feminist and otherwise, but in film, such as Laura Mulvey's and Peter Wollen's *Riddles of the Sphinx* (BFI, 1976), and in so-called 'third area' art work which used photographic practice, such as Sarah McCarthy's *The Milliner and the Student* (1978) and Marie Yates's *Image–Woman–Text* (1980; see Parker and Pollock, 1987). Both kinds of work identify the combinations of voyeurism and fetishism characteristically forming the production and consumption of the visual image. In the 1980s Marie Yates produced a serial work on woman, image and text, focusing on the function of narrative as a lure for the gaze, perpetually seeking what her texts exposed as 'the missing woman'. She links the pleasure of viewing to the necessity of the female image, both of which are denied in the effective construction of a critical, feminist viewing position. In a later work, *The Only Woman* (1985), Yates made a photographic multi-part work shaped according to Freud's thesis on 'Mourning and Melancholia', taking as its theme the daughter mourning a mother. While luring the spectator with heavily charged and emblematic images from a personal family album, the piece forced the viewer to confront the question of whose desire motivates the search for the woman in an IMAGE, a search which runs parallel with a desire for a complete story, and the achievement of distance at the end. Mitra Tabrizian has also taken on the relation of the gaze and subjectivity in works which disturb the identification of the look with MASCULINITY, through a calculated manipulation and proliferation of looks in her fictive and photographically contrived scenarios reminiscent of key cultural locations of looking and being on display – advertisement, fashion, cinema. No one owns the look; no one's identity is secured by an ideal mirror. The spectator is involved in being seen looking. The effect of this unsettling of the function of the image as both lure and fixer is to parade before the viewer a culturally generated repertoire of images through which the subject is positioned, differentiated, in relation not only to gender, but also to race and class. Thus Mitra Tabrizian uses psychoanalytical theory in making art-work which constitutes a cross-cultural and anti-colonial critique.

A major historical exhibition which took place first in New York (New Museum of Contemporary Art, 1984) and later in London (Institute of Contemporary Art, 1985), entitled *Difference: On Representation and Sexuality*, explored via the visual arts the 'complex terrain triangulated by the terms sexuality, meaning and language' (Linker, 1985, p. 5). Artists exhibiting were Ray Barrie, Victor Burgin, Hans Haacke, Mary Kelly, Silvia Kolbowski, Barbara Kruger, Sherrie Levine, Yve Lomax, Jeff Wall and Marie Yates; in addition there were videotapes and feature films. Lisa Tickner argued that 'The most important contribution of the feminism under consideration here is the recognition of the relations between representation and sexed subjectivity *in process* . . . The artists . . . hold the common aim of 'unfixing' the feminine, unmasking the relations of specularity that determine its appearance in representation' (Ibid., p. 28). Femininity, far from being the visual token which secures the fixed masculinity of the spectator, is undone, represented as mobile, fashioned, a matter of poses or 'masquerade', in which no real, innate or psychologically intrinsic subjectivity can be revealed. The feint of a fixed and eternal femininity, which is the effect of the visual image as object of beauty and pleasure, is systematically exposed. The subject of art is not the fetishized artist of art history's discourse, or that of Freud on Leonardo, but a culturally determined psychic process.

Mary Kelly's latest project, *Interim*, a multi-piece installation in four sections (Body, Money, History, Power), uses the art work as a signifying space for the older woman as the subject of desire. An ironic dedication of the work to 'Dora's mother', that is, the middle-aged woman with 'housewife's psychosis' dismissed by Freud in his famous case study (Freud, 1905) indicates the critical stance adopted towards the classic texts of psychoanalysis and an alignment with feminist theorists in France such as Cixous, Clément and Montrelay. Citing Montrelay's 'Inquiry into femininity' (1978), Kelly questions how women live their relation to the image when they exceed the culture's figurations of the feminine as object of male desire and exchange. Montrelay argues that the 'adult woman is one who reconstructs her sexuality in the field that goes beyond sex' (1978, p. 94). By generating imageries and discourses to utter the position of generations of women who encountered feminism and psychoanalysis in the aftermath of 1968, *Interim* achieves a significant reversal. Femininity is made to pass into historical discourse and into new relations of woman as subject rather than object of the look. The iconic passivity which characterized the representation of woman – so dramatically figured in Charcot's photographic staging of femininity as hysteria, *Iconographie de la Salpêtrière* (1878) and repeated in Freud's lack of interest in Dora's mother – is disrupted by women's discourse, a pleasure in the signifier, in 'theoretical as well as creative work, especially on sexuality itself' (Kelly, 1987, p. 12). Creative work is decisively shifted from Freud's use of art as evidence of the subject's past towards the production of knowledge for the subjects whose own political and psychic archaeology the installation undertakes. Interrogating femininity and its conditions within a historical and cultural frame can lead to elaborating strategies for changed relations to its own formation. It has been argued that the effect of such art work on its viewers/readers is comparable to the discourse of the analyst (Adams, 1991).

Feminist interventions in the contemporary production of art have in turn influenced the historical analyses of the art of women in the past. Feminist art histories examine women's representation of the feminine body, their specific relation to the gaze (Mulvey and Wollen, 1982; Kendall and Pollock, 1991). The further question of how women read art produced by men has led to the analysis of identification as a structure of viewing. Important work has been done to demolish a monolithic notion of woman as spectator by questioning the predominantly heterosexual character of analysis to date, which has operated a repression of lesbian subjectivity, the articulation of which as a viewing position has been mobilized for significant re-readings of the formations of masculinity from a feminist perspective (Leeks, 1990; Dawkins, 1991).

Feminist practice does not merely use or rely on psychoanalytical theory. In generating its own texts and imageries, art practice has offered theoretical advances as much as revised aesthetic pleasures addressed specifically to women whose subjectivity is at last being traced, promising – like analysis itself – the re-formulation of subjectivities for its novel signifying systems. The artist is not placed upon the couch, as Freud hypothetically placed Leonardo. Rather, Western culture's psychic investments are analysed and read against the grain of the current regime of sexual difference, which is secured around masculinity's castration crises and the anxieties of the phallus. Artistic practice allows femininity to be signified in its specificity and heterogeneity, marked by loss and formed by desire according to historically and culturally particular trajectories.

See also CASTRATION COMPLEX; FILM THEORY; MASQUERADE; PHALLOGO-CENTRISM; PHOTOGRAPHY; VOYEURISM/EXHIBITIONISM/THE GAZE.

BIBLIOGRAPHY

Adams, Parveen, 1991: 'The art of analysis: Mary Kelly's *Interim* and the discourse of the analyst', *October*, 58, pp. 81–96.
Bernheimer, Charles, 1987: 'Degas' brothels: voyeurism and ideology', *Representations*, 20, pp. 158–87.

Dawkins, Heather, 1991: 'Sexuality, Degas and women's history'. PhD thesis, University of Leeds.

Freud, Sigmund, 1905: 'Fragment of an analysis of a case of hysteria (Dora)', *SE*, 7, pp. 3–122.

Freud, Sigmund, 1908: 'Creative writers and day-dreaming', *SE*, 9, pp. 141–54.

Freud, Sigmund, 1910: *Leonardo da Vinci: a Memory of his Childhood*, *SE*, 11, pp. 59–138.

Kelly, Mary, 1983: *Post Partum Document*. London: Routledge.

Kelly, Mary, 1985: 'Desiring images/imaging desire', *Wedge*, 6, pp. 5–9.

Kelly, Mary, 1987: 'Invisible bodies: Mary Kelly's *Interim*', *New Formations*, 2, pp. 7–36.

Kelly, Mary, 1990: *Interim*. New York: New Museum of Contemporary Art.

Kendall, Richard, and Pollock, Griselda, 1991: *Dealing with Degas: Representations of Women and the Politics of Vision*. London: Pandora Press.

Kris, Ernst, 1952: *Psychoanalytic Explorations in Art*. London: Allen and Unwin.

Kristeva, Julia, 1980: *Desire in Language*, trans. L. Roudiez. Oxford: Basil Blackwell.

Leeks, Wendy, 1990: 'Ingres and the family romance'. PhD thesis, University of Leeds.

Linker, Kate, 1984: *Difference: On Representation and Sexuality*. New York: New York Museum of Contemporary Art; London: London Institute of Contemporary Art, 1985.

Montrelay, Michèle, 1978: 'Inquiry into femininity', *m/f*, 1, pp. 83–102.

Mulvey, Laura, 1987: 'Fears, fantasies and the male unconscious *or* "You don't know what is happening, do you, Mr Jones?"'. Parker and Pollock, 1987, pp. 125–7.

Mulvey, Laura, 1988: *Visual and Other Pleasures*. London: Macmillan.

Mulvey, Laura, and Wollen, Peter, 1982: *Frida Kahlo and Tina Modotti*. London: Whitechapel.

Nochlin, Linda, 1986: 'Courbet's *Origine du Monde*: the origin without an original', *October*, 37, pp. 76–86.

Pointon, Marcia, 1990: *Naked Authority: The Body in Western Painting, 1830–90*. Cambridge: Cambridge University Press, 1990.

Parker, Rozsika, and Pollock, Griselda, 1987: *Framing Feminism: Art and the Women's Movement, 1970–85*. London: Pandora Press.

Pollock, Griselda, 1988: *Vision and Difference: Feminism, Femininity and the Histories of Art*. London: Routledge.

Pollock, Griselda, 1990: 'Missing women: rethinking early thoughts on "Images of Women"', *The Critical Image*, ed. C. Squiers. Washington: Bay Press, pp. 202–19.

Rose, Jacqueline, 1986: *Sexuality in the Field of Vision*. London: Verso.

Silverman, Kaja, 1988: *The Acoustic Mirror*. Bloomington: Indiana University Press.

Simons, Patricia, 1988: 'Women in frames: the eye, the gaze and the profile in Renaissance portraiture', *History Workshop Journal*, 25, pp. 4–30.

AUTONOMY

Tickner, Lisa, 1988: 'Feminism, art history and sexual difference', *Genders*, 3, pp. 92–129.

GRISELDA POLLOCK

autonomy   Psychoanalysis has offered a radical challenge to post-Enlightenment conceptions of the rationality and autonomy of the self. Freudian theory postulates a dimension of unconscious process and DESIRE in the human psyche which can never be wholly amenable to rational understanding or control. Many human motives and actions can better be understood as the rationalizations of unconscious desire rather than as the outcome of conscious or rational intent.

An important strand in Freud's theories was his view that the aim of psychoanalysis as therapy was to increase the strength of the ego, via a process of understanding the unconscious compulsions, experienced as 'alien' to the self, which had dominated conscious life. Freud's conception of this increased 'autonomy' of the self was necessarily opposed to any view that the self could ever wholly attain conscious control over itself, or that the reasons and motives underlying human action could ever be wholly perspicuous. Nevertheless, a greater degree of autonomy might be achieved in so far as human beings could better learn to tolerate and understand the aspects of the psychical state which had formerly had such power over their lives.

However, Freud came to adopt a different view of the trajectory of male and female psychic development, and he depicted the 'path' to FEMININITY of the girl as more difficult than the 'path' to MASCULINITY of the boy. The fundamental reason for this, in Freud's later theories, was a crucial asymmetry in male and female psychic development. The 'task' for the boy was to convert his initial incestuous love for the mother into heterosexual love for a woman. The 'task' for the girl was more complex; since her first love-object was also a woman, the route to heterosexual love and object-choice involved an additional complexity. And since Freud believed that the girl was already 'castrated', the oedipal crisis in female psychic life was less severe, and therefore less likely to precipitate the sort of crisis in male development that led, through the CASTRATION COMPLEX, to the boy's relinquishing of his desire for his mother and his inheritance of the patriarchal right of his father.

Freud believed that the structural difference in the OEDIPUS COMPLEX for women and men led to more general differences in their psychic make-up: whereas a man of thirty would often seem to have before him a great number of possibilities, a woman of the same age might often

16

seem psychically more rigid, as if the difficult path to femininity had exhausted her possibilities of psychic development and freedom of action. He considered that for women the level of what is ethically normal is different from what it is in men: the female superego is less impersonal and independent of its emotional origins. Women show less sense of judgement; they are more influenced in their judgements by their emotions, and have less sense of justice than men.

Some feminist critics have accused Freud of simple misogyny in his account of female development. Others have argued that there may be an important half-truth in his view of female autonomy and development. Freud's view of women's development recapitulates a view which has been very common in Western philosophy (for example in the moral philosophy of Kant): that the crucial value in ethics is autonomy, and that women are less capable of this than men. A number of feminist philosophers and moral theorists have suggested that there is a clear masculine bias in this view. But they have suggested, too, that there may well be some important differences in the ways in which women and men think about moral issues and relate these to questions about the self and about autonomy.

OBJECT-RELATIONS THEORY has been used to theorize these differences and to attempt to explain how this stress on autonomy might be seen as masculine. As initially formulated by Guntrip, Fairbairn, Winnicott and others, object-relations theory paid little attention to questions of GENDER. CHODOROW (1978) however, put at the forefront of her work the fact that it has largely been women who have undertaken the primary care of children in infancy. It has therefore been in relation to the mother, she argued, that the tasks of separation and individuation must initially take place. Whereas Freud saw the psychic task of the girl as more difficult, Chodorow reversed this. The boy has a harder time trying to establish an identity as male, and to separate and individuate himself from the female-dominated world of the household; boys tend to develop a defensive stress on autonomy, conceived of as separation from others. The basic masculine sense of self is separate from the world, whereas the basic feminine sense of self is connected. Typical psychological problems for the male, therefore, will tend to revolve around questions of connectedness and intimacy, whereas those for the female will revolve around questions of separation and individuation.

Some feminists have found in Chodorow's work a basis for re-evaluating some common assumptions both in moral philosophy and in psychology. Gilligan (1982), for example, argued that the norms of moral development used in the work of Kohlberg (1981) as a yardstick for the moral development of children reflect a specifically masculine view of morality, which stresses an ethic of rights and rules, supposedly arrived at by a process of autonomous moral reflection and choice (*see* WOMEN'S PSYCHOLOGICAL DEVELOPMENT). A perspective typical of women, in which moral issues are thought of rather in terms of their effect on human relationships, is deemed by Kohlberg to be at a 'lower' developmental stage than the rule-based ethic more common to men. Flax (1983) has argued that the masculinity of philosophical theories can be understood in terms of norms of male psychic development resulting from women's monopoly of early infant care. Philosophical theories such as classical liberal individualism, which see the self as an isolated atom, not intrinsically connected to others, or theories which think of knowledge in terms of a radical separation between knower and known, can be seen as related to the typical defensive structures of the masculine unconscious, which stress autonomy, conceived of as separation from others, and involve a rejection and a distancing of the self from all that is seen as feminine (*see* PHILOSOPHY).

Some critics have pointed to the great difficulties in generalizing about male or female psychology and in relating such generalizations to an ahistorical model of the nuclear family. Others have noted the potential dangers in idealizing a notion of female 'connectedness' which have been implicit in some uses of Chodorow's theory. Still others have noted that there are traditions in Western philosophy which are very different from the liberal individualist traditions characterized as a paradigm of the ways in which philosophy should be seen as 'masculine'. Perhaps most importantly, writers influenced by the work of LACAN have queried the whole analytic framework of object-relations theory. Lacan argued that the notions of 'gender identity' and of 'the ego' used in object-relations theory should be rejected; in Lacanian theory, the idea of a coherent or unified ego is an illusion. French theorists such as KRISTEVA and IRIGARAY have tried, in different ways, to suggest that women, in order not simply to be 'spoken by' the law of the father, should create forms of female expression in the gaps in human psychic life created by the tensions between the realms of the 'Imaginary' (Irigaray) or the 'semiotic' (Kristeva) and the SYMBOLIC, which is irredeemably patriarchal.

Critics of those French feminist writings which have drawn on the writings of Lacan have been less than happy with their apparent total rejection of notions like 'autonomy' or 'identity' in the theorization of female subjectivity. They have recognized the acute problems of difference among women which are raised by notions such as 'identity', and recognized, too, that views of autonomy which postulate a wholly unitary, conscious and rational human subject have indeed been both masculine in many of their manifestations, and irrevocably fractured by any notion of the UNCONSCIOUS. The question has been raised, however, as to whether a viable feminist politics can dispense wholly with a concept of female autonomy, even if this concept urgently needs feminist reconstruction.

See also SCIENCE; SUBJECT; THEORY.

BIBLIOGRAPHY

Chodorow, Nancy, 1978: *The Reproduction of Mothering*. Berkeley: University of California Press.

Flax, Jane, 1983: 'Political philosophy and the patriarchal unconscious', *Discovering Reality*, ed. S. Harding and M. Hintikka. London: Reidel, pp. 245–82.

Gilligan, Carol, 1982: *In a Different Voice: Psychological Theory and Women's Development*. Cambridge, Mass.: Harvard University Press.

Kohlberg, Lawrence, 1981: *The Philosophy of Moral Development*. San Francisco: Harper and Row.

JEAN GRIMSHAW

B

Benjamin, Jessica (*b*. Washington DC, 17 January 1946). Jessica Benjamin's work in psychoanalytic feminism explores the problem of male domination and female submission. She views domination as a problem 'not so much of human nature as of human relationships' (1988a, p. 5). Her project, synthesized in the 1988 book *The Bonds of Love*, emerges from the American feminist tradition that employs OBJECT-RELATIONS THEORY to understand the social context of women's psychic development. She expands on the work of CHODOROW in pursuing the importance of PRE-OEDIPAL experiences in the development of GENDER identity. Rather than fixing on structural arrangements of parenting, Benjamin introduces the dual motives of self-assertion and recognition in the experience of infants with their caregivers. Her account of infant development draws on experimental research as well as on the clinical work of D. W. Winnicott and Margaret Mahler. She argues that the infant's wish for recognition of her independence binds her with a recognizing other, on whom she depends for validation of her independent striving. Dependence on a recognizing caregiver forces the infant to give up the wish for omnipotent control; the needs for AUTONOMY and for recognition are ideally held in tension and negotiated in social experience. This theoretical position stands in contrast to more traditional views, in which differentiation and strong ego boundaries are held up as the goal of healthy psychic development. Thus, Benjamin adds the domain of intersubjectivity – the impact of real relationships on psychic life – alongside the more closed system of intrapsychic FANTASY. Her position on the paradox of recognition draws from the Hegelian dialectic tradition, in particular from Hegel's account of master and slave. This influence of German political philosophy is rooted in Benjamin's doctoral studies in sociology and social theory and continues to distinguish her work from the French psychoanalytic school which posits meaning and LANGUAGE as inevitable mediators of relationships.

The issue of power and the potential for gendered subject positions of domination and submission become incorporated into Benjamin's account of development in the second year of life. Here the experience of boys and girls begins to diverge. The girl wishes for recognition of her agency and autonomy from one who is like herself and with whom she identifies. The mother's capacity to recognize her daughter's agency is limited by her cultural articulation as OBJECT of male desire rather than as subject who owns her own desire. (Thus Benjamin transforms the classic question, 'what do women want?' to inquire 'do women want?' (1988a, p. 86).) In foregrounding the subjective experience of DESIRE as central to an understanding of submission and domination, Benjamin re-asserts the erotic dimension of psychic life, something that the object-relations tradition in feminist theory tends to overlook. The mother's status as 'Object' plays out in her role as caregiver, which tends to be that of soother and pacifier. Such a caregiving other cannot fully recognize the girl's own self-assertion. She turns for this recognition to her father, who represents the excitement of the 'outside' and freedom from dependence on the powerful mother. Benjamin sees the girl's turn to her father not only as a hostile response to the mother, but also as an expression of love of the world, the wish for agency and autonomy. This position challenges Chodorow's notion that autonomy should be understood as a masculine, defensive reaction to early IDENTIFICATION with the mother (see MOTHER–DAUGHTER RELATIONSHIP).

Benjamin asserts that only an account of identification with the power of the father can explain the experience of desire in the psychic development of girls and boys. She sees the PHALLUS not as an intrinsic symbol of desire (taking issue here with Juliet MITCHELL), but rather as an emerging symbol of the father's ability to stand for separation from the mother. Both the girl and the boy seek recognition of their sexual agency from the father. But only the boy has his identificatory love confirmed by a father who recognizes him as being 'like me'. This allows the boy to maintain his sense of power but also results in a denial and devaluation of the dependence associated with the mother. For the girl, desire is missing because her identification with the father's power is denied. She is left with the wish to be chosen by the father, and he becomes the object of her ideal love. Submission is rooted in psychic compromise, that is, in the idealization of the man who is seen to represent power and desire. This fantasy becomes the basis for the girl's heterosexual love, foreclosing the possibility of autonomy or a 'desire of her own'. In locating the problem of gender domination and submission in the intersubjective sphere of social relationships, Benjamin's account avoids the problem of biologizing PENIS ENVY while at the same time recognizing and reconstructing the power of fantasy in the development of gender identity.

Benjamin's feminist vision allows for the possibility that women as well as men, mothers as well as fathers, might be articulated as figures of separation *and* attachment, and that girls as well as boys might make constructive use of their identifications with both mother and father. If the cultural and psychic splitting of the feminine as the symbol of attachment (which also carries the threat of fusion and annihilation), and the masculine as the symbol of separation (which carries the threat of loss of connection), could be repaired, children would not come into a social world in which one side of the sexual power relationship is devalued and subordinated to the other.

WRITINGS

1977: 'The end of internalization: Adorno's social psychology', *Telos*, 32, pp. 42–64.

1978: 'Authority and the family revisited; or, a world without fathers?', *New German Critique*, 13, pp. 35–58.

1986: 'The alienation of desire: women's masochism and ideal love', *Psychoanalysis and Women: Contemporary Reappraisals*, ed. Judith Alpert. Hilllsdale, NJ: Analytic Press, pp. 113–38.

1988a: *The Bonds of Love*. New York: Pantheon.

1988b: 'Jessica Benjamin' (Interview), *Women Analyze Women: In France, England and the United States*, ed. Elaine Hoffman and Lucienne J. Serrano. Hemel Hempstead: Harvester Wheatsheaf, pp. 317–33.

MAUREEN A. MAHONEY

biology Since the eighteenth century, biology has referred to the scientific study of organic life, the *logos* founding the law of nature. Biology can either be an open-ended scientific discipline, the 'study of life', or it can refer to a fixed and determined biological order.

Since its inception, psychoanalysis has made reference to the biological sciences. As a physician and neurologist, Freud was familiar with the natural and physical sciences of his day, and particular influences like Darwinism, and the physicalist school of Brücke, Bois-Raymond, Helmholtz and others are well documented (see Sulloway, 1979). There is a tension between the Freud who is in search of a biological bedrock, and the Freud who develops a field of psychoanalytic enquiry which reveals a malleable biology. For Freud, this tension, arguably, has never been entirely resolved, but the work of LACAN has been seen to clarify Freud's confusions in the move away from biology and towards the primacy of the symbol and language.

It has been disputed whether Freud's biological analogies function as metaphors or whether they imply a biological reality. Laplanche (1989) argues that Freud, in his ontogenetic account of the origin and development of the individual, only makes reference to a biological entity which exists prior to culture. Elsewhere, Laplanche suggests that Freud invents an organism based on a 'pseudo-biology', for example, where Freud states that the organism is in a state of autarky (that is, seeking only its own pleasure, without regard for external reality) (1911) or where the organism is said to be left entirely traumatized by the energy from the external environment (1920). Laplanche argues that such models are not empirically viable and can only serve as metaphors for the psyche.

Yet it is precisely at the interface between the organism as a biological entity and its emergence as a psychic and cultural being where questions concerning pre-given biological dispositions and the influence of anatomy on the distinctions between the sexes are raised. For Müller-Braunschweig (co-founder of the Institute for Psychotherapy, Berlin, in 1947), JONES, KLEIN and HORNEY, an innate masculine and feminine disposition corresponds to the biological male and female, whereas, for Freud, biological instincts are neither sexed nor gendered.

Freud rarely uses the term 'instinct'; however, the English translation of Freud has replaced the German *Trieb* ('drive') with the word 'instinct', which has led to a biologistic reading of Freud in the English-speaking countries. Despite the confusion between instinct and *Trieb*, Laplanche (1976) argues that a useful distinction between *Instinkt* ('instinct') and *Trieb* ('drive') can be maintained in reading Freud. The instinct applies to a pre-social biological order, whereas the DRIVE refers to the emergence of a sexuality which is not biologically determined, and is always psychically represented.

In Laplanche's reading of Freud, the crucial effect of deferred action (*Nachträglichkeit*) puts into question the distinction between the biological and the sexual order in the genetic account; for it introduces a temporal dimension which throws into crisis the linear order given to the sequence biological instinct → symbol and sexual drive. As the biological 'origin' is impossible to grasp in some state 'prior' to SEXUALITY, it can only be reconstructed retroactively, because drive, symbol and sexuality are already under way, which makes it difficult to locate when and where the process begins. Laplanche starts out with a fixed and pre-sexual biological order, but then corrects this initial account by pointing out that the biological processes, far from being sufficient, are found to be lacking in natural structure, are born premature and arrive maturationally too late, so that the representation of sexuality has already intervened, providing the support structure required to supplement biology. The biological order has somehow, from the 'first', begun to err from its course of 'proper' development.

Freud and Lacan both note the biological and physiological immaturity of the infant at birth, which leads to a nursling dependency lasting longer than in other mammals. This means that the infant, in attempting to satisfy any biological needs, is dependent on a response from a care-taker, who provides what Freud calls 'a secondary function of the high-est importance, that of communication' (1895, p. 315), supplying a representational structure to help organize the biological processes. Lacan identifies how the incompletion of physiological maturation results in the fact that, before the maturational development is complet-ed, the SUBJECT already encounters an image of illusory wholeness which differs from the physiological reality of neurological insufficiency and motor incoordination (*see* IMAGINARY). The pre-mature entry of the image has consequences for the biological oral, anal and genital stages of development which Freud describes, and which ANNA FREUD retains as biologically determined phases in development. Lacan argues that these stages are 'nothing other than images of the human body' (1988, p. 141), instinctual stages already sexualized and invested with FANTASY (Lacan 1977, p. 53).

Feminists have been troubled by the definition of biology as an essen-tial, innate, universal structure, that in principle cannot be changed, and that has been ideologically used to justify the inequality between the sexes on biological grounds (biologism). The genetic account (Laplanche) of sexuality's emergence from the biological order has been employed by feminists as it avoids biological ESSENTIALISM by showing how sexuality comes into being with the drive's representation in LAN-GUAGE. Here biological realities support the formation of sexuality, but do not determine the drive's structure and use.

There is some disagreement about how to conceptualize the relation between biology and culture. Juliet MITCHELL, in her reading of Freud via Lacan, emphasizes how the symbolic order emerges at the moment the object of need is lost. She stresses how the human order is severed from biology and uses this to show how psychoanalysis can contribute to feminist theory. In contrast, Jane Gallop (1989) challenges any clear division between biology and the cultural order, for such a distinction can collude with a violent split between the two fields, a split which his-torically has placed women on the side of nature, outside culture. For Gallop, it is the ideological use of biology which is oppressive to women, not biology itself.

Wariness about the ideological (mis)use of biology often leads to charges of biological essentialism, levelled not only at the fathers of psy-choanalysis, but also at French women analysts such as Julia KRISTEVA and Luce IRIGARAY. Kristeva has been questioned on her theory of the semiotic for its stress on the PRE-OEDIPAL, 'non-verbal', 'maternal space', which has been considered as biologistic for positing the BODY and FEMI-

NINITY in a state of nature (see Adams and Brown, 1979). In fact, Kristeva argues that the semiotic implies a mark, a trace, a facilitation which informs the disposition of drives. This is not an unmediated state of nature, since a 'trace' already implies an inscription which, furthermore, always figures in relation to a symbolic field, positioning a subject and directing the drives (Kristeva, 1989, p. 264). Irigaray has similarly been seen to appeal to a feminine nature outside the symbolic order. Her now famous 'two lips that caress' have been seen to imply an essential female biology (Sayers, 1982). However, Irigaray's description of two lips in perpetual interchange makes it clear that she is not referring to a literal biology (Montefiore, 1987, p. 149). She does not speak of biology, but of the imaginary, with all its rich philosophical and other connotations. Although Irigaray at moments appears to collapse the imaginary anatomy into a biological referent, this is strategic, a means of re-figuring morphology in a historical situation, which already equates the imaginary and the biological with respect to a male anatomy (Whitford, 1991).

Recent feminist work argues for the strategic importance of maintaining a tension between biology and culture, anatomy and representation. The critique of biological essentialism forces a decision between biology and culture, choosing culture instead of biology. This position keeps the two poles of the metaphysical divide in operation, for to deny biology is to retain its definition as an essential order, while placing it outside the cultural order. Rather than taking sides, feminists are attempting to keep biology and culture in tension by thinking them together, simultaneously challenging the definition of a fixed and determined biological order and avoiding the collusion with a violent break between them which historically, as Gallop argues, has tended to place women on the side of nature.

The radical implication of psychoanalysis for biology is the way it transforms the meaning of biology for sexuality. It puts into question the retrieval of a biological origin, for when the sexual drive begins cannot be located as a moment in time. It shows how the biological order is already open to the detours of the drive, already lacking in structure, supplemented by a symbolic system. This makes the distinction between a fixed biological infrastructure and the field of representation a false division, since biology is already transformed and figured through psychic and social forms of REPRESENTATION.

See also SEXUAL DIFFERENCE.

BIBLIOGRAPHY

Adams, Parveen, and Brown, Beverley, 1979: 'The feminine body and feminist politics', *m/f*, 3, pp. 35–50.

25

Freud, Sigmund, 1895: 'The project for a scientific psychology', *SE*, 1, pp. 283–397.

Freud, Sigmund, 1905: *Three Essays on the Theory of Sexuality*, *SE*, 7, pp. 123–245.

Freud, Sigmund, 1911: 'Formulations on the two principles of mental functioning', *SE*, 12, pp. 218–26.

Freud, Sigmund, 1920: *Beyond the Pleasure Principle*, *SE*, 18, pp. 1–64.

Gallop, Jane, 1988: *Thinking through the Body*. New York: Columbia University Press.

Gallop, Jane, 1989: 'Moving backwards or forwards', *Between Feminism and Psychoanalysis*. London: Routledge, pp. 27–39.

Kirby, Vicki, 1992: 'Corporeal habits: Addressing essentialism differently', *Hypatia*, 6, No. 3, pp. 4–24,

Kristeva, Julia, 1989: *Black Sun: Depression and Melancholia*, trans. Leon Roudiez. New York: Columbia University Press.

Lacan, Jacques, 1977: *Écrits: A Selection*, trans. Alan Sheridan. London: Tavistock.

Lacan, Jacques, 1988: *The Seminar of Jacques Lacan*. book 1, *Freud's Papers on Technique 1953–1954*, ed. Jacques-Alain Miller. Cambridge: Cambridge University Press.

Laplanche, Jean, 1976: *Life and Death in Psychoanalysis*. Baltimore: Johns Hopkins University Press.

Laplanche, Jean, 1989: *New Foundations for Psychoanalysis*. Oxford: Basil Blackwell.

Montefiore, Jan, 1987: *Feminism and Poetry: Language, Experience, Identity in Women's Writing*. London: Pandora.

Sayers, Janet, 1982: *Biological Politics: Feminist and Anti-Feminist Perspectives*. London: Tavistock.

Sulloway, Frank, 1979: *Freud, Biologist of the Mind*. London: Burnett Books.

Whitford, Margaret, 1991: *Luce Irigaray: Philosophy in the Feminine*. London: Routledge.

NICOLA DIAMOND

bisexuality   This term has at least three current meanings, and these can easily produce confusion. As used by Darwin and his contemporaries it represented an exclusively biological notion, synonymous with hermaphroditism, and referred to the presence within an organism of male and female sexual characteristics. This meaning persists. Secondly, bisexuality denotes the co-presence in the human individual of 'feminine' and 'masculine' psychological characteristics. Thirdly, and most commonly, it is used of the propensity of certain individuals to be sexually attracted to both men and women. On the face of it, the biological and psychological senses of the term seem clearly separable. For Freud, in the 'Three essays on the theory of sexuality', it was impossible to demonstrate any close connection between physical and psychical hermaphroditism (1905, p. 142), and later writers have gone further: Charlotte Wolff, for example, claims that the two concepts have nothing to do with each other (1977, p. 246). Accounts of this kind overlook, however, the extent to which BIOLOGY provided psychoanalysis with a powerful and potentially misleading model of SEXUAL DIFFERENCE. In biology, 'male' and 'female' are indispensable descriptive categories, and, used with appropriate caution of the human and other species, they specify material differences at the chromosomal, hormonal and morphological levels. The much looser psychological and social notions 'masculine' and 'feminine' have often been expected to perform a similar specifying and clarifying role, and 'bisexuality' has been thought of as a mildly paradoxical middle region between two otherwise straightforwardly polarized sets of characteristics. 'Bisexuality', by dissolving sexual difference for a minority of sexual constitutions, has in fact often reinforced a repressive binary view of SEXUALITY at large.

'I am accustoming myself', Freud wrote to the Berlin physician Wilhelm Fliess in 1899, 'to regarding every sexual act as a process in which four individuals are involved' (Freud and Fliess, 1985, p. 364). It was under the continuous influence of Fliess in the period 1896–1904 that Freud arrived at the view that all human beings were bisexually constituted. Early on, indeed, he proclaimed Fliess as the originator of the idea and defended him against such rival claimants as Otto Weininger, in whose *Sex and Character* (1903) the idea appears prominently. By 1905, however, Freud was already offering a much more detailed and circumspect history of the term (1905, p. 143), and was conscious that the sheer variety of human sexual preferences had become a fashionable topic for the *fin-de-siècle* European intelligentsia. The excitement displayed by Freud and Fliess at the 'discovery' of bisexuality should be seen in the context of its time, a period when the foundations of the modern science of sexology were being laid by such writers as Richard von Krafft-Ebing, Havelock Ellis and Magnus Hirschfeld.

One of Freud's difficulties lay in deciding on the relationship between bisexuality and the essential concept of REPRESSION. In 'A child is being beaten' he repudiates Fliess's view that 'with men, what is unconscious and repressed can be brought down to feminine instinctual impulses; and conversely with women' (1919, p. 201). But in 'Analysis terminable and interminable' matters are much less clear-cut: Freud, while still claiming to disagree with Fliess, allows that the repression of 'the attitude proper to the opposite sex' (1937, p. 251) plays a major part in the sexual development of males and females alike. One can readily understand Freud's hesitation: if repression became too plainly sexualized along the lines sketched by Fliess it became too 'biological' and therefore deficient as a mainspring of the 'psychical apparatus'. If, on the other hand, too little attention was paid to the conspicuous biological facts of possessing or not possessing a penis, the entire oedipal scenario – centred on castration fear – was in danger of losing its explanatory power (see PRIMARY CASTRATION). The uncertainty surrounding bisexuality stayed with Freud until the end of his life. In his last book, the posthumously published *An Outline of Psycho-Analysis*, he was still looking for a psychological model of sexual difference that would approximate to the 'great antithesis' between male and female, and still hindered in his search by a psychical bisexuality which 'embarrasses all our enquiries into the subject and makes them harder to describe'. The unsatisfactory Freudian exit from this embarrassment was unchanged from the period of the 'Three Essays': 'we call everything that is strong and active male, and everything that is weak and passive female' (1940, p. 188). Freud's desperate recourse at moments like this to commonplace opinion, and to gender stereotyping of the baldest imaginable kind, has only one advantage: it reminds his reader forcibly that masculine and feminine characteristics are constructed rather than innate, that these are fashioned from an original bisexual disposition common to both sexes and that members of both sexes are the receivers of a composite and ambiguous sexual inheritance.

The OEDIPUS COMPLEX, in Freud's account, can be resolved in a number of ways, and, unresolved, can have a number of grave consequences. From within the force-field of identifications, envies, anxieties, rivalries and attachments in which the child's relations with its parents develop, a lasting capacity for, say, heterosexual object-choice is by no means a straightforward achievement. But Freud's descriptions of the standard routes by which the complex can be resolved and firm sexual identity attained have a marked normative and normalizing air: from the original bisexual condition that all humans share, male children are expected to become masculine, female children feminine and all children, in due course, heterosexual adults. HOMOSEXUALITY and bisexuality, while perfectly ordinary and intelligible as responses to the oedipal situation, are almost unthinkable in orthodox Freudian terms as satisfactory solutions to it. Freud's insistence on the constitutional bisexuality of *homo sapiens*, and on the precariousness of early sexual development, might lead one to expect from psychoanalysis a spectrum of adult sexualities, across which a variety of factors – 'masculine' and 'feminine', active and passive, homosexual and heterosexual – would be variously conjoined. In such a spectrum, adult bisexuality might be expected to occupy a privileged place, as representing an unusual equilibrium between the

28

homosexual and heterosexual passions of childhood and a fertile contact with the primal polymorphousness of human DESIRE. But in the theorizing of Freud and his followers, very few adult sexualities are held to be worthy of detailed comment, and bisexuality is not one of them: it is vastly exciting as a putative point of departure for the adventure of sexual development, but almost negligible as a destination. In his paper 'Hysterical phantasies and their relation to bisexuality' he lays down the principle that 'in psycho-analytic treatment it is very important to be prepared for a symptom's having a bisexual meaning', and he offers a fragment of case material in support of this: 'the patient pressed her dress up against her body with one hand (as the woman), while she tried to tear it off with the other (as the man)' (1908, p. 166). But in this paper, and elsewhere, bisexuality in fact often appears as a secondary theoretical theme and is presented as having very limited etiological significance in the discussion of neurotic disorders (*see* SYMPTOM).

In the work of Freudians as different from each other as Melanie KLEIN and Jacques LACAN, Freud's view of bisexuality reappears for the most part as an unexamined working assumption. On finding that thinkers as original-minded as these have little of note to say on the subject, and are so little concerned to adjust Freud's own picture, we could easily assume that bisexuality was simply not problematic enough as a clinical or theoretical topic to warrant further attention. Klein's account of ego-formation and Lacan's account of subjectivity-in-process certainly seem to work smoothly without making detailed reference to MASCULINITY, FEMININITY and the fluid zone that lies between them. The beauty of the classic Freudian 'bisexuality' is perhaps simply that it offers a neutral-seeming ground on which gender-neutral models of the psyche may be erected. For feminism, however, this neutrality has often been a sham, a protective screen placed around a thoroughly monosexual and phallocentric theoretical position. Hélène Cixous, for example, has castigated the upholders of this 'bisexuality' for granting undeserved privileges to castration fear and for being seduced by a facile denial of sexual difference. In her essay 'The laugh of the Medusa' she calls for 'another bisexuality' which would multiply 'the effects of the inscription of desire over all parts of my body and the other body, indeed, this other bisexuality doesn't annul differences, but stirs them up, pursues them, increases them' (1975, p. 254). But elsewhere in feminist thinking, the concept, far from being de-phallicized and reinvigorated in this way, has remained under suspicion. Luce IRIGARAY, in her *Parler n'est jamais neutre*, has pointed out that in a monosexual economy bisexuality is not a genuine option (1985, pp. 275–6). Her work as a whole accepts, at least for polemical purposes, the notions 'masculine' and 'feminine' as traditionally dichotomized and proceeds to a massive revaluation of the feminine.

BISEXUALITY

For many feminists in the English-speaking world, bisexuality is tactically useful – as a way of pluralizing desire and calling the phallic dispensation into question – but still has little character or urgency as a political issue. And for many radical feminists bisexuality is of interest only as a staging-post on the way towards the individual woman's full self-discovery in LESBIANISM.

There have been moments when feminist and psychoanalytic views of bisexuality seemed about to converge fruitfully. During the heyday of the Bloomsbury group, for example, Virginia Woolf produced both proto-feminist polemic and an individual strain of bisexual and transsexual literary fantasy, and she did this in an intellectual context that was unusually responsive to Freud's teaching. But in general bisexuality is one of those areas where the encounter between feminism and psychoanalysis has yet to acquire seriousness and depth. Searching discussion of the theoretical issues involved is not encouraged by those writers who have appointed themselves the harbingers of a new age of ANDROGYNY. Elisabeth Badinter, for example, writing in an optimistic post-feminist vein (1989), speaks of a historic mutation in the sexual self-awareness of the human species: a 'resemblance model' of the sexes is proposed as an alternative to a now outmoded 'complementarity model', and a wide terrain of sexual indeterminacy is presented as a newly colonizable habitat for modern men and women. Badinter's work is a *tour de force*, but the bright androgynous future she foretells seems to be an over-reaction to the sexually ambiguous idols of Euro-American popular culture and the 'New Man' recently invented by the lifestyle magazines.

Within psychoanalysis itself, a new theoretical subtlety has appeared in the work of Robert Stoller in the United States and Christian David in France. What is impressive in the work of David in particular is that, while adhering strictly to the Freudian model, he is prepared to grant unusual weight to the social construction of sexual identities. His central contention is similar to that of Badinter, who quotes him, but in articulating it he sketches an exacting new programme of psychoanalytic research which would explore the dialectical equilibrium between masculine and feminine and the ways in which the unconscious reacts to new prompting from outside (David, 1975, p. 728). The most challenging new work on bisexuality is likely to be done at the interfaces between psychoanalysis, sociology and social anthropology. The primal 'psychical bisexuality' postulated by Freud will once more become absorbing as a theoretical topic only if it is studied in a wide variety of social dispensations, and only if analysts are prepared to be fully attentive to the findings of anthropology. For feminism, in Europe and the United States, the urgent political tasks that it currently faces are likely to make bisexuality remain a side issue for some time to come: the original material from which sexualities are made may well be bisexual, and bisexual conduct may well be an option for an increasing number of individuals, but the major problem is still that of understanding and counteracting the unjust privileges that Western societies still accord to the sexuality of the heterosexual male.

See also ANTHROPOLOGY AND CROSS-CULTURAL ANALYSIS; GENDER; HETERO-SEXUALITY.

BIBLIOGRAPHY

Badinter, Elisabeth, 1989 [1986]: *Man/Woman: The One is the Other*. Trans. Barbara Wright. London: Collins Harvill.

Cixous, Hélène, 1975: 'The laugh of the Medusa', *New French Feminisms*, ed. Elaine Marks and Isabelle de Courtivron. Trans. Keith Cohen and Paula Cohen. Brighton: Harvester, 1980, pp. 245–64.

David Christian, 1975: 'Rapport sur la bisexualité psychique', *Revue française de psychanalyse*, 5–6, pp. 695–856.

Freud, Sigmund, 1905: *Three Essays in the Theory of Sexuality*, SE, 7, pp. 123–245.

Freud, Sigmund, 1908: 'Hysterical phantasies and their relation to bisexuality', *SE*, 9, pp. 157–66.

Freud, Sigmund, 1919: ' "A child is being beaten": A contribution to the study of sexual perversions', *SE*, 17, pp. 175–204.

Freud, Sigmund, 1937: 'Analysis terminable and interminable', *SE*, 23, pp. 209–53.

Freud, Sigmund, 1940: *An Outline of Psycho-analysis*, SE, 23, pp. 141–208.

Freud, Sigmund, and Fliess, Wilhelm, 1985: *The Complete Letters* (1887–1904), trans. and ed. Jeffrey Moussaieff Masson. Cambridge, Mass. and London: Harvard University Press.

Irigaray, Luce, 1985: *Parler n'est jamais neutre*. Paris: Minuit.

Stoller, Robert, 1984: *Sex and Gender*. London: Maresfield.

Weininger, Otto,1906 [1903]: *Sex and Character*. London: Heinemann.

Wolff, Charlotte, 1977: *Bisexuality: A Study*. London: Quartet.

MALCOLM BOWIE

black feminist critique of psychoanalysis   The topic here is the (im)possibility (at this point in history and discourse) of appropriating – even of deploying – either traditional or continental psychoanalytic theory for black feminist critical and theoretical practices. Even the relationship of mainstream (white) feminist practice to (either traditional or continental) psychoanalytic theory is at best problematic and at worst a *mésalliance*. In the configuration of paradigms for political, historical and social agency, and in fact for any kind of counter-hegemonic practice, the politics of race certainly complicate those of GENDER, class and sexual orientation – those categories of difference, hierarchization, discrimination, exclusion and colonization (in all senses of the term: *colonus*, colony, culture, cultivation) in contemporary material life. The woman of colour occupies the liminal area under the sutures of class, race and gender: a dispersion of subject positions at conflict with legal institutions, family, social and state policies, and cultural norms and authority.

Oedipus (the ur-paradigm of psychoanalysis) is the figure of (universal) colonization *par excellence*: the attainment of the 'subject' (itself a problematic category) in the SYMBOLIC order requires a submission (for women a resignation) to 'the father's law' (it really makes no difference within this paradigm whether or not there is a gap between the African-American father and the Lacanian name-of-the-father, as has been claimed) organized around the master signifier, the PHALLUS and/or penis, which woman lacks but desires: the classic equation of phallus=lack= law=signifier. Even though LACAN insists that the phallus is not the penis, he still fails to prevent the collapse of the master signifier into the organ. In 'The meaning of the phallus' Lacan (1982) says – and here, as usual in psychoanalytic discourse, metaphors are quite revealing – that the phallus becomes the master signifier because of its 'turgidity', which suggests the 'transmission of vital flow' in copulation. Culture and cultural authority are thus encoded as transhistorical and inevitably masculine: all signifying practices are then consigned to a monolithic quasi-divine Symbolic order (abstracted from history) that evacuates all social and historical agencies, conflicts and practices. According to Freud in *Totem and Taboo* (1913), all culture originates in patricide – a 'universal' anchored in the psyche as the famous complex: this assertion is more or less an erasure of the specificity of cultural differences in the field of history. Ironically, this text is the closest traditional psychoanalysis gets to so-called theorizing about race. And despite claims to the contrary, we await the 'necessary' heteroglossia of a contemporary discourse that bridges race, gender, psychoanalysis and history.

Psychoanalysis has not hesitated to metaphorize woman as the 'dark continent' (Africa): the figure/witch of mystery to be explored, deciphered and colonized. And recently, certain feminisms have identified the colonial as coded female and advocated the theory of woman as primarily colony (Kipnis, 1988; Echols, 1989).

One could argue that oedipalization-as-colonization would yield useful paradigms for black feminist practice. The problem here is that for psychoanalysis oedipus operates as a master (and therefore universalist) narrative. And even today, the manner of inscribing the terms 'colonization' and 'de-colonization' in certain feminist discourses seems to signify a universalized index of 'subjecthood' – in both senses of the word: 'subject of knowledge and/or power' and 'subjected to various oppressions, regimes, or forces' (*see* SUBJECT). The way the term 'de-colonization' itself is circulated by avant-garde First World (feminist) theorists through their myriad analyses elides specific political conditions and geographic and historical practices. In discussions about heterogeneity and agency and in gestures toward 'global sisterhood', most First World (white) feminist theories propose the universally colonized 'woman' subjected to 'patriarchal oppression', ignoring the specific historical, social, political and economic conditions of women of colour. The point is that women of colour occupy the double axes of the commerce between 'feminist practice' and (de-)colonization. Strictly speaking, psychoanalytic theory has a logic of necessity (everything passes through patricide, oedipus and castration) that allows for no political or social intervention or change, and also a logic of contingency that cannot theorize historical, political or social specificity: the oedipal ur-paradigm folds all of material history into a transhistorical 'family romance', and specific investments by the subject are always interpreted as imaginary dependencies on oedipus. At this point one cannot help concluding, at least provisionally, that both logics of necessity and contingency have an exchange-value rather than a use-value, for black feminist practice.

See also ANTHROPOLOGY AND CROSS-CULTURAL ANALYSIS; BLACK FEMINIST PSYCHOTHERAPY; RACE/IMPERIALISM.

BIBLIOGRAPHY

Abel, Elizabeth, 1990: 'Race, class, and psychoanalysis? Opening questions', *Conflicts in Feminism*, ed. Marianne Hirsch and Evelyn Fox Keller. New York: Routledge, pp. 184–204.

Echols, Alice, 1989: *Daring to be Bad: Radical Feminism in America 1967–1975*. Minneapolis: University of Minnesota Press.

Fraser, Nancy, 1990: 'The uses and abuses of French discourse theories for feminist politics', *Boundary 2*, 17/2, pp. 83–101.

Freud, Sigmund, 1913: *Totem and Taboo*, SE, 12, pp. 1–161.

Iginla, Biodun, 1978: 'Woman and Metaphor', *Enclitic*, 2/1, pp. 27–37.

Kipnis, Laura, 1988: 'Feminism: the political conscience of postmodernism?', *Universal Abandon? The Politics of Postmodernism*, ed. Andrew Ross, pp. 149–66.

Lacan, Jacques, 1982 [1958]: 'The meaning of the phallus', *Feminine Sexuality: Jacques Lacan and the École Freudienne*, ed. Juliet Mitchell and Jacqueline Rose. London: Macmillan, pp. 74–85.

Laclau, Ernest, and Mouffe, Chantal, 1985: *Hegemony and Socialist Strategy: Towards a Radical Democratic Politics*. London: Verso.

Leland, Dorothy, 1989: 'Lacanian psychoanalysis and French feminism: toward an adequate political psychology', *Hypatia: A Journal of Feminist Philosophy*, 3/3, pp. 81–103.

BIODUN IGINLA

black feminist psychotherapy   Black feminist psychotherapy consists of the practical application of feminist ethics and psychotherapy principles in ways which are specifically sensitive to the realistic world-view and psychological realities of black women. This presumes that any theoretical orientation used, whether feminist or combining feminist with other theoretical frameworks, incorporates an understanding of the following factors: the unique African derivatives in the cultural distinctiveness of black women; the ways and means by which those cultural derivatives have been distorted and devalued by Western historians and social scientists as well as the covert reasons for doing so; the psychological task of being bicultural in an overtly and covertly antagonistic environment, together with the subsequent development of coping mechanisms designed to enhance survival in such an environment; and the ways in which those survival tools have been pathologized by traditional mental health approaches.

The psychological realities of black women have their origins in the requirement to cope with the negative effects of historical and contemporary environments. In such environments black women are held accountable to beauty standards based on the idealized image of white females, are institutionally devalued and face the multiple effects of race, gender and sexual orientation oppression. These oppressions result from the institutionalized practices of racism, sexism, HETEROSEXISM and HOMOPHOBIA in the United States. The consequence of these practices is that black women face a unique constellation of developmental tasks and difficulties, with clearly delineated risks to their optimal development. This legacy affects black women differently than the history of sexism and other forms of discrimination affect their white counterparts.

This warrants that black feminist psychotherapy must, by definition, understand the collective plight of black women and the individual black client in the context of (1) the prevailing racial reality, which includes a familiarity with the dominant American culture's view of black women's roles as distinct from its view of white women's roles; (2) the wide range of similarities and diversities that exist within black women as a group; and (3) the individual black female client's intrapsychic and familial endowments and personal history as they are embedded in the aforementioned context. Careful analysis of the developmental interactions of these variables promotes a more accurate understanding of an individual's view of the world, her strategies for negotiating both the world and her relationships with other persons, and any contributions she makes consciously or unconsciously to her own dilemma. If successful, the black woman as a client learns to discern the parameters of the negative, racist and patriarchal boundaries which traditionally define her, and undertakes the risky and difficult task of daring to step outside them. This initiates the process by which she begins to define and value all of her selves.

Black feminist therapy is distinguished from other approaches by the imperative to maintain simultaneously an explicit Afrocentric and gynocentric focus and contextual base, to validate and also be accessible to its consumers and to explicitly require cultural literacy of its practitioners. While other psychotherapy approaches may incorporate or leave room for these imperatives in practice, they are not generally given explicit attention in their theoretical constructs.

Ideally, Black feminist psychotherapy should validate what Johnson (1979, p. 113) refers to as the 'preciousness of black women's psyches'; it should bear witness to their struggles and should facilitate the process of healing in the direction of self-discovery, self-value and empowerment.

For a detailed discussion of African cultural derivatives, clinical problems and technical interventions in inter-racial and homogeneous psychotherapy dyads with black women, the reader is referred to Greene (1986, 1992) and Comas-Diaz and Greene (1992).

See also BLACK FEMINIST CRITIQUE OF PSYCHOANALYSIS; MICHIGAN PSYCHOANALYTIC COUNCIL; RACE/IMPERIALISM; WOMEN'S THERAPY CENTRE.

BIBLIOGRAPHY

Boyd, Julia, 1990: 'Ethnic and cultural diversity in feminist therapy: keys to power', *The Black Women's Health Book: Speaking for Ourselves*, ed. Evelyn C. White. Seattle: Seal Press, pp. 226–34.

Greene, Beverly, 1986: 'When the therapist is white and the patient is black: considerations for psychotherapy in the feminist heterosexual and lesbian communities', *Women and Therapy*, 5/2–3, pp. 41–65.

Greene, Beverly, 1992: 'Still here: a perspective on psychotherapy with African American women', *New Directions in Feminist Psychology*, ed. Joan Chrisler and Doris Howard. New York: Springer, forthcoming.

Comas-Diaz, Lillian, and Greene, Beverly, eds 1992: *Women of Color and Mental Health*. New York: Guilford Publications.

Johnson, Eleanor, 1979: 'Reflections: on black feminist therapy', *Conditions, 5, The Black Women's Issue*, 5, pp. 113–17.

BEVERLY GREENE

body, the   Although psychoanalysis is largely oriented to analysis and interpretation of psychical activities, and although the psyche is generally considered to be allied with mind, and opposed to the body, Freud and a number of other psychoanalysts have devoted considerable attention to the body's role in psychical life. Freud's own background in neurology, and his pre-psychoanalytic writings, especially *Project for a*

Scientific Psychology (1895a), make explicit his fascination with finding neurophysiological and biological bases of and correlations with psychical events. Even when his neurological orientation is gradually transformed into a more properly psychological project, starting with the *Studies on Hysteria* (1895b), Freud retains a commitment to a kind of psycho-physical dualism inherited from Cartesian philosophy, in which chemical and neurological processes are neither causes nor effects of psychological processes, but are somehow correlated with them. However, in spite of an avowed commitment to dualism – Freud retained the hope that one day medical science would discover the 'chemistry' of LIBIDO, but believed it could never replace psychological investigation – there are moments in his writings when he presents an (often implicit) critique and undermining of the assumptions governing dualism. These moments of (self-)critique can be located in his notions of the sexual drives and erotogenic zones, and in his understanding of the ego.

Freud does not assume a givenness or naturalness for the body: on his understanding, the biological body is rapidly overlaid with psychical and social significance, which displaces what may once (mythically) have been a natural body. Much of Freud's work, particularly on female SEXUALITY, makes biologistic presupppositions, yet he also presents alternative accounts of a socially, historically and culturally sexed body.

Both Freud and LACAN link the genesis of the ego in primary NARCISSISM – or the mirror stage (*see* IMAGINARY) – to two distinct but complementary processes. First, the ego is the product of a series of identifications with and introjections of the image of others, most especially the mother. These images are introjected into the incipient ego as part of its ego-ideal (the ego-ideal always being a residue of the subject's identificatory idealizations of the other). Second, the ego is an effect of a re-channelling of libidinal impulses in the subject's own body. The body is thus the point of junction of the social and the individual, the hinge which divides the one from the other. The ego is formed out of a blockage of libido that, until this time, had circulated in an untrammelled, objectless, formless, pleasure-seeking way. Until around six months, the infant does not have a unified, hierarchical relation to its body. It is not yet a subject over and above its various bodily experiences; it does not yet occupy a fixed and bounded space, the barrier provided by its own skin. In Lacan's terms, the child experiences its body as disunified and disorganized, a body in bits and pieces. It is a fragmented body, not yet organized by the distinctions between inside and outside, self and other, or active and passive. Lacan describes the infant at this stage as an 'hommelette', a subject-to-be, a psychical scrambled egg whose processes remain anarchical and chaotically unintegrated.

The child gradually becomes able to distinguish the self from the other, its body from the maternal body, its insides (bounded by the skin) from the outside. At around the same time, the sexual drives begin to emerge and to distinguish themselves in their specificity, first according to the particular sites or erotogenic zones of the body (oral, anal, phallic, scopophilic, etc.) from which they emanate; and then with particular sources, aims and objects (*see* DRIVE). Only now do objects acquire a status independent of the subject who is capable of locating its objects, including its own body, in space and time. The ego is not simply a condition of the separation of subject and OBJECT or self and other; it is a product of and not a precondition for the child's relations to its own body, the other and the socio-symbolic order (see OTHER/OTHER).

The ego is the meeting-point of two different psychical processes: a process of mapping the body and the circulation of libido on to the psyche; and a process of IDENTIFICATION with the image of another (or the image of itself as an other, as occurs in the mirror stage). In *The Ego and the Id* Freud claims that the ego must be considered a 'bodily ego', a 'surface projection' of the libidinal body, which he compares with the 'cortical homunculus' described by neurophysiologists (1923, p. 126).

The ego is like an internal screen on to which the illuminated images of the body's outer surface are projected. It is not a veridical map, a photograph, but a representation of its degrees of erotogenicity, of the varying intensities of libidinal investment in different body parts. The ego is an image of the body's significance or meaning for the SUBJECT; it is as much a function of FANTASY and DESIRE as of sensation and perception. Freud illustrates this with the example of hypochondria, in which the subject's attitude to the body is not congruent with the body's physiological condition. The subject libidinally over-invests a psychically significant region of the body, withdrawing libido from the erotogenic zones.

Lacan's account of the mirror stage describes the formative effect on the child's ego of the introjection of the externalized image of the child's own body. The ego is regarded as a tracing of the subject's perceived corporeality; it is not an outline or projection of the real body, the body of anatomy and physiology, but of an 'imaginary anatomy', here following the work of the neurophysiologists on the body schema (Schilder, 1978). The imaginary anatomy is an internalized image of the meaning that the body has for the subject, for others in its social world and for its culture as a whole. It is a shared and/or individualized fantasy of the body's form and modes of operation. This, Lacan claims, helps to explain the peculiar, non-organic connections formed in HYSTERIA and in such phenomena as the phantom limb. Hysterical paralyses, for example, do not follow the structure and form of organic paralyses, but popular or everyday concepts of how the body functions (see Lacan,

1953, p. 13). In the phenomenon of the phantom limb, a limb that has been surgically removed continues to induce sensations of pain. This pain clearly cannot be located in any real anatomy, for the limb to which it refers is no longer there. The absence of a limb is in this case as psychically invested as its presence. The phantom is a form of nostalgia, a libidinal memorial to the lost limb. Similarly, the hysterical SYMPTOM also conforms to an image of anatomy and the body that may often be at odds with physiology. This is strikingly clear in the case of anorexia nervosa, in which the subject's overweight body image is discordant with the reality of the body's real under-nourishment. Indeed, as Schilder (1978) and others argue, the body image extends far beyond the subject's skin, for it includes clothing, the surrounding environment, tools and implements, and even vehicles.

Freud's and Lacan's work on the psychical representations of the body, the cortical homunculus and the body image imply that the body is a pliable 'object', one which in its very biological form is dependent on the acquisition of a psychical image for voluntary behaviour. Human subjects need the mediation of such a psychical image of the body in order to link their wishes and desires to their corporeal capacities, making concerted action and rational thought possible.

If narcissistic identification with the image of the body is one major facet of the acquisition of bodily boundaries and a sense of stable, abiding identity, the other psychical process crucial to the child's growing sense of bodily autonomy derives from the various processes of sexualization that specific zones of the body undergo. Certain parts of the child's body are more eroticized than others. This is partly a function of biological privilege (for example, the sense organs and orifices are particularly well suited to act as erotogenic zones because they are thresholds of the body's interior and its exterior, sites for the perception of the external world and the reception of information); and partly a result of the individual's life history. Freud refers to this as 'somatic compliance': there are zones of the body privileged for the reception and transmission of sexual impulses through accident and contingency. A wound or scar, a history of various organic diseases, or even family myths about body parts all render these bodily zones more susceptible to sexualization, hystericization and fantasy. In a sense, one's psychical life history is written on and worn by the body, just as, in turn, the psyche bears the history of the lived body, its chance encounters, its punctures, transformations and extensions. The child's body becomes marked, privileged, established as a whole, libidinally intensified in an uneven layer across the body's edges and surfaces. Oral, anal and phallic drives are not biologically determined stages of human development (this reduces the drive to a form of instinct), but the results of processes of libidinal intensification which correlate with the acquisition of labile meanings for various body components. The establishment of imaginary sites and locations plays a central role in the constitution of the imaginary anatomy but this libidinal process must not be confused with an identificatory relation: the libidinal site comes to function as an erotogenic rim, a loop seeking an object (or several) to fill or satisfy it. There is no limit to the number of erotic zones in and on the body, nor any way of predicting which ones will dominate an individual's life.

Psychoanalytic theory has enabled feminists and others to reclaim the body from the realms of immanence and BIOLOGY, in order to see it as a psycho-social product, open to transformations in meaning and functioning, capable of being contested and re-signified. Feminists have stressed that the generic category 'the body' is a masculinist illusion. There are only concrete bodies, bodies in the plural, bodies with a specific sex and colour. This counterbalances psychoanalysis's tendency to phallocentrism, especially the ways it understands the female body. If the female body is castrated, this is not, contrary to Freud, simply a matter of seeing. Rather, we learn how to see and understand according to prevailing systems of meaning and value, not nature. If the body is plastic, malleable and amenable to social re-inscription, this means that the female body is *a priori* capable of being seen and understood outside the notion of castrated privation. This is only one of a number of possible meanings, but the very one men and women have up to now had little possibility of refusing.

Although psychoanalysts have discussed the body and the body image, Freud and Lacan do so largely in passing. Feminists, by contrast, have long disdained analysing and theorizing the body in so far as the body was the site of PATRIARCHY's most entrenched investments and, many feminists believed, had been so contaminated that women needed to aspire to intellectual, conceptual and transcendental positions rather than to reclaim the bodies by which patriarchy had constrained them. However, more recently, spurred at least in part by psychoanalytic theory itself, feminists have sought to re-evaluate the body beyond biologistic, essentialist and universalist presuppositions. While strongly influenced by psychoanalytic theory, feminists such as IRIGARAY and Gallop develop different understandings of corporeality, although both insist on two autonomous, sexually specific models of the body. Where Gallop tends to see the female body as a site of resistance, a kind of recalcitrance to patriarchal recuperation, but thereby silenced and refused representation, Irigaray sees the female body (like the male body) as sites for the inscription of social significances. Here it is not that the female body is silenced, but rather that it is 'spoken through', produced as such, by a wide variety of forces of social representation.

BODY, THE

Where psychoanalysis has always seen the two sexes on a single model, in which the presence or absence of the PHALLUS signified one's psycho-social and sexual position, feminists have insisted on the necessity of conceiving of (at least two) distinct types of imaginary anatomy, two sexually specific types of corporeal experiences, two modes of sexuality, two points of view and sets of interests, only one of which has been explored in its own terms in our history of thought. Both negatively and positively, psychoanalysis has provided a crucial moment in the recognition of women's corporeal submersion in phallocentric models – negatively in so far as it participated in and legitimized models of female corporeality as castrated; positively in so far as its insights provide a challenge to the domination of biology in discourses of the body.

See also ESSENTIALISM; PHALLOGOCENTRISM.

BIBLIOGRAPHY

Anzieu, Didier, 1990: *A Skin For Thought: Interviews with Gilbert Tarrab.* London: Karnac Books.

Freud, Sigmund, 1895a: 'The project for a scientific psychology', *SE*, 1, pp. 295–387.

Freud, Sigmund, 1895b: *Studies on Hysteria* (with Joseph Breuer), *SE*, 2.

Freud, Sigmund, 1905: *Three Essays on the Theory of Sexuality*, *SE*, 7, pp. 123–246.

Freud, Sigmund, 1914a: 'On narcissism: an introduction', *SE*, 14, pp. 67–104.

Freud, Sigmund, 1914b: 'Instincts and their vicissitudes', *SE*, 14, pp. 109–40.

Freud, Sigmund, 1923: *The Ego and the Id*, *SE*, 19, pp. 12–59.

Gallop, Jane, 1988: *Thinking Through the Body.* New York: Columbia University Press.

Irigaray, Luce, 1985: *Speculum: Of the Other Woman*, trans. Gillian Gill. Ithaca: Cornell University Press.

Lacan, Jacques, 1953: 'Some reflections on the ego', *International Journal of Psychoanalysis*, 34, pp. 11–17.

Lacan, Jacques, 1977: 'The mirror stage as formative of the function of the I . . . ', *Écrits: A Selection*, trans. Alan Sheridan. London: Tavistock, pp. 1–7.

Schilder, Paul, 1978: *The Image and Appearance of the Human Body.* Oxford: Basil Blackwell.

Voyat, Gilbert, ed. 1984: *The World of Henri Wallon.* New York and London; Jason Aronson.

ELIZABETH GROSZ

C

castration complex   The castration complex is, in a sense, the linchpin of psychoanalytic theory. It occurs during the PRE-OEDIPAL or narcissistic stage of infantile development and is inextricably connected to the OEDIPUS COMPLEX, in that the latter marks its resolution. It is thus closely associated with psychic phenomena that emerge from the oedipus complex, such as the notion of the superego with its concomitant production of guilt from the establishment of the paternal code of laws and prohibitions, all of which are based on acknowledging the primacy of the PHALLUS. Indeed, within this theoretical model, the successful achievement of sexual maturity requires as a universal norm the acceptance of castration. In its most literal sense this means that the girl must accept her definition as inferior, because she is anatomically castrated, lacking a penis, while the boy must accept the father's castrating 'no' to his incestuous wish for the mother, i.e. must accept that he is temporarily inferior to the phallically more powerful father. In its relation to theories about BISEXUALITY and the primacy of HETEROSEXUALITY, the castration complex therefore forms the essential background for Freud's theories on FEMININITY.

At the same time, the castration complex plays an integral part in the cultural regulation of the DEATH DRIVE and of the murderous fantasies located in the UNCONSCIOUS, and in so doing comes to serve as the central source for anxieties about the threat to the ego's sense of wholeness. Thus Freud concedes that 'castration can be pictured on the basis of the daily experience of the faeces being separated from the body or on the basis of losing the mother's breast at weaning. But nothing resembling death can ever have been experienced . . . I am therefore inclined to adhere to the view that the fear of death should be regarded as analogous to the fear of castration' (1926, pp. 129–30; *and see* BODY).

Freud discovered the castration complex in his case study on little Hans (1909) and formulated the concept for the first time in 'The sexual theories of children' (1908). His basic premiss being that all infants believe that every human being has a penis, he deduces that for both sexes a narcissistic self-validation is tied to the primacy of this organ. Hence, Freud's concept centres on castration fantasies of children as these involve the riddle of anatomical sexual differences. For children, the difference between boy and girl, he argues, can only be explained on the basis of castration, as this implies the presence or 'lack' of a penis. That is to say, during this phallic phase of genital organization there is only MASCULINITY, and the option is that of either having the masculine genital or of being castrated. At the same time, the penis-as-phallus assumes a central role in the integrity of the child's self-image, and the threat of losing this privileged organ becomes coterminous with the experience of a wound to its NARCISSISM.

According to classical psychoanalytic theory, the structure and effects of the castration complex vary for boys and girls. In the case of the boy, for the idea of castration to take effect, several events must coincide: the father's threat to punish him for masturbation, the sight of the disappearance of the penis in coitus if he watches his parents (the primal scene) and, above all, the sight of the absence of a penis in the woman. The boy fears that castration will be the paternal punishment for premature sexual activity, and the woman's lack of a penis seems to signify the castrated body he fears he may become. For him, the resolution of the castration complex also marks the completion of the oedipus complex.

A crucial point in Freud's formulation is that castration serves to transmit culture. By symbolically accepting the possibility of castration, the need to renounce his mother and to accept the primacy of the father's laws, the boy subjects himself to the cultural restraints that underlie all sociation, even as he knows that he will be the heir of patriarchal law (see PATRIARCHY). He embarks on the path to 'normal' manhood. Once symbolic castration has been accepted, the threatening paternal agency is de-personalized and exchanged for fear of the superego, an anxiety which is only neurotic when exaggerated. As Freud writes, 'castration anxiety develops into moral anxiety – social anxiety' (1926, p. 139). Attempts to reject castration take on various forms of neurosis, notably FETISHISM, uncanny doubling, and acknowledged or denied HOMOSEXUALITY (see FETISHIZATION; UNCANNY.)

The girl, who may feel that she has been robbed of her penis through her mother, in turn experiences her lack as a disadvantage which she must deny, compensate or seek to repair. The crucial difference is that, while for the boy bodily castration is a FANTASY and in accepting it he symbolically defers to the father, for the girl castration is a real and irrevocable situation. For her, accepting castration means acknowledging her lack of the phallus (that is to say, the lack of social power), as well as abandoning the inferior clitoris as a source of sexual satisfaction. Resolving castration leaves her with three choices: (1) she can despise and debase the feminine body and the social position of FEMININITY, which, according to Freud, will induce neurosis; (2) she can refuse to abandon the pleasures of the clitoris and thus, again neurotically, remain arrested in the pre-oedipal phase of masculinity; or (3) she can choose the 'healthy' or 'positive' oedipus complex. This third option lets her shift her desire from mother to father, wanting his phallus (PENIS ENVY), and then, by analogy, his child, to substitute for her own lacking member, re-finding in a lover the father she can now love with impunity. While for the boy accepting castration means leaving the oedipus complex, for the girl it means securing her in this position for life.

One of the theoretical problems inherent in Freud's definition is how the castration complex can be applied to both sexes when for the girl there appears to be no threat in losing something she never possessed. Psychoanalytic theorists have thus tried to re-formulate the castration complex so as to ground it on realities other than the threat of genital loss: the fear of castration has been seen as being on a par with any traumatizing experience of loss. August Stärcke, for example, suggested that breast-feeding and the subsequent weaning of the child could be seen as the model for all later experiences of castration. This primary castration, he felt, was the only real experience which could explain its universality; the deprivation of the maternal breast could be seen as that unconscious meaning underlying all thoughts, fears and desires that eventually emerge as the castration complex. Otto Rank, in turn, seeking an even more primal source, offered the thesis that separation from the mother during the trauma of birth and the physical reactions to this separation should be seen as the model for all later anxieties. For him, the fear of castration merely translates the fear of birth.

The most useful re-formulation of the castration complex for feminist discourse comes from LACAN, who shifts the focus from BIOLOGY to differences produced for both sexes by LANGUAGE. Rather than connecting castration with the absence or presence of an organ, he uses the term to refer to alienation in language, to subjection to the symbolic codes of culture. The crucial concept underlying his thinking is that any image of unity, such as that brought about by an identification with the PHALLUS, is an apotropaic gesture against the knowledge of the real void or LACK underlying all existence. Castration refers to all prohibition, all difference that underwrites the illusion of identity, the disharmony and asymmetry of which is bound to re-emerge in subsequent separation. Castration can thus be seen as signifying a primordial lack; and this enables Lacanians such as Ellie Ragland-Sullivan to argue that 'femininity and masculinity are Oedipal interpretations of Castration' (1987, p. 24).

With such re-formulations in mind, the castration complex can be seen not only as governed by the father's phallus, but also as emerging from the child's relation to the maternal body, for that, like the penis, is the source of ego stability. Here, too, castration refers to more than the loss of the male sex organ. The mother, in her function as symbiotic organizer, represents the source of plenitude, responding to all the child's demands and providing gratuitous and endless pleasure. But she also effects the separation between the child and its source of completion, in that her absence or her rebuke threatens to damage not so much a specific organ but rather the precariously attained image of the self as a coherent and stable entity obtained during the stage of primary narcissism.

However, the feminine body comes to function as a duplicitously pivotal site for other reasons as well. Not only does the boy notice the concrete anatomical lack of an organ in the female body (a threat to his own potency), but also there is the possibility that the maternal body, hitherto perceived as full, may itself have been damaged from the start (Pollock, 1988, pp. 138–9). The cultural construction of GENDER thus uses the feminine body as its privileged sign both for what the masculine subject is not, and for what it will become if it does not subject itself to cultural interdictions. At the same time, setting up the feminine body as the castrated Other, the source of the child's disappointment and the father's interdiction, implies a dangerous paradox. For if the male child's sense of wholeness is dependent not only on its possession of the phallus but also on its identification with the PHALLIC MOTHER, the discovery of her castration puts the entire process of narcissistic self-assurance into question.

Though he never elaborates on the interconnection between the fear of castration and the fear of death, Freud himself opens the way to yet another re-formulation of his pivotal concept, which is useful for feminist discourse in that it too moves the notion of castration away from the destiny of anatomical difference and the hierarchies this implies. As Pontalis suggests, Freud's privileging of the paradigm of castration anxiety based on sexual difference may reveal his wish: 'If only the whole affair could be taken care of by Oedipus, and by a conquering of Oedipus' (Pontalis, 1978, p. 90). For one could argue that castration effects a wound to narcissism in two senses: (1) in reference to the oedipal father, whose prohibition inserts the child into the SYMBOLIC order; and (2) in reference to real loss such as the actual death of a beloved person or the fact that from birth onwards, existence is coterminous with the actual threat of dying. Hence, the subject is also castrated in the real sense that growing means degeneration.

For a feminist discussion, there is a gain in rejecting the gendered concept of castration (in its contingency on the phallus), and adopting instead a concept of castration that refers to the fact of human mortality. Were the navel rather than the genitals to become the anatomical sign of lack (in the sense of losing the primordial mother at birth and the sense that each living body is inscribed with mortality), this would allow for the theoretical primacy of a non-gendered moment of loss: it would represent death's ubiquitous castrating threat to the subject, over and above both the lack of an organ and any alienation in language (Bronfen, 1989). Notions of domination and inferiority based on gender difference can then be shown to be secondary to a more global and non-individuated disempowerment before death.

See also BODY; PRIMARY CASTRATION; REAL; SEXUAL DIFFERENCE.

BIBLIOGRAPHY

Bronfen, Elisabeth, 1989: 'The lady vanishes: Sophie Freud and *Beyond the Pleasure Principle*', *South Atlantic Quarterly*, 88, pp. 961–91.

Freud, Sigmund, 1908: 'The sexual theories of children', *SE*, 9, pp. 205–26.

Freud, Sigmund, 1909: 'Analysis of a phobia in a five-year-old boy', *SE*, 10, pp. 3–150.

Freud, Sigmund, 1926: *Inhibitions, Symptoms and Anxiety, SE*, 20, pp. 75–176.

Kovel, Joel, 1985: 'The castration complex reconsidered', *Women and Analysis: Dialogues on Psychoanalytic Views of Femininity*, ed. Jean Strouse. Boston: G. K. Hall, pp. 136–43.

Pollock, Griselda, 1988: 'Woman as sign: psychoanalytic readings', *Vision and Difference: Femininity, Feminism and the Histories of Art*. London: Routledge, pp. 120–54.

Pontalis, J.-B., 1978: 'On death-work in Freud, in the self, in culture', *Psychoanalysis, Creativity, and Literature*, ed. Alan Roland. New York: Columbia University Press, pp. 85–95.

Ragland-Sullivan, Ellie, 1987: *Jacques Lacan and the Philosophy of Psychoanalysis*. Urbana: University of Illinois Press.

Stärcke, August, 1921: 'The castration complex', *International Journal of Psychoanalysis*, 2, pp. 179–83.

ELISABETH BRONFEN

Chodorow, Nancy Julia (*b*. New York, 20 January 1944). Nancy Chodorow is perhaps the best known author in the United States on the relationship between psychoanalysis and feminism. Her book *The Reproduction of Mothering: Psychoanalysis and the Sociology of Gender* (1978) signalled a paradigmatic shift in American feminist thinking with respect to the contribution of psychoanalysis to feminism, the underlying causes of women's oppression, differential development in boys and girls, and the reasons for women's desire to bear and rear children. In this work she introduced OBJECT-RELATIONS THEORY to American readers, to most of whom the work of Winnicott, Fairbairn, Guntrip and others was unknown.

As a sociologist and as a recently trained psychoanalyst, Chodorow argues against biologism, the ESSENTIALISM of Lacanian feminism, and the drive theory of both Freud and KLEIN. As a self-proclaimed 'object-relations feminist', the focus of her work has been on the development of self through relationship to others, and the conscious and unconscious experience of negotiating separation and connection in this development. Her writings privilege the PRE-OEDIPAL mother–child relationship as critical to the construction of self, in contrast to the Freudian and Lacanian focus on the primacy of oedipal phenomena and the role of the PHALLUS.

Chodorow is most commonly identified with her account of how women's universal responsibility for mothering creates asymmetrical relational capacities in girls and boys. Because of being mothered by someone of the same GENDER, girls, Chodorow argues, develop more fluid or permeable ego boundaries than boys, and a sense of self that is continuous with others. This sense of self-in-relationship and need for connection to others in turn underlies the desire to mother. By contrast, boys develop their sense of self in opposition to the mother through the establishment of more rigid ego boundaries and often a defensive denigration of that which is feminine or associated with the mother. Extrapolating from this developmental schema, Chodorow identifies men's fear of the pre-oedipal mother and of losing their sense of MASCULINITY as fuelling male dominance in society.

While her work has been criticized for being both overly deterministic in its reliance on the explanatory value of women's mothering and insufficiently attentive to differences among women, Chodorow, more than any other author, has been responsible for introducing psychoanalytic ideas into the heart of the feminist theoretical project in the United States. Although she has attained little visibility within the psychoanalytic establishment, her work has been widely influential among feminists in the humanities and social sciences, academics writing on gender and feminist psychotherapists.

See also AUTONOMY; MOTHER–DAUGHTER RELATIONSHIP; MOTHERHOOD; OBJECT-RELATIONS CRITICISM; PSYCHICAL REALITY; SCIENCE; WOMEN'S PSYCHOLOGICAL DEVELOPMENT.

WRITINGS

1978: *The Reproduction of Mothering: Psychoanalysis and the Sociology of Gender.* Berkeley: University of California Press.
1989: *Feminism and Psychoanalytic Theory.* New Haven: Yale University Press.

BIBLIOGRAPHY

Abel, Elizabeth, ed. 1982: *Writing and Sexual Difference*. Chicago: Chicago University Press.

Balbus, Issac, 1982: *Marxism and Domination*. Princeton: Princeton University Press.

Keller, Evelyn Fox, 1985: *Reflections on Gender and Science*. New Haven: Yale University Press.

O'Brien, Sharon, 1987: *Willa Cather: The Emerging Voice*. Oxford: Oxford University Press.

ILENE PHILIPSON

clinical perspectives   Although feminist therapy is now a burgeoning branch of therapeutic practice, particularly in the USA, clinicians as a group including many women (see Chodorow, 1989; Segal, 1990) are traditionally suspicious of feminism, in so far as political views are thought to be neurotic in origin, and therefore case material in the consulting room where the analyst aspires to be neutral and 'value-free'. Feminists have challenged the possibility of complete neutrality. If one group considers feminism as 'masculine protest', the other argues that 'normal' femininity may be pathogenic too. Clinicians sympathetic to feminism point out that analysts themselves are in theoretical disagreement over numerous issues. Since different theoretical accounts lead to different clinical interventions, these are not just academic questions (see Person, 1990).

Chodorow (1989) identifies three main types of response to the women's movement: first, the desire to exclude *any* non-analytic considerations; secondly, the resurgence of interest among orthodox psychoanalysts in questions of women's psycho-sexuality and psychology; thirdly, extensive theoretical revision, especially in the so-called 'cultural' schools of psychoanalysis. The theoretical pioneers belong in many cases to the generation of women who were feminists before they became practitioners: Jessica BENJAMIN, Nancy CHODOROW, Juliet MITCHELL. Other prominent feminist psychoanalysts write from a more clinical perspective: these include Jean Baker Miller, Carol Nadelson, Malkah Notman, Ethel Spector Person and Teresa Bernardez (see also the contributors to Alpert, 1986 and Bernay and Cantor, 1986).

There are a number of interconnected clinical issues affected by the feminist analysis of society, all related to the claim that psychoanalysis is not insulated from the rest of the world. Orthodox psychoanalysis focuses primarily on internal or intrapsychic conflicts. The environmental and cultural context that has produced them is often considered

47

irrelevant. However, the social changes in women's roles over the past century have had an effect on psychoanalytic evaluations. Women's desire to work, for example, may now be seen as a legitimate striving for growth and AUTONOMY (not to mention a response to economic necessity), and not simply as a defensive response to PENIS ENVY. Similarly, feminism could affect the analyst's perceptions of social reality, and by extension the diagnosis of what counts as pathology. Ethel Spector Person points out that 'some problems, experienced in terms of personal distress or shortcomings derive not from unconscious conflict or personal inadequacies but from pressing external circumstances' (Person, 1986, p. 136). The failure of psychoanalysis to take into account the extent to which present social structures limit a woman's real choices can lead to unhelpful clinical interventions (*see also* RAPE: POLITICAL PERSPECTIVES).

Feminist psychoanalysts point out that cultural stereotypes have an effect on psychoanalytic models and as a result on analytic interpretations. An analyst whose analysand conforms closely to cultural stereotypes may not investigate far enough, and may fail to see the neurotic reasons underlying the conformity. Conversely, the analyst who feels that the patient's responses (such as anger and aggression) are unfeminine may have difficulty in recognizing them, eliciting them or accepting their legitimacy. If the analyst does not take into account the cultural devaluation of women, interpretations run the risk of reinforcing a woman's own lack of self-esteem (Lerner, 1988). Or the analyst may be constrained by normative ideas of the role of MOTHERHOOD. Feminists have also been responsible for some re-thinking of clinical attitudes towards HOMOSEXUALITY. Increased awareness of the importance of the PRE-OEDIPAL period is leading to tentative revision of the theory and practice of analysis *vis-à-vis* homosexual object-choice (see Eisenbud in Alpert 1986; but *see also* LESBIANISM: CLINICAL PERSPECTIVES).

GENDER was previously not considered a crucial variable in the transference. The feminist account has highlighted questions of gender in the analytic encounter, and the way in which the male analyst/female analysand pair may re-enact the roles and stereotypes of male–female relationships in the wider society, and reinforce existing patterns of dominance and submission, autonomy and dependence (Lerner, 1988). Person (1989, ch. 10) points out that male analysts are more likely than female analysts to seduce their patients. The dynamic of the erotic transference depends on the gender of analyst and analysand. The male analyst may develop an intensely strong countertransference to a female patient, whereas a male patient with a female analyst may sometimes have difficulty forming an erotic transference at all (Person, 1989, ch. 10; see also discussion in Gornick, 1986). Lisa Gornick's discussion of transferential issues argues that 'the case of the woman therapist and the male patient throws into relief the ways in which psychoanalytic method relies on male authority, and suggests that for the woman practitioner, the therapeutic process needs to be conceptualised in new terms' (p. 282) (see also essays on transference and counter-transference in Bernay and Cantor, 1986).

Psychoanalysts influenced by feminism display on the whole a vivid awareness that new conflicts for both men and women may arise when social norms are in transition. They see their role as helping their patients to understand the psychic sources of the conflict rather than imposing choices or a way of life; at the same time, they recognize that they are not themselves immune from such conflicts.

See also BLACK FEMINIST PSYCHOTHERAPY; IRIGARAY; MICHIGAN PSYCHOANALYTIC COUNCIL; WOMEN'S THERAPY CENTRE.

BIBLIOGRAPHY

Alpert, Judith, ed. 1986: *Psychoanalysis and Women: Contemporary Reappraisals.* Hillsdale, NJ: Analytic Press.

Baruch, Elaine Hoffman, and Serrano, Lucienne J., eds. 1988: *Women Analyze Women: In France, England and the United States.* New York and London: Harvester-Wheatsheaf.

Bernay, Toni, and Cantor, Dorothy W., eds 1986: *The Psychology of Today's Woman: New Psychoanalytic Visions.* Hillsdale, NJ: Analytic Press.

Chasseguet-Smirgel, Janine, et al. eds 1970: *Female Sexuality: New Psychoanalytic Views.* Ann Arbor: University of Michigan Press.

Chodorow, Nancy J., 1989: *Feminism and Psychoanalytic Theory.* Cambridge: Polity Press (esp. chs 8, 9, 10).

Eisenbud, Ruth-Jean, 1986: 'Lesbian choice: transferences to theory', Alpert, 1986, pp. 215–33.

Gornick, Lisa K., 1986: 'Developing a new narrative: the woman therapist and the male patient', Alpert, 1986, pp. 257–86.

Lerner, Harriet Goldhor, 1988: *Women in Therapy.* Northvale, NJ: Jason Aronson.

Miller, Jean Baker, ed. 1973: *Psychoanalysis and Women.* Harmondsworth: Penguin.

Person, Ethel Spector, 1986: 'Working mothers: impact on the self, the couple and the children', Bernay and Cantor, 1986, pp. 121–38.

Person, Ethel Spector, 1989: *Love and Fateful Encounters.* London: Bloomsbury.

Person, Ethel Spector, 1990: 'The influence of values in psychoanalysis: the case of female psychology', Zanardi, 1990, pp. 305–25.

Segal, Hanna, 1990: 'Hanna Segal interviewed by Jacqueline Rose', in *Women: A Cultural Review*, 1/2, pp. 198–214.

Zanardi, Claudia, ed. 1990: *Essential Papers on the Psychology of Women.* New York: New York University Press.

MARGARET WHITFORD

49

clitoral hermeneutics   Though the term clitoral hermeneutics may not refer to a broadly recognized tendency or school within feminist psycho-analysis, one can none the less pinpoint the articulation of this expression in an essay by Naomi Schor entitled 'Female paranoia: the case for psychoanalytic feminist criticism' (Schor, 1981). Taking as her point of departure the critique of Freud's famous definition of the clitoris as a 'little penis' (Freud, 1933) or as an inadequate phallic projection in paranoid women (Freud, 1911), Schor notes that even feminist theorists such as Julia KRISTEVA and Luce IRIGARAY, concerned to redress the lacunae of masculinist psychoanalysis, have privileged a vaginal rather than a clitoral model of feminine JOUISSANCE. Schor credits Kristeva and Irigaray with the discovery of the female body as a material locus of semiosis – a positive site of theorization for feminist definitions of female SEXUALITY – but she criticizes them all the same for not having done enough to counter the historic devaluation of the clitoris. Irigaray, one could argue in response, has not so much under-appreciated the clitoris as she has chosen to accord a regime of interpretability to all female erogenous zones: from the vaginal lips which respond to each other to the non-localized, disseminated sensations of secretion and touch, a plurality of pleasures is construed. The clitoral hermeneutic emerges as inseparable from a hermeneutic of the female body as a non-totalized, pleasure-ready entity of surfaces and depths.

Schor eludes a reductive oppositionalism between clitoral and vaginal theories of female PLEASURE by equating the clitoris with the *detail* within the feminist body's figuration of corporeal literacy, that is, its theoretically transparent strategies for reading itself pleasurably. In her words, 'the clitoral school of feminist theory might then be identified by its practice of a hermeneutics focused on the detail, which is to say on those details of the female anatomy which have been generally ignored by male critics and which significantly influence our reading of the texts in which they appear' (1981, p. 216). As a poetic of the as yet unseen or ignored, clitoral hermeneutics thus emerges as the not-so-distant cousin of a feminist unconscious, de-repressed and made visible in a flash of interpretive insight or, alternatively, assimilated to a hitherto taboo lesbian erotics. *Qua* detail, the textually re-presented clitoris also comes to be associated with a repertory of images historically used to represent femininity: ornament, jewels, trinkets, make-up and masks.

Another approach to defining clitoral hermeneutics, one which corrects its Eurocentrically psychoanalytic and textual determination by means of the wider lens of cultural studies, is suggested by Gayatri Chakravorty Spivak (1981). Arguing that 'at least symbolic clitoridectomy has always been the "normal" accession to womanhood and the unacknowledged name of motherhood' (p. 181), Spivak recognizes none the less that in de-legitimating this real and symbolic practice, one falls inadvertently into the ideological trap of an 'inbuilt colonialism of First World feminism toward the Third' (p. 184). Spivak's emphasis on the controversial status of global clitoridectomy within feminist discourse implicitly calls for a reading of its psychosymbolic complexities in a wider material, political and cultural context.

BIBLIOGRAPHY

Freud, Sigmund, 1911: 'Psycho-analytic notes on an autobiographical account of a case of paranoia (dementia praecox)', SE, 12, pp. 1–84.
Freud, Sigmund, 1933: 'Femininity', SE, 22, pp. 112–35.
Gallop, Jane, 1989: 'The monster in the mirror: the feminist critic's psychoanalysis', Feminism and Psychoanalysis, ed. Richard Feldstein and Judith Roof. Ithaca, NY: Cornell University Press, pp. 13–24.
Schor, Naomi, 1981: 'Female paranoia: the case for psychoanalytic feminist criticism', Yale French Studies, 62, pp. 204–19.
Spivak, Gayatri Chakravorty, 1981: 'French feminism in an international frame', Yale French Studies, 62, pp. 154–84.

EMILY APTER

D

death drive (Freud)   In his late writings, Freud repeatedly addressed the question of how the ego responds to the phenomenon of fragmentation, destruction and decay. Though recognizing the certainty and inevitability of death, the ego nevertheless strives to circumvent the irrevocability of mortality by assuring itself that life can be preserved against the inevitability of dissolution (Freud, 1916). Thus the fear of annihilation, much like the fear of separation, is one of the most basic primal anxieties in forming human existence. It elicits a massive gesture towards self-preservation in an effort to conquer or at least control death.

Psychoanalysis locates death in several registers of the psychic apparatus. For one, the fatality of human bodily existence – decay and decomposition – demonstrates the way death gains presence in life in the realms of the real. For another, death is also articulated in the pure destructive force of the UNCONSCIOUS, that needs to be 'constrained' if any social or personal existence is to be upheld. An articulation of death in this psychic register involves an outwardly directed sadism or an inwardly directed MASOCHISM. At the same time, since culture, in order to support the interests of the group, must protect itself against the violence of real, natural materiality, as well as against destructive impulses originating from its individual members, Freud also locates an aspect of the death drive at the heart of guilt, in the subject's relation to cultural norms and laws. The superego functions as an agency that authorizes each individual to subject him- or herself to the interdictions of the community's laws. Yet – in one of Freud's many paradoxical turns during his elaboration of this theory – when the superego imposes too thoroughly on the ego's self-preservation, the result can be a 'pure culture of the death drive' (1923, p. 52).

Finally, death is also always implicated in the subject's narcissistically informed desire for PLEASURE. The subject's imaginary desire is most pronouncedly expressed in fantasies of wholeness and security gained by an appropriation of the beloved, modelled along the lines of the infant–mother dyad. Yet, as Freud (1920) argues, this sense of integral being is also reminiscent of a pre-natal stasis of inanimation and is thus a radical contradiction of the change and tension which constitutes life. At the same time, as LACAN has so insistently suggested, all self-constructions are illusions, based on an originary void, the experience of birth as loss, and are thus inextricably informed by another kind of death, namely that very LACK which they are meant to occlude. The death drive thus refers both to a reduction of tensions as a return to an initial inanimate state before life and also to that force which fragments, castrates and separates unities. Not only can the self be constructed only over an experience of division, but its preservation is contingent on preventing a short-circuit that would lead to a premature end, by means of repeated substitution and difference. Death, the opposite of life, emerges as its ground, its vanishing point *and* its sustaining force (*see* DEATH DRIVE (LACAN)).

Freud's introduction into psychoanalytic vocabulary of the opposition between a 'death drive' (*thanatos*) and the life drives (*eros*) proved controversial, and was denounced by his peers as being unscientific, untenable and unnecessary. Though issues of femininity are not directly at stake in his formulation of this concept, one implicit connection emerges from the fact that both 'death' and 'woman' function as Western culture's privileged tropes for the enigmatic and for alterity.

The analogy runs as follows: like the death drive, which articulates that death is not outside but rather inextricably inhabiting life, FEMININITY also is not a reassuringly canny opposite to MASCULINITY, but rather is inside the masculine, inhabiting it as 'otherness, as its own disruption' (Felman, 1981, p. 41). As manifestations of such a force of oscillation, both death and femininity not only call into question rigid categories, but also mark the absence of a fixed place within culture. They function as the foundation and condition of culture's representational systems, as *telos* and origin, yet themselves exist nowhere as reference for this representation (de Lauretis, 1984, p. 13).

It is worth summarizing Freud's arguments in 'Beyond the pleasure principle' (1920), his thanatogenic narration about the way that death comes into the world. Seeking to discover a function of the psychic apparatus that is beyond, i.e. more original than and independent of, the dominating pleasure principle, Freud's general assumption is that psychic processes are inscribed by a principle of constancy. Spurred on by an unpleasurable tension, their trajectory is a lowering of this tension, so that the most fundamental aim, he claims, is the avoidance of unpleasure or the production of pleasure. Pleasure and unpleasure are each understood as a quantity of excitation that is present in the mind but is not in any 'bound', and their interrelation is such that unpleasure corresponds to an increase, and pleasure to a diminution, in the quantity of excitation. Forced to recognize that the majority of mental processes are not accompanied by pleasure, Freud postulates a tendency towards the pleasure principle, which is, however, perpetually inhibited. Furthermore, because unrestrained pleasure, aimed only at individual self-preservation, would be ineffectual and dangerous for the collective social group, the reality principle dictates a deferral of pleasure and a limited tolerance of unpleasure (*see* DRIVE).

Attempting to delineate a function in the psychic apparatus which overrides this psychic dialectic of pleasure and self-preservation, Freud begins by discussing the origin of trauma. Traumas mark moments when the state of constancy cannot be attained and the ego's defences break down because the psychic apparatus, in a state of low cathexis, is unable to bind the dangerous, external energies. The result is a compulsion to return mentally to the situation in which the trauma occurred, in an endeavour to master the external stimuli retrospectively by producing the anxiety which will allow a psychic binding of these dangerous stimuli. It is in this compulsion to repeat experiences that cannot be contained within the dialectic play of pleasure/unpleasure that Freud tries to locate the 'beyond' of this system.

However, because the drives in the primary process are freely mobile, and need to be translated into bound drives in the secondary process, Freud distinguishes between the dominance of the pleasure principle and its subordination to the mastering or binding of excitations. The notion of repetition forms the crux of his argument. In an attempt to differentiate the repetition staged by the *fort–da* game of his grandson and the compulsive repetition of traumatized patients (1920, p. 35), Freud sees the former as a process of mastery, working on the level of secondary, bound processes, with repetition affording a pleasurable sense of identity; he sees the latter as instinctual, working on the premiss that experiences remain unbound.

To explain the connection between the 'instinctual' and the 'repetition compulsion', Freud offers a definition of drives that is clearly derived from his thanatogenic interest – 'an instinct is an urge, inherent in organic life, to restore an earlier state' (1920, p. 36). To define drives as an expression of the 'conservative nature' of all living organisms stands in seeming opposition to two tendencies Freud had previously ascribed to the economy of the psychic apparatus – a striving for self-preservation or immortality and instinctual repetition as an urge towards new formations and progress. Yet Freud pursues the notion of constancy in order to conclude that the aim of life cannot be a state never before attained but rather must be that initial state from which the living organism departed at birth and towards which it returns. Freud thus introduces a second paradox: even as the ego disavows its own mortality the primary processes are governed by conservative instincts that strive to return to a pre-animate state.

In 'The theme of the three caskets', Freud significantly connects femininity with the need to acknowledge mortality. In countless myths, the choice of the last of three women, surpassing the other two because she is most beautiful, coincides with the choice of death in a highly ambivalent form of wish-fulfilment (1913). Indeed, his decoding of the three objects of choice with which man is faced – 'the mother herself, the beloved who is chosen after her pattern, and finally the Mother Earth who receives him again' – can be read as a gender-oriented commentary on the thanatogeny, based on repetition and return, which he develops in *Beyond the Pleasure Principle* (1913, pp. 299, 301).

For Freud, repetition and death are connected with only such values as quiescence, stability, constancy. Repetition is seen as a move to an earlier position – the moment initiating each trauma and, in a more general sense, the initial point of transgression from an inanimate to an animate state. The satisfaction that repetition, informed by the death drive, affords is that it serves as a fulfilment of two fundamental desires: for an absence of tension and for the re-finding of lost wholeness. If we recall that the finding of a love-object is, in fact, a re-finding of the lost maternal body, another connection between the death drive and femininity emerges. The return to a prior state involves the maternal body in a threefold sense: as the real material body lost with birth, as the fiction of a whole body that the PHALLIC MOTHER represents during primary narcissism and in the image of which surrogate love-objects are chosen, and as trope for the dust to which the human being is forced to return.

Yet repetition can be located on the side of the sexual drives as well, given that it also refers to those processes that aim at fragmentation in an effort to achieve new forms. It is precisely in the two concepts 'tension' and 'desire for wholeness' that a second interconnection between death and repetition emerges, which involves difference and the detour deferring finality. For the sexual drives preserve life in the form of destruction and division, that is, by rupturing existing unions, disturbing the life-threatening short-circuit of stasis and creating new entities by virtue of transformation.

If the first type of repetition (stasis) works on the rhetorical premiss of tautology, striving for a transparent, identical relation between signifier and signified, the latter (rupture) involves difference, for it informs all moments of 'doubleness', of turning 'back' to some place or someone, or of repeating 'again'. That is to say, where the former transfers the unsteady, inconstant body back into a stabilized and static 'other' state, the latter transforms unstable material into new states, on the basis of destruction, in an effort at partial re-binding and re-stabilizing of the psychic apparatus, at re-contributing new energies. By implication, the notion so central to the sexual drives, namely castration, is also perceived as an analogue of death (Freud, 1923, p. 59). The first form of repetition sees death as a retrieval of lost wholeness and stability beyond life (figured in the maternal body before birth or the phallic mother), and thus supports NARCISSISM, implying that in its extreme form, as the myth shows, the exclusive desire for one's self ends in the stasis of death. The second form of repetition posits an expression of death in the form of dismemberment, in the disruption of any illusory stability afforded by narcissism, in the anxiety of losing any of the precious images or signifiers substituting for wholeness.

To point to a final link between Freud's concept of the death drive and issues of gender, one could evoke the cultural convention that the mother's gift of birth is also the gift of death, and that the embrace of the beloved also signifies a dissolution of the self. Woman functions as privileged trope for the uncanniness of unity and loss, of independent identity and self-dissolution, of the pleasure of the body and its decay. It is not without significance that Freud ends his speculative discourse on death by turning directly to poetry – to Aristophanes' tale about the androgynous origin of human sexuality (*see* ANDROGYNY). From this tale Freud concludes that while the prior state towards which the animate existence is driven is that of material death, the one it longs for is that of sexual wholeness. Birth thus inaugurates two moments of difference that mark a lack of wholeness: life, with death inscribed at its centre, and gender division, with femininity inhabiting masculinity. The challenge posed by Freud's formulation of a death drive resides in the fact that he ultimately binds all desire, whether sexual, aggressive or melancholic, to a desire for death. Given that woman is culturally constructed as the object of a plethora of contradictory desires, the death drive and the drive for femininity are readily aligned. At the same time, the radical subversion of fixed categories that are inherent to notions of the death drive also readily translates into the argumentative concerns of feminist theory.

BIBLIOGRAPHY

de Lauretis, Teresa, 1984: *Alice Doesn't: Feminism, Semiotics, Cinema.* Bloomington: University of Indiana Press.

Felman, Shoshona, 1981: 'Rereading femininity', *Yale French Studies*, 62, pp. 19–44.

Freud, Sigmund, 1913: 'The theme of the three caskets', *SE*, 12, pp. 289–301.

Freud, Sigmund, 1915: 'Thoughts for the times on war and death', *SE*, 14, pp. 273–302.

Freud, Sigmund, 1916: 'On transience', *SE*, 14, pp. 303–7.

Freud, Sigmund, 1920: *Beyond the Pleasure Principle, SE*, 18, pp. 1–64.

Freud, Sigmund, 1923: *The Ego and the Id, SE,* 19, pp. 1–66.

Freud, Sigmund, 1933: *New Introductory Lectures on Psychoanalysis, SE,* 22, pp. 1–183.

Laplanche, Jean, 1976: *Life and Death in Psychoanalysis,* trans. Jeffrey Mehlman. Baltimore: Johns Hopkins University Press.

Rose, Jacqueline, 1989: 'Where does the misery come from? Psychoanalysis, feminism and the event', *Feminism and Psychoanalysis,* ed. Richard Feldstein and Judith Roof. Ithaca: Cornell University Press, pp. 25–39.

ELISABETH BRONFEN

death drive (Lacan) Lacan's re-interpretation of Freud's thoughts on the death drive (*see* DEATH DRIVE (FREUD)) went through three different periods (*see* LACAN). In the first period, Lacan theorized clinical treatment as an intersubjectivity of the word reaching out to the other for recognition. The premiss of this theory is that LANGUAGE uses us to try to *re*-find the unificatory oneness of infantile pleasures lost in the deferral of *re*-presenting the thing (Lacan, 1977a). Symptoms were seen as non-symbolized parts of a subject's history to be integrated into the SYMBOLIC via the telling of a narrative or the recognition of Other DESIRE. In Lacan's re-reading of Freud on the *Wiederholungszwang* (repetition compulsion), it is not bad memories from inadequate parenting that are repeated in adult behaviour, but a piece of life retained and re-lived as *inertia* where memory has been unable to assimilate.

In the second period of Lacan's evolving theory of the death drive, the accent shifts from speech to language as a synchronic structure, a sense-less, mechanistic automaton, which produces nonsensical meaning as its effect. Lacan has shifted from a phenomenological view of language to a structuralist one, wherein language is a differential system of elements (Lacan, 1977b). The death drive is identified as a mask of the Symbolic order, covering over the fact that the SUBJECT is not there as a presence but lives in the Symbolic as a discontinuity (Miller, 1985–6: (unpublished)). As he elaborated his theory of the death drive in the 1950s and 1960s, Lacan conceptualized the 'second death', the first being the animal death of the body. In Lacan's theory of the second death the subject is eclipsed behind the signifier, thus being castrated or alienated within the language imposed on the biological organism. Henceforth language is not spoken *by* the subject, but 'speaks' the subject.

In his third period of re-thinking the death drive, Lacan hypothesized that the Other has a traumatic element at its very centre, an irreducible kernel which each person is unable to relinquish. Infant life is character-ized by losing 'objects', the breast, daytime voices, the mother's familiar face, and so on. Lacan argues that the subject is constituted from this paradox: objects with which infants identify were never possessed in the first place, and were always already radically lost. Yet, loss is at the heart of language, being, representations, desire and BODY, and thus the death drive – JOUISSANCE effects that coalesce around loss – is central to life. The *objet a* is any filler of a void in being, which, because of its indispensable function in filling up that void, quickly provides a consistency, palpable in repetitions. We pursue objects which sustain our fantasies, but the origins of FANTASY or experience are unknown and can only ever be encountered as a boundary beyond which nothing can be said. We never become one with the OBJECT desired in a way that eradicates the void. Even those things that give PLEASURE in a first moment give reality or 'death' in a second moment of repetition (Lacan, 1986). That is, repetition, by definition, can never re-find the same pleasure. For Lacan, the 'end' of analysis was to identify the object of fundamental fantasy as whatever idealizes or seems to fill out a lack in the Other, and to let it go.

Lacan's re-definition of fantasy as a cover over the void that inserts death into life is of a piece with his emphasis on the REAL as that which gives rise to culture out of the fundamental lack of a 'sexual rapport' (Lacan, 1975). This Lacanian theory has been read literally by post-structuralist feminists who have taken Lacan to mean that people do not have sexual relations (Jardine, 1985, p. 163). Rather, Lacan links the idea of an unbridgeable void between the sexes (usually denied or idealized) to a death drive in culture which he attributes to an impossibility of Oneness in any union, be it of a couple, of a group, or between oneself and the object sought to give a pleasure of constancy.

'Beyond the pleasure principle' (Freud, 1920) lies a mortified enjoyment, or *jouissance*, by which the death drive can be related to the Real. Lacan argued that the Real bespeaks loss as traumatic material that cannot drop out of memory, nor assimilate itself to fantasy or thought. But how are we to recognize this Real which is 'not there'? By the *jouissance* effects that place rigidity, negative affects, painful impasses, in our lives as absolutes, things we cannot change by willpower or concentrated efforts. Feminism has not yet grappled with this aspect of Lacan, except in so far as the Real has been dismissed. Following the lead of French intellectuals, philosophers and feminists such as Derrida, Lyotard, Deleuze, Guattari, Cixous, Kofman and others, many feminists have accepted post-structuralist notions of Lacan as a phallocrat, one who spoke a master discourse.

In fact, Lacan's reading of the death drive as a desire to repeat patterns by which one hopes to achieve *jouissance*, leading to endless repetitions of finite desire, is a more useful theory for feminists than Freud's (Lacan, 1977c, ch. 4, pp. 42–52).

Woman is man's symptom, Lacan argued, but not the reverse, because gender fictions are not taken on symmetrically (Ragland-Sullivan, 1991). Moreover, the male's attachment to the mother as a primary object – which is lost, was never possessed, but which he tries to retain or find in relations to other women – gives feminists a way to re-think masculinist aggressivity, desire and the quest for *jouissance* as a guarantee for living against the death effects of loss. At the very place where the male subject is suffering the greatest loss, he creates the fantasy which enables him to persist with his Imaginary identity.

The value of this idea for feminism, therefore, lies in its potential to explain male aggression that causes female suffering. Both are controlled by unconscious fantasies, whose function is to hide the palpable void of nothingness and meaninglessness – death – at the centre of apparent meaning or appearance.

See also OTHER/OTHER; SYMPTOM.

BIBLIOGRAPHY

Freud, Sigmund, 1920: *Beyond the Pleasure Principle*, SE, 18, pp. 1–64.

Jardine, Alice, 1985: *Gynesis*. Ithaca: Cornell University Press.

Lacan, Jacques, 1975: *Le Séminaire*, book 20: *Encore*, ed. Jacques-Alain Miller. Paris: Seuil.

Lacan, Jacques, 1977a [1953]: 'The function and field of speech and language in psychoanalysis', *Écrits: A Selection*, trans. Alan Sheridan. London: Tavistock, 1977, pp. 30–113.

Lacan, Jacques, 1977b [1957]: 'The agency of the letter in the unconscious or reason since Freud', *Écrits*, pp. 146–78.

Lacan, Jacques, 1977c [1964]: *The Four Fundamental Concepts of Psychoanalysis*, ed. Jacques-Alain Miller, trans. Alan Sheridan. London: Hogarth Press.

Lacan, Jacques, 1986: *Le Séminaire*, book 7: *L'Éthique de la psychanalyse*, ed. Jacques-Alain Miller. Paris: Seuil.

Miller, Jacques-Alain, 1985–6: *Extimité*. (His course for the year, unpublished.)

Miller, Jacques-Alain, 1989: 'To interpret the cause: from Freud to Lacan', *Newsletter of the Freudian Field*, 3, Nos 1 and 2, pp. 30–50.

Ragland-Sullivan, Ellie, 1991: 'The sexual masquerade: a Lacanian theory of sexual difference', *Lacan and the Subject of Language*, ed. Ellie Ragland-Sullivan and Mark Bracher. New York: Routledge, pp. 49–80.

ELLIE RAGLAND-SULLIVAN

depression Epidemiological research in Spain and the United States has arrived at the conclusion that twice as many women as men suffer from depression (Boyd and Weissmann, 1981; Hirschfield and Cross, 1982). The concept of depression used in the assessment is psychiatrically defined. Some female analysts (Notman, 1989; Bleichmar, 1991) have stressed that there are parallels between the concept of FEMININITY in our society and the character of depressive illness, and that the seeds of depression are already present in the development of the feminine.

The concept formulated by psychoanalysis extends from the psychodynamics of depressive experience as a component of human development in general, to the related reactions of mourning for the loss of a loved OBJECT, to depression as a regressive syndrome to be found in all neurotic, psychotic and borderline illnesses.

Depression has been a fundamental concept in the clinical and theoretical development of psychoanalysis in general. Where Abraham (1982 [1924]) had placed emphasis on the regressiveness of drives, today, under the influence of ego psychology in the United States, depression is seen as a basic ego reaction (Bibring, 1953). Interest centres on the comprehension and description of the various ego regressions able to cause changes in the ego and the superego. The depressive affect can be ascribed to a temporary ego regression; the psychotic depression, with its loss of self-esteem, to a lasting and far-reaching one.

Abraham separates compulsive neurosis from melancholia in maintaining that the compulsive neurotic regresses to a later anal phase (to which retention is central) whereas the melancholic regresses to an earlier one (where expulsion is significant). A further regression to the oral–sadistic phase of the development of the LIBIDO allows the re-incorporation (i.e. INTROJECTION) of the expelled object. The process of introjection typical of melancholic illness, consisting of a narcissistic IDENTIFICATION with the abandoned object, allows, on the one hand, through a form of self-reproach, an indulgence in revenge upon the loved object, and, on the other, a protection from total destruction. According to Abraham, a combination of four factors can induce a state of melancholia: a developmental increase of oral-eroticism, a particular fixation of libido at the oral stage, a deep narcissistic wound through a disappointment in love before the resolution of the OEDIPUS COMPLEX and the repetition of this process in later life.

Freud (1917) compares the effects of mourning and melancholia and starts out by noting that both exhibit the same phenomena, an exception being the lowering of self-esteem in the melancholic illness, which is absent from mourning. Both mourner and melancholic have lost interest in the external world; they are unable to choose a new love-object and their life participation is much reduced. Where the cause of mourning is the loss of a real object, for melancholia the catalyst is a narcissistically experienced rejection from the loved object, whereby an already existing

60

ambivalence attendant upon relation to objects is intensified. Freud describes the central mechanism of melancholic illness as a movement of regression from an original narcissistic object-choice to a narcissistic identification, a substitute for the original attachment. The libido that has been released is not directed to a new object but rather taken back into the ego where it induces an identification of the ego with the abandoned object. The forsaken object transforms itself into an agency within the ego, which becomes restricted by this change. According to Freud, whereas in mourning it is the object-world that becomes impoverished, in melancholia it is the ego. For Freud as well as for Abraham, melancholia is essentially characterized by a high degree of narcissistic vulnerability, an intolerance in the face of aggressive instinctual drives and an abandonment of the disappointing love-object because of the former narcissistic identification with it.

Among modern writers, it is Edith Jacobson (1971) and Margaret Mahler (1968) in particular who have pointed to conflicts with aggressive drives. Jacobson, furthermore, stresses the narcissistic injuries arising out of relations to objects. For Melanie KLEIN, an innate DEATH DRIVE lies at the centre of psychic development, which is directed by the self against the loved object too. In the depressive position, the infant is aware of the co-presence of love and hate, and experiences depression over its own destructiveness. In her view, the early operations of the depressive position become re-activated in the unconscious fantasies, conflicts and dreams of the adult depressive patient. Jacobson starts out from the premiss that disappointment at the oedipal stage re-activates regressive pre-genital conflicts, and that these disappointments can become a model for adult depression. René Spitz (1965) points to the similarities and differences of anaclitic depression in infancy (i.e. arising from the child's dependency upon the mother) and later depressive illness. Without specifically intending to, the above-mentioned analysts, starting out from a parallel between femininity and depression, construct an infantile prototype that is typically feminine.

There is disagreement between psychoanalysis and ego psychology on the aetiology of depression; whereas the first tends to eliminate as causes any conflictual situations that occur in the sixth year, the second assumes that the life-cycle as a whole has a significance for the establishment of a theory of depression, and that early infantile stages need to be linked to crucial phases in women's later life.

KRISTEVA (1989 [1987]) argues that a woman is at a disadvantage as against a man, because she has to separate herself from her mother without the compensation of a substitute mother in the future. It is important, too, to draw attention to a feminine depressive reaction which often occurs without being noticed, in many cases hiding behind

DEPRESSION

a psychosomatic symptom, proneness to accident or the breakdown of a partnership. It is a question of the difficulty women have in separating from a partner, even though they realize that the relationship has been damaging and self-limiting over the years. Chasseguet-Smirgel (1981 [1964]) points to an infantile prototype which, if it is to account sufficiently for this depressive reaction, must be linked with later conflicts and attempts by women to solve them. Because the girl, in the primal scene, has experienced the mother as a castrating figure like the father, she fears that, in identifying with her, she will, in coitus, devour the father's penis. These aggressive and anal-sadistic fantasies induce specifically feminine guilt feelings, which lead to emotional and intellectual impediments in later life. If an envisaged separation is experienced as a recurrence of old aggressive conflicts and guilt feelings (i.e. as a castration), a depressive reaction will follow. If, however, in adult life new and different experiences are brought into contact with aggression not identical with its infantile precursors, separation is lived through as self-justified, in which case, it will result in mourning but not depression.

See also CASTRATION COMPLEX; DRIVE; FANTASY; NARCISSISM; SEDUCTION THEORY; UNCONSCIOUS; WOMEN'S PSYCHOLOGICAL DEVELOPMENT.

BIBLIOGRAPHY

Abraham, Karl, 1982 [1924]: 'Versuch einer Entwicklungsgeschichte der Libido auf Grund der Psychoanalyse seelischer Störungen', *Gesammelte Schriften*, vol. 2. Frankfurt am Main: Fischer Verlag, pp. 3–145.

Bibring, Edward, 1953: 'The mechanism of depression', *Affective Disorders*, ed. P. Greenacre. New York: International Universities Press, pp. 13–48.

Bleichmar, Dio Emilce, 1991: 'La depresion en la mujer', *Colección Fin de siglo*, 17.

Boyd, John, and Weissmann, Michael, 1981: 'Epidemiology of affective disorder: a re-examination and future directions', *Archives of General Psychiatry*, 38, pp. 1–39.

Chasseguet-Smirguel, Janine, 1981 [1964]: *Female Sexuality: New Psychoanalytic Views*. London: Virago.

Freud, Sigmund, 1917: 'Mourning and melancholia', *SE*, 14, pp. 237–58.

Haynal, André, 1985 [1976]: *Depression and Creativity*. New York: International Universities Press.

Hirschfield, Richard, and Cross, Charles, 1982: 'Epidemiology of affective disorders: psychological and social risk factors', *Archives of General Psychiatry*, 39, pp. 35–46.

Jacobson, Edith, 1971: *Depression: Comparative Studies of Normal, Neurotic and Psychotic Conditions*. New York: International Universities Press.

Kristeva, Julia, 1989 [1987]: *Black Sun: Depression and Melancholia*, trans. Leon C. Roudiez. New York: Columbia University Press.

Mahler, Margaret (1968): *On Human Symbiosis and the Vicissitudes of Individuation*. New York: International Universities Press.

Notman, Malkah T., 1989: 'Depression in women', *Psychiatric Clinics of North America*, 12/1, pp. 221–30.

Spitz, René, 1965: *The First Year of Life: Deviant Development of Object-Relations*. New York: International Universities Press.

MECHTHILD ZEUL
(*trans. Elizabeth Wright*)

desire   The important discussions of desire for feminism stem less from antiquity (Plato and Aristotle) than from the early Christian era, especially Augustine, whose conceptions partly derive from theirs. In Augustine (*De doctrina christiana*) desire is 'primitive' with the soul because it is a motive force which leads the soul to God, linking things future (hope), things present (perception) and things past (memory). Involvement with objects of desire apart from God are errors; but the cardinal desire whose prime motivation is leading the ascent to the Good (Aristotle) or to God (Augustine; Malebranche) is not. This fundamental conception holds sway well into the early modern era, when Protestantism reverses directions, emphasizing less the ascent to Supreme Being than God's desire for those below. This radical re-orientation in the active direction of desire partakes of a larger theological shift from a God existing 'above' us (the supposed *aim* of all desires) to a God who makes *us* the aim of *His* universal desire (Lacan, 1982). The two ontotheologies position 'woman' differently. In the classic paradigm, the 'feminine' object provides a means of access, or ascent to the Good: desire for her leads one 'higher', as Beatrice does Dante. The post-Reformation paradigm grants the feminine 'object' (defined as per Freud 1915, as the means for attaining an aim) no special status (*see* OBJECT).

This Protestant emphasis is radicalized in the Enlightenment, and culminates in Hegel, where the spatio-temporality of *human* desire first receives its radical definition: in Hegel's *Encyclopedia* the 'aim' of 'our' desire (previously God or Sovereign Good) is definitively lost, is at best unknowable, or is known only to the imagination. In defining *human* desire, Hegel distinguishes it from animal *need*: *human* desire is historical, deferred and unsatisfiable in character by definition. This analysis of desire was to open the door to both marxist and Freudian speculations on the nature of desire and its link to unconscious processes. But there is another side, stressed in *The Phenomenology* (bk II, chs 1, 2), which proved decisive for subsequent thought. In this text, there is one form of *human* desire which is 'satisfiable': human desire is capable of achieving its own self-certainty through the relation to the desire of an other, human, historical, desire. Self-certainty is assurance about one's identity in relation to an ego-ideal, the (narcissistic) equation of self with ideal realized through one's reflected image in the mirror or the other (Kojève, 1977, pp. 26–7).

It must be noted that desire (*Begierde*) is hardly Freud's word (*Wunsch* or *Lust*). Hegel's discussion of desire is, none the less, pertinent for psychoanalysis (via LACAN) and, by extension, for feminism (MITCHELL, 1966; IRIGARAY, 1985), though it stems less from his emphasis on the split between animal (ahistorical)/human (historical) desire, than from his interpretation of *human* desire as desire for *recognition*, especially in the master/slave dialectic stressed in Kojève's *Introduction to the Reading of Hegel* (1977, pp. 3–9, 25–43).

According to Kojève, Hegelian *desire* is the desire to have one's own desire recognized by the other, and thus to make desire represent a certain *value*: in other words, desire, as *human* desire (*Begierde*), is constituted under the mediation of values, which is 'to desire a desire', that is, 'to want to substitute oneself for the value desired by this desire' (Wilden, 1980, p. 66). Since the ultimate value for Hegel is self-consciousness or at least self-certainty, one's own desire would be autotelic/autoerotic (object-less) in character: desire is finally for oneself. Thus one wants to be a value for the other such that this value equals his quintessential desire, narcissistic in nature, which is the desire for himself (Roudinesco, 1990, p. 144).

One 'recognizes' the other only to the extent that one re-discovers oneself in him or her: summing up Hegelian desire, Kojève (1977, p. 6) frames the man/woman relation purely in terms of recognition. Ragland-Sullivan (1989, p. 40), however, sees 'the lineaments of Janus-like narcissism and aggressiveness . . . in the all-pervasive human desire for recognition'. According to Kojève, 'Man will risk his biological *life* to satisfy his *nonbiological* desire . . . the being that is incapable of putting its life in danger in order to attain ends that are not immediately vital – i.e., the being that cannot risk its life in a fight for *Recognition*, in a fight for pure *prestige* – is *not* a truly *human* being' (p. 41, emphasis in original). Since recognition cannot be obtained from a dead body, aggression must stop short of biological death; yet one must yield to the other, and the master/slave dialectic is thus established on the basis of the desire for desire. This is where the Hegelian–Kojèvian desire is directly relevant to feminism. Woman, no longer valued for her role in biological reproduction, is valued only if she becomes the instrument of man's self-representation, that is, only if she is caught in the dialectic of desire and made subject to the ego's imaginary aggressiveness. By accenting the masculine subject in the structure of desire-as-recognition, Kojève refers SEXUAL DIFFERENCE away from 'preservation of the species', biological reproduction, into the pleasure of the DEATH DRIVE. The desire for stasis is turned inside out and becomes an aggressive rage for a control to ensure constancy, leading to the relation of servitude and domination, 'the battle of the sexes', with woman dominated.

The Kojèvian reading of Lacan's *desire* has, to a certain extent, been misread, especially in reference to the woman. For Lacan desire-as-recognition remains critical for the history of oppression of women, because it arranges the sexes in an imaginary symmetry, as it does all egos, when in fact, owing to its inherent aggressiveness and its structures of domination and servitude, dissymmetry prevails. By bringing in *unconscious desire* Lacan thought not to eliminate 'conscious desire' but to analyse it, designating its roots in the linguistic structures of unconscious desire, especially its desire not to know its own desire. He puts the Kojèvian–Hegelian structure into the framework of an overall critique of NARCISSISM and the aggressiveness of the ego constituted exclusively as if it were a structure of pure consciousness (1977, p. 307).

In resorting to Hegelian desire-as-recognition Lacan fills in a certain gap apparent in Freud: Freud comments regularly *on*, but apart from 'On narcissism' (1914) does not do a general analysis *of* how narcissistic desire fundamentally affects all human relations (between the sexes, between self and other) and skews them in the direction of a single form of relation, domination and servitude. Lacan showed (ironically in the light of Hegel's own definition of human desire as historical) how imaginary (conscious/ego) desire dramatically suspends the historicity of desire, once it finds accomplishment in self-certainty. On the one side, the structure generates the Other, unknowable, as the crucial and ultimate source for recognizing one's own desire (as 'the desire of/for the Other'), and on the other, conscious desire is treated by Lacan as a SYMPTOM of the desire not to know one's *unconscious desire*, potentially intersubjective in character. Both are read through the construction of *fantasies* created through signs.

Following Freud (as well as Hegel before Kojève), Lacan sees the historicity of *desire* as bound to the signifying relation. Freud's *Wunsch* seeks 'fulfilment' rather than 'satisfaction' by dint of its *mode of signification*: signs, forms and symptoms restore a link to an *unconscious* past wish, which, in fact, does not even perhaps come into existence outside such a deferred attribution of signification (Roudinesco, 1990, p. 146). *Lust*, as passion or penchant, is also linked to such structures of repetition 'forward' in that the subject moves from a state of unpleasurable tension forward into a state of PLEASURE (see Freud 1920, p. 24), but less as the absolute correlation of the future with a past (as in Augustine) than as a past created retroactively (see Žižek 1989, pp. 12–14). As distinct from Kojève, the link between the two lies, precisely, not in consciousness, but in the UNCONSCIOUS, where desire finds 'fulfilment' in hallucinatory perceptions, phantasms and other devices which are *signs* of a JOUISSANCE (once experienced) inaccessible to consciousness. Such unconscious effects are due to the fundamental prohibition (of incest) formed in relation to the threat/incentive of the CASTRATION COMPLEX. The male must sacrifice his mother's love for his patrimony, requiring that he understand and assume his desire as nothing other than exchange, the substitution of another woman for his mother. This desire is to be satisfied only by substituted signs. In traditional readings of Freud the dynamically repressed tokens of desire are the ideational representatives of instincts; the unconscious and its 'contents' remain unknowable, inaccessible to conscious perception as well as to knowledge, conscious or unconscious. But in this conception, desire is accessed by reference not to content (i.e., the mother), but to the value-charge, carried in the *form* (dream, FANTASY), in which the unconscious desire is expressing itself.

Thus 'conscious' desire (for self-certainty), whose 'signs' are representatives of the power of REPRESENTATION to deny need and dependency on the other's love, to dominate the other and distribute self-consciousness through him or her, cannot claim to have its desires freed from the unconscious. For such representatives are 'at home in the unconscious, where [they] cause desire according to the structure of the phantasy', that is, as *objets petits a* (Lacan, 1977, p. 312), tied to desires for forbidden others (especially the mother).

The universal Other does not satisfy, finally, the desire for recognition; only the labour of translation, anxious interpretation of 'signs' from it are obtained (*see* OTHER/OTHER). Re-worked psychoanalytically by Lacan, then, 'Hegelian desire' (consciousness) is a drive to elevate the desire for self-certainty: to deny *need*, to obtain a 'gain . . . over anxiety with regard to need' (Lacan, 1977, p. 312), as well as *demand*, which is a request for presence or absence, for proof of love from the Other, originally the mother, then the absent father. Conscious desire occupies a place between the dependency of need and the dependency of asking love from the other (demand): the ego wants to be Master. Yet such a consciousness must encounter the unconscious. For the subject embroiled in the dialectic of the desire for recognition, 'there [is always] the phantom of the Omnipotence, not of the subject, but of the Other in which his demand is installed' (Lacan, 1977, p. 312). Thus one asks of the Other, 'Che vuoi?' – 'what does It want?' – in order to find out what one wants oneself, but the answer is never the direct (IMAGINARY) mirroring that the conscious ego desires; it requires a symbolic, linguistic, rhetorical translation. The result is that one can best tell what one wants by asking 'What do *You* want?' or better yet, with the help of an analyst, 'What does he want of me?'

This involvement of the Other in the nature of desire links Lacan's concept of the PHALLUS (as the principal precipitate of his admixture of Freudian unconscious and Hegelian conscious desire) to feminism. As signifier of desire, the phallus is read both imaginarily and symbolically. The imaginary reading indicates the re-emergence of Hegelian desire in the form of the phallus, which marks the 'transcendence of human desire beyond organic need' (Casey and Woody, 1983, p. 83); the symbolic reading presents SEXUALITY as determined, the phallus as a medium of symbolic exchange which makes of man and woman two non-natural categories, attempting to 'play themselves out as a masquerade around reified myth and inexplicable desires' (Ragland-Sullivan, 1989, pp. 42–3; see MASQUERADE). Thus the implications of Lacan's revision of Kojève are of critical interest to contemporary feminism, for Lacan materially worked out the structure of the-desire-for-desire in terms of the phallus such that, when woman attempts to enter the game of desire-as-recognition, she must, 'in order to be the phallus, [i.e.] the signifier of the desire of the Other . . . reject an essential part of femininity, namely all her attributes in the masquerade. It is for that which she is not that she wishes to be desired as well as loved. But she finds the signifier of her own desire in the body of him to whom she addresses her demand for love' (Lacan, 1977, p. 290). Feminists have made the effort to re-write the phallic character of this central image of desire. Hélène Cixous, utilizing a poetic Imaginary, replaces the phallus with a laughing vagina (1988, pp. 245–64) and more symbolically with a 'feminine' economy ('luminous parataxis') of style and grammar in writing (pp. 25–6), opposed to masculine styles of 'reduction' ('scenes of castration') (see FEMININE ECONOMY). Symbolically, too, Irigaray elaborates the phallus as that which has the structure of the commodity (1985, p. 83). She also tries to re-work the imaginary and symbolic figures of desire (metonymy and metaphor), locating a feminine desire in 'the looking glass', like Hegel, but 'from the other side' (pp. 9–33), reversing the patriarchal interpretation.

See also REAL.

BIBLIOGRAPHY

Casey, Edward, and Woody, J. Melvin, 1983: 'Hegel, Heidegger, Lacan: dialectic of desire', *Interpreting Lacan*, vol. 6: *Psychiatry and the Humanities*, ed. William J. Kerrigan. New Haven and London: Yale University Press, pp. 75–112.

Cixous, Hélène, 1988: 'Extreme fidelity', *Writing Differences: Readings from the Seminar of Hélène Cixous*, ed. Susan Sellers. New York: St Martin's Press, pp. 9–36.

Copjec, Joan, 1989: 'Cutting up', *Between Feminism and Psychoanalysis*, ed. Teresa Brennan. London: Routledge, 1989, p. 238.

Freud, Sigmund, 1914: 'On narcissism' *SE*, 14, pp. 69–102.
Freud, Sigmund, 1915: 'On instincts and their vicissitudes', *SE*, 14, pp. 109–40.
Freud, Sigmund, 1920: *Beyond the Pleasure Principle*, *SE*, 18, pp. 1–64.
Grosz, Elizabeth, 1990: *Jacques Lacan: A Feminist Introduction*. London and New York: Routledge.
Hegel, G. W. F., 1910: *The Phenomenology of Mind*, trans. J. B. Baillie. London: George Allen and Unwin.
Hegel, G. W. F., *The Encyclopedia*.
Irigaray, Luce, 1985: 'The looking-glass, from the other side', *This Sex Which Is Not One*, trans. Catharine Porter. Ithaca, NY: Cornell University Press, pp. 9–33.
Kojève, Alexandre, 1977: *Introduction to the Reading of Hegel. Lectures on The Phenomenology of the Spirit*, ed. Alan Bloom. Ithaca, NY and London: Cornell University Press.
Lacan, Jacques, 1977: 'Subversion of the subject and dialectic of desire', *Écrits: A Selection*, trans. Alan Sheridan. London: Tavistock, pp. 293–325.
Lacan, Jacques, 1982: 'A love letter', *Feminine Sexuality: Jacques Lacan and the École Freudienne*, ed. Juliet Mitchell and Jacqueline Rose. New York: Pantheon, pp. 149–61.
Kristeva, Julia, 1980: *Desire in Language*. New York: Columbia University Press.
Mitchell, Juliet, 1966: *Women: The Longest Revolution*. New York: Pantheon.
Ragland-Sullivan, Ellie, 1989: 'Seeking the third term', *Feminism and Psychoanalysis*, ed. Richard Feldstein and Judith Roof. Ithaca, NY and London: Cornell University Press, pp. 40–64.
Roudinesco, Elisabeth, 1990: *Jacques Lacan & Co: A History of Psychoanalysis in France*, trans. Jeffrey Mehlman. Chicago: University of Chicago Press.
Žižek, Slavoj, 1989: *The Sublime Object of Ideology*. London: Verso.
Wilden, Anthony, 1980: *System and Structure*. London: Tavistock.

JULIET FLOWER MACCANNELL

Deutsch, Helene (*b*. Przemsyl, Poland, 9 October 1884; *d*. Boston, USA, 29 March 1982). The life and career of Helene Deutsch, one of Freud's most distinguished disciples and analysands, and an early campaigner for women's rights, stand in marked contradiction to her theoretical position on the psychology of women. She helped to create the Vienna Psychoanalytic Institute in 1925, formulating its training programme and serving as its director for ten years before achieving eminence in the United States. In an interview (*New York Times*, 1972) she described herself as a lifelong feminist, yet her insistence on NARCISSISM, MASOCHISM and passivity as the essential traits of FEMININITY has consistently annoyed the women's movement. Deutsch on the whole buttressed Freud's theories about women: in her schema, passivity and masochism follow from an infantile IDENTIFICATION on the part of the girl with the mother, based on fantasies of a painful labour and menstruation (Deutsch, 1944–5, p. 150), and later from the wish for the completely passive, receptive vagina to be awakened and subjugated by the penis.

It is the infantile, sadomasochistic conception of coitus and the equation of the mother's breast with the father's penis which provides the mature female with her model of femininity. The sexual act can assume its significance for the woman only if it is not 'transformed into the un-act of erotic play or sexual equality' (1930, p. 50). Passive, masochistic pleasure and the hope of a child are the woman's rewards. Indeed, Deutsch sees the pains of labour as an 'orgy of masochistic pleasure'.

Passivity and masochism by definition precluded the development of intellectuality in the ideal 'feminine erotic' type, rendering these women 'helpmates' and 'ideal collaborators' (Deutsch, 1944–5, p. 191–2); the 'intellectual' woman, on the other hand, 'is masculinized' (pp. 290–1). It is for these views that Deutsch is usually dismissed by feminist writers. However, her autobiographical writings and clinical papers offer an alternative perception of feminity, albeit one that never moves far beyond the Freudian model. Webster (1985) notes that Deutsch rejects PENIS ENVY as the central organizer of female personality, although the clitoris is seen as an inadequate and masculine outlet for aggression in masturbation. Thus, while buttressing Freud's view of basic female masochism as aggression against the self, Deutsch consistently treats masochism as a neurotic symptom in her patients to be controlled (Webster, 1985, p. 555); and, rather than invoking penis envy, she gives a biological explanation (a conclusion even more offensive to some). She sees narcissism, when not excessive, as a positive source of ego strength, helping to negate masochism. Together with passivity, masochism is associated with regressive feelings of dependency on the mother and examined (in 1944–5) in a way consistent with some recent trends in feminist studies. The girl's struggles with her unresolved oedipal and pre-oedipal conflicts are discussed in the context of mother–adolescent daughter relationships.

In Deutsch's autobiography (1973) she strongly implies that her emotional dependence on Freud inhibited her intellectual freedom (Roith, 1987, p. 50), a factor she was able to recognize in her later years. Her work elaborated on, yet conformed to, his basic approach.

WRITINGS

1930: 'The significance of masochism in the mental life of women', *International Journal of Psycho-Analysis*, 9, pp. 48–60.

DISAVOWAL

1944–5: *The Psychology of Women: The Psychoanalytic Interpretation*, 2 vols. New York: Grune and Stratton.
1965: *Neurosis and Character-Types: Clinical Psychoanalytic Studies*. New York: International Universities Press.
1972: Interview in *The New York Times*, 13 Feb.
1973: *Confrontation with Myself: An Epilogue*. New York: Norton.

BIBLIOGRAPHY

Roazen, Paul, 1985: *Helene Deutsch*. New York: Anchor Books.
Roith, Estelle, 1987: *The Riddle of Freud: Jewish Influences on his Theory of Female Sexuality*. London and New York: Tavistock.
Webster, Brenda S., 1985: 'Helene Deutsch: a new look', *Signs*, 10, 31, pp. 553–71.

ESTELLE ROITH

disavowal   The concept of disavowal (also translated as negation or denegation) refers to those utterances of an analysand where something is affirmed in the same gesture that it is denied. Since for Freud drives are active, affirmative and positive, a tension is created between conscious and unconscious: for the UNCONSCIOUS, negation does not exist. There is an ambivalent relationship between a SUBJECT and a given desire. Contradictions of this kind are typical of many psychic disorders, in which a subject is placed in a dilemma of choice between mutually exclusive desires.

In his article 'Negation' Freud uses the concept to describe psychic processes in which a subject can give clear expression to desires, thoughts and feelings that were hitherto repressed, even as it continues to repel or resist them, by disavowing that they are its desires. 'Negation is a way of taking account of what is repressed; indeed, it is actually a removal of the repression, though not, of course, an acceptance of what is repressed.' The psychic defence against endangering repressed material works by virtue of duplicity, for disavowal assists in undoing one of the consequences of REPRESSION, 'namely, the fact that the subject-matter of the image in question is unable to enter consciousness' (Freud, 1925, p. 236). What results is an intellectual acceptance of what is repressed, even as the repression is maintained.

The enmeshing of affirmation with disavowal, due to which repressed material can make its way into the conscious on the condition that it is denied, links this psychic articulation to other concepts involving ambivalence. One could name FETISHISM, where the castration of the feminine body can be affirmed via negation, and the UNCANNY, as the

70

moment where the negated repressed (any previous experience of castration), returns in the compulsion to repeat (*see* CASTRATION COMPLEX).

What is relevant for feminist discourse is that among the cases in which Freud discusses the process of disavowal are those involving his treatment of HYSTERIA. The resistance his female patients showed to recognizing memories that emerged was such that even at the core of a recollection, the woman would disavow it in the act of reproduction (1895, p. 289). Feminists such as Mitchell have re-formulated hysteria, seeing it as a strategy of feminine resistance: 'Hysteria is the woman's simultaneous acceptance and refusal of the organisation of sexuality under patriarchal capitalism. It is simultaneously what a woman can do both to be feminine and to refuse femininity, within patriarchal discourse' (Mitchell, 1984, p. 290). Thus, for women, disavowal inscribes a form of self-articulation which has particular consequences for their mental health.

BIBLIOGRAPHY

Freud, Sigmund, 1895: *Studies on Hysteria, SE*, 2.
Freud, Sigmund, 1925: 'Negation', *SE*,19, pp. 235–9.
Green, André, 1986: 'Negation and contradiction', *On Private Madness*. London: Hogarth Press, pp. 254–76.
Kofman, Sarah, 1985: *The Enigma of Woman: Woman in Freud's Writings*. Ithaca: Cornell University Press.
Mitchell, Juliet, 1984: *Women: The Longest Revolution. Essays in Feminism, Literature and Psychoanalysis*. London: Virago.
Thom, Martin, 1981: '*Verneinung, Verwerfung, Ausstossung*: A problem in the interpretation of Freud', *The Talking Cure: Essays in Psychoanalysis and Language*, ed. Colin MacCabe. London: Macmillan, pp. 162–87.

ELISABETH BRONFEN

drive   Sexual drives need to be carefully distinguished from (biological) instincts. Strachey, Freud's English translator, collapsed two terms Freud clearly separated, *Trieb* ('drive') and *Instinkt* ('instinct'), translating them both as 'instinct', and thus creating major confusions about Freud's understanding of SEXUALITY and its relation to BIOLOGY. As a general rule, 'instinct' should be understood as 'drive'. Whereas the drive always and only refers to the sphere of sexuality, the instinct refers to self-preservation, a biological need. Both imply endogenous impulses which direct the SUBJECT to an OBJECT of satisfaction.

Freud's careful distinction mirrors the opposition he sets up between ego instincts and erotic or libidinal drives. The sexual drives mimic the biological instincts, which set up the bodily zones, organs and processes the drives will utilize to gain sexual (though not necessarily or exclusively genital) satisfaction. The physiological maturation of oral, alimentary, bowel and bladder functions provide the raw materials out of which the drives will emerge, yet the drives are a deviation from the instincts. The separation of erotic/libidinal relations from self-preservative instincts is the consequence of a LACK or absence of a predetermined or given object. A lack of object at an instinctual level would be life-endangering: if the requirements of the instincts are not satisfied, this will eventually lead to the death of the organism. Yet this lack of object enables the drive to insinuate itself into the bodily zones previously dominated by instincts. This may explain why the sexual drives emerge only from six months of age, when the child is capable of recognizing the absence of the breast. Lack initiates the first psycho-sexual stage, which Freud calls sensual sucking. It is no longer the real object, milk, the child seeks in sucking at the breast; it sucks for PLEASURE even when it is full. The process of sucking is eroticized. All sexual drives follow this patter of re-traversing bodily paths that have in some way been singled out by various biological processes.

Freud defines three major characteristics of all the drives: they are derived from and supported by instincts; they have no pre-given objects; and they are dominated by an erotogenic zone (see Freud, 1905, pp. 182–3). The drive has no fixed object, or a vast range of interchangeable objects. The child may get oral satisfaction from any suckable object, whether it provides nutrition or not. Sexual drives are all localized in particular regions of the BODY – in the first instance, the orifices, but as Freud claims, any part of the body, including the entire surface of the skin, and any internal organs, even the brain itself, can become an erotogenic source.

The extreme pliability and flexibility in the range, scope and form of sexual drives implies their openness to historical transformations. Human sexuality is not fixed, regulated by biology, directed towards (heterosexual) copulation and reproduction, as is commonly assumed (*see* HETEROSEXUALITY). Any part of the body can be eroticized and become the source of a sexual drive. Moreover, the concept of the drive is one which problematizes the binary oppositions between mind and body, nature and culture, for it entails both terms. The drive may thus prove a strategically vital term in various feminist challenges to the governing concepts and methods within the history of Western thought.

BIBLIOGRAPHY

Freud, Sigmund, 1905: *Three Essays on the Theory of Sexuality*, SE, 7, pp. 123–245.

Freud, Sigmund, 1914: 'Instincts and their vicissitudes', *SE*, 14, pp. 114–40.
Laplanche, Jean, 1976: *Life and Death in Psychoanalysis*. Baltimore: Johns Hopkins University Press.
Laplanche, Jean, 1989: *New Foundations for Psychoanalysis*. Oxford: Basil Blackwell.

ELIZABETH GROSZ

E

<hr>

écriture féminine *Écriture féminine* is experimental writing, initially French, whose impulse is to inscribe FEMININITY. It writes that for which there is as yet (in phallocentric culture) no language, and which has been marginalized, silenced and repressed in the masculine SYMBOLIC order. Its context is the range of feminist moves to produce discursive spaces, in and from which feminine difference and desire may be creatively articulated. Its earliest exponents, in the mid-1970s (such as Hélène Cixous and Xavière Gauthier), were associated with *Psychanalytique et politique* ('Psych et po') and its publishing house, *des femmes*, but the link was never determinant; nor was there ever a homogeneous movement. Heterogeneity was paramount. This misleading term *écriture féminine* has tended to become reified in (largely American) commentaries, and also to generate a bewildering array of translations. In fact the writers in question have only rarely, if ever, used the term themselves. It is a question of the feminine process and practice of writing, even though the nature of the feminine remains an open question (*see* FEMININE ECONOMY).

Some posit women's irreducible difference from men, others argue that men also may produce feminine texts. KRISTEVA, who is dismissive of *écriture féminine* but whose privileged concept of the semiotic is comparable, and who has argued against positive difference and for an atopic sexuality beyond sexual identity, suggests that men rather than women have more closely approached this creative 'feminine' linguistic horizon. Cixous, possibly the most seductive and challenging practitioner of *écriture féminine*, finds it impossible to define or theorize. Her resistance to theorization identifies THEORY as phallocratic, symptomatic of a deadly desire to master, to impose exclusory reason and to deny difference, which this writing challenges. She also insists on its political potential: it is 'precisely the very possibility of change'; it 'cannot fail to be more than subversive' (1981, pp. 249, 258).

The subversive impulse works provisionally, strategically and playfully with masculine theories: Freud, LACAN and Derrida all figure. Difference and deconstruction are part of this writing's challenge to logocentrism, particularly Cixous's and Irigaray's; but its engagement with psychoanalysis is perhaps prior. Where psychoanalysis had posited that woman does not exist, or defined woman in terms of man, this writing may affirm women's positive difference and aims to articulate embodied female/feminine subjectivity. It counters Lacanian JOUISSANCE with insistence on women's, and in particular the mother's, desire (*see* MATERNAL VOICE); and on the idea that provisional definitions of the feminine begin with *jouissance*, in order that this, the repressed of Western culture, may return. Underlying this practice is the assumption that the text and the psyche are isomorphic (the 'text of her self': Cixous, 1981, p. 250): hence both the possibility and the importance of experimenting to produce feminine texts which inscribe an 'other' language. The linguistic horizon of these texts is a writing which some describe as closer to the (mother's) voice, to the flesh and rhythm of our earliest awareness of LANGUAGE than is conventional writing (*see* PRE-OEDIPAL). The texts are characterized by play, disruption, excess, gaps, grammatical and syntactic subversion, ambiguities; by endlessly shifting register, generic transgressions; by fluid figurative language and myths. They are anti-authoritarian, questioning, unsettling.

Cixous's 'Laugh of the Medusa' (1981) and *Sorties* (Cixous and Clément, 1986, pp. 61–132) are habitually cited as examples. Other women writers of women's desire include Marguerite Duras, Josette Féral and Jeanne Hyvrard; past texts which might be read in similar terms include the work of Woolf, H. D. and Colette; male writers of the 'feminine', that is, what is culturally dissident and marginal are said to include Genet, Lautréamont, Artaud and Joyce. IRIGARAY questions such 'master thinkers' as Plato and Freud in psychoanalytic dialogues that undermine, parody, mime, and dislocate their writing about women, challenging their authority.

Laughter is one significant way in which *écriture féminine* may be said to inscribe the BODY. At times this practice is characterized by commentators as 'writing the body' or 'writing through the body': the latter characterization is more accurate, although its implicit identification of writing and the body as *the* salient feature is problematic without further elaboration of the nature of the body in question. When not lamenting *écriture féminine*'s supposed mystification and lack of political purchase, critics focus reservations on the texts' insistence on the body, particularly the maternal body, arguing that this reduces the feminine to an essentialist location in female anatomy and also to a celebration of MOTHERHOOD (a powerful site of women's oppression). However, the body in these texts is not biologically determined; nor does this writing claim unmediated access to the body. The body is always already a cultural artefact, inescapably mediated, and it largely figures metaphorically, anti-naturalistically, morphologically and strategically in these texts, as a challenge to the Cartesian mind–body split and to all binary logic (*see* PHILOSOPHY). It is a site of REPRESSION as well as oppression, whose textual return is to be celebrated as a fundamental aspect of the potentially liberated creative textual power of lived feminine subjectivity. The body also functions figuratively as what cannot be unified or categorized, what has been excluded or unvoiced. This writing does not promote a utopian notion of an ideal, unmediated coincidence of body, subjectivity and language, although it may explore the fantasy; rather, it keeps difference and the UNCONSCIOUS in play. Nor does it claim to operate beyond the existing cultural and linguistic order in some pure new space (as some critics suggest); rather, it is produced from its extreme margins and from its gaps and interstices.

Critics of these unsettling texts also question the strategic purchase of disruption, suggesting that this seems to collapse into the old identification of the feminine and disorder; likewise their characteristic challenges to reason, which may seem to leave in place the old *logos*–masculine and *pathos*–feminine equation. The recurring question these texts confront is how to write the not-yet-thought-or-said; but this is also the question to the reader.

See also AUTONOMY; FEMINISM OF DIFFERENCE; PHALLOGOCENTRISM.

BIBLIOGRAPHY

Atack, Margaret, and Powrie, Phil, eds, 1990: *Contemporary French Fiction by Women: Feminist Perspectives*. Manchester: Manchester University Press.

Cixous, Hélène, 1976: *LA*. Paris: Gallimard.

Cixous, Hélène, 1981 [1975]: 'The laugh of the Medusa', trans. K. Cohen and P. Cohen, *New French Feminisms*, ed. Elaine Marks and Isabelle de Courtivron. Brighton: Harvester, pp. 245–64.

Cixous, Hélène, with Clément, Catherine, 1986 [1975]: *The Newly Born Woman*, trans. B. Wing. Minneapolis: University of Minnesota Press.

Irigaray, Luce, 1985a [1974]: *Speculum of the Other Woman*. Trans. Gillian C. Gill. Ithaca, NY: Cornell University Press.

Irigaray, Luce, 1985b [1977]: *This Sex Which Is Not One*, trans. C. Porter with C. Burke. Ithaca, NY: Cornell University Press.

Jones, Ann Rosalind, 1981: 'Writing the body: toward an understanding of *l'écriture féminine*', *Feminist Studies*, 7/2, pp. 247–63.

Sellers, Susan, 1991: *Language and Sexual Difference: Feminist Writing in France*. London: Macmillan.

Shiach, Morag, 1991: *Hélène Cixous: A Politics of Writing*. London: Routledge.

ELIZABETH GUILD

essentialism   The term essentialism in feminist theory is taken on the one hand as biological or psychical determinism and on the other as denying the possibility of historical changes occurring in the structures of subjectivity. This term gave rise to a debate that can be organized in four different phases: (a) the pre-feminist critiques of Freud's theories of 'female sexuality'; (b) the feminist critiques of the same; (c) the post-Lacanian debate on 'the feminine'; and (d) the recent developments over the 'female feminist' subject.

It is significant to note that each of these phases also provides different definitions, intellectual locations, theoretical developments and solutions for the problem of 'essentialism' itself. Accordingly, each phase also names and situates quite differently the feminist debate: in a Freudian perspective the problem is 'female sexuality', whereas for Lacanian feminists the focus is more on 'femininity' or 'the feminine' (see FEMININITY).

Thus, there is not one, single, fixed frame of reference for the problem of essentialism; rather, it should be located in the paradoxical junction of two important aspects of feminist thought: on the one hand the inevitable feminist confrontation with psychoanalysis (Brennan, 1989), and on the other the recurrent use of essentialism as a term of pejoration in feminist theory. As recent feminist analyses have pointed out (Schor, 1989; Fuss, 1989) the anti-essentialist crusade against the allegedly reactionary implications of the term acts as if essentialism had an essence of its own. Following these analyses, it is important to de-essentialize essentialism as a problem area in feminist enquiry.

The pre-feminist critiques of Freud's theories of 'female sexuality'

To the extent that the psychoanalytic theory and practice of the unconscious de-naturalizes sexuality, it contributes to the critique of 'human nature' as a set of essential categories and attributes. It also challenges the classical distinction between nature and culture; feminists have argued that this had comforted Western culture in its belief in the 'natural', that is, the inevitable and therefore historically invariable structure of its kinship system, myths, symbols and representations of sexual difference, thereby providing the material and symbolic means of perpetuating its white, middle-class, masculine consciousness (see IDEOLOGY).

The emphasis thus placed on the social construction of the SUBJECT as a cultural entity did not, however, result in the psychoanalytic rejection of essentialism, but merely in its displacement elsewhere. In Freud's theory the burden of nature, seen as biological or anatomical determinism, is shifted on to the woman. By asserting that the LIBIDO is one and that it is masculine in both sexes, Freud defined the female as lacking in essential human attributes, keeping her tied to BIOLOGY, that is, the reproduction of the species. He thus confined woman to a subordinate position *vis-à-vis* the masculine norm that governs the constitution of the subject.

This position was challenged well before the first systematic feminist critiques and from within the psychoanalytic movement itself. It was pointed out that the Freudian theorization of the libido led to a new female 'essence', to the woman as mark of absence, mystery, radical difference, devalued otherness. As such, it was seen as upholding the common belief in the predominance of the masculine as the standard-bearer of the human and therefore as perpetuating the classical dichotomies between the sexes, which psychoanalysis had challenged elsewhere. Freud's re-essentialization of woman as the unconscious of man, deprived of a SEXUALITY of her own, subordinate to and indexed on biology or anatomy, was rejected in favour of the idea of the specificity and autonomy of the female libido, especially in its PRE-OEDIPAL phase (see also HORNEY, KLEIN, JONES). Freud's phallocentred account was replaced with a notion of female vaginal sexuality, which was not modelled on the male penis-centred development. Contrary to JUNG, however, who went so far as to uplift the specific female essence to the rank of one of the fundamental principles in the organization of psychic, intellectual and cosmic life, these critics of Freud remained close to the fundamental insight of psychoanalysis, merely challenging the emphasis on keeping woman confined to a subordinate position (*see* CLITORAL HERMENEUTICS).

The feminist critiques of Freud's theories of 'female sexuality'

The first systematic critique of Freud within feminist theory was inaugurated by Simone de Beauvoir. This critique took the form of a double-edged rejection, on the one hand of the biologically deterministic or naturalistic assumptions about women, and on the other of the constant subjection of women to a male model of psychic development. Special emphasis was placed on criticizing notions such as penis envy, castration and the woman's inability to sublimate, which results in her allegedly stunted superego (see SUBLIMATION).

De Beauvoir also identified as the crucial issue the role of necessary 'other' that woman has to play in psychic, mental, social and cultural life. She pointed out the genderized structure of the dialectical opposition between man as the representative of culture and woman as the repository of nature. In de Beauvoir's analysis, otherness is synonymous with inferiority to the masculine as the human norm: that in this 'difference' PATRIARCHY should have located woman's essence is, for de Beauvoir, a central point of concern (see FEMINISM BEFORE PSYCHOANALYSIS).

Following de Beauvoir, all the major texts of the second feminist wave perpetuated the rejection of psychoanalysis on the grounds of its essentialist, that is, biologically deterministic, view of women. They opposed to its emphasis on desire a political theory based on the will to change, where the idea of socio-cultural influences, as opposed to the biological construction of differences, plays a crucial role. The de-essentialization of woman is therefore seen as part of a political process aimed at the attainment of equality through the overthrowing of patriarchy. The latter is seen not only as a socio-political system, but also as a psychic order. Rejecting the UNCONSCIOUS as an ideology-laden notion and stressing instead the importance of volition, radical feminists argue that identity – in the sexual, psychic and social senses – is the effect and the reflection of a power system where the masculine dominates. They consequently argue that the very structures of identity can be subverted by introducing concrete changes in the social division of labour between the sexes, especially in relation to reproduction. They also oppose to the psychoanalytic notion of the cure the practice of 'consciousness-raising' as a counter-strategy that allows for the exploration of women's preconscious wishes and desires, while avoiding the trappings of the psychoanalytic situation.

The terms of the debate on essentialism shifted in the mid-1970s under the joint impact on the one hand of Lacanian psychoanalysis and on the other of new trends in feminist thought. Central to the latter is the revalorization of female sexual identity and more particularly of MOTHERHOOD. Contesting the belief that motherhood is the symbol of the women's confinement to their biological function, thinkers like Rich and CHODOROW argued for its positive value as a female experience, as opposed to the institution of motherhood, which upholds the patriarchal order. They also stressed the need to reach a more equitable division of social roles between the sexes in the field of reproduction. What does remain as a steady feature of feminist thought is the suspicion of the role of the unconscious in the construction of identity: whereas Rich assimilated it to creativity, Chodorow ignored it altogether in favour of a sociological approach to the construction of identity. This led to charges of psychological essentialism (see Rose, 1986).

The post-Lacanian debate on 'the feminine'

Juliet MITCHELL in her landmark text (1974) argues that Lacan's return to Freud could help rid psychoanalysis of the remaining traces of biological determinism. The emphasis LACAN places on LANGUAGE as the site of inscription and constitution of the subject as a split, sexually differentiated being, led him to assert the priority of cultural and symbolic structures in the process of constitution of the subject (see PHALLOGOCENTRISM). Mitchell defends Lacanian psychoanalysis as an accurate description of the ways in which PATRIARCHY essentializes woman as the other, elevating this sexual dichotomy to the rank of a symbolic, that is both psychic and social, law.

Subsequent feminist discussions reviewed and adjusted Mitchell's position. In her outstanding analysis, Rose (1986) shifted the emphasis in Lacan's work away from the adequate description argument; she stresses instead the extent to which Lacanian analysis can be useful for feminism by undermining any claim to a fixed and steady identity, through its emphasis on the specular game of identifications that lies at the heart of its (im)posture.

Other feminists followed the prompting of the French theorists of SEXUAL DIFFERENCE and criticized Lacan accordingly. IRIGARAY points out that Lacan refuses any specificity to the female subject and re-essentializes the feminine as LACK or symbolic absence. Lacan defines the feminine as non-represented, either by lack or by excess of the phallic order: it is signified by exceeding the boundaries of the order of REPRESENTATION. Through Lacan this definition of the feminine as lack, excess and absence entered post-structuralist thought and nurtured a whole philosophical debate against metaphysical essentialism (see Spivak, 1983).

Theorists of sexual difference, such as Irigaray, and spokeswomen of the ÉCRITURE FÉMININE movement, like Cixous, stressed that, by positing a single structure of symbolic operations as the law of psychic, mental and social life, Lacan elevates phallogocentrism to the rank of a necessity: the evidence he draws from structural anthropology about exogamy leads him to argue for the inevitability and the universality of the patronymic kinship structures. They oppose to it their own re-elaborations of the feminine. Irigaray argues that woman is not representable (as opposed to not being represented), in that she defies the system of representation based on phallogocentric premises. Woman is the mark for another system: Irigaray defends the idea of a female symbolic as a radically different system of theorization of the subject. Difference is not understood here, as in de Beauvoir, as a mark of inferiority, but rather as a positive source of alternative values.

The term 'essentialism' becomes most widely operational in feminism in the controversy that opposed the new theorists of sexual difference to the de Beauvoir-style radical materialists (see Delphy, 1984; Plaza, 1978; Wittig, 1980); it entered English-speaking feminism through the influence that both schools of thought exercised in the late 1970s. Some have argued that what is really at stake in this controversy is, first, a culture-specific understanding of the mechanism or technology of gender (see de Lauretis, 1988), and secondly, different definitions of the very concept of 'materialism' (see Braidotti, 1989).

The centre of the radical materialists' attack was the emphasis placed on the bodily self; they follow de Beauvoir in declaring the body a dangerous concept in that it is so imbued with patriarchal dualistic assumptions that it offers no liberating potential for women. Similarly, they dismiss sexual pleasure as a source of alternative knowledge and identity. They reject the emphasis on sexuality as the mainstay of identity in favour of the social construction approach (see Adams and Brown, 1979). The assertion of sexual difference was thus dismissed as 'neo-feminine', 'pre-feminist' and essentialist. Wittig (1980) claims that the whole category of 'woman' is a patriarchal construction and as such it is imbued with logocentric assumptions; she suggests that the term be abandoned as implicitly essentialist, and be replaced by the position of a 'minority-subject', immune from the MASQUERADE of femininity meant as both a social and a psychic construct. Wittig proposes instead the term 'lesbian' as the antithesis to woman, thereby disconnecting lesbian from female sexuality (*see* LESBIANISM; WOMAN-IDENTIFIED WOMAN/RADICAL LESBIANISM).

Recent developments over the 'female feminist subject'

After a long period of polemic, the discussion took new forms. One of these is Foucault-style feminism, which approaches psychoanalysis genealogically, as the descendant of the scientific discourse of medicine and psychiatry. Following Foucault, de Lauretis (1987) and Butler (1990) argue that psychoanalysis creates the very categories of 'sexuality' and 'desire' which it purports to analyse. This approach, in which discourse-analysis replaces the critique of ideology, redistributes the terms of the debate. By stressing the historical nature of the very idea of 'essentialism', these feminists argue for a more specific location of the terms of reference, allowing them to bypass sterile oppositions and open up new perspectives.

The main impact of this Foucauldian approach was to force a reconsideration of the term 'materialism', in contrast to the marxist definition and in a way that echoes the 'bodily matter' of *écriture féminine*. Foucault stressed the corporeal materiality of the subject as the site of struggles over both knowledge and power, that is, disciplining, controlling and naming. De Lauretis (1987) deconstructs the subject 'woman' into a continuing definition of identity, describing GENDER as a process based on 'experience', as both a semiotic and material force, arguing instead for the multiplicity of meanings, positions and discourses for the female feminist subjects, in terms of the technology of the sexed subject.

ESSENTIALISM

Similarly, Haraway (1991) stresses the role gender plays in combating the pervasive biological determinism used in defining sexual differences, arguing for the 'situated' positioning of women in multinational science- and technology-mediated social, cultural and technical systems.

For Butler (1990), feminist theory assumes and implies a subject 'woman' who is the bearer of essential attributes and is the subject for whom political representation is sought. She argues that this notion is normative and exclusionary and that it conceals the multiplicity of inter-secting axes which define woman: class, race, sexual choice. 'Gender identity' discourse is intrinsic to the fiction of heterosexual coherence and calls for production of narrative legitimacy for a whole array of non-coherent genders. The emphasis thus placed on the narrative or figurative structure of gender is noteworthy.

At the end of the essentialism debate women have learned to look upon gender as a performative notion, which constitutes the very identi-ty of woman which it purports to both analyse and politicize.

See also BIOLOGY; FEMINISM OF DIFFERENCE; POSTMODERNISM.

BIBLIOGRAPHY

Adams, Parveen, and Brown, Beverly, 1979: 'The feminine body and feminist politics', *m/f*, 2, pp. 43–61.
Braidotti, Rosi, 1989: 'The politics of ontological difference', Brennan, ed., pp. 89–105.
Braidotti, Rosi, 1991: *Patterns of Dissonance: A Study of Women in Contemporary Philosophy*. Cambridge: Polity Press.
Brennan, Teresa, 1989: 'Introduction', *Between Psychoanalysis and Feminism*, ed. T. Brennan. London and New York: Routledge, pp. 1–23.
Butler, Judith, 1990: *Gender Trouble*. London and New York: Routledge.
de Lauretis, Teresa, 1987: *The Technologies of Gender*. Bloomington: Indiana University Press.
de Lauretis, Teresa, 1989: 'The essence of the triangle or, taking the risk of essentialism seriously: feminist theory in Italy, the US and Britain', *Differences*, 2, pp. 3–37.
Delphy, Christine, 1984: *Close to Home: A Materialist Analysis of Women's Oppression*, trans. and ed. Diana Leonard. London: Hutchinson.
Fuss, Diana, 1989: *Essentially Speaking*. London and New York: Routledge.
Haraway, Donna, 1991: 'Gender for a Marxist dictionary: the sexual politics of a word', *Simians, Cyborgs, and Women*, ed. D. Haraway. London: Free Association Books, pp. 127–48.
Irigaray, Luce, 1985: *Speculum of the Other Woman*. Ithaca, NY: Cornell University Press.
Mitchell, Juliet, 1974: *Feminism and Psychoanalysis*. London: Allen Lane.
Moi, Toril, 1985: *Sexual/Textual Politics*. New York: Methuen.
Plaza, Monique, 1978: 'Phallomorphic power and the psychology of woman', *Ideology and Consciousness*, 4, pp. 4–36.

Rose, Jacqueline, 1986: 'Femininity and its discontents', *Sexuality in the Field of Vision*. London: Verso, pp. 83–103.

Schor, Naomi, 1989: 'This essentialism which is not one: coming to grips with Irigaray', *Differences*, 2, pp. 38–58.

Spivak, Gayatri Chakravorty, 1983: 'Displacement and the discourse of women', *Displacement: Derrida and After*, ed. Mark Krupnick. Bloomington: Indiana University Press, pp. 169–97.

Whitford, Margaret, 1991: *Luce Irigaray: Philosophy in the Feminine*. London: Routledge.

Wittig, Monique, 1980: 'The straight mind', *Feminist Issues*, 1, pp. 103–11.

ROSI BRAIDOTTI

F

fantasy In the common-sense view, we simultaneously live in two distinct worlds. One is mental, private, 'internal'. The other is physical, public, 'external'. Gilbert Ryle, however, noted a lacuna in this view: that the transactions between private and public realms remain mysterious, since by definition they belong to neither (Ryle, 1963, p. 14). It is to this 'mysterious' area of transaction that psychoanalysis allows access through the theory of the UNCONSCIOUS, that which posits 'the idea of another locality, another space, another scene, *the between perception and consciousness*' (Lacan, 1977, p. 56; italics in original). Fantasy, 'the fundamental object of psychoanalysis' (Laplanche and Pontalis, 1986, p. 14), is rooted in this 'transactional' space.

Unlike most other animals, the human infant is born into a state of nursling dependency in which it is incapable of actively seeking its food. Nourishment must be brought to it, as when the mother provides the breast. Freud hypothesizes that when hunger reasserts itself the suckling initially has no recourse but to seek to repeat the original experience of satisfaction in fantasy: 'The first wishing seems to have been a hallucinatory cathecting of the memory of satisfaction' (1900, p. 598). The origin of fantasy here is inseparable from that of autoerotic SEXUALITY. The child's lips 'behave like an erotogenic zone, and no doubt stimulation by the warm flow of milk is the cause of the pleasurable sensations' (1905, p. 181). After its hunger has been satiated, and after the breast has been withdrawn, the infant may nevertheless continue to suck. Initially associated with the ingestion of food, sucking has now become 'sensual sucking', a pleasure in its own right; consequently, 'the need for repeating the sexual satisfaction now becomes detached from the need for taking nourishment' (p. 182). We may see in this account the Lacanian schema according to which DESIRE insinuates itself between 'need' and 'demand'. The infant's need for nourishment is satisfied when the milk is provided; the infant's demand that its mother care for it is also met in that same instant. Desire, however, is neither for a thing (here, the milk) nor for a person, but for a fantasy – the mnemic traces of a lost OBJECT.

The above scenario might suggest a simple parallel: on the one hand need, directed towards a real object; on the other hand desire, directed towards a fantasized object. A fantasy, however, is not to be defined simply as the mental image of a desired object; it involves the total context and activity in and through which the object may be attained. The 'hallucinatory cathecting' of which Freud speaks will comprise: 'several representative elements linked together in a short scene, an extremely rudimentary scene, . . . for example, a breast, a mouth, a movement of a mouth seizing a breast' (Laplanche, 1976, pp. 60–1). Fantasy, then, is not simply a matter of summoning imaginary objects, it is a matter of staging, of *mise-en-scène*. That the subject may play more than one part in the staging of desire is shown in Freud's essay, '"a child is being beaten": a contribution to the study of the origin of sexual perversions' (1919, pp. 175–204). The paper begins with Freud's observation that many of those who seek treatment for HYSTERIA or obsessional neurosis confess to the (often masturbatory) fantasy that a child is being beaten. Freud finds that this fantasy emerges in three phases, in each of which the subject occupies a different role. The first phase, sadistic and consciously remembered, expresses hostile rivalry towards a sibling and takes the form: 'My father is beating the child whom I hate.' The second phase, masochistic and repressed, is expressed as: 'I am being beaten by my father.' The final form of the fantasy, again conscious, is: 'A child is being beaten.' Although all three forms express the same incestuous desire, the part taken by the SUBJECT differs. The 'mature' form of the fantasy constructs a theatre in which the subject is the audience ('I am probably looking on,' the patient tends to reply when asked how she or he figures in the scene). This impartial attitude however merely serves to conceal the intermediate stage of the fantasy, the unconscious masochistic IDENTIFICATION with the child being chastised – by a beating which both represents and is punishment for the forbidden gratification. In the original form, which Freud says may initially have been less a fantasy than a simple wish, the subject is again on stage but is now identified with the agent of the punishment (*see* SADOMASOCHISM; PERVERSIONS).

Freud first speaks of fantasy in relation to daydreams. He finds that the diurnal reverie, like the nocturnal dream, is a scenario for the fulfilment of a wish. Like the dream, much of the material of the daydream originates in early childhood; daydreams 'stand in much the same relation to the childhood memories from which they are derived as do some of the Baroque palaces of Rome to the ancient ruins whose pavements and columns have provided the material for the more recent structures' (1900, p. 492). The main difference between daydreams and nocturnal dreams is that the former are subject to conscious processes of 'secondary elaboration' which impose a narrative coherence lacking in dreams. This is why the daydream may seem relatively resistant to the mutability of subject position described in Freud's essay 'A child is being beaten'. The reverie differs from the dream, however, not in kind but in degree. For example, we might ask if the adolescent who daydreams about a rock star is in the audience, by the star's side or identified with the star.

The daydream represents only the conscious extremity of a transformational continuum of fantasy structures and materials which appear in a variety of conscious, pre-conscious and unconscious formations. Freud found fantasy behind the hysterical symptom: for example, 'a fantasy of prostitution, of street-walking, might be discovered beneath the symptom of agoraphobia' (Laplanche and Pontalis, 1986, pp. 14–15). He believed that such cultural manifestations as 'art' represent the more or less elaborately disguised expressions of unconscious fantasies (see, for example, 'Creative writers and day-dreaming', 1908). He also found fantasy in the delusional fears of paranoiacs. His essay 'A case of paranoia running counter to the psychoanalytic theory of the disease' concerns a woman who, while lying with her lover, is alarmed by a sound, 'a kind of knock or click'. The noise appears to her to have come from the direction of a heavy curtain. Her delusions of persecution begin with her conclusion that the sound was that of a camera shutter, and that her lover had conspired to have her photographed in 'a particularly compromising position which he wished to record' (1915, pp. 264–5). Freud's conclusion in this particular case identifies a special category of fantasies:

> Among the store of unconscious fantasies of all neurotics, and probably of all human beings, there is one which is seldom absent and which can be disclosed by analysis: this is the phantasy of watching sexual intercourse between the parents, of seduction, of castration, and others – 'primal phantasies' . . . The accidental noise was thus merely playing the part of a provoking factor which activated the typical phantasy of overhearing which is a component of the parental complex. (1915, p. 269)

Freud was led to explain the apparent universality of the primal fantasies, which seem always to have been in place in the history of any subject whatsoever, regardless of individual circumstances, by suggesting they might be transmitted by hereditary factors. Laplanche and Pontalis (1986) have objected that we do not need to invoke phylogenetic inheritance to explain the ubiquity of the primal fantasies. All of them devolve upon major enigmas in the life of a child, enigmas concerning origins: origin of the subject, of the subject's sexuality and of sexual difference. These 'typical' fantasies are the precipitate of the early familial complex in which each child finds itself, at once irreducibly unique in its historical, cultural and biographical detail, and universally shared – in that each newcomer to the world confronts an adult world it does not understand (Laplanche, 1989, pp. 90–2). A fundamental consequence is that sexual identity itself is produced through the agency of fantasy.

Psychoanalysis deconstructs the positivist dichotomy in which fantasy is seen as an inconsequential addendum to 'reality'. It reveals the supposedly marginal operations of fantasy to be constitutive of our identity, and to be at the centre of all our perceptions, beliefs and actions. There is no possible state of unambiguous and self-possessed lucidity in which the external world is seen for, and known as, simply what it is. The 'real world' is not all that is real for us, a fact emphasized by Freud in the concept of PSYCHICAL REALITY. Psychoanalysis, then, contradicts the popular belief that fantasies are nothing but wishful scenarios in which a simple subject gains a simple object denied to it in 'real life.' Fantasy is a complex articulation of both the subject and its unconscious desire in a shifting field of wishes and defences (see DISAVOWAL; PROJECTION; SUBLIMATION).

The psychoanalytic problematization of fantasy has been important to recent feminist cultural theory, and in reading texts against the grain. For example, it has helped in questioning the assumption that female readers of the Mills and Boon, and Harlequin, type of romantic fiction simply identify with the heroine, and that such fiction can only represent dominant heterosexual norms (Kaplan, 1986, p. 151). Here, theories of unconscious fantasy may be used to disengage the complex and often contradictory levels of subject position and meaning imbricated in an apparently simple text – for instance, to read unconscious homoeroticism inscribed between the lines of a consciously heterosexual narrative (see LITERATURE; READING AS/LIKE A WOMAN). The psychoanalytic theory of fantasy has been especially important to feminist FILM THEORY. Here, for example, it has helped combat 'the emergence of a theoretical orthodoxy' (Cowie, 1989, p. 128) in which all of classic Hollywood cinema is seen as an instrument of patriarchy, for the projection of a pathological and oppressive 'masculine gaze'.

See also REPRESENTATION; SYMPTOM; VOYEURISM/EXHIBITIONISM/THE GAZE.

BIBLIOGRAPHY

Cowie, Elizabeth, 1989: discussion contributions to *Camera Obscura*, 20, 21. Baltimore: Johns Hopkins University Press.
Freud, Sigmund, 1900: *The Interpretation of Dreams*, SE, 4, 5.
Freud, Sigmund, 1905: *Three Essays on the Theory of Sexuality*, SE, 7, pp. 124–248.
Freud, Sigmund, 1908: 'Creative writers and day-dreaming', *SE*, 9, pp. 141–53.

Freud, Sigmund, 1915: 'A case of paranoia running counter to the psychoanalytic theory of the disease', *SE*, 14, pp. 261–72.

Freud, Sigmund, 1919: '"A child is being beaten": a contribution to the study of the origin of sexual perversions', *SE*, 17, pp. 175–204.

Kaplan, Cora, 1986: '*The Thorn Birds*: fiction, fantasy, femininity', *Formations of Fantasy*, ed. V. Burgin, J. Donald and C. Kaplan. London and New York: Methuen, pp. 143–66.

Lacan, Jacques, 1977: *The Four Fundamental Concepts of Psychoanalysis*, ed. Jacques-Alain Miller, trans. Alan Sheridan. London: Hogarth Press.

Laplanche, Jean, 1976: *Life and Death in Psychoanalysis*. Baltimore: Johns Hopkins University Press.

Laplanche, Jean, 1989: *New Foundations for Psychoanalysis*. Oxford: Basil Blackwell.

Laplanche, Jean, and Pontalis, Jean-Baptiste, 1986: 'Fantasy and the origins of sexuality', *Formations of Fantasy*, ed. V. Burgin, J. Donald and C. Kaplan. London and New York: Methuen, pp. 5–27.

Ryle, Gilbert, 1963: *The Concept of Mind*. Harmondsworth: Penguin.

VICTOR BURGIN

fashion   In the 1960s the early women's liberation movement rejected fashion with anger, an anger informed by its alienation from the idea of FEMININITY. Women produced fashion, but they did not own it; they had to buy it, actually and metaphorically. Bra-burning was a media hype, but at early women's liberation demonstrations in the USA high heels, handbags and hairsprays were symbolically discarded into specially provided trash cans. This rejection of fashion was part of a wider movement against consumerism influenced by writers like Herbert Marcuse and Betty Friedan; the latter's *The Feminine Mystique* (1963) identified women in particular as victims of consumerism. In the 1970s some feminist writers analysed fashion in more depth, but the debate was largely an extension of the debate on PORNOGRAPHY and did not draw on psychoanalysis. Rather than trying to understand its appeal to women, it made a critique of fashion. It was only in the 1980s that the specific conjunction of feminist and psychoanalytic theory facilitated a more rigorous enquiry into women's fashion, but it remains an under-explored area.

At the turn of the century Thorstein Veblen (1899) had analysed women's fashion as an impediment which debarred them from useful work and obliged them to consume, vicariously, for the male head of the household. Within the psychoanalytic canon only J. C. Flugel (1930), a psychoanalyst and old-fashioned dress-reformer, turned his attention to fashion in a more benign analysis. In the field of semiotics

Roland Barthes's important discussion of 1950s fashion captions (1985) designated the world of fashion as essentially arbitrary and meaningless, resisting cultural analysis and actively seeking to obscure its own significance.

Yet the conjunction of feminist and psychoanalytic theory, in particular as it developed in the 1980s, found a way of scaling the barricades put up by fashion in its fight against meaning. Specifically, this conjunction has been useful in making links between fashion and the cultural construction of a gendered identity. The BODY is of critical importance, both in fashion and in psychoanalysis. Psychoanalysis suggests that picturing the body is fundamental to the construction of a gendered identity, while fashion allows the displacement of feelings about the body on to dress. Feminist theory has made a connection between SEXUALITY on the one hand and REPRESENTATION and the entire field of the visual (*see* IMAGE) on the other. Once women's fashion is identified as a field of representations of the female body it then becomes a significant text of how the dominant culture constructs femininity and how that representation is addressed to women. Fashion is the guided tour of feminine 'difference', a text not simply of a finished femininity but of the formation of that femininity (Evans and Thornton, 1989, 1991).

Within this field the fashionable woman's role is that of a performer, or masquerader, who both flaunts her femininity and holds it at a distance (see MASQUERADE). Through fashion she takes control of the mask, or disguise, of femininity. This representation, which is both excess and denial, may contain elements of illusion, artifice and even violent eroticism, as in Elsa Schiaparelli's collaborations with the surrealist Salvador Dali in the 1930s, notably her Shoe Hat ensemble and Tear Dress.

Both fashion and SURREALISM have in common the FETISHIZATION of the female body, a practice which Baudrillard (1988) has identified as intrinsic to fashion in Western consumer capitalism. However, his treatment of FETISHISM conflates the marxist and the psychoanalytic usage of the term. David Kunzle (1980) discusses the corset as liberating but avoids any reference to psychoanalysis. In her reply, Valerie Steele (1985) redresses the balance but, like Baudrillard, makes no distinction between commodity fetishism and its psychoanalytic counterpart. However, despite the problems of historicity, the question of the fetishistic function of dress makes us acknowledge that, in displacing our interest from the body on to dress, clothing can supplement the body and make good a LACK.

The degree to which phallicism enters into fashion is also apparent in the female 'power-dressing' of the 1980s, the adaptation of masculine tailoring to signify control, restraint and sobriety, which sets up femininity against the other of MASCULINITY. Yet if fashion is the field in which such binary oppositions are constructed, it is also an arena in which they may be contested. Designers like Vivienne Westwood and the Japanese Rei Kawakubo of Comme des Garçons produced a series of designs in the 1980s which undid the clichés about the female body and which were predicated on an idea of the wearer's autonomous and subjectively defined sexuality.

The use of psychoanalysis by feminists has enabled critics to look at fashion in terms of the gaze (see VOYEURISM/EXHIBITIONISM/THE GAZE) and women's NARCISSISM, although it is arguable that theories of spectatorship are unhelpful in understanding how women look at pictures in fashion magazines, perhaps the only field of popular culture which generates images of women for women.

BIBLIOGRAPHY

Barthes, Roland, 1985: *The Fashion System*, trans. Matthew Ward and Richard Howard. London: Jonathan Cape.
Baudrillard, Jean, 1988: 'Towards a critique of the political economy of the sign', *Selected Essays*, ed. Mark Poster. Cambridge: Polity Press.
Evans, Caroline, and Thornton, Minna, 1989: *Women and Fashion: A New Look*. London: Quartet.
Evans, Caroline, and Thornton, Minna, 1991: 'Fashion, representation, femininity', *Feminist Review*, 38, pp. 48–66.
Flugel, John C., 1930: *The Psychology of Clothes*. London: Hogarth Press.
Friedan, Betty, 1963: *The Feminine Mystique*. London: Victor Gollancz.
Kunzle, David, 1980: *Fashion and Fetishism: A Social History of the Corset, Tight-Lacing and Other Forms of Body Sculpture in the West*. New York: Rowman and Littlefield.
Steele, Valerie, 1985: *Fashion and Eroticism: Ideals of Feminine Beauty from the Victorian Era to the Jazz Age*. Oxford: Oxford University Press.
Veblen, Thorstein, 1899: *The Theory of the Leisure Class*. New York: Macmillan; New York: Viking Press, 1953.

CAROLINE EVANS

feminine economy This term is a translation from the French *économie féminine*, which causes two problems: the first is the familiar one that *féminin* may be translated either as *female* (and suggest it is natural to the sex) or as *feminine* (and suggest culturally gendered) and both have controversial implications; the second, less obvious, problem is that *économie* is used more happily in a metaphorical sense than *economy* is. However, *economy* can refer not only to the production and distribution of goods and services within society, but also to the psychic organization of individuals. Freud uses the term economy in his metapsychological writings; his deployment of economic metaphors such as investment and disinvestment can be related to a scientific and 'masculine' desire for quantification. The expression *économie féminine* is associated with Hélène Cixous: she suggests that for some time there have existed two distinct economies (masculine and feminine), and that such a situation is not essential but rather subject to change (see Cixous, 1986).

The masculine economy is an economy of appropriation which can usefully be related to capitalism, presupposing some kind of allocation of property rights (mine and thine) and assuming that individuals behave rationally, in that they calculate to bring about desired outcomes on the basis of mathematical probabilities, using as much data as it has been economic to acquire (another calculation). Emotional relationships can be perceived in terms of investment (for instance, of time and energy as well as of material goods) in the expectation of finally profiting from that investment by increased pleasure, ego-massaging and other personal services. Cixous gives the example of Don Juan as a figure who treats personal relationships economically.

Cixous refers particularly to the economic context in the psychoanalytic sense. She argues that psychoanalysis describes the traditional man who wants to 'gain more masculinity: plus-value of virility, authority, power, money or pleasure, all of which reinforce his phallocentric narcissism at the same time' (Cixous, 1986, p. 87). I would translate 'plus-value' as 'surplus value' since this term is used in marxist contexts, and such a translation brings out Cixous's analogy between two kinds of *homo economicus*: capitalist man described by Marx and psychoanalytic man described by Freud.

A feminine economy would embrace uneconomic (or 'otherly' economic) behaviour, and may also be referred to as a gift economy. The form of gift-exchange may of course conceal obligation and economic self-interest, as Marcel Mauss has pointed out. Cixous suggests that while there is no absolute free gift, yet there can be a gift which does not involve a profitable (supplementary) return: 'all the difference lies in the why and how of the gift, in the values that the gesture of giving affirms, causes to circulate; in the type of profit the giver draws from the gift and the use to which he or she puts it . . . She is able not to return to herself, never settling down, pouring out, going everywhere to the other' (Cixous, 1986, p. 87). Luce IRIGARAY has also suggested that women subvert what she calls the *hommosexual* economy (founded on men exchanging women) by maintaining another kind of commerce among themselves. Both argue that the different feminine relation to castration means a more supple relationship to (emotional and material) property, that can stand separation and detachment, and can bear the freedom of the other.

These proposals and similar ones have proved controversial. Feminists have argued that men's exploitation of women, for example women's 'gift' of unpaid domestic labour, must not be confused with any notion of essential feminine generosity. But Jacques Derrida suggests in his essay on Nietzsche that the gift, 'the essential predicate of woman' (Derrida, 1979, p. 121) is precisely that which cannot be thought in terms of essence or being. The feminine economy is, I would claim, a necessary utopic horizon or moment of radical destructuring which should accompany the more everyday and patient labour of feminist struggle.

See also ANTHROPOLOGY AND CROSS-CULTURAL ANALYSIS; ÉCRITURE FÉMININE; FEMININITY; FEMINISM OF DIFFERENCE; JOUISSANCE; MASCULINITY.

BIBLIOGRAPHY

Cixous, Hélène, 1986 [1975]: *The Newly-Born Woman* [*Sorties*], trans. Betsy Wing. Manchester: Manchester University Press, pp. 63–132.

Derrida, Jacques, 1979 [1978]: *Spurs: Nietzsche's Styles*, trans. Barbara Harlow. Chicago: University of Chicago Press.

Irigaray, Luce, 1985 [1977]: *This Sex Which Is Not One*, trans. Catherine Porter with Carolyn Burke. Ithaca, NY: Cornell University Press.

On Feminine Writing: A Boundary 2 Symposium, ed. Verena Andermatt Conley and William V. Spanos, 1984: *Boundary 2*, 12/2.

JUDITH STILL

femininity Freud considered BISEXUALITY (1931) and phallic sexual monism (1905) to be fundamental preliminary steps in a woman's accession to femininity. Every woman was first a little man. Her entry into 'normal' femininity is only a matter of the correct proportioning of repression of clitoral sexuality to mirror the masculine model. Excessive repression of clitoral activity sets the woman on the road to hysterical neurosis; refusal to abandon masculinity turns the woman towards a complex of virility (Freud, 1933).

The painstaking evolution towards femininity thus presupposes that the little girl does belong to both realms: the masculine first, and then, but only secondarily, the feminine. In her reliance on a rigorous analysis of Freud's writings, Kofman (1980) considers that what maintained Freud in the impasse where he defines femininity as dependent upon a former masculinity, and the woman as incomplete compared to the man, is that insurmountable 'rock' of his ultimate reference to biology.

She asserts that while much of Freud's work clearly demonstrates that he quite readily questioned the authority of the father, he none the less was unable to 'lift the veil off the enigma of femininity'. In positing the unveiling of a forbidden sexual desire as the consequence of an enigma being resolved, she affirms that it was impossible for Freud to solve the question of femininity because 'dis-covering the Mother would have been tantamount to incest' (p. 113).

For Jones, on the other hand, accession to femininity does not depend on a phallic phase, but 'develops progressively from the promptings of an instinctual constitution' (Jones, 1935, p. 273). He creates a specific field for early or precocious femininity. In his theoretical opposition to Freud, Jones relies on the anatomical constitution to assert that from the start the girl 'is more feminine than masculine . . . concerned more with the inside of her body than the outside' (p. 265). He attempts to rehabilitate the woman by ceasing to view her as an *'homme manqué'* or an incomplete being (Jones, 1935). However, his reference to real genital organs and his insistence on biological sexual bipolarity render him ever more blind to the SYMBOLIC articulation of the SUBJECT and keep him in the IMAGINARY that is the body, as Lacan defined it (1977). He accordingly condemns the woman to the fate of reproducer. Furthermore, any logical clinical argumentation, concerning for example transsexuals, becomes impossible, as does any discussion of the LACK, to which Freud had obviously given thought.

Lacan, in radically leaving aside all reference to biology, defined the field of the feminine in stating that the woman is 'not entirely' within the phallic function, in the phallic effects of the signifier and the Symbolic (quoted in Mitchell and Rose, 1985, pp. 137–48). Femininity is here characterized by its failure in relation to the rules defined by the phallus as the representative of the lack: to be a woman is not only to be situated within the phallic as subject of language, but also to be one who cannot trust LANGUAGE or bring herself to make phallic laws the sole foundation of the meaning of her life.

For Freud (1931, 1933), the stages in the constitution of the woman being require that the girl surmount two difficulties before puberty: a change in erogenous zone from the clitoris to the vagina, and a change in love-object from the mother to the father. The change of *object* is facilitated by the girl's discovery of her 'castration', after which she develops an intense hatred of her mother, whom she blames for not giving her a penis (*see* PENIS ENVY). As for the change in erogenous zone, the mother's frustration of the girl's active masturbatory clitoral activity causes the activity to be partially repressed, leaving room for the libido's passive tendencies that allow for the transfer from the clitoris to the vagina. The passage to a passive position *vis-à-vis* the mother paves the way for accusations of seduction in reference to the body-care the mother had previously given to her child (*see* SEDUCTION THEORY); thus it reinforces the hate felt towards the mother. Freud writes that during this period, the little girl discovers not only that her mother has deprived her of the male penis, but that the mother herself does not have one, a situation that further discredits the mother in the girl's eyes.

It may be assumed that the close relation to the mother's body and the care given to the young child by the mother resulted in sporadically unifying the body of the girl. But, at the outset of the phallic phase, after anal toilet training, the child ceases to be 'mothered'. She is then beset by anxiety caused by the wandering of DRIVE within her which she attributes to *jouissance* demanded by her mother. Is the hate for her mother not caused by the state of disarray in which the little girl now finds herself as a result of the prohibition placed on the clitoral activity that was enabling her to centre drive around an organ? More precisely, is there not an underlying, deeper hate, that of femininity, handed down as a legacy from the mother – that field of capture by the 'other' *jouissance*, as Lacan (1975, p. 69) stated? At that age, the child has not yet developed the strategies of the letter whereby the feminine body asserts itself as phallus, thereby linking the subject to that other *jouissance* (*see* JOUISSANCE).

Lacan (1987) as reported by Miller (1988), relates the concept of letter to the REAL of the *jouissance* as that which ruptures the cohesion of the system of 'seeming', of the Symbolic. In order to address femininity more precisely Apollon (1990) develops the notion of letter as a writing that constitutes the body as a place for the return of *jouissance* precluded from the living being by the law of the Symbolic. In resorting to the 'blow by blow' strategy of the letter (Cantin, 1990), the feminine contrasts with the masculine and its linear logic of the signifier (Bergeron, 1990a).

The little girl, therefore, does not reproach her mother for depriving her of a penis; rather, she faults her for not having been given the phallus, that signifier linking every human, the mother first, to the authority of the law of the Symbolic. The phallus safeguards the little girl against the 'unlimitedness' of *jouissance* (Lacan, 1975, p. 13) and against the hole of the absence of the Other (see OTHER/OTHER). That is precisely what the girl solicits in turning to the father. Confronted with the never-fulfilled demand of the mother, she turns to the demand of the father embodying the phallic limit. But her relation to maternal *jouissance* remains consequently in abeyance, keeping the girl short of the phallic.

After advancing the view that what puts an end to the oedipus complex for the boy and procures him a strong internalized superego is the castration complex, Freud (1924) suggests that for the girl it is the castration complex, through 'penis-envy', that causes her to enter into the oedipus complex. But as her relation to *jouissance* is not centred on an organ subject to castration, the girl will have a weak superego that responds solely to external pressure such as education and the threat of loss of love, and that compromises her social participation and moral values (*see* CASTRATION COMPLEX; OEDIPUS COMPLEX).

Chasseguet-Smirgel (1964) sees penis envy, which she refuses to interpret as a virile demand, at the root of the conflictual outcome of the woman's fate. For her a woman's social participation too often reflects the thoughts of a master and lacks subjective originality. She contends that in the phallic phase, the girl, narcissistically injured by the all-powerful mother, turns to the father for the penis that will make her both different from and independent of the mother, a 'woman'. But, despite her highly interesting clinical observations that clearly portray the symbolic character taken on by the penis in feminine fate, Chasseguet-Smirgel is caught in the trap set by the theory of object relation, that of the final reference to anatomical constitution. A biological explanation in which lack of satisfaction is not conceived as something at the very foundation of human and social life, but rather, is related to the non-possession of an organ, sustains the Freudian impasse of the penis envy which creates a dialectic of power and guilt between beings.

In his approach to femininity, Freud looked for the equivalent of an organ in the woman's body that would operate as a marker against the emptiness. While he did have a primary intuition of another *jouissance* in woman, he set it on the level of penile *jouissance*, to the point of establishing, in some of his writings, as noted by Kofman, a physical reality of the girl's castration, 'as if loudly proclaiming the primacy of the phallus would cover over and finally do away with the surprising, ghastly and fascinating character of feminine sexuality in its difference' (1980, p. 160). But in her endeavour to provide a place for femininity, Kofman appears, like many other authors, to reduce femininity to feminine sexuality. In contrast, Montrelay (1977) considers that SEXUALITY contributes to sustaining the REPRESSION of precocious femininity.

What specificity of the feminine unconscious enables us to grasp that trace of dissatisfaction sustaining the gap in the feminine demand? In her initial approach to the question, Montrelay, relying on Lacanian theory, defines the UNCONSCIOUS as a structure or combination of desires articulated as representations depriving the subject of a part of *jouissance*, the loss of which is the price of REPRESENTATION. She then introduces a new point of view that links the modalities of feminine desire both to Freud's phallocentrism and to the concentricity espoused by Jones and his followers. Although contradictory, the two aspects coexist in the feminine unconscious; it is the interplay of their forces that structures the unconscious and their incompatibility that creates its specificity. Montrelay defines femininity as the set of oro-vaginal and anal drives that resist repression during the process of symbolization. The subject, whether man or woman, is defined as the effect of unconscious representation, the effect of the signifier. 'The feminine body', writes Montrelay, 'as a non-repressed object . . . experienced as real and immediate, constitutes a blind spot in the symbolic processes' (1977, p. 70). Precocious feminine drives circumscribe a 'dark continent', a place excluded from the symbolic economy, that is, unrepresentable and outside the meaning proposed by the relation to the phallus. The real woman is a woman who has 'forgotten her femininity'. Forcing repression of early femininity, the oedipus complex institutes symbolic castration in the woman and imposes relinquishment of the real *jouissance* of the primary 'insatiable organ-hole' which was reducing the world to the 'lawless' condition of archaic drives.

Under the effect of the law introduced by the father, it is therefore through 'masquerade' (Riviere, 1929) that 'the woman will reject an essential part of her femininity' (Lacan, quoted in Mitchell and Rose, 1985, p. 84), as a disguise and masking of that Thing insisting in her body as a 'tidal wave of drive', to quote the words of one patient in treatment. Passage through conformity to cultural ideals is the price exacted to be inscribed in DESIRE, to be signifier of a desire which is other. Yet, constructed on the very foundation of this precocious femininity, the narcissistic image of the woman horrifies. This is no doubt how Marilyn Monroe, the incarnation of femininity, could provoke adulation and violent rejection at one and the same time (*see* MASQUERADE).

Clinical research (Bergeron, 1990b) enables us to posit that, while the boy has the penis to enable him to centre his erogenous zones under the axis of the phallus, it is the word of the father that inscribes a limit on the body of the girl. The signifier of the father's word, manifesting his love for his girl in the absence of sexual lust, situates her as subject in the order of language, and manages the libidinous writing of her body by uniting it under a distinct ego. The limiting of the Other's *jouissance* insisting in the girl-child's body inscribes the mark of lack and situates the girl in the register of desiring subject. It therefore appears that femininity is constituted from this construction of the BODY that defines the relation of the girl to an unnameable *jouissance*. It follows that a failing in the father may result in psychosis or in HYSTERIA.

Freud states that the girl's evolution towards femininity takes place through passage from active to passive, from the mother to the father, and terminates in the establishment of the 'feminine situation' in the mutation of penis envy into baby wish, the baby being the symbolic equivalent of the penis (1937, 1925). To equate femininity with feminine sexuality on the strength of reproductive function, and reduce it to the object of masculine FANTASY, is to attempt to limit excess in femininity by circumscribing it entirely within the field of the phallus.

Kofman criticizes Freud's identification of the feminine with the maternal and his dismissing of every other substituting derivative of penis envy as 'offspring' incompatible with femininity. However, from that very excess in femininity, something, 'a work', can be made through a linking of that other *jouissance* sustaining the feminine subject to the symbolic and to culture. The child, upon whom the woman leaves her traces, should not be the 'work' of its mother. Today's authors, artists, physicians and other prominent women testify to how, relying on the letter of the body where the *jouissance* of the Real is excluded but returns, they have taken it upon themselves to produce a new object of desire which sustains social life. The feminine thus reveals itself in the connection with the Real of a *jouissance* that must be inscribed in a somewhere that forcibly will be a 'no man's land'.

See also MASCULINITY.

Note: English translations of quotations from French works are by the present author.

BIBLIOGRAPHY

Apollon, Willy, 1990: 'The Freudian Writing', paper given at the fifteenth annual meeting of the International Association for Philosophy and Literature, University of California at Irvine.
Bergeron, Danielle, 1990a: 'The letter against the phallus', *American Journal of Semiotics*, 7/3, pp. 27–33.
Bergeron, Danielle, 1990b: 'Le Féminin, un espace autre pour le désir', *Revue Santé mentale au Québec*, 15/1, pp. 145–64.
Cantin, Lucie, 1990: 'The feminine thing', *American Journal of Semiotics*, 7/3, pp. 35–41.
Chasseguet-Smirgel, J., 1964: 'La Culpabilité féminine', in *La sexualité féminine: Recherches psychanalytiques nouvelles*, Petite bibliothèque Payot, pp. 143–202.
Freud, Sigmund, 1905: *Three Essays on the Theory of Sexuality*, SE, 7, pp. 123–246.
Freud, Sigmund, 1924: 'The dissolution of the oedipus complex', SE, 19, pp. 173–82.
Freud, Sigmund, 1925: 'Some psychical consequences of the anatomical distinction between the sexes', SE, 19, pp. 241–60.
Freud, Sigmund, 1931: 'Female sexuality', SE, 21, pp. 223–46.
Freud, Sigmund, 1933: 'Femininity', SE, 22, pp. 112–35.
Freud, Sigmund, 1937: 'Analysis terminable and interminable', SE, 23, pp. 209–54.
Jones, Ernest, 1935: 'Early female sexuality', *International Journal of Psychoanalysis*, 16, pp. 263–73.

Kofman, Sarah, 1980: *L'Énigme de la femme*. Paris: Galilée. Trans. Catherine Porter, 1985: *The Enigma of Woman: Woman in Freud's writings*. Ithaca: Cornell University Press.

Lacan, Jacques, 1975: *Le Séminaire*, book 20: *Encore*. Paris: Seuil.

Lacan, Jacques, 1977a: 'The agency of the letter in the unconscious or reason since Freud', *Écrits: A Selection*, trans. Alan Sheridan. London: Tavistock, pp. 146–78.

Lacan, Jacques, 1977b: 'The mirror stage as formative of the function of the "I"', *Écrits: A Selection*, pp. 1–7.

Lacan, Jacques, 1987: 'Lituraterre', *Ornicar*, 41, pp. 5–13.

Miller, Jacques-Alain, 1988: 'Remarques et questions', in 'Lacan et la chose japonaise', *Analytica*, 55, pp. 95–112.

Mitchell, Juliet, and Rose, Jacqueline, 1985: *Feminine Sexuality: Jacques Lacan and the École Freudienne*. New York: Norton.

Montrelay, Michèle, 1977: 'Recherches sur la fémininité', in *L'Ombre et le nom*. Paris: Minuit, pp. 56–81.

Riviere, Joan, 1929: 'Womanliness as Masquerade', *International Journal of Psychoanalysis*, 10, pp. 303–13.

DANIELLE BERGERON

feminism before psychoanalysis One of the themes of contemporary feminism is the argument that 'there has always been a women's movement'. This view suggests that although it is not until the nineteenth century that specific feminist organizations can be identified in Britain, North America or Europe, there was nevertheless always feminist thinking – in the sense that, since Mary Wollstonecraft's *A Vindication of the Rights of Woman* (1792), women in many societies have protested against women's social and sexual subordination and powerlessness. To locate feminism as the product of a particular historical period or culture is therefore a hazardous exercise, since too precise a location can exclude the various other forms of feminism that existed in diverse contexts.

Given this qualification, it is nevertheless the case that feminism as the term is generally understood emerged as a response to the social transformation of the West in the nineteenth century. As societies industrialized, so many of the traditional assumptions about women and men were questioned. The extension of democratic citizenship to men brought with it demands from women that they too should be allowed to vote, enter politics and the professions, own property and assume personal responsibility for their lives. Many feminist battles of the late nineteenth century were therefore around the issues of reproduction and education. Without the freedom to control their fertility and without access to the means of acquiring the qualifications necessary in an increasingly meritocratic society, women recognized that they would never be able to occupy anything except an increasingly powerless social position. Middle-class women in Britain, Germany, the United States and France all began to organize themselves in order to gain a place in the new social order.

Yet just as white middle-class women joined together to make their demands, so working-class women, and black women in the United States, also fought for improvements related to their interests. As many feminist historians have now shown, there is a long and articulate tradition of collective action by working-class women and women of colour.

These different traditions within the history of feminism frequently contained views which were incompatible. The British suffragette movement is one instance of the dissent within a single feminist alliance, and provides an example of the way in which feminists could often disagree passionately with each other about the cause of women's subordination. This tradition of dissent has continued into the twentieth century; today it is accepted by feminists that feminism is a broad-based movement containing women with very different ideas. Among the many differences that exist, one has remained constant: the reasons that women advance for their subordination. In the recent wave of feminism (dating from around the mid-1960s) radical feminists identified men as 'the main enemy'. In various forms this argument suggested that men, in part because of their fear of women, and particularly their fear of women's capacity to bear children, deliberately ensure that women's interests are subordinated to their own. What emerges from this determined – and concerted – action is a situation in which in every society and every culture women are significantly less able than men to assert their own interests. PATRIARCHY, the argument continues, is universal and trans-cultural.

The assertion of the universal subordination of women is, however, unacceptable to many other feminists, who have pointed out the many differences in condition and experience between women. Class and ethnic distinctions both contribute, they point out, to considerable discrepancies in the lives of women and structure the alliances and associations that are as much with men (and against other women) as they are with women. Ethnicity, nationalism, and political and religious differences all contribute to the construction of social identity, an identity which is derived from sources other than simply that of biology.

But the part played by BIOLOGY in the construction of MASCULINITY and FEMININITY remains contested grounds for feminists. At the beginning of *The Second Sex* Simone de Beauvoir wrote that 'one is not born, but rather becomes, a woman' (1964, p. 249). What de Beauvoir attempted to do was to show how women were socially constructed and were taught to become feminine in ways which she saw as negative and constraining. The book is a powerful assertion of women's right to independence, autonomy and self-determination. As such, it stands very much within that tradition of nineteenth-century feminism which saw women's escape from their social subordination as lying in their rejection of femininity and the adoption of masculinity and the masculine. Being like a man seemed to offer a release from all that was confining and limiting about the traditional place of women.

The Second Sex, first published in 1949, is unarguably one of feminism's great, and central, texts. Nevertheless, it encapsulates clearly the contradictions and problems within feminism. In it, the main issue of the relationship of biology to human personality is both denied and claimed. De Beauvoir argues that men, and masculinity, are 'essentially independent' just as women, and femininity, are 'essentially dependent' (1964, p. 477). De Beauvoir's account of human reproduction (which includes a description of the active sperm and the passive ovum) is as much an essentialist argument as those of earlier critics of feminism who had claimed that women were limited *by nature* in the capacity for rational thought.

The relationship between feminism and biology has always been an uneasy one, and de Beauvoir demonstrates this particularly clearly. What she does about biology, and biological difference, is largely to deny its possibilities. She is therefore especially concerned to deny the positive rewards of MOTHERHOOD and maternity. The sections of *The Second Sex* which deal with 'the mother' paint a picture of motherhood which is irredeemably damaging to women. From the moment of conception, the mother becomes a slave to the foetus. After the birth of the child, the mother is never free from care, concern and the drain of physical and emotional demands. Maternity, de Beauvoir concludes, is 'a strange mixture of narcissism, altruism, idle daydreaming, sincerity, bad faith, devotion, and cynicism, (1964, p. 484). Dismissive of the more positive possibilities of motherhood, de Beauvoir remains firmly committed to a view of maternity which sees it as a state through which women are robbed of their freedom and individuality. The woman, who has a personality and a history, becomes through motherhood nothing but the general cipher of 'the mother'.

This perception of motherhood (and with it, of course, of the specific biological capacity of women) has largely been resisted by feminism. What has emerged in the decades after de Beauvoir is an argument which claims that it is not motherhood *per se* which oppresses women but the oppressive conditions of motherhood under patriarchy. Adrienne Rich in *Of Women Born* (1979) argued passionately for the re-claiming by women of motherhood. The isolation of women in the nuclear, patriarchal household, the modern technology of childbirth and the exclusive female responsibility for children were all factors which she identified as contributing towards the cost to women of bearing children. For Rich, one of the most important projects of feminism was to change the particular circumstances of mothers – and women – in patriarchy and to give a new, positive, meaning to the 'feminine' and 'femininity'.

For de Beauvoir, such a project would have been impossible, since she saw little of value in the feminine. For her, femininity was a male construct, a learned incapacity by women to realize their independence and their autonomy. Women, de Beauvoir argued, would always be objects, never subjects. Until women could learn to abandon the NARCISSISM, triviality and essential 'bad faith' that de Beauvoir identified as their central characteristics, they would never escape from the kind of unrealized, and partial, existence that she saw as the lot of women.

A central problem with this argument (as with all feminist campaigns which seek to improve the situation of women through the replication of male experience and behaviour) is the assumption that women and men have fixed and distinct sexual and social identities. In her vivid and fierce attacks on femininity, de Beauvoir (and others like her) inevitably assume masculinity to be an unproblematic state, representing an ideal of human achievement. Even when she is most critical of men, and male writers, de Beauvoir nevertheless accepts their masculinity as given. What is not at issue is the way in which men, just as much as women, have potentially bisexual desires and capacities for a wide variety of emotional inclinations. For men, as for women, there are numbers of social demands and social expectations which effectively prevent or inhibit the development of anything other than a rigidly 'male' or 'female' person. De Beauvoir, like many feminists of both the nineteenth and twentieth centuries, assumes that men, and masculinity, are the universal norm of human achievement and aspiration. It is only through being like men, according to de Beauvoir, that women can be free.

What led de Beauvoir to take such a rigid view of human development was in part her rejection of psychoanalysis. This position (which de Beauvoir maintained throughout her life) was based on her view that the UNCONSCIOUS did not exist as a meaningful influence on human action. As far as she was concerned, all adult human action could be freely chosen; people did not act, in her view, as a result of emotional patterns that they had learned (or failed to learn) in infancy and childhood. Thus adult women and men could choose what kind of life they would live; all that was needed was critical, and rational, intelligence.

This radical refusal of the part played by an individual's emotional history in her/his actions made de Beauvoir's thesis difficult for many women (and feminists) to accept. Her work rightly pointed to the constraints and demands placed on women by the ideology of feminin- ity, but at the same time what remained tendentious was the part that biology did play in the construction of women (and men). In rejecting the positive possibilities of motherhood and yet at the same time unequivocally pointing women towards HETEROSEXUALITY as the 'nor- mal' form of sexual desire and sexual relationship, de Beauvoir seemed to be leaving women in some kind of androgynous never-never land, in which the relationship of heterosexual desire to the possibility of reproduction, among other things, was never discussed or even enter- tained. It was logically internally consistent for de Beauvoir to argue that women who accepted or desired motherhood were embracing their own secondary situation, but this consistency still did not offer, as psychoanalysis could, an explanation of the genesis of DESIRE.

In much feminist writing prior to the impact of psychoanalysis on femi- nism there is an assumption, voiced most coherently by de Beauvoir but also to be found in the work of others, that current ideologies of femin- inity have to be described, analysed and above all refuted. Viola Klein's *The Feminine Character* (1979) gives a persuasive account of the way in which femininity was constructed (from the early nineteenth century onwards) as a discourse which could legitimate and rationalize the subor- dination of women. From theories of women's intellectual inferiority to those which stated the essential emotional instability and fragility of women there emerged a taken-for-granted assumption that women and men had fixed natures. Feminists had to challenge these ideas and the insti- tutional practices to which they gave credibility. As Viola Klein and many other feminists recognized, women had to fight for intellectual recognition, for professional training and for access to the most elementary rights of citizenship. None of these rights, assumed by men to be the natural con- comitant of masculinity, were easily given to women. Inevitably, therefore, women had to deny that they were in any sense different from men. Being able to do as well as men at the tasks men did was, as many feminists per- ceived it, a step towards emancipation and independence.

De Beauvoir provided an original, systematic and passionate attack on the enfeebling and restricting ideas about women common to Western bourgeois societies in the early and mid-twentieth century. Yet in doing so, she presented an argument which trapped both women and men in a straitjacket of over-determined difference. More than that, she contributed to the continuation of the age-old idea – constructed and defended by patriarchy – that men are the universal human being and women the deviant other. The question of the extent to which male being, and experi- ence, can contain and know all varieties of human emotional and sexual relationships was barely allowed. Given even less credence was the way in which all human beings, male and female, became adult through primary relationships with people of both sexes. The recovery of the mother and the father for the construction of the adult self of both sexes was only to be accomplished by later generations of feminists.

BIBLIOGRAPHY

Blair, Deirdre, 1990: *Simone de Beauvoir: A Biography*. London: Cape.
Coward, Rosalind, 1984: *Female Desire*. London: Paladin.
de Beauvoir, Simone, 1964 [1949]: *The Second Sex*. Toronto: Bantam Books.
Gordon, Linda, and Dubois, Ellen, 1983: 'Seeking ecstasy on the battlefield: danger and pleasure in nineteenth century feminist thought', *Feminist Review*, 13, pp. 42–55.
Evans, Mary, 1985: *Simone de Beauvoir: A Feminist Mandarin*. London: Tavistock.
Klein, Viola, 1979: *The Feminine Character*. London: Routledge.
Liddington, Jill, and Norris, Jill, 1978: *One Hand Tied Behind Us: The Rise of the Women's Suffrage Movement*. London: Virago.
Rich, Adrienne, 1979: *Of Woman Born*. London: Virago.
Sayers, Janet, 1986: *Sexual Contradictions*. London: Tavistock.
Walby, Sylvia, 1990: *Theorizing Patriarchy*. Oxford: Basil Blackwell.
Wollstonecraft, Mary, 1975 [1792]: *A Vindication of the Rights of Woman*. Harmondsworth: Penguin.

MARY EVANS

feminism of difference   The term 'difference' is particularly significant in feminist discussions of ESSENTIALISM; it is a nodal point in debated relations between psychoanalysis and politics; and it is an index of the plurality of feminisms. Acknowledgement of specific differences among women has become an increasingly insistent aspect of feminist discourse in all domains.

Initially the function of difference in Anglo-American and French feminism was to replace equality as a leading idea. Less emphasis was to be placed on equality with men, more on women's difference from them, thereby moving beyond a principle of identity, and beyond negative difference (women are different, that is, not men), towards ways of thinking difference positively and, later, deconstructively, in terms other than those of the founding hierarchical oppositions of Western thought. However, even when 'woman' and 'man' were understood as cultural constructions rather than essentialist categories, the conceptual framework was characteristically empirical, and the relativity and radical potential of 'difference' for thinking about GENDER were not fully realized. Nor were its political implications: while invoking 'experiential diversity' (Barrett, 1987, p. 39), arguments failed adequately to acknowledge situational differences among women.

Subsequently other 'feminisms of difference' have emerged, such as a radicalization of post-structuralist difference. However conceptually powerful the function for feminists of Derridean *différance* as a means of fundamentally re-conceptualizing gender identities and relations, the political impulse of these feminisms requires that theories of difference be supplemented by theories of agency, concerned with the ideological, cultural, social and political differences towards which feminisms work. Closely related is the question many feminists of difference put to post-structuralism's difference: what are the implications for feminist politics of its habitual metaphorization of 'women', the 'feminine', as the 'figure of difference'?

A further development has been the combining of post-structuralist linguistics, PHILOSOPHY and psychoanalytic thought with theories of SEXUAL DIFFERENCE. Sexual identity and subjectivity, like meaning, are theorized as differential, positional, and constituted in LANGUAGE; differences between one subject and an 'other' can coexist with inner difference. At stake here are the implications for SEXUALITY and sexual identity of this shifting, differing subjectivity, and of the idea that difference founds the SYMBOLIC, rather than resulting from it. Theories of sexual difference encompass the debated question of the possibly irreducible differences between masculine and feminine libidinal economies (as currently constructed) and therefore of differences between masculine and feminine language (see Braidotti, 1989; Irigaray, 1985).

Difference has also come to operate as a challenge to the sexual *indif*ference characteristic of phallocentrism (see for instance Irigaray, 1984). Here its force is markedly ethical and political, while converging on psychoanalysis: feminist theorists argue against masculine indifference and for recognition both of the other (subject) as woman and also of the otherness/difference of the other woman.

See also FEMININE ECONOMY; PHALLOGOCENTRISM; SUBJECT.

BIBLIOGRAPHY

Barrett, Michèle, 1987: 'The concept of "difference"', *Feminist Review*, 26, pp. 29–41.
Braidotti, Rosi, 1989: 'The politics of ontological difference', *Between Feminism and Psychoanalysis*, ed. Teresa Brennan. London: Routledge, pp. 88–105.
Irigaray, Luce, 1984: *Éthique de la différence sexuelle*. Paris: Minuit.
Irigaray, Luce, 1985 [1977]: *This Sex Which Is Not One*, trans. C. Porter with C. Burke. Ithaca, NY: Cornell University Press.

ELIZABETH GUILD

feminist cinema   The term 'feminist cinema' assumes, as Kuhn (1982, pp. 3–18) points out, a connection between 'two sets of practices': feminism and film-making. It further assumes that interventions in the cultural sphere can produce changes in the social sphere, either by bringing women's experience, hitherto marginalized, to the centre of film narrative, or, through a manipulation of the film apparatus, by effecting changes in the very construction of gendered subjects.

Certainly feminists, together with other women, have regarded film as an effective tool for social and cultural change since the earliest days of the cinema. The National American Woman Suffrage Association, for example, collaborated on such films as *Votes for Women* (1912) and *Your Girl and Mine* (1914) (Bataille, 1973). Lois Weber (USA, 1882–1939) made over fifty 'morality message films' between 1913 and 1934, many of them addressing women's issues. *His Brand* (1913) is the allegorical story of a cowboy who brands his wife on the breast, while *Where Are My Children?* (1916) is a fiction film which decries abortion but calls for the legalization of birth control (Heck-Rabi, 1984, pp. 53–71). Germaine Dulac (France, 1882–1942), popularized as the 'mother of surrealism', experimented with a number of technical devices in her films to portray the complex psychology of her frequently female characters (Flitterman-Lewis, 1990). And the writer and patron of the arts, Bryher (the chosen name of Annie Winnifred Ellerman: United Kingdom, 1894–1983), together with Kenneth Macpherson, began *Close-up* (1927–33), the first English-language film journal, as a way of promoting film's potential as an emancipatory educational and artistic medium. As these early examples suggest, feminist and other woman film-makers worked – and continue to work – primarily in three genres: documentary, fiction or narrative, and avant-garde film.

While early film-makers occasionally put film to feminist use, a substantial and explicitly feminist cinema awaited the second wave of the women's movement in the late 1960s and early 1970s. Most feminist film-makers of the following decade worked within the genres of the documentary and the fiction film; their projects were, for the most part, recuperative and their aesthetics were largely realistic. As de Lauretis points out (1987, p. 128), 'immediate documentation for purposes of political activism, consciousness-raising, self-expression' motivated films like *Janie's Janie* (dir. Geri Ashur, USA, 1971), which used *cinéma verité* techniques to convey the empowerment of a working-class welfare mother, and *Union Maids* (dir. Jim Klein, Julia Reichert and Miles Mogulescu, USA, 1976), an 'oral history' of women labour organizers in 1930s Chicago; 'the search for "positive images" of woman' motivated fiction films like *Girlfriends* (dir. Claudia Weill, USA, 1977), an exploration of women's friendship in the face of marriage and other life changes, and *My Brilliant Career* (dir. Gillian Armstrong, Australia, 1979), the story of a young woman's decision to devote herself to writing rather than to marriage (based on the novel by Miles Franklin).

However, it is feminist avant-garde film which has most consistently engaged with psychoanalysis. Germaine Dulac's *La Souriante Mme Beudet* (The Smiling Mme Beudet, 1923), is an exploration of the fantasy life of an unhappy provincial housewife, while her *La Coquille et le clergyman* (The Seashell and the Clergyman, 1927, based on a screenplay by Antonin Artaud), an 'examination of the very mechanisms of unconscious desire' (Flitterman-Lewis, 1990, p. 130), was the first surrealist film. Maya Deren (USA, 1917–61), film-maker, photographer, choreographer and anthropoplogist, drew extensively upon Freudian dream symbols in such films as *Meshes of the Afternoon* (1943) and *Ritual in Transfigured Time* (1946). In their films Dulac and Deren rejected logical narrative development and attempted instead to construct a 'pure cinema', based on image and movement, through which the 'inner life' could be visually reflected on the screen. Dulac's claim that 'Movement, and only movement, was the basis of my psychological technique' (quoted in Flitterman-Lewis, 1990, p. 58) also applies to Deren's aesthetics.

Feminist avant-garde film of the later 1970s and 1980s abandoned the project of *reflecting* an *a priori* unconscious, and sought instead to expose and to interfere with the ways in which the film apparatus, like other systems of representation, contributes to the construction of gendered subjects in PATRIARCHY. Highly influenced by the emerging field of feminist FILM THEORY – itself influenced by developments in post-1968 semiotics, psychoanalysis and structural marxism – the later feminist avant-garde film focused on issues relating to spectatorship (including voyeurism and FETISHISM), PLEASURE, and DESIRE. Yvonne Rainer's *Film About a Woman Who . . .* (USA, 1974) in its self-conscious use of intertitles, its refusal of narrative and its suspension of identifiable familial relationships, anticipated many of these concerns and, though not an avowedly feminist film, was praised by such feminist film critics as the editors of *Camera Obscura* who saw it as an important 'break from illusionist practice' providing 'distanciation which insures room for critical analysis' (1976, p. 59). Laura Mulvey's influential 1973 essay, 'Visual pleasure and narrative cinema' (1989; first published in *Screen*, 1975), drew upon psychoanalysis to problematize the possiblility of a female spectatorship (describing 'woman as image, man as bearer of the look') and to call for a film practice which would destroy the pleasure arising from traditional filmic solutions (premissed upon narcissistic and fetishistic scopophilia) to the problem of woman's castration. The essay 'appropriates' psychoanalytic theory 'as a political weapon, demonstrating the way the unconscious of patriarchal society has structured film form' (1989, p. 14). Mulvey's own film, *Riddles of the Sphinx* (UK, 1976, dir. with Peter Wollen), links the Oedipus myth with such devices as direct address to the camera, a 360-degree panning shot and montage to 'shift narrative perspective to the mother in the Oedipal triangle' (Mulvey, 1989, pp. 177–8) and thus point to the repression of woman's discourse in patriarchy. Other 'theory films' of the period include *Thriller* (dir. Sally Potter, UK, 1979) and *Sigmund Freud's Dora: A Case of Mistaken Identity* (dir. Anthony McCall, Claire Pajaczkowska, Andrew Tyndall and Jane Weinstock, USA, 1979).

Feminist film theorist de Lauretis, following Johnston, has argued that a women's cinema is characterized in terms of address; that is, it addresses the spectator as female (1987, p. 135). Furthermore, a feminist cinema must not forfeit pleasure, which is 'vital for the cinema's survival and its development as a political weapon' (Johnston, 1976, p. 50). While avant-garde film, like other avant-garde practices, has limited audience appeal, many feminist film-makers have incorporated avant-garde self-consciousness and techniques into more accessible and/or mainstream films for women. Michelle Citron's *Daughter-Rite* (USA, 1978) uses voice-over narration (diary excerpts), the looping and syncopation of home-movie footage, and staged *verité* scenes to explore the tensions in mother–daughter relationships. Lizzie Borden's *Born in Flames* (USA, 1983) draws upon the science-fiction genre in its decentring of narrative and its exploration of the function of REPRESENTATION in constructing political subjectivity, while her *Working Girls* (USA, 1986) de-fetishizes the female body through a refusal of the traditional shot-reverse shot establishment of cinematic identity and through an emphasis instead upon a constitutive female gaze. More recently, feminist film-makers like Trinh T. Minh-ha have turned their attention to deconstructing the documentary, and especially the ethnographic, film, inaugurating a feminist film theory and practice rooted in post-coloniality. *Reassemblage* (dir. Minh-ha, USA, 1982), a 'documentary' film of Trinh's (herself born in Vietnam) visit to an African village, deconstructs an aesthetics of authenticity by 'refusing to naturalise the "I"' (Minh-ha, 1989, p. 147). *Surname Viet Given Name Nam* (dir. Minh-ha, USA, 1989) similarly problematizes ethnic, race and gender identity through a series of highly aestheticized and convincing, yet impossible, 'talking heads' interviews.

Emerging debates within feminist film theory and critical practice focus upon issues relating to historicity (Doane, 1990) and authorship (Silverman, 1988; Mayne, 1990). These issues locate feminist film within a larger cinematic apparatus of accreditation and distribution.

See also FETISHIZATION; GENDER; IMAGE; RACE/IMPERIALISM; SURREALISM; VOYEURISM/EXHIBITIONISM/THE GAZE.

BIBLIOGRAPHY

Bataille, Gretchen, 1973; 'Preliminary investigations: early suffrage films', *Women and Film*, 1, pp. 42–4.

Camera Obscura, ed. 1976: 'Yvonne Rainer: interview', *Camera Obscura*, 1, pp. 79–96.

de Lauretis, Teresa, 1987: *Technologies of Gender: Essays on Theory, Film, and Fiction*. Bloomington: Indiana University Press.

Doane, Mary Ann, 1990: 'Remembering women: psychical and historical constructions in film theory', *Psychoanalysis and Cinema*, ed. E. Ann Kaplan. New York and London: Routledge, pp. 46–63.

Flitterman-Lewis, Sandy, 1990: *To Desire Differently: Feminism and the French Cinema*. Urbana: University of Illinois Press.

Heck-Rabi, Louise, 1984. *Women Filmmakers: A Critical Reception*. Metuchen, NJ and London: Scarecrow Press.

Johnston, Claire, 1976: 'Towards a feminist film practice: some theses', *Edinburgh Magazine*, 1, pp. 50–9.

Kuhn, Annette, 1982: *Women's Pictures: Feminism and Cinema*. London: Routledge and Kegan Paul.

Mayne, Judith, 1990: *The Woman at the Keyhole: Feminism and Women's Cinema*. Bloomington: Indiana University Press.

Minh-ha, Trinh T., 1989: 'Outside in inside out', *Questions of Third Cinema*, ed. Jim Pines and Paul Willemen. London: BFI Publishing, pp. 133–49.

Mulvey, Laura, 1989: 'Visual pleasure and narrative cinema', *Visual and Other Pleasures*. London: Macmillan, pp. 14–26.

Silverman, Kaja, 1988: *The Acoustic Mirror: The Female Voice in Psychoanalysis and Cinema*. Bloomington: Indiana University Press.

JO-ANN WALLACE

feminist history   Feminist history has been slow to draw on psychoanalysis, which is odd given the (to some extent) shared preoccupations of psychoanalysis and the women's movement. Who women were was of absorbing interest to the women's liberation movement in Britain and the United States in the late 1960s and early 1970s. The first British national women's liberation conference, held in 1970 at Ruskin College, Oxford, was a history conference. If feminist scholarship in the US was literary and radical feminist, then English feminist scholarship was historical, its polemic socialist and humanist. Women's history in the early 1970s sprang from that utopian and romantic disposition – 200 years old – which sought to tell women's stories in their own words, to invent new vocabularies for women, and to re-map the divisions between the personal and political. This disposition reaches back at least to the feminism of Mary Wollstonecraft, which struggled to reconcile a reformed femininity with the revolutionary notion of a democratic political subject (Kaplan, 1986a, c). Feminist history's first self-designated task – to recover women's experiences – involved, and was swiftly followed by, the ambition to transform the whole body of historical knowledge (Hufton and Scott, 1983).

That first wish of feminist history – to fill the gaps and silences of written history, to uncover new meanings for FEMININITY and women, to propel SEXUALITY to the forefront of the political mind – shares some of the intentions and scope of psychoanalysis. Whether the UNCONSCIOUS is traced through the familar routes of the early Freud, via slips, jokes, dreams and symptoms, or installed in primal fantasy as Melanie KLEIN suggested, or inferred, following Jacques Lacan, from the gaps, silences, absences in speech, what is central to both feminism and psychoanalysis is the discovery of a subjective history through IMAGE, symbol and LANGUAGE. In the foundation of psychoanalysis, there is a close proximity between the concept of the unconscious and the unspoken histories of women's lives. In an encyclopedia entry of 1923, Freud begins with the relationship between doctor (Josef Breuer of Vienna) and patient (Anna Q.) as the 'best way of understanding psychoanalysis' (Freud, 1923, p. 193). By listening to the hysteric and allowing her to speak, Freud uncovered the place of memory and female desire in the aetiology of hysteria, and shifted the constellation of neurosis from women's bodies to the centre of psychic life (Rose, 1986).

The coincidence of the appearance of psychoanalysis with the gathering of the women's movement in Europe and the United States at the turn of the twentieth century explains the intermittent, if sometimes antagonistic, fascination between the two (like the feminists, Freud referred to his movement as 'the cause' in the early twentieth century). For both Freud and feminism, femininity was a problem to be deciphered and understood. Twice during the twentieth century psychoanalysis and feminism have considered and debated the question of femininity and SEXUAL DIFFERENCE. Psychoanalysis, preoccupied with the power of unconscious desire and sexuality in the formation of the subject, began to debate the possibility and meaning of female desire, issues which had preoccupied feminists since at least the seventeenth century, only after the First World War. During the 1920s and 1930s femininity arose as a problem for psychoanalysis: how does a woman come into being? is a woman born or made? (Mitchell, 1983). Feminism in the 1920s was also arguing about the nature of woman, this time as a political subject. Should women collectively demand what they want as 'women', as 'workers', as 'mothers' or as 'citizens'? Within psychoanalysis, the debate about femininity was suspended, replaced by an increasing focus on MOTHERHOOD. The women's movement, too, faded during the 1930s, surpassed by the political urgency of unemployment and fascism, but also undermined from within by irresolution and conflict about women's proper place and what women should want.

By the 1970s the protagonists were differently aligned, the debate between psychoanalysis and feminism more direct. In the United States, radical feminism rejected Freud, seeing psychoanalysis as diagnosing a problem – femininity – whose political solution – feminism – it either ignored or repressed. (For a radical feminist history see London Feminist History Group, 1983.) In England, on the other hand, some feminists who had read Freud and Marx drew on Lacan's reading of Freud to explain the constitution of female subjectivity in and through language. The difficulty for historians was how to reconcile this notion of a sexed speaking subject with historical materialism's privileging of class (Lewis, 1985). Some managed it. Cora Kaplan's essay on three centuries of women poets in England and the United States, noting the very high proportion of women's poems which have been about the right to speak and write, suggested that women's poems – romantic and lyric – use metonymy as a 'way of referring to experience suppressed in public discourse' (Kaplan, 1986, p. 93). Luisa Passerini's work on memory and subjectivity in fascism and autobiography, Sally Alexander's on identification and unconscious FANTASY in early nineteenth-century radical movements and Alex Owen's exploration of women's mediumship and spiritual possession as forms of resistance and female power in the nineteenth century all employ a psychodynamic notion of subjectivity (Passerini, 1987; Alexander, 1984; Owen, 1989); while Carolyn Steedman (1984) interrogates dreams, memories and family stories to give an account of the reproduction of mothering in the 1940s and 1950s as a process which failed. Poverty, absence and envy shape female desire in Steedman's acid yet poignant counter to the nostalgia of men's autobiographies which have imprinted a sentimental portrait of mothering on working-class experience in the twentieth century.

And yet, feminist history's interest in Freud and psychoanalysis constantly meets those resistances in the wider profession excavated and eloquently challenged by Peter Gay (Gay, 1986; Ashplant, 1988). Historians, he discovers, resist in particular any deliberate use of psychology and psychoanalysis because of its ahistoricism, its inapplicability to anything other than neuroses or the irrational, and its individualism; and anyway, they ask, how can we analyse the dead? Gay – rare among historians in having undergone a training analysis – asks for a 'welding' of historical method with psychoanalysis's scheme of human nature and development. The historian can, he suggests, interpret dreams, read private journals as though they were free association, understand public documents as condensations of wishes and exercises

110

in denial; he can tease out the unconscious fantasies underlying popular novels and art (Gay, 1984).

The unconscious fantasies underlying fascism (psychoanalysis has been allowed to explore the 'irrational' in history) have drawn feminist historians since the coming-of-age of the children of those regimes in 1968. The urgent task of Maria-Antonetta Macchiocchi was to uncover the extent and causes of women's consent to fascism, in order to place women 'as protagonists, who are responsible, and in any case never innocent' (1979, p. 80). And in this cause she evokes – though not as a psychoanalyst, only as a political militant – female MASOCHISM and the DEATH DRIVE. The problem of consent, argues Macchiocchi, lies within the psychic structures of femininity. There was no rational reason for women's support for fascism under the Duce. Their labour was grossly exploited, their sons killed, their husbands symbolically castrated; they were enjoined in a marriage with Mussolini which was sexless, chaste and death-like.

Fascism's repudiation of femininity and women's consent are the concerns of Claudia Koonz's study of women in the Third Reich (Koonz, 1987). No one was innocent, Koonz argues. While women took no part in the planning of the 'final solution', nor – except for a few thousand camp guards and matrons – did they administrate murder, almost as many women as men voted for the National Socialist Party between 1930 and 1932; and they supported the women's bureau under Hitler for as long as it advocated the dream of family and home. Psychoanalysis implicitly informs Koonz's analysis of the Nazi state. National Socialism constituted a social order founded on gender and race, on eugenics and genocide. Whatever its contradictions in practice, the heart of its vision lay in 'a dream of a strong man and a gentle woman, cooperating under the stern guidance of an orderly state' (Koonz, 1987, p. xx).

Theweleit's study (1987) of the Freikorps literature (the Freikorps were the volunteer armies of 1918–23 which, he claims, prefigured the Nazis) assumes that these men meant what they said. What they spoke about was their hatred of women, their dread of women's bodies and sexuality and their wish to kill them. Anti-semitism discovers its emotional source in this revulsion which itself springs from the PRE-OEDIPAL infant and its fear of being engulfed, swallowed up, sucked in by the mother's body. Theweleit thinks that these fantasies belong to all men, whereas Barbara Ehrenreich points out in her introduction first, 'that not all men murder', and secondly, that 'these Freikorpsmen do not emerge on the plain of history fresh from the pre-oedipal nursery of primal emotions, but from the First World War' (Theweleit, 1987, vol. 1, p. xvi).

If we follow the logic of fascism's deathly antinomy, the full horror of its unconscious repertoire, then it is easier, perhaps, to understand the recent withdrawal from sexual difference by some feminist historians. Two influential books refuse the 'monotony' of a psychoanalytic understanding of sexual difference. Joan Scott (1988) moves in favour of deconstruction, which evacuates the SUBJECT from the centre of both history and language. The concept of GENDER, divested of any notion of psychic subjectivity, adjudicates the various meanings assigned to sexual difference, class or race (although race, as in most North American and European feminist history, is muted). Denise Riley (1988) prefers the discursive construction of the category 'women' in the hope, following Foucault, of an eventual dissolution of all identities. The problem is that what is lost with the unconscious is the psychic instability of sexual identities. The place of the psychoanalytic notion of sexual difference in historical work – its repetitions, refusals and engagements – seems to follow unconscious rather than historical time (for further thoughts on time and women's history see Kristeva, 1981).

See also FEMINISM BEFORE PSYCHOANALYSIS; MATERIALIST FEMINIST CRITICISM; RACE/IMPERIALISM.

BIBLIOGRAPHY

Alexander, Sally, 1984: 'Women, class and sexual difference: some reflections on the writing of a feminist history', *History Workshop Journal*, 17, pp. 125–49.
Ashplant, Tim, 1988: 'Psychoanalysis and historical writing', *History Workshop Journal*, 26, pp. 102–19.
Freud, Sigmund, 1923: Two encyclopaedia articles, (A) psychoanalysis, *SE*, 18, pp. 235–54.
Gay, Peter, 1985: *Freud for Historians*. Oxford: Oxford University Press.
Gay, Peter, 1984, 1986: *The Bourgeois Experience, Victoria to Freud*, vol. 1: *Education of the Senses*; vol. 2: *The Tender Passion*. Oxford and New York: Oxford University Press.
Hufton, Olwen, and Scott, Joan, 1983: Survey articles on 'Women in history': no. 1, 'Early modern Europe'; no. 2, 'Women in history: the modern period', *Past and Present*, 101, pp. 125–41 and 141–57.
Kaplan, Cora, 1986a: 'Wild Nights', *Sea-Changes: Culture and Feminism*. London: Verso, pp. 31–56.
Kaplan, Cora, 1986b: 'Language and Gender', *Sea-Changes*, pp. 69–74.
Kaplan, Cora, 1986c: 'Pandora's Box', *Sea-Changes*, pp. 147–76.
London Feminist History Group, 1983: *The Sexual Dynamics of History: Men's Power, Women's Resistance*. London: Pluto Press.
Kelly-Gadol, Joan, ed. 1984: *Women, History and Theory*. Chicago: Chicago University Press.
Koonz, Claudia, 1987: *Mothers in the Fatherland: Women, the Family and Nazi Politics*. London: Methuen.

Kristeva, Julia, 1981: 'Women's time', trans. A. Jardine and H. Blake, *Signs*, 7, pp. 13–35.

Lewis, Jane, 1985: 'The debate on sex and class', *New Left Review*, 149, pp. 108–30.

Macchiocchi, Maria-Antonetta, 1979: 'Female sexuality in fascist ideology', *Feminist Review*, 1, pp. 68–72.

Mitchell, Juliet, 1983: 'Introduction', *Feminine Sexuality: Jacques Lacan and the École Freudienne*, ed. J. Mitchell and J. Rose. London: Macmillan, pp. 1–26.

Owen, Alex, 1989: *The Darkened Room: Women, Power and Spiritualism in Late Victorian England*. London: Virago.

Passerini, Luisa, 1987: *Fascism and Popular Memory: The Cultural Experience of the Turin Working Class*. Cambridge: Cambridge University Press.

Riley, Denise, 1988: '*Am I That Name?*': Feminism and the Category of Women in History*. London: Macmillan.

Rose, Jacqueline, 1986: 'Femininity and its discontents', *Sexuality and the Field of Vision*. London: Verso, pp. 83–103.

Scott, Joan Wallach, 1988: *Gender and the Politics of History*. New York and London: Columbia University Press.

Steedman, Carolyn, 1984: *Landscape for a Good Woman*. London: Virago.

Theweleit, Klaus, 1987, 1989 [1977, 1978]: *Male Fantasies*, 2 vols. Vol. 1: *Women, Floods, Bodies, History*; vol. 2: *Male Bodies: Psychoanalysing the White Terror*, trans. Erica Carter, Stephen Conway and Chris Turner. Cambridge: Polity Press.

SALLY ALEXANDER

fetishism   A concept borrowed from the study of primitive religions, fetishism is first described in Freud's 'Three essays on the theory of sexuality' (1905), but receives its most complete treatment in his relatively late essay, 'Fetishism' (1927). Fetishism is there defined as an exclusively masculine perversion which consists in deriving sexual gratification from the association of a female sexual object with a fetish, generally an inanimate or partial OBJECT, e.g. fur and velvet, feet, a shoe, a certain 'shine on the nose', a plait of hair. The presence of a fetish is the condition of the male pervert's sexual desire and satisfaction, indeed his very HETEROSEXUALITY, for the male fetishist is in fact a failed homosexual.

Because the psychoanalytic literature has generally borne out Freud's restriction of this perversion to men – there are few recorded cases of female fetishism – the concept of fetishism is of special interest to feminists: Freud's reconstruction of the aetiology of the fetishist's aberrant object-choice is key to understanding not merely perversion as such, but, more to the point, Freud's views on SEXUAL DIFFERENCE, masculine sexual development, female anatomical inferiority, gendered subjectivity and normative heterosexuality.

FETISHISM

How and why does a man become a fetishist? The answer to this question lies in raising another question: what is a fetish? The fetish is a substitute for the mother's missing penis; it commemorates the scene where the little boy sees the mother's genitals and simultaneously denies his perception of her castration, lest the same fate befall him. It is a scene of radical and redemptive disidentification between the male child and his mother, which precipitates his rude awakening from a dream of undifferentiation and his uneasy entry into the binary sexual universe of normative SEXUALITY. The fetish is a curious and fascinating compromise formation between the horrified recognition of female castration and its vehement denial, or DISAVOWAL. More precisely, the fetish commemorates the last percept prior to the little boy's traumatic loss of illusions regarding maternal anatomy, power and identity. Hence the fetish is almost always linked metonymically, rather than strictly metaphorically, to the female genitalia: it is not necessarily a conventional phallic symbol, but a part of the body (the foot) or an inanimate object (underclothes) contiguous to the female genitals. But the substitute is never the same as the original, and the original is a fiction; in the fetish what is preserved is the fantasy of a hidden maternal penis, an imaginary PHALLUS that is the source of the so-called phallic mother's omnipotence (*see* PHALLIC MOTHER).

The aetiology of fetishism rests upon, but also serves to anchor, some of the most controversial axioms of psychoanalysis: female castration, male castration anxiety, the OEDIPUS COMPLEX and phallocentrism, as well as oculocentrism, the primacy of the visual. Fetishism (like PENIS ENVY) is the linchpin of Freud's privileging of the phallus, and privileging the phallus underwrites the IDEOLOGY of GENDER and the hegemony of heterosexuality. At the same time, the hypothetical scene of fetishism attests to the extreme fragility of Freudian theories of sexual differentiation, and especially of the development of male heterosexual desire, for what the fetish advertises is the little boy's *uncertainty* over maternal lack; it is a testimony to the ultimate undecidability of female castration. The mark of fetishism is a perpetual oscillation between two logically incompatible beliefs: woman is and is not castrated. Or, in the words of Octave Mannoni's celebrated patient: '*Je sais bien, mais quand même . . .*' (I know, but nevertheless . . .) (1969).

It is, then, no accident that the earliest connection between feminism and fetishism was made in the context of Derridean deconstruction, which can be said to be the supreme contemporary philosophical form of fetishism, in that it promotes the fetishist's undecidability and mad logic to the status of a powerful strategy for undoing Western metaphysics, and the PHALLOGOCENTRISM it entails. Kofman (1981) was the first to draw out the implications of Derrida's generalized fetishism for a

FETISHISM

feminist re-reading of Freud, but she did so at the cost of neutering fetishism. The feminist reading of fetishism has in typically fetishist fashion oscillated between two contradictory positions: appropriation, a 'perversion-theft' (Schor, 1985 [1986]), attempts to elaborate theories of female fetishism; and rejection, for it must never be forgotten that fetishism is bound up with the most primal form of misogyny, the 'aversion, which is never absent in any fetishist, to the real female genitalia' (Freud, 1927, p. 154), and thus irrecuperable as such by feminism.

The case *for* female fetishism has been made from three distinct but occasionally overlapping perspectives. The first, which is essentially political, takes fetishistic oscillation as a paradigm for a typically deconstructive strategy of pressing claims for equal rights while asserting sexual difference (Berg, 1982). The second, which is more purely textual, involves attending to instances of fetishism both in women's writing (Schor, 1985 [1986]) and in male-authored representations of women (Schor, 1988–9; Apter, 1991). Thus, Apter re-writes the entire history of fetishism in psychiatry by tracing it back not to Freud, but to Clérambault, Freud's contemporary and Lacan's teacher. What makes Clérambault important for feminist appropriations of fetishism is that his fetishist patients were women. Basing herself on the fiction of Maupassant and the art work of Mary Kelly, Apter hypothesizes that collecting memorabilia is the specifically female form of both the psychoanalytic and marxian forms of fetishism. The third mode of appropriating fetishism for feminism involves re-reading Freud in such a manner as to tease out from his theories of female development a framework for articulating fetishism and lesbian sexuality. This is accomplished by tracking the play of disavowal in female sexual development. For if castration anxiety and the oedipal renunciation it calls for are the little boy's lot, there is nothing specifically masculine about disavowal and the splitting of the ego (Freud, 1940) which structure fetishism. Female disavowal, whatever its form, differs, however, in one crucial respect from its masculine counterpart: the castration that is disavowed is not the mother's, but the daughter's (Grosz, 1991). Women can, according to Grosz's reading of Freud, disavow their own castration through NARCISSISM (the woman turns her own body into the phallus), HYSTERIA (the woman phallicizes a part of her own body) and the 'masculine complex' (the woman takes her love object for the phallus). The female homosexual is a successful female fetishist.

The trend towards appropriating fetishism for feminism is controversial even within lesbian theory. Thus, taking issue with the appropriators, Garber (1990) questions the 'fetish envy' of certain feminists who would more or less covertly bring back penis envy and thus collaborate

115

in the reinforcement of the 'ideology' of heterosexuality. In contradistinction to the Freudian model, which pins the fetish on the female body, the evidence provided by the eminently fetishistic transvestism in both early English drama and recent pop videos strongly suggests that the fetish is always the phallus. Female fetishism is invisible, untheorizable because it coincides with the norm of phallocentrism, which is to say the fetishization by the culture of the phallus *on men*.

The convergence of Freud's theorization of psychic fetishism with Marx's theory of commodity fetishism in the nineteenth century points up the historicity of the concept and the phenomenon, both of which seem bound up with the history of capitalism in its ascending and triumphant phases. So widespread is fetishism and the morcelization it entails in the field of nineteenth-century French representations of FEMININITY, that it pervades even female self-representation (Solomon-Godeau, 1986). Historicizing the conceptualization of fetishism in psychoanalysis as a nineteenth-century and especially *fin-de-siècle* perversion of Enlightenment anthropology, although it may not offer a way out of the current debates, may contribute to enabling feminists to find a way of theorizing sexual difference and sexuality beyond the eminently fetishistic regimes of high and late capitalism.

See also CASTRATION COMPLEX; FETISHIZATION; LACK; LESBIANISM; PERVERSION; PHOTOGRAPHY.

BIBLIOGRAPHY

Apter, Emily, 1991: 'Splitting hairs: female fetishism and post-partum sentimentality in Maupassant's fiction', *Eroticism and the Body Politic*, ed. Lynn Hunt. Baltimore: Johns Hopkins University Press, pp. 164–90.
Berg, Elizabeth, 1982: 'The third woman', *Diacritics*, 12, pp. 11–20.
Freud, Sigmund, 1905: *Three Essays on the Theory of Sexuality*, SE, 7, pp. 125–248.
Freud, Sigmund, 1927: 'Fetishism', *SE*, 21, pp. 147–58.
Freud, Sigmund, 1940: 'The splitting of the ego', *SE*, 23, pp. 271–8.
Garber, Marjorie, 1990: 'Fetish envy', *October*, 54, pp. 45–56.
Grosz, Elizabeth, 1991: 'Lesbian fetishism?', *differences*, 3/2, pp. 39–54.
Kofman, Sarah, 1985 [1981]: *The Enigma of Woman*, trans. Catherine Porter, Ithaca, NY: Cornell University Press.
Kofman, Sarah, 1981: 'Ça cloche', *Les Fins de l'homme: A partir de Jacques Derrida*, ed. Philippe Lacoue-Labarthe and Jean-Luc Nancy. Paris: Galilée, pp. 89–116.
Mannoni, Octave, 1969: 'Je sais bien, mais quand même . . . ', *Clefs pour l'imaginaire ou l'autre scène*. Paris: Seuil, pp. 9–33.
Schor, Naomi, 1985: 'Female fetishism: the case of George Sand', *Poetics Today*, 6, pp. 301–10; repr. 1986, *The Female Body in Western Literature*, ed. Susan Suleiman. Cambridge, Mass.: Harvard University Press, pp. 363–72.

Schor, Naomi, 1988–9: 'Fetishism and its ironies', *Nineteenth-century French Studies*, 17, pp. 89–97.

Solomon-Godeau, Abigail, 1986: 'The legs of the Countess', *October*, 39, pp. 65–108.

NAOMI SCHOR

fetishization   That process by which an object – an inanimate object, a part of a body or the whole of a body – becomes psychically invested with the value and significance of the fetish. The fetishist demands, in spite of recognizing its impossibility, that there be a maternal phallus. He simultaneously affirms and denies that the mother is castrated. He accepts maternal castration in so far as he provides a fetishistic substitute for the 'missing' maternal phallus; yet he also denies the mother's castration by putting the fetish in place of the PHALLUS. In Freud's writings, the fetishist disavows what he sees – the absence of the phallus – and in its place, he positions a substitute (e.g. shoes, underwear, raincoats, fur, etc.), usually the last thing a small boy sees before the horror of the *nothing*. FETISHISM enables the boy, unlike the hetero- and homosexual resolutions of the OEDIPUS COMPLEX, both to remain within the intimacy of his PRE-OEDIPAL attachment to the phallic mother (through denial of her castration, and thus a refusal to recognize the possibility of his own) and yet also to accept the father's law and thus to enter into symbolic, oedipal relations, and develop his sense of MASCULINITY. In this way, he avoids psychosis. Fetishism is, for Freud, a uniquely masculine phenomenon: the oedipal girl has no need, no motive to disavow the mother's castration. It is more likely that, if she is to disavow castration, it will be with reference to herself (*see* DISAVOWAL).

Fetishization functions in analogous fashion to the processes of hystericization: both make a part or a whole of the body into a phallus. They eroticize, even give a genital meaning to, non-genital parts of the BODY. The two, however, differ; for, in the case of hystericization, one (commonly a woman) makes a part of *oneself* function as a phallus; while in the case of fetishization one (always a man) makes a part of *another's* body into a phallus. Fetishization renders the OBJECT into an image of another, genital object, thereby sexualizing it and making it into an appropriate or worthy object of DESIRE for the SUBJECT. It thus describes a common male mode of objectification of women's bodies. This may explain the frequent use of this concept in feminist FILM THEORY and feminist analyses of PORNOGRAPHY: it describes not only how men

117

may objectify women, but also the threat posed for phallic masculinity in the very conception of women as castrated.

See also HYSTERIA; PERVERSION.

BIBLIOGRAPHY

Apter, Emily, and Pietz, William, eds 1990: *Fetishism as Cultural Discourse,* Ithaca: Cornell University Press.
Freud, Sigmund, 1927: 'Fetishism', *SE,* 21, pp. 147–58.
Lacan, Jacques, and Granoff, Wladimir, 1956: 'Fetishism: the symbolic, the imaginary and the real', *Perversions, Psychodynamics and Therapy,* ed. M. Balint. London: Hogarth Press.
Lewin, Bertram D., 1933: 'The body as phallus', *Psychoanalytic Quarterly,* 3, pp. 24–47.

ELIZABETH GROSZ

film theory   With the question: 'What contributions can Freudian psychoanalysis make to the knowledge of the cinematic signifier?' Metz (1975) launched a new era of psychoanalytic film theory. Earlier film theories had stressed either the inherent realism of the medium, or a contrary formalism. In the late 1960s, however, structuralist theorists had investigated the extent to which cinema could be considered a coded language.

In 1975, the heyday of Lacanian psychoanalysis, Metz's new question proceeded from the post-structuralist assumption that film's signifying systems could not be empirically observed as structures, nor could they be considered apart from the human subjects constructed by cinema's signifying system. His answer to the question of the contribution of Freudian psychoanalysis to the knowledge of the cinematic signifier was the book *The Imaginary Signifier* (1977). Previous film theory had not been able to explain adequately the specificity of the film medium without going overboard in its claims to 'capture' or reproduce reality. What Metz's Lacanian-inflected theory offered was a new definition of the ephemeral but powerful pleasures of a medium. For example, in his definition of cinema's 'imaginary signifier', the cinematic image is defined paradoxically as both more real and less real – more real in its unprecedented 'perceptual wealth', less real in the fact that what we perceive is never really present with us as we gaze upon it – hence the very term 'imaginary signifier'. This insight into what seemed to be a founding contradiction of the medium liberated theory from the necessity of choosing between earlier aesthetico-theoretical poles: between realism on the one hand and SURREALISM or expressionism on the other.

Male psychoanalytic theorists such as Metz, Baudry (1986) and Comolli (1980) described the subject effect of the medium, especially in its narrative forms, as similar to the SUBJECT of psychoanalysis; that is, as the effect of splitting, division and loss parallel to the subject's entrances into the Symbolic. In this system, the experience of the basic filmic apparatus was seen as a kind of imaginary union, and film narrative as compensation for the split subject and the lost object.

These theorists stress the compensatory structure of the medium, its perpetual need to make up to the subject 'lacks' that would be too traumatic to face. Compensations include: Metz's various descriptions of the specific nature of cinematic voyeurism and the DISAVOWAL structure of FETISHISM at the heart of the cinematic impression of reality; Comolli's analyses of the ways in which technological innovations come to fill in lacks in the previous regime of REPRESENTATION; Baudry's analyses of the basic technological apparatus as an imitation of the psychical apparatus; and Dayan (1976) and Oudart's (1977–8) analysis of the 'system of suture' of shot-reverse-shot editing, or continuity editing in general, which functions to smooth over the spectator's perceptions of a discontinuous, fragmented imaginary world.

Feminist film theorists of the late 1970s tended to accept the basic psychoanalytic paradigms, but they did not assume that these pleasures were eternal and universal. Noting that the ideal viewing subject constructed both by psychoanalytic film theory and by the realist narratives of the influential Hollywood classical cinema was male, they questioned a system of pleasure geared to the gaze of male viewers (*see* VOYEURISM/EXHIBITIONISM/THE GAZE).

Mulvey's enormously influential article of 1975 (reprinted in Mulvey, 1989) began by launching the feminist critique of the visual pleasures of narrative film. Mulvey argued that these were constructed to reassure male subjects of their integrity when confronted with sexual difference. Though she writes in Lacanian terms of the IMAGINARY and SYMBOLIC, the central argument of her essay returns to the terms of Freud's essay on FETISHISM as a means of describing the ways in which narrative cinema resolves the crisis of castration for the masculine viewing subject. According to Mulvey's application of Freud, the sight of the woman precipitates an oedipal crisis in the masculine subject resolved by a re-staging of loss that masters its trauma. Mulvey re-deploys Metz's general description of cinema as fetishistic disavowal in very specific terms: the sight of the woman in the film precipitates a crisis resolved through FETISHIZATION of the woman's body. Thus the excessive glamorization of female stars endemic to cinema compensates for and disavows the truth of her 'lack'.

Voyeuristic investigation and punishment accomplishes a similar function. The series of 'looks' which animate film narratives are especially charged when investigating the woman. Voyeurism is activated as a general pleasure of film viewing, but always as a protective 'avenue of escape' for the male viewer whose distance from the castrated site of LACK is assured. Thus, while accepting psychoanalytic tools for the analysis of the subject-effect of cinema, Mulvey uses these very tools to challenge psychoanalysis's patriarchal assumptions. For Mulvey, if the purpose of the entire system of narrative cinema was to reassure the psyche of traumatized male viewers, then this system – erected at the expense of female subjectivity, on the central assumption of female 'lack' – must be destroyed.

All subsequent feminist film theory working within a psychoanalytic tradition has begun with Mulvey's articulation of the patriarchal gaze of narrative cinema. In the mid-1970s the tendency was to view a masculine visual pleasure invested in the classical Hollywood narrative and in the objectification of women against a radical avant-garde seen as destructive of these 'bad' objectifying pleasures. In the intervening years, however, and with the growth of a large body of feminist theory and criticism aimed at deepening the appreciation of how SEXUAL DIFFERENCE affects the visual pleasures of cinema, this relatively simple dichotomy between patriarchal pleasures and an assumed feminine displeasure (and thus a necessary radical destruction of PLEASURE) has seemed inadequate.

Many feminist film theorists and critics have questioned Mulvey's somewhat rigid pleasure/unpleasure dichotomy while others have turned away from the basic oedipal model of the 'normal' male as ideal viewer of film. Rose (1988), for example, explains the extreme aggressivity towards the heroine of Hitchcock's *The Birds* in terms of the paranoia inscribed in complex systems of point-of-view shot.

Other theorists have sought to examine the diverse ways in which mainstream films have constructed often contradictory feminine viewing subjects under different historical conditions. Doane's (1987) book-length study of the woman's film of the 1940s represents one important direction of this enterprise in seeking to define the spectator constructed by the textual configurations of the genre. To Doane this spectator is constituted in structures of pathos and loss which work to reconcile her to the dominant social order and her position under patriarchy.

Others have sought to understand better the diverse and not necessarily oedipal 'negotiation' of pleasure by different social and cultural groups under different historical conditions. These theorists and critics have offered descriptions of historical periods (Petro, 1989), of the existence of entire genres such as soap operas (Modleski, 1982), and of the position of the female spectator of cinema.

On a more purely theoretical level, de Lauretis (1984) advanced the notion of the construction of women spectators through oscillation between masculine and feminine discursive positions. She also introduces the important concept of the social experience of historical women brought to the viewing situation, a concept deployed in a wide variety of ways by feminist theorists and critics. In another vein, Silverman (1988) has explored the theoretical parameters of Mulvey's original project of delineating masculine visual pleasure. But in doing so she discovers moments of rupture in which the mastery of the male gaze fails to deny lack and encounters a breakdown of its mastery. Silverman's work goes on to theorize within the domain of the Symbolic what Mulvey and other theorists have attributed to the imaginary or the pre-oedipal: a NEGATIVE OEDIPUS COMPLEX which tells the female version of oedipal desire in the daughter's relation to the mother. Silverman finds the articulation of this complex in avant-garde feminist films such as Mulvey and Wollen's *Riddles of the Sphinx*.

Many of the threads of feminist film theory were pulled together in a single volume of the journal *Camera Obscura* (Bergstrom and Doane, 1989) organized around the question of the female spectator. Over fifty feminist film theorists and critics in the USA, Canada, Britain, Germany, Italy and Australia responded in short essays to a series of questions posed by the editors. The sheer number of responses by critics and theorists who engaged with this question is remarkable, attesting to the mainstreaming of feminist concerns within many of the countries represented (especially the United States) and to the diversity of investigations carried out in relation to a basic matrix of psychoanalytic and feminist concerns. Although it is clear from the responses that there is little agreement about the goals of feminist film theory and criticism, it is equally clear that many of the insights of the initial feminist critique of psychoanalytic and semiotic film theory have been expanded to include a wide variety of other differences: race, class, ethnicity and sexual orientation.

See also FEMINIST CINEMA; LACAN; OEDIPUS COMPLEX.

BIBLIOGRAPHY

Baudry, Jean-Louis, 1986: 'The apparatus: metapsychological approaches to the impression of realism in the cinema', *Narrative, Apparatus, Ideology: A Film Theory Reader*, ed. Philip Rosen. New York: Columbia University Press, pp. 299–318.

Bergstrom, Janet, and Doane, Mary Ann, eds 1989: *Camera Obscura: A Journal of Feminism and Film Theory*, 20–1.

Comolli, Jean-Louis, 1980: 'Machines of the visible', *The Cinematic Apparatus*, ed. Teresa de Lauretis and Stephen Heath. New York: St Martin's Press, pp. 438–50.

FRENCH-INSPIRED CRITICISM

Dayan, Daniel, 1976: 'The tutor code of classical cinema', *Movies and Methods*, ed. Bill Nichols. Berkeley: University of California Press, pp. 438–51.

de Lauretis, Teresa, 1984: *Alice Doesn't: Feminism, Semiotics, Cinema*. Bloomington: Indiana University Press.

Doane, Mary Ann, 1987: *The Desire to Desire: The Woman's Film of the 1940s*. Bloomington: Indiana University Press.

Metz, Christian, 1977 [1975]: *The Imaginary Signifier: Psychoanalysis and the Cinema*, trans. Annwyl Williams, Ben Brewster and Alfred Guzetti. Bloomington: Indiana University Press.

Modleski, Tania, 1982: *Loving with a Vengeance: Mass-produced Fantasies for Women*. New York: Methuen.

Mulvey, Laura, 1989 [1975]: 'Visual pleasure and narrative cinema', *Visual and Other Pleasures*. Bloomington: Indiana University Press, pp. 14–26.

Oudart, Jean-Pierre, 1977–8: 'Cinema and suture', *Screen*, 17/4, pp. 35–47.

Petro, Patrice, 1989: *Joyless Streets: Women and Melodramatic Representation in Weimar Germany*. Princeton: Princeton University Press.

Rose, Jacqueline, 1988: 'Paranoia and the film system', *Feminism and Film Theory*, ed. Constance Penley. New York: Routledge, pp. 141–58.

Silverman, Kaja, 1988: *The Acoustic Mirror: The Female Voice in Psychoanalysis and Cinema*. Bloomington: Indiana University Press.

LINDA WILLIAMS

French-inspired criticism   'Inspired' articulates a relationship between (Anglo-)American feminisms and French psychoanalytic, post-structuralist feminisms. Their initial encounters in the mid-1970s tended to be cast in terms which marked hesitation or suspicion and a politically complex relationship. Gradually a creative relationship developed, but it is asymmetrical, in that others tend to negotiate with French theories more than the French with the theories of others. As French theories have grown more familiar to feminist audiences elsewhere, owing both to increasing availability in translation and to mediation by anglophone feminists, critical recognition and a sense of invigoration often outweigh resistance, appropriation or assimilation.

The feminism that has evolved out of the encounter characteristically focuses on questions of feminine subjectivity and LANGUAGE. The feminist literary criticism typically explores connections between theories of language, textuality, gendered subjectivity and psychoanalysis – both primarily Freudian (for instance, Jacobus) and Lacanian (for instance, Rose and Gallop).

In Britain Juliet MITCHELL was early influential, as has been her collaboration with Rose (1982) and Rose's own work on psychoanalysis, feminism and cultural theory (Rose, 1986). The journals *Screen* and *m/f* have also been important critical mediators between materialist and psychoanalytic theory. Feminists in Britain such as Parveen Adams, Teresa Brennan, Laura Mulvey and Margaret Whitford continue to engage with French psychoanalytic theory in such fields as film, cultural theory and PHILOSOPHY. In the United States, not least perhaps for institutional reasons, the particularly dynamic focus for French theory has tended to be literary criticism, supplementing the rather scant French work in this domain.

Until the late 1970s American feminist critical practice was traditionally socio-historical and reformist, concerned with women's cultural oppression and engaged in recuperating lost writing by women in feminist 'thematics' and in constructing a feminist literary history and canon (*see* OBJECT-RELATIONS ORIENTED CRITICISM). American feminist psychoanalysis had not yet taken a Lacanian turn; OBJECT-RELATIONS THEORY and sociology dominated. Nor had psychoanalysis and feminist literary criticism significantly converged: criticism tended to work with empiricist, untheorized concepts of 'women' and lacked adequate theories of signification, REPRESENTATION and subjectivity.

It was French psychoanalytic theory, just preceded in its journey across the Atlantic by deconstruction, that made the difference to this critical practice, in that it radicalized the dominant empiricism. Felman's explorations of psychoanalysis and reading/writing and Spivak's translation of and continuing critical engagement with Derridean writing are two significant instances of cross-fertilization (see Felman, 1985 and Spivak, 1987). Deconstruction seemed to offer new theories of language and textuality, challenging the assumptions on which the critical tradition had implicitly relied, and to suggest sophisticated and seductive modes of reading and critical practice (see particularly Johnson, 1981). It also put in question such categories as 'feminine' and 'masculine', and the opposition between the terms, with which criticism had tended to operate (see Gallop, 1982). At the same time, resistance to French theories was giving way to discussion of FEMININITY and SEXUAL DIFFERENCE in the light of psychoanalytic theories, drawing critically both on Freud and LACAN and on feminist theorists' problematization of their work (*see* LITERARY AND TEXTUAL CRITICISM; READING AS/LIKE A WOMAN).

French theories of the feminine, perhaps particularly those which have critically engaged with Lacanian versions, have played a decisive role in new thinking about subjectivity and language (see Rose, 1986) and also in challenging traditional philosophy. In this broad context French-inspired criticism is by now widespread. The following exemplify significant positions and strands, but do not speak for the plurality of practices.

Mediation of, and commentary on, French theories, continues to be important. While interested in the interplay of literary criticism, psychoanalysis, feminism and difference, they continue to problematize the issues without specific involvement in literary critical practice. Toril Moi has been influential in providing a critical version of French feminist theory as embodied in the work of IRIGARAY and Cixous and as powerfully but problematically articulated by KRISTEVA; her materialist, anti-essentialist introduction to feminist theory (one of the earliest), though somewhat partial and polarized, is cogent and forceful (Moi, 1985).

There is a broad community of feminist critics whose work strategically engages with French theory; it includes such critics as Shoshana Felman, Jane Gallop, Mary Jacobus, Teresa de Lauretis, Nancy K. Miller, Naomi Schor and Gayatri Spivak. Characteristics of their work are a double exploration, in which psychoanalytic and feminist discourses put each other in question, and in turn (re-)read and are (re-) read by literary texts; a preoccupation with the difference that feminism makes in the domain of aesthetics; and a theoretical and political attentiveness to the status of their own reading and writing. These critics vary considerably in their relations to French theory. Some work primarily on French texts, others on English; some on the canon, others explore the margins; some choose male-authored texts, others female-authored – but all theorize the objects of their discourse and their relation to them, not least in terms of theories of sexual difference and gendered subjectivity. Some are still in part committed to the earlier practice of 'feminist critique' while negotiating carefully with the French, particularly with theories of sexual and textual difference. Schor, for instance, has explored the (im)possibilities of representation of the female protagonist in French realist writing through readings energized by psychoanalytic feminist criticism, and elsewhere sets out to read 'double', questioning psychoanalytic theories of sexual difference through insistently historicized readings of textual difference. Felman, Gallop and, increasingly, Jacobus are primarily psychoanalytic in emphasis. Felman, an early radical mediator, is a subversive critic, particularly interested in transference, subjectivity and sexual difference. Gallop and Jacobus exemplify the poles of the psychoanalytic trend. While Jacobus is a self-effacing writer, erudite and scrupulous in her engagement with literary texts, with psychoanalytic theory (particularly Kristeva's), and with the work of other feminists, Gallop's style strategically plays its part in engaging the reader in her arguments for a different sexual economy. She performs a more polemically, politically disruptive, feminist intervention in her debates with authoritative figures and texts. Her writing incorporates acute critical investigation and confessional exploration of her transference as reader, particularly of Lacan. More than most American feminists, Gallop engages with Lacan, particularly with respect to the question of the BODY – 'all that in the organism which exceeds, and antedates consciousness or reason or interpretation' (1988, p. 13). Nancy Miller both explores the formation of the female critical subject and develops a subtle, historically specific feminist poetics (*see* PERSONAL/AUTOBIOGRAPHICAL CRITICISM). De Lauretis's work engages with ideology, semiotics and psychoanalysis and, in keeping with the political edge of her feminist position, sceptically questions the limits of the notion of sexual difference (1987). Alice Jardine's *Gynesis* (1985) deconstructively questions the male French masters' putting of 'woman' and 'the feminine' into the philosophical, psychoanalytic and literary discourses of modernity, and traces its implications for feminist thought, both French and American. Her perspective indicates the distance that American feminist thinking may travel from its empirical, materialist origins through encounters with French ideas.

French theories of (gendered) subjectivity and sexual difference, whether of a primarily psychoanalytic or deconstructive turn, are by now influential in American feminist literary critical practice and critiques of representation. The encounter between two such different traditions, as the proliferation of challenging and theoretically innovative texts suggests, has been more fruitful than negative, despite some feminists' reservations.

BIBLIOGRAPHY

de Lauretis, Teresa,1987: *Technologies of Gender*. London: Macmillan.
Felman, Shoshana, ed. 1977: *Yale French Studies*, 55–6.
Felman, Shoshana, 1985 [1978]: *Writing and Madness*, trans. M. N. Evans with S. Felman and B. Massumi. Ithaca, NY: Cornell University Press.
Gallop, Jane, 1982: *The Daughter's Seduction: Feminism and Psychoanalysis*. Ithaca, NY: Cornell University Press.
Gallop, Jane, 1988: *Thinking Through the Body*. New York: Columbia University Press.
Jacobus, Mary, 1986: *Reading Woman: Essays in Feminist Criticism*. London: Methuen.
Jardine, Alice, 1985: *Gynesis: Configurations of Woman and Modernity*. Ithaca, NY: Cornell University Press.
Johnson, Barbara, 1981: *The Critical Difference: Essays in the Contemporary Rhetoric of Reading*. Baltimore and London: Johns Hopkins University Press.
Miller, Nancy K., 1988: *Subject to Change: Reading Feminist Writing*. New York: Columbia University Press.
Miller, Nancy K., ed. 1986: *The Poetics of Gender*. New York: Columbia University Press.
Mitchell, Juliet, and Rose, Jacqueline, eds 1982: *Feminine Sexuality: Jacques Lacan and the École Freudienne*. London: Macmillan.

Moi, Toril, 1985: *Sexual/Textual Politics: Feminist Literary Theory*. London: Methuen.

Rose, Jacqueline, 1986: *Sexuality in the Field of Vision*. London: Verso.

Schor, Naomi, 1985: *Breaking the Chain: Women, Theory, and French Realist Fiction*. New York: Columbia University Press.

Spivak, Gayatri Chakravorty, 1987: *In Other Worlds: Essays in Cultural Politics*. New York: Routledge Chapman and Hall.

ELIZABETH GUILD

Freud, Anna (*b.* Vienna, 3 December 1895; *d.* London, 9 October 1982). Anna Freud's chief contributions to psychoanalysis have been collected in the eight volumes of her *Writings* and put into practice at the Anna Freud Centre, London (formerly the Hampstead Clinic), where she and her partner Dorothy Burlingham did pioneering work in child analysis and exploration of normal child development. While the other two of the three British schools of psychoanalysis (the Kleinians and the Middle Group) have had indirect influence on feminism, Anna Freud's group has not. Her work has been seen simply as an extension of her father's.

Anna Freud did adopt the Freudian formulations so many current feminists have refused: she had an instinctual drive theory as well as an ego psychology and she took structural (id, ego, superego) theory for granted: she did not emphasize PRE-OEDIPAL over oedipal dynamics: she wrote extensively about PENIS ENVY and masturbation conflicts. She was, further, a critic of feminism, and considered that phrases like 'the social construction of gender' ignored both the anatomical distinctions between the sexes and intra-psychic conflicts. None the less, her work has much to offer feminists, as some recent clinical contributors to *The Psychoanalytic Study of the Child*, a journal she co-founded in 1945, have recognized.

Of greatest importance is the fact that Anna Freud never assumed a monolinear model of human development. Each person develops along a plurality of 'developmental lines' (from autoerotism to object-love; from inter- to extra-family love; from bodily dependence and uncontrol to control and self-care; from play to work; etc.) and each employs a variety of the defences described in *The Ego and the Mechanisms of Defence* (1966) on the different lines. A woman's adult character is a registration of her courses along all these lines, and any psychopathology in her can either lie primarily in one line or be the product of uneven progress among several. This general theory implies, for example, that for some women penis envy will be critical, and for others it will be relatively minor, fleeting; in some, mother-love will be reproduced, while in others father-love will dominate, and in still others sibling rivalry fills the clinical picture; some will be crucially shaped by specific traumas or handicaps or over-reliance on a single defence; others, by specific identifications or by cultural and multi-cultural milieus. All stages of life have important roles in character achieved and also in psychopathology.

Anna Freud argued strongly against privileging any line of development or life-stage (including the first, the pre-oedipal) in theory and against neglecting any in therapy. This general approach, which was multi-causal and anti-reductionistic, could be of great importance to feminism. Had her work been less conventionally normative, it would have been truly radical, and perhaps would have been more clearly recognized as feminist in theoretical spirit.

See also FREUD'S FEMALE PATIENTS/FEMALE ANALYSTS.

WRITINGS

1966: *The Ego and the Mechanisms of Defence.* New York: International Universities Press.

1966–80: *The Writings of Anna Freud*, 8 vols. Madison, Conn.: International Universities Press.

Sandler, Joseph, et al. 1980: *The Technique of Child Analysis: Conversations with Anna Freud.* Cambridge, Mass.: Harvard University Press.

BIBLIOGRAPHY

Memorial issues dedicated to Anna Freud: *Bulletin of the Hampstead Clinic*, 6 (1983); *International Journal of Psycho-Analysis*, 64 (1983); *Psychoanalytic Study of the Child*, 39 (1984).

Young-Bruehl, Elisabeth, 1988: *Anna Freud: A Biography.* New York: Summit Books.

Young-Bruehl, Elisabeth, 1989: 'Anna Freud for feminists', *Mind and the Body Politic.* London: Routledge, pp. 170–97.

ELISABETH YOUNG-BRUEHL

Freud, Sigmund (*b*. Freiberg, Moravia, 6 May, 1856; *d*. London, 23 September, 1939).

Life and Work

Sigmund Freud began his career as a neurologist, publishing papers from the early 1880s onwards, but soon suspected that many patients treated for organic, neurological disorders were suffering from psychologically induced symptoms. In the mid-1880s he travelled to Paris to study under the most eminent psychologist of the day, Charcot, at his clinic in La Salpêtrière, where he was treating hysterics by means of hypnosis. What interested Freud was the way Charcot could treat apparently organic illnesses by purely verbal, non-organic techniques; Charcot's hysterics, it seems, merely *imitated* organic illness, but needed altogether different therapeutic treatment.

With the publication of his first major text (with Breuer, 1895), the *Studies on Hysteria*, psychoanalysis as such was born. The 'Studies' were made up of the analyses of five female hysterics, the best known being Breuer's patient, 'Anna O.' – Bertha Pappenheim (one of Germany's first feminists of the twentieth century), a most intelligent woman, who suffered from a number of incapacitating symptoms. She described her treatment as 'the talking cure', a phrase Freud considered particularly apt for describing psychoanalysis. The 'Studies' introduced a number of the key concepts Freud was to develop over the next thirty years: his notion of the splitting of consciousness and the over-determination of hysterical and neurotic symptoms anticipated his later understanding of the unconscious; he developed a notion of a non-genital sexuality (a preliminary to his more developed conception of infantile sexuality), and the concepts of TRANSFERENCE, COUNTERTRANSFERENCE and resistance to psychotherapeutic treatment, all of which emerged as major themes. He argued that HYSTERIA was the result of psychological conflict which was unable to gain expression except through corporeal symptoms. The hysteric was expressing in bodily form the various psychical conflicts tormenting her. By remembering and verbalizing these conflicts, the analysand was able to gain relief from the symptoms (*see* SYMPTOM).

The two themes dominating the 'Studies', the splitting of consciousness and the frustrations of the analysand's sexual life, became the cornerstones of psychoanalysis and the objects of investigation of his next major writings. In 1900, Freud published his most famous and respected text, 'The interpretation of dreams', outlining his understanding of the unconscious; and in 1905, he published the 'Three essays on the theory of sexuality', containing his hypothesis of a sexuality that exists in infantile life, whose form will provide the outline for adult sexuality.

If the first phase of Freud's work dates from 1895 until about 1910, his middle period culminates around 1915, when he published the 'Papers on metapsychology', in which he presented a theoretical discussion and analysis of the concepts upon which he had to rely in his case studies. These papers, together with his papers on psychotherapeutic technique, were crucial in establishing the theoretical and practical validity of psychoanalysis as institution, body of knowledge and mode of treatment. They included papers on repression, the unconscious, mourning and melancholia, and NARCISSISM. The final phase of his work dates from about 1919 until his death. During these years he explored a number of new postulates (including the concept of the DEATH DRIVE and the UNCANNY) developed new models or topographies of the psychical agencies, and analysed culture and works of ART. He also returned to a number of elements of his earliest works – the concept of the ego, sexuality, and particularly the question of female sexuality, which he began to explore in detail only after 1924 (see Freud, 'The dissolution of the oedipus complex', 1924; 'Some psychical consequences of the anatomical distinction between the sexes', 1925; 'Female sexuality', 1931; and 'Femininity', 1933).

Basic Concepts

Freud's great contributions to twentieth-century thought and to contemporary feminist theory were his various accounts of SEXUALITY and the UNCONSCIOUS. He provided a number of sometimes incompatible models of the psychical functioning of subjects, in which the agencies constituting subjectivity are analysed one way or another in a changing set of schemas, whose utility was judged from the point of view of capacity to explain clinical data. Feminist theory found some ready-made ingredients in Freud's writings of direct relevance to their explorations of women's oppression; but in turn, it had to devise a series of procedures by which to appropriate psychoanalytic theory for its own purposes, techniques of reading and theory production that were methodologically and politically risky in so far as feminists either risk being appropriated into the theoretical system, or else remain outside it, unable to utilize its insights to their own advantage. Where psychoanalysis is of theoretical use to feminist theory, it entails a feminist re-working or re-deployment of psychoanalytic principles and techniques against its own explicit pronouncements and underlying presumptions.

To explain what Freud meant by sexuality, his notion of PLEASURE must be elucidated. Pleasure and its opposite, pain, are defined in biological terms. For Freud, pain is the increase in tension within the organism. While a certain level of tension is necessary to maintain life, beyond this threshold the increase in tension leads to pain. Pleasure is simply the removal or easing of that tension. Upon satisfaction, tension is diminished and pleasure experienced (Freud, *Project for a Scientific Psychology*, 1950; 'Instincts and their vicissitudes' 1915, pp. 111–40). The sensations of hunger are based on physiological tensions that increase over time. These tensions strive for food as the object to bring pleasure and thus relief. However, the biological functions regulating pleasure and pain cannot be identified with sexuality, which is a psychical re-tracing of biological instincts (see Freud, 1905, pp. 181–2).

Sexuality is in no sense 'natural' or innate, instinctive or regulated by
BIOLOGY, but is pleasure, derived from a wide variety of sources, and
directed, not to a real object but to a LACK or an absent, that is, a fantasmatic OBJECT (Freud, 1905, p. 222). Sexual drives, which find their
source in the child's erotogenic zones, libidinally invest the child's body
with an unevenly distributed flow of intensities, creating privileged loci
for the expression of (sexual) DESIRE (*see* BODY).

Freud thus posits an infantile sexuality preceding adult genitality, and
an unconscious that cannot be considered submerged consciousness.
These two notions radically de-stabilized prevailing conceptions of sexual identity and human subjectivity. Sexual identity could no longer be
considered innate, pre-given, the result of biological or hormonal factors; instead, adult genitality is the result of the repression of infantile
polymorphous perverse sexual drives. The sexes are not simply born
biologically different. Their differences are re-inscribed, given new
meaning and preferred paths of development according to cultural
requirements through the mediation of the OEDIPUS COMPLEX. Although
Freud did not recognize it in these terms, the oedipus complex is regarded by many feminists as the culmination point of the child's induction
into patriarchal social values, the point at which the boy acquires the
characteristics of masculinity, and the girl the features of femininity.
MASCULINITY and FEMININITY, in accordance with patriarchal misconcep-
tions of femininity, are constructed according to the presence and
absence of a single defining term, the very term that designates male
superiority: the PHALLUS.

The phallus and the oedipus complex are crucial in both the establishment of the child's sexual identity and the construction of the unconscious. The division between consciousness and the unconscious appears
only as a result of the creation of the censor, the barrier that prevents
unconscious wishes and impulses gaining access to consciousness (*see*
REPRESSION). The censor or superego is the result of the child's (more
clearly the boy's rather than the girl's) resolution of the oedipus complex. When the boy is threatened with castration for his various infantile
attempts at seduction of the mother (outlined in Freud's case study of
little Hans, 1909), he renounces his sexual desire for the mother and
converts it into an identification with the authority of the father. The
oedipus complex forms the nucleus of the unconscious, and attracts into
the unconscious all subsequent experiences that recall the repressed
complex (*see* SEDUCTION THEORY).

The oedipus complex and its resolution are also crucial to the psychical position of the adult. It is what enables the distinction between neurosis and psychosis to be drawn. Neurosis is not the opposite of
normality, but of PERVERSION: the neuroses repress precisely what the

130

perversions express. Paradoxically, 'normality' is the ideal balance between the expression and the repression of perverse impulses. Depending on whether the child accepts the father's prohibition on access to the mother or not, the child will retain or abandon its perverse infantile condition; and depending on whether the repression of the desire for the mother is successful or not, the child will become a more or less neurotic individual. However, where repression fails to function, where the child repudiates or forecloses the father's oedipal interdict, failing to register the prohibition psychically, the child may remain in a psychotic connection to the PHALLIC MOTHER.

Freud presented a number of different accounts of psychical agencies: topographical (in which temporal relations are presented in spatial terms); dynamic (in terms of forces and impulses); and economic (in terms of quantities of energy). In what might be called his first topography, the unconscious is sharply separated from both the preconscious and consciousness. The energies regulating the unconscious and the conscious–preconscious systems are quite different: the first is regulated by the 'primary processes', which seek the immediate gratification of wishes independent of the constraints of reality; while the second is regulated by the 'secondary processes' in which gratification is deferred in accordance with the dictates of the reality principle (see Freud, 1900, ch. 7). This model is difficult to compare with his second topography, developed in *The Ego and the Id* (1923), in which the psyche is now described in terms of the distinction between the id, the ego and the superego. The id corresponds to a series of biologically given processes, impulses and wishes which strive for conscious expression. The impulses of the id are regulated by the functioning of the ego: as mediator between the id and reality, the ego's function is to restrain the id into accepting compromise satisfaction in the face of a hostile social world. The superego is a modification of the ego which functions to judge the performance of the ego, and, where necessary, to effect repressions of id impulses, creating an unconscious portion of the id. These two topographies, by no means exhaustive of Freud's understanding of the unconscious, provide much of the terminology and conceptual framework for feminist analyses of subjectivity.

Freud and Feminism

Without the willingness and desire to be analysed on the part of those hysterics first treated by Freud, psychoanalysis would not have been possible. Their speech is the foundation of analysis, even though his treatment of many female patients leads to his most spectacular failures. This paradoxical relation between hysteria and psychoanalysis has provided a densely compressed emblem of the continuing ambivalence between psychoanalytic and feminist theory.

If hysterical patients helped to make psychoanalysis possible, female analysts, who featured prominently within psychoanalytic institutions almost from the start, helped refine and develop psychoanalysis in various directions, particularly regarding Freud's conceptions of women's sexuality and development (see FREUD'S FEMALE PATIENTS/FEMALE ANALYSTS). From the 1920s through the 1930s, a number developed highly critical reactions to Freud's accounts of the female oedipus complex and female sexuality; indeed, the end of his paper on 'Femininity' (1933) is a response to many of these criticisms.

Probably the most articulate and sophisticated of Freud's 'feminist' colleagues was Karen HORNEY, who, along with Helene DEUTSCH and Ernest JONES, participated in a series of interchanges in the *International Journal of Psycho-Analysis*. Horney does not deny the value and importance of psychoanalytic theory, but challenges Freud's characterization of femininity (Horney, 1926). She claims that it is partial and value-laden, representing men's interests. Unlike most contemporary feminists, she seems committed to creating a genuinely neutral and universal scientific account, rather than developing women's perspectives.

The next wave of feminist reaction to psychoanalysis did not come until the late 1960s, when feminism (re-)emerged as a political movement addressing the politics of THEORY as well as the status of women. This development was marked by a series of critiques of and disagreements with psychoanalysis from the left in general (this was the era of anti-psychiatry) and from many feminists. Greer, Millett, de Beauvoir, Friedan, Weisstein (see Mitchell, 1974) condemned Freud's account of the oedipus and castration complexes and PENIS ENVY. They accused Freud of biologism, of limiting women's social possibilities through biological suppositions and of explicitly upholding male supremacism.

This hostility to psychoanalysis continues today among many Anglo-American feminists; but, under Lacan's influence in France, psychoanalysis became recognized as a tool in analysing the construction of subjectivity and was thus seen as an ally in revolutionary struggle. Lacan's interpretation of Freud, and his 'distinction' between the penis (an organ) and the PHALLUS (a sign) inspired a number of French feminists, including the group *Psychanalyse et politique* (see ÉCRITURE FEMININE), through which Juliet Mitchell's text, *Psychoanalysis and Feminism* (1974) became possible. MITCHELL spearheaded a new, positive response to Freud in claiming that Freud did not specify what women should be, but provided a 'scientific' description of how women are constructed in patriarchal culture. Mitchell's defence of Freud was vital in so far as it signalled the need to reconsider the question of how to interpret Freud, and use his work to explain facets of women's oppression; yet it was also problematic in so far as it left unquestioned Freud's presumptions about the *inevitability* of his oedipal mode. Her more recent work (Mitchell and Rose, 1982) makes it clear that without some account of the social constitution of masculinity and femininity and a concept like the unconscious, feminists cannot explain the transmission of patriarchal social values from one generation to the next.

Other feminists – Julia KRISTEVA, Hélène Cixous, Michèle Montrelay, Sarah Kofman, and Luce IRIGARAY – remain highly critical of psychoanalytic presumptions about femininity, using psychoanalysis in the service of feminism rather than criticizing feminists from a psychoanalytic perspective (as Mitchell does). They claim that psychoanalysis is not a science of human subjects, but rather a description of *male* subjects and perspectives. This means that, while it cannot be ignored by feminists (for it describes what PATRIARCHY expects and men require of women), it is unable to recognize and explain either sexual difference or femininity. Nevertheless, Freud's work enables unknown spaces to be developed by feminists using Freudian concepts like PRE-OEDIPAL sexuality, the movement of desire, and the unconscious to unsettle other terms, like the phallus, in his system (*see* FEMININE ECONOMY). These spaces may be read as symptoms of, or clues about, a concept of woman and femininity different from Freud's model of castration, lack or absence.

WRITINGS

1900: *The Interpretation of Dreams, SE*, 4 and 5.
1905: *Three Essays on the Theory of Sexuality, SE*, 7, pp. 123–245.
1909: 'Analysis of a phobia in a five-year-old boy', *SE*, 10, pp. 1–149.
1915:' Papers on metapsychology', *SE*, 14, pp. 105–260.
1923: *The Ego and the Id, SE*, 19, pp. 12–59.
1924:'The dissolution of the oedipus complex', *SE*, 19, pp. 173–82.
1925: Some psychical consequences of the anatomical distinction between the sexes', *SE*, 19, pp. 241–58.
1931:' Female sexuality', *SE*, 21, pp. 221–43.
1933: 'Femininity', *SE*, 22, pp. 112–35.
1950: *Project for a Scientific Psychology, SE*, 1, pp. 281–397.
and Breuer, Joseph, 1895: *Studies on Hysteria, SE*, 2.

BIBLIOGRAPHY

Horney, Karen, 1926: 'The flight from womanhood', *International Journal of Psycho-Analysis*, 7, pp. 324–39.
Irigaray, Luce, 1985 [1974]: *Speculum of the Other Woman*, trans. Gillian Gill. Ithaca, NY: Cornell University Press.
Jones, Ernest, 1961: *The Life and Work of Sigmund Freud*. New York: Basic Books.

FREUD'S FEMALE PATIENTS/FEMALE ANALYSTS

Kofman, Sarah, 1985: *The Enigma of Woman*. Ithaca, NY: Cornell University Press.

Mitchell, Juliet, 1974: *Psychoanalysis and Feminism*. London: Allen Lane.

Mitchell, Juliet, and Rose, Jacqueline, eds 1982: *Feminine Sexuality: Jacques Lacan and the École Freudienne*. London: Macmillan.

ELIZABETH GROSZ

Freud's female patients/female analysts   For the feminist, the fact that many if not most of Freud's early patients were women has required complex interpretation. So has the fact that the psychoanalytic profession, from its early days, has had many more women members than any comparable profession. Over the period 1920–80, 17 per cent of analysts in the US and 27 per cent in Europe were women (compared with 4–7 per cent women doctors and 1–5 per cent women lawyers for the same period); in the period between the world wars, 30 per cent of analysts were women, the high point being 40 per cent in London (Chodorow, 1987, 1989). Two questions are provoked by these recognitions: is psychoanalysis a symptom of women? Secondly, is the psychoanalytic profession one that is peculiarly receptive both to women's traditional skills and to women shifting from traditional roles to non-gender-linked professional occupations? The two questions might be tied together with a third: is the distinctive method of training in psychoanalysis – whereby every practitioner must start off as a patient, and every patient is, just by being a patient, engaged in the process that leads to professional qualification – one that allowed women in particular to find in psychoanalysis an answer to the woman question and a vocation that was psychically and socially congenial; one indeed, for many, that had the character of destiny?

Freud was greatly indebted to his early female patients in at least three distinct ways. First, they showed him how and how not to construct his theory and therapy of the neuroses. Deeply sympathetic as he so often was to their neurotic misery, a great admirer of their characters, which he regarded as grossly maligned by contemporary theories of the hereditary degeneracy of the hysteric, his sympathetic identification with the traumatic events that he pieced together as the causes of their troubles was absolutely necessary to the foundation of psychoanalysis: it allowed him to hear what they were saying. The extent of the sympathetic identification can be gauged from the first theory of the causation of the neuroses, the SEDUCTION THEORY. In this account of the violent introduction of SEXUALITY into the pre-sexual innocence of childhood,

Freud identified both with the victim of violation and, less immediately, less consciously, with the violator – wasn't his own penetrative method a repetition of this violation, he reflected? Even with this theory, however, Freud was well aware of the connivance and mutuality of these early perverse sexual relations; at the same time as he proposed the theory of seduction, he was coming to terms with, and eschewing responsibility for, the sexual fantasies and repudiated thoughts of these self-same female patients about him, namely, the transference (Freud, 1895a, p. 301; *see* HYSTERIA; TRANSFERENCE/COUNTERTRANSFERENCE).

These early patients not only showed Freud the way to his theory; but they also helped him make a living and establish himself in the wealthier bourgeois circles of Vienna. He had been guided by that most exemplary of patients, Breuer's Anna O., in reality Bertha Pappenheim, whose later career was so intriguingly different from the severity and misery of her youthful neurosis: she became a social worker, founder of the League of Jewish Women and champion of orphans and abandoned girls. Some of Freud's early patients were rich and distinguished members of European high society. Frau Emmy von N., the first of Freud's lengthy case histories in 'Studies on hysteria', was in reality Fanny Moser, the aristocratic widow of a wealthy industrialist, a salon hostess at her castle on a Swiss lake, an admired eccentric, philanthropist and patron of the arts. The true identity of another early patient, Frau Cäcilie M., whom Freud called his teacher and who prompted Breuer and Freud to write their 'Preliminary communication' in 1892, was Baroness Anna von Lieben, a member of the wealthy Jewish aristocracy. Freud's treatment of her and of her close friend Elise Gomperz not only taught him much but also created and consolidated contacts that the poor young doctor of a lower-middle-class family would not otherwise have had.

The intricate overlap between his family, his circle of friends and his patients both complicated and stimulated the development of Freud's work. The dream of Irma's injection of 1895, in which he discovered that dreams had a meaning and that they were wish-fulfilments, paraded a series of female patients whose treatments were worrying him. Behind these patients lay two different scenes: the scene of doctors violating the female patient, both surgically and sexually, and the scene of a father's sexual relations with his daughters – Freud's relations with his own daughters. The scene of medical violation was symbolized by Emma Eckstein, whose life had been put in danger by Freud's friend Fliess's surgical incompetence, and yet who was to remain one of Freud's most important, challenging and faithful patients, who before 1895 had given Freud a hint of the importance of wish-fulfilment in psychotic episodes, of the significance of the erotic transference and the mechanism of deferred action in the genesis of symptoms, and who was over the next few years to reveal to Freud the interweaving of sadistic fantasy and reality in her mental life. By late 1897, Emma Eckstein had shown Freud the way of the future for both his theory and his professional relations, by shifting from being a patient to being an analyst and taking on her own patients for psychoanalytic treatment. She was the first trained analyst.

The other great theme of the dream of Irma's injection, the father who seduces his own daughters, was to be transformed in Freud's development into the OEDIPUS COMPLEX, in which it is the little boy rather than the father who seduces the mother, at the risk of punishment from the interdicting father. But in reality, Freud found a way to preserve the father–daughter theme of the dream: his daughter Anna, centre of attention of the dream while still unborn, became his faithful Cordelia and Antigone, the unmarried virgin priestess of the psychoanalytic movement. She too, like Emma Eckstein, decided to become an analyst. Indeed, so did all the children of the medical figures who appeared in the dream; Robert Fliess, Marianne Rie-Kris, Margarethe Rie-Nunberg, Robert Breuer (albeit briefly) and Anny Rosenberg-Katan. The dream announced that the ignorance of the fathers would be visited upon the children.

In Freud's biography, there were in Ernest JONES's view two distinctive female figures: the sole sexual object he could contemplate, a gentle feminine woman; and the woman of a more intellectual and perhaps masculine cast (Jones, 1953–7, vol. 2, pp. 468–9). Among the latter Jones listed Freud's sister-in-law, Minna Bernays, then, in chronological order, Emma Eckstein, Loë Kann, Lou Andreas-Salomé, Joan Riviere, Marie Bonaparte – and we should add Anna Freud. Whereas Freud's close relations with men were likely to be riven with rivalry and eventual definitive breaches, he had the gift of sustained long-term relationships with these women. Yet these were not makeshifts or pale reflections of men. What distinctively marked them was their lack of erotic tension. Of course, many of these women felt most comfortable addressing him, as Loë Kann and Hilda Doolittle did, as father, although at least some of them also could happily address him as mother. The playful positive transference they shared suited them all, not least Freud. How directly Freud was affected by the positive erotic transference of many of these women patients can be gauged from his candid paper on transference-love in 1915: 'when a woman sues for love, to reject and refuse it is a distressing part for a man to play; and, in spite of neurosis and resistance, an incomparable magic emanates from a woman of high principles who confesses her passion' (Freud, 1915, p. 170). And, from the 1890s on, he had depicted the fate of women's sexuality as being essentially a tragic one, to be sympathized with, and sometimes to be protested at: 'women, when they are subjected to the disillusionments of marriage, fall ill of severe neuroses which permanently darken their lives' (Freud, 1908, p. 195). Women were doubly cheated in Freud's view of his society's sexual mores: first, by being rendered neurotic by the disillusionment and impotence visited upon them by their husbands, secondly, by the social demand for sexual abstinence (Freud, 1895b, p. 111).

Yet, despite his sympathy with the sexual plight of women, despite his acquaintance with and complicity in the explicit erotic transference, despite his growing conviction that neurosis stemmed from the arousal of repressed sexual memories, Freud's early sexual theories blithely ignored the distinction between masculine and feminine sexuality, except in so far as he wished to maintain and develop a theory of universal BISEXUALITY. What is remarkable about his theory of sexuality was how little attention it paid to the most fundamental distinction in human life, that between male and female (Freud, 1933, p. 113). Perhaps it was this claim that human sexuality, with its early developmental foci on areas other than the genitals, with its indiscriminate attachment to and taking up of objects, is much larger than the distinction between the sexes, that attracted women thinkers and students (*see* FEMININITY).

However, these women followers did not always become the intellectual collaborators that Minna Bernays and Emma Eckstein had been in the early days, or that Lou Andreas-Salomé and Anna Freud became later on. Lou joined Freud's psychoanalytic cause in 1912, and was greeted enthusiastically as a fresh and novel guarantor of its validity, with her wide literary reputation and her respected former relationship with Nietzsche; she soon became the only colleague who truly understood him and his psychoanalysis. Her writings focused on female sexuality, on love and on questions of NARCISSISM and SEXUAL DIFFERENCE, and also – overlapping more with Anna than Sigmund here – on beating fantasies, anal sexuality and masochism (*see* SADOMASOCHISM). Freud called her the 'poet of psychoanalysis', and he permitted her to moderate his hostility to broad syntheses and philosophical speculation.

No other colleague but Anna was as loved by or as intimate with Freud as Lou, but several, all women, became his close colleagues and friends. Mutual liking and respect, though never close friendship, characterized his relations with Helene DEUTSCH, whose early feminism and radical politics came to be channelled, with her training as a psychiatrist and her analysis with Freud in 1918–19, into her becoming one of the most important of the Viennese analysts of the 1920s. Her most solid and also most controversial work, however, was the study she had begun in the early 1920s, alongside Freud, of female sexuality, culminating in her

The Psychology of Women (1946), seen by many feminist critics as *plus royaliste que le roi*. It was certainly true that those prominent women theorists of female sexuality whose writings were generally in agreement with Freud's views were also members of his inner circle: besides Deutsch, there was Jeanne Lampl-de Groot, analysed by Freud in the early 1920s and a close colleague, friend and correspondent throughout the late 1920s and 1930s; Ruth Mack Brunswick, whose analysis with Freud continued over many years, beginning in 1922, and who effectively collaborated with him not only in the treatment and study of the Wolf-man, but also in developing their views on femininity. Then there was Marie Bonaparte, who graduated rapidly from being Freud's prized analysand of 1925 to being a dependable friend and unstinting benefactor, and who followed Freud in his explorations of the theory of femininity and of the concept of the death instinct (*see* DEATH DRIVE (FREUD)). Marie Bonaparte was to be a great power in the world of psychoanalysis, helping found the Société Psychanalytique de Paris, and continuing to exert, with her close friend ANNA FREUD, considerable influence throughout the psychoanalytic movement for some thirty years.

Anna Freud perhaps best exemplifies the relation of colleague and disciple to the founder of psychoanalysis. Even before she was born, as we have seen, this last child was identified in Freud's dreams with the creation of psychoanalysis. As she came of age, she increasingly shared her problems with her father, and, at the same time, studied his writings. Working as a teacher, she had already decided she wanted to be an analyst; but Freud dissuaded her from this, and took her into analysis in 1918. Her first patients were the children of her dead sister and great rival Sophie. She wrote her first paper, based, although covertly, on her own beating fantasies, and presented it for membership to the Vienna Psychoanalytic Society. A further episode of analysis with her father in 1924 failed, as did Marie Bonaparte's analysis, to 'drive her libido from the hiding place into which it has crawled', as Freud put it (see Gay, 1988, pp. 440–1). Yet, as he well knew, he had been entirely complicit in her attaching herself to her old Lear–Oedipus, as he had always manoeuvred things such that none of the suitors for the princess's hand appeared entirely satisfactory.

None the less, Anna Freud made the most of her fairy-tale destiny. Her father's mouthpiece, his nurse, his adviser, his dutiful daughter indeed; but also the innovator in child analysis in Vienna and the author of a definitive study of the ego's mechanisms of defence in 1936. Her life was always devoted to preserving her father's heritage, as she fought to find sufficient space in the Kleinian British Society, and throughout the international psychoanalytic community manoeuvred to win every political conflict and issue of the next forty years.

The example and figure of Melanie KLEIN, Anna's great theoretical and technical rival in child analysis, always provokes the query whether proximity to Freud always made it too difficult for his disciples, male or female, to find their own style and creative lode. Yet the example of Klein, together with Lou, Anna Freud, Helene Deutsch and the others, also provokes the question whether being female was not a more likely way to find creative and professional fulfilment in analysis than being male. 'Women always make the best psychoanalysts – until they fall in love, and then they make the best patients.' Thus Hitchcock's Hollywood dictum about analysis in *Spellbound*. A reversed version *might* be closer to the truth: 'It's the best patients who make the best psychoanalysts – and it takes a woman to be a good patient.'

See also FREUD.

BIBLIOGRAPHY

Appignanesi, Lisa, and Forrester, John, 1992: *Freud's Women*, London: Weidenfeld and Nicolson.

Assoun, Paul-Laurent, 1983: *Freud et la femme*. Paris: Calmann-Levy.

Chodorow, Nancy, 1987: 'Psychoanalyse und Psychoanalytikerinnen. Der Beitrag der Frauen zur psychoanalytischen Bewegung und Theorie', *Psyche*, 41, pp. 800–31.

Chodorow, Nancy, 1989: 'Seventies questions for thirties women: gender and generation in a study of early women psychoanalysts', *Feminism and psychoanalytic theory*. Cambridge: Polity Press, pp. 199–218.

Freud, Sigmund, 1895a: *Studies on Hysteria* (with Joseph Breuer), SE, 2.

Freud, Sigmund, 1895b: 'On the grounds for detaching a particular syndrome from neurasthenia under the description "anxiety neurosis"', *SE*, 3, pp. 85–118.

Freud, Sigmund, 1908: '"Civilized" sexual morality and modern nervous illness', *SE*, 9, pp. 177–204.

Freud, Sigmund, 1915: 'Observations on transference-love', *SE*, 12, pp. 157–71.

Freud, Sigmund, 1933: 'Femininity', *SE*, 22, pp. 112–35.

Gay, Peter, 1988: *Freud. A Life for our Time*. London: Dent.

Jones, Ernest, 1953–7: *Sigmund Freud: Life and Work*, 3 vols. London: Hogarth Press.

Livingstone, Angela, 1984: *Lou Andreas-Salomé: Her Life and Writings*. London: Gordon Fraser Gallery.

Swales, Peter J., 1986: 'Freud, his teacher, and the birth of psychoanalysis', *Freud Appraisals and Reappraisals: Contributions to Freud Studies,* vol. 1, ed. Paul E. Stepansky. Hillsdale, NJ: Analytic Press, pp. 3–82.

Swan, Jim, 1974: *Mater* and Nannie: Freud's two mothers and the discovery of the Oedipus complex', *American Imago*, 31, pp. 1–64.

JOHN FORRESTER

G

gender   Gender as a category emerges within feminist psychoanalytic discourse at the site of a series of debates about how and where to formulate the problem of cultural construction. Is gender *acquired* in the course of socialization and the internalization of norms, or is gender part of a linguistic network that precedes and structures the formation of the ego and the linguistic subject? For the most part, OBJECT-RELATIONS THEORY tends to argue that gender is a set of roles and cultural meanings acquired in the course of ego formation within family structures, and that significant changes in child-rearing practices and kinship organization can alter the meaning of gender and close the hierarchical gap between the genders of 'man' and 'woman' (see Chodorow, 1978). As an English term, 'gender' is used within some Anglo-American feminist theory, but does not usually appear within a Lacanian analytic discourse. Feminists re-working the Lacanian tradition tend to refer to SEXUAL DIFFERENCE, the primary form of linguistic differentiation that belongs to the SYMBOLIC and which conditions, regulates and institutes the speaking SUBJECT. Although LACAN comes to distinguish between the subject and the ego, it is clear that neither construct can exist prior to its marking by sex. Whereas most theorists of gender presume a subject who takes on a gender in the course of its development, the Lacanian view insists that the subject itself is formed through a subjection *to* sexual difference (for an exception see Wittig, 1985). Whereas gender appears to be a cultural determination that a pre-existing subject acquires, sexual difference appears to constitute the matrix that gives rise to the subject itself.

When 'gender' is used in feminist analysis, it is almost always defined in relation to 'sex': gender is the cultural or social construction of sex. The distinction between sex and gender has received consequential formulations in Simone de Beauvoir's *The Second Sex* ('One is not born, but rather becomes, a woman': de Beauvoir, 1952, p. 301) and in cultural anthropology where gender does not reflect or express sex as a primary given, but is the effect of social and cultural processes (Ortner and

Whitehead, 1981, p. 1). As a sociological or anthropological category, gender is not simply 'the gender one is', i.e. man or woman, but rather a set of contingent meanings that sexes assume in the context of a given society (see Scott, 1988).

The 'sex/gender system' is a coinage that anthropologist Gayle Rubin offered to explain the variable ways that kinship organizations produce gendered beings out of sexed bodies: 'Every society also has a sex/gender system – a set of arrangements by which the biological raw material of human sex and procreation is shaped by human, social intervention and satisfied in a conventional manner, no matter how bizarre some of the conventions may be' (Rubin, 1974, p. 165). Rubin's essay takes its bearings in relation to the work of Claude Lévi-Strauss (1969; see especially final chapter) and Jacques Lacan (1977a, b), and constitutes a specific effort to re-work the theoretical alignment of structural linguistics with a psychoanalytic account of the Symbolic. Her argument questioned the alleged universality of Lévi-Strauss's analysis of kinship relations in which he outlined the universal or permanent Symbolic structures that require every nascent human to submit to the incest taboo in order to enter into kinship and the cultural status of the human subject. Only through subjecting incestuous impulses to this taboo do 'subjects' emerge; as a result, human subjects emerge upon the condition that they are first gendered through kinship relations. In other words, to accede to the status of a speaking 'I', one (of course, there is not yet a 'one', although the temporal fiction of explanation requires this grammar) must first be positioned within kinship, i.e. become a daughter, sister, brother, son. These positions are secured, as it were, through the effectivity of the incest taboo, that is, the prohibition against certain incestuous unions that is effected through a compulsory *differentiation* among family members. Kinship relations can thus be understood as the enactment of this differentiating prohibition. 'I' only become a coherent and viable 'I' to the extent that I am differentiated from (prohibited from desiring or becoming) the members of my kinship group – family or clan (*see* ANTHROPOLOGY AND CROSS-CULTURAL ANALYSIS).

Significantly, the law of kinship produces human subjects, i.e. speaking beings, through differentiating between genders by means of the prohibition not only of incest, but also HOMOSEXUALITY; gendered subjects are thus produced through a series of generative prohibitions which regulate not only sexual behaviour, but sexual DESIRE itself. Part of the Lacanian contribution to this theory consists in the following suggestion: the 'I' is a coherent and viable 'I' to the extent that it effects an IMAGINARY identification with the parent of the same sex, and displaces its desire for the parent of the opposite sex on to a substitute for that parent. Of course, for 'the girl' matters are more difficult since she must effect a double renunciation: first, she must renounce her desire for the mother (the mother is understood psychoanalytically as the primary object) and then displace the ostensibly consequent desire for her father. Men have it easier, needing only to displace that desire for the mother. Of course, this account is highly debatable, since it presumes, first, a primary homosexuality on the part of women that is denied to men, and second, that women will not only deny the desire for the mother, but will be required to deny any desire for a substitution for the mother as well (*see* MOTHERHOOD; MOTHER–DAUGHTER RELATIONSHIP).

It appears, then, that it is only through subjection to this process of heterosexualized gendering that viable or coherent human subjects are produced. One is a 'man' to the extent that one does not desire other men, but desires only those women who are substitutes for the mother; one is a 'woman' to the extent that one does not desire other women (one has transformed the spectre of that desire into an 'identification') and desires only those men who are substitutes for the father. Indeed, 'one' is not a one, that is, a speaking, human subject, except through subjection (the French *assujettissement* might more accurately be translated as 'subjectivation') to this heterosexual imperative.

A significant difference emerges between feminist theorists based on object relations and those grounded in Lacan with respect to the effectivity of this primary prohibition. Object-relations theorists tend to confirm that this process whereby the differentiating norms of kinship are internalized actually works, that is, that the prohibitions are binding. On the other hand, feminist theorists such as Jacqueline Rose (1986) argue that the internalization of norms in the construction of gender is bound to fail. In so far as prohibitions are internalized, they produce a domain of unconscious fantasy that calls into question the stability of the very identification that the prohibition compels: 'the unconscious constantly reveals the "failure" of identity' (Rose, 1986, pp. 89–91).

The contestation of stable gendered positions is conceived yet differently by Rubin. Whereas Lévi-Strauss described the structures of kinship as *universal*, Rubin argues persuasively that those very structures are culturally variable and historically contingent. She claims that there are cultures in which kinship does not produce human subjects through the strict legislation of heterosexuality, and that kinship structures have a historical future which suggests a relaxation and revolution of the rules of kinship (Rubin, 1974, p. 199). Informed by feminist and gay cultural movements, the future of kinship relations could lead to the de-stabilization and 'overthrow' of gender itself. In this sense, Rubin is perhaps closer to those object-relations theorists who maintain that changes in family structures and co-parenting arrangements can effectively produce an equality between women and men.

At least two problems emerged in the context of Rubin's analysis. First, if feminists are to take Lacan seriously, gender cannot be said to be the cultural construction of sex, for 'sex' is established through the linguistic effect of sexual difference, and this effect is coextensive with LANGUAGE, and, hence, culture as such. Whereas Rubin presumes that gender is produced through various practices that regulate kinship relations, Lacan privileges the initiation into *language* as the primary process by which sexual difference is required and constituted. If the Lacanian scheme is right, gender cannot be overthrown, and the very wish to do so is a provisional fantasy inevitably thwarted by the Symbolic, i.e the constitutive constraints of language itself. Secondly, biological 'sex' is not a given, since there is a politically informed history of the biological sciences which articulates the putative 'facticity' and 'materiality' of sex (see Ortner and Whitehead, 1981). Not only have several writers, including Wittig and Foucault, argued that sex is a political category and not a biological given, but even within Lacanian theory, it is unclear that recourse to a pre-symbolic 'biology' is possible, since there is no direct, i.e. non-fantasmatic, access to that which precedes language. This latter point suggests that the sex/gender distinction, operative in sociological (Chodorow, 1978) and anthropological (Ortner and Whitehead, 1981) discourse, comes under critical pressure from the Lacanian view that sex is always marked within the matrix of sexual difference, and recourse to sexual difference can take place only within and as language. In so far as language designates cultural significance, sexual difference emerges simultaneously with culture itself. This calls into question the notion of a pre-cultural sex that must be made over into a culturally contingent 'gender'. Such a view has critical implications for any effort to consider 'gender' as that into which one is socialized, for the 'one' is always already marked by sexual difference, constituted, as it were, in culture as a sexed being prior to the process called 'socialization'.

On the other hand, a strength of Rubin's revision of Lacanian theory is that it challenges the way in which compulsory HETEROSEXUALITY is installed as a permanent feature of the Symbolic, and questions whether that naturalization of heterosexuality misreads the workings of kinship outside the framework provided by Lévi-Strauss. Moreover, in so far as the Lacanian scheme concentrates on the oedipal drama as that which articulates sexual difference, it misses the variations on how prohibitions, identifications and desires are constituted in contestation of the heterosexualizing norm. To accept that norm as the invariant Symbolic instituted in the rules of language implies that the only contestation of those norms will take place in the Imaginary and through FANTASY (*see* Rose, 1986), but that the norm will remain the invariable norm by virtue of which every such contestation takes place.

143

GENDER

If the strength of Rubin's critique is to be retained, it must be reformulated in a theory that both acknowledges the cultural primacy of the Symbolic – that fact that we are born into and through sexual difference – but also locates an historical specificity and contingency to that very Symbolic domain. To that end, the term gender remains an important reminder of the variable and contestatory modes of masculine and feminine psychic life as well as those forms of psychic life and SEXUALITY which either fail to fit squarely into those conventional domains or which cross those domains in ways that call for a new sexual vocabulary (*see* FEMININITY; LESBIANISM; MASCULINITY; SADOMASOCHISM).

To the extent that genders have remained binary within certain Western cultures, they have appeared to naturalize the distinction between men and women. Freud argued that this distinction is an unstable one, and that sexed positions stabilized through the 'accomplishment' of heterosexuality are in no way guaranteed (1905, pp. 233–7). Freud reviewed the possibilities of other developmental trajectories, such as various forms of inversion and modes of anatomical hermaphroditism. The development of stable genders within the binary frame of 'man' and 'woman' thus presupposes the effective exclusion of these other developmental possibilities. Conversely, we might well argue that the de-pathologization of these other modalities of gender is opening up the terrain of gender beyond the heterosexual matrix and the binary logic which supports it.

BIBLIOGRAPHY

de Beauvoir, Simone, 1952 [1949]: *The Second Sex*, trans. H. M. Parshley. New York: Random House.

Butler, Judith, 1990: *Gender Trouble: Feminism and the Subversion of Identity*. New York: Routledge

Chodorow, Nancy, 1978: *The Reproduction of Mothering: Psychoanalysis and the Sociology of Gender*. Berkeley: University of California Press.

Foucault, Michel, 1978: *The History of Sexuality*, vol. I. London: Allen Lane.

Freud, Sigmund, 1905: *Three Essays on the Theory of Sexuality*, SE, 3, pp. 123–246.

Lacan, Jacques, 1977a [1953]: 'The function and field of speech and language in psychoanalysis', *Écrits: A Selection*, trans. Alan Sheridan. London: Tavistock, pp. 30–113.

Lacan, Jacques, 1977b [1958]: 'The signification of the phallus', *Écrits: A Selection*, trans. Alan Sheridan. London: Tavistock, pp. 281–91.

Lévi-Strauss, Claude, 1969 [1949]: *The Elementary Structures of Kinship*, trans. J. H. Belle and J. R. von Sturmer. London: Eyre and Spottiswoode.

Ortner, Sherry B., and Whitehead, Harriet, 1981: *Sexual Meanings: The Cultural Construction of Sexuality*. Cambridge: Cambridge University Press.

Rose, Jacqueline, 1986: 'Femininity and its discontents', *Sexuality in the Field of Vision*. London: Verso, pp. 83–103.

Rubin, Gayle, 1974: 'The traffic in women: notes on the "political economy" of sex', *Toward an Anthropology of Women*, ed. Rayne R. Reiter. New York: Monthly Review Press, pp. 157–210.

Scott, Joan W., 1988: 'Gender as a useful category of analysis', *Gender and the Politics of History*, ed. Joan W. Scott. New York: Columbia University Press, pp. 28–52.

Wittig, Monique, 1985: 'The mark of gender', in *Feminist Issues*, 5/2 (Fall), pp. 3–12.

JUDITH BUTLER

gerontophobia   Defined in *The Oxford Companion to Medicine* as a 'morbid dislike of old people; alternatively, a dread of growing old' (Walton et al., 1986, p. 475), the term 'gerontophobia' was first introduced in American gerontological circles, where it met with much resistance. J. H. Bunzel (1972) explained that he and his colleagues had developed gerontophobia as a sociological concept, identifying fear and hatred of older people in the United States as a dangerous 'mass neurosis with the seat in the individual' (p. 116). Although Bunzel insisted that gerontophobia is fundamentally sociological in nature, it is obviously laden with psychological overtones in its specification of the origin of the fear of ageing in the individual psyche.

Instead of gerontophobia, the term 'ageism' took hold and is widely used today. Coined by American psychiatrist Robert N. Butler (1969), ageism is defined in *The Encyclopedia of Phobias, Fears, and Anxieties* as a 'stereotyping of old people' which results in discriminatory practices in order 'to avoid primitive fears of aging' (Doctor and Kahn, 1989, p. 12). Even here a psychological dimension is invoked. Ultimately the term 'ageism' was favoured over 'gerontophobia', in part because it gives a more sociological than psychological explanation of the phenomenon, and in so doing helps relieve researchers in gerontology from the burden of being implicated in prejudice against their own subject of research – the processes of ageing and the elderly as a group.

The dynamic relation between the psychological bases of fears of ageing in the individual and the social and cultural construction of ageing and the elderly remains to be carefully worked out. The distinction offered by the American social gerontologist Erdman Palmore (1990) is unacceptable on theoretical and factual grounds. He defines gerontophobia as an actual illness, as an extreme negative form of the widespread 'mild' prejudice against the elderly (pp. 38–9). But prejudice against the elderly is hardly mild. Gerald Gruman (1978) has offered a trenchant analysis of the cultural origins of ageism. What needs investigating is the extent to which fear of ageing is unconscious.

What is the relation of gerontophobia to psychoanalysis? First, Freudian psychoanalysis, as a theory concerned primarily with the early years of life (infancy and childhood, the PRE-OEDIPAL and oedipal phases), does not contain an explicit theory of ageing in general or of gerontophobia in particular. It has been argued, however, that Freudian psychoanalysis is itself complicit with the prevalent REPRESSION of ageing and oppression of the elderly in Western culture; in this view Freudian psychoanalysis is a symptom of gerontophobia and produces it as well (see Woodward, 1991). On the other hand, in the psychoanalytic life-course theories of Carl JUNG (1955), Erik Erikson (1959), and David Gutmann (1987), ageing is seen as a normal process which offers possibilities for psychic growth and development. Gutman explicitly challenges the catastrophic or gerontophobic view of ageing as one of decline only. The theories of both Jung and Gutmann, however, are strongly driven by stereotypes of MASCULINITY and FEMININITY.

Second, the analytical concepts and concerns of Freudian psychoanalysis and its descendants can be deployed to understand the working of gerontophobia, including analyses of anxiety in relation to ageing as castration, fears of the fragmenting body, narcissistic wounds to the ego and the specular body, unconscious denial of ageing and aggressive PROJECTION of it on to others, oedipal or generational conflict in late life, and the ageing body as phobic object (see Woodward, 1991).

Third, feminist critiques of Freudian and Lacanian psychoanalysis lead us to ask to what extent gerontophobia may be gendered, directed more towards women and the ageing female body than towards men and the ageing male body. The intersection of gerontophobia and sexism remains to be explored from a psychoanalytic point of view. In general, feminist contributions to psychoanalysis in terms of age-related categories have concentrated on the mother–daughter relation in the early years and have ignored the older woman.

Pioneering feminist Simone de Beauvoir herself makes the case for a psychoanalytic reading of gerontophobia in *The Coming of Age* (1978), a book which has been seriously neglected. She argues that no matter what the social and cultural context for every person, 'age brings with it a dreaded decline'; 'old age in others also causes an instant repulsion' (p. 60).

In old age women are subject to a double marginality at the very least, one that feminist critiques of psychoanalysis can help explain. First, the male fear of woman as the all-engulfing mother is exacerbated when women grow old; moreover, in psychoanalysis the attraction to the mother is taboo, and the older woman necessarily occupies the position of the mother or grandmother. Second, the connection between SEXUALITY and identity needs to be thought through in terms of the place of the post-menopausal woman in psychoanalysis. De Beauvoir (1978) offers this analysis (which is itself symptomatic of gerontophobia): 'as men see it, a woman's purpose in life is to be an erotic object, when she grows old and ugly she loses the place allotted to her in society: she becomes a *monstrum* that excites revulsion and even dread' (p. 184). Third, and perhaps most importantly, the consequences of the dread of ageing for feminism itself need to be addressed. Activist lesbian Barbara Macdonald (1983) has offered the most incisive indictment of what she refers to as the ageism of the woman's movement. The emphasis on *sisterhood*, she argues, reinforces and produces mistrust and divisions between younger and older women: 'youth is bonded with patriarchy in the enslavement of the older woman. There would, in fact, be no youth culture without the powerless older woman' (p. 39). (See also Alexander et al., 1986; Rosenthal, 1990.)

See also BODY; CASTRATION COMPLEX; HOMOPHOBIA; MOTHER–DAUGHTER RELATIONSHIP; NARCISSISM; OEDIPUS COMPLEX.

BIBLIOGRAPHY

Alexander, Jo; Berrow, Debi; Domitrovich, Lisa; Donnelly, Margarita; and McLean, Cheryl, eds 1986: *Women and Aging.* Corvallis, Oregon: Calyx.

Beauvoir, Simone de, 1978 [1970]: *The Coming of Age,* trans. Patrick O'Brian. New York: Warner.

Bunzel, Joseph H., 1972: 'Note on the history of a concept – gerontophobia', *The Gerontologist*, 12, pp. 116 and 203.

Butler, Robert N., 1969: 'Ageism: another form of bigotry', *The Gerontologist*, 9, pp. 243–6.

Doctor, Ronald M., and Kahn, Ada P., 1989: *Encyclopedia of Phobias, Fears, and Anxieties.* New York: Oxford University Press.

Erikson, Erik, 1959: *Identity and the Life Cycle.* New York: International Universities Press.

Grumann, Gerald J., 1978: 'Cultural origins of present-day "Age-ism": the modernization of the life cycle', *Aging and the Elderly: Humanistic Perspectives in Gerontology*, ed. Stuart F. Spicker, Kathleen Woodward and David D. Van Tassel. Atlantic Highlands, NJ: Humanities Press, pp. 359–87.

Gutmann, David, 1987: *Reclaimed Powers: Toward a New Psychology of Men and Women in Later Life.* New York: Basic Books.

Jung, Carl Gustav, 1976 [1955, 1956]: *Mysterium Conjunctionis: An Inquiry into the Separation and Synthesis of Psychic Opposites in Alchemy*, trans. R. F. C. Hull. Princeton: Princeton University Press.

Macdonald, Barbara, with Rich, Cynthia, 1983: *Look Me in the Eye: Old Women, Aging and Ageism.* San Francisco: Spinster's Ink.

GERONTOPHOBIA

Palmore, Erdman B., 1990: *Ageism: Negative and Positive*. New York: Springer.

Rosenthal, Evelyn R., ed. 1990: *Women, Aging and Ageism*. New York: Haworth.

Walton, John, Beeson, Paul B., and Bodley Scott, Ronald, 1986: *Oxford Companion to Medicine*. Oxford: Oxford University Press.

Woodward, Kathleen, 1991: *Aging and Its Discontents: Freud and Other Fictions*. Bloomington: Indiana University Press.

KATHLEEN WOODWARD

H

heterosexism   'Heterosexism' is a term that has enjoyed widespread currency in the field of lesbian and gay politics since the mid-1970s. It is strictly Anglo-American in origin and application, taking the form of a specification of the wider, generic term 'sexism'. In order to understand the discursive claims of the concept of 'heterosexism' it is first necessary to understand something of this prior concept 'sexism', which is frequently used to refer descriptively to all aspects of discrimination and prejudice rooted in beliefs about supposedly innate GENDER disparities. Jokes about women drivers are thus deemed 'sexist' because their humour resides in assumed notions about female technological incompetence, 'dizziness', and so on. It can be ascribed to individuals, or groups, or whole societies. It offers no theory to explain the phenomena which it depicts; rather, it is closely discursively aligned with radical feminist explanations of gender disparities and inequality by reference to 'the patriarchy', understood as the source of all basic power relations in society (see PATRIARCHY).

In the early 1970s many lesbians and gay men who were involved in the emergence of the modern gay movement came from political backgrounds which were heavily informed by radical or revolutionary feminism. Others were more influenced by varieties of anarchist thought and socialist feminism and these tendencies have competed for hegemony within the field of lesbian and gay politics, much as they have competed within the broad field of the women's movement. The term 'sexism' has always presented problems in lesbian and gay theory, since it *only* operates at the level of gender, and is blind to discrimination and prejudice organized around SEXUALITY. Sexism is often held to be a property of men, in relation to women; its relation to anti-gay attitudes is very uncertain. In this respect sexism has clearly moved into the linguistic mainstream of Anglo-American society, to the extent that it expresses a widespread cultural acknowledgement that the social and economic position of women is unacceptable. It is far from clear that the acceptance of HOMOSEXUALITY is as widespread, and indeed, the rarity of the

149

everyday use of the word 'homophobia' strongly suggests the extent of continued anti-gay prejudice (*see* HOMOPHOBIA).

This problem is what the term 'heterosexism' is intended to rectify. It offers a legitimating descriptive concept of specific kinds of discrimination and prejudice organized around sexuality. 'Heterosexism' might thus be defined as prejudice and discrimination against lesbians and gay men based on notions of innate heterosexual superiority. At its most common, 'heterosexism' identifies the tendency to systematically ignore or forget the existence of lesbians and gay men. In another vein, a piece of legislation such as Section 28 of Britain's 1988 Local Government Act, which discriminates against lesbians and gay men, might be termed 'heterosexist'; likewise, anti-gay jokes, or a failure on the part of programme-makers to acknowledge lesbians and gay men as part of the national television audience, and so on. Like 'sexism', heterosexism may be revealed either as presence or as absence. Furthermore, just as the concept of sexism relies upon a radical feminist theory of gender differences and inequalities, so the concept of heterosexism tends to rely upon a rather similar theory of anti-gay prejudice and discrimination, which it finds rooted in a massive homophobia. Given the close links in this theoretical/discursive formation with radical feminist thought, it is easy to understand how heterosexism tends to be seen as a target susceptible to political interventions. For example, it is believed that heterosexism might be remedied by anti-heterosexist education, on a par with the pedagogic aims of anti-sexist education, which is now a commonplace part of many training schemes for statutory and voluntary sector employees, especially in relation to equal opportunities programmes.

Heterosexism is thus a crucial term within a type of politics which aims to introduce positive images of lesbians and gay men into the field of secondary education, and which also wishes to establish the issue of anti-gay discrimination and prejudice as a serious national issue. In this latter respect it has undoubtedly proven strategically useful, but it is doubtful whether it has much theoretical purchase. Certainly the whole concept of heterosexism betrays a significant lack of interest in the psychic dimensions of the phenomena which it describes. Its model of culture and of the individual is completely 'culturalist' and contains no account of conflict or ambivalence, let alone the workings of the UNCONSCIOUS. This is hardly surprising, given the explicit hostility of radical and revolutionary feminism to psychoanalysis, which it dismisses *tout court* as patriarchal, sexist and probably heterosexist. Yet psychoanalysis has much to say about sexual anxiety, including heterosexual anxieties concerning homosexuality, although this is a significantly under-developed area within the literature of psychoanalysis.

In conclusion, the concept of heterosexism is symptomatic of a particular tendency within modern lesbian and gay political culture. It is intended to specify a type of sexism that affects lesbians and gay men, either by denigrating their sexuality or by denying its existence. While it can usefully draw attention to particular instances of discrimination or prejudice, it is unable to distinguish between neurotic behaviour on the part of a given individual, and the complex historical legacy of cultural boundaries drawn between supposedly licit and illicit sex. Indeed, it lacks any explanation of the varieties and degrees of heterosexist practices and beliefs. Its principal use has been in relation to institutions such as education and local government, as a means to draw attention to systematic forms of anti-gay discrimination and prejudice, as instituted within the school curriculum, for example, or in a refusal to recognize the legitimacy of lesbian and gay relationships for the purposes of obtaining pension rights for same-sex spouses. Perhaps the main significance of the term lies in the way it draws attention to the paucity of contemporary analysis in mainstream political or psychoanalytic theory of how heterosexuality forms social identities that are consciously or unconsciously conceived in relations of opposition rather than complementarity to homosexuality. Psychoanalysis will in any case doubtless find many conflicting forces at work in the fantasies and neuroses that shape the unacceptable attitudes and behaviours which for convenience's sake we may designate as heterosexist.

See also HETEROSEXUALITY; LESBIANISM; WOMAN-IDENTIFIED WOMAN/RADICAL LESBIANISM.

BIBLIOGRAPHY

Fuss, Diana, 1989: Essentially Speaking: Feminism, Nature and Difference. New York: Routledge.
Lewes, Kenneth, 1988: The Psychoanalytic Theory of Male Homosexuality. New York: Simon and Schuster.
Sedgwick, Eve Kosofsky, 1990: Epistemology of the Closet. Berkeley: University of California Press.
Weeks, Jeffrey, 1985: Sexuality and its Discontents: Meanings, Myths and Modern Sexualities. London: Routledge and Kegan Paul.

SIMON WATNEY

heterosexuality   'From the point of view of psycho-analysis,' Freud wrote in 1915, in a footnote addition to the 'Three essays on the theory of sexuality', 'the exclusive sexual interest felt by men for women is . . . a problem that needs elucidating . . . ' (Freud, 1905, p. 146, n. 1, added 1915). Writing in the wider context of the peculiarities of object-choice,

HETEROSEXUALITY

Freud noted that, whereas the ancient world laid stress on the sexual instinct in all its vicissitudes, the modern world despises the instinctual activity and finds excuse for it 'only on the merits of the object' (p. 149, n. 1, added 1910) (*see* OBJECT).

This is a profoundly radical position, though one often ignored or rejected in the subsequent history of psychoanalysis, because it problematizes heterosexuality at the same time as it potentially validates its supposed polar opposite, HOMOSEXUALITY. Both heterosexuality and homosexuality can be traced back to the constitutional BISEXUALITY of all human beings. Both are treated as potential limitations on the range of sexual choices, compromise formations shaped in complex psychic processes rather than the inevitable outcome of a pre-given instinct or 'an attraction that is ultimately of a chemical nature' (Freud, 1905, p. 146, n. 1). As the reference to the ancient world suggests, there is an implication in what Freud writes here that cultural norms have a vital part to play in delimiting SEXUALITY in this way. The categories of 'heterosexuality' and 'homosexuality', and the supposed exclusivity and polarity they suggest, need interrogation, and cannot be taken for granted.

Words, Freud once remarked, were originally magic. If not magical in their impact, the emergence of the two terms 'heterosexuality' and 'homosexuality' mark a crucial stage in the modern definition and delimitation of sexuality, which in turn provide an essential backcloth to Freud's own endeavours. The two terms were coined by the same person, Karl Maria Kertbeny, and were first used publicly by him in 1869 (Katz, 1990, p. 12). The context in which they emerged is critical: they were deployed in relation to an early attempt to put on the political agenda in Germany the repeal of the anti-sodomy legislation. They were part of a wider effort, subsequently taken up by the developing discipline of sexology, to define 'homosexuality' as a distinctive form of sexuality, a benign variant in the eyes of the embryonic law reformers, against the potent but unspoken and ill-defined norm of 'normal sexuality' (another of Kertbeny's neologisms). Hitherto, sexual activity between people of the same biological sex had been dealt with under the catch-all category of sodomy, generally seen as a potential in all sinful creatures. Early propagandists were anxious to suggest that homosexuality was a distinct mark of a particular type of person. As Michel Foucault has noted, the sodomite was seen as a temporary aberration, whereas the homosexual belonged to a species (Foucault, 1979).

The deployment of these terms must be seen, therefore, as part of a major effort at the end of the nineteenth century and the beginning of the twentieth to define more closely the types and forms of sexual behaviour and identity, in which homosexuality and heterosexuality became key oppositional terms. In the process, however, the implica-

152

tions of the words subtly changed. Homosexuality, instead of being seen as a benign variant as the coiner of the term intended, became a medico-moral description in the hands of pioneering sexologists such as Richard von Krafft-Ebing. The ever-widening categorization of sexual perversities became a means of defining the norm more closely. Heterosexuality, as a term to describe the hitherto untheorized norm, slowly came into use in the early twentieth century – more slowly, it should be noted, than its partner word: a norm rarely needs an explicit descriptor.

Freud's own work can be seen as in part a dialogue with this wider sexological effort. Sexology took upon itself two distinct tasks. First, it attempted to define the key characteristics of what constituted normal MASCULINITY and FEMININITY, seen as distinct characteristics of biological men and women. In this process it relied heavily on post-Darwinian evolutionary biology, and on subsequent discoveries concerning the chromosomes and hormones (Freud's 'chemicals'). Secondly, by cataloguing the infinite variety of sexual practices, it produced a hierarchy in which the abnormal and the normal could be distinguished. For most of the pioneers, the two endeavours were closely linked: heterosexual object-choice was closely linked to normal genital intercourse. Other sexual activities were either accepted as fore-pleasures or condemned as aberrations and perversions.

Freud consciously problematizes these links. In his first major statement on sexuality, the 'Three essays' (1905), he begins with a discussion of homosexuality, thus severing the expected connection between sexuality and heterosexual object-choice, and continues with a discussion of the PERVERSIONS, so breaking the automatic link between PLEASURE and genitality. The accomplishment of heterosexual object-choice, if ever fully achieved, linked to the genital organization of sexuality, must be understood as the culmination of a process of development, not assumed as a starting-point. Though never departing from his belief that in the end a biological explanation might exist for the form of object-choice assumed by an individual, Freud, unlike his contemporaries, did not take BIOLOGY as the starting-point for understanding heterosexuality. We need, on the contrary, to 'loosen the bond that exists in our thoughts between instinct and object' (1905, pp. 147–8). They are merely 'soldered' together in a process of psychic development.

For Freud, of course, the mechanism by which heterosexual (like homosexual) object-choice was achieved was the OEDIPUS COMPLEX, the central phenomenon of early childhood (1924). It marks the end of autoeroticism, and the achievement of true object-relatedness. It is abolished in the UNCONSCIOUS by the threat or perception of castration, and survives only in traces of pathological psychic structures. For heterosexual object-choice to occur, the child's narcissistic libido must be strong enough to outweigh the strength of earlier object cathexes and identifications. But this is by no means a foregone conclusion. To attain the anatomically appropriate gender identification, as a man or woman, and the culturally necessary genital organization of sexuality in the interest of procreation, is a hazardous and trauma-prone process (particularly for the young girl), and even when apparently achieved is constantly open to disruption. Adult sexuality only emerges by 'a series of developments, combinations, divisions and suppressions which are scarcely ever achieved with ideal perfection' (Freud, 1913, p. 180).

This does not mean, however, that Freud does not think a heterosexual resolution necessary. When all the proper qualifications are made, Freud does insist that a heterosexual object-choice is the most appropriate. A development assumes a norm, and for Freud this could only be heterosexuality as the guarantee of reproduction and the survival of the species. Running through his writings on sexuality are two themes: the unstructured and polymorphous nature of infantile sexuality; and the necessity of abandoning this in the accession to heterosexual masculinity and femininity. Freud is saying simultaneously that GENDER and sexual identifications are precarious, provisional and continually undermined by the play of desire, and that they are necessary and essential, the guarantee of mental and social health. The latter argument has been the starting-point for most subsequent psychoanalytical writings on heterosexuality, which increasingly from the 1940s assumed heterosexuality as the given state from which homosexuality was a by-product as the result of trauma.

Heterosexuality, thrown into sharp relief by its deviant 'other', homosexuality, remains the norm of our culture, and the unspoken taken-for-granted of almost all our discussions of sexuality. The procreative emphasis to which Freud was heir has shifted, and the aberrant forms that he sought to explore as dispassionately as possible have increasingly been integrated into heterosexuality as aids to pleasure and the success of loving relations. But the centrality of heterosexuality has rarely been questioned. Its aetiology is rarely explored, almost a century after Freud began his work. Only under the impact of contemporary feminism has its role as a power relationship been explored and challenged (see HETEROSEXISM). The study of heterosexuality as a historically specific organization of sexuality, embedded in social institutions and practices, is still in its infancy (Rich, 1980; Katz, 1990).

Yet the issues raised by Freud are as potent as ever. When Alfred Kinsey suggested in the late 1940s that sexuality was not a pre-given destiny but a continuum he was, despite his own rejection of psychoanalysis, and the widespread disregard of his findings by analysts at the time, fully in line with Freud's work. The idea of seeing sexuality in this way is still, apparently, a threatening one. The full complexities of gender, and the precarious nature of sexual identity, remain to be explored. In this task the work of Freud still provides a radical point of departure.

BIBLIOGRAPHY

Foucault, Michel, 1979: *The History of Sexuality*, vol. 1: *An Introduction*. London: Allen Lane.

Freud, Sigmund, 1905: *Three Essays on the Theory of Sexuality*, SE, 7, pp. 123–245.

Freud, Sigmund, 1913: 'The claims of psycho-analysis to scientific interest', *SE* 13, pp. 165–92.

Freud, Sigmund, 1924: 'The dissolution of the oedipus complex', *SE*, 19, pp. 173–82.

Katz, Jonathan Ned, 1990: 'The invention of heterosexuality', *Socialist Review*, 21/1, pp. 7–34.

Rich, Adrienne, 1980: 'Compulsory heterosexuality and lesbian existence', *Signs*, 5/4, pp. 631–60.

Weeks, Jeffrey, 1986: *Sexuality*. Chichester and London: Ellis Horwood and Tavistock.

JEFFREY WEEKS

homophobia   The popularization of the concept of 'homophobia' is generally attributed to George Weinberg (1972), and was elaborated as a reaction to the view that HOMOSEXUALITY was a problem of mental health. In response to a new spirit of self-affirmation among homosexuals, Weinberg argued that the real problem was not homosexuality but society's reaction to it. This took the form, he suggested, of a phobia, prevalent among most non-homosexuals. Homophobia was defined as 'the dread of being in close quarters with homosexuals' (Weinberg, 1972, p. 5), inculcated in early life, which produced a revulsion towards homosexuals and often a desire to inflict punishment or retribution on them. Among homosexuals themselves this led to a chronic self-denial and a flight into guilt.

The relation of this concept to psychoanalysis is complex. Weinberg himself argued that psychoanalysis was itself a major agent for the reproduction of homophobia (1972, p. 23). At the same time, however, roots of the idea can be found in psychoanalytical writings themselves. As a contemporary analyst has put it, 'irrational, anxious, hostile responses may be activated not only amongst people who are threatened by their own homosexual impulses, but also in any one whose aggressive and sexual feelings are barely repressed' (Friedman, 1988, p. 187).

155

HOMOPHOBIA

As a tactic in the campaign for homosexual rights the concept of homophobia has many 'splendid ironies' (Plummer, 1981, p. 62). Whereas traditionally the homosexual was regarded as sick, now it is those hostile to homosexuality who are thus labelled. Whereas homosexuals were often seen as having an irrational fear of the opposite sex, now heterosexuals can be portrayed as having their own fear, 'homosexual panic'.

There are certain problems with the concept. It stays, for example, within the problematic of mental illness, simply reversing the terms. Linked with this is an inevitable tendency to individualize the question of hostility towards homosexuality, making it 'a problem of personalities rather than societies' (Plummer, 1981, p. 63).

Weinberg himself recognized these problems to some extent. He listed a number of motives for homophobia, including religious injunctions, the secret fear of being homosexual, and the threat to values, particularly those relating to family life. Such explanations are clearly social and historical in focus rather than psychological. The concept of homophobia as it has developed so far has done little to explicate the complexities of the relationship between these social processes and the structuring of sexed and gendered personalities. But then, it could be argued, neither has orthodox psychoanalysis, which has only been minimally concerned with exploring the irrational fear of homosexuality (Friedman, 1988, p. 266).

It is perhaps as a *descriptive* term that the concept of homophobia has most value. It directs our attention to a widespread problem in modern society, a generalized hostility towards homosexuality expressed in a variety of forms ranging from personalized violence and media prejudice to legislative and judicial practice. The concept of homophobia can be seen as a borderline one, bridging the psychic and the social. It poses questions for both which need urgent attention.

See also HETEROSEXISM; HETEROSEXUALITY; LESBIANISM.

BIBLIOGRAPHY

Friedman, Richard C., 1988: *Male Homosexuality: A Contemporary Psychoanalytical Perspective.* New Haven and London: Yale University Press.

Plummer, Kenneth, 1981: 'Homosexual categories: some research problems in the labelling perspective of homosexuality', *The Making of the Modern Homosexual,* ed. Kenneth Plummer. London: Hutchinson, pp. 53–75.

Weinberg, George, 1972: *Society and the Healthy Homosexual.* New York: St Martin's Press.

JEFFREY WEEKS

homosexuality   Erotic relations between people of the same biological sex have a long history. The history of 'homosexuality' as a concept is, however, relatively short. The term itself was not invented until 1869; it first appeared in English in the 1890s, when used by the pioneering sexologist Havelock Ellis. While the idea of homosexuality frequently occurs in Freud's work, his preferred term is 'inversion', etymologically connected with the older, and more heavily value-laden term 'perversion'. The appearance of neologisms such as 'homosexuality', and the battle over the use of terms, is more than a matter of alternative labellings. It signals a struggle over meaning, in which psychoanalysis played a key role.

Freud's own work was decisively influenced by the sexological debate on homosexuality that was in full swing by the time he penned his early thoughts on the topic in the *Three Essays on The Theory of Sexuality* (1905). It was estimated by the German sexologist Magnus Hirschfeld that over a thousand articles on the subject appeared between 1898 and 1908, a crucial period in the development of psychoanalysis, and the various themes and tensions displayed in them are duly reflected in Freud's own speculations.

Three key questions deeply troubled the early sexologists: what *was* homosexuality? What caused it? And what were its implications for the health, social functioning and sense of self of the individual? Freud engaged with all of these. His main concern was not, however, with homosexuality as a social or medical problem, but with the psychic mechanisms of homosexual object-choice, and with the light that these threw on general psychic mechanisms. So Freud consciously distanced himself from many of the favoured ideas of his contemporaries.

Homosexuality, he believed, could not be regarded as a 'degeneracy', a favoured late nineteenth-century term to describe the abnormal. This was, in his opinion, a condemnation instead of an explanation. Such concepts were inadequate because inverts showed no other signs of mental or social 'inefficiency' apart from their sexual preferences. Moreover, the hypothesis of an original polymorphous perversity in both race and individual necessitated the abandonment of such loaded terms.

Similarly, he found the distinction between acquired and congenital inversion, one much favoured by people like Havelock Ellis, a fruitless one, given the widespread nature of homosexuality and the existence of non-absolute forms. Homosexuality could not be explained in terms of male souls in female bodies, or vice versa, as the pioneering writer on homosexuality Karl Heinrich Ulrichs had argued in the 1860s. Nor did homosexuals, he argued, constitute a 'third' or 'intermediate' sex, as Hirschfeld believed. The general explanation had to be found in the universal BISEXUALITY of human beings, not in the biology or hormonal make-up of a distinct group of people.

Starting with a notion of the original undifferentiated nature of the LIBIDO, Freud argued that homosexuality was a peculiarity of object-choice, not of a constitutionally given perverse instinct. The implication of this was that homosexuality could not be easily or straightforwardly separated off from HETEROSEXUALITY, for that too depended on a reduction in the range of object-choice. Both were compromise formations, both demanded explanations. Everyone, he wrote in his essay on Leonardo (1910), was capable of a homosexual object-choice, while sublimated homosexual feeling was an important factor in binding groups together.

The answer to the 'mystery' of homosexuality had to be sought in the general theory of the psychic apparatus, in the complex processes through which the human animal acquired sexed and gendered identities. The detailed explanation of why some people became homosexual and others did not varied considerably, however, in Freud's work (Lewes, 1988). In *Three Essays on the Theory of Sexuality*, (1905), he expressed the belief, repeated in subsequent work, that homosexuality in the male derived from the boy's refusal to relinquish his first love-object, the mother, his subsequent unconscious IDENTIFICATION with her and his consequent search for love-objects that resembled himself. This overlapped with an alternative explanation offered in the case study of Little Hans (1909) and in the essay on Leonardo (1910), where the young male, horrified by the discovery of the 'castrated' mother, rejects her and seeks a compromise figure in a 'woman with a penis', a feminine boy. In the case study of the Wolf-man, on the other hand, the child's discovery of the castrated mother propelled him into identification with his father, having earlier identified with the mother's passivity in relation to men (1918). Finally, in his paper on 'Certain neurotic mechanisms in jealousy, paranoia and homosexuality' (1922), Freud elaborated a fourth theory. Here an intense love for the mother is transformed into intense jealousy of siblings, and then into feelings of homosexual love through the process Freud called 'reaction formation'.

These explanations related almost entirely to male homosexuality, which was Freud's main concern, as it was for his contemporaries. They could not be simply reversed to explain lesbianism, which had to be understood in relation to the prolonged and painful process whereby FEMININITY was precariously achieved (*see* LESBIANISM).

Clearly Freud was reluctant to offer a monocausal explanation of homosexuality. This reflected his wider belief that homosexuality itself could not be regarded as a unitary phenomenon: what was thrown together for analytical purposes may derive from a number of processes of psycho-social inhibition, as indeed heterosexuality does. Should homosexuality therefore be regarded as on a par with heterosexuality?

At this point a fundamental ambiguity in the psychoanalytical explanation of homosexuality emerged. Freud favoured law reform, and his attitude towards his homosexual patients was generally humane. He rejected, for example, any idea that his young lesbian client was 'in any way ill', and throughout his writings he is extremely cautious about the effectiveness or desirability of a 'cure' for inversion. But inevitably there are certain normative assumptions in his work, which are best summed up in his famous letter to the American mother of a young homosexual. Homosexuality is assuredly no advantage, he wrote. But it is nothing to be ashamed of, it is not a vice, nor a degradation; it is not an illness: 'we consider it to be a variation of the sexual function produced by a certain arrest of the sexual development' (Freud, 1961, p. 277). Here we have, on the one hand, the demythologizing effect of Freud's theory of psycho-sexual mechanisms; and on the other a clear normative stance, for an 'arrest' presupposes a 'normal' development. Whatever the logic of the theory of the UNCONSCIOUS, and the acknowledgement of the fluidity of object-choice, Freud in the end does believe that the notion of development must imply a norm, and for him that norm can only be the necessity of heterosexual object-choice in the interests of reproduction (*see* OBJECT).

Freud's work opened the way to much less enlightened views than his own. From the 1940s, as the epicentre of psychoanalysis moved to the USA and ego psychology, with its emphasis on an adjustment to cultural norms, became dominant, a hostile tone became more pronounced. With this went an explicit abandonment of key elements of Freudian theory. Thus both I. Bieber (1962) and C. W. Socarides (1978), who published substantial studies of male homosexuality in the 1950s and early 1960s, rejected the central idea of bisexuality. Instead of seeing an original bisexuality of which both heterosexuality and homosexuality were in complex ways derivatives, such writers saw heterosexuality as the given natural state, from which homosexuality emerged as a result of a developmental blockage of the heterosexual impulse. In place of Freud's emphasis on it as a dispersed potentiality, homosexuality became a mark of and explanation for a pathologized type of individual (Lewes, 1988).

The alternative streams of psychoanalysis did little to redress the balance. Lacanianism has had little to say on the topic, and in the well-known dictionary by Laplanche and Pontalis (1980), homosexuality is dealt with only under the heading of 'perversion'. For Wilhelm Reich, the resolution of the OEDIPUS COMPLEX into genital heterosexuality was a natural development; only inhibition by socially oppressive forces could

159

prevent its natural, healthy efflorescence. Until recently, only in the radical psychoanalysis of Herbert Marcuse, in the 'anti-oedipal' writings of Gilles Deleuze and Felix Guattari and Guy Hocquenghem, and to some extent in post-Lacanian feminist writings, was there a clear emphasis on the positive merits of homosexuality as a sexual preference (Weeks, 1985).

Not surprisingly, when a new homosexual militancy developed in the 1970s psychoanalysis became a major target. A new theoretical tendency stressed the 'social construction' of the category of 'the homosexual' itself, a historic process designed to privilege heterosexuality. This was seen as in part the product of the socially controlling work of the sexologists, to which Freud's work was assimilated as a central moment (Weeks, 1985).

Such work has been very important in demonstrating the importance of historical processes and social definitions in shaping our concepts of the sexual norms. 'Homosexuality' and 'the homosexual' are increasingly seen as arbitrary sub-divisions of what is actually a flux of sexual possibilities. Ironically, it is the work of Freud himself which in part opened up such perspectives. The question remains open as to whether, freed of its normative overlay, psychoanalysis can contribute further to the understanding of the shaping of sexed identities as part of the complex dialogue of the social and the psychic.

See also HETEROSEXISM; HOMOPHOBIA; LESBIANISM.

BIBLIOGRAPHY

Bieber, Irving, et al. 1962: *Homosexuality: A Psychoanalytic Study*. New York: Basic Books.

Dollimore, Jonathan, 1991: *Sexual Dissidence: Augustine to Wilde, Freud to Foucault*. Oxford: Clarendon Press.

Freud, Ernst, ed. 1961: *Letters of Sigmund Freud 1873–1939*. London: Hogarth Press.

Freud, Sigmund, 1905: *Three Essays on the Theory of Sexuality*, SE, 7, pp. 123–245.

Freud, Sigmund, 1909: 'Analysis of a phobia in a five-year-old boy', *SE*, 10, pp. 1–150.

Freud, Sigmund, 1910: *Leonardo da Vinci and a Memory of his Childhood*, SE, 11, pp. 59–137.

Freud, Sigmund, 1918: 'From the history of an infantile neurosis', *SE*, 17, pp. 13–124.

Freud, Sigmund, 1922: 'Some neurotic mechanisms in jealousy, paranoia and homosexuality', *SE*, 18, pp. 221–33.

Laplanche, Jean, and Pontalis, Jean-Baptiste, 1980: *The Language of Psycho-Analysis*. London: Hogarth Press.

Lewes, Kenneth, 1988: *The Psychoanalytical Theory of Male Homosexuality*. London: Quartet.

Socarides, Charles W., 1978: *Homosexuality*. New York and London: Jason Aronson.

Weeks, Jeffrey, 1985: *Sexuality and its Discontents: Meanings, Myths and Modern Sexualities*. London: Routledge and Kegan Paul.

JEFFREY WEEKS

Horney, Karen (*b*. Eilbeck, Germany, 15 September 1885; *d*. New York City, 4 December 1952). Karen Horney has had a profound influence on psychoanalytic theories of FEMININITY, both within feminism and outside it, although like most women psychoanalysts of her generation, she was not interested in a feminist agenda. In her first article, written in response to one by Karl Abraham on the female CASTRATION COMPLEX (Abraham, 1922), Horney proposed one of the first systematic arguments against Freud's theory that PENIS ENVY constituted the central organizing force in female development, thereby helping to inaugurate what came to be known as the Freud–Jones debate (Horney, 1924). In this and in later, more polemical papers she argued that masculine narcissism was responsible for the assumption that the female feels her genital to be inferior and that male envy and fear of the female's reproductive capacity is the motive behind this assumption (Horney, 1926, 1932, 1933).

Horney found that, while the pre-oedipal girl with her hidden genitals is at a real anatomical disadvantage compared with the boy, and that envy of his ability to see, touch and display his genital is to be expected, this envy is neither the result nor the cause of the castration complex. On the contrary, this early stage is normally left behind without trauma as the small girl, guided by an intrinsic pleasure-oriented femininity in which the clitoris and the vagina play an integrated role, turns towards her father with a wish for his child. Thus the penis is desired libidinally for pleasure rather than narcissistically as a possession. The castration complex occurs only in the presence of a 'profound disappointment' or other disturbance when the girl, fantasizing that she is being castrated, identifies with her father instead of with her mother and regresses defensively to her earlier, PRE-OEDIPAL stage, while a 'second root' of the complex takes the form of a wishful fantasy of castration through violent intercourse with him. Thus penis envy in the post-oedipal female is a secondary and defensive formation; it is 'wounded womanhood' which gives rise to the castration complex (Horney, 1924, p. 63).

Horney's thesis was strongly supported by JONES and others, including KLEIN (1975) who credited her with the first examination of the oedipal sources of the castration complex in females. Horney propounded astonishingly advanced theories of male envy and fear of women, of the social determinants of penis envy and of a primary and active femininity. After her emigration to the United States in 1932, she came to focus on social, non-libidinal determinants of neurosis in both sexes, which eventually led her out of the Freudian camp altogether. Fliegel (1973) has shown, however, that Horney's 1924 paper almost certainly prompted Freud's major essay 'Some psychical consequences of the anatomical distinctions between the sexes' (1925), in which he revised his theory of symmetry between the sexes. Later, in 1935, Freud criticized attempts to 'establish a neat parallelism' between BIOLOGY and the psyche without reference to the mediating agency of the UNCONSCIOUS (Freud, 1971), a criticism recently revived in the context of Lacanian readings of Freud (Mitchell and Rose, 1982).

See also NARCISSISM; PLEASURE.

WRITINGS

1924: 'On the genesis of the castration complex in women', *International Journal of Psycho-Analysis*, 5, pp. 50–65.

1926: 'The flight from womanhood: the masculinity complex in women, as viewed by men and women', *International Journal of Psycho-Analysis*, 7, pp. 324–39.

1932: 'The dread of women: observation on a specific difference in the dread felt by men and by women respectively for the opposite sex', *International Journal of Psycho-Analysis*, 13, pp. 348–60.

1933: 'The denial of the vagina', *International Journal of Psycho-Analysis*, 14, pp. 57–70.

1967: *Feminine Psychology*. London: Routledge and Kegan Paul.

BIBLIOGRAPHY

Abraham, Karl, 1922: 'Manifestations of the female castration complex', *International Journal of Psycho-Analysis*, 3, pp. 1–22.

Fliegel, Zenia Odes, 1973: 'Feminine psychosexual development in Freudian theory: a historical reconstruction', *The Psychoanalytic Quarterly*, 42, pp. 385–408.

Freud, Sigmund, 1925: 'Some psychical consequences of the anatomical distinction between the sexes', *SE*, 19, pp. 248–58.

Freud, Sigmund, 1971: Letter to Karl Müller-Braunschweig, 21 July 1935, *Psychiatry*, 34, pp. 328–9.

Klein, Melanie, 1975: 'Early stages of the Oedipus complex', *Love, Guilt and Reparation and Other Works, 1921–1945*. New York: Delta, pp. 186–98.

Mitchell, Juliet, and Rose, Jacqueline, 1982: *Feminine Sexuality: Jacques Lacan and the École Freudienne*. London: Macmillan.

ESTELLE ROITH

hysteria Psychoanalysis was born with Freud's treatment of the illness then named 'hysteria' (from the Greek *hysteros* 'womb'), a uterus thought to be 'wandering', a malady as old as Hippocrates and the subject of the oldest known medical text (1900 BC; see Wajeman, 1988, p. 2). Before Freud, Charcot had been a pioneer in seeing hysteria as a disease, like other diseases; perhaps this viewpoint directed him away from its prolific, multiform nature. Reducing hysteria to one indivisible entity, Charcot attributed it to neurological affliction, but Breuer and Freud went further than Charcot to consider hysteria a 'psychic' disease with sexual disturbance in its aetiology. Freud discovered that hysteria owed its cause to the complexity of SEXUALITY (Freud, 1905), later claiming to have found biological 'homosexual' tendencies in hysterics.

LACAN translates Freud's find, the hysteric's sexual oscillation between women and men, into *the* quintessential question about GENDER, divided artificially by the effects of IDENTIFICATION and LANGUAGE that constitute a sense of being in the form of totalized gender concepts of male and female (Lacan, 1968). The hysteric's gender question – 'Am I a woman or a man?' – links sexuality to identity: her discourse reveals the fundamental impossibility of reducing identity to gender in the first place. For Lacan, there is no signifier, symbol or archetype adequate to re-present the difference between the sexes (Lacan, 1975, p. 74).

Freud described the relationship between libidinal problems and organic symptoms by focusing on the displacement of sensation or erotogeneity onto the hysteric's body. Monique David-Ménard has attempted to amend Freud's associational theory of hysterical symptoms by a semi-Lacanian interpretation of why the hysteric is disgusted with her sexual body: her *jouissance* has been negated such that her body is unsymbolized in the world (David-Ménard, 1989, pp. 89, 99; Freud, 1893, 1905). David-Ménard argues that Freud did not account for the hysteric's divided subjectivity or the effects of language on BODY; her distinction between the hysterogenic and erotogenic body is meant to fill in this gap in the theory of hysteria. Freud sought to substantialize the unconscious and homogenize the psychic and the somatic (David-Ménard,1989, p. xi). The hysterogenic body is produced when the sexualization of the erotogenic body has been somehow disrupted, making the hysterogenic body a prosthesis for the lack of an erotogenic one. Cure lies in the realm of movement of the language of *jouissance*, felt as an antithesis to the hysterical paralysis of negation. But from a Lacanian perspective, while the hysteric's dilemma lies in her not knowing whether to identify her body with that of a man or woman, its *cause* is the inadequacy of gender identity to support the anatomical difference between the sexes. Hysteria manifests the pattern of a daughter who identifies with her father, in opposition to identifying

163

with her mother. The hysteric is not disgusted by her sexual body *per se*, but by the effort of others to pin her down as a sexual body in terms of a gender identity for which she lacks a signifying basis (see Ragland-Sullivan, 1989).

The importance of such a thesis for an understanding of hysteria lies not only in its theory of *cause*, but also in its clinical description which views hysterical conversion symptoms as a relation between suffering and language. Although symptoms obviously change in form and content, Lacan argued that Freud's discovery of the UNCONSCIOUS as sexuality was this: a few precise structurings of desire (e.g. the OEDIPUS COMPLEX) are determined by certain identifications to a lack-in-being-and-in-knowledge. These structures show up in language as *jouissance* properties which under the patriarchal dimension (the *père-version*), are defined as neurosis (hysteria and obsession), perversion and psychosis. Lacan placed knowledge of the something else on the side of woman or the feminine: the hysteric's solution goes against the normative one of believing in cultural stereotypes, adapting to the Symbolic *père-version*, aiming, rather, at the Real father or the *jouissance* of the impossible. In its very impossibility, her quest reveals a LACK in DESIRE, a flaw in culture, and in knowledge. Not surprisingly, she has a certain subversive attitude towards norms. Lacan hypothesized that the hysteric's particular dignity comes from her ability to elevate a suffering life to a worthy position, despite the fact that her body is constantly invaded by anxiety and affect that others more successfully repress. In a more general sense, Lacan saw the hysteric as embodying the quintessence of the human subject because she speaks, as agent, from the lack and gaps in knowledge, language and being. In her 'being' she reveals the incapacity of any human subject to satisfy the ideals of Symbolic identifications.

Sarah Kofman has read Freud in a Derridean mode (Kofman, 1985). Where Freud claims that the sight of female genitalia causes castration fright for the male (1927, pp. 154-5), Kofman thinks he is describing his own horror and pleasure in relation to them in his theories of male castration anxiety and female PENIS ENVY (1985, p. 85). Lacan advances feminist theory beyond a literal biological reading of Freud, arguing that the culturally imposed sexual divide is the cause of a fundamental split in the subject that sets both males and females on a pathway of incompletion. His concern is not only to ascertain the *cause* of suffering, but also to find more efficacious ways of treating it. For example, anorexia, bulimia and *complaint* (lack of direction) are seen as modern manifestations of hysteria and treated in Lacanian clinics (see Cereda, 1982-).

Lacan sees hysteria as an oscillation of sexual identification that points to the Real impasse that makes all of language and knowledge a MASQUERADE around a sexual harmony which is not One

(Ragland-Sullivan, 1991). In so far as hysteria is constituted by identification, language and the mother's desire as it refers to a signifier for a *name*, Lacan argues that hysteria is the condition of the division of any speaking, desiring subject. When pushed beyond the limits of their control of language and affect, any person (except the psychotic, already living in a state of fragmentation) can be hystericized. This fundamental split, absent in psychosis (autism being a pole of psychosis), points to hysteria as a precise identificatory problematic, one that establishes a social link – discourse – because her identification with the lack in things points to a structure in knowledge that is itself an enigma. Cixous and Clément see the hysteric as a threshold figure for women's liberation and as a form of resistance to patriarchy. While Cixous argues that the 'hero' of women's writing in the twentieth century is the hysteric, Clément, insisting that the hysteric is a victim rather than a hero, maintains that women must act collectively (Cixous and Clément, 1986).

Lacan's contribution to feminism lies in his making a science of the REAL out of the enigmas such as hysteria that he finds in life and logic, even going so far as to describe Socrates and Hegel as hysterics. Lacan reserved his greatest praise for the *truth* of hysteria as a structure which speaks dissatisfaction with knowledge as it stands, in any age. He argued, moreover, that knowledge – cultural, academic, clinical – can only advance in so far as the hysteric's question prevails over the master's answer.

See also DISAVOWAL; MITCHELL; PSYCHICAL REALITY; SEDUCTION THEORY.

BIBLIOGRAPHY

Cereda (*Le Centre de Recherche sur l'Enfant dans le Discours analytique*), 1982–: Continuing series of publications on Lacanian analysis of children. Paris: Navarin, diffusion Seuil.

Cixous, Hélène, and Clément, Catherine, 1986: *The Newly Born Woman*, trans. Betsy Wing. Manchester: Manchester University Press.

David-Ménard, Monique, 1989: *Hysteria From Freud to Lacan*, trans. Catherine Porter. Ithaca, NY: Cornell University Press.

Freud, Sigmund, 1893: 'On the psychical mechanism of hysterical phenomena', *SE*, 2, pp. 19–47.

Freud, Sigmund, 1905: 'Fragment of an analysis of a case of hysteria', *SE*, 7, pp. 1–122.

Freud, Sigmund, 1927: 'Fetishism', *SE*, 21, pp. 145–59.

Hunter, Dianne, 1985: 'Hysteria, psychoanalysis and feminism: the case of Anna O.', in *The (M)other Tongue: Essays in Feminist Psychoanalytical Interpretation*, ed. Shirley Nelson Garner, Claire Kahane and Madelon Sprengnether. Ithaca, NY and London: Cornell University Press, pp. 89–119.

Kahane, Claire, and Bernheimer, Charles, eds, 1985: *In Dora's Case: Freud–Hysteria–Feminism*. New York: Columbia University Press.

Kofman, Sarah, 1985: *The Enigma of Woman: Woman in Freud's Writings*, trans. Catherine Porter. Ithaca, NY: Cornell University Press.

Lacan, Jacques, 1968: 'Bisexualité et différence des sexes', *Scilicet*, 1, pp. 85–96.

Lacan, Jacques, 1975: *Le Séminaire*, book 20: *Encore*, ed. Jacques-Alain Miller. Paris: Seuil.

Ragland-Sullivan, Ellie, 1989: 'Dora and the name-of-the-father: the structure of hysteria', *Discontented Discourses*, ed. Marleen Barr and Richard Feldstein. Urbana and Chicago: University of Illinois Press, pp. 208–40.

Ragland-Sullivan, Ellie, 1991: 'The sexual masquerade: a Lacanian theory of sexual difference', *Lacan and the Subject of Language*, ed. Ellie Ragland-Sullivan and Mark Bracher. New York: Routledge, pp. 49–80.

Wajeman, Gérard, 1988 [1982]: 'The hysteric's discourse', trans. Thelma Sowley, *Lacan Study Notes*, nos. 6–9.

ELLIE RAGLAND-SULLIVAN

I

identification The process or effect of identifying with others (a) through lack of awareness of separation or difference, (b) as a result of perceived similarities, or (c) through INTROJECTION of the other within the ego as a reaction to loss.

Freud (1900) first discussed identification as involved in hysterical symptoms and dreams through the adoption of similarities perceived in others. Later he used the term to refer to the narcissistic response to object loss in DEPRESSION, whereby the LIBIDO – and with it the abandoned OBJECT (both hated and loved) – are withdrawn into the ego (1917). Later still he implied that this involves regression from libidinal object ties, to oral incorporation of the object – that is, to an original form of emotional tie preceding and initially indistinguishable from object-love (1921, 1923).

Identification became central to Freud's later theory of mind as structured into id, ego and superego via the oedipus and castration complexes. He argued that the id's oedipal cathexis (or libidinal investment) of the mother or father adds a hostile colouring to the child's already existing identification with the other parent – the wish to replace this parent in relation to the other sexually desired parent. This desire, however, is abandoned because the ego constructs the girl's lack of a penis as signifying castration. Object-cathexis is accordingly replaced by intensified, de-sexualized and sublimated identification, that is, by introjection of the father's or parents' authority within the ego to form the basis of the superego (see Freud, 1924).

Feminists differ in their development of these ideas. MITCHELL (1974) and others argue the value of Freud's oedipus and castration complex account of identification in explaining the beginnings of the child's situation of itself as a sexed subject in relation to the law of the father as signified by the PHALLUS. They thereby also adopt Lacan's critique of the adaptationist project of American ego psychology in fostering the ego's parental identification via transference identification with the analyst. In

167

this they specifically make use of Lacan's insistence on the self-alienation involved in such identification and its prototype in the infant's narcissistic mis-identification of itself with its mirror image and with its reflection in the DESIRE of the other (Lacan, 1977). Lacan's work has also been used by feminists (see Mitchell and Rose, 1982) to reiterate Freud's account of the centrality of SEXUAL DIFFERENCE to SUBJECTIVITY, and to emphasize the resulting precariousness of sexed identity, given its basis in mis-recognition and shifting identification with others. By contrast, others assume either that sexed identity is pre-given or that it is forged in girls through PRE-OEDIPAL identification with the mother and in boys through repudiation of such identification (see Chodorow, 1978). In this some adopt Freud's (1923) account of identification prior to object-love as developed by many post-Freudians (see Sayers, 1991) who, overlooking Freud's (1923) implication that such 'primary identification' is initially with the father, assume that it initially involves lack of awareness of separation of self and mother, a state of mind variously celebrated (Irigaray, 1985) and deplored (Ernst, 1987) within feminist theory and therapy.

See also CASTRATION COMPLEX; LACAN; NARCISSISM; OEDIPUS COMPLEX; SUBLIMATION; TRANSFERENCE/COUNTERTRANSFERENCE.

BIBLIOGRAPHY

Chodorow, Nancy, 1978: *The Reproduction of Mothering*. Berkeley: University of California Press.

Ernst, Sheila, 1987: 'Can a daughter be a woman?', *Living with the Sphinx: Papers from The Women's Therapy Centre*, ed. Sheila Ernst and Marie Maguire. London: Women's Press.

Freud, Sigmund, 1900: *The Interpretation of Dreams*, SE, 4, 5, esp. pp. 149–51.

Freud, Sigmund, 1917: 'Mourning and melancholia', *SE*, 14, pp. 237–60.

Freud, Sigmund, 1921: *Group Psychology and the Analysis of the Ego*, SE, 18, pp. 105–10.

Freud, Sigmund, 1923: *The Ego and the Id*, SE, 19, pp. 12–66.

Freud, Sigmund, 1924: 'The dissolution of the oedipus complex', *SE*, 19, pp. 173–9.

Irigaray, Luce, 1985 [1977]: *This Sex Which Is Not One*, trans. Catherine Porter with Carolyn Burke. Ithaca, NY: Cornell University Press.

Lacan, Jacques, 1977 [1949]: 'The mirror stage as formative of the function of the I as revealed in psychoanalytic experience', *Écrits: A Selection*, trans. Alan Sheridan. London: Tavistock, pp. 1–7.

Mitchell, Juliet, 1974: *Psychoanalysis and Feminism*. London: Allen Lane.

Mitchell, Juliet, and Rose, Jacqueline, 1982: *Feminine Sexuality: Jacques Lacan and the École Freudienne*. London: Macmillan.

Sayers, Janet, 1991: *Mothering Psychoanalysis*. London: Hamish Hamilton.

JANET SAYERS

ideology   The concept of ideology has come to feminism essentially from marxist thought, which further complicates its intrinsic complexity. In classical marxism the notion has a twofold relationship, with power and with illusion. The philosophical, religious and moral ideas in people's heads are not what determine the course of history, but distorted reflections of their material life-process (Marx and Engels, 1977, p. 47) (*see* FEMINIST HISTORY). Through these ideas they fight out the decisive historical conflicts that arise from social and economic contradictions but the true nature of which is opaque to them (Marx and Engels, 1977, p. 53; Marx, 1968, pp. 181–2). At the same time, ideology also serves to keep conflict at bay: for the ruling class's control over material production gives it control over mental production, hence over the ideas of those who lack the means of mental production (Marx and Engels, 1977, p. 64). The concept therefore aims in part to explain why individuals and social groups assent to social systems that run directly counter to their own well-being and freedom. Hence it is not surprising that it should have seemed useful to some feminists; yet in so far as it deals with consciousness (ideas and beliefs), the concept seemed inadequate to explain the behaviour patterns and desires that shape the relationships between women and between women and men, through which the power of PATRIARCHY is exercised.

It had been developed by Althusser, however, along lines that seemed to address this problem. First, he stressed that ideology, like other superstructures, though determined 'in the last instance' by the economic, could not be reduced to economic determinants: it was 'relatively autonomous' (Althusser, 1977, pp. 111–12). Secondly, drawing on LACAN, he argued that the ideological process was *unconscious*. Ideology is not primarily a matter of conscious belief: it is the name of the process by which actual individuals are transformed into subjects. They are inserted from, and even before, birth into certain institutions whose characteristic rituals and discourses furnish them with their identity, and teach them to act so as spontaneously to reproduce the dominant social relations – that is, those of capitalism. The possibility of a general theory synthesizing this conception with the psychoanalytic theorization of the construction of subjectivity (and hence of GENDER difference) was importantly investigated by, for instance, Juliet MITCHELL and Michèle Barrett, and 'ideology' was thus a key notion in this marxist feminist project. Other feminists, however, such as Parveen Adams, queried the term's epistemological implications, and by extension the whole theoretical project of marxist feminism. Drawing on the post-Althusserianism of Hindess and Hirst, Adams rejected the term 'ideology' in so far as it denotes a REPRESENTATION of a prior reality (whether the economic, patriarchy or some synthesis of the two). This move made it possible to argue that sexual differences were 'generated in various discursive and social practices' rather than these practices being held to represent or reflect an already existing sexual division between men and women, a notion deemed residually essentialist. Whatever the force of this analysis it is probably fair to say (as Barrett herself has suggested) that the status and utility of the term 'ideology' are nowadays problematic, for feminism in particular. The possibility (and the value) of a feminist/marxist synthesis appears now more remote, both as feminist theory develops (seeking importantly to accommodate race) and as the political and theoretical crisis of marxism continues. In turning away from marxism, some feminists have turned towards Foucault, who eschews the term 'ideology' because it seems to postulate both an opposing term, 'science' or 'truth', and a bearer or 'subject' of ideology, two notions he seeks to discard. Yet although some feminists have likewise deemed the notion of the SUBJECT an obstruction, it has equally been pointed out, by Rosi Braidotti (1987), that they have not the same stake as male theorists in the evacuation of the subject, women having been denied subjectivity throughout history. In any case, one may think that the notion of ideology, despite its attendant problems, will remain relevant as long as the discrepancy between the situation of being oppressed and taking action to remove that oppression continues to exist and to perplex.

See also ESSENTIALISM; RACE/IMPERIALISM.

BIBLIOGRAPHY

Adams, Parveen, 1979: 'A note on the distinction between sexual division and sexual differences', m/f, 3, pp. 51–7.
Althusser, Louis, 1977: For Marx, trans. Ben Brewster. London: Verso.
Althusser, Louis, 1984a: 'Ideology and ideological state apparatuses', Essays on Ideology, trans. Ben Brewster. London: Verso, pp. 1–60.
Althusser, Louis, 1984b: 'Freud and Lacan', Essays on Ideology, pp. 141–71.
Barrett, Michèle, 1988: Women's Oppression Today, rev. edn. London: Verso.
Braidotti, Rosi, 1987: 'Envy: or, with your brains and my looks', Men in Feminism, ed. Alice Jardine and Paul Smith. New York and London: Methuen, pp. 233–41.
Eagleton, Terry, 1990: The Ideology of the Aesthetic. Oxford: Basil Blackwell.
Foucault, Michel, 1980: Power/Knowledge: Selected Interviews and Other Writings 1972–1977, ed. Colin Gordon. New York: Harvester Wheatsheaf.
Marx, Karl, 1968: Preface to 'A contribution to the critique of political economy, Selected Works, Marx and Engels, London: Lawrence and Wishart.
Marx, Karl, and Engels, Friedrich, 1977: The German Ideology, ed. C. J. Arthur. London: Lawrence and Wishart.
Mitchell, Juliet, 1975: Psychoanalysis and Feminism. Harmondsworth: Penguin.
Žižek, Slavoj, 1991: For They Know Not What They Do: Enjoyment as a Political Factor. London: Verso.

MICHAEL MORIARTY

image Derived from the Latin *imago*, meaning 'likeness', *image* is as much an abstract concept as a simple referential noun. As such, it has a lengthy philosophical pedigree extending from Aristotle ('It is impossible to think without a mental picture') to, for example, Heidegger, Husserl, Merleau-Ponty, Sartre and Wittgenstein. In modern aesthetic theory, interrogations of the image and its relation to the problematics of representation *per se* have been undertaken, most prominently, by Nelson Goodman (1976) and E. H. Gombrich (1956). At stake in much of the philosophical discourse on the image is the enigma of its ontology, particularly since concepts of imagery embrace a host of different manifestations, for example, mental images, hallucinations, literary and verbal images, visual images, and so forth (Mitchell, 1980, 1986). These are themselves imbricated with questions of knowledge, perception, LANGUAGE and consciousness. Moreover, the history of philosophical speculation on the nature of visual imagery is inseparable from iconoclastic debates in which, at least as far back as the Old Testament and, even more influentially, with Plato, visual imagery has been associated both with idolatry (mistaking the image for what it represents) and with processes of mystification that blur the boundaries of the real and its simulacrum – 'idols of the mind'.

Within psychoanalytic theory, the concept of the imago derives from JUNG, and posits an internalized and imaginary REPRESENTATION of a (typically) familial figure (Laplanche and Pontalis, 1973). On the other hand, psychoanalytic readings of the visual image may be dated from Freud's study of Leonardo, wherein the interpretation of the image is thought to provide access to the psychology of its maker (Freud, 1910). More recently, feminist and deconstructive revisions of psychoanalytic theory and the Western philosophic tradition have put in question the privileged status of the visual itself, linking specularity, visuality, the gaze and the image with the patriarchal unconscious (Kofman, 1985) and also with the spurious spectacle of commodity culture in capitalism (IRIGARAY, 1985a, b).

Both psychoanalytic and traditional iconoclastic critiques of visual imagery are of some relevance for feminist interrogations of visual imagery (whether high- or mass-cultural), in so far as one of the primary areas of investigation focuses on the ways by which visual imagery, in tandem with other signifying systems, operates to produce and reproduce concepts of GENDER and SEXUALITY. Furthermore, to the extent that visual imagery is implicated in a dense matrix of ideological formations, including those of gender, critical work on the image has sought to expose the ideological through a form of critical hermeneutics (Berger, 1972). In this respect, feminist critiques have shifted from an initial (generally empirical) consideration of 'images of women' (Hess and

Nochlin, 1972; Baker and Hess, 1973) to a more complex and nuanced consideration of the issue of 'woman as image' (Pollock, 1988; Nochlin, 1989). This latter enterprise has been variously influenced by semiotics and by psychoanalysis (Cowie, 1977, 1978; Mulvey, 1974; Rose, 1986) and takes as its starting-point a rejection of the notion of mimetic and figural visual imagery as natural (as opposed to cultural and conventional), transparent (as opposed to mediated), or able to solicit universalized readings (as opposed to subjective and gendered ones). Concomitantly, one of the consequences of the analysis and critique of (figurative) visual representation is a form of feminist iconoclasm, premissed on the belief that any and all images of the woman are inescapably complicit with a patriarchal scopic regime that figures the feminine as either fetish or object. Such an analysis underpins those feminist arguments against censorship which maintain that distinctions between 'good' and 'bad' or 'true' and 'false' images of women are meaningless (Kuhn, 1985). Thus, while deconstructions of woman-as-image have been an important theme within one strand of contemporary feminist art production (notably that of Cindy Sherman and Barbara Kruger), there have also emerged significant and theoretically influential art practices that refuse the mimetic image of the woman altogether (e.g. Mary Kelly). Drawing variously upon these different approaches, critical, politicized, and preeminently feminist analyses of visual imagery have thus become crucial elements in fields such as art history, communications, film and PHOTOGRAPHY, cultural studies and semiotics – and, of course, within contemporary art practice itself.

See also ART; FETISHISM; FETISHIZATION; IDEOLOGY; PATRIARCHY; VOYEURISM/EXHIBITIONISM/THE GAZE.

BIBLIOGRAPHY

Baker, Elizabeth C., and Hess, Thomas, eds 1973: *Art and Sexual Politics*. New York: Macmillan.
Berger, John, 1972: *Ways of Seeing*. Harmondsworth: Penguin.
Broude, Norma, and Garrard, Mary D., eds 1982: *Feminism and Art History*. New York: Harper and Row.
Cowie, Elizabeth, 1977: 'Women, representation and the image', *Screen Education*, 23, pp. 15–23.
Cowie, Elizabeth, 1978: 'Woman as sign', *m/f*, 1, pp. 49–63.
Freud, Sigmund, 1910: *Leonardo da Vinci and a Memory of his Childhood*, SE, 11, pp. 59–137.
Goodman, Nelson, 1976: *Languages of Art*. Indianapolis: Hackett.
Hess, Thomas B., and Nochlin, Linda, 1972: *Woman as Sex Object: Studies in Erotic Art 1730–1970*. New York: Art News Annual.
Irigaray, Luce, 1985a: *This Sex Which Is Not One*, trans. Catherine Porter with Carolyn Burke. Ithaca, NY: Cornell University Press.

Irigaray, Luce, 1985b: *Speculum of the Other Woman*, trans. Catherine Porter. Ithaca, NY: Cornell University Press.

Kofman, Sarah, 1985: *The Enigma of Woman: Woman in Freud's Writings*, trans. Catherine Porter. Ithaca, NY: Cornell University Press.

Kuhn, Annette, 1985: *The Power of the Image: Essays on Representation and Sexuality*. London: Routledge and Kegan Paul.

Laplanche, Jean, and Pontalis, Jean-Baptiste, 1973: *The Language of Psychoanalysis*. London: Hogarth Press.

Mitchell, W. J. T., 1986: *Iconology: Image, Text, Ideology*. Chicago: University of Chicago Press.

Mitchell, W. J. T., ed. 1980: *The Language of Images*. Chicago: University of Chicago Press.

Mulvey, Laura, 1989: 'Visual pleasure and narrative cinema', *Visual and Other Pleasures*. London: Macmillan, pp. 14–26.

New Museum of Contemporary Art, 1984–5: *Difference: On Representation and Sexuality*. New York: New Museum of Contemporary Art.

Nochlin, Linda, 1989: *The Politics of Vision*. New York: Harper and Row.

Pollock, Griselda, 1977: 'What's wrong with "images of women"?', *Screen Education*, 24, pp. 25–33; repr. *Framing Feminism: Art and the Women's Movement 1970–1985*, ed. Roslika Parker and Griselda Pollock. London: Pandora Press, 1987.

Pollock, Griselda, 1988: *Vision and Difference*, London: Routledge.

Rose, Jacqueline, 1986: 'Sexuality in the field of vision', *Sexuality in the Field of Vision*. London: Verso, pp. 224–33.

ABIGAIL SOLOMON-GODEAU

Imaginary, the   While elaborating three different theories of the mirror stage (between the 1930s and 1980), Lacan developed in the 1950s a theory of the Imaginary order and thereby caused the French adjective *imaginaire* to take on new meaning as a substantive. By Imaginary Lacan does not mean the richness of imagination as a source of love (Kristeva, 1987); nor FANTASY which, for Lacan, arises from a LACK in identity and a subsequent quest for 'objects' meant to fill that lack; nor the poetic, which reveals a flight from ontology; but rather a belief in images that cover over the veiled object that promises JOUISSANCE (Lacan, 1973; Žižek, 1989).

In Lacan's first elaboration of the mirror stage, he saw the BODY *qua* organism as a given that puts on an image of its species. In tune with the phenomenological psychology of Henri Wallon (1984) in which the social intersects with the biological, Lacan's mirror phase neonate bridges the gap between a prematurity in motor skills and neurophysiological development at birth by identifying with *images* on which perception depends and which excite the nervous system. An incipient ego takes on its first form through mental identifications.

173

IMAGINARY, THE

In his 1949 *écrit* Lacan dated the mirror stage as beginning at around six months of age. Although he paid tribute to KLEIN for discovering the function of the 'Imaginary primordial enclosure formed by the *imago* of the mother's body', his own theory evolves away from Klein's OBJECT-RELATIONS THEORY, according to which an infant identifies with the mother through part objects or in a holding environment (Lacan, 1977a, p. 20). In his 1932 doctoral thesis he proposed that narcissistic pathology was caused by identificatory relations, rather than by biological or environmental defects (Lacan, 1975a). From the moment an infant is captivated by an image of the human body and imagizes itself as a whole entity, paradoxically dependent upon others whose judgements and responses do or do not validate illusions of being, NARCISSISM will be subject not only to paranoia, but to the full range of human affects.

The Imaginary order, then, is the domain of transference relations. But it goes far beyond Freud's description of transference – a positive or negative pathology – that arises within psychoanalysis to reveal affective conflicts which remain unresolved from childhood (*see* TRANSFERENCE/COUNTERTRANSFERENCE). Lacan describes transference as a drama where narcissism and aggression, love and hate, play themselves out (Lacan, 1991, pp. 199–213). As a narcissistic structure, Imaginary relations – be they between individuals or societies – are governed by jealousy, competition and aggressivity, mediated through idealization, love and the rationalizations which Lacan calls misrecognition. Although consensus between people seems to offer a guarantee of certainty and stability, Imaginary collusions continually break down.

Lacan advanced a second theory of the mirror stage according to which the SYMBOLIC dimension imposes language as a mask on the body, weaving it as text (Lacan, 1973, pp. 206–11). We take on identities, just as we take on body images. Each of us tries to become whole or ideal in the eyes of others on the basis of a desire to be thought of in certain ways, which others can never validate as fully true. Lacan says the mirror is a wall and, thus, it tells a lie of the illusion of completeness, from which all later anticipations of unity or union will arise as fantasy efforts at resolution, be they issues of SEXUAL DIFFERENCE, identity, DESIRE, social being, IDEOLOGY, and so on. The wall appears to be a mirror because the forms of the world – LANGUAGE, objects and others – resonate with Imaginary material whose prototypes are unconscious fixations.

In Lacan's third elaboration of the mirror stage, he returns to Freud's concept of repetition in *Trieb* as the libidinal glue that gives consistency to being and body. He argues that humans value consistency over all else, even though the repetitions required to maintain illusions of consistency leave them symptom-ridden and unfree (Lacan, 1966, p. 853).

Even though the ego can be unravelled or 'shaken', the illusion of its fixity is the anchor from which people guarantee their existence as creatures of certainty tinged with doubt. But since no so-called autonomous ego is adequate to its task of self-maintenance, we look to others to verify our illusions.

In Lacanian theory Woman (as a mythical cultural construct) is confused with mother at the level of primordial ur-objects that cause desire. Because these pre-specular objects – the breast, voice, gaze, and so on – are radically lost, but none the less constitute a foundation of the REAL, the Imaginary confusion of mother with primordial loss rules out the possibility of Woman becoming a totalized Symbolic signifier, an organizing symbol of power. Lacan's later theory that Woman is a symptom of *man*'s refusal to believe that lack and loss are organizing agents of being and language might be seen as a reply to Luce Irigaray's castigation of the early Lacan, whom she reads literally (Imaginarily) as showing the female lacking a penis in the mirror (IRIGARAY, 1987).

The *objet a* – a plus value or excess in *jouissance* – enters the fantasy as '*the object which causes the desire of a subject and limits its jouissance*' (Brousse, 1987, p. 116). Lacan called the *objet a* an axiom, without an effect of meaning, but functioning to sustain the illusion of meaning and truth that permits the subject to define his or her *jouissance*. In so far as the *objet a* is split off from the Symbolic, it returns in the Real to split the subject beyond the fantasy, causing discontinuity in seeming unities.

The importance of the Imaginary for feminism lies in Lacan's explanation of how sexual difference first comes to be constituted by the effects of division, language and identification imposed on an infant by others. Jacqueline Rose (1986, pp. 167–98) pursues the question of the relation of the Imaginary to identification in Lacanian theory, suggesting that desire becomes more important than IDENTIFICATION. She would find her answer in Lacan's elaboration of topology and the Real from 1974 on, where identification is no longer a matter of collusion or merger with images, objects and fictions, but identification with the *objet a* that causes desire, itself lost in the drive for a totality which is lacking. In so far as *jouissance* gives a libidinal consistency to fantasies, desires and drives, at this level the subject is the *objet a*, sub-ject of one's own gaze, for example. By definition, desire can never reach the goal of oneness with others or the universe. In so far as male and female experiences of identification constitute radically different relations to the Real, feminism can re-think the Imaginary in relation to the Real (Lacan, 1975b, p. 73). The effort to maintain consistency is attributable not to the Imaginary *per se*, but to the emergence of the Real in the *jouissance* effects that bespeak loss. These effects of displeasure provide the ego with an illusion of continuity

INTROJECTION

in space and time by repetition: oscillating between a sense of being and of nothingness, the subject as *objet a* is a response of the Real as discontinuity that shatters the body's sense of itself as a whole, an Imaginary signifier. The consistency that the Imaginary gives and the repetition of its habitual identifications make it conceal both the mode of its own productions and also the Real which speaks from inscriptions on the body (Ragland-Sullivan, 1988). Hence, the Real blocks Imaginary consistencies, showing the inadequacy of the Imaginary to cover over the palpable void of loss.

BIBLIOGRAPHY

Brousse, Marie-Hélène, 1987: 'Des fantasmes au fantasme', *Lacan*, ed. Gérard Miller. Paris: Bordas, pp. 107–22.
Irigaray, Luce, 1987 [1974]: *Speculum of the Other Woman*, trans. Catherine Porter. Ithaca, NY: Cornell University Press.
Kristeva, Julia, 1987: *Tales of Love*, trans. Arthur Goldhammer; intr. Otto Kernberg. New York: Columbia University Press.
Lacan, Jacques, 1966 [1964]: 'Du "Trieb" de Freud et du désir du psychanalyste', *Écrits*. Paris: Seuil, p. 853.
Lacan, Jacques, 1975a [1932]: *De la psychose paranoïaque dans ses rapports avec la personnalité, suivi de premiers écrits sur la paranoïa*. Paris: Seuil.
Lacan, Jacques, 1975b [1972–3]: *Le Séminaire*, book 20: *Encore*, ed. Jacques-Alain Miller. Paris: Seuil.
Lacan, Jacques, 1977a [1966]: 'Aggressivity in psychoanalysis', *Écrits: A Selection*, trans. Alan Sheridan. London: Tavistock, pp. 8–29.
Lacan, Jacques, 1977b [1966]: 'The function and field of speech and language in psychoanalysis', *Écrits*, pp. 30–113.
Lacan, Jacques, 1977c [1964]: *The Four Fundamental Concepts of Psychoanalysis*, trans. Alan Sheridan. London: Hogarth Press.
Lacan, Jacques, 1991 [1960–1]: *Le Séminaire*, book 8: *Le Transfert*, ed. Jacques-Alain Miller. Paris: Seuil.
Ragland-Sullivan, Ellie, 1988: 'A writing of the Real', *Visible Language*, 22/4, pp. 483–95.
Rose, Jacqueline, 1986: *Sexuality in the Field of Vision*. London: Verso.
Wallon, Henri, 1984: *The World of Henri Wallon*, ed. Gilbert Voyat. New York: J. Aronson.
Žižek, Slavoj, 1989: *The Sublime Object of Ideology*. London: Verso.

ELLIE RAGLAND-SULLIVAN

introjection　Introjection describes the opposite process to that of PROJECTION. It refers to the way the subject in FANTASY 'takes into itself' objects from the 'outside' world and, henceforth, preserves them 'inside' the self.

176

Ferenczi (1909) coined the term 'introjection'; Freud developed the concept and sometimes used it interchangeably with the term 'incorporation' (specifically, incorporation refers to corporeal fantasies of taking objects into the body). In 'Mourning and melancholia' (1917), Freud notes how a loved OBJECT is taken into the SUBJECT only when the object is lost through death or absence. This shows that if introjection is to take place, the capacity to symbolize experience needs to be developed as a way of coping with separation and loss. For it is only via the REPRESENTATION of the object in its absence that the symbol can come to replace the loss as a memory which is, from then on, registered psychically. Melanie KLEIN subsequently linked the process of introjection with the emergence of the depressive position.

In 'Group psychology and the analysis of the ego' (1921), Freud describes how the subject introjects others and, in doing so, identifies with them. The connection between introjection and IDENTIFICATION implies that the introjection of others can become a part of the subject's ego, which then takes on the character of these identifications. In contrast, *The Ego and the Id* (1923) gives an account of the formation of the superego as an introjection of parental figures whereby the superego remains alien to the ego in the way that the superego functions as a critical agency (see Heimann, 1942).

Feminists have not made much use of the term 'introjection'. However, the concept has important implications for understanding the creation of woman's image, for it can explain how such an image is altered and formed with introjections taken from the 'outside', and the role perception plays in the process. In particular, introjection can account for the way that projections of male fantasy on to the woman can be assimilated into the woman's ego or remain alien to it. Women can perceive themselves as 'lacking' in relation to the man, and can feel alien and objectified in relation to themselves. The process of introjection forces one to consider that the change feminists seek can not be brought about solely by a transformation in the external situation; it also requires an intra-psychic re-structuring and, in consequence, an alteration of the woman's self-image.

See also PROJECTIVE IDENTIFICATION; SUBLIMATION.

BIBLIOGRAPHY

Abraham, Nicholas, 1986: *The Wolf Man's Magic Word*. Minneapolis: University of Minnesota Press.
Ferenczi, Sandor, 1909: 'Introjection and transference', *First Contributions to Psychoanalysis*. London: Hogarth Press, pp. 35–93.
Freud, Sigmund, 1917: 'Mourning and melancholia', *SE*, 14, pp. 237–58.

Freud, Sigmund, 1921: *Group Psychology and the Analysis of the Ego*, SE, 18, pp. 69–143.

Freud, Sigmund, 1923: *The Ego and the Id*, SE, 19, pp. 12–66.

Heimann, Paula, 1942: 'A contribution to the problem of sublimation and its relation to processes of internalization', *International Journal of Psychoanalysis*, 23, pp. 8–17.

Kristeva, Julia, 1989: *Black Sun: Depression and Melancholia*. New York: Columbia University Press.

NICOLA DIAMOND

Irigaray, Luce (*b.* Belgium, 1932). Irigaray is a psychoanalyst who became well known as an outspoken feminist and critic of psychoanalysis with the publication of her second book, *Speculum*, in 1974. She immediately lost her post in the Department of Psychoanalysis at Vincennes and, in her own words, was 'put into quarantine' by the psychoanalytic establishment. In particular she was censured for being politically committed by psychoanalysts who thought that being a psychoanalyst precluded political commitment. As Irigaray points out, such a position is itself politically determined (1981b, p. 58). What is interesting about Irigaray's critique is that it is a critique from *within* psychoanalysis. She uses psychoanalytic theory against itself to put forward a coherent explanation for theoretical bias in terms of unconscious FANTASY, splitting, resistance and defences in the discourse of psychoanalysis. Thus she is not simply hostile to psychoanalysis; in fact, she speaks of Freud in most positive tems as an 'honest scientist' who went as far as he could, but whose limitations need to be identified and not turned into dogma.

In summary, the main points of her critique of Freud are as follows. First, psychoanalysis is unaware of the historical and philosophical determinants of its own discourse. Secondly, psychoanalysis is itself governed by unconscious fantasies which it has not been able to analyse. Thirdly, it is patriarchal: it reflects a social order which does not acknowledge what it owes to the mother. As a consequence of these factors, its phallocentric bias is taken for universal truth; psychoanalysis is blind to its own assumptions. For example, Freud takes the development of the little boy as the norm, and assumes that a similar model of development must apply to the little girl; her difference is subsumed under male parameters. Irigaray is also critical of the way in which psychoanalysis is transmitted – from father to son – with a premium on IDENTIFICATION with the father and devotion to his law (an identification and devotion that her critique of LACAN put into question).

Her relation to Lacan is equally complex. Lacan's structural reading of Freud, the emphasis on the role of LANGUAGE in the formation of the UNCONSCIOUS and in the acquisition of SEXUAL DIFFERENCE, undoubtedly made her own psychoanalytic readings possible. In addition, Lacan was one of her mentors; she had attended his seminars at the École Normale Supérieure and he was in charge of the Department of Psychoanalysis at Vincennes. His rejection of her was particularly painful, but Lacan did not easily tolerate theoretical deviations. Irigaray attacks Lacan for what she sees as his ahistoricism and social conservatism (see 'Così Fan Tutti' in *This Sex Which Is Not One*, 1985b), and indicts some of the cornerstones of his theory: the primacy of the PHALLUS, and his conceptualization of the imaginary body of the mirror stage as a male body. The title of her 1974 book, *Speculum*, refers to the mirror used by doctors for examining the internal cavities of the body. Playing on the idea of the mirror, she points out that Lacan's mirror can only see women's bodies as lacking, as a 'hole'; to see what is specific to women's bodies, he would have needed a mirror that could look inside. The mirror, of course, is the mirror of THEORY, or discourse (see Irigaray, 1985a and the powerful essay 'The poverty of psychoanalysis', 1991a).

Irigaray has made a specific, but until now relatively unnoticed, theoretical contribution to psychoanalytic theory in two areas (*see also* LESBIANISM for an account of her critique psychoanalytic approaches to female homosexuality). The first is that of psycholinguistics. Irigaray's first book was a thesis on the language disturbances of senile dementia (*Le Langage des déments*, 1973). She claims to have discovered, quite unexpectedly, that there were significant differences between the impairments of women's speech and those of men's speech. The aim of *Le Langage des déments* was to provide a grammar of dementia, which would lead to a clinical definition based on the nature of the linguistic disturbance, in addition to the physiological factors registered by medical investigation. Her analysis argued that, allowing for loss of memory and physical deterioration, the most serious malfunction in senile dementia is the loss of the ability to respond to another speaker, and to generate new responses to others and to the world. Stereotyped or 'dead' language takes over. Her patients have little or no metalinguistic ability, and cannot use the corpus of language as an object to be manipulated. Further work of this kind was undertaken with schizophrenic patients, and with analysands diagnosed as hysterical or obsessional (see *Parler n'est jamais neutre*, 1985c). It was this research which provided the groundwork for her attempts to define sex in language. Irigaray hypothesizes that so-called neutral language is in fact always sexuate (see 'Le Sexe linguistique', 1987b).

Irigaray's second contribution to psychoanalytic theory involves the question of the parameters of the psychoanalytic session: the GENDER of the analyst/analysand; the disposition and layout of the room, with the analyst seated behind the couch; non-verbal factors and so on (see three articles in particular: 'Le Praticable de la scène', 1985c, pp. 239–52; 'The limits of the transference', 1991b; 'The gesture in psychoanalysis', 1989b). Of the many issues raised by these papers, two are of particular interest here. First, the question of separation and merging in relations between women, which has been much discussed in the feminist psychoanalytic literature (*see* OBJECT-RELATIONS THEORY) is located as an issue in analysis between women. Secondly, Irigaray raises the possibility that classical psychoanalytical interpretations in analysis with women could block rather than release their DESIRE. If psychoanalytic theory is not sexually neutral, but in fact specific to men, the model may be inadequate for women, and its imposition could have the effect of further reinforcing their position in PATRIARCHY. Irigaray's ambivalence towards psychoanalysis is clear. She spells out its dangers for women. On the other hand, she suggests, implicitly or explicitly, that women should begin to theorize alternative psychoanalytic models more appropriate for them (*see* MICHIGAN PSYCHOANALYTIC COUNCIL; WOMEN'S THERAPY CENTRE).

However, Irigaray's theory is not limited to psychoanalysis. She has produced a kind of psychoanalysis of culture, which starts from the premiss that Western culture is built on matricide. More ancient than the parricide of Freud's 'Totem and taboo' is the murder of the mother. Irigaray's cultural analysis can be divided into two aspects: the deconstruction of patriarchal theory and the exploration of alternatives to patriarchy.

Her diagnosis of patriarchy is that it is a symbolic order which is sexually *indifferent*, that is to say, which does not recognize sexual difference: in this hom(m)osexual economy, there are only men, either men possessing a phallus/penis, or castrated and defective men. The other sex is defined in terms of its relation to men: as mother, virgin or whore, for example; but not in relation to itself. Women have no identity *as women*. This sexual indifference is far-reaching: it is embodied in language, in REPRESENTATION, in theory, in scientific knowledge, in PHILOSOPHY and in psychoanalysis, yet it remains unrecognized, because women's difference is never symbolized. Irigaray argues for the necessity of women's symbolic representation. (For a full account see Grosz, 1989 and Whitford, 1991.) It is this more constructive aspect of her theory which is often regarded as utopian in its willingness to imagine a post-patriarchal future. Her work in the 1980s, particularly *Éthique de la différence sexuelle* (1984), *Sexes et parentés* (1987a) and *Le Temps de la différence* (1989a), provides a vision of a future in which women will take their place in the making of culture and society, and will have a language, a religion and an economy of their own. The essential condition of a socially embodied sexual difference would be a maternal genealogy coexisting with the paternal genealogy (*see* MOTHER–DAUGHTER RELATIONSHIP).

Paradoxically, despite her fame and undoubted stature as a theorist, Irigaray's work has not so far had a major impact on feminist theory. Various factors are responsible for this lack of impact: for example, the fact that most of her work has still not been translated into English; the difficulty of reading her often enigmatic writing; lack of familiarity with the continental philosophical tradition; and above all, the accidents of reception (she was dismissed as 'essentialist' long before her major work, *Speculum*, had even been translated, and this no doubt discouraged more serious and detailed consideration). Her fate has been to be endlessly footnoted, but seldom understood. She has often been reduced to a representative of 'French feminism', that catch-all phrase concealing a multitude of differences, as is gradually becoming clear (see Grosz, 1989). There may be in addition two theoretical reasons for Irigaray's relative lack of influence. The first is a widespread and persistent suspicion that psychoanalysis is one of the patriarchal theoretical systems which entrap women. The second is an equally widespread fear that the assertion of women's difference – even when it is not reducible to biologism – merely reinforces traditional gender divisions and cannot be liberating for women. So far, it has been mostly in feminist literary theory that her work has had most influence (see FRENCH-INSPIRED CRITICISM).

Her work does not lend itself to easy summary, in that its whole aim is to disturb the categories and concepts with which we are familiar. Much of it is written in a poetic and allusive style from which it is difficult to extract theoretical statements (see in particular 'And the one doesn't stir without the other' (1981), *The Marine Lover of Friedrich Nietzsche* (1991c), *Passions élémentaires* (1982), and *L'Oubli de l'air* (1983)). For this reason, no doubt, it has given rise to numerous conflicting interpretations.

Materialist feminists (Moi, 1985; Plaza, 1978), because of their theoretical orientation, have tended to be unsympathetic to Irigaray's psychoanalytically inspired critique of culture. They see it as ahistorical and universalizing and, even if unwittingly, as an ally of patriarchy, since it leaves the dimension of power untouched. Psychoanalytically oriented feminists give different readings. Feminists influenced by object-relations theory have not yet engaged with Irigaray at a theoretical level. In Lacanian accounts, Irigaray is accused of not recognizing the necessity for symbolic castration (see Ragland-Sullivan, 1986; Rose, 1986; Silverman, 1988). According to this critique, she is calling for a regressive (and impossible) return to a PRE-OEDIPAL closeness with the mother which would, it is argued, cut women off from language and the SYMBOLIC altogether. (For a counter-argument, see Whitford, 1991.) However, critics who see her work as merely a celebration of femininity miss the more sombre aspects of her analysis – her stress on the DEATH DRIVE, on conflicts between women, and on women's own hatred of other women and of the mother. In Irigaray's picture, women are not just innocent victims. A more subtle account is provided by Gallop (1982, 1983), who attempts a more psychoanalytic reading of Irigaray's text; rather than explaining to the reader the limitations of Irigaray's theory, she seeks to identify the desire at work in the text, thus providing an Irigarayan reading of Irigaray herself. Gallop sees Irigaray as deploying strategies which intervene in patriarchal discourse and destabilize it, loosening the rigidity of 'phallomorphic' logic.

There has so far been relatively little discussion of Irigaray's relation to her theoretical predecessors. It is either argued that Irigaray is philosophically naive, and has not understood the work of influential modern theorists such as Derrida and Lacan, or it is argued that, on the contrary, she is a too faithful disciple of these same (male) thinkers. Both these views have tended to be more partisan than well informed. One exception is Grosz's brief account (1990) of Irigaray and Lacan, but there is virtually nothing on Irigaray's debt to Derrida, Hegel, Heidegger, Nietzsche or Levinas, to mention only the most obvious theoretical influences. The best introductory piece still remains Carolyn Burke's 1981 article, 'Irigaray through the looking glass'.

WRITINGS

1973: *Le Langage des déments*. The Hague: Mouton.
1981a [1979]: 'And the one doesn't stir without the other', *Signs*, 7/1, pp. 60–7.
1981b: *Le Corps-à-corps avec la mère*. Montreal: Éditions de la pleine lune.
1982: *Passions élémentaires*. Paris: Minuit.
1983a: *L'Oubli de l'air chez Martin Heidegger*. Paris: Minuit.
1983b: *La Croyance même*. Paris: Galilée.
1984: *Éthique de la différence sexuelle*. Paris: Minuit.
1985a [1974]: *Speculum of the Other Woman*, trans. Gillian C. Gill. Ithaca, NY: Cornell University Press.
1985b [1977]: *This Sex Which Is Not One*, trans. Catherine Porter with Carolyn Burke. Ithaca, NY: Cornell University Press.
1985c: *Parler n'est jamais neutre*. Paris: Minuit.
1987a: *Sexes et parentés*. Paris: Minuit.
1987b: 'Le Sexe linguistique', special issue of *Langages*, no. 85, March, ed. Irigaray.
1989a: *Le Temps de la différence: pour une révolution pacifique*. Paris: Librairie générale française.

1989b [1987]: 'The Gesture in Psychoanalysis' trans. Elizabeth Guild, *Between Feminism and Psychoanalysis*, ed. Teresa Brennan, London: Routledge, pp. 127–138.

1990: *Je–Tu–Nous*. Paris: Grasset.

1990, ed.: *Sexes et genres à travers les langues*. Paris: Grasset.

1991a [1985]: 'The Poverty of Psychoanalysis', trans. David Macey with Margaret Whitford, *The Irigaray Reader*, ed. Margaret Whitford, Oxford: Blackwell, pp. 79–104.

1991b [1985]: 'The Limits of the Transference', trans. David Macey with Margaret Whitford, *The Irigaray Reader*, ed. Margaret Whitford, Oxford: Blackwell, pp. 105–17.

1991c [1980]: *Marine Lover of Friedrich Nietzsche*. Trans. Gillian C. Gill, New York: Columbia University Press.

BIBLIOGRAPHY

Burke, Carolyn, 1981: 'Irigaray through the looking glass', *Feminist Studies*, 7/2, pp. 288–306.

Gallop, Jane, 1982: *Feminism and Psychoanalysis: The Daughter's Seduction*. London: Macmillan.

Gallop, Jane, 1983: '*Quand nos lèvres s'écrivent*: Irigaray's body politic', *Romanic Review*, 74, pp. 77–83.

Grosz, Elizabeth, 1981: *Sexual Subversions: Three French Feminists*. Sydney: Allen and Unwin, chs 4, 5.

Grosz, Elizabeth, 1990: *Jacques Lacan: A Feminist Introduction*. London: Routledge, pp. 167–83.

Hypatia: A Journal of Feminist Philosophy, 1989: 3/3, special issue on French feminism.

Moi, Toril, 1985: *Sexual/Textual Politics: Feminist Literary Theory*. London: Methuen, ch. 7.

Plaza, Monique, 1978: '"Phallomorphic power" and the psychology of "woman"', *Ideology and Consciousness*, 4, pp. 4–36.

Ragland-Sullivan, Ellie, 1986: *Jacques Lacan and the Philosophy of Psychoanalysis*. Urbana and Chicago: University of Illinois Press.

Rose, Jacqueline, 1986: *Sexuality in the Field of Vision*. London: Verso, ch. 2.

Silverman, Kaja, 1988: *The Acoustic Mirror: The Female Voice in Psychoanalysis and Cinema*. Bloomington: Indiana University Press, ch. 5.

Whitford, Margaret, 1991: *Luce Irigaray: Philosophy in the Feminine*. London: Routledge.

Whitford, Margaret, ed. 1991: *The Irigaray Reader*. Oxford: Basil Blackwell.

MARGARET WHITFORD

J

Jones, Ernest (*b.* Gowerton, South Wales, 1 January 1879, *d.* London, 11 February 1958). Ernest Jones played a crucial formative role in the development of psychoanalysis. He founded the American Psycho-Analytical Association in 1911, and the London Psycho-Analytical Society in 1913 (which later was reconstituted as the British Psycho-Analytical Society). He also founded *The International Journal of Psycho-Analysis*, and was its first editor (from 1920 to 1929). Jones claimed to be the first psychoanalyst to undergo a 'didactic' or 'training' analysis, though critics since have suggested that his reasons for entering analysis with Sándor Ferenczi in 1913 may well have been equally primed by his intense personal difficulties with his long-term partner, Loë Kann (Paskauskas, 1985, pp. 285–99).

Jones is frequently portrayed paradoxically as both a superb diplomat and a ruthless autocrat. He is given credit for convincing the British Medical Committee in 1928 that psychoanalysis was a legitimate scientific activity, and for preventing the British Psycho-Analytical Society from dividing irreparably over the 'controversial discussions' between Kleinians and their critics (see Brennan, 1988). Conversely, he is accused of shrewd manoeuvring to rid himself of potential rivals and consolidate his personal power (Roazen, 1976, pp. 349–50). Even his magisterial *Life and Work of Sigmund Freud* (Jones, 1953, 1955, 1957) has been criticized for manipulation and invention of evidence to consolidate his own importance; for example, many critics now view his account of Ferenczi's final mental state as seriously flawed if not fabricated (Jones, 1957, pp. 188–90; cf. Masson, 1984, pp. 174–87).

Despite such paradoxes, Jones was never a simple guardian of Freudian orthodoxy. This is nowhere better illustrated than in his discussion of SEXUALITY and SEXUAL DIFFERENCE, in which he went to great lengths to criticize Freud's theories. Crucial in this respect is his 1927 paper, 'The early development of female sexuality' (Jones, 1948, pp. 438–51). In this, he supports the criticisms of DEUTSCH, HORNEY and

184

Klein on Freud's views of female sexuality, and argues both for a separation of female from male sexual development and for the specific formative role of the clitoris and vagina in early female infantile psychosexuality. He also suggests that Freud seriously over-estimates the fear of castration, which, even for men, at best constitutes only a partial threat. He maintains that there is, rather, a more basic fear, shared by male and female alike: namely, the total loss of the capacity (including opportunity) for sexual enjoyment. He calls this 'aphanisis' (a Greek term meaning 'extinction'), which, in his opinion, best reflects the conscious avowed intention of most adults to prevent children from having any sexual gratification at all.

See also CASTRATION COMPLEX; KLEIN.

WRITINGS

1923, 1951: *Essays in Applied Psycho-Analysis*, 2 vols. London: Hogarth Press.
1953, 1955, 1957: *The Life and Work of Sigmund Freud*, 3 vols. Vol. 1: *The Young Freud (1856–1900)*; vol. 2: *Years of Maturity (1901–1919)*; vol. 3: *The Last Phase (1919–1939)*. London: Hogarth Press.
1948: *Papers on Psycho-Analysis*. London: Baillière, Tindall and Cox.

BIBLIOGRAPHY

Brennan, Teresa, 1988: 'Controversial discussions and feminist debate', *Freud in Exile: Psychoanalysis and its Vicissitudes*, ed. Edward Timms and Naomi Segal. New Haven and London: Yale University Press, pp. 254–74.
Brome, Vincent, 1983: *Ernest Jones: Freud's Alter Ego*. New York and London: Norton.
Masson, Jeffrey, M., 1984: *The Assault on Truth: Freud's Suppression of the Seduction Theory*. London: Faber.
Paskauskas, R. Andrew, 1985: 'Ernest Jones: a critical study of his scientific development (1896–1913)'. PhD thesis, University of Toronto.
Roazen, P., 1976: *Freud and His Followers*. Harmondsworth: Penguin.

MARTIN STANTON

jouissance   French term for extreme pleasure that has no adequate equivalent in English, current in Anglo-American psychoanalytic discourse with respect to the Other and woman (*see* OTHER/OTHER). *Jouissance* means the usufruct or surplus value of an object or property (*jouir de* something implies the ability to profit from it, whether owned or not). It also connotes the bliss of sexual orgasm. Psychoanalytically *jouissance* is opposed to 'LACK'. In Freud's terminology it is closest to 'wish-fulfilment' (1900, p. 122) disguised in dreams, where it is barred by oedipal regulations. Indeed, in Freud's work, only the pre-totemic father of the primal horde in *Totem and Taboo* (1913, pt IV) could really be said to *jouir*, either in the sense of profiting exclusively from the collective wealth of the community, or in the sense of exclusive sexual enjoyment of the women of the horde. His sons, for example, having engaged in patricide and cannibalism to secure his *jouissance* for themselves, discover they cannot enjoy the fruits of their crime. Thus they proscribe sexual relations with their female relatives, assigning to an animal totem the sacred task of representing (by forbidding its consumption) their cannibalized father. Only once a year do the sons re-enact (and then only figuratively) the bliss of identification with the enjoyment of their father-figure/animal god at a communal feast, which compensates for their self-imposed sacrifice at all other times and joins all in communal 'bliss' as well as in a community of equally shared guilt for their misdeeds. While this is proto-oedipal in structure, the centrality of *jouissance* is far more pronounced than in oedipus.

The two frames (the PRE-OEDIPAL and oedipal) in fact both locate *jouissance* in the pre-oedipal – father and infant. Within oedipus, lack and DESIRE predominate, except in FANTASY. The inverse is the case for the pre-oedipal Other of *jouissance* (the father of 'totem and taboo'). It/he/she demands the sacrifice of one's LIBIDO (one's wants and desires as subjects) so that one can identify with the Other's *jouissance*. The oedipal Other's desire means, conversely, that *jouissance* is located on the side of the subjects, not the Other or father: 'castration means that *jouissance* must be refused, so that it can be reached on the inverted ladder of the law of desire' (Lacan, 1977, p. 324). Under oedipus, to be a 'man' means to identify with the lack in the Other (i.e. to accept castration). However, the woman, who does not finally, LACAN suspects, accept her castration (1982, p. 151), herself becomes the site of *jouissance*, the one to be reached by this 'inverted ladder' of the law of desire. The oedipal Other's desire is a defence (*défense*) and prohibition (*défense*) against going beyond a certain limit in *jouissance*.

Defining pre-oedipal and oedipal *jouissance* with emphasis on the man and male libido has consequences for feminism, which understands 'woman's' *jouissance* quite diversely. IRIGARAY (1985, pp. 357–60) tries to define a 'hysterical' *jouissance* that would not be 'paternal' in character, though it remains 'unrepresentable'. Cixous employs an alternative strategy (1990, *passim*), creating vivid images of feminine *jouissance* at every level, from material to ideal, but which always have to be read upside down, bisexually, or in reverse. KRISTEVA (1980, pp. 242, 247–9) only intimates or alludes to a feminine *jouissance*, specified as 'maternal'. She assigns *jouissance* to that portion of woman that exceeds the bounds of oedipal laws, especially the law of language: it remains almost within her range of vision and experience, but can never be articulated within oedipus, where the woman is imprisoned. This is close to Lacan (1982) but differs in one critical feature: for Lacan 'woman' does not ex-sist within the masculine set, she in-sists from beyond a totaliz-ing, phallic world of masculine things. The *jouissance* of woman is less what remains free of or goes beyond *language* and *the law* than what exceeds the phallic fantasy of totalization on the part of the male, of his version of 'the' woman. The PHALLUS stands for man's lack of *jouissance*; or, unconditional fulfilment simulates a perfection of being for him, and therefore stands as recompense for his loss (*see* OTHER/OTHER for relation of *jouissance* to *objet a*). The Kristevan woman who exists fully within the oedipal framing also accepts her loss of *jouissance*, and thus is not distinguished from the male except by her greater awareness of the loss, owing to her being less compensated by the addition of phallic power.

In the topology of superego/ego/id, Freud (1923, p. 28) made an important move linking the contemporary superego, which is narcissis-tic (*see* SUBLIMATION), more closely to the id than the oedipal superego, in so far as it is involved with *jouissance* or the pleasure principle. This principle, allied to the death drive (*see* DEATH DRIVE (FREUD)), rules the id; but the id now stands on equal footing with the superego in issuing commandments. Its imperative ('Enjoy!') is strictly opposed to that of the superego of lack, which commands the sexes to desire, not to enjoy each other. Even such demands for 'sacrifice' as are made by the narcis-sistic or id-driven superego are, Lacan discovered (1966), covertly com-mands to enjoyment – not one's own immediate enjoyment, but the 'bliss' of communal union with the Other. The sadistic superego (named after the French writer whose categorical imperative was framed as the reciprocal right of each to enjoy the body of the other) calls the SUBJECT to become the OBJECT of enjoyment; the oedipal superego of lack requires that one not become the object of its enjoyment. Under the sadistic superego, SEXUAL DIFFERENCE is not an issue as it is for the oedipal, so that the contours of the Sadean world are not markedly gendered.

See also LACAN; MASOCHISM; REAL; SYMPTOM.

BIBLIOGRAPHY

Bergeron, Danielle, 1990: 'The letter against the phallus', *American Journal of Semiotics*, 7/3, pp. 35–42.
Cixous, Hélène, 1981: 'The laugh of the Medusa', *New French Feminisms*, ed. Elaine Marks and Isabelle de Courtivron. New York: Schocken Books, pp. 245–64.
Cixous, Hélène, 1990: 'The two countries of writing', *The Other Perspective in Gender and Culture: Rewriting Women and the Symbolic*, ed. Juliet Flower MacCannell. New York: Columbia University Press, pp. 191–208.
Freud, Sigmund, 1900: *The Interpretation of Dreams*, SE, 4, 5.
Freud, Sigmund, 1913: *Totem and Taboo*, SE, 13, pp. 1–161.

JUNG, CARL GUSTAV

Freud, Sigmund, 1923: *The Ego and the Id, SE,* 19, pp. 3–68.

Irigaray, Luce, 1985: *Speculum of the Other Woman,* trans. Gillian C. Gill. Ithaca, NY: Cornell University Press.

Kristeva, Julia, 1980: *Desire in Language.* New York: Columbia University Press.

Lacan, Jacques, 1966: 'Kant avec Sade', *Écrits.* Paris: Seuil, pp. 765–90.

Lacan, Jacques, 1977: 'The subversion of the subject and the dialectic of desire', *Écrits: A Selection,* trans. Alan Sheridan. London: Tavistock, pp. 293–325.

Lacan, Jacques, 1982: 'A love letter', *Feminine Sexuality: Jacques Lacan and the École Freudienne,* ed. Juliet Mitchell and Jacqueline Rose. New York: Pantheon, pp. 149–61.

JULIET FLOWER MACCANNELL

Jung, Carl Gustav (*b.* Kesswil, Switzerland, 26 July 1875; *d.* Küsnacht, Switzerland, 6 June 1961). Jung is the founder of analytical psychology, a school of psychology that trains Jungian analysts in many major cities of the world, including Zurich, Tel Aviv, Berlin, London, New York, Boston, Chicago, Dallas, Los Angeles and San Francisco.

Typical methods in Jungian analysis used to help move a patient towards the goal of individuation (see below) are 'active imagination' and 'amplification' of dream and/or fantasy images. In contrast to Freud, with whom Jung corresponded and collaborated from about 1906 to 1913, Jung emphasized the positive function of religion (not 'creeds') in human psychic life and downplayed the role of sexuality. It might be fair to say that where Freud divinized SEXUALITY, Jung eroticized divinity. (See, for example, vol. 5 of the *Collected Works, Symbols of Transformation.*)

Some major concepts of analytical psychology are: the *archetype* (a universal predisposition to form images, a structural aspect of the psyche, personal and collective, the 'imprinter'); *archetypal images* (symbols with numinosity; symbols that mediate opposites in the psyche, often found cross-culturally in religious art, mythology, fairy tales; the 'imprint'); *complex* (often likened to a sub-personality, 'split-off' psychic fragments incompatible with the ego); *individuation* (becoming who one is intended to be, differentiating oneself from unconscious compulsions and sub-personalities); *shadow* (the repressed side of the personality, often experienced as negative, also acting as a sub-personality); *anima* (the feminine aspect of a man's psyche, personal and collective, both a complex and an archetypal image; able to act as sub-personality); *animus* (the masculine aspect of a woman's psyche, personal and collective, complex and archetypal image, able to act

188

as sub-personality); *trickster*; *child*; *Wise Old Woman*; *Wise Old Man*; and *Self* (the central archetypal image governing the individuation process, symbolized by mandalas, the union of male and female, totality, unity).

Jung was not a feminist, although many women have become Jungian analysts and/or followers. For these women, both first-generation (e.g. Von Franz, 1972; Emma Jung, 1957) and contemporary Jungian theorists (e.g. Leonard, 1982; Ulanov, 1971), Jung's psychology – especially his emphasis on integrating the contrasexual other (for women, animus; for men, anima) and his appreciation of the 'feminine' – can give a sufficient framework for liberating women psychologically and spiritually from culturally imposed role definitions, or from self-imposed psychological straitjackets. In the works of these authors, varying degrees of awareness of the effect of patriarchal society on women's self-esteem are present.

In opposition to the above-named theorists, some contemporary feminist theologians have found Jung's theories to be part of the continuing problem of PATRIARCHY, reifying an illusory and romantic conception of women (e.g. Ruether, 1983; Daly, 1979; Goldenberg,1990). The usefulness of Jung's psychology for women is thus highly controversial and women's theoretical stances on the matter vary widely. Many feminists hold the position of these feminist theologians.

A third, more moderate group of feminist theorists has tried to point out Jung's own sexism (including his veneration of the 'feminine', which exemplifies the ubiquitous and thus invisible influence of patriarchy on most Western thought, at the same time as they retain helpful aspects of his theory (e.g. Goldenberg, 1979; Lauter and Rupprecht, 1985; Wehr, 1987; Young-Eisendrath, 1984). In the early work of Goldenberg, and the works of Wehr, Lauter and Rupprecht, for instance, feminist critique focuses on Jung's understanding of the archetype. These authors attempt to contextualize the archetype: rather than understanding the archetype as in any way an 'eternal and static form' producing 'eternal images', they show that whatever is 'archetypal' (numinous, awe-inspiring) in human life is dependent on its context for its being perceived that way – a reading that seems entirely congruent with much of Jung's own, especially later, attempts at understanding the 'archetype' and its effects. They also note problems with Jung's *psychological* model of balance and harmony in a *social* situation of an imbalance of social power and esteem between the sexes. For example, to have as a goal 'harmony' between the 'feminine' and the 'masculine' aspects of the personality in patriarchal societies where the far greater proportion of poor people are women, and where misogyny is still alive and well, is to romanticize a social situation that needs addressing in far more concrete ways. An awareness and critique of patriarchal societies' misogyny needs to become part of Jungian lore in order for Jungian psychology really to address contemporary women's needs; a greater dimension of political and social awareness needs to be evident in Jungian theory.

Jungian psychology evokes an extraordinary richness of imagery. Its use of active imagination, and its trust and respect for the unconscious as source of creativity, wisdom and spiritual insight, do not disempower women by forcing them into a mould in which they do not belong. Individuation, ideally, allows one to become who one is 'meant to be' – an empowering goal for anyone.

WRITINGS

1972–83: *Collected Works*, ed. Sir Herbert Read, Michael Fordham and Gerhard Adler, trans. R. F. C. Hull. Princeton: Princeton University Press.

BIBLIOGRAPHY

Daly, Mary, 1979: *Gyn/Ecology: The Metaethics of Radical Feminism*. Boston: Beacon Press.

Goldenberg, Naomi, 1979: *Changing of the Gods: Feminism and the End of Traditional Religions*. Boston: Beacon Press.

Goldenberg, Naomi, 1990: *Returning Words to Flesh: Feminism, Psychoanalysis and the Resurrection of the Body*. Boston: Beacon Press.

Jung, Emma, 1957: *Animus and Anima: Two Essays*. Zurich: Spring Publications.

Lauter, Estella, and Rupprecht, Carol Schreier, 1985: *Feminist Archetypal Theory: Interdisciplinary Re-Visions of Jungian Thought*. Knoxville: University of Tennessee Press.

Leonard, Linda, 1982: *The Wounded Woman: Healing the Father–Daughter Relationship*. Boston: Shambala Publications.

Ruether, Rosemary, 1983: *Sexism and God-Talk: Toward a Feminist Theology*. Boston: Beacon Press.

Ulanov, Ann Belford, 1971: *The Feminine in Jungian Psychology and in Christian Theology*. Evanston, Ill.: Northwestern University Press.

Von Franz, Marie Louise, 1972: *The Feminine in Fairy Tales*. New York: Spring Publications/The Analytical Psychology Club of New York.

Wehr, Demaris, 1987: *Jung and Feminism: Liberating Archetypes*. Boston: Beacon Press.

Young-Eisendrath, Polly, 1984: *Hags and Heroes: A Feminist Approach to Jungian Psychotherapy with Couples*. Toronto: Inner City Books.

DEMARIS S. WEHR

K

Klein, Melanie   (*b*. Vienna, 30 March 1882, *d*. London, 22 September 1960). Melanie Klein is perhaps best known for her invention of play analysis, a technique for psychoanalysing children which revolutionized child analysis. Her work with children enabled her to contribute to psychoanalytic understanding of the PRE-OEDIPAL psyche, and her followers later formed one of the three British 'schools' of psychoanalysis (the others are the Anna Freudians and the Middle Group). Klein's model of mental organization sets up the life and death instincts as opposing principles. Her key concepts of the paranoid-schizoid and depressive positions are formulations of the mechanisms employed by the rudimentary ego to deal with conflict between the two drives. As *positions*, rather than developmental stages, they are descriptions of mental structures which can be found in the adult as well as the child psyche.

The paranoid-schizoid position is described in 'Notes on some schizoid mechanisms' (1946; reprinted in Mitchell, 1986). It develops the theory of the child's earliest relationships to part-objects (e.g. to the ideal or persecutory breast). The paranoid-schizoid phase is described as dominated by persecutory mechanisms and mechanisms of splitting. Under the impact of anxiety, the primitive ego fragments and disintegrates. Its fear is of annihilation and death. Splitting, PROJECTION and INTROJECTION are the early mechanisms of defence, which organize the internal chaos in a primitive but life-preserving way. Both the ego and its OBJECT may be split into ideal and destructive parts. Through PROJECTIVE IDENTIFICATION, the primitive self attempts to get rid of unwanted parts of the self, or to separate off the good parts of the self in order to protect them and avoid internal conflict. The mother's body is fantasized as being full of, and identified with, the child's projected parts.

The concept of the depressive position is introduced in 'A contribution to the psychogenesis of manic-depressive states' (1935; reprinted in Mitchell, 1986). The depressive position signals the transition from seeing the mother as a part-object to seeing her as a whole object, and understanding that feelings of love and hate are directed at the same person. When the child realizes that its feelings of destructive and sadistic hatred are directed against the loved mother, it may feel guilt and loss, and a need to attempt reparation. There is a constant fluctuation between persecutory anxiety, the fear of retaliatory attack from the hated object, and depressive anxiety, when love and a desire to restore what has been damaged is uppermost. The depressive position is crucial to Kleinian theory, displacing the Freudian centrality of the OEDIPUS COMPLEX. It opens up, as the oedipus complex could not, the possibility of understanding women's early PRE-OEDIPAL relationship with the mother.

Klein is most likely to appeal to those with some experience of therapy or analysis. She has a gift for providing a language to talk about the fluid and mobile experiences of non-verbal affect. Her conceptualization offers a rich 'descriptive phenomenology' (Mitchell, 1986) of the intuitive identifications, non-verbal communication and fusional, merged relationships on which successful clinical practice is based.

Klein's direct influence on feminism seems to have been slight; few theoretical essays situate themselves within a specifically Kleinian perspective. (For some exceptions, see Dinnerstein, 1978; Chernin, 1986; Bower, 1986.) However, a few significant theorists do use aspects of Klein's work, without necessarily committing themselves to her overall theoretical framework (see Moi, 1982; Kristeva, 1989; Brennan, 1992). Her indirect influence, however, has been enormous.

The main current of feminist psychoanalytic thought in the USA, OBJECT-RELATIONS THEORY, owes its major theoretical reference points to the work of Klein's followers. Unlike Klein, it plays down the instinctual drives and focuses primarily on the child's relations with real or fantasied others. But what it gains in attention to social reality, it loses in its under-estimation of the power and autonomy of unconscious FANTASY. Feminists have usually preferred Freudian or Lacanian theory to Klein, because her work appears to locate FEMININITY and feminine heterosexual desire in innate drives. Nor does she explicitly engage with the social structures that subordinate women: she is not a feminist. Feminists attempting to theorize *social* change find her drive theory inadequate. However, Klein is important for feminists in several ways. First, she opposed Freud's theorization of female SEXUALITY in terms of a single, masculine, model. Secondly, her stress on the pre-oedipal period, and her analytic work with young children, focusing on the early parent–child relation and the child's fantasies about the mother's body, was a crucial enabling factor in feminist accounts of the MOTHER–DAUGHTER RELATIONSHIP. Thirdly, in addressing both the destructive and the reparative aspects of the psyche, her work enables feminist theory to move beyond victimology to examine the more problematic

192

aspects of women's psyche and behaviour, such as their aggression, their paranoia or DEPRESSION and their SADOMASOCHISM. It puts into question the picture of women as solely self-sacrificing and caring, allowing them to have powerful sexual, aggressive and destructive drives; it thus raises questions about the traditional construction of femininity and masculinity which subvert its own biologism.

See also OBJECT-RELATIONS ORIENTED CRITICISM.

WRITINGS

1988a: *Love, Guilt and Reparation and Other Works 1921–1945*. London: Virago.
1988b: *Envy and Gratitude and Other Works 1946–1963*. London: Virago.
1989a: *The Psycho-Analysis of Children*. London: Virago.
1989b: *Narrative of a Child Analysis*. London: Virago.

BIBLIOGRAPHY

Bower, Marion, 1986: 'Daring to speak its name: the relationship of women to pornography', *Feminist Review*, 24, pp. 40–55.
Brennan, Teresa, 1992: *The Interpretation of the Flesh*. London: Routledge.
Chernin, Kim, 1986: *The Hungry Self: Women, Eating and Identity*. London: Virago.
Dinnerstein, Dorothy, 1978: *The Rocking of the Cradle and the Ruling of the World*. London: Souvenir Press. (Published in the USA as *The Mermaid and the Minotaur: Sexual Arrangements and Human Malaise*. New York: Harper Colophon, 1977.)
Grosskurth, Phyllis, 1986: *Melanie Klein: Her World and Her Work*. London: Maresfield Books.
Hinshelwood, R. D., 1989: *A Dictionary of Kleinian Thought*. London: Free Association Books.
Kristeva, Julia, 1989 [1987]: *Black Sun: Depression and Melancholy*. New York: Columbia University Press.
Mitchell, Juliet, ed. 1986: *The Selected Melanie Klein*. Harmondsworth: Penguin.
Moi, Toril, 1982: 'Jealousy and sexual difference', *Feminist Review*, 11, pp. 53–68.
Sayers, Janet, 1986: *Sexual Contradictions: Psychology, Psychoanalysis, and Feminism*. London: Tavistock, ch. 5.
Sayers, Janet, 1987: 'Melanie Klein, psychoanalysis and feminism', *Feminist Review*, 25, pp. 23–37.
Segal, Hanna, 1981: *Melanie Klein*. Harmondsworth: Penguin.
Women: A Cultural Review, 1990: 'Positioning Klein', 1/2.

MARGARET WHITFORD

Kristeva, Julia (*b*. Bulgaria, 1941). Julia Kristeva is a literary and cultural theorist, a linguist and a practising psychoanalyst. Her work combines two usually disparate projects: the scientific study of LANGUAGE and sign-systems initiated by the Swiss linguist, Ferdinand de Saussure; and Sigmund Freud's project of developing a psychology of the UNCONSCIOUS and of human SEXUALITY. Kristeva's writings focus on the point of overlap between psychoanalysis and semiotics, the notion of the *speaking subject*, the SUBJECT as a speaking, meaning-producing and meaning-deforming desiring being. She explores how psychoanalytic theory contributes the notion of the split subject (the subject divided between consciousness and the unconscious) to theories of REPRESENTATION, signification and meaning production; and conversely, how semiology and theories of representation contribute to and enrich psychoanalytic concepts of subjectivity by making language one of the necessary conditions of human existence.

In her earlier writings (for example, 1984a), Kristeva utilizes Freudian concepts of infantile sexuality, particularly the distinction between PRE-OEDIPAL, polymorphous perverse, anarchic sexuality and oedipalized, phallic, genitally oriented adult sexuality, as well as the distinction between the conscious and the unconscious, to explain the ways in which the speaking subject is constituted as such, and the ways in which it is able to speak, to produce, transform and subvert signs and sign systems. The speaking subject is, for Kristeva, the commonly unacknowledged condition of the functioning of all psychical, social and signifying practices. In her earliest writings (1976, 1980, 1984a) she is committed to a 'Freudo-marxist' framework, which is marked by the desire to provide a cohesive account of psychical and socio-political existence, integrating psychoanalysis with marxism, supplementing psychoanalysis with a social and historical dimension, and marxism with an understanding of individuality, DESIRE and psychological functions. By linking marxism to psychoanalysis through the mediation of semiotics, Kristeva hoped to show that both psychical and social relations are always necessarily signifying relations. The mode of production is also always a mode of signification; the libidinal economy is simultaneously a system of meaning.

The child's earliest pre-oedipal sexual phases are correlated with what Kristeva calls 'the semiotic', the unspoken and unrepresented conditions of signification. Kristeva distinguishes the semiotic from the SYMBOLIC, the order of social and signifying relations, of law, language and exchange. Both the semiotic and the Symbolic are necessary for the continuing functioning of the three orders of human existence Kristeva is concerned to link: the psychical functioning of the individual; the ordered and ordering structure of social institutions and ensembles; and the coherent meaningful functioning of discourses and texts.

To explain her notion of the semiotic, Kristeva refers to what Plato, in the *Timaeus*, calls the *chora*. The *chora* is 'receptacle, unnameable, improbable, hybrid, anterior to naming, to the one, to the father and consequently maternally connoted' (Kristeva, 1980, p. 133). The *chora* is the site of the undifferentiated bodily space the mother and child share. A site for the production of the matrix/womb and matter, the *chora* is the unnameable, unspeakable corporeality of the inextricably tangled mother/child dyad which makes the semiotic possible.

The semiotic is a set of pre-signifying impulses and drives that chaotically circulate in and through the infant's body; the Symbolic consists in the replacement of these polymorphous body impulses and libidinal drives through their hierarchical subsumption in the OEDIPUS COMPLEX, through which these impulses are harnessed in social production. The symbolic is the domain of propositions and positions, the site for the creation of unified texts, cultural representations and knowledges; the semiotic is the undirected and uncontrolled input of the repressed impulses, energies and spasms of the infant in the first case, and later, of the subject in moments of crisis and psychical upheaval. Although the Symbolic is formed through the REPRESSION and SUBLIMATION of the semiotic it is unable to exist – it has no 'raw materials' or energetic force – without the semiotic, which must thus be considered logically prior. However, the distinction between the Symbolic and the semiotic is retrospective: the semiotic can only be discerned through its Symbolic overlay. The semiotic (mythically, retroactively) precedes and exceeds the Symbolic, overflowing and problematizing its boundaries. In the broadest terms, the semiotic is the input of the undirected body, while the symbolic is the regulated use and organized operations of that body in social production. It is only through the Symbolic that we can have access to the semiotic; the former provides the latter with a voice and a mode of representation.

Although it is necessary for the Symbolic, the semiotic cannot be articulated within it or acknowledged by it. It threatens to undermine and de-stabilize the rule-governed operations of the Symbolic, resisting its rules and norms. Governed by the primary processes, which seek immediate gratification of what may be anti-social impulses, the semiotic is the raw data of corporeal forces and energies organized by the law-abiding and rule-governed secondary-process activities of the Symbolic. The maternally defined semiotic is the prop or support of, as well as the site for, the disruptive transgression of the paternal, patriarchally regulated Symbolic. It remains incompletely contained by the Symbolic, and is manifested in the 'physicality' or 'materiality' of textual production: it is a materiality that, like the primary processes or the repressed, threatens to return, disrupting signifying conventions. The semiotic must be renounced and transcended in order for the pre-oedipal child to acquire a stable social or Symbolic position as a unified (masculine or feminine) subject. But this subsumption of the semiotic in the Symbolic is never complete or finalized.

There are two strategic moments in the infant's life – termed by Kristeva 'thetic' – in which the semiotic is provisionally ordered and unified to provide the stability required by the Symbolic. The thetic, as an anticipation in the semiotic of its later Symbolic overlay, occurs in two phases: what Freud describes as primary narcissism and LACAN calls the mirror-stage; and what Freud calls the oedipus complex and Lacan the Name-of-the-Father. The mirror stage initiates the child into the field of elementary signifiers; but the subject's definitive separation from the immediacy of its experiences is secured only with the oedipus complex, where the child is able to designate and replace its experiences with representations. If the mirror stage generates a field of signifiers (marked by Saussurean 'pure difference'), the CASTRATION COMPLEX generates signs (the combination of signifier and signified), which organize and give meaning to these signifiers, making discourse possible. The castration threat and the resolution of the oedipus complex re-structure the primitive 'identity' and rudimentary vocalic oppositions established in the mirror stage according to the demands of coherence and order. In uncritical agreement with Lacan, Kristeva asserts that this occurs through the child's relation to the PHALLUS.

Kristeva utilizes these concepts to analyse the production and disruption of meaning in various signifying systems. Although she focuses mainly on literary texts, she has also used these concepts to discuss the visual arts and music. ART is an index of social stability. Upheavals or radical ruptures in artistic norms neither cause nor reflect social upheavals; rather, they anticipate and accompany them. Revolutions in poetic language are no less symbolically de-stabilizing than economic upheavals. Kristeva refuses to accept the reductionism common in many versions of marxism in which socio-cultural products are seen merely as by-products or effects of class struggle. She grants a relative autonomy to signifying practices, for the mode of production always implies a mode of sign production as a necessary accompaniment (Kristeva, 1976, p. 64). Ruptures at the level of signifying practice, for example, in the poetry of Mallarmé, the plays of Artaud or the writings of Joyce, are symptomatic of broader ruptures at the level of socio-economic relations; crises in representation signal cracks in the functioning of the Symbolic that may also indicate points of political vulnerability.

If art in its broadest sense is a privileged object of investigation in all her writings, Kristeva has always placed special emphasis on the most extreme points of disruption within artistic practices in those critical moments she designates as 'avant-garde'. Avant-garde texts, she claims, de-stabilize the pretensions of the subject to identity and of the text to coherent meaning. These radical signifying practices put their own symbolic requirements into question, pressing sometimes beyond the tolerable limits of intelligibility. It is thus that '*jouissance* works its way into the social' (Kristeva, 1984, p. 80). But the texts of the avant-garde not only introduce JOUISSANCE to the social: they make it exceed the boundaries of identity and coherence. Avant-garde practices are mong those rare social instances in which the semiotic transgresses the Symbolic, gaining the upper hand, creating historical transformations of the social and signifying order. The avant-garde text puts into question the repressive powers of the Symbolic by capturing and expressing the otherwise unarticulated *jouissance* of semiotic impulses, and by making explicit the social investments in the repression and subordination of the semiotic (*see* SURREALISM).

Kristeva is interested both in understanding how the semiotic becomes amenable to Symbolic codification, and, conversely, in those moments (witnessed in avant-garde texts) where the semiotic overflows its Symbolic containment. This project of seeking out the symptoms and signals of revolutionary rupture in subjectivity, textuality and sociality is framed by an implicitly marxist notion of IDEOLOGY and revolutionary social change. As her work develops, this framework begins to dissolve, and is replaced by a growing commitment to psychoanalytic discourses, accompanied by what many consider to be a de-politicization or aestheticization of her prior interest in class struggle and revolutionary social change, and its alignment with women's struggle for social, psychical and sexual AUTONOMY. While her allegiances to a marxist framework seem to diminish, her relations to feminism remain ambiguous and ambivalent. On the one hand, she is clearly interested in many of the major commitments of contemporary feminism (maternity, female sexuality and desire, egalitarian struggles and struggles for the recognition of sexual difference); at the same time, she refuses to label herself a feminist and remains highly critical of feminist uses of the category of 'woman' (Kristeva, 1981). She refines and develops her analyses of maternity and the pre-oedipal mother–child relation in develoing a number of new interests – her notions of abjection, the establishment of an 'herethics' and the concept of the imaginary father.

Like the semiotic, the abject is both precondition and sporadic accompaniment of subjectivity and Symbolic functioning (Kristeva, 1982), manifesting itself in various cultural taboos, in literary texts as well as in religious rituals and doctrine. Neither subject nor object, the abject makes clear the impossible and untenable identity of each. If the object secures the subject in a more or less stable position, the abject signals the fading or disappearance, the absolute mortality and vulnerability of the subject's relation to and dependence on the OBJECT. The abject is an impossible object, still part of the subject: an object the subject strives to expel but which is ineliminable. In ingesting objects into itself or expelling objects from itself, the 'subject' can never be distinct from these 'objects'. These ingested/expelled 'objects' are neither part of the BODY nor separate from it. The abject (including tears, saliva, faeces, urine, vomit, mucus) marks bodily sites which will later become erotogenic zones (mouth, eyes, anus, nose, genitals). The subject must expel these abjects to establish the 'clean and proper' body of oedipalization. Yet they can never be expelled, for they remain the preconditions of corporeal, material existence. Utilizing the work of cultural anthropologist Mary Douglas on the distinction between the clean and the unclean, Kristeva examines three major expressions of the abject in social life, in the various cultural, social and psychical taboos erected to deal with food, death and SEXUAL DIFFERENCE. The abject is undecidably both inside and outside (like the skin of milk); dead and alive (like the corpse); autonomous and engulfing (like infection). It signals the precarious grasp the subject has over its identity and bodily boundaries, the ever-present possibility of sliding back into the corporeal abyss out of which it was formed (*see* UNCANNY).

While not explicitly feminist in its orientation, Kristeva's analysis of abjection nevertheless provides a series of insights and reflections of great consequence for feminist theory. Most particularly, Kristeva clearly explains the costs and the conditions of the acquisition of culture and a Symbolic position: the subject does not develop naturally, nor is he or she merely the effects of 'conditioning' or upbringing. Rather, Symbolic subjectivity is founded on a constitutive repression (of the maternal, the *chora*, the semiotic, the abject).

Like the abject, pregnancy is a borderline state in which there is an indistinction between subject and object. Kristeva brings together her interest in questions of social transgression, especially in religious and poetic texts, through her readings of religious representations of maternity, for example, the cult of the Virgin Mary ('Stabat Mater', in Moi, 1987). Religion is a privileged domain of her researches, for it symbolically recuperates a usually repressed *jouissance*: religion provides one of the few social institutions which tolerates, even encourages, the experience and articulation of commonly unspoken pre-oedipal or semiotic elements, such as religious ecstasy. Religious discourses, for example, those surrounding the Virgin Mary, are among the few that provide social and signifying space where a representation of the maternal debt remains tolerable. Yet there is an unrepresented element of maternity which religious discourses and Symbolic rituals have been unable to harness (*see* MATERNAL VOICE).

The sphere of ethics, which for a number of years was obscurely confused with politics in French theory, is, Kristeva claims, heir to the libidinal excesses that religous discourses have inherited but not adequately expressed. Such a conception of ethics would not be based on Kantian imperatives, on universal moral commands; it is an 'herethical ethics', an ethics of heresy, an ethics of love (see Kristeva, 1987). Love is here understood as a transference relation based on the structures of primary NARCISSISM. In the same way that she uses religious discourses, abjection and poetic texts, she uses the discourses of love as a means by which the earliest, pre-oedipal or semiotic contributions to the Symbolic can be elucidated.

It is from this perspective that she introduces her heretical notion of the 'imaginary father', the third term mediating between mother and infant, into the Imaginary rather than into the Symbolic order as Lacan does, insisting, against Lacan, that the father plays a crucial role in establishing the child's narcissistic relations. The imaginary father is not the punitive law-giver who regulates the Symbolic; the imaginary father is the position that the father occupies in the mother's desire, a position which displaces the child as the mother's phallus (see Kristeva, 1984b, p. 23). He embodies love. This love, fellow-feeling (*agape*) rather than desire (*eros*), cannot be represented by the pre-oedipal mother, who is 'too close' to the child to provide it with a means of positioning itself. Her love hovers between a dangerous fusional overwhelming of the child (the PHALLIC MOTHER of psychosis) and abandonment. In a different way, the love of the Symbolic father cannot represent unconditional profusion, for the Symbolic father, perhaps best represented by the God of Judaeo-Christian scripture, is abstract and judgemental. Only the love founded on the child's relation to the imaginary father can give the child value, the ability to detach itself from its potentially crippling dependence on the mother, and allow it to gain a place as a signifying subject.

Kristeva's works have prompted widespread criticism from feminists. She has been accused of anti-feminism because of her refusal of the category of woman, which involves, she believes, an ESSENTIALISM and singularity that belie the subject's complex constitution. In shifting the problematic from an analysis of sexual difference to that of a sexual differentiation within each individual, male or female, she has been accused of advocating ANDROGYNY, of neutralizing concrete women's experiences and social contributions, and of reducing women to the maternal function. However justified these objections may be, nevertheless her works have provided far-reaching insights, methods and objects of analyses for many feminist projects: for psychoanalytic feminists, her investigations of the pre-oedipal have provided more depth and detail to the period commonly valorized as feminine or proto-feminist; for literary feminists, she has provided a mode of textual interrogation that seeks out the corporeal, material contributions of the drives to textual production, a means, in the wake of the death of the author, of introducing a notion of the Derridean trace in explicitly sexual terms – in short, every text contains traces or residues of the repressed semiotic. For feminist cultural theorists, she has demonstrated that all cultural production requires an understanding of psychical and signifying elements; and for feminists committed to developing therapies and therapeutic procedures, she has provided a way of analysing culture always in relation to psychology and signification without reducing culture to these constitutive elements.

See also FRENCH-INSPIRED CRITICISM; LITERARY AND TEXTUAL CRITICISM; POSTMODERNISM.

WRITINGS

1976: 'Signifying practice and mode of production', Edinburgh Review, 1, pp. 64–77.
1980: Desire in Language, trans. Leon S. Roudiez. Oxford: Basil Blackwell.
1981: 'Interview', m/f, 5, pp. 158–63.
1982 [1980]: Powers of Horror: An Essay on Abjection, trans. Leon S. Roudiez. New York: Columbia University Press.
1984a [1974]: The Revolution in Poetic Language, trans. Margaret Waller. New York: Columbia University Press.
1984b: 'Julia Kristeva in conversation with Rosalind Coward', ICA Documents, special issue on 'Desire', pp. 22–7.
1987 [1983]: Tales of Love, trans. Leon S. Roudiez. New York: Columbia University Press.
1987: The Kristeva Reader, ed. Toril Moi. Oxford: Basil Blackwell.

BIBLIOGRAPHY

Douglas, Mary, 1966: Purity and Danger: An Analysis of the Concept of Pollution and Taboo. London: Routledge and Kegan Paul.
Grosz, Elizabeth, 1989: Sexual Subversions: Three French Feminists. Sydney: Allen and Unwin; Boston: Unwin Hyman.
Jardine, Alice, 1985: Gynesis: Configurations of Women and Modernity. Ithaca, NY: Cornell University Press.
Lechte, John, 1990: Julia Kristeva. London: Routledge.
Moi, Toril, 1985: Textual/Sexual Politics: Feminist Literary Theory. London: Methuen.

ELIZABETH GROSZ

L

Lacan, Jacques (*b*. Paris, 13 April 1901; *d*. Paris, 9 September 1981).

Life and work

Jacques Lacan began his career in 1932 as the *chef de clinique* of psychiatry at the Sainte-Anne, the major psychiatric hospital serving central Paris. His doctoral dissertation had been on the subject of paranoid psychosis. Though influenced by Gaëtan G. de Clérambault's work on the criminally insane, it departed from theories of organic causality then current in medicine (Lacan, 1975a). De Clérambault had found a *common* element in the psychoses – 'mental automatism' or the idea that troubling thoughts and words were imposed on the patient by others – and assumed an organic origin. Lacan's *new* thesis was that mental hallucinations were not caused by organic dysfunction or social distress, but were connected to 'personality', a concept he was later to drop. In 1975 Lacan explained his reluctance to publish his thesis. There is no *relationship* between personality and paranoia because they are the same thing (Lacan, 1976, p. 7), this being in accordance with his later stress on the gaze as the primordial agent of castration, judgement and idealization installed prior to the subject of the unconscious (*see* VOYEURISM/EXHIBITIONISM/THE GAZE).

In his doctoral thesis, Lacan studied Aimée, who suffered from a narcissistic disorder. He defined it as her remaining tied up in symbiotic relations with women in her life, such that she could not distinguish between her *unconscious* fantasies of whom she would like to be (her ideal ego), and actual persons seeming to embody these ideals (ego ideals) (Freud, 1921). In paranoia, the subject comes to believe that another has stolen the subject position that rightfully was hers or his. This lack of delineation between IMAGINARY and SYMBOLIC materials led Lacan to hypothesize the REAL as an order constituted in its own right, distinct from reality. Whether the Real returns as a moment of blockage in the memories of everyday life or in hallucinations that bespeak psychosis, Lacan discovered the cause of psychosis to be the foreclosure of a signifier for a name of one's own. In neurosis and perversion, identity coheres in discrete ensembles of differentials (including body image, name, ideals, family history, intentionality of desire). But in psychosis these 'concrete pieces' return in the Real as voices or shattered body images, bespeaking a confusion and commingling of identities, bodies, properties and destinies. During a psychotic episode, disasters occur in which the subject kills him- or herself; or, as in the case of Aimée, tries to kill the ideal, the movie actress, with whom she had identified in fantasy. Out of these ideas, Lacan evolved new theories about how being is constituted, how language is acquired, how the SEXUAL DIFFERENCE is constituted in such a way as to give rise to culture, and so on. He gradually found the essentially traumatic character of human SEXUALITY – choosing one GENDER identity over another – to lie in identification with loss.

The newness of his thesis stemmed from his exhaustive study of the mental phenomena of paranoid delusions. Much like FREUD, who discovered the UNCONSCIOUS by paying serious attention to hysterical women speaking about their symptoms, Lacan's treatment of female psychotics showed that psychoanalysis could turn away from the study of a person's individual's relationship to his or her unconscious in order to consider how the social is placed within the individual and, in turn, how the individual is positioned within the social. In working with female patients, Lacan arrived at the cause of psychotic suffering: foreclosure of the signifier for difference that he called the paternal metaphor or Name-of-the-Father.

Lacan was a leader in psychoanalysis in France from the beginning of his career (G. Miller, 1987, p. 185). Fluent in German, he had access to Freud's texts (most of them then unpublished in French) in a way most of his colleagues did not. From 1949 on he had been given the task of developing formal training programmes for analysts within institutional settings. This very activity led to his critique of formalist training methods, which he came to see as blocking the development of Freud's discovery of the savage power of the unconscious. After the International Psychoanalytic Association 'excommunicated' him in 1963, Lacan sought other ways of training analysts and transmitting psychoanalysis as a logical field in its own right.

Lacan's ideas did not take on a radical cast until he began to attend Alexandre Kojève's lectures on Hegel, to meet with the surrealist circle of writers, painters and philosophers, and to publish short essays in Surrealist journals (*Le Minotaure, Cahiers de l'art*; see SURREALISM). Although Lacan gave papers at international psychoanalytic congresses, universities and in various other invited settings (papers that were published from 1926 onwards in psychoanalytic journals, art or philosophy journals and university collections), he was unlike Freud in that Freud published his letters and major texts from the beginning of his career; Lacan did not bind together his many papers in one collection until he was 65 years of age. Jacques-Alain Miller, the literary and intellectual inheritor of Lacan's work, has discerned three periods of Lacan's teaching: (1) 1953–64, when he elaborated the reading of Freud he had been developing since the 1920s and 1930s at the Hôpital Sainte-Anne and worked on the formula of the unconscious as structured like a language; (2) 1964–74, when he set forth his most widely diffused and characteristic concepts at the École normale supérieure and the Law Faculty adjacent to the Sorbonne and Panthéon and added his basic mathemes; and (3) 1974–81, when he re-worked his category of the Real and developed his theory of a mathematical topology based on the Borromean knot or chain of the Real, Symbolic and Imaginary orders.

In Lacan's first period, his key statement concerns the *function* and *field* of speech and language in psychoanalysis. Lacan proposes that humans, both male and female, are *alienated* within the field of LANGUAGE and *separated* from this field by whatever libidinal consistencies they identify with to fill up the LACK. So affixed are individuals to language that even their symptoms are structured by the traumatizing effects of loss and language in childhood. In so arguing, Lacan pushed psychoanalysis away from the empiricist, developmental, positivistic theories of experience through which psychology retains the idea of consciousness of self. Along with his rejection of the ego as a synthesizing agent, Lacan argued that developmental psychology was an attempt to answer the enigma of what a child is by a theory which equates the development of intelligence with language acquisition (observational journals of Darwin, Piaget and others). From his doctoral thesis onwards, Lacan had urged analysts to re-think the problem of what causes 'development'. He argued that psychic causality does not lie in organodynamism, but in a psychogenesis not reducible to biological development.

Lacan follows Freud's texts in pointing to the child as an enigma, in the sense that Freud described the 'infantile' as that which does not develop, nor speak its FANTASY. What does develop is the SYMPTOM, which Lacan named as the fourth order of the particular outcome of the knotting of the Real, Symbolic and Imaginary in each life, structured as a response to the mother's desire and the signifier for a Father's Name (Lacan, 1976). Based on this idea, Lacan said there is only psychoanalysis of a subject, not of a child or adult as such. While psychologists talk of 'self' knowledge, Lacan argued that there is no consciousness or perception preceding consciousness, only a series of emergent forms. The infant anticipates its image in the forms of the world around it, which, in turn, make it possible for an infant to recognize itself in an IMAGE. What we take to be self-knowledge is actually a *mé-connaissance*, a mistaking of the image for the thing itself. Lacan's Imaginary dimension displaces the Freudian idea of developmental stages; his counter-theory is that we depend on others and on a universe of language which diversifies and multiplies our needs.

Lacan posits the particularity of what causes each person to desire (or not). DESIRE resides within the 'self' circuit, Lacan argues, because our primary desire is for satisfaction or JOUISSANCE, not for the objects or things we assume will fulfil it. But to get the simplest satisfaction, even food, we must negotiate by submitting ourselves to another who speaks and looks. This requirement for satisfaction turns need into DESIRE, so that DRIVE enters the game, turning the issue of need into a dialectical one (J.-A. Miller, 1988, pp. 108–9). Thus, we re-find the *function* of our organs in language, where the signifier is *incorporated*, materializing or corporifying language by the Real.

In his second period of teaching, from 1964 until 1974, Lacan was rejected for criticizing standard theories of the ego, and for bringing the social into the individual via language. Although the ostensible reasons given were his practice of short-time sessions and his charismatic presence, he had called into question the sacred theories of classical psychoanalysis: biological drive theory and ego defence theory. For him, the ego is a narcissistic formation whose structure and function link it to the DEATH DRIVE as an 'agency' of resistance, clinging to the Real of libidinal consistency or *jouissance* over any possibility of change through re-constituting language and desire. But what does Lacan mean by structure? Lacan described structure as the Real itself in play in analytic experience (1975b, p. 14), in whatever concerns the speaking SUBJECT, whose living body has been taken over by the Symbolic, cut by the spoken (*le dit*) (Skriabine, 1990). When language works strangely in autism or psychosis, it tells Lacanians that the signifier *qua* name has not, in this case, been attached to images or to the BODY. In neurosis, on the other hand, the 'subject' functions *because* it is linked together in three associative orders that cohere in a linking of three constituted orders: the Real, the Symbolic and the Imaginary.

In the third period of his teaching, Lacan called into question what we usually term 'mind', making it a metaphor for an individual's identifications with language, images and others. By arguing that the Symbolic and Imaginary constitute, not only the subject, but also the Real of the drive, Lacan shows how mind and body are linked via desire and *jouissance*, thus obviating, not only the mind/body dualism of centuries of Western thought, but also the phenomenological split between the subject of consciousness and the object in the world. Persons identify in moments of time with language, with images, or with the *jouissance* effects of the Real. The subject is consistent in the Imaginary, fading in the Symbolic and absolute in the Real. The subject dwells – *qua* object – in the gaps between signifiers, materializing language with *jouissance* effects.

Lacan gradually pieced together an understanding of Freud's classical diagnostic categories out of this early find, such that each human's being is a *cause* that co-joins desire, knowledge, language and *jouissance* in precise ways depending on how identity was first structured to relate gender to language and body. This in turn gives rise to three ways of relating to desire – neurosis, perversion, psychosis – which are not continuous one with the other. One cannot destroy the unconscious desire that one lives from, nor can one pass from one desiring structure to another in analytic treatment, although one can learn to put one's symptoms to creative use.

Lacan and feminism

What is perhaps most relevant for feminism in Lacan's theory is his formalization of a logical subject, not a biological one. His problematizing of Freud argues that males and females both pay a price for being constituted as social creatures, each sex cohering as an identity only by losing something: there is no norm wherein neither sex suffers, only a caricatured MASQUERADE of sexual difference imposd by the particularities of a mother's desire functioning in relation to a Father's Name. For Freud, sexual excitation (which Lacan translates as *jouissance* or the satisfaction of the drive) is what draws the sexes together; not the genitals *per se*. Individuals are drawn towards other people, not by a biological urge, but in reference to the 'object' of desire or mark of lack Lacan called the PHALLUS or paternal metaphor. By 'phallus' Lacan means a pure signifier, a third term of reference for the lack that circumscribes the subject position imposed on an infant by a mother's desire in so far as it does – or does not – refer the infant away from her body and being, towards language and culture. A foreclosure or loss of the mother as absolute presence or primary object is necessary lest a psychotic structure be laid down, such that desire cannot be achieved and drive turns back on to the body rather than aiming out towards the world.

Lacan explains that the sexual difference – what he calls sexuation – is established as an asymmetry between the masculine and feminine positions (Lacan, 1975b, p. 73). Although males may claim the first position that Freud mythologized as the primordial father, it is a paradoxical lie (Freud, 1913, pp. 149–50, 159–50). So, a second masculine position is adopted which gives consistency to the sense of being whole:

by identifying themselves as an exception to the rule of lack – i.e. by not being like the mother who differs from them – males identify with the group, the whole, the inside. That they are exceptions – an imaginary lie – to the rule of loss defines the outside for males in terms of a limit. Because of this Lacan sees male sexuality as perverse, a FETISHIZATION of Woman who becomes a 'symptom' for men – of Otherness, the outside, the unconscious. Women, by contrast, identify with a logic of the particular by not undergoing an identificatory confusion with a phallic signifier, the signifier for difference itself. The feminine position is therefore subversive of patriarchal closures.

Freud's hypotheses about the male impasse of castration anxiety *in relation to other men* (Freud, 1937, p. 250) can be read as the problem of identifying with the group as the primary meaning of MASCULINITY, and the female impasse of PENIS ENVY as desire to know what one *is* within a group of the whole (Lacan, 1975b, p. 74). To understand Lacan's contribution to feminism, one must grasp that he reads Freud as having uncovered a *logic* of the unconscious which touches on the Real whose fundamental axiom is this: culture arises from the fact that 'there is no sexual relation', no signifier adequate to represent the difference between the sexes (1975b, p. 35). With this theory, the feminist challenge of understanding how one may fight sexist oppressions shifts away from totalizing concepts such as gender or PATRIARCHY to the Real of impasses and the drive for satisfaction. Heterosexual or homosexual, we are drawn to each other sexually because we are not whole and because we are not the same. If one is 'grounded' in the body, in the flux of desire and moments of *jouissance,* the totalizing concept of gender would render Imaginary 'the disputed question of equality versus difference' (Adams and Cowie, 1990, p. 5).

Identity is thus a desiring position whose parameters are much broader than language, sexuality or gender *per se.* Identity is not one with itself, because it starts with a prior lack in it: loss of the mother as primary object of mental and physical fusion and, therefore, loss of certainty. The one who does not differentiate away from the mother never assumes an identity demarcated by having acquired its own name, 'self' fictions, particular history and unique body images. This is the one Lacan calls psychotic: the one who learned no diacritical gender position in the first six years of life, and so in fundamental psychotic fantasy is *both/and*; man and woman. By discovering that the irrational – psychosis – is entirely rational once its causes are understood, Lacan linked up many areas of study usually thought to be separate from one another: sexuality, sexual difference, drive, libido, the relation of the individual to the cultural, and so on. Starting with the theory that psychosis is rational and working through perversion and neurosis to what we call the 'normative', Lacan re-defines the 'norm' in terms of structure, not content. The unconscious, re-defined by Lacan, is not only the gaps or negativities or lacks in being and language, but also carries the weight of the void which drives us to identify with Imaginary theories of consciousness. Having no depth, the Lacanian unconscious is assimilated to the interiority of the subject whose external surface is the body which, indeed, closes out the unconscious, trying to erase the gaps that Lacan defines as the home of the subject.

WRITINGS

Note: For an explanation of the policy followed in the citation of works by Lacan see p. xii of this Dictionary.

1973: 'L'Étourdit', *Scilicet*, 4, pp. 5–52.
1975a; *De la psychose paranoïaque dans ses rapports avec la personnalité suivi de Premiers écrits sur la paranoïa. Le Champ freudien*; series directed by Jacques Lacan. Paris: Seuil.
1975b: *Le Séminaire*, book 20: *Encore*, ed. Jacques-Alain Miller. Paris: Seuil.
1976: *Le Séminaire*, book 23: 'Le sinthome', *Ornicar?*, 6, pp. 3–20.

BIBLIOGRAPHY

Adams, Parveen and Cowie, Elizabeth, 1990: *The Woman in Question*. Cambridge, Mass.: MIT Press.
Borch-Jacobsen, Mikkel, 1991: *Lacan: The Absolute Master*. Stanford, California: Stanford University Press.
Bowie, Malcolm, 1991: *Lacan*. London: Fontana.
Freud, Sigmund, 1913: *Totem and Taboo*, SE, 13, pp. 1–161. London: Hogarth Press.
Freud, Sigmund, 1921: *Group Psychology and the Analysis of the Ego*, SE, 18, pp. 65–143.
Lee, Jonathan Scott, 1990: *Jacques Lacan*. Boston: Twayne Publishers.
Macey, David, 1983: 'Fragments of an analysis: Lacan in context', *Radical Philosophy*, 35, pp. 1–9.
Miller, Gerard, 1987: *Lacan*. Paris: Bordas.
Miller, Jacques-Alain, 1988: 'Cause et consentement', unpublished course.
Roudinesco, Elisabeth, 1990 [1986]: *Jacques Lacan & Co.: A History of Psychoanalysis in France*. Trans. Jeffrey Mehlman. London: Free Association Books.
Sauret, Marie-Jean, 1990: 'La question du développement de l'enfant', *traVaux*, 5, pp. 108–9.
Skriabine, Pierre, 1990: 'La Clinique de Lacan et la topologie', *traVaux*, 5, p. 63.

ELLIE RAGLAND-SULLIVAN

lack Psychoanalytic lack is problematic for feminism in three areas: (1) woman's PSYCHICAL REALITY; (2) woman's epistemology, the question of lack in her knowledge and perception of her sex; (3) politically, in relation to DESIRE and JOUISSANCE in the Lacanian system, which opens feminine psychical reality on to the politics of GENDER arrangements between the sexes.

One: feminine access to SEXUALITY is complicated by how the presence or absence of the penis in boy, girl and mother is conceived, and also by the inflated attributes granted to the father's (unseen) organ. Threatened with castration or absolute lack the boy can make the protective side-step of identifying with the father's imaginary potency, supported by the latter's 'lack' (understood as a mere 'hiding' of his power and enjoyment). The girl, however, is said by Freud to desire a penis and thereby to foreclose any transformation of her lack into the positive phallic strength open to the boy. 'Identification' with the father would masculinize her, but leave her still biologically the site of physical lack; accepting her lack without IDENTIFICATION with paternal phallic power leaves her lacking symbolically. Attributing a penis to the mother, with whom she could identify, leads to a different, inverted impasse (Adams, 1989, pp. 248ff.): she actually sees the mother, who does not have 'it' on her body, and either accepts and identifies with the mother's impotence or assumes she has 'it' elsewhere in a hidden, fetishized form (see FETISHISM; FETISHIZATION; PHALLUS).

Two: in the epistemological and perceptual field, feminism revolts against 'originary absence' derived from the male sex organ as primary reference point. Cixous (1981, 1990) construes the phallic power attributed to the father's hidden organ as a purely political structure based on a willed (and highly anxious) refusal to see the positive potency in the female sex organ (1981, p. 255). Undermining the notion of 'lack' altogether, she strives to re-orient all symbolic systems towards this 'Medusa's head' which, ironically, is where Freud locates, eventually, the boy's perception of the threat of castration rather than in the ideal(istic) identification with the father's oedipal lack or his phallic threats. Similarly, Irigaray (1985, p. 83) argues for a primary re-orientation, with woman symbolizing her 'own relationship to beginning' as a maternal 'imaginary' rather than a paternal 'symbolic' (in quotation marks).

Three: the political effects of PENIS ENVY and the phallic Imaginary/Symbolic set-up of feminine psychical reality are evaluated against a reading of how the structure of the phallic supplementation that crowns the boy's realization of lack depends on a misreading of the father's position as a hidden positivity. Once the father, or in Lacan's terms the Other, is understood to be the site of a radical and irremediable lack (even behind the phallic veil) the boy's identification is rendered as problematical as the girl's. It may even grant her epistemological as well as experiential priority, since she is rendered more able to understand how the lack in the Other frees her, as subject, to enjoy. Moreover, this makes women closer to the truth of the 'lack' in human culture as a (not) whole, not-all.

See also LACAN; OTHER/OTHER; PRIMARY CASTRATION; REAL; SYMPTOM.

BIBLIOGRAPHY

Adams, Parveen, 1989: 'Of female bondage', Between Feminism and Psychoanalysis, ed. Teresa Brennan. London and New York: Routledge, pp. 247–65.
Cixous, Hélène, 1981: 'The laugh of the Medusa', New French Feminisms, ed. Elaine Marks and Isabelle de Courtivron. New York: Schocken, pp. 245–64.
Cixous, Hélène, 1990: 'The two countries of writing', The Other Perspective in Gender and Culture: Rewriting Women and the Symbolic, ed. Juliet Flower MacCannell. New York: Columbia University Press, pp. 191–208.
Freud, Sigmund, 1940: 'The Medusa's head', SE, 18, pp. 273ff.
Irigaray, Luce, 1985: Speculum of the Other Woman, trans. Gillian Gill. Ithaca, NY: Cornell University Press, 1985.

JULIET FLOWER MACCANNELL

language   The linguistic studies that have had the greatest impact on feminist consciousness (Lakoff, 1975; Daly, 1978; McConnell-Ginet, 1980) dealt primarily with nomenclatures and vocabularies – 'women's language' – and only rarely with those language structures that are useful for psychoanalytic practice. Attention to language in feminism has meant hoping for the emancipation of women, as in Lakoff (1975) who conceives the mapping of 'genderlects' as eventually liberatory. Many feminists, like Christian, decry theoretical attention to language, considered as a patriarchal discourse, for undermining concerns for GENDER and ethnicity and their 'dynamic' uses of language (1989, p. 68). Psychoanalytic feminists like CHODOROW (1989) often consider language use subsequent to the more important sexual agenda set by object relations. Nor has feminism found a place in those general theories of language, like Chomsky's 'Cartesian Linguistics', that have raised hopes they could provide a bridge between global linguistic/grammatical 'deep structures' (taken to be similar to the UNCONSCIOUS) and more local social movements like the women's movement. Speech act theory, following Austin and Searle, has not been well articulated either to psychoanalysis or to feminism, primarily because it posits an unproblematic unity between the speaker's intention and the intention embodied in the speech act (Salecl, 1990, p. 45). Post-Saussurean linguistics (Benveniste, 1971, and Jakobson, 1963) has been more promising in its emphasis on the *grammatical paradigms* (conjugation of I/you/he) as sets of formal subject positions that model the relations of gender, and has helped feminists clarify questions of the feminine subject position, but not necessarily with reference to psychoanalysis and the unconscious. Benveniste's attention to the situation of the subject of the enunciation, beyond that of the subject of the statement, has also been useful to feminist critics in distinguishing male-oriented statements from feminine narrative modes.

Yet only the updated forms of ancient Greek diagnostics (semiotics) and the medieval trivium (logic, rhetoric and grammar) have proved of significance for both feminism and psychoanalysis, by treating those aspects of language that link the two most profoundly. Semiotics, the study of signifying practices that denote a discordance between apparent and possible meanings, can be said to encompass rhetoric and grammar (Saussure, 1966, p. 16; Peirce, 1955, p. 106, though they have more directly contributed concepts and methods to psychoanalysis and feminism).

The fact that psychoanalysis had its origins in the observation of a crucial disparity between the discourse of hysterical young women and the things their bodies were acting on and acting out (as Anna O.'s fantasmatic childbearing disclosed her dismaying desire for Doctor Breuer) set language, feminism and psychoanalysis into a virtually inextricable relation. The approach to language Freud evolved through the 'Studies on hysteria' (1895) and then 'The interpretation of dreams' (1900) implied a re-evaluation of the status of speech as relating to the BODY that diverged radically from classical conceptions of speech as directly reflective of thought, a move paralleled by Saussure's *Course* (1966).

The idea of a second, supplementary discourse (hinted at through gestures, tonalities, body postures, etc.) which provides not just 'another point of view' on a primary speech event but additional information about another powerful scene in a patient's life is quite radical from the perspective of traditional linguistic and rhetorical theory. The act of bridging a gap between two discourses with a neurosis, a dream, an enunciation, a parapraxis, a work of art (which all attempt to suture two discourses together in a compromise formation) takes precedence over the primary discourses themselves. Such speech events 'recreate a harmony with a Real' (Lacan, 1977d, p. 22), the REAL being *de facto* barred from perceptual language. These harmonizings differ from traditional 'allegorical' or 'figural' interpretation (Auerbach, 1959) which demand that an intellect, human or divine, translates correctly between two disjunctive realms, ideal and real, spiritual and temporal, while indicating their absolute disjunction. For psychoanalysis, relating primary and secondary processes is not an intellectual but a practical act, aimed at realizing an articulation to DESIRE; as such it is always a mistranslation whose primary focus is not on the Real but on its avoidance.

The earliest notices of the importance of language for Freud hailed psychoanalysis as *a rhetoric* – 'a science of tropes' (Trilling, 1951, p. 103) – the science of acts of misnaming. But Lacan (esp. 1977b, pp. 40ff.) insisted on a less platonic emphasis on naming, and drew attention instead to such things as the empty subject of speech and the 'full' word, the importance to gender division of the grammatical forms of active and passive voice (1978, p. 192), and the political power of tropes (metaphor and metonymy) in the fundamental economy of the Western psyche.

Freud's discovery that body and speech combined in ways not provided for by classical rhetoric and physics meant that a new hybrid form of expression was continually being produced at the site of neurotic, psychotic and even artistic speech. This is because language, as we know it, both literally and figuratively, is geared to a perceptual consciousness (Freud, 1940, p. 164; Muller, 1978, p. 23) that cannot account for primary processes (strictly off-stage) in their specific relation to conscious expression. Dislodging an essentially perceptual understanding of language based on figure and the visual (a tradition from the Greeks to Heidegger, for whom 'saying' is a 'showing', and 'disclosed being' is a manifestation in the symbolic order (1971, p. 134)), was crucial to Freud, because the analysis of speech in psychoanalysis needs a language addressed to more than the organs of perception. Freud (1940, pp. 193–4) wrote that, in addition to the 'attributes (qualities) of the object under examination which are presented directly to our perception, we have to discover something else which is more independent of the particular receptive capacity of our sense organs and which approximates more closely to what may be supposed to be the real state of affairs. . . . Reality will always remain "unknowable"' (1940, pp. 196–7). Freud's approach was to articulate a primary verbal discourse, openly avowed and expressed, and another discourse – a radically different scenic drama – that was being indicated in a singularly expressed set of verbal, gestural, intonational and other signifying practices. This other tongue demanded far more sophisticated and complex analyses than those offered by traditional rhetorical readings or hermeneutic unveilings. Words had to be seen against the backdrop of a body that was also saying something, in another mode, about itself and its needs and desires. That this speaking body was, for the early Freud, most often a woman's was decisive for aligning woman with the major discourse of the unconscious, and for feminist adoption or rejection of this equation.

The patient's discourse is, for Freud, radically doubled; but this is not a simple contradiction of the 'real state of affairs', rather its perpetual negation, the expression of a desire not to know, or even to murder a thing (nature, a wish, an event – the trauma) that is unfaceable. Such discourse requires less a hermeneutic or logical analytic method than a symptomatology. LACAN (1977a, p. 149) thus linked Freudian practice to Ferdinand de Saussure's new linguistics – the 'science of signs in society' – which re-united the study of language with the ancient art of *semeiology*, symptom-reading in Greek medicine. Semiology replaces the opposition literal/figurative (physical sign/mental figure or concept) with the co-determinacy of signifier/signified. Semiologically, primary processes (Freud's discovery) could be examined from the point of view of the signifier: i.e. REPRESSION proper would refer less to an original absence of meaning or to the absolute substitution of one meaning for another, than to the mis-translation of one signifier by another, which becomes its 'signified', although a 'signified' without any significance outside the sign-relation.

Freud thus developed the analysis of speech beyond Aristotelian rhetoric (as well as Aristotelian catharsis – the 'talking cure'). Feminist literary criticism, for example, has strained to liken condensation and displacement in the dream to metaphor (as negation) and metonymy (as continual substitution); yet distinctions made within the linguistic/rhetorical system always collapse in primary process itself, which is without negation.

A rhetorical orientation has inspired feminists in literary study, though the source is often more Nietzschean than psychoanalytic (Kofman, 1980; Berg, 1982). However, Lacan's use of tropology to re-frame key concepts in Freud has had the greatest significance for feminism. He re-defined Freud's stress on the determinative role of the father in rhetorical terms: paternity owes its impact to its metaphoric nature. Like metaphor, paternity is considered more purely inferential because it is dependent on the absolute elision of its primary, material referent; metonymy, or change of name, is likened to maternity, in contrast, because it presumes the existence of an original or primary referent, socially censured or tabooed, to which all its manifestations – objects, names, or letters – must always refer and thereby 'increase its presence' (Lacan, 1977a, p. 156). The oppression of a real or natural maternal presence by a hypothetical father is an effect of the predominance of metaphoric over metonymic modes in our culture, despite the fact that the 'spiritual' or paternal cannot 'live without the letter' though the reverse is the case (Lacan, 1977a, 156–8).

Feminists reacted to Lacan's designation of the metaphor of paternity and began to consider support for metaphor support for male dominance; Kristeva's feminism, like Derrida's grammatology, emphasizes metonymy in an effort to supplant/supplement the metaphoric-paternal by the metonymic-maternal. However, Lacan was criticizing less the power of metaphor *per se* than an imbalance between literal and figurative: turning the inference of metaphor into a 'proper name' is crucial to male dominance. When the patronym – the 'name of the father' – founds 'property' it becomes a dispossession of the woman, the mother and sister. Without a real or literal ballast (like the maternal body) the phallic version of metaphor ascribes unlimited powers to the mere signifier of MASCULINITY.

Feminist objections to the primacy of the phallic signifier in Lacan's theories have thus been plentiful, but few feminist linguists have offered systematic alternatives to Lacan's. This is in part because feminist theory, in taking language as the primary indicator of the presence of patriarchal values and of a sexually divided economy, has tended to direct its energies towards reforming language use, rather than the structure of articulation among symbol, fantasy and signifier (especially their knotting in the unconscious). Feminists (Kristeva, 1980; Irigaray, 1985; Cixous, 1990) emphasize that metonymic connection, feminine JOUIS-SANCE and the desire of the mother (all opposing the name of the father) are the leftover or excess residue unaccounted for by masculine/metaphoric language. Cixous (1990) sees in the twists of poetic language hidden resources for extracting 'other' meanings from the unconscious to contest any exclusively phallic definition of the signifier which, if liberated from patriarchal narrowness, could prove liberatory for both sexes, and especially for women. But by and large, the most elaborated counter-theories of language from feminism still play off the Lacanian insights, rather than seeking alternative theories.

For Chomsky (1978, p. 5) the grammar of a language is an 'unconscious' of sorts, being a knowledge without self-awareness of its existence. This internalized body of knowledge ('a mental grammar') is a matrix from which 'the set of sentences that are described by the grammar' (p. 6) can be infinitely generated. Although the language so generated is infinite, the grammar's capture by a finite brain limits and specifies sound, structure and meaning. Rejecting the view that the purpose of language is communication (p. 16), Chomsky argues that this mental grammar 'has a higher degree of reality' (p. 8) consisting of its access to the 'ideal homogeneous speech community' (p. 5) from which the ideal speaker can be unproblematically abstracted, without regard to SEXUAL DIFFERENCE or other forms of inter-subjective articulation. Thus, his theory would count Freud's practical reading of the unconscious through parapraxes, dreams, etc. as mistakes or misconstructions of universal grammar (Smith, 1978, pp. x–xi).

Grammatically, the most psychoanalytically inspired feminist innovations have come from IRIGARAY, whose resistance to male dominance

213

takes the form of strong interference with grammatical structures, especially the expected male designation of the determinative 'third person' form. Recently, Ducrot's modifications of speech act theory have also been described as potentially significant for feminism (Salecl, 1990, pp. 45–8). The speaker is the articulator of the network of symbolic values, but it also articulates an 'I' (a shifter) of discourse to the system of symbols as the bearer of an essential LACK or emptiness. Since the signifier introduces an element of suspense that requires prospective and retroactive links with other signifiers to produce its meaning and significance, even the straightest discourse cannot fail to incite, if only minimally, its hearer to take up a fantasy position in relation to the (empty) speaker of the discourse (Lacan's 'Che vuoi?' or 'What do you want?') and to oneself as articulated to the desire of the fantasmatic Other dimly adumbrated by the act of speech ('What does he want *of me*?' or 'Where do I fit in to the signifying place established by the signifier?') (Salecl, 1990, p. 50; Lacan, 1977c, p. 313).

See also FEMININE ECONOMY; HYSTERIA; PATRIARCHY; PHALLUS; SYMPTOM.

BIBLIOGRAPHY

Auerbach, Erich, 1959: 'Figura', *Scenes from the Drama of European Literature*, trans. Willard Trask. New York: Meridian, pp. 11–76.
Benveniste, Emile, 1971: *Problems in General Linguistics*. Miami: Miami University Press, 1971; 1st edn Paris: Gallimard, 1966.
Berg, Elizabeth, 1982: 'The third woman', *Diacritics* 12/2, pp. 11–20.
Cameron, Deborah, ed. 1990: *The Feminist Critique of Language: A Reader*. London: Routledge.
Chodorow, Nancy, 1989: *Feminism and Psychoanalytic Theory*. New Haven and London: Yale University Press.
Chomsky, Noam, 1978: 'Language and unconscious knowledge', Smith, 1978, pp. 3–44.
Christian, Barbara, 'The race for theory', *Changing Our Own Words*, ed. Cheryl A. Wall. New Brunswick and London: Rutgers University Press, pp. 67–79.
Cixous, Hélène, 1990: 'The two countries of writing', *The Other Perspective in Gender and Culture: Rewriting Women and the Symbolic*, ed. Juliet Flower MacCannell. New York: Columbia University Press, pp. 191–208.
Daly, Mary, 1978: *Gyn/Ecology: The Metaethics of Radical Feminism with a New Intergalactic Introduction by the Author*. Boston: Beacon Press.
Ducrot, Oswald, 1986: *Le Dire et le dit*. Paris: Minuit.
Freud, Sigmund, 1895: *Studies in Hysteria* (with Josef Breüer), *SE*, 2, pp. 37–59.
Freud, Sigmund, 1900: *The Interpretation of Dreams*, *SE*, 4, 5.
Freud, Sigmund, 1905, *Jokes and their Relation to the Unconscious*, *SE*, 8, pp. 3–238.
Freud, Sigmund, 1940: *An Outline of Psychoanalysis*, *SE*, 23, pp. 139–207.

Heidegger, Martin, 1962 [1927]: *Being and Time*, trans. John Macquarrie and Edward Robinson. New York: Harper and Row.

Irigaray, Luce, 1985 [1977]: 'The Looking-Glass, from the other side', *This Sex Which Is Not One*, trans. Ithaca, NY: Cornell University Press, pp. 9–33.

Jakobson, Roman, 1963: *Essais de linguistique générale*. Paris: Minuit.

Kofman, Sara, 1980: 'The narcissistic woman: Freud and Girard', *Diacritics*, 10/3, pp. 36–45.

Kristeva, Julia, 1980 [1977]: *Desire in Language*. New York: Columbia University Press.

Lacan, Jacques, 1977a: 'The agency of the letter in the unconscious or reason since Freud', *Écrits: A Selection*, trans. Alan Sheridan. London: Tavistock, pp. 146–78.

Lacan, Jacques, 1977b: 'Function and field of speech in language', *Écrits*, pp. 30–113.

Lacan, Jacques, 1977c: 'Subversion of the subject and dialectic of desire', *Écrits*, pp. 293–325.

Lacan, Jacques, 1977d: 'From love to the libido', *Four Fundamental Concepts of Psychoanalysis*, trans. Alan Sheridan. London: Hogarth Press, pp. 187–202.

Lakoff, Robin, 1975: *Language and Women's Place*. New York: Harper and Row.

McConnell-Ginet, Sally, 1980: *Women and Language in Literature and Society*. New York: Praeger.

Muller, John, 1978: 'Language, psychosis, and the subject in Lacan', Smith, 1978, pp. 21–32.

Peirce, Charles Sanders, 1955 [1897–1910]: 'Logic as semiotic: the theory of signs', *Philosophical Writings of Peirce*, sel. and ed. Justus Buchler. New York, Dover, pp. 98–119.

Salecl, Renata, 1990: '"Society doesn't exist"', *American Journal of Semiotics*, 7/1–2, pp. 45–52.

Saussure, Ferdinand de, 1966 [1905]: *Course in General Linguistics*, trans. Wade Baskin. New York: McGraw-Hill.

Smith, Joseph, ed. 1978: *Psychoanalysis and Language*, vol. 3 in 'Psychiatry in the Humanities'. New Haven and London: Yale University Press.

Trilling, Lionel, 1951: *The Liberal Imagination*. New York: Viking.

JULIET FLOWER MACCANNELL

lesbianism   Freud confines his speculations on female homosexuality to 'The psychogenesis of a case of homosexuality in a woman' (1920) and to the footnotes of 'Fragment of an analysis of a case of hysteria' (1905b). He attributes both cases to the woman's 'masculinity complex' rather than to a desire originating from within the libidinal vicissitudes or economy of FEMININITY itself, which helps explain his near oversight of Dora's 'gynaecophilia' even though it is supposedly 'the strongest unconscious current in her mental life' (1905a, p. 120–1). The aim and object of female homosexuality are understood by Freud to be the same as those of male heterosexuality. Dora is said to harbour an unconscious 'revenge fantasy', as the result of disappointed love for her father whom she renounces along with all men, repressing her (wounded) femininity in favour of an aggressive identification with masculinity. Likewise, in 'Psychogenesis' (1920), Freud explains the attraction of his young woman patient to an older woman of supposed ill repute as not only a retaliatory displacement of disappointed love for her father but also a displaced DESIRE for her brother, whose bodily likeness Freud detects in the forbidden woman. In this case there is no trace of female–female desire; rather, female homosexuality is likened more precisely to male homosexuality.

Perhaps it is because Freud understands female homosexuality as a recovery of masculinity that he does not regard it as pathological and that he prescribes no therapy. He does, however, classify it as a 'PERVERSION', since, like male homosexuality, female homosexuality constitutes a sexual practice which does not serve the normal (natural) aim of SEXUALITY (reproduction). To distinguish homosexuality from other perversions (e.g. FETISHISM), he also classifies it as an 'inversion', referring to the 'inverted' relation between physical and psychical sexual identity which is normally one of coincidence. Though he explicitly rejects anatomical determinism as a cause of HOMOSEXUALITY (see Freud, 1905b), he none the less notes the 'masculine' physique of his lesbian client and he does not rule out the consideration of constitutional factors (whatever they may be). In observing, without considering the cultural and social privileging of MASCULINITY, that only female 'inverts' take on the psychical or mental attributes of the opposite sex, Freud exposes his teleological view of SEXUAL DIFFERENCE.

Freud's view of female homosexuality was eventually challenged by sociologists, social psychologists and psychiatrists writing in the 1950s, who came to see it as a legitimate choice of lifestyle and cultivation of personal identity rather than as an untreatable 'perversion' (Garner, 1989). But it was much later before psychoanalysis reconsidered its view of lesbianism; even proponents of the 'cultural school' of psychoanalysis, such as Karen HORNEY, continued to defer to Freud's 'masculinity' theory of female homosexuality (Garner, 1989).

The 1970s saw the emergence of various psychoanalytically informed feminist analyses of female sexuality, including those by Adrienne Rich, Dorothy Dinnerstein and Nancy CHODOROW, which emphasize the homoerotic mother–daughter bond of the PRE-OEDIPAL phase, overlooked by Freud, as a constitutive determinant of female sexual difference, though not always emerging in lesbianism (Garner, 1989). Feminist therapist Phyllis Chesler criticizes psychoanalysis's misunderstanding of lesbians as maladapted and advocates widespread lesbian practice as effective treatment of women's sexual repression and domination by male sexuality (Chesler, 1972). Another clinician, Charlotte Wolff, draws upon Freud's theory of innate BISEXUALITY to judge the superior 'virility' and the more fluid exchange between masculine and feminine identity of lesbians, concluding that they are more healthily independent, more varied in their personal relationships and better adapted to HETEROSEXUALITY than 'normal' women (Wolff, 1971).

French analyst and theorist Luce IRIGARAY is perhaps the single most important contributor to the psychoanalytic theory of female homosexuality. Her close, subversive reading of Freud's writing on femininity and her poetic extension of psychoanalytic figures of sexual difference offer powerful negative and positive critiques of the speculative discourse on lesbianism. Irigaray's concern is at once theoretical and therapeutic, employing various counter-strategies of rhetoric to tease the unthought and the invisible of lesbianism out of Freud's text as well as to prompt the (lesbian) reader to re-view and see beyond her psychoanalytic/patriarchal imaginary.

Combining deconstructive and psychoanalytic readings of Freud, Irigaray exposes 'female homosexuality' for the fetish figure it is: instead of signifying a truly heterogeneous sexuality or sexual practice, with a specifically female aim and object, it is a 'hom(m)osexualized' figure, a woman with a man's desire for a woman-phallus or PHALLIC MOTHER, whose masculine MASQUERADE serves to veil the (double) LACK projected on to the lesbian body by the anxious gaze of the male voyeur-theorist (*see* VOYEURISM/EXHIBITIONISM/THE GAZE). Irigaray shows how psychoanalysis, blinded by discursive structures of phallocentrism, cannot envisage the circulation of PLEASURE between women unmediated and unmobilized by male desire. In theory, psychoanalysis prohibits female auto- and homoeroticism, content to see women's sexuality subjected to men's sadistic and scopophiliac drives. This discursive hom(m)osexualization of woman by psychoanalysis, its expropriation and/or REPRESSION of the woman's perspective in the imaging and symbolization of her sexuality, substantially contribute to her suffering from an insufficient sense of sexual self worth. While psychoanalysis would attribute this suffering to the normal process of becoming feminine, thus covering up the prohibitions it imposes on female self-love, Irigaray exposes these prohibitions and their damaging effects, calling for adequate treatment of female narcissism (Irigaray, 1985a).

But just as psychoanalytic theory may, if pressed, reveal discursive mechanisms which oppress women by alienating them from themselves and from each other, so also does it point to the site of trans-formation/transfiguration – which is why Irigaray reads so closely. Locating totalizing tropes, rhetorical gaps, logical inconsistencies where the 'other woman' could emerge, with other desires, other fantasies, an other libidinal economy, which are easily recuperated by the phallic order of representation, Irigaray uncovers discursive potential for criti-cal, curative treatment of psychoanalysis's hom(m)osexualized female. Working through the dominant images of male desire, Irigaray replaces the negative figures of femininity with positive ones, reconstructed from deconstructed phallomorphic figures. In place of one, visible, erect organ standing for the whole/hole of sexual pleasure, she presents a figure of many and multiplying female sex organs and erogenous zones, fluid in shape, size and number as well as in their interaction with them-selves and those of the other sex(es). Neither reduced to one (phallic) sex, nor lost to polymorphous perversity, her female sex comprises one and more sexualities, encompassing auto-, homo- and heterosexuality (Irigaray, 1985b). Elsewhere, she presents the image of women's lips touching/speaking, suggesting an embodied discourse-caress in place of the repressed or sublimated sexuality of masculine discourse. A specifically female figure, the conversing/caressing two lips belonging to either or both oral and vaginal erogenous zones, signifies women's auto- and homoerotic desire without signalling phallic intervention. Raised to the order of the symbolic, this image could enter women's dialogue into discursive practice. 'I/you touch you/me' recovers and re-presents a *parler entre femmes*, encompassing and transforming the 'I love you' of patriarchal lover's discourse and its colonizing, masculine speaking sub-ject (Irigaray, 1985c, p. 209). For auto- and homoerotic discourses to be produced among women, for women, Irigaray foresees the need for sep-arate existence, at least temporarily, so that women 'discover the love of other women while sheltered from men's imperious choices that put them in the position of rival commodities' (Irigaray, 1985b, p. 33).

Judith Butler draws upon Irigaray's critique of female hom(m)osexu-ality and Michel Foucault's critique of the repressive thesis in her analy-sis of compulsory heterosexuality. Like Irigaray, Butler reads the figure of the female hom(m)osexual in psychoanalysis as symptomatic of its blind subscription to patriarchal biases prohibiting the representation of all sexualities, sexual practices and sexual relations conceivable within its system. Like Foucault, she interprets 'the law of incest' as a mythic construct which structuralist theories of anthropology and psychoanaly-sis use to explain and naturalize a patriarchal discursive order (*see* ANTHROPOLOGY AND CROSS-CULTURAL ANALYSIS). Also like Foucault, she sees this 'law' as generative, not repressive, as constructing and producing transgressive homosexuality as well as sanctioned heterosexuality.

Consequently, she rejects the idea that there is female homosexuality prior to oedipalization which must be recovered and released. Recourse to the notion of a female unconscious or a female imaginary is only necessary to gay liberation if the law is conceived to be a rigid and universal determinism. Instead of attempting to re-present a wholly other imaginary–symbolic order, she would foreground under-represented heterogeneity within the existing order, calling for a new and more complete constellation of differing and/or multiple sexual practices, relations and identifications so as to supplement and de-centre the dominant and reductive Hegelian opposition of masculine/feminine, hetero/homo. Butler argues that it is more effective to think of lesbianism as a parody of heterosexuality and to stage it as a sexual strategy rather than to regard it as a marginalized and repressed, other sexuality. Just as femininity is the 'masquerade' which preserves and protects the mythos of an autonomous masculinity and therefore possesses the power to unveil those myths, so also is lesbianism the 'masquerade' that preserves or subverts heterosexuality.

Clearly much work remains to be done by feminist lesbians to determine whether or not psychoanalysis can be fruitfully appropriated and elaborated for the purpose of theorizing lesbian sexuality, for articulating the specificity of lesbian desire.

See also FEMININE ECONOMY; HETEROSEXISM; HOMOPHOBIA; LESBIANISM: CLINICAL PERSPECTIVES; WOMAN-IDENTIFIED WOMAN/RADICAL LESBIANISM.

BIBLIOGRAPHY

Butler, Judith, 1990: *Gender Trouble: Feminism and the Subversion of Identity*. New York: Routledge.
Chesler, Phyllis, 1972: 'Lesbians', *Women and Madness*. New York: Harcourt Brace Jovanovich, pp.182–205.
Freud, Sigmund, 1905a: 'Fragment of analysis of a case of hysteria', *SE*, 7, pp. 3–122.
Freud, Sigmund, 1905b: *Three Essays on the Theory of Sexuality*, *SE*, 7, pp. 125–248.
Freud, Sigmund, 1920: 'The psychogenesis of a case of homosexuality in a woman', *SE*, 18, pp. 145–72.
Garner, Shirley Nelson, 1989: 'Feminism, psychoanalysis, and the heterosexual imperative', *Feminism and Psychoanalysis*, ed. Richard Feldstein and Judith Roof. Ithaca: Cornell University Press, pp. 164–84.
Irigaray, Luce, 1985a: 'Female hom(m)osexuality', *Speculum of the Other Woman*, trans. Gillian Gill. Ithaca: Cornell University Press, pp. 98–104.
Irigaray, Luce, 1985b: 'This sex which is not one', *This Sex Which Is Not One*, trans. Catherine Porter with Carolyn Burke. Ithaca: Cornell University Press, pp. 23–33.
Irigaray, Luce, 1985c: 'When our lips speak together', *This Sex Which Is Not One*. Ithaca: Cornell University Press, pp. 205–18.

LESBIANISM: CLINICAL PERSPECTIVES

Roof, Judith, 1989: 'The match in the crocus: representations of lesbian sexuality', *Discontented Discourses: Feminism, Textual Intervention, Psychoanalysis*, ed. Marleen S. Barr and Richard Feldstein. Urbana: University of Illinois Press, pp. 100–16.

Ryan, Joanna, 1983: 'Psychoanalysis and women loving women', *Sex and Love: New Thoughts on Old Contradictions*, ed. Sue Cartledge and Joanna Ryan. London: The Women's Press, pp. 196–209.

Wolff, Charlotte, 1971: *Love Between Women*. New York: Harper and Row.

DIANNE CHISHOLM

lesbianism: clinical perspectives   'Lesbians' do not figure in psychoanalytic texts, whereas 'female homosexuals 'do. This difference in terminology marks an important divide between self-proclaimed and ascribed identities. It also reflects the refusal of the major psychoanalytic organizations to train lesbians (and gay men). This exclusion is part of the unchallenged pathologization of lesbianism that has held sway since Freud.

Freud expounded his main ideas on the subject in 'The psychogenesis of a case of homosexuality in a woman' (1920). Unlike later writers, he insisted that his patient was not ill, nor neurotic, and he also expressed his doubts about attempts to cure HOMOSEXUALITY. Freud saw his patient's homosexual love in terms of the crushing disappointment that her adolescent longings for her father suffered when her mother became pregnant by him. 'Furiously resentful and embittered' (1920, p. 157), she rejected not only her father, but also men in general, and her femininity. For Freud, the young woman's very active and intense pursuit of her beloved is a 'masculine' (p. 154) style of loving, and he describes her as 'changing into a man' (p. 158). He thus ties object-choice to the mental characteristics (MASCULINITY or FEMININITY) of the SUBJECT. This reflects not only the dualisms of active/passive, masculine/feminine, male/female, that so bedevil Freudian theory, but also the much wider cultural difficulty of understanding a female sexuality that is desiring, overt, initiating and directed towards another woman, in any other than 'male' terms (*see* MASQUERADE).

Freud abruptly terminated this analysis, apparently in response to the woman's sweeping repudiation of men which, he felt, transferred to him, rendered all his efforts useless. Freud's own account of this ending, and his pique at his patient, raise many important countertransference issues, which for historical reasons were unlikely to have been addressed at the time. Subsequently, however, there are no discussions about countertransference issues with lesbian patients, which perhaps indicates what an area of unconscious difficulty this is for many practitioners. It remains an urgent area for exploration (*see* TRANSFERENCE/COUNTERTRANSFERENCE).

The masculinization of homosexual women was developed much further in the 1920s and 1930s. Whereas Freud had emphasized the disappointment of felt heterosexual desire in the context of long-standing bisexual attachments, female homosexuality now became seen as a defence against basic heterosexual wishes. Homosexual women were described as being in flight from the terrors of heterosexual incestuous desires, abandoning the father as love-object and unconsciously identifying with him instead. This came to mean that within psychoanalytic theory a woman could only either *be* or *have* a woman; she could not do both. The major feminist criticism of this position is provided by Butler (1990), who questions the account of GENDER identity as built on prohibition, loss and IDENTIFICATION within the fixity of a binary and heterosexist framework (*see* HETEROSEXISM).

DEUTSCH (1933) disputed the attribution of masculinity, while retaining Freud's notions of bisexual oscillation between the parents. She saw female homosexual relationships as involving reciprocal mother–child dynamics, based on both PRE-OEDIPAL love and later heterosexual difficulties that caused a return to the mother.

Most of the ideas about female homosexuality were put forward in the context of the early debates about female sexuality, and subsequent to these, very little attention was paid to the subject. McDougall (1979) provides the most extensive modern account, incorporating and extending many of the foregoing ideas. Starting from the premiss that a homosexual woman's identity is 'fictitious' (p. 206), and that it is an illusion for a woman to believe that she can be the true sexual partner of another woman, she constructs a developmental scenario, in which homosexuality is necessary for psychic survival: she sees 'the' homosexual woman as having unconsciously identified with her father, while consciously denigrating or dismissing him as a love-object. The mother is seen as all powerful, controlling and idealized. The daughter desires, and often has, an exclusive relationship with her, in which she runs the risks of engulfment. The idealized aspects of the mother are carried over into homosexual relationships, which are used as a 'manic screen against depressive feelings and persecutory fears' (p. 210).

McDougall's clinical descriptions are rich and vivid, but her theorizing suffers from her attempt to universalize and typify on the evidence of five, allegedly very similar, patients. Not only is the existence of significant clinical variety ignored, but so also is the existence of nonclinical populations of lesbians, who do not show the acute disturbances she describes. McDougall also shows an unquestioning acceptance of existing heterosexual and gender relationships: for her, homosexuals disavow the difference between the sexes, and she has no other way of understanding the social construction of either gender or gender non-conformity (*see* DISAVOWAL).

Lesbianism is conspicuous by its absence in all the major feminist psychoanalytic writings. Feminist object-relations theorists have tentatively cast lesbian relationships within the framework of mother–daughter dynamics, a perspective that is explored and questioned by Ryan (1983). To date there has been no major attempt to go beyond criticism and re-work psychoanalytic thinking about lesbianism, but the new phenomena of practising lesbian psychotherapists and an analytically oriented counselling service for and by lesbians and gay men – Project for Advice, Counselling and Education (PACE) – provide fertile ground for such developments. The diversity of lesbian identities and sexualities needs to be recognized psychoanalytically, freed of conventional categorizations, as does the nature of the inner resources that allow many lesbians to live loving and creative lives.

See also BISEXUALITY; HETEROSEXUALITY; HOMOPHOBIA; LESBIANISM; MOTHER–DAUGHTER RELATIONSHIP; WOMAN-IDENTIFIED WOMAN/RADICAL LESBIANISM.

BIBLIOGRAPHY

Butler, Judith, 1990: *Gender Trouble: Feminism and the Subversion of Identity.* New York: Routledge.

Deutsch, Helene, 1933: 'Homosexuality in women', *International Journal of Psycho-analysis*, 14, pp. 34–56.

Freud, Sigmund, 1920: 'The psychoanalysis of a case of homosexuality in a woman', *SE*, 18, pp. 145–72.

McDougall, Joyce, 1979: 'The homosexual dilemma', *Sexual Deviation*, ed. I. Rosen. Oxford: Oxford University Press, pp. 206–45.

Ryan, Joanna, 1983: 'Psychoanalysis and women loving women', *Sex and Love*, ed. Sue Cartledge and Joanna Ryan. London: The Women's Press, pp. 196–209.

JOANNA RYAN

libido This is primarily a Freudian term, but it has also passed into more general psychoanalytic usage, with considerable change in meaning. Freud, in the *Three Essays on the Theory of Sexuality* (1905), saw libido as the force by which the sexual instinct is represented in the mind. Libido was conceived of in quite physical terms, as something that could vary quantitatively and that was subject to accumulation and discharge. It was also mobile, becoming fixated to or abandoning objects. Libido was finite in its amounts, so that if some was directed inwards, less was available for outward cathexis; if more was expended on sexual gratification, less was available for SUBLIMATION.

For Freud there was only one libido, 'invariably and necessarily of a masculine nature' (1905, p. 219), under which both male and female sexuality were subsumed. This conception has frequently been criticized as more appropriate to male SEXUALITY than female.

The most radical alterations in libido theory came with the development of object-relations theory, and the criticism of ideas of DRIVE or instinct. The quantitative formulation of libido as energy was dropped, but the notion of libido was retained, as object- rather than pleasure-seeking, reflecting the urge to be and to develop as a person through object relationships.

See also OBJECT; PLEASURE.

BIBLIOGRAPHY

Freud, Sigmund, 1905: 'Three Essays on the Theory of Sexuality', SE, 7, pp. 123–245.

JOANNA RYAN

literary and textual criticism   Literary criticism became textual with the advent of structuralism, which put the emphasis upon LANGUAGE as a system. An author's language could no longer be regarded as a privileged reflection of reality but was rather seen as a situated production: the text was not simply attributed to the individual author but to the system in power which gave him, and sometimes her, a position and a code from which to speak, to write and to read (*see* IDEOLOGY; READING AS/LIKE A WOMAN). Roland Barthes's (1977) proclamation of the 'Death of the Author' opened a space for the reader's production of the text, entitling her/him to disregard or subvert the author's intention as it might be historically deduced, focusing instead on an excess of meaning as a side-effect of any text production.

Whereas in belletristic and later humanist criticism such an excess was seen as deriving from the genial practice of an author, the rich harvest of his sovereign imagination, psychoanalysis provided for this excess of meaning a less honorific explanation via its materialist theory of the UNCONSCIOUS. In a manner analogous to Freud's theory in *The Interpretation of Dreams* (1900), meaning was seen as inherently unstable, subject to pressure from the unconscious, resulting in unexpected shifts (displacement) and blockages at nodal points (condensation); DESIRE cannot name itself except by means of substitution. Such a perpetual figuration of desire called for a new mode of interpretation, a sexual/textual reading practice that challenges the subject positions of reader and writer alike. It took some time for psychoanalytic criticism to shed a thematic and psychological author-based approach and to develop a textual criticism whose object was no longer the individual psyche but the trans-individual unconscious (for a critical survey of schools and tendencies, see Wright, 1984).

A textualized psychoanalytic criticism, inspired by French post-structuralism, including essays by Lacan and Derrida (see Mehlman, 1972), was closely followed by an influential volume inaugurating a dialectical exchange between psychoanalysis and literature, where psychoanalysis points to the unconscious of LITERATURE, and literature to the unconscious of psychoanalysis (see Felman, 1977, pp. 5–10). Literature was to be probed for its theories and structures of the mind, showing there was theory in fiction, while psychoanalysis was to be investigated for its literariness, its slippage of meaning, showing there was fiction in THEORY (for a general demonstration of this dialectical textual practice see Bowie, 1987). In challenging the assumption of the authority of psychoanalysis over literature, Felman paved the way, via a Lacanian notion of transference, for a psychoanalytic reading practice. It is the clinical practice of psychoanalysis as much as its innovative theories which has led to the understanding of the principle of a textual reading. Moreover, the insights gained, the transference relation and the dialogic nature of the psychoanalytic session are shared by all schools, in that this dialogue is seen as 'performative' rather than 'informative' (Felman, 1987, p. 121; *see* TRANSFERENCE/COUNTERTRANSFERENCE).

Initially psychoanalytic criticism and feminist criticism joined forces rather reluctantly, because of feminist suspicions of psychoanalysis (*see* FEMINISM BEFORE PSYCHOANALYSIS). A specifically psychoanalytic textual feminist criticism did not develop until the early 1980s (Gaudin et al., 1981), when it was described as showing a certain 'theoretical instability': 'those theoreticians who have contributed to articulating psychoanalysis and feminism are not necessarily or primarily interested in literary criticism (Mitchell, Dinnerstein, Irigaray); conversely, those who have contributed to articulating psychoanalysis and literature are not necessarily or primarily feminists (Felman)' (Schor, 1981, p. 204). The situation thus polarizes into, on the one hand, a search for psychoanalytic themes in literary texts and, on the other, a literary analysis of theoretical texts, particularly those of Freud and LACAN and their commentators (for recent examples of the former, see Hirsch, 1989; for the latter, see Gallop, 1985). Schor (1981, p. 205) argues for and sketches out 'a new feminist thematics grounded in feminist hermeneutics', which entails a subversive reading of Freud's texts in order to recover the (inadvertent) contribution of women (patients) to psychoanalytic theory. This kind of enterprise is well illustrated in a recent collection of articles on Freud's unresolved problem case history of Dora (Bernheimer and Kahane, 1985). This collection makes plain that HYSTERIA, far from being merely a pathology, is first and foremost a position in desire, common to all (lacking) subjects: the body speaks without being understood, refusing the place assigned to it in the oedipal triangle (see Evans, 1989; Hunter, 1985).

From the early 1980s onwards feminist criticism inspired by French feminist writing began to join forces with American feminist criticism, and thereby helped to politicize psychoanalytic criticism, challenging its (phallocentric) theory in a new practice of writing, inspired partly by Derridean deconstruction, emphasizing the displacement of meaning, and partly by Lacanian psychoanalysis, emphasizing the construction of the (gendered) subject in language (Jacobus, 1986). Literary and textual criticism began to flourish in the twin discipline of feminism and psychoanalysis, developing a certain astringency and political relevance, especially where it included a controversial position *vis-à-vis* psychoanalytic theory and the theories of feminine subjectivity this theory espouses, in some cases turning from Freud to KLEIN (*see* OBJECT-RELATIONS ORIENTED CRITICISM), in others launching a general critique of psycho-analysis (*see* FRENCH-INSPIRED CRITICISM; ÉCRITURE FÉMININE; MATERIALIST CRITIQUE OF PSYCHOANALYSIS). Paradoxically, psychoanalysis was taken over by the literary institution at the same moment as it was being challenged by feminists outside it, as Rose (1986) points out. She critically investigates the ideological representations of woman in patriarchal discourse, discerning the operation of key fantasies at the core of the social; this makes it imperative to retain a concept of the unconscious as a radical tool of criticism, instead of idealizing it as an infallible source of rebellious energy.

Gallop (1987) aptly sums up two 'theoretical double dates' effected by psychoanalytic criticism, in that 'we not only find feminism joining hands with psychoanalysis, but behind that more obvious couple . . . we might possibly glimpse the coming together of post-structuralism and American feminist social science, a pair that has rarely been known to speak' (p. 316). This link has been brought about by challenging the objectivity of theory in the sciences via the use of OBJECT-RELATIONS THEORY as derived in particular from the thought of Klein. The result has been an influential form of textual criticism in feminist attacks, first, on the traditional logocentric and androcentric mode of scientific investigation (Fox Keller, 1985; Harding, 1986) which suppresses the subjectivity of its investigators, and, second, on the patriarchal family unit for its institutionalization of the mother and consequent suppression of her subjectivity (Chodorow, 1978). Object-relations oriented criticism, as an

225

outcome of this challenge, interrogates texts for their repression of the PRE-OEDIPAL moment and specifically for the significance of the MOTHER–DAUGHTER RELATIONSHIP (Abel, 1989), neglected and implicitly devalued in Freud's theory (*see* FEMININITY; OEDIPUS COMPLEX; MATERNAL VOICE). Recent anthologies have been landmarks of this kind of criticism (see Garner et al., 1985; Miller, 1986), joining forces with French-inspired criticism in a common endeavour to recover the repressed traces of a feminine subjectivity, with particular focus on the 'M(other)' (*see* MOTHERHOOD). Feminism has here had some success in influencing its other, psychoanalysis, so that the flow has not been only one-way. There is evidence that it is not only philosophers and literary critics who have undertaken a thoroughgoing revision of Freud's theories of femininity (Kofman, 1985) and the maternal (Sprengnether, 1990), but that psychoanalysts are attempting reconstructions of Freudian theory, re-thinking its (male) authoritarian structures (*see* BENJAMIN), changes that can also carry over into the consulting room (Baruch and Serrano, 1988).

A sexual/textual feminist practice thus implies a re-reading and re-writing of Freud's texts in conjunction with (other) literary and cultural texts (*see* ART; FILM THEORY; PHILOSOPHY; PHOTOGRAPHY; SURREALISM) in order to expose and protest against the marginalization of women. Women rebel against always being seen as 'ground' for the masculine 'figure', as passive foil to male activity and creativity, in the same way as people of subject race are denied free definition (Johnson, 1989; *and see* BLACK FEMINIST CRITIQUE OF PSYCHOANALYSIS; RACE/IMPERIALISM). This endeavour to find a new space for woman has led to the impasse of ESSENTIALISM, particularly as engaged in by those feminist thinkers working at the forefront of new ways of conceptualizing femininity. IRIGARAY, KRISTEVA and Cixous and Clément (1986) have endeavoured to theorize a pre-symbolic space conducive to and enabling for feminine SEXUALITY, but the writing practice they have employed in order to produce a woman's language (ÉCRITURE FÉMININE; FEMININE ECONOMY), has been seen by some feminists as leading to its own undoing: it implies the reversal of the binary – and hence the privileging of woman or the feminine position – thereby threatening to undermine the deconstructive project and, in the present historical situation, maintain women's marginality and institutional impotence.

The aporia of the woman reader/critic is perhaps well illustrated by Jane Gallop's reading practice cum literary and textual criticism (Gallop, 1985): she attempts a feminist reading which is neither a reading of a woman's text nor a reading for the representation of woman, but one which relinquishes a position of command in order to write from a subjective and vulnerable position, one which refuses to make a distinction between subject and object. Gallop tries to read not master-

fully, but transferentially, attending to slippages of meaning in the text
(be they produced by author, typesetter or reader), treating these as
effects of 'the fading author', resurrected by the desiring reader, for
whom the author is the 'subject-presumed-to-know' in the transference
relation. We have come round full circle, then: the author is uncannily
alive, producing ideological effects which require a symptomatic analysis. Gallop's polyphonic reading (she includes other interpreters and
practitioners of Lacan's theory) is a political one in so far as her emphasis throughout is on the relations of production, thus displaying an
explicit and implicit critique of power relations, including her own
(ironical) mastery of critical ploys. The aporia is that feminists, in
deconstructing the author-itarian position, cannot really afford to relinquish it, and hence specific strategies are required to walk this particular
tightrope (see, for instance, Spivak, 1987; Brennan, 1989).

See also PERSONAL/AUTOBIOGRAPHICAL CRITICISM.

BIBLIOGRAPHY

Abel, Elizabeth, 1989: *Virginia Woolf and the Fictions of Psychoanalysis.*
Chicago: Chicago University Press.

Barthes, Roland, 1977: 'The death of the author', *Image–Music–Text*, ed.
Stephen Heath. London: Fontana/Collins, pp. 142–8.

Baruch, Hoffman, and Serrano, Lucienne J., eds 1988: *Women Analyse Women:
In France, England and the United States.* New York: Harvester Wheatsheaf.

Benjamin, Jessica, 1990: *The Bonds of Love: Psychoanalysis, Feminism and the
Problem of Domination.* London: Virago.

Bernheimer, Charles, and Kahane, Claire, eds 1985: *In Dora's Case:
Freud–Hysteria–Feminism*, 2nd edn. New York: Columbia University Press.

Bowie, Malcolm, 1987: *Freud, Proust and Lacan: Theory as Fiction.*
Cambridge: Cambridge University Press.

Brennan, Teresa, ed. 1989: *Between Feminism and Psychoanalysis.* London:
Routledge.

Chodorow, Nancy, 1978: *The Reproduction of Mothering: Psychoanalysis and
the Sociology of Gender.* Berkeley and Los Angeles: University of California
Press.

Cixous, Hélène, and Clément, Catherine, 1986: *The Newly Born Woman.*
Manchester: Manchester University Press.

Evans, Martha Noel, 1989: 'Hysteria and the seduction of theory', *Seduction
and Theory: Readings of Gender, Representation and Rhetoric*, ed. Dianne
Hunter. Urbana and Chicago: University of Illinois Press, pp. 73–85.

Felman, Shoshana, ed. 1977: *Literature and Psychoanalysis: The Question of
Reading: Otherwise, Yale French Studies*, 55–6.

Felman, Shoshana, 1987: *Jacques Lacan and the Adventure of Insight:
Psychoanalysis in Contemporary Culture.* Cambridge and London: Harvard
University Press.

Freud, Sigmund, 1900: *The Interpretation of Dreams, SE*, 4, 5.

LITERATURE

Gallop, Jane, 1985: *Reading Lacan*. Ithaca, NY and London: Cornell University Press.

Gallop, Jane, 1987: 'Reading the mother tongue: psychoanalytic feminist criticism', *Critical Inquiry*, 13, pp. 314–29.

Garner, Shirley Nelson; Kahane, Claire; and Sprengnether, Madelon, eds 1985: *The (M)other Tongue: Essays in Feminist Psychoanalytic Interpretation*. Ithaca, NY and London: Cornell University Press.

Gaudin, Colette et al., eds 1981: *Feminist Readings: French Texts/American Contexts, Yale French Studies*, 62.

Harding, Sandra, 1986: *The Science Question in Feminism*. Ithaca, NY and London: Cornell University Press.

Hirsch, Marianne, 1989: *The Mother–Daughter Plot: Narrative, Psychoanalysis, Feminism*. Bloomington: Indiana University Press.

Hunter, Dianne, ed. 1985: 'Hysteria, psychoanalysis and feminism: the case of Anna O', in Garner et al. 1985, pp. 89–115.

Jacobus, Mary (1986): *Reading Woman: Essays in Feminist Criticism*. London: Methuen.

Johnson, Barbara, 1989: 'Is female to male as ground is to figure?', *Feminism and Psychoanalysis*, ed. Richard Feldstein and Judith Roof. Ithaca, NY and London: Cornell University Press.

Keller, Evelyn Fox, 1985: *Reflections on Gender and Science*. New Haven and London: Yale University Press.

Kofman, Sarah, 1985: *The Enigma of Woman: Woman in Freud's Writings*, trans. Catherine Porter. Ithaca, NY and London: Cornell University Press.

Mehlman, Jeffrey, ed. 1972: *French Freud: Structural Studies in Psychoanalysis, Yale French Studies*, 48.

Miller, Nancy K., ed. 1986: *The Poetics of Gender*. New York: Columbia University Press.

Moi, Toril, 1985: *Sexual/Textual Politics*. London: Methuen.

Newton, Judith, and Rosenfelt, Deborah, eds 1985: *Feminism and Social Change: Sex, Class, and Race in Literature and Culture*. London: Methuen.

Rose, Jacqueline, 1986: *Sexuality in the Field of Vision*. London: Verso.

Schor, Naomi, 1981: 'Female paranoia: the case for psychoanalytic feminist criticism', Gaudin et al., 1981, pp. 204–19.

Spivak, Gayatri Chakravorty, 1987: 'Feminism and critical theory', *In Other Worlds: Essays in Cultural Politics*. New York and London: Methuen, pp. 77–92.

Sprengnether, Madelon, 1990: *The Spectral Mother: Freud, Feminism, Psychoanalysis*. Ithaca, NY and London: Cornell University Press.

Wright, Elizabeth, 1984: *Psychoanalytic Criticism: Theory in Practice*. London: Methuen.

ELIZABETH WRIGHT

literature   A psychoanalytical approach and a feminist approach can of course be taken to any work of literature. The works selected here are exemplary ones by women which have been written in the light of both psychoanalysis and feminism, and which to some extent interpellate a reading subject cognizant of both discourses. A major issue in literature written by women (and particularly by feminists) is the depiction of GEN- DER roles and especially that of women. A number of feminist writers choose to show women who are victims of PATRIARCHY, some of whom collude in their own victimization, partly on account of the ideological (as well as material) structures which dominate in their lives, partly out of laziness (a disinclination to engage with the public sphere) or, worse, out of a masochistic and self-destructive tendency. Presenting negative images of women living secondary lives may be problematic enough, but can be justified politically as a consciousness-raising exposure of female oppression. To reveal the part women play in collaborating with their oppressors, with the conditions of their oppression, and even in oppress- ing men by their very weakness, is inevitably more problematic since it may seem to play into the hands of the enemy, albeit enlightening for women if true. Accounts of small- or large-scale female heroism have sometimes seemed more liberating, providing role models or at least pleasurable fantasy experiences less pacifying than conventional women's romantic fiction. Psychonanalysis enters the scene not only in informing the content and structure (for instance, the representation the- matically or formally of the problematic construction of feminine identi- ty), but also in terms of the reading effect which involves something like the psychoanalytic transference (*see* TRANSFERENCE/COUNTERTRANSFER- ENCE).

Simone de Beauvoir is inevitably read in the light of feminism since *The Second Sex* (first published in 1949) made her the mother of modern feminism. She is a mother idealized and then reviled by her daughters for her lack of perfection (see Moi, 1986); her fiction is often judged severely for its own apparent harshness towards female SEXUALITY and towards those female characters who cling to conventional feminine roles, women who deceive themselves and make themselves and others unhappy just as much as, or more than, they are deceived and made unhappy by men. De Beauvoir's fiction is an example of feminist writing which suggests to women readers that they should take their destinies into their own hands, a process of rational self-determination that excludes props such as psychoanalysis. In *The Mandarins* (1954) she presents a psychoana- lyst, Anne Dubreuilh, who adopts a sceptical distance to the psychoana- lytic cure. She worries that 'cure' means resignation and adaptation to material social conditions which should perhaps instead be acknow- ledged as unacceptable. The help which she nevertheless continues to offer, for example to those returning from Nazi camps, seems no more than a palliative. Male characters (such as Anne's husband and his friend

Henri) engage in political activity in an attempt to address injustice on a world scale; even though these attempts are not always successful, Anne herself appears to value them more highly than her own work, which seeks to restore equilibrium for individuals. The presentation of her troubled relationship with her own daughter also undermines any grand therapeutic claims for analysis, as well as suggesting the harm that mothers (even relatively enlightened mothers) can do their children. The major advantage of psychoanalysis in the novel seems to be that it offers an independent career for Anne; this helps to prevent her from falling into the trap of dependency. Women (such as Paule in *The Mandarins*) who live only in relation to their male partners, and who create a cult of eternal unchanging love with which they seek to bind their men, are doomed to unhappiness, if not mental breakdown, in Beauvoir's fiction.

Margaret Atwood engages explicitly and implicitly with feminism in all her writings. Her novels and poems are woman-centred, and treat a variety of dilemmas familiar to women today in which relationships are central: women's relation to their parents, particularly to their mothers, their relation with brothers, husbands, lovers and female friends. The exploration of these relationships always involves a painful but therapeutic attempt to construct a psychic map, to retrace a woman protagonist's history in all its enigmatic complexity. Atwood often focuses on the choice between a career, particularly that of an artist, and conventional femininity or motherhood, creativity and procreation. She compares words to unborn babies or sometimes to aborted babies. Atwood also, more controversially, emphasizes the problems not only of being, but also of feeling like, a victim, in particular, the danger of feeling complacent in victimhood. She makes this point in relation not only to gender but also to ethnicity, by writing as a Canadian woman, a situation which she designates as 'paranoid schizophrenia' (1970, p. 62), with the United States just across the border. There is a trap of binary thinking in which women (or the colonized) are seen as innocent and male colonizers are seen as criminals. Atwood's representation of women, with her implicit invocation of 'solutions', seems far more nuanced (or hazy) than de Beauvoir's, although she too has been criticized by feminist readers for her willingness to represent women characters as 'imperfect' (see Atwood, 1982).

Atwood's writing engages with psychoanalysis in its exploration of forms of self-abuse and fragmentation: madness, eating disorders (for example, *Lady Oracle*, 1977), religion and indeed the MASQUERADE of FEMININITY itself. Women's relationship with their own appearances through dressing up, making up and gazing into their mirrors, as well as their often fictitious constructions of themselves in LANGUAGE (derived from others) is seen to be a kind of alienation. In *Surfacing* (1973) a descent into madness, into a PRE-OEDIPAL, pre-linguistic, order, appears to be necessary before the female protagonist can re-receive her (dead) mother and father and re-enter the SYMBOLIC order. Atwood, like Marguerite Duras, obsessively re-works a family romance, which is, or effectively becomes, autobiographical. For Atwood the situation of a female subject is a schizophrenic or amputated one, and encourages split Manichean thinking, but the direction of her work is towards a position beyond fragmentation and madness.

The writing and cinema of Duras demand to be read psychoanalytically. The most famous psychoanalytical reading of her work is Lacan's analysis of *The Ravishing of Lol V. Stein* (1964), which he calls a '*délire cliniquement parfait*', a mania which is clinically perfectly accurate (Lacan, 1965). He claims that Duras understands or at least can illustrate his theories even though she has not read his work. Madeleine Borgomano, Marcelle Marini and Michèle Montrelay, among others, have all produced psychoanalytic studies of Duras. Her relationship to feminism is more problematic. One approach has been to claim her writing as ÉCRITURE FÉMININE, partly because of the same qualities which seem to demand a psychoanalytic reading (Foucault and Cixous, 1975). Another approach is to focus on her female characters as a depiction of a certain kind of feminine pathology under given socio-political circumstances, thus bringing her closer to de Beauvoir and Atwood.

Duras's writing meanders, but like the discourse of the analysand it is always looping back on itself; her style also, like that of the analysand, has empty spaces or gaps and frequent moments of disjunction. Her characters repeatedly claim that '*Il faut se perdre*': they lose themselves (their rational monitoring selves) in madness, alcohol, music and desire. They re-enact compulsively a moment or scene: in *Moderato Cantabile* (1958) a man and a woman re-live in their imaginations a crime of passion half witnessed; in *Lol V. Stein* Lol repeats in her mind the moment when her lover is taken from her by another woman. Duras's own oeuvre repeats obsessively the story of her origins: the story of a crazed mother (her own) both nourishing and devouring, both adored and hated by her children, a woman (herself) who abandons herself to love and becomes like 'nothing' at the heart of the story, or a lover who may be capable through his self-abandonment of becoming other, of merging with that feminine. The woman who appears over and over again in many guises in Duras's work is invaded and voided by lover, but is also a source of desire and can inspire a feminization of her lovers.

Duras's writing can be claimed for *écriture féminine* because of its seemingly uncensored relation to the BODY, to sexuality and to PLEASURE, its representation of DESIRE which '*va jusqu'au bout*' (goes to the limit) which is not held back by 'economic' considerations, which imposes itself as necessary. Her writing is traversed by otherness, such as the madness of the mute beggarwoman or of the vice-consul in *Le Vice-Consul*; their shrieks of pain or peals of laughter echo through the text. The body erupts in this way via the voice and then in convulsive vomiting, like a hysterical mime of passion in the sense of both love and suffering unto death. The superabundant generosity of Duras's female characters who give themselves and yet always have more to give is reminiscent of the FEMININE ECONOMY evoked by Hélène Cixous.

Angela Carter writes in a fantastic vein, self-consciously filling old bottles with new wine in the hope that she will destroy some of the outmoded forms of the masculine Imaginary. In *The Magic Toyshop* (1982) phallic might, oedipal rivalry and feminine passivity or masochism are shown in a ludicrous light; Leda's swan is a lumbering goose-like sham which fails to ravish her. But gender positions are not so much overturned as revealed as unheroic and shabby; myths are debunked, but domestic thraldom remains potent. *The Bloody Chamber* (1981) is even more fantastic and radical in its re-writing of fairy tales, a traditional repository of wish-fulfilment and dream resolutions: while the Bluebeard figure of *The Magic Toyshop* is finally castrated and destroyed by a younger male rival, that of 'The bloody chamber' (the title story) is shot by a PHALLIC MOTHER who rides in to save her daughter from execution. The latter story ends with the daughter happy in the maternal home with a piano-tuner as her gentle lover, who is metaphorically castrated in that, blind, he was unable to play the phallic role of saving her from her husband and is in the spell of her piano-playing as well as in her pay. Both blood and (bed)chambers are re-claimed for the feminine in *The Bloody Chamber*, which regularly refers to menstruation and maternity, and which explores – on the level of FANTASY – women's own capacity for cruelty and varied erotic pleasures.

The gender positions of *The Bloody Chamber* are mutable and shifting; the PHALLUS can pass from a male to a female character and back, and some episodes take place in an IMAGINARY order in which both female and male are transformed into beasts and hence have little access to symbolization, thus not being subject to the Law of the Father. In patriarchal mythology animality can represent male sexuality (from the many disguises of the rampant Zeus to Beauty's taming of the Beast) even while unbridled female sexuality is often figured in animal terms. Carter mimics folklore's strategies of containing women by accusing them of witchcraft or vampirism, or by telling them not to stray from the path lest they see a naked man (about to become a wolf) or, like Atwood, by deploying the imagery of the tangled forest to suggest a dangerous domain outside the law: in Carter's 'The Erl-King' (in *The Bloody Chamber*) the forest is slimy, decaying, oozing and dark, threatening to enclose and devour you. The menace of loss of self is nightmar-ishly related to the maternal vagina; yet the heroine of 'The Erl-King' not only enjoys the ecstasy of her vertiginous and violent couplings in the woods, but also strangles her lover, thereby releasing all the young girls whom he changed into birds. Daughter and mother are thus bond-ed in the forest of the Imaginary; the heroine is a young girl and yet her murdered lover calls her 'Mother'. The Erl-King is a representative of paternal law in his role of marking girls with his love-bite and then imprisoning them, and yet as dream lover he is sexually ambiguous as befits the Mother's son.

A more radical and experimental writer than any of those so far men-tioned, Monique Wittig employs literary and linguistic shock tactics as part of the war against PATRIARCHY. Presenting radical lesbian alterna-tives, she defies socially accepted and deeply rooted norms. She asserts that part of her work as a writer is the destruction of GENDER in lan-guage, since grammar is the mark of what appears to be an ontological distinction between the sexes and, more importantly, contributes to engineering it. While she maintains that economic and political change is essential, she argues that this alone would not be enough and not even possible since language does not simply reflect the material situation, but also acts on it. In *Les Guérillères* (1969) she evokes a fantasy all-female community, loving, playing and fighting. She intersperses the text with lists of women's names inscribed in capital letters and with large perfect circles, the symbol of the vulva. The narrative itself is in the form of a circle, beginning with the end; this enables her to universalize *elles* as the absolute subject of the world, so that when *ils* are introduced two-thirds of the way through the book they appear, in a reversal of the usual situation, as the particular exception to the general rule of *elles*.

In *The Lesbian Body* (1973) Wittig scars *j/e*, claiming that the bar through the I is a sign of excess which exalts it to the point where it can lesbianize love, gods, men and women. The bar has also been read as representing the implicit schizophrenic or split nature of any female who attempts to constitute herself as the subject of her own discourse (Wenzel, 1981). This lesbianization of amorous myths (including those of Isis and Osiris, or Ulysses and Penelope) is necessary in order to counteract the use which has long been made of them in the attempt to poeticize heterosexual oppression. Wittig lovingly and ferociously lingers on every element of the female body: its organs, sensations, func-tions and the mucous fluids which flow from it. For Wittig the latest revival of myths to bolster up heterosexual male power in the face of challenge from feminists, lesbians and gay men is to be found in struc-turalism and, particularly, in Lacanian psychoanalysis. The latter attempts to impose a single invariant unconscious that denies material historical change and the reality of class struggle, women being a social class and not a biological sex. Psychoanalysis makes HETEROSEXUALITY (and SEXUAL DIFFERENCE) appear necessary to the Symbolic order, to meaning, language and society. In fact, she claims, compulsory heterosexuality is only necessary to the continuation of male economic, political and social power (Wittig, 1980).

Wittig consistently depicts a world of women without men in which sexual difference is irrelevant; she therefore parts company from those feminists for whom it is all-important. She deplores any attempts to re-valorize womanhood, femininity or MOTHERHOOD and indeed claims that 'lesbians are not women' (Wittig, 1980, p. 110) since the term 'woman' only makes sense in opposition to (and dependence on) the term 'man'. She also attacks the privileging of parts of the female anatomy; in *Les Guérillères* the exaltation of the vulva is a transient stage and in *The Lesbian Body j/e* and *tu* tear each other apart, enacting the fragmentation of the female body, only to put each other back together again, just as Wittig attempts to break down patriarchal IDEOLOGY and reconstruct new erotic discourses.

The twentieth century has witnessed a remarkable flowering and dissemination of women's writing alongside other improvements in women's circumstances. Woman-centred literature provides particular pleasures for women readers, whether it be the pleasure of recognition experienced by early readers of Beauvoir's *The Woman Destroyed* or the revolutionary excitement of many American feminists when reading Wittig in translation in the 1970s (see Wenzel, 1981). However, much animosity has also characterized women's reception of women's writing. Atwood has herself attacked feminist writers and critics for their desire to see stereotypical representations of women as natural forces, or for awarding points to women writers according to their conformity or non-conformity to an ideological position (Atwood, 1982). A psychoanalytical approach can help to elucidate what is at stake in women's investments as readers and writers.

See also FRENCH-INSPIRED CRITICISM; IMAGE; LITERARY AND TEXTUAL CRITICISM; OBJECT-RELATIONS ORIENTED CRITICISM; READING AS/LIKE A WOMAN.

BIBLIOGRAPHY

Atwood, Margaret, 1970: *The Journals of Susanna Moodie*. Oxford: Oxford University Press.

Atwood, Margaret, 1973: *Surfacing*. London: André Deutsch.

Atwood, Margaret, 1977: *Lady Oracle*. London: André Deutsch.

Atwood, Margaret, 1982: *Second Words: Selected Critical Prose*. Toronto: Anansi.

Beauvoir, Simone de, 1982 [1954]: *The Mandarins*, trans. Leonard M. Friedman. London: Fontana.

Beauvoir, Simone de, 1972 [1949]: *The Second Sex*. Harmondsworth: Penguin.

Carter, Angela, 1981: *The Bloody Chamber*. Harmondsworth: Penguin.

Carter, Angela, 1982: *The Magic Toyship*. London: Virago.

Duras, Marguerite, 1958: *Moderato Cantabile*. Paris: Minuit.

Duras, Marguerite, 1966 [1964]: *The Ravishing of Lol V. Stein*, trans. Richard Seaver. New York: Grove Press.

Fallaize, Elizabeth, 1988: *The Novels of Simone de Beauvoir*. London: Routledge.

Foucault, Michel, and Cixous, Hélène, 1975: 'À propos de Marguerite Duras', *Cahiers Renaud-Barrault*, 89, pp. 8–22.

Hill Rigney, Barbara, 1987: *Margaret Atwood*. Basingstoke and London: Macmillan.

Lacan, Jacques, 1965: 'Hommage fait à Marguerite Duras du Ravissement de Lol V. Stein', *Cahiers Renaud-Barrault*, 52, pp. 7–15.

Moi, Toril, 1986: 'She came to stay', *Paragraph*, 8, pp. 110–120.

Wenzel, Hélène V., 1981: 'The text as body/politics: an appreciation of Monique Wittig's writings in context', *Feminist Studies*, 7, pp. 264–87.

Wittig, Monique, 1973 [1969]: *Les Guérillères*, trans. D. Le Vay. New York: Avon Books.

Wittig, Monique, 1976 [1973]: *The Lesbian Body*, trans. D. Le Vay. New York: Avon Books.

Wittig, Monique, 1980: 'The Straight mind', *Feminist Issues*, 1, pp. 103–11.

JUDITH STILL

M

---

m/f An independently financed feminist journal published in England from 1978 to 1986. The original editorial group consisted of Parveen Adams and Elizabeth Cowie, who remained as editors throughout the history of the journal, and Rosalind Coward, who served as an editor for the first two issues. Beverley Brown joined the group later in 1978 and continued as editor until 1985.

m/f's project is best characterized as a questioning of the category 'woman'. This description may appear at first tautological – with what else would a feminist project concern itself if not woman? – but the work of *m/f* helps us to see that much of feminism had been about what is done to women, what acts of oppression are performed on women, without stopping to question our understanding of the object which is supposed to be acted upon. It is not that this other work proceeded in the absence of some notion of woman – a core of unvarying, essential traits were tacitly or implicitly assumed to be characteristic of the feminine – but this notion was not itself the object of feminist analysis. By shifting the focus of its investigation to the very category woman, *m/f* not only began an exploration of one of the fundamental, unthought categories of feminist theory, it also re-conceived the way woman entered into and inhabited the social sphere.

m/f rejected the notion that woman possessed certain eternal traits which she was then forced or induced to sacrifice (or 'repress') as the price of her entry into a 'patriarchal' society; in other words, it rejected the notion that woman *as woman* was prevented from entering society, which could thus be said to perform an erasure or distortion of the feminine. *m/f* argued instead that society – the concrete social practices which constitute it – constructs categories of 'the woman' that are specific within each practice. This argument not only denies that there is a single or concerted cause of the social positioning of women; it also denies that there is a single effect: the 'oppression of women' or the 'repression of the feminine'. What this argument discovers, rather, is a number of different effects, not all of which can be defined as oppressive, since in constructing the concept of woman, any practice must also construct the modes of her viability, her power.

m/f's rigorous analyses of the constructed place of woman in specific practices – psychoanalytic, cinematic, legal, political, etc. – gave the journal a wide-ranging scope and a kind of concreteness that was much admired. But even as its attention to concrete *practices* was praised, its lack of attention to concrete *individuals* was sometimes criticized. It must be pointed out, however, that this inattention was not an over-sight, but a matter of policy: *m/f* did not take the concrete individual to be the proper focus of political analysis. This position was arrived at by two separate theoretical paths. First, the analyses of social practices inspired by the work of Michel Foucault committed the journal to the position that a particular practice need not necessarily define the individual as an agent of its functioning. Second, the journal's commitment to Freudian–Lacanian psychoanalysis obliged its recognition of the *limitations* of the concrete, fully determinate individual. It is the partially *in*determinate subject, which exceeds the concrete individual, that is the focus of psychoanalysis. Both these paths led, for similar reasons, to *m/f*'s suspicion of the category of experience that is often privileged in other feminist analyses.

The twin focus of *m/f* on social theory and psychoanalysis generated a number of positions that are still central to feminist debates. The urgen-cy of its critiques of ESSENTIALISM and of the categories of the concrete individual and experience remains unabated.

BIBLIOGRAPHY

Copies of *m/f*, issues 1–12, may be obtained by writing to: *m/f*, 24 Ellerdale Road, London NW3 6BB, UK.

Adams, Parveen, and Cowie, Elizabeth, eds 1990: *The Woman in Question*. London: Verso; Cambridge, Mass.: MIT Press.

JOAN COPJEC

masculinity   Why do men want? Feminist theory has been satisfied that it understands *what* men want reasonably well enough. It turns to psy-choanalysis for a deeper explanation of the *why* of men's desires.

Psychoanalytic feminism's re-telling of the oedipal tale to emphasize the social construction of GENDER identity and the family has problema-tized and developed a critique of masculinity which would have been quite puzzling to Freud, for whom it was female rather than male devel-opment that was problematic (Friedman and Lerner, 1986).

'Pre-' is woman's time. Just as in the phylogenetic story of 'mankind', 'prehistory' refers to a more matrifocal era, before the linguistic law of the written record inscribed history as male by forgetting women's oral history, so in psychoanalysis's ontogenetic tale the 'pre-oedipal' designation obscures the central matrifocality of the early years of development, considering them as mere prelude to the ostensibly more crucial patrifocal period of gender formation. Feminist mother-oriented psychoanalysis denaturalizes male gender identity development by emphasizing the trauma of the break from and subsequent repressions of the memory of the feminine past required for the male ego to maintain its myth of autonomous self-creation and independence (Chodorow, 1978). The son's identification with the father, his willingness to trade present pleasure for the promise of future power, introduces an ethic of delayed gratification which serves both patriarchal and capitalist imperatives. While for Freud male identity is the primary norm, masculinity here appears reactive, fragile, never quite completely attained. Aggressive masculinity is now defence or protest against feminine identification (Brod, 1987).

Feminism's insistence on the personal as political means that the father's absence from the mother–child dyad cannot be accepted as a biological given, but must be understood as part of PATRIARCHY, as a consequence of the father's flight from the family in order to seek power in the external world. The father forces not only his own absence, but the son's as well. Before the OEDIPUS COMPLEX there is the Laius complex. This is the father's fear of the son's impending ascension to power, and his banishing him as a defence against this threat. Father and son therefore tragically do not recognize each other when they meet at the crossroads. Many of our founding myths express this violence of fathers against sons, whether it be Laius against Oedipus, Abraham against Isaac, or the Christian God the Father against Jesus. Feminism has argued that Freud's SEDUCTION THEORY covers up the violence of the fathers against the daughters (Benjamin, 1988). Does the tale of the revolt of the sons against the father in the primal horde cover up the violence of the father against the sons?

According to the myth, Laius seeks to kill Oedipus because of the Delphic Oracle's prophecy that his son would kill him, conveying the curse placed on Laius by Pelops for Laius' abduction of Pelops' son Chrysippus. Euripides, among other contemporaries, named Laius the father of homosexuality because of this episode, while other versions of the tale give the motivation for the abduction as Laius' lack of an heir, rather than sexual attraction. Homophobic and pro-natalist norms curse the house of Laius because of his non-(re)productive sexuality, a curse which persists into the post-Oedipal generation. Its last victim is

Oedipus' daughter/sister Antigone, who is entombed for mourning her brother, a victim of patriarchal/fratricidal war, and for attempting to uphold the law of the family against that of the state, embodied by her king/uncle/father-in-law-to-be Creon (*see* HOMOPHOBIA; HOMOSEXUALITY).

New feminist psychoanalytic insights into masculinity are central in diverse fields of inquiry: e.g. film criticism, where the construct of the 'male gaze' which takes pleasure in voyeuristic control is a central paradigm of contemporary discourse; theories of fascism, which argue that mass society's displacement of the family as the primary site of acculturation leads to a 'fatherless society' dominated by diffuse aggression not integrated into the psyche; and political theory, in feminist critiques of the relegation of women's labour to a devalued private sphere (Mitscherlich, 1969; Theweleit, 1987, 1989).

See also FANTASY; FEMININITY; HETEROSEXISM; HETEROSEXUALITY; MASQUERADE; MEN IN FEMINISM; VOYEURISM/EXHIBITIONISM/THE GAZE.

BIBLIOGRAPHY

Benjamin, Jessica, 1988: *The Bonds of Love: Psychoanalysis, Feminism, and the Problem of Domination*. New York: Pantheon.

Brod, Harry, ed. 1987: *The Making of Masculinities: The New Men's Studies*. London and Boston: Unwin Hyman.

Chodorow, Nancy, 1978: *The Reproduction of Mothering: Psychoanalysis and the Sociology of Gender*. Berkeley: University of California Press.

Friedman, Robert M., and Lerner, Leila, eds 1986: *Towards a New Psychology of Men: Psychoanalytic and Social Perspectives*. The Psychoanalytic Review: A Special Issue, 73/4.

Mitscherlich, Alexander, 1969: *Society without the Father: A Contribution to Social Psychology*, trans. Eric Mosbacher. New York: Harcourt, Brace and World.

Theweleit, Klaus, 1987, 1989: *Male Fantasies*, 2 vols: vol. 1 trans. Stephen Conway, vol. 2 trans. Erica Carter and Chris Turner. Minneapolis: University of Minnesota Press.

HARRY BROD

masochism　Emphasizing the passive character of masochism and the active one of sadism, Freud developed a theme Lacan would later contradict: masochism as the return of sadism against the self (Freud, 1915; *see* SADOMASOCHISM). Freud distinguished three forms or stages in the drives of masochism and sadism: erotogenic, moral and feminine (Freud, 1924). Whereas he readily described 'moral masochism' as the need for punishment, the feeling of guilt, the fear of failure, a response to the superego or a negative therapeutic reaction, the feminine and erotogenic were far more troublesome. Freud called masochism the 'expression of the feminine essence' within the cadre of the psychic BISEXUALITY of man and woman. But he never found a cause for the linkage between the feminine, the erotic and passivity, except in NARCISSISM, which he called a pathology, and the DEATH DRIVE, if one finds an analogy between this drive and resistance to change (Freud, 1937, p. 252).

According to LACAN, Freud's opposition of sadism and masochism was too simple a dichotomy. Freud's effort to isolate masculine/feminine difference partakes of a similar error. To counter Freud's view of active and passive denoting literal sexual positions, Lacan argued that generalized oppositions are totalizing Imaginary views that try to impose a consistency on the inconsistencies between partners, as well as within a person's own libidinal economy. In the latter the preferred position of lover or beloved bespeaks a relation between DESIRE and knowledge within differential structures of neurosis, PERVERSION or psychosis.

Lacan, re-thinking both 'drive' and theories of subject/object, argued that sadism is a DISAVOWAL of masochism. A normative masochism – the norm pointing to myths and fictions by which a person or culture coheres – is the most radical of perversions, in so far as a subject tries to identify with the Other as a law of unity and certainty. Such a *père-version* is not gender-specific, but describes those who seek identification with social conventions and LANGUAGE, as in the masculine fantasy of feminine masochism (Lacan, 1977b, pp. 192–3), where narcissism and perversion join hands in a master (*m'être/maître*) discourse, so that the alienated subject finds authority in the Other presumed to know, without knowing it him/herself (Lacan, 1977a, ch. 18) (*see* OTHER/OTHER).

Where Freud explained the FANTASY of 'a child is being beaten' in relation to the OEDIPUS COMPLEX and perverse fantasies associated with it (Freud, 1919), Lacan translated this fantasy as a masculine SYMPTOM, finding there a 'my father is beating me' fantasy of the male neurotic. But the male symptom also touches the female in so far as the primary composition of all clinical structures is masochism: IDENTIFICATION (or not) with the father's name entails a certain identification with loss of forbidden satisfaction, loss of mother *qua* primary object of Oneness. For Lacan, obsessional neurosis is the ur-type of masochism, and sadism a defence against it. Caricaturing the normative male's symptoms, the obsessional punishes *women* for subverting his illusion of being *all* to his mother, for shaking his fantasy of an essence of *Woman* who should be still and quiet lest she subvert his identification with stasis. Lacan formulates as prototypical of obsessional neurosis Freud's moral masochism, calling it 'cowardice' or inaction (Bautista et al., 1990, p. 113). Such masochism dwells in the realm of the voice: the voice and the gaze create the ideal ego and superego by marking the BODY through the mortification of fictions governing one's SEXUALITY, and this produces problems of gender identity. The obsessional believes he is the PHALLUS, the object of desire that can fill the Other's LACK and thus speaks the word of law.

The paradox of the obsessional's masochism shows a double irony: by clinging to the primary *lost* OBJECT, the mother, he is tied to the REAL and thus identifies with death or loss. Masochism, seen in this light, does not concern sexual pleasure *qua* PLEASURE, but JOUISSANCE or the death drive seen in the fixity of narcissism. Whereas sadists intervene in the field of the Other to fill in the gap left by the primary object through identifying with the father's law, masochists identify with *jouissance*, with the Real of their suffering, which is the fundamental truth of the dissatisfied human subject – the loss of the undifferentiation that a union with the mother represents. For Lacan, Freud's 'feminine masochism' becomes a response to the paradox of an Other *jouissance*: the human hope for completeness is based on a structural refusal to relinquish the loss of the mother as imagined primary object. Lacan's discovery of the links between the Real, the death drive, primary masochism and the feminine are an advance over Freud's biological arguments: woman is seen as inseparable from this primary object that causes both sexes to desire. This theory of a topological structuring wherein primary masochism is linked to women because, and only because, they are for ever after inter-locked with a structural reality means that the Real of loss has implications for every person, whether male or female.

Feminist theorists working after Freud and Lacan have attempted to shift the problem of masochism to GENDER (an Imaginary for Lacan). Kaja Silverman (1988) for example, sees masochism in all its forms as an integral and sustaining part of the Symbolic order, contributing to the oppression of women. In the case of female masochists the fantasies of submission and degradation show the female subject as reducing herself to an even lower symbolic position than the male in male fantasies (Silverman, 1988, p. 60). In Silverman's view this shifts the power from the father to the mother. Male masochists, on this model, would reject the power of the Symbolic order as such: masochism takes more violent and pathological forms in the male, since it blatantly calls into question his identification with the patriarchal masculine position. Silverman's view is based on the premiss that the SYMBOLIC order can be separated out from the IMAGINARY and REAL, and, furthermore, that masochism in all its forms is somehow prior to it. In the Lacanian perspective masochism arises from the Real and the Imaginary as interpreted by the Symbolic. The Symbolic therefore creates and thus precedes masochism, case by case, whether in male fantasy or in female acting-out of this fantasy.

241

MASQUERADE

BIBLIOGRAPHY

Bautista, B. et al., 1990: 'Le Masochisme dans la névrose', *Traits de perversions dans les structures cliniques*, ed. Dominique Miller and Guy Trobas. Paris: Navarin, pp. 108–20.

Freud, Sigmund, 1905: *Three Essays in the Theory of Sexuality*, SE, 7, pp. 123–245.

Freud, Sigmund, 1915: 'Instincts and their vicissitudes', *SE*, 14, pp. 109–40.

Freud, Sigmund, 1919: '"A child is being beaten": A contribution to the study of sexual perversions', *SE*, 17, pp. 175–204.

Freud, Sigmund, 1924: 'The economic problem of masochism', *SE*, 19, pp. 159–70.

Freud, Sigmund, 1937: 'Analysis terminable and interminable', *SE*, 23, pp. 209–54.

Krafft-Ebing, Richard von, 1897–9: 'Beiträge zur Kenntnis des Masochismus', *Arbeiten aus dem Gesammtgebiet der Psychiatrie und Neuropathologie*. Leipzig: Barth.

Lacan, Jacques, 1977a: *The Four Fundamental Concepts of Psychoanalysis*, trans. Alan Sheridan. London: Hogarth Press.

Lacan, Jacques, 1977b [1973]: 'From love to the libido', *Four Fundamental Concepts*, pp. 187–200.

Silverman, Kaja, 1988: 'Masochism and male subjectivity', *Camera Obscura*, 17, pp. 31–66.

ELLIE RAGLAND-SULLIVAN

masquerade   The status of the term 'masquerade' in feminism and psychoanalysis is extremely problematic in so far as it is at once a kind of 'fetish' of feminist discourse (given intellectual currency by feminist thinkers such as Luce IRIGARAY (1985), Michèle Montrelay (1977), Mary Ann Doane (1982, 1988–9) and Judith Butler (1990), among others) and a *bête noire* of political critiques of femininity. Feminism's continued engagement with the term may in part be traced to its pedigree, which stems from an essay entitled 'Womanliness as a masquerade' originally published in *The International Journal of Psycho-Analysis* in 1929 by Freud's distinguished woman colleague and occasional translator, Joan Riviere. That Riviere was a professional woman in a man's world, struggling to establish novel ways of thinking femininity as a psycho-social construction despite the patently phallocentric *doxa* of psychoanalysis in the 1920s and 1930s, lends a political pathos to the reading of her essay. The fact that she self-referentially pictured the career woman at a speaking engagement behaving in a parodically 'feminine' manner (flirting with her male audience, performing a pantomime of FEMININITY so as to assuage male fear of so-called 'women with a

MASCULINITY complex' (Rivière, 1986, p. 37), may be disheartening for a feminism seeking to shed outmoded stereotypes of the feminine mystique, but it also offers a brilliantly performative rendering of the masquerade's circularity as a philosophical and psychoanalytical discourse. In its emphasis on gender play-acting and the sartorial projection of a feminine superego (see Copjec, 1989), the masquerade offers a liberatory avenue leading away from biological ESSENTIALISM: woman can play the woman or not as she so pleases.

Drawing on a philosophical legacy (Nietzsche and Georg Simmel) that treats the mask or the veil as a particularly appropriate signifier of hypostasized Woman, Riviere develops the notion of womanliness as a feint or cover-up coequal with the social constructions enabling femininity to be pretended into existence. There is no absolute femininity beneath the veil, only a set of ontologically tenuous codes that normatively induct the feminine subject into the social practice of 'being' woman through mimesis and parroting. As Riviere argued in a canonically cited passage:

Womanliness therefore could be assumed and worn as a mask, both to hide the possession of masculinity and to avert the reprisals expected if she was found to possess it – much as a thief will turn out his pockets and ask to be searched to prove that he has not stolen the goods. The reader may now ask how I define womanliness or where I draw the line between genuine womanliness and the 'masquerade'. My suggestion is not, however, that there is any such difference; whether radical or superficial, they are the same thing. (Riviere, 1986, p. 38)

Articulating the 'there is no there there' nature of femininity, Riviere points feminism towards a configuration of gender that would no longer necessarily stipulate womanliness as a psychoanalytic fixture. The discourse of masquerade, like the discourse of femininity which it apes, inverts and refracts (as in a hall of mirrors), would endure in this 'future perfect' theatre of gender only as a kind of atavism evocative of what woman was once thought to 'be': a symbolic sheath or cover for the elusive ideal PHALLUS that neither sex ever possesses (LACAN), an impersonation of the maternal phallus desired by the male subject (a fetish), or a defensive strategy improvised to disguise the dormant power of the female agent in a system where feminine power is denied by PATRIARCHY (*see* PHALLIC MOTHER).

In addition to its enlistment within theories of anti-essentialism, the notion of masquerade has been applied in GENDER studies to examine the history of travesty, cross-dressing and what Judith Butler has characterized as the 'psychic inculcation of compulsory heterosexuality'. 'The donning of femininity as a mask', Butler maintains, 'may reveal a refusal of a female homosexuality and, at the same time, the hyperbolic incorporation of that female Other who is refused' (Butler, 1990, p. 53).

See also HETEROSEXISM; HETEROSEXUALITY; LESBIANISM.

BIBLIOGRAPHY

Butler, Judith, 1990: *Gender Trouble: Feminism and the Subversion of Identity*. New York and London: Routledge.

Copjec, Joan, 1989: 'The sartorial superego', *October*, 50, pp. 57–96.

Doane, Mary Ann, 1982: 'Film and the masquerade: theorizing the female spectator', *Screen*, 23/3–4, pp. 74–87.

Doane, Mary Ann, 1988–9: 'Masquerade reconsidered: further thoughts on the female spectator', *Discourse 2/1*, pp. 42–54.

Gaines, Jane, and Herzog, Charlotte, 1990: *Fabrications: Costume and the Female Body*. New York and London: Routledge.

Heath, Stephen, 1986: 'Joan Rivière and the masquerade', *Formations of Fantasy*, ed. Victor Burgin, James Donald and Cora Kaplan. London and New York: Methuen, pp. 45–61.

Irigaray, Luce, 1985 [1974]: *Speculum of the Other Woman*, trans. Gillian Gill. Ithaca, NY: Cornell University Press.

Kaplan, Louise J., 1991: 'Masquerades', *Female Perversions: The Temptations of Emma Bovary*, New York: Doubleday, pp. 237–83.

Lacan, Jacques, 1982: 'The meaning of the phallus', trans. Jacqueline Rose, *Feminine Sexuality: Jacques Lacan and the École Freudienne*, ed. Juliet Mitchell and Jacqueline Rose. New York: Norton, pp. 74–85.

Montrelay, Michèle 1977: *L'Ombre et le nom: sur la féminité*. Paris: Minuit.

Riviere, Joan, 1986 [1929]: 'Womanliness as a masquerade', *Formations of Fantasy*, ed. Victor Burgin, James Donald and Cora Kaplan. London and New York: Methuen, pp. 35–44; first published *International Journal of Psychoanalysis*, 10 (1929).

EMILY APTER

materialist critique of psychoanalysis   In addition to the liberal bourgeois political tradition, the two theories or systems of thought that have had most influence on Anglo-American feminism are marxism and psychoanalysis. Ironically, these are also theories that have been pitted against each other since their inception, in spite of numerous attempts, feminist and non-feminist, to weave the insights and analytical methods of each into a single system. The 'materialist' critique of psychoanalysis generally refers to the marxist historical (or dialectical) materialist critique of the systems of thought and analysis developed by Sigmund Freud and his followers.

Materialism, as a philosophical concept, has a long and complex history of multiple meanings, as Raymond Williams has pointed out (1976, pp. 163–7). Reduced to its simplest relevant terms, modern philosophical materialism argues, as against theological or spiritual explanations, for the physical origin and causality of nature and human life and, in a corollary argument, for a corresponding mechanical description of human life, moral behaviour and social organization. Karl Marx accepted the first premiss, but rejected the corollary in favour of a historical materialism that recognized human agency and considered it a primary force. Friedrich Engels generalized Marx's notion of the human activity of production and its determinative nature into dialectical materialism (the laws of historical development and of all natural and physical processes).

Marx's materialism is often contrasted with philosophical idealism, particularly that of Hegel, whereby ideas, or consciousness, are seen to be the fundamental and originating activity from which all else derives. In a famous passage from *The German Ideology*, Marx argues: 'The ruling ideas are nothing more than the ideal expression of the dominant material relations, the dominant material relations grasped as ideas' (Marx and Engels, 1976, p. 59). Thus, with regard to psychology itself, Marx and Engels's comment (1976, p. 37) that 'it is not consciousness that determines life, but life that determines consciousness' is understood as a rejection of any analysis that takes consciousness as its explanatory starting-point. For Marx the history of industry is 'man's psychology present in tangible form', and any psychology that ignores this history cannot become a genuine science (1975, p. 354; Bottomore, 1983, p. 402).

The historical debate about the status of psychoanalysis within marxism played itself out in the Soviet Union of the twenties, in the form of a discussion of the relative merits of objective (materialist, behavioural) psychology, most notably represented by I. P. Pavlov (1850–1936) and the behaviourist school, and subjective or Freudian psychology. In 1927 V. N. Volosinov published *Freudianism: A Marxist Critique* which was, at the time, the most comprehensive and popular marxist critique of Freudian psychoanalysis. He rejected psychoanalysis in favour of an objective, 'scientific' psychology, the one that was ultimately accepted by the USSR in 1950, when Pavlovianism was declared the only acceptable psychological approach for marxism–leninism and remained so until after Stalin's death in 1953 (Bottomore, 1983, p. 403).

Volosinov's critique, though based on an incomplete corpus of Freud's works, presents what still seems to be the basic marxist objection to Freudian psychoanalysis: that, in psychoanalysis, a person's consciousness is shaped, not by his or her historical existence, but by his or her biological being. In characteristic orthodox fashion, Volosinov pro-claims Freudian psychology to be a symptom of crisis and decline in twentieth-century bourgeois philosophy, a crisis whereby, in the face of declining historical significance, bourgeois thinkers elevate the isolated and abstract biological organism to the role of central hero, a sort of surrogate for history (Volosinov, 1976, p. 11). Other, more specific, objections include: Freud's disregard of sociology in favour of the indi-vidual organism and its psyche (p. 24); the subjectivity of Freud's method and his reliance on myth (p. 24); and finally, the bourgeois scientific claim to a higher level of ideological neutrality for SCIENCE, and psychology in particular, in matters of world outlook and social orienta-tion (p. 25). Ironically, what have been regarded as Volosinov's greatest contributions to both marxism and psychoanalysis, his focus on lan-guage as units of social exchange and his anticipation of structuralist analysis, are precisely what the French psychoanalyst Jacques LACAN later understood to be already contained in Freud's work and which Lacan claimed to be elaborating upon in his own theory of psychoanaly-sis (Volosinov, 1976, pp. 117–48).

Since the work of several members of the group of German left intel-lectuals known as the Frankfurt School (Theodor Adorno, Erich Fromm, Max Horkheimer and Herbert Marcuse) and Wilhelm Reich's *The Mass Psychology of Fascism*, most Western marxists have incorpo-rated Freudian insights into their analyses to understand the relations between the individual subject, IDEOLOGY and historical process. The phenomenon of fascism in Europe represented a challenge for marxist theorists, who had difficulty accounting for the mass popular support it received. Thus, subsequent work focused on developing within marxism a theory of LANGUAGE and the SUBJECT, and the role of ideology in dialec-tical materialism. The advent of structuralism and Lacan's reinterpreta-tion of Freud greatly facilitated these developments by laying the foundation for a materialist theory of the subject. As Rosalind Coward and John Ellis point out, Lacan's emphasis on the materiality of the signifier (language) and his analysis of the determining force of the sym-bolic system upon the human subject prepare 'a route for an elaboration of the subject in the social process, the subject demanded by dialectical materialism' (Coward and Ellis, 1977, p. 93). Louis Althusser and Etienne Balibar also used psychoanalytic insights about language and the subject to develop a structuralist theory of ideology, arguing that there were epistemological analogies between Freud and Marx, among which figured the concepts of over-determination and displacement (Althusser and Balibar, 1979, pp. 188, 243). Feminists drew from Lacan and French post-structuralist thought (Althusser and the deconstructive analyses of Jacques Derrida in particular) to help bridge the gap between materialist feminism and psychoanalysis, though rather more successfully in France and Britain than in the US or elsewhere. French feminists such as Hélène Cixous and Luce IRIGARAY were thus able to critique Freudian ideology by means of the Symbolic practice of ÉCRITURE FÉMININE.

Nevertheless, Fredric Jameson, perhaps one of the most influential marxist critics in the United States today, points out that analogies are insufficient to produce an adequately historicized psychoanalysis, or theory of DESIRE (Jameson, 1981, p. 68). Although he argues for the necessity in marxist interpretation for such a theory of desire and for a notion of the UNCONSCIOUS, he takes psychoanalysis to task for the way it 'remains locked into the category of the individual subject' (p. 68) and insists on the need for a theoretical account in terms of the collective. Indeed, he suggests that psychoanalysis, with its narrative of REPRESSION, revolt and libidinal transfiguration through the liberation of desire, should be treated within marxism as a powerful allegory of revolution (1981, p. 67).

Raymond Williams, Britain's most influential contemporary marxist thinker, argued, in agreement with the Italian materialist Sebastiano Timpanaro, that psychoanalysis suffers from an insufficiently examined dual claim: on the one hand it presents its concepts as 'findings', scientific facts based on empirical evidence, while on the other hand it speculates on a more literary (some would say mythic) level that has not been subjected to scientific examination (Williams, 1980, pp. 117–18). He calls for a 'rigorous theoretical and historical critique of psychological theory as mixed "science" and "ideology"' (p. 119), a critique that has been performed in large part by contemporary psychoanalytic feminists in their analysis of Freud's patriarchal biases.

The most radical (post-)marxist critique of psychoanalysis today can be found in the work of Gilles Deleuze and Félix Guattari, whose *Anti-Oedipus* (1983) attacks psychoanalysis for focusing exclusively upon the family narrative. Deleuze and Guattari set forth a model of production rather than representation, arguing that, in psychoanalysis, the unconscious 'ceases to be what it is – a factory, a workshop – to become a theater, a scene and its staging' (p. 55). The replacement of production by representation, the theatricalization of desire, 'raises the familial relation to the condition of a universal metaphoric structural relation' (p. 307), a relation they playfully and sarcastically refer to as 'mommy–daddy–me'. The critique of Deleuze and Guattari thus converges, in part, with several themes in the materialist feminist and Third World critiques of psychoanalysis: that it depends upon a historically and ethnographically limited notion of the (nuclear) family (whose only child is, of course, male) and elides the specificities of the historical, economic, political and social context that informs any given domestic or kinship arrangement.

Marxist or materialist feminists, like psychoanalytic feminists, have had to revise and critique their modifier – that is, the position from which they approach feminism – to produce specifically feminist analyses of their subject of inquiry, be it historical process or the psyche. For the most part, marxist feminist critique, in its bid for a more comprehensive explanatory theory of the oppression of women, has focused on psychoanalytic feminism rather than on specifically non-feminist Freudian or Lacanian psychoanalysis. Indeed, the materialist critique has been able to accommodate more readily than psychoanalysis the interrelations of class, race and gender that structure the material conditions and consciousness of women throughout the world. Today, most feminists recognize the need for a materialist critique – with the exception of US liberal feminism, for whom marxism is, for obvious reasons, inimical. Yet, like their predecessors, few feminist theorists have relinquished the possibility of weaving together the explanatory powers of both marxism and psychoanalysis in the face of a necessity to account for both the historical conditions of women and the specificities of individual female subjects.

See also MATERIALIST FEMINIST CRITICISM.

BIBLIOGRAPHY

Althusser, Louis, and Balibar, Etienne, 1979: *Reading Capital*. London and New York: Verso/NLB.

Bottomore, Tom, ed. 1983: *A Dictionary of Marxist Thought*. Cambridge, Mass.: Harvard University Press; Oxford, Basil Blackwell.

Coward, Rosalind, and Ellis, John, 1977: *Language and Materialism: Developments in Semiology and the Theory of the Subject*. London and New York: Routledge and Kegan Paul.

Deleuze, Gilles, and Guattari, Félix, 1983: *Anti-Oedipus: Capitalism and Schizophrenia*. Minneapolis: University of Minnesota Press.

Freud, Sigmund, 1961: *Civilization and its Discontents*, ed. James Strachey. New York and London: Norton.

Jameson, Fredric, 1981: *The Political Unconscious: Narrative as a Socially Symbolic Act*. Ithaca, NY: Cornell University Press.

Marcuse, Herbert, 1966: *Eros and Civilization: A Philosophical Inquiry into Freud*. Boston: Beacon Press.

Marx, Karl, 1975: *Early Writings*, intr. Lucio Colletti. New York: Vintage Books.

Marx, Karl, and Engels, Frederick, 1976: *Collected Works*, vol. 5: *Marx and Engels 1845–1847*. New York: International Publishers.

Reich, Wilhelm, 1970: *The Mass Psychology of Fascism*. New York: Simon and Schuster.

Timpanaro, Sebastiano, 1975: *On Materialism*. London and New York: Verso/NLB.

Volosinov, V. N., 1976: *Freudianism: A Marxist Critique*, ed. Neal H. Bruss. New York and London: Academic Press.

Williams, Raymond, 1976: *Keywords: A Vocabulary of Culture and Society*. New York: Oxford University Press.

Williams, Raymond, 1980: *Problems in Materialism and Culture*. London: Verso/NLB.

CARLA FRECCERO

materialist feminist criticism   Materialist feminist criticism assumes that women's experiences differ as they are influenced by social, racial, sexual and economic conditions. It analyses women's oppression in the past and the present by addressing issues in these and other categories. Critics who use the approach assert that women are not the same either across cultures or within a culture, and hence are not configured in exclusively similar ways; they view the differences among women as produced by the material conditions in which women are placed. This approach is therefore anti-essentialist and anti-idealist, eschewing universal categories such as 'woman' or 'patriarchy' and advocating an interventionist politics with social change as its goal.

Materialist feminist criticism is a product of two related developments in this century. In the late 1970s and early 1980s, socialist feminists in Britain and France articulated the theoretical relations between marxism and feminism (see Kuhn and Wolpe, 1978; Barrett, 1980; Delphy, 1984). While these critics differ in the degree to which they accept marxism as appropriate for feminist analysis, in their own way each extends the marxist problematic of economic and class oppression to women. The word 'materialist' is used to mark this extension. By the time the feminist challenge to marxism was discernible, an internal critique of economism within marxism had also contended that the economy was not the sole or final determinant of history. This critique is associated most fully with Althusser, whose consideration of the relative autonomy of the superstructure and the concomitant role of IDEOLOGY permitted individual experience to be analysed as a complex effect of interacting forces (Althusser, 1971). Culture then came to be seen as a material practice which shaped and was shaped by constructions of such categories as 'experience', 'meaning' and 'language'.

These developments within marxism were also affected by a break with the humanist view of the 'individual' and a Freudian view of the 'self' occasioned by the Lacanian account of the 'subject'. Althusser

249

adapted the notion of the subject as produced through its entry into the Symbolic Order to claim that one becomes a SUBJECT through being 'interpellated', or hailed, within a discursive context (1971, pp. 170–7). Although the 'subjects' produced by the two theories differ in many ways, the materialist notion of its relation to LANGUAGE was influenced by the work of Lacan (Coward and Ellis, 1977). Developments such as these in marxism, feminism and psychoanalytic theory enabled European feminists, especially those such as Catherine Belsey, Rosalind Coward, Cora Kaplan, Juliet MITCHELL, and Jacqueline Rose working in Britain, to address issues of sex, class and DESIRE in their criticism. The work of American feminists during the 1970s and 1980s was, on the other hand, influenced more often by Freud than by Marx or Lacan.

A theoretical account of materialist feminism is offered in the introduction to Newton and Rosenfelt's collection of essays (1985), which includes British and American critics addressing issues of sex, class and race in literature and culture. Newton and Rosenfelt emphasize the multiple concerns of the approach in its attention to gender and other categories of identification, its consideration of history and society as well as LITERATURE and its analysis of the textual inscriptions of culture (see FEMINIST HISTORY). Interpreting history as a process of transformation rather than a static or linear account of oppression or triumphs, they conclude that social change should not be conceived or produced only by women who are white and privileged, and that unequal power relations should be reconstructed for all of the oppressed (pp. xix–xxvii). Materialist feminism therefore becomes a way of addressing a range of oppressions while remaining attentive to GENDER. It also tries to correct the white, middle-class orientation of much feminist work done in this century, which has insufficiently addressed the needs of most of the world's women – especially those beyond the triangle of French, British and American critics most engaged in producing it.

This criticism is only beginning to be practised more widely outside of Britain, its concerns often being addressed by those who do not directly associate themselves with the label. The recent critical movements of new historicism (in America) and cultural materialism (in Britain) share many of its methods and assumptions, especially the claim that history and literature be analysed in relation to the contexts of their production and reproduction. Yet some critics who want to maintain a connection between feminism and marxism have objected that the practice of materialist feminism is now becoming too diffuse and eclectic, with the result that its most radical features are being recuperated (Hennessy and Mohan, 1989). The objection arises in part because those who practise the approach differ about whether their use of a materialist understanding of history implies support for marxist economic and political forms of organization.

In addition to a sometimes uneasy alliance with marxists and socialists, materialist feminists take up varying positions in relation to postmodernism. The distrust of absolutes, the scepticism about truth and meta-narratives associated with POSTMODERNISM are described by Catherine Belsey as providing a climate in which feminist criticism can flower, since both undermine rationalism and empiricism (1991, p. 262). Others disagree, asserting that a politically committed feminism is incompatible with some of the assumptions of postmodernism. Sabina Lovibond (1989) argues that feminists should not abandon the impulse to 'enlighten' and reconstruct sensibility that they inherited from Enlightenment modernism.

Not all of those who have applied postmodern or poststructuralist strategies to feminism could be described as materialist feminists, for critics who use this approach are especially aware of their work as an act of political intervention. Acknowledging their alignment with the political goals of feminism, they write and teach from a critical perspective directed to social change. So if materialist feminists address the implications of historical analysis and critical theory more often than earlier feminists did, they are also concerned about the political effects of histories and theories in ways that many current critics are not.

It is in this last respect that the emphases of materialist feminism and psychoanalysis diverge, because the assumptions and goals of the former are directed beyond the psychic and the personal to the social and political. Yet since they assent to the feminist dictum that 'the personal is political', materialist feminists do resist a simple opposition between the psychic and social or the sexual and political (Adams and Cowie, 1986, pp. 8–10). They may instead adapt Freudian concepts of the UNCONSCIOUS and Lacanian notions of desire and the subject to consider larger sites of activity. Materialist feminism has no implicit creed or unitary project, no required text or founding mother, yet its analyses of the differences among women often include, as well as critique, the insights of psychoanalysis.

See also ESSENTIALISM; FEMINISM OF DIFFERENCE; LACAN; MATERIALIST CRITIQUE OF PSYCHOANALYSIS; PATRIARCHY; RACE/IMPERIALISM; THEORY.

BIBLIOGRAPHY

Adams, Parveen, and Cowie, Elizabeth, 1986: 'm/f: Interview 1984', m/f, 11/12, pp. 5–14.
Althusser, Louis, 1971: 'Ideology and ideological state apparatuses (notes towards an investigation)', Lenin and Philosophy and Other Essays. New York: Monthly Review Press, pp. 127–86.

Barrett, Michèle, 1980: *Women's Oppression Today: Problems in Marxist Feminist Analysis*. London: Verso.

Belsey, Catherine, 1991: 'A future for materialist feminist criticism?', *The Matter of Difference: Materialist Feminist Criticism of Shakespeare*, ed. Valerie Wayne. Hemel Hempstead: Harvester Wheatsheaf; Ithaca, NY: Cornell University Press, pp. 257–70.

Coward, Rosalind, and Ellis, John, 1977: *Language and Materialism: Developments in Semiology and the Theory of the Subject*. London: Routledge and Kegan Paul.

Delphy, Christine, 1984: *Close to Home: A Materialist Analysis of Women's Oppression*, ed. and trans. Diana Leonard. Amherst: University of Massachusetts Press.

Hennessy, Rosemary, and Mohan, Rajeswari, 1989: 'The construction of woman in three popular texts of empire: towards a critique of materialist feminism', *Textual Practice*, 3/3, pp. 323–59.

Kuhn, Annette, and Wolpe, AnnMarie, eds 1978: *Feminism and Materialism: Women and Modes of Production*. London and Boston: Routledge and Kegan Paul.

Lovibond, Sabina, 1989: 'Feminism and postmodernism', *New Left Review*, 178, pp. 5–28.

Newton, Judith, and Rosenfelt, Deborah, 1985: 'Introduction: towards a materialist-feminist criticism', *Feminist Criticism and Social Change: Sex, Class and Race in Literature and Culture*, ed. Judith Newton and Deborah Rosenfelt. New York and London: Methuen, pp. xv–xxxix.

Omvedt, Gayle, 1986: '"Patriarchy:" the analysis of women's oppression', *The Insurgent Sociologist*, 13/3, pp. 30–50.

VALERIE WAYNE

maternal voice   Neither psychoanalysis nor feminism has comfortably been able to assume a maternal voice. In psychoanalytic theories, the child is the subject of study. The mother exists only in relation to her child; as object of DESIRE and FANTASY she may be idealized or disparaged, but she remains distant and mystified. She cannot be the subject of her own discourse. Psychoanalytic feminism has added the female child to the male but has not been able to adopt or to inscribe the perspective of the adult woman, especially that of the mother. Its strong dependence on a psychoanalytic framework has actually been a barrier to feminism's understanding and articulation of the maternal.

In Freud's writings, the mother's presence is persistent, though submerged, always in the interstices of his argument; often, as in the Dora case, the mother is the one familial figure eliminated from consideration altogether. For LACAN, language itself is the name-of-the-father; acceding to the SYMBOLIC means transcending maternal silence and the mother's materiality. The articulation of a maternal voice thus remains an impossibility. If the story of development, as told in psychoanalytic theories, rests on a process of separating from the mother, the mother's own part in that process – her own desire or anger – is erased from REPRESENTATION. Feminist theory, relying on psychoanalysis for its account of subject formation, continues, disturbingly, to represent the mother as the ground against which the female subject develops. Much feminist writing is shaped by maternal idealization and PROJECTION, permeated with desire for maternal approval, with fear of maternal power, with anger at maternal powerlessness: it is informed by a child-centred primary-process perspective (Chodorow and Contratto, 1982).

In 'Stabat mater', a text with two voices, one theoretical, the other disruptive, personal, marginal, Julia KRISTEVA (1986) experimentally writes the maternal. As the semiotic, pre-Symbolic voice of the PRE-OEDIPAL, this pre-linguistic maternal voice becomes in Kristeva's writings a privileged space of dissidence and subversion. Literary critics, however, turning to women's literary texts, have attempted to find a maternal voice within LANGUAGE and from within maternal experience, even if they have found it necessary to push against the bounds of psychoanalytic theory in their explorations (Suleiman, 1985). A mother-inclusive feminism might challenge the place of the father as a necessary third term in the process of subject formation (Sprengnether, 1989). It might conceive of development other than as a process of separation from a neutral background occupied by a passive 'good-enough' mother, of subjectivity other than as dependent on objectification. It might begin with the mother, rather than with the child (Ruddick, 1989; Hirsch, 1989).

Critics have cautioned, however, that concentrating on the maternal returns feminism to biologism, as well as to the dream of an idealized maternal voice speaking only to women (Kahane, 1988). This need not be so, if maternity is historicized and politicized from within feminism and if maternal voices are heard.

See also MOTHERHOOD; MOTHER–DAUGHTER RELATIONSHIP; OBJECT-RELATIONS ORIENTED CRITICISM; PHALLIC MOTHER.

BIBLIOGRAPHY

Chodorow, Nancy, and Contratto, Susan, 1982: 'The fantasy of the perfect mother', Feminism and Psychoanalytic Theory, ed. Nancy Chodorow. Cambridge: Polity Press, pp. 79–96.
Hirsch, Marianne, 1989: The Mother/Daughter Plot: Narrative, Psychoanalysis, Feminism. Bloomington: Indiana University Press.
Kahane, Claire, 1988: 'Questioning the maternal voice', Genders, 3, pp. 82–91.

Kristeva, Julia, 1986 [1977]: 'Stabat mater', *Tales of Love*, trans. Leon Roudiez. New York: Columbia University Press, pp. 234–63.

Ruddick, Sara, 1989: *Maternal Thinking: Toward a Politics of Peace*. Boston: Beacon Press.

Silverman, Kaja, 1988: *The Acoustic Mirror: The Female Voice in Psychoanalysis and Cinema*. Bloomington: Indiana University Press.

Sprengnether, Madelon, 1989: *The Spectral Mother: Freud, Feminism, Psychoanalysis*. Ithaca, NY: Cornell University Press.

Suleiman, Susan, 1985: 'Writing and motherhood', *The (M)other Tongue: Essays in Feminist Psychoanalytic Interpretation*, ed. S. N. Garner, C. Kahane, and M. Sprengnether. Ithaca, NY: Cornell University Press, pp. 352–77.

MARIANNE HIRSCH

men in feminism   Although the possibility of 'male feminism' has been on the agenda since the current wave of feminism began, it is only in recent years that the question of men in feminism has been theorized in psychoanalytic terms and given rise to the emergent discipline of 'men's studies'. The most important collection of essays in this field is Alice Jardine and Paul Smith (1987), and the *locus classicus* Stephen Heath's opening declaration: 'Men's relation to feminism is an impossible one . . . Men have a necessary relation to feminism – the point after all is that it should change them too . . . and that relation is also necessarily one of a certain exclusion – the point after all is that this is a matter *for women*' (p. 1). Heath attacks psychoanalysis's role in the oppression of women and warns of the danger that 'male feminism' might repeat those same phallocentric moves, suggesting that male interest in feminism could be 'pornographic', a re-bonding of men around women. For Heath the centrality of the PHALLUS and castration to psychoanalysis must be historicized, and in this process feminism is a 'necessary lever on psychoanalysis that forces it into truth' (p. 23). Feminism has taught men that the personal is political; but there can be no equivalent of writing the female body for men (no equivalent of the feminist quest for a woman's writing), except perhaps in the case of gay men (p. 25). Heath proposes 'admiration' as the proper male response to feminism: an acceptance of the irreducible separation of women and men leading to an ethics of SEXUAL DIFFERENCE.

Heath's essay ends with a biographical reference to his mother's hospitalization; male feminists in the US have competed with each other in the confessional mode. In Linda Kauffman's recent collection (1989), Joseph Allen Boone tries to put back the me in me(n), proposing a 'personalizing' discourse (*see* PERSONAL/AUTOBIOGRAPHICAL CRITICISM), in opposition to the supposed abstractions of Heath's 'theorizing'. Boone also calls attention to the differences between men, in particular the presence of gay men in feminism, which he claims women such as Elaine Showalter have failed to address. If feminist men could come together as a 'community with phalluses' (and not as a 'community as phallus') then they would be a threat not to feminism but to PATRIARCHY (p. 177). Toril Moi gives a sceptical, European response to Boone in the same volume, recognizing a man's right to call himself feminist, but insisting on the parochialism of North American academics who fail to see feminism in the context of other political struggles, such as anti-racism, and are obsessed with male professional hierarchies (pp. 185–8).

Boone himself cites Cixous's dictum that 'men still have everything to say about their sexuality' (p. 176). It seems likely, however, that 'men in feminism' are inevitably paralysed by their fear of appropriating feminist language. Volumes such as Chapman and Rutherford (1988) reveal that, although the necessary debate on masculinity is inspired by feminism, it will take place in men's studies rather than in feminism itself.

See also MASCULINITY.

BIBLIOGRAPHY

Chapman, Rowena, and Rutherford, Jonathan, eds 1988: *Male Order: Unwrapping Masculinity*. London: Lawrence and Wishart.
Jardine, Alice, and Smith, Paul, eds 1987: *Men in Feminism*. London: Methuen.
Kauffman, Linda, ed. 1989: *Gender and Theory: Dialogues on Feminist Criticism*. Oxford: Basil Blackwell.

PAUL JULIAN SMITH

Michigan Psychoanalytic Council   The Council is a feminist-inspired training institute, the first in the United States, designed by a core women's studies group composed of feminist mental health professionals interested in psychoanalysis, including one man (Gordon, 1990), together with other professional men and women. In addition to integrating a feminist perspective in the required curriculum for candidates, this core group, which had struggled with the challenges open to psychologists interested in psychoanalysis (Meisels, 1989), instituted a series of changes in the structure and process of the new organization in order to promote the participation of women in teaching and training roles and to alter the hierarchies and distribution of power in training institutes that generate sexism, inequality and conformity (Bernardez, 1990).

255

Some of the changes introduced increase critically the number of women active in the organization. Others are intended to live up to the radical nature of psychoanalysis (Karon, 1989), to democratize the process and organization and to bring it into line with more collaborative, egalitarian views of training and education. It was accepted from the outset that all of the main health professionals would be eligible for membership and for analyst/faculty status. In addition to psychologists and psychiatrists, this would include social workers and psychiatric nurses who have been denied access to traditional psychoanalytic institutes and are still kept from training. Since the great majority of nurses and social workers are women, the presence of women in large numbers both as faculty and as trainees was thus insured.

The Council's by-laws mandate that women occupy half of the executive and Board positions in the organization and that this ratio be maintained throughout in the composition of committees. In addition, the participation of candidates in the Board and the Training Committee was institutionalized so that they would have influence in the decisions concerning admission policies, curriculum and training issues. This attempt to involve candidates from the very beginning in crucial aspects of the training is intended to restore the responsiveness and mutuality of the training relationship (Cunningham, 1990). In traditional institutes, candidates, most of whom are seasoned professionals, were subject to a very passive and conformist role, infantilizing them and denying them input in their own education.

An affirmative action committee, originated by the feminist group which instituted and negotiated the changes in the structure of the organization, was institutionalized as permanent (Tenbusch, 1990). Its functions were: (1) maintaining awareness of the goals of affirmative action for women and minorities; (2) creating regulations and by-laws that would promote equality; and (3) preventing prejudicial behaviour in the organization and its process.

In the institute, any analyst in the faculty can analyse candidates. This is distinctly different from institutes belonging to the American Psychoanalytic Association, where a 'caste' system operates: training analysts, separated from the rest, have the power to analyse candidates and decide matters in the educational committees. This situation has resulted in these analysts (with no demonstrable superiority over other analysts), accumulating an unusual amount of power, being subject to no checks and balances and dictating the fate of the careers of the candidates. This repetition leads to self-serving aims and the development of 'followers', with consequent negative influences in the analysis of candidates, who are not free to disregard the positions of their own analysts and to criticize them. In contrast the institute's candidates choose their own analysts (rather than being assigned them), who do not participate in any way in decisions concerning the educational status or certification of their analysands.

Because the conduct of the organization was likely to reflect the influences and biases of the society at large, the process and practice of decision-making in the organization had to be altered. The daily conduct of business was subject to analysis to protect the rights of candidates and to alter standard practice when necessary. One of the first position statements was on HOMOSEXUALITY: discrimination against gay men and lesbian women in the institute was ruled as inadmissible (Tenbusch, 1990).

The curriculum was to take precedence over other aspects of training. The aim was to introduce innovations into psychoanalytic education as had been originally envisioned by the founder group of the Council and others (Meisels and Shapiro, 1990) but never put into practice, and to integrate feminist theories of development and of clinical practice, now required courses. Teaching the views of male development from a feminist perspective is also included, as are feminist critiques of Freud's cases. A clinical perspective conscious of the issues of GENDER is to be taught, as well as contributions from other schools of psychoanalysis that have hitherto been considered deviant primarily because they have emphasized the male bias in traditional theories. Thus there are clinical seminars emphasizing feminist views of transference and countertransference as modified by the gender of the analyst and conscious of the most common gender biases encountered in analysts of both sexes (Bernardez, 1987) (see TRANSFERENCE/COUNTERTRANSFERENCE). The teaching of this curriculum is done by equal numbers of men and women. Maintaining this ratio of women teachers does not guarantee a feminist perspective, since not all women teachers are feminists, but it does ensure the visibility and influence of woman's viewpoint. The requirements for supervision also expect the candidate to have at least two supervisors of different gender. Particularly in the supervision of candidates who are analysing women patients, the woman supervisor may offer a less traditional vision, one more aware of the impact of gender-role socialization in both sexes.

Finally, a programme of seminars, workshops and presentations by women who have contributed to psychoanalysis, and who reflect in their theory and practice the missing aspects of theorizing from a woman-centred perspective, was instituted to disseminate and discuss feminist perspectives and the work of ignored female psychoanalytic pioneers.

The above changes in curriculum, structure, hierarchy and process of operation in accordance with a feminist perspective in theory and practice, defines the institute as a feminist institute.

MITCHELL, JULIET

BIBLIOGRAPHY

Bernardez, Teresa, 1987: 'Gender-based countertransference of female therapists in the psychotherapy of women', *Women, Power and Therapy*, ed. M. Braude. New York: Haworth Press, pp. 25–39.

Bernardez, Teresa, 1990: 'Feminizing psychoanalysis: the process and experience of integrating a feminist curriculum in a new psychoanalytic institute', paper presented at the annual Women Studies Conference, Michigan State University, 21 April 1990.

Cunningham, Anne, 1990: 'Experiences of a woman candidate in helping to found a new psychoanalytic institute', paper presented at the annual Women Studies Conference, Michigan State University, 21 April 1990.

Gordon, Norman, 1990: 'A re-education gender-wise', paper presented at the annual Women Studies Conference, Michigan State University, 21 April 1990.

Karon, Bertram, 1989: 'The state of the art of psychoanalysis: science, hope and kindness in psychoanalytic technique', *Psychoanalysis and Psychotherapy*, 7, pp. 99–115.

Meisels, Murray, 1989: 'Envy and political conflict in psychoanalysis: implications for the Michigan practitioner', paper presented at the Michigan Psychoanalytic Council, E. Lansing, 23 April 1989.

Meisels, Murray, and Shapiro, Esther R., eds 1990: *Tradition and Innovation in Psychoanalytic Education: Clark Conference on Psychoanalytic Training for Psychologists*. London: Lawrence Erlbaum Associates.

Tenbusch, Lynne, 1990: 'The women's group: an exploration of the impact of a group of feminists on the development of a psychoanalytic training group', paper presented at the Women Studies Conference, E. Lansing, 21 April 1990.

TERESA BERNARDEZ

Mitchell, Juliet (*b.* 1940, New Zealand). Juliet Mitchell is best known for *Psychoanalysis and Feminism* (1974), a book instrumental in reintroducing Freud to Anglo-American feminism which, through reactive misinterpretation, had become negatively disposed to his work. In their gross misreading of psychoanalytic theory, leading feminists such as Betty Friedan, Germaine Greer, Eva Figes, Shulamith Firestone and Kate Millett assume, Mitchell argues, that Freud prescribes the SEXUAL DIFFERENCE that PATRIARCHY institutes, and that he subscribes to either biological or cultural determinism. They fail to see and to appropriate his revolutionary analysis of the UNCONSCIOUS, his exposure of unconscious structures which engender DESIRE and reproduce patriarchal (sexed) power relations. Mitchell's purpose was to clarify the radical elements of Freud's psychoanalysis in the belief that his theories of the unconscious and sexual difference provided the basis for the most comprehensive ideological analysis of patriarchal society and the conceptual groundwork for its eventual overthrow. Her stimulating defence of Freud helped to generate a 'vast industry of psychoanalytically-inspired feminist texts' in the mid to late 1970s (Grosz, 1990, p. 21).

While restoring Freud to Anglo-American feminism, Mitchell brings continental marxist feminism to psychoanalysis. Her collection of essays, *Women: The Longest Revolution* (1984), traces her thought from an early critical engagement with Althusser in the years before the emergence of the women's movement to her later engagement with Lacan's Freudianism, inspired by her contact with *Psychanalyse et politique*, the marxist section of the *Mouvement de libération des femmes*. Both Althusser and LACAN frame her re-reading of Freud in *Psychoanalysis and Feminism*, though she makes explicit references only to Lacan. Her introduction to *Feminine Sexuality: Jacques Lacan and the École Freudienne* (1982), a collection of essays she edited with Jacqueline Rose, defends Lacan in much the same way as she had earlier defended Freud. Both texts read as a defence of Lacan's anti-humanist Freud; the difference between them lies in the greater scope of the earlier text, which historicizes Anglo-American feminism in the context of the 'debased' psychoanalysis of post-Freudians (the biologistic essentialism of Karen HORNEY, the moralistic psychologism of Helene DEUTSCH, the originary femininity of Melanie KLEIN), and of leftist libertarians (Wilhelm Reich, R. D. Laing), whose radical humanism profoundly influenced the women's movement.

In *Psychoanalysis and Feminism*, Mitchell understands the particular task of psychoanalysis to be the deciphering of our acquisition of the ideas and laws of society through the unconscious. Psychoanalytical theory provides feminism with an understanding of how patriarchy is reproduced in the history of the individual. Following Freud's observation that ontogeny recapitulates phylogeny, Mitchell proclaims that the law of the unconscious, the law of the symbolic father, reflects the law of civilization, which is necessarily patriarchal. To know how this law constitutes the human subject is to know how women are subjected to patriarchy. Psychoanalysis understands the making of the SUBJECT in terms of sexual difference, by differential subjection of girls and boys to the Law through symbolic castration and the repudiation of FEMININITY. To know how masculine and feminine subjects are unconsciously and historically engendered within the organizing structures of patriarchy is to know how women are necessarily, psychologically, made powerless and oppressed.

Psychoanalysis and Feminism is divided into three parts. The first part reviews the breadth of the work Freud devoted to theorizing the unconscious and SEXUALITY, emphasizing how a woman is made through the CASTRATION COMPLEX and its resolution. Contrary to the mistaken

259

assumption that Freud formulates the development, vicissitudes and evolution of the one, male sex and that he maps out the transcendental trajectory of the unified ego, Mitchell, following Lacan, stresses how sexual difference is at the root of ego formation, and how this difference is itself not an essence but the product of a complex and conflictual process.

Crucial to Mitchell's defence of Freud is her assertion that his analysis of the girl's symbolic castration is descriptive and not prescriptive; yet her 'objective' re-presentation affirms, unnecessarily, the negative normative consequences of this castration. Rather than questioning the structural conditions that, accordingly, ensure anatomical man's inheritance of a phallic–symbolic power and woman's corresponding exclusion from the orders of power, she accepts these conditions – as if knowledge of how patriarchy is secured in the psychology of women were, in itself, a subversive achievement, a satisfying compensation for femininity. Her failure to question further is perhaps most obvious in her discussions of NARCISSISM, PRE-OEDIPAL sexuality and the castration complex: she flatly reiterates the discriminatory process in which the boy copes with the threat of castration by making positive identifications with the father and the phallic/male model of the universe, while the girl merely assumes her castrated, de-narcissisized state, her alienation from a universe bereft of positive feminine images. From this 'description' it is not clear how the girl finds a way out of her infantile narcissism in any positive sense. Whereas the boy incorporates positive, powerful images of the father, of maleness in general, in the making of an ego-ideal, and later, a cultural superego, the girl, having but the debased, phallic-less image of the mother from which she abjectly detaches herself, could only be plunged into interminable melancholia.

Neither the first part nor the second (the part which reviews the radical psychologies of Reich and Laing and the anti-Freudianism of Anglo-American feminists, including Simone de Beauvoir) prepares the reader for the final chapter of the last part entitled 'Cultural Revolution', where Mitchell argues that women as a group can collectively dismantle patriarchy. Here her feminism draws more support from dialectical materialism and from a marxist belief in the inevitable historical demise of the patriarchal nuclear family (which capitalism makes redundant), than from a radical psychoanalysis. It is difficult to see how women, whose very selfhood, according to Mitchell, is constituted by the laws and ideas of patriarchy, are able to restructure their political unconscious simply by conscious knowing and re-conceptualizing. Mitchell's resolute belief in the necessity and universality of the phallic-symbolic, in the law of the father, gravely undermines her call for women's structural transformation of society (Grosz, 1990, p. 23).

In *Feminism and Psychoanalysis: The Daughter's Seduction* (1982) Jane Gallop asks Mitchell what it means to present a feminism that is, in the last analysis, unchanged by psychoanalysis, that has not built a political practice on its theories and that does not even question its own unconscious desire in/for psychoanalysis. Gallop argues that Mitchell embraces a feminism whose 'utopic rationalism' resembles the social engineering of the feminisms she criticizes, implying that Mitchell's problem is her anthropological and sociological overvaluation of the PHALLUS as Father, as Patriarch, neglecting the Lacanian emphasis on the phallus as LANGUAGE.

Mitchell's introduction to *Feminine Sexuality* does not add substantially to her pro-Freudian thesis of *Psychoanalysis and Feminism*, but elaborates Lacan's emphasis on the radically split subject, the centrality of the castration complex, the construction (as opposed to the naturalness) of sexual difference, the primacy of the Law of the Father, and the structural 'patrocentrism' of the human subject, all of which, as she sees it, contribute significantly to feminism's demystification of sexed subjectivity. The later essays of *Women: The Longest Revolution* focus on feminist psychoanalytic literary criticism, on the role of women's narrative in the 'longest revolution'. Against Julia Kristeva's observation that women's experimental writing is more often pathological than avantgarde, Mitchell affirms the female novelist's 'discourse of hysteria' as women's symbolic mode for negotiating self-representation in patriarchal culture. The novelist's/hysteric's voice is 'woman's masculine language' talking about female experience, simultaneously accepting and refusing femininity under patriarchy (Mitchell, 1984, pp. 289–99). Mitchell presents this hysterical writing practice as non-neurotic and transformative, as the site of women's cultural resistance. But however positive this new literary focus, Mitchell does not tell us (1) how we can decipher *semiotically* the difference between symptomatic text production and revolutionary text production, (2) how textual hysteria can mobilize collective (and not just individual) reserves of unconscious resistance, or (3) how hysteria breaks out of patriarchal ideology, if at all. Does hysterical text production destroy and replace phallocentric structuring of the subject or does it reactively re-produce another discursive formation within the same domain of the law of the father? Mitchell's conviction that the woman's hysterical novel is revolutionary does not dissolve doubt either that textual hysteria is more than women's bourgeoisification of the female subject in patriarchy or that the hysterical female subject is not a revolutionary subject at all but a figure of profound ambivalence, a divided 'self' which 'knows' the redundancy of patriarchal identity in capitalist free economy but which cannot abandon it. But while Mitchell's work is not beyond criticism, its significance in re-initiating feminist negotiations with psychoanalysis cannot be over-estimated.

WRITINGS

1971: *Women's Estate*. Harmondsworth: Penguin.
1974: *Psychoanalysis and Feminism*. London: Allen Lane.
1984: *Women: the Longest Revolution: Essays in Feminism, Literature and Psychoanalysis*. London: Virago.
1986: 'Juliet Mitchell' (interview), *Women Analyze Women*, ed. Elaine Hoffman Baruch and Lucienne J. Serrano. Hemel Hempstead: Harvester, pp. 209–20.
ed. 1986: *The Selected Melanie Klein*. Harmondsworth: Penguin.
with Ann Oakley, eds 1986: *What is Feminism?* Oxford: Basil Blackwell.
with Jacqueline Rose, eds 1982: *Feminine Sexuality: Jacques Lacan and the École Freudienne*. New York: Norton.

BIBLIOGRAPHY

Gallop, Jane, 1982: *Feminism and Psychoanalysis: The Daughter's Seduction*. London: Macmillan, ch. 1.
Grosz, Elizabeth, 1990: *Jacques Lacan: A Feminist Introduction*. London: Routledge, ch. 1.

DIANNE CHISHOLM

mother–daughter relationship   Feminism has focused attention on the maternal line or genealogy, and on relations between natural or spiritual mothers and daughters. On the publication of Adrienne Rich's *Of Woman Born* in 1976 there was immediate and wide-ranging interest in this previously unexplored relationship, which began to be examined not only in fiction, poetry and autobiography, but across a variety of academic disciplines: sociology, anthropology, theology, history, philosophy, psychology, psychoanalysis and literary criticism. Of these the most significant is perhaps psychoanalysis.

The OEDIPUS COMPLEX is central to orthodox Freudian theory. But the oedipal triangle involves mother, father and son, and the link between the oedipus complex and PATRIARCHY has now been extensively argued. Only late in his career did Freud see clearly that the daughter's relation to her mother was not symmetrical to that of the son (see Freud, 1925, 1931). Since for both daughter and son the mother was the first love-object, the son's HETEROSEXUALITY was congruent with his deepest and earliest passions, while the daughter was required to turn away from her mother. The importance of the PRE-OEDIPAL mother–daughter relationship was the crucial psychoanalytic discovery which enabled feminist theory to focus on and re-valorize what is specific to the daughter's relation to her mother.

Feminist psychoanalytic accounts fall roughly into three groups: (1) Jungian accounts; (2) revisionary Lacanian accounts; (3) Freudian or neo-Freudian accounts.

The first group analyse symbols and archetypes. They draw on the model created by JUNG and others in their studies of the archetype of the Great Mother and the Eleusinian mysteries. The emphasis is placed on the continuity between mother and daughter. Nor Hall's book, *The Moon and the Virgin* (1980), for example, is not so much psychoanalytic theory as an attempt to re-valorize femininity in cultural terms through the use of maternal symbols.

The most important figure in the second type of account is Luce IRIGARAY. Central to Irigaray's work is the notion of the maternal genealogy and its absence in Western thought. Her critique of Freudian theory (1985) points out that this absence is detrimental for both mother and daughter. The mother cannot transmit to her daughter a culturally accessible and respected image of woman, while the daughter can only see her mother in one of two ways: either as a PHALLIC MOTHER, a terrifying figure of omnipotence whom the daughter must flee to ensure some autonomy and identity for herself, or as a castrated mother (see CASTRATION COMPLEX), a mother lacking or deficient with whom the daughter does not wish to identify, and from whom she turns, in humiliation and hatred, to the father. Although Irigaray's essay 'And the one doesn't stir without the other' (1981) has sometimes been read as a lyrical celebration of the mother–daughter relationship, in fact it is more accurately interpreted as the daughter's struggle for life and AUTONOMY, for freedom from a paralysing and life-denying mother. The food and protection which the mother offers bring not the longed-for nurturance, but a poisoned and imprisoning embrace. Irigaray concludes that patriarchy functions by separating women from each other, and by suppressing the possibility of the maternal genealogy. The establishment of symbolic mother–daughter relationships is essential to women's autonomy and identity, *as women and not just as mothers.* Horizontal relations between women – sisterhood – will only be possible if the vertical relationship – the maternal genealogy – has been given cultural recognition, if, that is, women's desire for, and love of, the mother is given a voice. The strength of Irigaray's account is that it recognizes women's ambivalence towards their mothers, without blaming mothers as individuals. The responsibility is transferred to the patriarchal SYMBOLIC order. In her later work, Irigaray has started exploring mythological archetypes. This links her to Jungian-inspired writing, with which otherwise she would seem to have very little in common.

The third group includes the work of BENJAMIN, CHODOROW, Dinnerstein, Flax and Miller. All of these converge in their agreement about the significance of the fact that it is *women* who mother. Whereas boys *differentiate* themselves from the mother in order to establish their GENDER identity, girls perceive themselves as *the same as* their mother, and as a result often have difficulty in achieving a separate identity at all. They may turn to their father (as Freud had suggested) as a protection from an engulfing symbiosis with the mother. These accounts describe with great subtlety the quality and nature of women's relationships with their mothers. Their phenomenology of the mother–daughter relationship shows existing psychoanalytic theories of the ego to be inadequate to describe the particularity of women's experience and women's psyche: women's ego boundaries tend to be more fluid than men's, their sense of separateness more precarious and their sense of self more relational. Although the second and third types of accounts have different theoretical presuppositions, there is general agreement about the clinical symptoms: women's tendency towards merged or fusional relationships which indicate a failure to separate from the mother at an unconscious level, or to develop a defined sense of self-identity.

A number of overlapping problems with these accounts can be identified. First, there is some oscillation between a celebration of women's relational skills and a recognition that these may often depend on the sacrifice or loss of self-identity and autonomy. This oscillation creates problems for feminist accounts of MOTHERHOOD. It is pointed out that there are two perspectives on the mother–daughter relationship, the mother's and the daughter's. Chodorow and Contratto (1989) argue that most feminist theory (not to mention most psychoanalytic theory) is child-centred. (This may be true even if the feminist is herself a mother. Maternal guilt may lead her to see only the child's needs, to the neglect of her own.) They find a disturbing convergence between the dominant cultural view that mothers should be totally self-sacrificing, and feminist fantasies about the ideal mother (*see* MATERNAL VOICE). Hirsch (1989) also notes that it seems difficult to integrate the daughter's point of view with the mother's: they appear to be mutually exclusive. Secondly, different theorists draw varying social conclusions. The step from psychoanalytic model to social or political model is not a self-evident one, and it is not clear, for example, that shared parenting (Chodorow, Dinnerstein) is a completely adequate response to patriarchal structures. Similarly, it is necessary to take into account historical variation. In addition, there is a general absence of reference to black or non-Western women in feminist psychoanalytic literature, which raises some questions about the limitations of the proposed models. (One exception is Hirsch's (1989) interpretation of Toni Morrison's novel *Beloved* in terms of Jocasta's story.) There are many black women's narratives about the mother–daughter relationship (for one example among many see Walker, 1983), but they are more likely to take a fictional or auto-biographical form, and in general black women have not up to now regarded psychoanalysis as central to their self-understanding (*see* BLACK FEMINIST PSYCHOTHERAPY). A further, and more far-reaching, critique is made by Hirsch (1981), who points out that all the feminist psychoana-lytic perspectives are dependent on the androcentric parameters of male theorists. She argues that there is a need to transform the paradigms more radically, and to invent new theoretical frameworks which will go beyond patriarchal myths and perceptions. This would involve concep-tualizing the mother–daughter relationship outside the terms of the oedipus and the castration complexes, and it is not clear yet whether this is a regressive FANTASY of return to the pre-oedipal (as orthodox Lacanians would argue), or a genuine glimpse of a post-patriarchal future.

See also KLEIN; KRISTEVA; OBJECT-RELATIONS THEORY; WOMEN'S PSYCHOL-OGICAL DEVELOPMENT.

BIBLIOGRAPHY

Benjamin, Jessica, 1980: 'The bonds of love: rational violence and erotic domi-nation', *The Future of Difference*, ed. Hester Eisenstein and Alice Jardine. Boston: G. K. Hall, pp. 41–70.

Chodorow, Nancy, 1978: *The Reproduction of Mothering: Psychoanalysis and the Sociology of Gender*. Berkeley: University of California Press.

Chodorow, Nancy, and Contratto, Susan, 1989: 'The fantasy of the perfect mother', *Feminism and Psychoanalytic Theory*, ed. Nancy J. Chodorow. Cambridge: Polity Press, pp. 79–96.

Dinnerstein, Dorothy, 1978: *The Rocking of the Cradle and the Ruling of the World*. London: Souvenir Press. (Published in the USA as *The Mermaid and the Minotaur: Sexual Arrangements and Human Malaise*. New York: Harper Colophon, 1977).

Feminist Studies, 1978: Special issue, 'Toward a feminist theory of mother-hood', 4/2.

Flax, Jane, 1980: 'Mother–daughter relationships: psycho-dynamics, politics and philosophy', *The Future of Difference*, ed. Hester Eisenstein and Alice Jardine. Boston: G. K. Hall, pp. 20–40.

Freud, Sigmund, 1925: 'Some psychical consequences of the anatomical distinc-tion between the sexes', *SE*, 19, pp. 241–60.

Freud, Sigmund, 1931: 'Female sexuality', *SE*, 21, pp. 221–46.

Hall, Nor, 1980: *The Moon and the Virgin: Reflections on the Archetypal Feminine*. New York: Harper and Row.

MOTHERHOOD

Hirsch, Marianne, 1981: 'Mothers and daughters: a review essay', *Signs*, 7/1, pp. 200–22.

Hirsch, Marianne, 1989: *The Mother/Daughter Plot: Narrative, Psychoanalysis, Feminism*. Bloomington: Indiana University Press.

Irigaray, Luce, 1981 [1979]: 'And the one doesn't stir without the other', *Signs*, 7/1, pp. 60–7.

Irigaray, Luce, 1985 [1974]: *Speculum of the Other Woman*, trans. Gillian C. Gill. Ithaca, NY: Cornell University Press.

Kristeva, Julia, 1989 [1987]: *Black Sun: Depression and Melancholia*, trans. Leon C. Roudiez. New York: Columbia University Press.

Miller, Jean Baker, 1978: *Toward a New Psychology of Women*. Harmondsworth: Penguin.

Rich, Adrienne, 1976: *Of Woman Born: Motherhood as Experience and Institution*. New York: Norton.

Sage: A Scholarly Journal on Black Women, 1984: 'Mothers and daughters I', special issue, 1/2.

Sage, 1987: 'Mothers and daughters II', special issue, 4/2.

Walker, Alice, 1983: *In Search of Our Mothers' Gardens*. London: The Women's Press.

MARGARET WHITFORD

motherhood   Classical Freudian/Lacanian psychoanalysis has little place for a theory of motherhood. In the OEDIPUS COMPLEX, development depends on surpassing the mother–child dyad; with the real or fantasized intervention of the father, social being begins. The mother's role is essentially to be outgrown: proximity to her or the desire of her (in LACAN, both a passive and an active genitive) betokens fixation or even psychosis. Motherhood is the goal of female development; but only via a series of losses, relinquishing the preferred erotic organ, the first-desired parent and, finally, the wish for a penis, in favour of a compensatory desire for a child from the father or husband. The girl's PRE-OEDIPAL period is extended: her attachment to her mother is given up only at the moment of the CASTRATION COMPLEX, when she blames her mother for her 'inadequate genital' and abandons clitoral masturbation. The baby as penis substitute is more nearly gratifying if, being male, it carries the prized object. Freud argues that the most perfect love bond is that between mother and son; as IRIGARAY points out, this directs all women to end up as Jocasta.

Ernest JONES and Karen HORNEY offered alternative theories, suggesting that the girl's early knowledge of the vagina gives the desire for a child primacy over PENIS ENVY. This argument, however, retains the stress on genital difference as basic to gender development. Melanie KLEIN explores the first months of life, identifying an oedipal complex in the pre-genital period. Infants of both sexes have destructive impulses against actual or potential children 'inside' the mother. Development proceeds by a struggle with such aggressions and the growing ability to 'restore' the mother's wholeness through guilt and reparation. Feminist psychoanalytic theory has been much influenced by both sides of this theory.

Psychoanalysis began to concern itself with mothering, in a prescriptive mode, in the 1940s with the popularization in Britain of the work of Donald Winnicott and John Bowlby. Bowlby's theories of attachment and loss, based in a combination of Kleinian psychoanalysis and ethology, argued that even brief separation from the mother or mother-figure could cause serious psychological and social damage. Winnicott's theories are more measured and exploratory, but he suggests that a too-experienced mother may 'castrate' her child by the over-skilful anticipation of its needs; his appealing term 'good-enough mothering' actually leaves little space for maternal skill, knowledge and experience.

Essentially, psychoanalysis has two problems with motherhood, both of which often implicate psychoanalytic feminists too. First, even when paternalistic it always views motherhood from the child's position, whether current or recollected. Secondly (and connectedly) it is rarely exempt from mother-blaming. Where the mother is studied, her position of power is seen through a child's retrospective gaze, which makes it difficult either to incorporate her political powerlessness or to take seriously the rational and conscious procedures of mothering. Feminist sociologists have contributed to researching the daily conflicts, pleasures and challenges of mothering as motivation in action (see Oakley, 1981; Statham, 1986). Clearly, motherhood is more than just 'experience and institution' (Rich, 1976) but a theory is likely to be partial in both senses if it excludes these two aspects.

As far as feminist attitudes to motherhood are concerned, two main stages emerge in the post-1970 period. In the 1970s women mainly rejected PATRIARCHY by refusing reproduction: they had neither time nor inclination to consider motherhood. Around 1980, as a generation of intellectual women entered their thirties, motherhood became an urgent practical and theoretical option and a central issue in cultural feminism.

Back in 1949, de Beauvoir had denounced maternity as 'narcissism, altruism, idle day-dreaming, sincerity, bad faith, devotion and cynicism' (1972, p. 528). In the early 1970s, abortion and contraception were rallying issues. The *Nouvel Observateur* of 5 April 1971 published a manifesto signed by 343 women, many of them famous, claiming to have had illegal abortions; it was this publicity that really got the French women's movement off the ground. Shulamith Firestone demanded 'the freeing of women from the tyranny of reproduction' (1971, p. 221) as the base-line for a feminist revolution. As late as 1978, when attempting to form 'a feminist theory of motherhood', the authors of *Feminist Studies* gave a lurid and Beckettian picture of motherhood as inextricably tied to death.

The next stage is typified by Dowrick and Grundberg (1980), in which fifteen women relate why they are or are not mothers by choice. Rich (1976) is the best known of a large number of feminist books about motherhood which blend the confessional with the analytical. Curiously, they are split along gender lines. The mother–daughter relation continues to be represented almost solely by daughters: compilations like Friday (1977) and Arcana (1979) sketched a reparative emancipation that tried hard to be a different kind of mother-blaming, offering her entry to the sisterhood. Meanwhile, mothers of sons represented their problems and feelings in a startling variety of modes – Lazarre (1976), Rich (1976), Kristeva (1986), Arcana (1983), Kelly (1983), Collange (1987) – as if the crisis for feminism must always be about the masculine and how it enters our bodies. More recently, the mother–daughter bond has entered both theoretical and confessional feminist discourse, the latter most strikingly in fiction and letters; but the passions and conflicts of mothering daughters are still little documented.

Feminist psychoanalytic writing on motherhood now falls into two camps, roughly split down the familiar Anglo-American/French divide. Among the former, two studies have been widely influential: Dinnerstein (1976) and CHODOROW (1978). Both attribute the production of GENDER to the effect of early upbringing by women. Dinnerstein (Kleinian and polemical) argues that our divisive (hetero-sexual habits and political madness can be traced to pre-verbal resentment of an all-powerful mother. Chodorow claims that, since mothers cathect sons oedipally and sexually and daughters pre-oedipally and narcissistically, mothering reproduces itself: girls develop greater skills of connectedness and nurturance, boys struggle all their lives with a trauma of separation. Both argue for changes in Western child-rearing, perhaps too confident that social changes (themselves hardly straightforward) can have a direct influence on psychical structures. If these are versions of mother-blaming, they are imaginative and optimistic ones. Meanwhile, feminist psychotherapists, whose research generally derives from eating-disorder therapy (very much a daughters' disease) defend the resented mother in terms of her too being a misloved, ill-nurtured daughter under the skin. In Eichenbaum and Orbach (1983), for instance, each woman's cure will depend on constructing an endless genealogy of daughters struggling against mother-blaming by blunting generational difference.

The problems remain. How is feminism to identify a maternal subject incorporating the two 'unknowns': the mother's knowledge and the mother's desire? French post-Lacanian feminists attempt the latter. In their search for a representable femininity which displaces phallocentrism, Cixous, Irigaray and KRISTEVA look to a language (written, spoken, or something else) of female bodily identity. The connectedness of mother and daughter, the fluidity of women's JOUISSANCE and plurality of its organs, the ecstasy of birth, the idea of a matriolatry free of Christianity's virginity cult, an utterance tied to the maternal/pre-oedipal – all these are ways of putting desire outside the symbolic. Two criticisms may be made: first, that woman here remains the crazy Other, functioning familiarly somewhere below the waist; second, that, as an elaborate metaphor, this rhetoric cannot escape a fixity as dangerous as its abstraction (see Stanton, 1986).

Can the mother never be the 'subject presumed to know'? Psychoanalysis, even feminist psychoanalysis, seems stuck with retrospection as long as she remains Jocasta. Two writers suggest ways in which we might begin to combine the maternal with knowledge: O'Brien (1981), arguing that 'the biological process of reproduction is a material substructure of history', suggests 'an aspect of human understanding that might be called reproductive consciousness' (p. 188); and Ruddick's concept of 'maternal thinking' (1989) sketches philosophical and practical qualities, however ideal, which inform the processes of motherhood. Other feminists turn to the current wave of reproductive technologies and their legal outgrowths and see not just a further encroachment of the masculine into our bodily space but a possible and disturbing 'deconstruction of motherhood' (Stanworth, 1987).

See also FEMININE ECONOMY; MOTHER–DAUGHTER RELATIONSHIP.

BIBLIOGRAPHY

Arcana, Judith, 1979: *Our Mothers' Daughters*. Berkeley: Shameless Hussy.
Arcana, Judith, 1983: *Every Mother's Son*. New York: Anchor/Doubleday.
Beauvoir, Simone de, 1972 [1949]: *The Second Sex*, trans. H. M. Parshley. Harmondsworth: Penguin.
Chodorow, Nancy, 1978: *The Reproduction of Mothering: Psychoanalysis and the Sociology of Gender*. Berkeley and Los Angeles: University of California Press.
Chodorow, Nancy, and Contratto, Susan, 1989 [1982]: 'The fantasy of the perfect mother', *Feminism and Psychoanalytic Theory*, Nancy J. Chodorow. Cambridge: Polity Press, pp. 79–96.
Collange, Christiane, 1987: *I'm Your Mother*, trans. Helen McPhail. London: Arrow.
Dinnerstein, Dorothy, 1976: *The Mermaid and the Minotaur: Sexual Arrangements and Human Malaise*. New York: Harper and Row.

MOTHERHOOD

Dowrick, Stephanie, and Grundberg, Sybil, 1980: *Why Children?* London: The Women's Press.

Eichenbaum, Luise, and Orbach, Susie, 1985 [1983]: *Understanding Women.* Harmondsworth: Penguin.

Feminist Studies, 1978: special issue, 'Toward a feminist theory of motherhood', 4/2.

Firestone, Shulamith, 1971: *The Dialectic of Sex.* London: Jonathan Cape.

Friday, Nancy, 1979 [1977]: *My Mother, My Self.* London: Fontana.

Kelly, Mary, 1983: *Post-Partum Document.* London: Routledge and Kegan Paul.

Kristeva, Julia, 1986 [1977]: 'Stabat mater', trans. Léon S. Roudiez, *The Kristeva Reader*, ed. Toril Moi. Oxford: Basil Blackwell, pp. 160–86.

Lazarre, Jane, 1976: *The Mother Knot.* New York: McGraw-Hill.

Oakley, Ann, 1981: *From Here to Maternity.* Harmondsworth: Penguin.

O'Brien, Mary, 1981: *The Politics of Reproduction.* London and New York: Routledge and Kegan Paul.

Rich, Adrienne, 1976: *Of Woman Born.* New York: Norton.

Ruddick, Sara, 1986: *Maternal Thinking.* Boston: Beacon.

Stanton, Domna, C. 1986: 'Difference on trial: a critique of the maternal metaphor in Cixous, Irigaray and Kristeva', *The Poetics of Gender*, ed. Nancy K. Miller. New York: Columbia University Press, pp. 157–82.

Stanworth, Michelle, ed. 1987: *Reproductive Technologies.* Cambridge: Polity Press.

Statham, June, 1986: *Daughters and Sons.* Oxford: Basil Blackwell.

NAOMI SEGAL

N

narcissism   The love of one's own self-image. The myth of Narcissus
tells the story of a young man who falls in love with his own reflection,
ignoring Echo, the fairest of all maidens. Nemesis finally punishes
Narcissus's cruelty by paralysing him into a position of contemplating
only his own face in a pool of water. Fascinated by his image, he pined
away and died (Ovid, *Metamorphoses* 3, 339–510). Havelock Ellis
linked autoeroticism (obtaining sexual satisfaction from one's own body
on one's own) to perverse and totalitarian character; Paul Näcke used
Ellis's work in 1899 to describe a particular perversion – of one who
treats his body as he would a sexual object – using the word
Narzissismus (Laplanche and Pontalis, 1973, p. 257).

Freud first picked up the term to try to account for various libidinal
states he considered pathological, using it alternately of homosexual
object-choice and of Schreber's 'narcissistic psychosis' (1911b). In 'On
narcissism: an introduction' (1914) and 'Mourning and melancholia'
(1917), Freud placed narcissism within the whole of psychoanalytic
theory, at a theoretical turning-point between his first and second
topologies. By linking narcissism to identificatory investments in others,
Freud distinguished as early as 1911 between a primary narcissistic
state, where an infant's libido is entirely focused on itself, and a secondary narcissism in which LIBIDO is withdrawn from the persons it is
invested in and returned again to its own ego. He described primary
narcissism as an indifferentiation between ego and id, characterized by a
total absence of object relations in sleep and dreams, as also in new-
borns, psychotics, melancholics, and those in mourning (1911a).
Although Freud saw narcissism as an autoerotic pathology once he had
proposed the id, ego and superego agencies, he nevertheless regarded
narcissistic identifications as a mechanism by which mental functioning
worked. Narcissism creates the forms that make INTROJECTION and PRO-
JECTION intelligible, as well as the 'magic thinking' of children and primi-
tives (1914, p. 75). He made a distinction between infantile narcissism,
described as an investment in the self as an ideal ego, and the objects of

271

libidinal energy in the outside world that he called ego-ideals (Freud, 1921).

LACAN re-cast Freud's theories of narcissism from his first and second topologies to argue that his theory of the ego was incomplete. He drew attention to the impossible leap Freud made from a narcissism (where autoerotic drives would provide quantitative energy unified into primal fantasies of PLEASURE) to a secondary narcissism formative of an ego which would be cognizant of others. According to Lacan, Freud failed to find the link between the ego's narcissistic efforts to preserve the biological individual and the eroticism of the sex drives, because Freud's insistence on the pathology of narcissism blocked his understanding of the normative role narcissism played in constituting and then maintaining ego-function. Narcissism results from identifications with images and words that are linked to the BODY to form a seemingly consistent entity. Primary narcissism, for Lacan, entails the creation of a corporeal image, and secondary narcissism concerns the dialectic of love and aggression in all human relations. Identification with objects is another process where the narcissistic ego can screen out the splits and gaps in language and being. No analytic cure, no freeing up of the possibility of re-constituting one's own DESIRE, can occur without cutting into narcissism (be it normative or neurotic) in order to separate the ego from the SYMPTOM (Lacan, 1988, ch. 11).

In contrast, Anglophone psychoanalytic theory has remained faithful to Freud's view of narcissism as inherently pathological. Two celebrated analysts who have re-defined narcissism within this purview are Heinz Kohut and Otto Kernberg. Although Kohut follows Lacan's 1949 mirror-stage theory to argue for a normative functioning of narcissism at the level of infant identification with the parents, his texts divide people into patients who have a narcissistic disorder and analysts who possess the empathy to help them cure this disorder. He equates primary narcissism with IDENTIFICATION, finding the cause of later personality disorders in bad mother-mirroring and inadequate father-ideal (Kohut, 1978). Otto Kernberg (1975) aligns his view of narcissism with an ego-psychology OBJECT-RELATIONS THEORY. Narcissistic disorders appear in borderline conditions where PRE-OEDIPAL conflicts are repressed and internalized objects are disturbed.

In the 1930s Lacan began his return to contradictory thoughts in Freud, claiming that the inadequacies of ego psychology had brought about a dynamic REPRESSION of Freud's structural unconscious. Unlike Kohut and Kernberg, who conflate IDENTIFICATION and narcissism, Lacan elaborates them as two different functions. Identifications are so powerful because they cover over what lies behind them: a void. In this sense the narcissistic ego is not a pathological self-preoccupation, but an

IDEOLOGY in which people (not in a psychotic state) believe in order to bridge the gaps between (1) a Symbolic order whose systems are inadequate to hide the discontinuities that emanate from the Real, and (2) Imaginary consistencies that depend on misrecognitions and the structure of fiction.

Lacan's reading reverses Freud's theory of narcissism by attributing the formation of the ego as a narcissistic structure to the process of identification with others *outside* the self. Captivated by the other's IMAGE, or by one's own image as reflected in others, humans cohere as seeming unities, although they are paradoxically dependent on others for any acquisition of a fundamental or primary narcissism and for verification of this first narcissism in a secondary narcissism of identification with others. Forever after, identification will serve as a buffer between the IMAGINARY and the REAL, the means by which narcissism is regulated as the basis of belief in an ego entity thought to cohere within the world of others.

Although narcissism is not in and of itself pathological, Lacan read the Narcissus myth as a depiction of the relation between the fragmented body – the voice, the gaze – in its relation to Imaginary transference love and the JOUISSANCE of the Real. Humans literally die from identifying with the sameness of someone else's desires and being: psychosomatically, affectively or, in the most extreme case of structural indifferentiation, psychosis. Yet identification with others not only connects narcissism to desire as the *cause* of DRIVE, but also separates individual narcissism from the weight of the superego (as parental and cultural judgements). We confront this paradox: narcissistic fixations make us all subjects of our pathologies – separated/alienated – but without narcissism, we lack the necessary illusion of *being* from which we live by desiring and speaking.

According to Kofman (1985), Freud's theory can be deconstructed by showing that Freud uses words in a mirror of his own narcissism. Freud claimed that *man* over-values a loved object by transferring his originary narcissism to the sexual OBJECT, thus impoverishing his own ego as regards libido (1914, p. 88). Love-objects become substitutes, new ideal egos, for the narcissistic perfection of childhood in which he was his own ideal (1914, p. 94); beautiful women, for example, cannot renounce their narcissism to love others. Hence, when men choose to love narcissistic women, rather than nurturing, anaclitic ones, they are troubled by their own choice and envious of the beloved's consistent narcissism (1914, pp. 88–9). According to Jacques Derrida (1979), Freud reveals *himself* to be the male fascinated with his own double; likewise, Freud's picture of the narcissistic woman repeats his fascination with the double.

NARCISSISM

However, this does not invalidate Freud's speculations – clearly historically biased – on the asymmetrical relations between women and men. For Lacan, Freud erred in confusing narcissistic identity with the UNCONSCIOUS, placing them both within FANTASY and opposing them to reality. Lacan's importance for feminism is his linking of GENDER to the DEATH DRIVE; ego-fixity functioning as resistance to change through identifications with *jouissance* effects emanating from the Real. These maintain the MASQUERADE around a fundamental void between the impossibly totalized male identity and the female one. The value of Lacan's theory of narcissism for feminism lies in his postulating identity fixity – which is never one with gender, anatomy or libido – as the enemy of change.

See also OTHER/OTHER.

BIBLIOGRAPHY

Derrida, Jacques, 1979: *Spurs: Nietzsche's Styles*, trans. Barbara Harlow. Chicago: University of Chicago Press.

Ellis, Havelock, 1898: 'Autoeroticism: a psychological study', *Alienist and Neurologist*, 19: 260–99; cited in Laplanche and Pontalis, 1973, *The Language of Psychoanalysis*, p. 47.

Freud, Sigmund, 1911a: 'Formulations concerning two principles of Mental Functioning', *SE*, 12, pp. 213–26.

Freud, Sigmund, 1911b: 'Psychoanalytic notes upon an autobiographical account of a case of paranoia (dementia paranoides)', *SE*, 12, pp. 1–84.

Freud, Sigmund, 1914: 'On narcissism: an introduction', *SE*, 14, pp. 67–104.

Freud, Sigmund, 1917: 'Mourning and melancholia', *SE*, 14, pp. 237–60.

Freud, Sigmund, 1921: *Group Psychology and the Analysis of the Ego, SE*, 18, pp. 88–145.

Kernberg, Otto, 1975: *Borderline Conditions and Pathological Narcissism*. New York: Aronson.

Kofman, Sarah, 1985: *The Enigma of Woman: Woman in Freud's Writings*. Ithaca, NY, and London: Cornell University Press.

Kohut, Heinz, 1978: *The Search for the Self: Selected Writings of Heinz Kohut, 1950–1978*, 2 vols, ed. R. H. Ornstein. New York: International Universities Press.

Lacan, Jacques, 1988 [1975]: *The Seminar*, Book 1: *Freud's Papers on Technique* (1953–1954), trans. John Forrester. New York: Norton.

Laplanche, Jean 1976: *Life and Death in Psychoanalysis*, trans. Jeffrey Mehlman. Baltimore: Johns Hopkins University Press.

Laplanche, Jean, and Pontalis, Jean-Baptiste, 1973: *The Language of Psychoanalysis*. London: The Hogarth Press and the Institute of Psycho-Analysis.

ELLIE RAGLAND-SULLIVAN

negative oedipus complex   The negative form of the OEDIPUS COMPLEX occurs when the infant incestuously desires the parent of the same sex, and wishes to destroy the parent of the opposite sex. The negative form of the complex remained conceptually undeveloped until Jeanne Lampl-de Groot defined it in 1927 as primary in the oedipal development of women (1973). She pointed out that the girls' desire of their mothers could not be confined to a PRE-OEDIPAL phase, and indeed continued throughout their development. She used this insight to expose the inadequacies of 'castration' as a general principle to explain infantile development, and to argue for a fresh look at the dynamics of the MOTHER–DAUGHTER RELATIONSHIP.

In contrast, Freud (1919) and Sachs (1923) regard the negative form of the oedipus complex as a defence against castration anxiety through regression to pre-oedipal oneness with the mother. The persistence of this accounts for the aetiology of 'perversions', particularly HOMOSEXUALITY. According to this thesis, homosexuals do not cease to be sexually aroused by the opposite sex, but simply repress and displace the excitement to the same sex. They identify with the parent of the opposite sex while gratifying themselves with someone of the same sex (Fenichel, 1946, p. 331). Such gratification is viewed as constantly undermined by the 'castration' threat which it has supposedly displaced: 'The male develops anxiety due to fears of penetration by the more powerful male (father); the female fears rejection by the more powerful female (mother) . . . Homosexual acts in the oedipal form are attempts to insure dependency and to attain power through the seduction of the more powerful partner' (Socarides, 1978, p. 95).

Feminists have pointed out that this thesis poses a much easier 'resolution' for men than for women. First, the little girl is supposed to conclude that she is already castrated, so permanently disadvantaged, whereas boys are only threatened with the punishment. Even if she accepts this interpretation, it still makes it especially difficult to identify with the father, as opposed to the mother, as guarantor of the law, stability and gratification. Instead, it is argued that 'Girls do not "reject" their mother and women in favour of their father and men, but remain in a bisexual triangle throughout childhood and into puberty' (Chodorow, 1978, p. 140). Finally, it is also questioned whether the 'negative charge', or fear and anxiety that supposedly provoke homosexual identification, actually derives from the oedipus complex at all. Kleinians, for example, argue that all erotic and aggressive drives retain pre-oedipal features of fragmentation and splitting (Klein, 1975, vol. 1). This undermines the very notion of a unilinear, unambivalent or permanently heterosexual resolution of the oedipus complex following the positive line.

See also CASTRATION COMPLEX; PERVERSION.

275

NEGATIVE OEDIPUS COMPLEX

BIBLIOGRAPHY

Chodorow, Nancy, 1978: *The Reproduction of Mothering: Psychoanalysis and the Sociology of Gender*. Berkeley: University of California Press.

Fenichel, Otto, 1946: *The Psychoanalytic Theory of Neuroses*. London: Routledge and Kegan Paul.

Freud, Sigmund, 1919: '"A child is being beaten": a contribution to the study of the origin of sexual perversions', *SE*, 17, pp. 175–204.

Klein, Melanie, 1975: *The Writings of Melanie Klein*, 4 vols. London: Hogarth Press.

Lampl-de Groot, Jeanne, 1973 [1927]: 'The evolution of the oedipus complex in women', *The Psychoanalytic Reader*, ed. Robert Fliess. New York: International Universities Press, pp. 180–94.

Sachs, Hanns, 1923: 'On the genesis of perversions', Socarides, 1978, pp. 531–46.

Socarides, Charles W., ed. 1978: *Homosexuality*. New York and London: Jason Aronson.

MARTIN STANTON

O

object   In everyday use, the word 'object' tends to be applied only to inanimate material things. In psychoanalytic theory, however, the term may equally be used of a person, an attribute of a person or a product of FANTASY. For Freud, the 'object' is first the object of the 'instinct' or DRIVE – a drive whose 'source' is in a bodily excitation, whose 'aim' is to eliminate the consequent state of tension and whose 'object' is the more or less contingent agency by which the reduction of tension is achieved. In Freud's succinct definition: 'The object of an instinct is the thing in regard to which or through which the instinct is able to achieve its aim' (1915, p. 122). The original object is an object of the self-preservative instinct alone. The neonate must suckle in order to live. The source of the self-preservative drive here is hunger, the object is the milk and the aim is ingestion. However, ingestion of milk and excitation of the sensitive mucous membranes of the mouth are inseparable events. Fed to somatic satisfaction, and after the nipple has been withdrawn, the infant may nevertheless continue to suck. The act of sucking, functionally associated with the ingestion of food, has become 'sensual sucking', enjoyed as a pleasure in its own right. It is here that the sexual drive first emerges, separating from the self-preservative instinct in a process termed 'anaclisis' or 'propping'. The original somatic experience of satisfaction survives as a constellation of visual, tactile, kinaesthetic, auditory and olfactory memory traces, and it is from this mnemic complex that the first object of LIBIDO is formed. This object, the 'breast', does not yet correspond to the external anatomical organ of later knowledge; it rather belongs to the order of fantasy and is internal to the SUBJECT. Nor is it yet a whole object: it is 'partial', both in the sense that it is the object of a 'component' instinct, the oral drive, and in the sense that it is fragmentary. After Freud the idea of the 'part-object', a real or fantasmatic object of instinctual attachment during about the first six months of life, subsequently represented through substitutions, was elaborated as a fundamental concept in Kleinian OBJECT-RELATIONS THEORY. As already observed, the object 'breast' – a complex of mnemic elements initially associated with feeding – comes to play the part in respect of the sexual drive that the milk played in regard to the self-preservative drive. This is to say there is a metonymical displacement of object from 'milk' to 'breast', and a metaphorical shift of aim from 'ingestion' to 'incorporation'. According to Laplanche, however, in this early state of apprehension, in which no 'self' has yet formed as distinct from the (m)other, 'there is a sort of coalescence of the breast and the erogenous zone', as a result of which 'we pass from "ingest" not to "incorporate" but to the couple "incorporate/be-incorporated" [such that the subject] loses its place: is it this time on the side of that which eats, or the side of that which is eaten?' (Laplanche, 1980, p. 62).

In 'Three essays on the theory of sexuality', Freud wrote: 'At a time at which the first beginnings of sexual satisfaction are still linked with the taking of nourishment, the sexual instinct has a sexual object outside the infant's own body in the shape of his mother's breast. It is only later that the instinct loses that object, just at the time, perhaps, when the child is able to form a total idea of the person to whom the organ that is giving him satisfaction belongs . . . the sexual instinct then becomes auto-erotic, and not until the period of latency has been passed through is the original relation restored . . . The finding of an object is in fact a refinding of it' (1905, p. 222). Autoerotism is in effect imposed on the infant through weaning (see Mitchell, 1974, pp. 22–3). In autoerotism, the 'component instincts' (oral, anal, phallic) seek satisfaction on the same sites of the body ('erotogenic zones') at which excitation occurs, without recourse to an external object. Thumb-sucking is a familiar form of autoerotic behaviour, representing an enactive recollection of previous satisfaction at the breast. In Freud's account of the subsequent development of SEXUALITY, the passage from infantile autoerotism to adult 'object-choice' is described as routed by way of NARCISSISM. The bodily experience of the neonate is fragmentary, a shifting constellation of sites of excitation. The sense of a unitary corporeal identity is not innate but must be achieved. The phase of 'narcissism' coincides with the emergence of a sense of a coherent ego (which, Freud stresses, is a 'body-ego') through the agency of an internalized self-representation.

The primacy of vision in this process, which takes place somewhere between age six and eighteen months, has been emphasized by LACAN in his concept of the mirror stage (Lacan, 1977; and *see* IMAGINARY). A newly unified sexual drive now takes as its object the child's own body *as a totality*. The subsequent object-choice of a whole *other* person is made by analogy with this first relation to a self perceived as a whole. The word 'choice' here does not imply a conscious decision. The type of object that will consistently be selected by the subject rather *imposes* itself as a result of decisive contingencies in the subject's early history.

The misrecognition and idealization of self and other endemic to the mirror stage henceforward marks object-choice and extends its determinants beyond the parameters of instinct alone: adding the object of 'love' to the object of the drive (Freud described the tendency of many men to separate the elements of idealization and of drive and assign them to different women, to form the dichotomy 'virgin'/'whore' (1912, pp. 177–90). Freud categorized object-choice in terms of two basic types: anaclitic and narcissistic. An anaclitic choice is made on the basis of a real or imagined resemblance of the object to an early object of need (a 're-finding', for example, of the mother or father); a narcissistic choice is based on a (mis)recognition in the other of what the subject imagines itself to be, or wishes to become. In the last analysis, what the subject comes to recognize as desirable in the other is a reflection of her or his own internalized object representations. With some variation in detail, most psychoanalytic accounts of the unfolding of sexual life against the backdrop of functional need follow the progression described above: from the earliest oral relation, through 'autoerotism' and 'narcissism', to adult 'object-choice'. This is not, however, to be understood as an inexorable developmental sequence, the final 'stage' of which definitively supersedes all the earlier ones. For example, in the object-choice of a given individual adult there might be a combination of anaclitic and narcissistic elements, and object-related activity might alternate with autoerotism. A complete picture of individual object-choice would also include consideration of the respective parts played by the elements of HETEROSEXUALITY and HOMOSEXUALITY, which are never fully mutually exclusive.

In a general feminist context, the word 'object' may readily be associated with the expression 'sex object'. Here the word takes an everyday pejorative sense to connote the reduction of a person to the status of a thing. The technical sense of the term in psychoanalytic theory carries no such connotation. Some confusion has resulted from the use of such expressions as 'object of the male gaze' in the wake of Laura Mulvey's application of psychoanalytic theory to analyse the 'objectification' of women in visual images (Mulvey, 1989, pp. 6–26; *and see* VOYEURISM/EXHIBITIONISM/THE GAZE). The difficulties arise when some of those who adopt Mulvey's psychoanalytic terminology apply it in an essentially empirical sociological setting – equating sexuality with GENDER and leaving out that which is most fundamental to psychoanalysis: the UNCONSCIOUS. In its accounts of the infant at the breast, of the active–passive duality of the drives, of narcissism and the mobility of the subject in fantasy, psychoanalysis consistently demonstrates that there is no objectification without IDENTIFICATION The separating-out of subject and object is a process that cannot be theorized without involving each with the other. Clearly, this does not help eliminate the offensive reductionism at issue, but it makes greater demands on the theory which would explain it.

See also OTHER/OTHER.

BIBLIOGRAPHY

Freud, Sigmund, 1905: *Three Essays on the Theory of Sexuality*, SE, 7, pp. 124–248.
Freud, Sigmund, 1912: 'On the universal tendency to debasement in the sphere of love', *SE*, 11, pp. 177–90.
Freud, Sigmund, 1915: 'Instincts and their vicissitudes', *SE*, 14, pp. 109–40.
Lacan, Jacques, 1977 [1949]: 'The mirror stage as formative of the function of the I as revealed in psychoanalytic experience', *Écrits: A Selection*, trans. Alan Sheridan. London: Tavistock, pp. 1–7.
Laplanche, Jean, 1980: *La Sublimation*. Paris: Presses Universitaires de France.
Mitchell, Juliet, 1974: *Psychoanalysis and Feminism*. London: Allen Lane.
Mulvey, Laura, 1989: *Visual and Other Pleasures*. London: Macmillan.

VICTOR BURGIN

object-relations oriented criticism For feminist literary critics and theorists, object-relations theory's focus on the female subject and its lucid explanation of differences between female and male development and adult personality, offers a number of useful strategies for exploring differences between feminine and masculine writing practices. Feminist OBJECT-RELATIONS THEORY itself emerged in the 1970s and early 1980s as a psychoanalytic theory particularly in tune with feminist values and ideals. Discovering the pre-oedipus, Freud claimed, 'was like the discovery, in another field, of the Minoan–Mycenean civilization behind the civilization of Greece'. This archaeological image suggests the mythic power, for feminists, of imagining the PRE-OEDIPAL – its mystery, its unavailability to conscious memory, its promise of a space of alternative values, its subversive challenge to oedipal PATRIARCHY.

Although the work of Melanie KLEIN, Margaret Mahler and D. W. Winnicott has inspired several literary studies, feminist literary critics followed with special eagerness the revisionary efforts of Nancy CHODOROW, Dorothy Dinnerstein, Jane Flax, Jessica BENJAMIN and Carol Gilligan and the distinctive shapes of FEMININITY they identified: the powerful and lasting effects of the submerged pre-oedipus, women's fluid ego boundaries and relationally structured identities, the complicated negotiations and multiple repressions by which women reach adulthood, and their ambivalent but determining mother–daughter bonds.

Feminist literary critics, interested in identifying characteristically feminine literary traits, came to see in the texts of women writers reflections of the personality structures theorized in object-relations psychoanalysis. Diverse aspects of literary production revealed such parallels and formed the focus of critical exploration: the formation of a female tradition; female authorship and the female signature; characteristically feminine plot structures; the relationships between female characters, especially mothers and daughters, sisters and friends; the hypothesis of a characteristically female language and style; the relation of GENDER and genre, gender and reading (*see* READING AS/LIKE A WOMAN).

Yet object-relations theories did more than provide a suggestive methodology with which to read women's writing. By positing the pre-oedipal as a mythic female space, they pointed to an alternative to patriarchy and the logos, to a world of shared female knowledge and experience in which subject–object dualism, separation, AUTONOMY and power relations might be re-envisioned. Thus, object-relations critics counter Freudian and Lacanian theories of writing. For them, the process of imagination and the activity of fabulation are motivated not by phallic LACK but by plenitude, not by castration but by connection, not by loss but by a longing to re-experience a symbiotic closeness with the mother. Even the struggle against maternal identification reveals at the heart of women's writing a profound and continued, if ambivalent, interconnection between mother and daughter (*see* MOTHER–DAUGHTER RELATIONSHIP).

Most literary studies influenced by object relations focus on the novel. That may be because the novel both narrates the story of development and places that story in the context of familial connections. Critics have found, for example, that the relations of mothers and daughters, sisters, and female friendships, often expressed in palimpsestic plots which communicate multiple and contradictory messages, displace heterosexual love plots from the centre of women's fictions, disrupting their seemingly smooth surfaces to reveal the repressed content beneath (Miller, 1981; Hirsch, 1981). Such subversive strategies allow women writers to inscribe into their plots their own rebellious relation to male literary tradition and their own self-identification as female, a self-identification arrived at through affiliation with other women. An analytic strategy which reads for sub-plots and female characters marginal to the central plot obviously is more appropriate for the work of some writers than others. Modernist and post-modern women writers – e.g. Virginia Woolf, Colette, Willa Cather, Doris Lessing, Toni Morrison, Margaret Atwood, Simone Schwartz-Bart, Jamaica Kincaid, Maxine Hong Kingston – have enjoyed the richest readings. Not only does the work of these writers intersect with the development of psychoanalysis, but the women's movement from the 1920s on has allowed a more sustained and less submerged focus on female relationships in women's fictions, thereby inviting an object-relations approach. Some feminist critics of Shakespeare, however, have used the insights of object-relations theory to explore MASCULINITY, especially its formation in relation to the early mother (Kahn in Garner et al., 1985; Adelman, 1991).

A number of other literary concerns intersect with the images of gender difference identified by feminist object-relations theorists. The shift of allegiance from father to mother and the oscillations between attachment and separation identified in object-relations theories can offer a model with which to study a dynamics of literary influence different from Harold Bloom's masculine 'anxiety of influence' (Gilbert and Gubar, 1979). Reader-response critics have found greater capacities for empathy and identification in women readers and in women's representations of reading. Theorists of genre have revealed a characteristically female *Bildungsroman* with development progressing towards affiliation rather than autonomy, with a less definitive shift from mother to father, and a less linear move towards adulthood (Abel et al., 1983). Others have identified a female elegy whose goal is not separation but continued remembrance and relation (Schenck, 1986). The act of writing itself can be seen as simultaneously depending on merging and separating, just like the developmental rapprochement phase (Johnson, 1987). The interpersonal rather than the solitary dimensions of writing also emerge through an object-relations approach (Perry and Brownley, 1984).

Most challenging to feminist critics has been the attempt to identify a distinctively female relation to language, a feminine sentence or style. Here again, object-relations theory has been helpful, particularly to Joan Lidoff (1986) and Margaret Homans (1986). Lidoff controversially describes the imagery, structure, style, character, plot and tone of Woolf's *To the Lighthouse* as pervaded by the presence of a lost mother and therefore shaped by a female sense of fusion, of lack of separation, boundary or division. Homans finds in Chodorow a feminine complement to the Lacanian masculine-based story of language. As opposed to the son who moves unproblematically into the Symbolic, the daughter retains a connection to the literal, pre-Symbolic language of the mother. Though socially and culturally suppressed, this literal language remains subversively present in the work of women writers even as they must enter the Symbolic realm of literary language and tradition.

Considered by feminist theorists a particularly 'American' brand of feminist criticism, object-relations criticism has been consistently questioned by Lacanian feminists for assuming too unproblematic and too unified a notion of the SUBJECT; for positing an idealized female realm, outside of patriarchal discourse; for postulating a female language unmarked by castration, difference and the unconscious; and for defining a maternal figure and a mother-tongue not sufficiently 'other' (*see* ÉCRITURE FÉMININE). Other critiques have come from within the 'American' feminist scene itself. In fact, the very notion of 'object relations' and the theoretical conceptions of subject formation that it inspires perpetuate a hierarchical division between subject and object and make it difficult to envision a truly different form of interrelation – a mutual recognition between subjects – and a different form of subjectivity that might not be based on objectification. Related is the recognition that any form of criticism inspired by object relations would focus on the figure of the child and not the mother. For object-relations psychology, the mother necessarily remains the idealized or degraded object and cannot be a subject in her own right (*see* MATERNAL VOICE; MOTHERHOOD). But if object-relations criticism is not as vital in the early 1990s as it was a decade ago, it is no doubt primarily because the spectre of 'essentialism' has inhibited research about gender difference. Object-relations theory and criticism have posited the category 'woman' and the notion of gender difference as if they were self-evident, leaving little space for the articulations of differences among women, whether they be historical differences or differences determined by class, race, ethnicity or sexual preference (*see* FEMINISM OF DIFFERENCE; RACE/IMPERIALISM). Still, positing a notion of intersubjectivity, reinforcing a sense of commonality and encouraging allegiances among women has given literary critics a powerful feminist voice and a rallying point which shares both the strengths and the pitfalls of other aspects of cultural feminism. Despite what may now look like idealism and perhaps even ESSENTIALISM, this criticism has facilitated a sustained study of women writers unprecedented in its focus and depth.

See also LITERARY AND TEXTUAL CRITICISM; WOMEN'S PSYCHOLOGICAL DEVELOPMENT.

BIBLIOGRAPHY

Abel, Elizabeth, 1989: *Virginia Woolf and the Fictions of Psychoanalysis.* Chicago: University of Chicago Press.

Abel, Elizabeth, Hirsch, Marianne, and Langland, Elizabeth, eds 1983: *The Voyage In: Fictions of Female Development.* Hanover and London: University Press of New England.

Adelman, Janet, 1991: *Smothering Mothers: Some Origins of the Female Site of Origins in Shakespeare.* New York and London: Routledge.

Gardiner, Judith Kegan, 1982: 'On female identity and writing by women', *Writing and Sexual Difference*, ed. E. Abel. Chicago: University of Chicago Press, pp. 177–92.

Garner, Shirley Nelson, Kahane, Claire, and Sprengnether, Madelon, eds 1985: *The (M)Other Tongue: Essays in Feminist Psychoanalytic Interpretation.* Ithaca, NY: Cornell University Press.

Gilbert, Sandra, and Gubar, Susan, 1979: *The Madwoman in the Attic: The Woman Writer and the Nineteenth-Century Literary Imagination.* New Haven: Yale University Press.

Hirsch, Marianne, 1981: 'Incorporation and repetition in *La Princesse de Clèves*', *Yale French Studies*, 62, pp. 67–87.

Hirsch, Marianne, 1989: *The Mother/Daughter Plot: Narrative, Psychoanalysis, Feminism.* Bloomington: Indiana University Press.

Homans, Margaret, 1986: *Bearing the Word: Language and Female Experience in Nineteenth-Century Women's Writing.* New Haven and London: Yale University Press.

Johnson, Barbara, 1987: 'Mallarmé as mother', *A World of Difference.* Baltimore: Johns Hopkins University Press.

Lidoff, Joan, 1986: 'Virginia Woolf's feminine sentence: the mother–daughter world of *To the Lighthouse*', *Literature and Psychology*, 32/3, pp. 43–59.

Miller, Nancy K., 1981: 'Emphasis added: plots and plausibilities in women's fiction', *PMLA*, 96/1, pp. 36–48.

Perry, Ruth, and Brownley, Martine Watson, eds 1984: *Mothering the Mind: Twelve Studies of Writers and their Silent Partners.* New York: Holmes and Meier.

Schenck, Celeste, 1986: 'Feminism and deconstruction: re-constructing the elegy', *Tulsa Studies in Women's Literature*, 5/1, pp. 13–27.

MARIANNE HIRSCH

object-relations theory   A post-Freudian branch of psychoanalysis evolving initially in Britain that takes as its primary field of study the relation between mother and infant in the first year of life. Object-relations theory assumes that from birth, the infant engages in formative relations with 'objects' – entities perceived as separate from the self, either whole persons or parts of the body, either existing in the external world or internalized as mental representations (*see* OBJECT). Because object-relations theory privileges the maternal object as central to the vicissitudes of the developing self, it has offered feminists an alternative paradigm to the Freudian OEDIPUS COMPLEX with its emphasis on the father, the PHALLUS and castration. Yet its primary focus on pre-verbal infantile experience in the mother–child dyad and its consequent lack of attention to the network of signification in which both mother and infant move also raise problems for feminism (*see* PRE-OEDIPAL; MOTHER-HOOD).

Object-relations theory can be said to derive from the work of Melanie KLEIN, who, through play therapy with children in the late 1920s, transformed the oedipal drama by making the mother its central figure and thus permanently altered the direction of British psychoanalysis. Although much of Klein's work relied on Freud's dual DRIVE theory, Klein re-defined the drives by foregrounding destructive impulses and their attachment to objects, especially the prototypical object, the breast. Condensing the time frame of the Freudian phases of psycho-sexual development to the first year of life, Klein described an infant inundated by its fantasies of aggression against the body of the mother, which in turn provoked persecutory fantasies of retaliation, guilt and a desire to make reparation.

What is particularly relevant for feminists is that in contrast to the Freudian notion that 'the little girl is a little man' until the CASTRATION COMPLEX, Klein (1928) proposed a primary FEMININITY phase for both sexes. In Klein's view, original joy in the feminine is strong for male and female; both identify with the mother. But in the male this identification leads to a femininity complex – a frustrated desire for a special organ of conception – provoking envy, rivalry and even hatred of women because of his disadvantage. Thus Klein theorizes a path of male development that presents womb envy as an analogue of Freud's concept of PENIS ENVY in the girl. Given this valorization of the maternal body, the girl's over-estimation of the penis is for Klein a result of dread of injury to her own sexual organs, an imagined maternal retribution for her aggressive wishes against the mother; similarly, the boy's castration anxiety is not attributed to fear of the father, but is a punishment for a fantasied destruction of the mother's body, which contains the father's penis. Indeed, there is virtually no operative father in Klein's formulations, except in so far as the paternal principle is already in the body of the mother. Even in the formation of the superego, the site of paternal law for both Freud and LACAN, Klein makes the mother central, deriving it from oral incorporation of the good/bad breast.

Klein's work gave rise to the school of British object-relations theory, its most prominent theorists being W. R. D. Fairbairn, Harry Guntrip and D. W. Winnicott. But object-relations theory after Klein significantly re-defined the relation between mother and infant by making the actual environment and the nature of maternal care the primary influences on the developing self. Shifting attention from the Kleinian dichotomy between reality and FANTASY to the relation between external and internal reality, a reality unproblematized by the mediation of LANGUAGE or the UNCONSCIOUS, object-relations theory posits a maturational self that develops through real relations with external objects. If not rejecting outright Klein's emphasis on the drives, aggression and fantasy

285

as Fairbairn does (see below), object-relations theory nevertheless downplays it and situates fantasy as an ego function, an effort to deal with the drives rather than a representation of them.

Object-relations theory's most radical departure from Freud and Klein was Fairbairn's re-definition of LIBIDO as object-seeking rather than pleasure-seeking (1941, 1944). Fairbairn, whose ideas were expounded and extended by Guntrip (1961), argued that this object-seeking impulse is an adaptation for man's survival similar to the instinctual programming of lower animals (1946, p. 140), that from birth the ego strives towards objects; but unlike Freud, he maintains that this movement is impelled not by erotic desire but by a desire for a relationship. Thus erotic PLEASURE is placed in a different register, as 'a signpost to the object' (1941, p. 33) rather than as an end itself: erogenous zones are used by the object-seeking ego as points of contact or modes of relatedness. Fairbairn substitutes the capacity for intimacy and mutuality for the Freudian goal of genital primacy (1941, p. 34) and derives aggression from frustrations in relatedness. The infant develops from 'primary identification', a state of IDENTIFICATION with the object (1941, p. 48), to mature dependence, marked by co-operation and exchange with differentiated others, through a renunciation of compulsive attachments to external and internal objects, the latter defined as pathological compensatory substitutes for relations to external objects in the real world.

Fairbairn's stages anticipate those of Margaret Mahler, the most important object-relations theorist in the United States, for whom the child at birth is not differentiated from the maternal body, but gradually moves from a state of merger to symbiosis to separation and individuation (1975). Although feminist object-relations theorists such as Nancy Chodorow and Jessica Benjamin challenge object-relations theory for valorizing separation and autonomy, Fairbairn's emphasis on mutuality and a relational ego and Mahler's theorization of symbiotic fusion between mother and infant significantly contributed to feminist formulations (see below).

The object-relations theorist most closely linked to Klein is D. W. Winnicott, a pediatrician whose clinical work with mothers and infants formed the basis of his contributions to theory. For Winnicott, a baby is born with inherited potential, which is realized through the mother's patterns of holding. The mother is thus a supplementary ego for the infant; her perceptions are mirrored to the infant who utilizes this mirroring to organize its own perceptions (1967). As a 'good enough mother' (1960a) she provides the infant with an experience of continuous being; if she impinges too much or is absent, the infant develops a distorted or false self (1960b). Yet while Winnicott states there is no baby, only the mother–infant dyad which produces a subjectivity that is a consequence of their interrelations, it is the mother alone who bears responsibility for the dyadic relation. It is she who sustains the infant's illusion of omnipotence by providing the object of the infant's need so quickly that there is no experience of a gap between desire and gratification. Only when omnipotence is a fact of infantile experience, when the infant has been under the illusion that external reality corresponds to its own capacity to create, can it make creative use of the world (1967). The maternal devotion which allows this sensitive manipulation of the dyadic relation is presented by Winnicott as an instinctive response to the rhythm of the infant; 'the good enough mother', by a graduated failure of adaptation, allows the infant to realize separation, to enter that intermediate area between subjective and objective, the transitional space (1951), in which all creative gestures are initiated, and to use the transitional object, an unchallengeable first possession between the thumb and teddy bear, between oral eroticism and object relations. While this vision of perfect complementarity reveals its own underlying desire for the more than good enough mother, these concepts have been usefully extended by feminist theorists (see below).

Winnicott's formulations, like Fairbairn's, are deeply problematic, not only in their focus on the mother as the origin of the self and their lack of attention to maternal ambivalence and aggressivity, but in their exclusion of the cultural context of meaning in which the mother and infant move, a symbolic network structured along the axis of the masculine subject which holds them both. What is the effect of language on the maternal mirror? How do internalized cultural codes influence maternal perception of the infant and vice versa? Winnicott recognizes the importance of the 'environmental provision' (1971a), but like the other object-relations theorists does not interrogate the effect of already constituted cultural meanings on that provision.

What distinguishes feminist object-relations theory is its location of GENDER issues in the first year of life and its questioning of the biological inevitability of mother-dominated childhood rather than its historical contingency. The most influential early feminist studies to use object-relations theory were Dorothy Dinnerstein's *The Mermaid and the Minotaur* (1977) and Nancy Chodorow's *Reproduction of Mothering* (1978), both of which described the social denigration of women and the pervasive sexual malaise it engenders as inevitable consequences of women's exclusive mothering. Both called for joint parenting by men and women as a means of disrupting the historical propagation of women's oppression, and thus both texts were justifiably criticized for the basically heterosexual orientation of their discussion and the exclusion of lesbians from their model solution. *The Mermaid and the Minotaur*, strongly influenced by Kleinian concepts of infantile fantasy, argues that because a woman is the first object from whom the infant has to wrest a separate subjectivity, women in general become the bearers of infantile ambivalence, archaic representatives of a fearsome nature magically construed as female that has to be overcome by both male and female children. It is because only women's hands rock the cradle that public power has concentrated in the hands of men, perpetuating the gender-marked split between love and work, emotion and reason. *The Reproduction of Mothering*, also tracing the difference in male and female gender identity to woman-dominated parenting, argues that because a mother is of the same gender as her daughter, she treats her daughter as an extension of herself, creating a deeper identification in her daughter than in her son, whom she experiences as different. The son is encouraged to repudiate his primary identification with the mother, but the daughter continues in her earliest relational mode, developing an ego marked by permeable boundaries. Although separation and individuation consequently remain problematic issues for female development, CHODOROW valorizes the relational ego with its more fluid boundaries. As a result of an energetic separation from the mother, men tend to have more firm ego boundaries, but MASCULINITY has a reactive and defensive quality. Men tend to deny connection and to project their defensive needs as desirable cultural qualities: autonomy, independence, objectivity. While Chodorow (1989) uses Fairbairn's and Winnicott's ideas to applaud the imaginative and feminine ability to enter into the world of the other, she continues to point out the essential ambivalence in woman's ego experience, which is also threatened by a lack of AUTONOMY and the dissolution of self into others. Women's mothering itself shares this ambivalent position as it often generates pleasure and fulfilment at the same time that it is fundamentally related to women's secondary position in society and to the fear of women in men. Jane Flax (1980) also has stressed the difficulties women have in recognizing differences from other women and argued that women's empathic self rests on the repression of selves bound up with autonomy, aggression, intellectual mastery and active desire.

Other feminist theorists have confronted the idealization of masculinity as well as the re-valuation of femininity in order to elaborate a critique of individualism that has been enabled by object relations. Evelyn Fox Keller (1985) censures the idealization of autonomous thinking in SCIENCE and in the tradition of Western rationality generally. Gilligan (1982) describes philosophy's gender-based hierarchy of moral values that ranks individual responsibility higher than collective and/or interpersonal, that assumes the masculine affinity for independence superior to co-operation (*see* WOMEN'S PSYCHOLOGICAL DEVELOPMENT). Benjamin (1988) has continued the thesis of Dinnerstein's admonitory text, arguing that the idealization of autonomy in denying dependency leads to domination; for since the mother continues to be needed, independence comes to mean possessing and controlling the needed object, leading to the domination of woman by man. This structure of gender domination is materialized in the instrumentalism that pervades our socio-economic relations. Another pernicious effect of a symbolic order structured by the phallus is that women, objects rather than subjects, lack an image of their own desire and thus tend to seek separateness and recognition through a love for the powerful father that becomes masochistic. Arguing against the phallic mode of psychic structuring that equates separation, agency and DESIRE with the father and confirms patterns of domination, Benjamin proposes an alternative structuring of the psyche, through the object-relations concept of 'intersubjectivity', and utilizes Winnicott's ideas about transitional phenomena and the maternal holding environment to describe a space of containment in which women can experience their own inner desire.

While the intersection of feminism and object-relations theory has provoked complex cultural analyses, these contributions can also be criticized – for an ESSENTIALISM about a female nature no less insidious for being culturally determined, for an idealization of the PRE-OEDIPAL mother–daughter bond as essentially outside the effects of the paternal law, for its reliance on a heterosexual model of parenting that also subtends the object-relations school in general, and for a perspective that does not take sufficient account of the effects of the unconscious on interpersonal experience.

See also MATERNAL VOICE; MOTHER–DAUGHTER RELATIONSHIP; MOTHERHOOD; OBJECT-RELATIONS ORIENTED CRITICISM; PERSONAL/AUTOBIOGRAPHICAL CRITICISM.

BIBLIOGRAPHY

Benjamin, Jessica, 1988: *The Bonds of Love: Psychoanalysis, Feminism and the Problem of Domination*. New York: Pantheon.
Chodorow, Nancy, 1978: *The Reproduction of Mothering: Psychoanalysis and the Sociology of Gender*. Berkeley: University of California Press.
Chodorow, Nancy, 1989: *Feminism and Psychoanalytic Theory*. New Haven: Yale University Press.
Dinnerstein, Dorothy, 1976: *The Mermaid and the Minotaur: Sexual Arrangements and Human Malaise*. New York: Harper and Row.
Fairbairn, W. R. D., 1941: 'A revised psychopathology of the psyche and psychoneuroses', Fairbairn, 1952, pp. 28–58.
Fairbairn, W. R. D., 1944: 'Endopsychic structure considered in terms of object-relationships', Fairbairn, 1952, pp. 82–132.
Fairbairn, W. R. D., 1946: 'Object-relationships and dynamic structure', Fairbairn, 1952, pp. 137–51.

Fairbairn, W. R. D., 1952: *An Object Relations Theory of the Personality*. New York: Basic Books.

Flax, Jane, 1980: 'Mother–daughter relationships: psychodynamics, politics, and philosophy', *The Future of Difference*, ed. Hester Eisenstein and Alice Jardine. New Brunswick and London: Rutgers University Press, pp. 20–40.

Gilligan, Carol, 1982: *In A Different Voice: Women's Conceptions of the Self and Morality*. Cambridge, Mass.: Harvard University Press.

Guntrip, Harry, 1961: *Personality Structure and Human Interaction*. New York: International Universities Press.

Keller, Evelyn Fox, 1985: *Reflections on Gender and Science*. New Haven: Yale University Press.

Klein, Melanie, 1928: 'Early stages of the oedipus conflict', *The Selected Melanie Klein*, ed. Juliet Mitchell. Harmondsworth: Penguin, 1986, pp. 69–83.

Mahler, Margaret, et al. 1975: *The Psychological Birth of the Human Infant*. New York: Basic Books.

Winnicott, D. W., 1951: 'Transitional objects and transitional phenomena', Winnicott, 1971b, pp. 1–25.

Winnicott, D. W., 1960a: 'The theory of the parent-infant relationship', Winnicott, 1965, pp. 37–55.

Winnicott, D. W., 1960b: 'Ego distortion in terms of true and false self', Winnicott, 1965, pp. 140–52.

Winnicott, D. W., 1965: *Maturational Processes and the Facilitating Environment*. New York: International Universities Press.

Winnicott, D. W., 1967: 'Mirror role of mother and family in child development', Winnicott, 1971b, pp. 111–18.

Winnicott, D. W., 1971a: 'Creativity and its origins', Winnicott 1971b, pp. 65–85.

Winnicott, D. W., 1971b: *Playing and Reality*. London: Tavistock.

CLAIRE KAHANE

oedipus complex The oedipus complex is traditionally seen as the central or 'nuclear' complex (*Kernkomplex*) around which Freudian theory revolves. It is supposed to account for the infant's negotiation of incestuous desires for its parents, which includes both erotic and destructive components, as well as concomitant guilt and fear of reprisal. The positive oedipus complex involves the infant's incestuous desire for the parent of the opposite sex. The NEGATIVE OEDIPUS COMPLEX concerns the infant's DESIRE for the parent of the same sex. In traditional formulations, the infant is portrayed as discovering, exploring and passing through the complex during a specific phase of development called the 'oedipal phase', that is, between three and five years old. The complex therefore serves to further the child's psychic growth and consolidate its ego and superego functions, as well as help orient its sexual proclivities. During this phase, each individual is supposed to acquire some effective relation through knowledge to the law that governs the child/mother/father triad, and thus opt for the one prescribed route out of the complex: renunciation of incestuous desire and identification with the parent of the same sex. The law then operates within the infant through the superego, and freedom of erotic choice outside incest develops within the ego.

It is quite clear that such a traditional formulation of the oedipus complex is vitiated by major paradoxes, which many psychoanalytic and feminist critics have set out to expose. First, there is the total ignorance and suppression of the mother, who is accused either of promoting incestuous desire or of encouraging regression. Secondly, there is the acceptance of the father's rights over the mother, and the erection of patriarchal law as a universal and normative principle that determines psycho-sexual development. Finally, the phallogocentric government of all psycho-sexual relationships excludes anything specifically feminine: the PHALLUS and castration, for example, determine not only the constitution of SEXUAL DIFFERENCE, but 'knowledge' of it, and its supposed heterosexual 'resolution'.

Freud's view

The oedipus complex is inspired by the tragedy of King Oedipus recounted in the Theban cycle of legends. In this, Oedipus progressively discovers the chain of past events which have brought a plague upon his kingdom. He realizes that an old man he had previously murdered at a crossroads was Laius, his father, and that Jocasta, his wife and the mother of his children, is indeed also his own mother. When the truth dawns, he blinds himself and flees the kingdom (see MASCULINITY).

Freud has a special and lasting concern with this story. His first direct reference to Oedipus comes in a letter to his friend Wilhelm Fliess dated 15 October 1897, in which he discusses the special power of one of Sophocles' plays on the subject, *Oedipus Rex*: 'A single idea of general value dawned on me. I have found, in my own case too, [the phenomenon of] being in love with my mother and jealous of my father, and I now consider it a universal event in early childhood . . . ' (Freud, 1985, p. 272). At this time, however, these observations are about *one* 'idea of general value' among others. More prominent is his concern with the other side of incest, that is, the sexual abuse of children by parents, and whether patients' accounts of this are real or FAN-

TASY. Furthermore, *Oedipus Rex* is just one play among others mentioned, such as Grillparzer's *Die Ahnfrau* and Shakespeare's *Hamlet*. Even when he does give it pride of place for the first time in 'The interpretation of dreams' (1900), he still cites it in general comparison with *Hamlet*, *Timon of Athens* and *Macbeth*.

Freud's concern with Oedipus only became associated with 'complexes' through reading and debate with JUNG. Jung was the first person to link the word-association technique with the complex nature of recalling the past: 'such a recollection', Jung wrote in 1905, 'which is composed of a large number of component ideas, is called a *complex of ideas*. The cement that holds the complex together is the *feeling-tone* common to all the individual ideas, in this case unhappiness' (Jung, 1973, 2, p. 321, italics in original). By posing an oedipus 'complex of ideas', therefore, Freud was able to cement together positive and negative aspects of incest and its prohibition in such 'feeling-tones' as helplessness, castration anxiety and PENIS ENVY. His first use of the term 'oedipus complex' is in 'A special type of object choice' (1910), though previous references to the character of Oedipus are later expanded in footnotes to refer to the complex. In this context, it is important to note that his first reference to the 'nuclear complex' (*Kernkomplex*) in 'The sexual theories of children' (1908) does not actually refer to the oedipus complex, but is retrospectively related to it. In general terms, therefore, Freud's early work on SEXUALITY refers surprisingly little to Oedipus, and even less to the oedipus complex (cf. 'Three essays on the theory of sexuality', 1905). The oedipus complex was only firmly identified as the 'nuclear complex' when Jung started to question Freud's sexual aetiology of the neuroses. By 1920, it had become the shibboleth that distinguished adherents to psychoanalysis from its opponents.

Ironically, by the time Freud finally formalized the oedipus complex as central to his structural theory in *The Ego and the Id* (1923), other analysts had already filled in the apparent gaps with their own misreadings and assumptions, and had started to question both the temporal and the psycho-sexual framework. Not surprisingly, therefore, much of the later critical work on the oedipus complex displays only tenuous textual links with Freud.

Criticisms of Freud's view

It is possible to distinguish three main trends of critical reaction to Freud's view of the oedipus complex, each of which has had a very different impact on feminist theory: the *cultural* critique, which focuses both on the internal dynamics of the Oedipus cycle and its lack of cultural universality; the *Lacanian* critique, which points to the absence of an adequate account of the Symbolic in Freud's formulation, and attempts to provide it; and finally, the *Kleinian* critique, which questions the structure, timing and importance of the oedipus dynamic, arguing instead for more emphasis on the PRE-OEDIPAL.

A frequent preliminary to the cultural critique is the comment that Freud distorted or misread the original story. It is suggested, for example, that he overlooked the fact that Laius, Oedipus's father, had also intended to kill his son to prevent the oracular curse becoming true (Devereux, 1953). This is sometimes taken further, and seen to indicate that Freud could not face up to his own father's past: furthermore, as, according to some sources, Laius 'invented' homosexual paedophilia, it is even suggested that Freud repressed the fact that fathers sexually abuse sons (Krüll, 1986, pp. 61–3). Such literary criticism rests mainly on the assumptions that the Oedipus cycle constitutes a complete textual body, that Freud was aware of this, and that variant or free associative readings are impossible. In fact, besides Aeschylus, Euripides and Sophocles, at least ten other contemporary Greek authors contributed accounts of the Oedipus cycle, and offered many variants, including the assertion that Oedipus did not blind himself, that his sons were born not from Jocasta, but from another wife, and that he was killed by Laius's avenging furies. Even if Freud were aware of this wider context, it seems wiser to conclude that his elaboration of the oedipus complex drew selectively and free-associatively from the Theban body of texts.

The main line of the cultural critique of the oedipus complex argues that it is limited to Western culture, drawing its inspiration from the anthropological studies conducted by Malinowski, Mead, Reich and Roheim in the 1920s and 1930s which debated the cogency of the oedipus complex in matriarchal societies. Claude Lévi-Strauss (1969) suggests this debate is outmoded, and attempts to vindicate Freud by arguing that different family or power structures are secondary in the oedipal dynamic. Primary, rather, are incest taboos, which universally structure sexual difference (*see* ANTHROPOLOGY AND CROSS-CULTURAL ANALYSIS).

The Lacanian critique builds on Lévi-Strauss's intervention, and adds a dual definition of the oedipus complex's articulation of the incest taboo. First, it claims that the complex structures the infant's confrontation between DESIRE and the law. It is important to note here that the law pre-determines the emergence of the infant's desire, just as the oracle pre-determines the story before Oedipus arrives on the scene (Lacan, 1988, 2, pp. 229–33). This structuration of the confrontation between desire and the law itself contains components that mutually interrelate to progress the infant through the complex: crucial here are the imago of the fragmented body, the mirror stage and the disc game (Lacan, 1966, 1977).

Secondly, as a result of this structuration, the infant acquires language and temporalization, which locate, pin down (*capitonner*) and cover desire. According to LACAN, the main problem with Freud's formulation lies in the inadequacy of the terms adduced to analyse these linguistic and temporal aspects of the complex. Freud appeals only to a pre-oedipal imaginary register and post-oedipal real, but has an inadequate grasp of the symbolic register which articulates the two (cf. Laplanche, 1981). Furthermore, Freud has not fully explored the radical new form of temporality he discovered with *Nachträglichkeit* (deferred action or 'afterwardsness'), and frequently lapses back into a notion of real as opposed to symbolic or lived time (Lacan, 1977, p. 48). Hence Freud's misguided need in 'Totem and taboo' (1912–13) to argue for the existence of a real patricide in ancient history to provide an origin for the oedipal process.

The Kleinian critique shares this concern about the temporality of the oedipus complex, but wishes rather to locate its emergence in the first year of life. Klein's reasons for this derive mostly from clinical observation, but in fact oblige major theoretical revisions of the complex (Klein, 1975, vol. 1). She maintains that the infant not only expresses violent aggression during this early period, but also experiences guilt which may be interpreted as a precursor of the superego. At this stage, though, the child has no access to the genital components that Freud associated with the oedipal phase, but is bound within an oral and anal universe in which aggressive drives split off or fragment the objects that deny gratification. For KLEIN, then, the oedipus complex does not primarily focus on the father, or the penis, or the symbolic phallus, or the threat of castration. It focuses rather on the mother and the breast, which are good objects if they are gratifying, or bad objects if they are denying. Moreover, the aggressive fantasies that accompany the denial of the breast are oral and not phallic. Even when the father and his penis enter the scene, they follow the same figuration as breast fantasies, and are fantasized as sucked for gratification or experienced as denying (Klein, 1975, vol. 1, pp. 370ff.).

Klein has inspired the feminist critique by BENJAMIN (1990), CHODOROW (1978), and Dinnerstein (1976) of the prescribed role of the mother in the oedipus complex. They appeal to Klein to expose an implicit moralism in Freud's oedipus formulation, which degrades the mother, her body and her mothering into complexual material which has to be 'resolved' according to a purportedly superior patriarchal law. To accept Freud means not only to institute a one-way process away from the primal relationship with the mother, but also to view the mother as a site for regressive and 'bad' feelings: 'The myth of the good paternal authority that is rational and prevents regression purges the father of all terror and . . . displaces it onto the mother, so that she bears the badness for both of them' (Benjamin, 1990, p. 136).

Conclusions

As a consequence of this intense and varied criticism, many perceive a diminution in the importance of the oedipus complex for psychoanalytic and feminist theory. Instead, debate is shifted to the pre-oedipal and early oedipal stages, and attempts are made to re-map the infant's development here in non-sexist terms. Particularly important here is the re-valorization of the mother, and of the infant's early relationship to her. Some, like IRIGARAY (1985), choose to focus on the infant's entry into sexual difference, and argue that there is space to elaborate a new language for women (*parler-femme*) which enjoys the fluidity of the imaginary and refuses to be subsumed in a fixed and closed symbolic order. Others, like Jean Laplanche (1989), argue for a primal 'priority of the other', in which the child receives messages from the mother that it cannot understand. The breast, for example, is not just a source of nourishment or comfort, but an erotic object in an adult world that the child senses but cannot process.

In rebuttal, defenders of the oedipus complex have focused on its consolidation of the superego. Janine Chasseguet-Smirgel (1985) suggests that the oedipus complex articulates a progression from the ego-ideal, which omnipotently idealizes 'oneness' with the mother, to the superego, which facilitates more realistic and differentiated perceptions of her. Some feminists have rejected this re-formulation because it denies that the father might also be an object of idealization incorporated in the ego-ideal (Benjamin, 1990, pp. 148–54). They propose instead a final ironic twist to this version of the story: perhaps Oedipus himself confused the ego-ideal with the superego, and so idealized his father as the guarantor of family law and harmony, rather than realistically recognizing him to be the vehicle of tragedy.

See also HETEROSEXUALITY; PSYCHICAL REALITY; SEDUCTION THEORY.

BIBLIOGRAPHY

Benjamin, Jessica, 1990: *The Bonds of Love: Psychoanalysis, Feminism, and the Problem of Domination*. London: Virago.

Chasseguet-Smirgel, Janine, 1985: *The Ego-Ideal*. London: Free Association Books.

Chodorow, Nancy, 1978: *The Reproduction of Mothering: Psychoanalysis and the Sociology of Gender*. Berkeley: University of California Press.

Devereux, George, 1953: 'Why Oedipus killed Laius: a note on the complementary oedipus complex in Greek drama', *International Journal of Psycho-Analysis*, 34, pp. 132–41.

Dinnerstein, Dorothy, 1976: *The Mermaid and the Minotaur: Sexual Arrangements and Human Malaise*. New York. Harper.

Freud, Sigmund, 1900: *The Interpretation of Dreams*, SE, 4, 5.

Freud, Sigmund, 1905: *Three Essays on the Theory of Sexuality*, SE, 7, pp. 123–245.

Freud, Sigmund, 1908: 'On the sexual theories of children', *SE*, 9, pp. 205–26.

Freud, Sigmund, 1910: 'A special type of object-choice made by men', *SE*, 11, pp. 163–76.

Freud, Sigmund, 1912–13: *Totem and Taboo, SE*, 13, pp. 1–161.

Freud, Sigmund, 1923: *The Ego and the Id, SE*, 19, pp. 3–68.

Freud, Sigmund, 1985: *The Complete Letters of Sigmund Freud to Wilhelm Fliess 1887–1904*, trans. and ed. Jeffrey M. Masson. Cambridge, Mass. and London: Harvard University Press.

Irigaray, Luce, 1985 [1977]: *This Sex Which Is Not One*, trans. Catherine Porter. Ithaca, NY: Cornell University Press.

Jung, Carl-Gustav, 1973 [1906]: 'A psychological diagnosis of evidence', *Experimental Researches, Collected Works of C. G. Jung*, 2, ed. Leopold Stein with the collaboration of Diana Rivière. London: Routledge & Kegan Paul, pp. 318–32.

Klein, Melanie, 1975: *The Writings of Melanie Klein*, 4 vols. Vol. 1: *Love, Guilt and Reparation*; vol. 2: *The Psycho-Analysis of Children*; vol. 3: *Envy and Gratitude*; vol. 4: *Narrative of a Child Analysis*. London: Hogarth Press.

Krüll, Marianne, 1986: *Freud and his Father*, trans. A. J. Pomerans. London, Hutchinson.

Lacan, Jacques, 1977 [1966]: *Écrits: A Selection*, trans. Alan Sheridan. London, Tavistock.

Lacan, Jacques, 1988 [1975, 1978]: *The Seminar of Jacques Lacan*, 2 vols, ed. Jacques-Alain Miller, trans. J. Forrester and S. Tomaselli. Cambridge: Cambridge University Press.

Laplanche, Jean, 1981: *Problématiques IV: L'Inconscient et le ça*. Paris: Presses Universitaires de France.

Laplanche, Jean, 1989 [1987]: *New Foundations for Psychoanalysis*, trans. D. Macey. Oxford: Basil Blackwell.

Lévi-Strauss, Claude, 1969: *The Elementary Structures of Kinship*. London: Eyre and Spottiswoode.

MARTIN STANTON

Other/other Lacan's concept of the Other, although it refers essentially to the SYMBOLIC order of language and speech, does not have a single meaning; it allows for more than one reading, and must be rigorously distinguished from the concept of other – with a small 'o' – which designates the relation to the specular other, the other who resembles the self, an imaginary relation which originates in what LACAN in 1936 called 'The mirror stage', and which describes the relation of the child to his image.

The relation to the specular other

The image which the child sees may be narcissistic, but it is genuinely other in that its new wholeness does not correspond to the child's fragmented experience of its body. Between the body that is still subject to the fragmentation of the drives and its image in the mirror there is a fundamental disparity, a discrepancy which means that, via his image, the child relates to himself as if to another. If he is to assume the image and recognize himself in it, the image needs to bear sufficient resemblance to him, but it must also offer, at a distance, the otherness of a complete, unified body image, which will ground the child's hope for an anticipated mastery; the fiction of this mastery will become the basis of the ego. The narcissistic identifications linked to this body image, and the jubilation and aggressivity which accompany them, will leave their mark on all subsequent relations with others (Lacan, 1977, p. 307).

In 1938, in a fundamental text on the Family, Lacan illustrates the narcissistic and competitive structure of the IMAGINARY relation to the other, with reference to what he calls the 'Intrusion Complex', that is, the child's 'discovery that he has brothers' (sisters, other children in the nursery school), and the consequent realization that he will have to share the mother – or father. When the age difference between the children is no greater than two months, one finds reactions in which a kind of communication is displayed: taking turns, provocations, ripostes, gestures of transitivism. When the age difference is greater, then one finds attempts at seduction, exhibitionism or despotism, in which each child identifies with his rival in an Imaginary duplication.

These situations imply two principal types of outcome. In one type, the child may attempt to claim sole possession of the mother, to the exclusion of the other child(ren), and may even be bent on the latter's destruction, passing from the passional 'you are me', to the exclusive 'either you or me'. If the Imaginary relation becomes arrested at this stage, it will always take a dangerously aggressive form, acting out perverse libidinal drives, particularly of a sadistic or masochistic kind (*see* MASOCHISM). In the second type, the child is oriented towards others, whom he discovers as 'objects' to be known, and, while the other child is still seen as a rival, it is in a contest where agreement and recognition are not excluded. It is within the framework of this fratricidal drama, whatever its outcome, that the ego and the OBJECT are structured, via the mediation of the relation to the (specular) other (Lacan, 1987, p. 48).

The symbolic Other

In opposition to this other and to the ego constituted in the Imaginary relation, Lacan proposed the Symbolic pair of Subject and Other, which he defined in 1955 as 'the place where is constituted the I who speaks with the one who hears' (Lacan, 1981, p. 309).

In the following year, in his commentary on 'The purloined letter' with which the French edition of *Écrits* opens, he broke with the two principal reference points of his previous research – phenomenology and history – and began to put forward a conception of the speaking subject as the effect of an autonomous Symbolic syntax, engendered by the structure of LANGUAGE, the 'signifying chain' as he calls it. This chain constitutes the field of the UNCONSCIOUS, and governs all speaking subjects, unbeknown to them: it shapes their destiny, binds their desires, determines their fantasies, and marks indelibly the SUBJECT which it brings into existence. Unaware of the extent to which his speech is spoken from the Other scene of the signifying chain, the subject, then, is split between what he *says* and what *is said*, a split which Lacan formulates as the split between the subject of the utterance and the subject of the statement.

The central meaning of the concept of Other lies in its designation of the unconscious as a site signifying the subject, a site structured like a discourse (Lacan, 1977, p. 193). However, this Symbolic Other must be linked to the Other as transcendent or absolute pole of the address, summoned each time that a subject speaks to another subject (Lacan 1981, pp. 286–7). Absolute pole of the address, but also Witness of the Truth, the Other is not a real interlocutor: it is essentially the Symbolic place required by the speech of the subject, where the subject both *is*, and at the same time *is not*, in so far as he is constituted by LACK in the Other.

The Symbolic Other is supposed to occupy the place of JOUISSANCE itself. However, when Lacan, in his Seminar on 'The ethics of psychoanalysis', refers to *jouissance* as a concept, he posits that *jouissance* cannot be completely translated into words. *Jouissance* always leaves a 'remainder' which cannot be spoken; it is to this remainder that we must attach the well known concept of *objet-a*, to which Lacan assigns the function of cause of DESIRE.

Once the subject has been constituted in speech, the Other will never exhaust the 'real' of *jouissance*; the signifier which would put this *jouissance* into words will always be lacking. For this reason, Lacan marks the place of the Other with a bar, connoting fissure or loss, which he writes as a matheme $S(\cancel{A})$, meaning: 'signifier of A [Other] insofar as it is barred'. It is through the barred Other that the status of truth is revealed as that which can never be entirely spoken; and in addition, Lacan maintains that the 'woman part' of speaking beings entertains a privileged relation with the barred Other.

Finally, even if the Other is not a real interlocutor, it can be embodied, not only in the maternal Other, but also in the Other sex which, despite the claims of tradition, is not necessarily the female sex: 'Man, a woman, they are only signifiers. It is from that, from speech in its incarnation as one sex or the other, that they derive their function. The Other, in my terms, can therefore only be the Other sex' (Lacan, 1975, pp. 39–40).

If, on the one hand, Lacan is careful not to hypostatize SEXUAL DIFFERENCE, it is none the less true that the function of that which exceeds all discourse is characterized as 'feminine', thus leaving open for contemporary debate the question of what links women to 'the feminine', and as a result the question of their position in discourse as speaking subjects.

See also FEMININITY.

BIBLIOGRAPHY

Lacan, Jacques, 1977 [1966]: *Écrits*, trans. Alan Sheridan. London: Tavistock.
Lacan, Jacques, 1975: *Le Séminaire*, book 20: *Encore*. Paris: Seuil.
Lacan, Jacques, 1981: *Le Séminaire*, book 3: *Les Psychoses*. Paris: Seuil.
Lacan, Jacques, 1987: *Les Complexes familiaux dans la formation de l'individu: Essai d'analyse d'une fonction en psychologie*. Paris: Navarin.

MARIE-CLAIRE BOONS-GRAFÉ
(trans. Margaret Whitford)

P

patriarchy The problem with discussions of patriarchy is the ambiguity of the referent. Patriarchy can be defined in different ways, according to the theoretical framework in which the term is employed. The most general definition is that it is a term – either descriptive or explanatory – which refers to the hierarchical organization of the relations between the sexes. However, 'the domination of women by men' is a description which could cover the whole of human history, which reduces its explanatory value in specific historical situations.

The term 'patriarchy' has a pre-feminist history in a number of theories which have been important for feminism, particularly marxism, psychoanalysis and anthropology. In each, it has a different definition and function. In marxism, the focus is the relation between patriarchy and private property; in psychoanalysis, it is the role of the patriarchal family in the formation of sexual identity; in anthropology, it is patriarchy as it operates through kinship structures across a wide range of different societies. The parameters of modern discussions are set to a substantial extent by the history of debates in the late nineteenth and early twentieth centuries, when marxism, psychoanalysis and anthropology were in process of formation (Coward, 1983). As a result, there is a considerable problem of articulation between different accounts of patriarchy, which surfaces in the tension between materialist and psychoanalytic accounts in feminist theory (*see* ANTHROPOLOGY AND CROSS-CULTURAL ANALYSIS; MATERIALIST CRITIQUE OF PSYCHOANALYSIS). While anthropological and marxist feminists have often accused psychoanalysis of positing timeless universal structures of human experience, neglecting history, culture and society, the psychoanalytic perspective in turn may see materialist accounts as economist or reductive, *reducing* PSYCHICAL REALITY to the mere reflection of external, material and historical circumstances.

The theory of patriarchy which re-launched the concept for specifically feminist purposes was put forward by Kate Millett in 1969. This was a general theory which sketched out the dominance of men in all areas of social, cultural and political life. Arguments soon developed about the status of patriarchy as an analytic category, and its relation to marxist categories such as capitalism and class (for a review of the arguments, see Barrett, 1981; Walby, 1990). A debate arose over priority: was it class or GENDER that had analytic primacy? Patriarchy as an explanatory concept was rejected by many feminists, for several reasons: it was seen as an ahistorical explanation; it appeared to posit 'woman' as a universal category, irrespective of differences of class, race or ethnicity; it appeared to be a form of ESSENTIALISM or biological determinism. The apparent universality and inevitability of patriarchy seemed to put men's domination of women into the category of the immutable and natural, rather than that of the socially variable and constructed. In addition, early feminist theories of patriarchy tended to posit a single explanatory principle or cause for women's oppression, whether this was the institution of HETEROSEXUALITY (Adrienne Rich), the BIOLOGY of reproduction (Shulamith Firestone) or RAPE (Susan Brownmiller). In response it was argued that because of their position *within* patriarchy, it was impossible for women to get outside it to assess whether sexual differences played a causal role in the establishment of patriarchy or whether they were produced by it, so that the quest for the ultimate origin of patriarchy was doomed to failure.

The problems of theorizing patriarchy led to attempts to develop more sophisticated accounts, initially dual systems theory, which treated capitalism and patriarchy as co-existent but analytically independent, followed by attempts to offer more complex models with a larger number of causal elements. Sylvia Walby (1990), for example, has argued that there are six main structures constituting a patriarchal system; paid work, housework, SEXUALITY, culture, violence and the state. Psychoanalytic theory, on this account, deals with only one aspect of patriarchy, specifically the reproduction and perpetuation of patriarchy in the UNCONSCIOUS (an aspect which is no more than a subset of Walby's third structure, sexuality).

While arguments about the status of patriarchy as a concept were being extensively debated by radical feminists on the one hand and socialist feminists on the other, the status of psychoanalysis as an explanatory theory was also in process of modification. Psychoanalysis had originally been seen by Kate Millett as a version of patriarchal IDEOLOGY. Although she accepted that this was so partly despite Freud's intentions, and recognized the potentially revolutionary nature of his discoveries about the human psyche, she argued that, in practice, psychoanalysis provided ideological support for the forces of conservatism, particularly in the USA. For example, Freud's account of the evolution of human society equates the (hypothetical) transition from matriarchy to patriarchy with the advent of civilization. He saw matriarchy as an inferior form of social organization (see Freud, 1913, 1939; Spreng-nether, 1990 gives a recent feminist discussion of Freud's patriarchal bias.)

Leaving aside Freud's excursions into evolutionary theory, however, the term 'patriarchy' in most recent feminist accounts of psychoanalysis has come to take on a quite precise meaning: the internalized law of the (Symbolic) father and the oedipal structure of human subjectivity. To put it in Lacanian terms, it is the necessity for the phallic signifier and the name-of-the-father in the maintenance of the SYMBOLIC order and the defence against psychosis. The re-consideration of psychoanalysis by feminism came about largely through Lacan's re-reading of Freud (see LACAN). Both Juliet MITCHELL in Britain and Luce IRIGARAY in France drew on Lacanian theory, whether to confront the rejection of psycho-analysis by feminism or to use it as a feminist resource (see also KRISTEVA). Lacan's theory paradoxically suggests at one and the same time (a) that sexual identities are the result of a process of construction and are not naturally or biologically given, so that identities formed in patriarchy are a construct, and thus, in theory, modifiable; and (b) that each individual has to insert him- or herself into a Symbolic order which already exists, so that the possibility of modifying patriarchy is so mini-mal as to be virtually non-existent. This contradiction has dominated discussions in feminist psychoanalytic theory since the 1970s.

Mitchell (1974) argued that psychoanalysis provides an invaluable description of the mechanisms by which patriarchy perpetuates itself, but also that the law of the father in unconscious structures is the pre-condition of human society itself. She thus appears to reproduce the Lacanian contradiction, arguing both that the OEDIPUS COMPLEX is the only entry into human culture, so that patriarchy is universal, co-exten-sive with human history, and also that we can overthrow patriarchy (in its other meaning, perhaps, of social and political domination by men?). In so far as Mitchell located capitalism at the economic level and patri-archy at the ideological level, leaving out the question of a possible material base for patriarchal relations, she was putting forward a ver-sion of dual systems theory, which once more raises the question of the relationship between the two systems. Irigaray (1985) analyses the unconscious historical and cultural determinants of psychoanalytic dis-course. Her approach is more radical than Mitchell's, in that she chal-lenges the necessity of the monolithic law of the father. She evades the problems of the dual systems approach by focusing entirely on the Symbolic order, suspending the question of the articulation of symbolic and material, which is then left untheorized, as in Mitchell's account. Given the polarizations in which the patriarchy debate has developed, this has meant that her work has been interpreted by materialist feminists as essentialist, but the problems of her theory lie elsewhere: in the impossibility of finding a position *outside* patriarchy from which to contest it; the contradiction of challenging patriarchy from within (which seems to promise psychosis rather than a different order); and the unimaginable transition to a new Symbolic order.

Some feminists have seen Lacanian theory as a reiteration of the inevitability of patriarchy. The patriarchal Symbolic order seems to be the condition of sanity, and the role of the PHALLUS seems therefore impossible to challenge (see Rose, 1986). Others have optimistically suggested that the relation between the primacy of the phallus in the Symbolic order and the domination of women by men in social and economic terms is a contingent relation: there may be no necessary and inevitable link between the two (Ragland-Sullivan, 1986; possibly Mitchell, 1974). Yet others have questioned the domination of the phallic signifier and considered the possibility that we might have more than one symbolic economy (Irigaray). The articulation of materialist and psychoanalytic accounts of patriarchy is a continuing issue.

BIBLIOGRAPHY

Barrett, Michèle, 1981: *Women's Oppression Today: Problems in Marxist Feminist Analysis*. London: Verso.
Coward, Rosalind, 1983: *Patriarchal Precedents: Sexuality and Social Relations*. London: Routledge and Kegan Paul.
Freud, Sigmund, 1913: *Totem and Taboo*, SE, 13, pp. 1–164.
Freud, Sigmund, 1939: *Moses and Monotheism*, SE, 23, pp. 1–138.
Irigaray, Luce, 1985 [1974]: Speculum of the *Other Woman*, trans. Gillian C. Gill. Ithaca, NY: Cornell University Press.
Millett, Kate 1970: *Sexual Politics*. New York: Doubleday.
Mitchell, Juliet, 1974: *Psychoanalysis and Feminism*. London: Allen Lane.
Pateman, Carole, 1988: *The Sexual Contract*. Cambridge: Polity Press.
Patriarchy Conference, 1978: *Papers on Patriarchy*. Brighton: PDC and Women's Publishing Collective.
Ragland-Sullivan, Ellie, 1986: *Jacques Lacan and the Philosophy of Psychoanalysis*. Urbana and Chicago: University of Illinois Press.
Rose, Jacqueline, 1986: *Sexuality in the Field of Vision*. London: Verso.
Sprengnether, Madelon, 1990: *The Spectral Mother: Freud, Feminism and Psychoanalysis*. Ithaca, NY: Cornell University Press.
Walby, Sylvia, 1990: *Theorizing Patriarchy*. Oxford: Basil Blackwell.

MARGARET WHITFORD

penis envy The concept of penis envy (*Penisneid*) occupied an extremely important place in Freud's account of the development of

FEMININITY. Most importantly, it was used by him to explain what he believed was the little girl's relinquishment of her PRE-OEDIPAL attachment to the mother, together with her renunciation of the clitoris as an erotogenic zone in preference for the arguably more passive vagina (this entails the cessation of masturbatory activity), and the replacement of her infantile NARCISSISM with a lasting feeling of inferiority. First mentioned by Freud in 'On the sexual theories of children' (1908), penis envy was allied to his theory of the little girl's CASTRATION COMPLEX in 'On narcissism' (1914). Freud later argued that this discovery of castration – or anatomical LACK – forces the little girl into the OEDIPUS COMPLEX and DESIRE for the paternal penis. Yet 'normal' femininity is only fully established if the wish for a male child replaces the desire for the father's penis (see 'On the transformation of instinct, as exemplified in anal erotism' (1917). If this substitution did not occur, Freud believed there were two other possible responses: either the girl will develop as sexually inhibited and neurotic; or, if she does not relinquish her first wish to grow into a boy, she will develop a 'masculinity complex' (Freud, 1931).

Some of the most influential of early reactions to Freud's theory appeared in the 1920s and 1930s; HORNEY, DEUTSCH, KLEIN and JONES all variously took issue with Freud's notion of penis envy. Deutsch (1944) questioned the extent to which the pre-oedipal attachment to the mother was relinquished by the little girl (in fact, this was a view which Freud himself seemed prepared to reconsider near the end of his career). Horney (1967) attacked the Freudian fatalism which presented penis envy as inevitable. She saw the male attribution of penis envy to women as a consequence of both fear of women and envy of their reproductive power. Klein argued in 1928 that it was the deprivation of the breast, rather than the discovery of her lack of a penis, which first turned the little girl against the mother and towards the father (Klein, 1988a). Later, in 1957, tracing penis envy back to the child's original envy of the mother's breast, Klein stressed the oral nature of the little girl's desire (Klein, 1988b). Jones (1948) also challenged the assumption that penis envy was a primary symptom, that which drives the little girl into femininity.

The theory of female penis envy was a crucial factor in the initial rejection of Freud and psychoanalysis by the Anglo-American feminism of the early 1970s, after Freud was denounced as 'counterrevolutionary' in Millett's *Sexual Politics* (1969, pp. 176–208). But MITCHELL (1974) helped to change feminist attitudes to the term by stressing its relationship to a PSYCHICAL REALITY: 'we are talking not about an anatomical organ, but about the ideas of it that people hold and live by' (p. xvi). This re-interpretation of penis envy was influenced by the work of LACAN, who re-defined the distinction between the sexes in terms, not of the presence or absence of the penis, but of the subject's relation to the PHALLUS (a distinction between the anatomical organ and its symbolic equivalent is indeed implicit in Freud's reference to the girl's acceptance of a baby as a substitute penis). Lacan (1977) defined the phallus as a signifier of DESIRE (in its relation to lack) which, by implication, neither sex possesses. But several later feminist critiques of Lacan's work have argued that the male continues to enjoy a special relationship to this privileged, albeit symbolic, term.

Although their perspective differs from that of Lacanian feminists, some feminist psychoanalysts (e.g. Chasseguet-Smirgel, 1970; Chodorow, 1978; Torok, 1970) have also defended penis envy as necessary, in order to enable the little girl to separate from the mother. More influential in feminist circles recently, however, has been emphasis on the inconsistencies of a theory of femininity *erected* on the desire *to be like a man*. Yet such critiques may be said to repeat the ESSENTIALISM of early opposition to Freud's theory of femininity. IRIGARAY states that penis envy guarantees a phallocentric 'law of the same' which attempts to eliminate the threat of SEXUAL DIFFERENCE. She sees the masculine 'allegation' of female penis envy as a response to the gaping 'nothing to see' of the female genitals; that is, as an attempt by men to accord a privileged value to the penis and to deny the possibility of woman having any other desire (1985, pp. 55–60). Kofman too attributes the charge of penis envy to men's horror of the female organs. She argues that in Freud, an appeal to biology always conceals what is most suspect in his work (indeed, it has been suggested that penis envy allows Freudian theory to become complete by projecting its own incompleteness upon woman; Jacobus, 1986). For Kofman (1985), penis envy asserts a universal *rejection* of femininity rather than the means to its 'normal' expression.

BIBLIOGRAPHY

Chasseguet-Smirgel, Janine, 1970: 'Feminine guilt and the oedipus complex', *Female Sexuality*, ed. J. Chasseguet-Smirgel, pp. 94–134. Ann Arbor: University of Michigan Press.

Chodorow, Nancy, 1978: *The Reproduction of Mothering: Psychoanalysis and the Sociology of Gender*. Berkeley: University of California Press.

Deutsch, Helene, 1944: *The Psychology of Women*. New York: Grune and Stratton.

Freud, Sigmund, 1908: 'On the sexual theories of children', *SE*, 9, pp. 205–26.

Freud, Sigmund, 1914: 'On narcissism', *SE*, 14, pp. 67–102.

Freud, Sigmund, 1917: 'On the transformation of instinct, as exemplified in anal erotism', *SE*, 17, pp. 125–34.

Freud, Sigmund, 1931: 'Female sexuality', *SE*, 21, pp. 221–43.

Horney, Karen, 1967: *Feminine Psychology*. London: Routledge and Kegan Paul.

PERSONAL/AUTOBIOGRAPHICAL CRITICISM

Irigaray, Luce, 1985 [1974]: *Speculum of the Other Woman*, trans. Gillian C. Gill. Ithaca, NY: Cornell University Press.

Jacobus, Mary, 1986: *Reading Woman: Essays in Feminist Criticism*. London: Methuen.

Jones, Ernest, 1948: 'Early female sexuality', *Papers on Psychoanalysis*, pp. 485–95. London: Ballière, Tindall and Cox.

Klein, Melanie, 1988a [1928]: 'Early stages of the oedipus conflict', *Love, Guilt and Reparation and other works 1921–1945*, pp. 186–98. London: Virago.

Klein, Melanie, 1988b [1957]: 'Envy and gratitude', *Envy and Gratitude and Other Works 1944–1963*, pp. 176–235. London: Virago.

Kofman, Sarah, 1985: *The Enigma of Woman: Woman in Freud's Writings*, trans. Catherine Porter. Ithaca, New York: Cornell University Press.

Lacan, Jacques, 1977: 'The signification of the phallus', *Écrits: A Selection*, trans. Alan Sheridan. London: Tavistock, pp. 281–91.

Millett, Kate, 1969: *Sexual Politics*. London: Abacus.

Mitchell, Juliet, 1974: *Psychoanalysis and Feminism*. London: Allen Lane.

Torok, Maria, 1970: 'The significance of penis envy in women', *Female Sexuality*, ed. Janine Chasseguet-Smirgel. Ann Arbor: University of Michigan Press, pp. 135–70.

PHILIPPA BERRY

personal/autobiographical criticism Historically, feminist theory has built out from the personal: the witnessing 'I' of subjective experience. The notion of the 'authority of experience' founded a central current in feminist theory in the 1970s and continues – dismantled and renovated – to shape a variety of theoretical discourses in the 1990s. If one of the original premises of 1970s activist feminism, emerging out of 1960s slogans, was that 'the personal is the political', 1980s critical feminism has made it possible to see that the personal is also the theoretical.

In the 1970s, however, academic women in the USA did not locate their writing in that autobiographical ground. In literary studies, the works of pioneering critics like Kate Millett, Elaine Showalter, Sandra Gilbert and Susan Gubar, Annette Kolodny and Judith Fetterley were clearly fuelled by a profound understanding of the intellectual and political consequences that follow from taking the personal as an epistemological category and the experience of gender politics as an analytic one. But working within the university system, they translated those subjective insights, as did most feminists of that generation, into the 'objective' academic prose PhDs are trained to produce.

By the early 1980s, with the growing recognition of feminist scholarship as a body of knowledge with a vast literature of its own, and the 'theory' frenzy that affected most academic writing, this self-neutralization became a protocol. Academic women wanting jobs and tenure conformed to the critical plausibility of their scene and cohort, which required an objective style. At the same time, however, experiments in autobiographical or personal criticism were also taking place and came to compose a contrapuntal voice in dialogue with the newly authorized discourse. Rich (1979) is the key precursor figure here. This polemical, overtly political and often anecdotal criticism, which was visibly shaped by the intensity of personal experience, tended to occur in occasional writing: for feminist sponsored sessions at professional meetings, at Women's Studies conferences, in feminist anthologies, newsletters, etc.

Getting personal in criticism typically involves a deliberate gesture of self-figuration, an autobiographical performance in writing, although the degree and form of disclosure necessarily vary widely in style and tone: at one end of the scale, one might place, for instance, Barbara Johnson's 'Gender theory and the Yale school' – her third-person walk-on part from the authorizing groves of professional life; at the other, a fully elaborated critical narrative like Rachel M. Brownstein's ironic reading-memoir, *Becoming a Heroine*, Jane Tompkins's manifesto for a 'new personalism', 'Me and my shadow', or Eve Kosofsky Sedgwick's mixed genre, erotic self-portrait 'A poem is being written'.

But are autobiographical and personal criticism the same thing? Caws (1990) argues that this 'participation in the subject seen and written about' does not necessarily require autobiographical self-representation (p. 2); its defining feature entails the mixing of text and critic, and the marking of that interaction in voice, tone, and attitude. DuPlessis (1990) describes a practice, her own, that combines both Caws's sense of personal criticism and Miller's (1991) of autobiographical acts: essays, she writes, 'in which elements of guarded, yet frank autobiography, textual analysis, and revisionary myth-making suddenly fused into a demanding voice, with a mix of ecstatic power over cultural materials and mourning for the place of the female in culture' (p. viii). Autobiographical or personal, this mode of criticism, by its displacement of boundaries and its demands on the reader, raises crucial questions about GENDER and the constitution of cultural authority.

Personal criticism takes many forms: self-narrative woven into critical argument, like Alice Walker's revision of Woolf through her daughter's eye in 'One child of one's own' (1983); the interleaving of autobiographical and political analysis like Carolyn Heilbrun's 'Woman as outsider' (1979) or Marianne Hirsch's daughter/mother introduction to *The Mother/Daughter Plot* (1990); the insertion of framing or interstitial material, like Jane Gallop's *Thinking Through the Body* (1988). Personal criticism may mean liminal or punctuating self-portrayal, along the lines of Barthes's 'biographeme', volatile signifiers of a recollected but dispersed biographical subject: Naomi Schor's prefatory invocation of her father's craft in *Reading in Detail* (1987). Experiments in form like DuPlessis's feminist classic 'For the Etruscans' (1990), or Patricia Williams's (1989) montage of personal and legal anecdote, 'On being the object of property' also depend on the expanded cultural material engendered by these autobiographical critical acts – as does the full-scale interdigitation of personal and theoretical arguments that characterizes Carolyn Steedman's auto- and biographical *Landscape for a Good Woman* (1987) and Miller's *Getting Personal* (1991). Finally, autobiographical criticism has produced entire collections of cultural criticism articulated through personal narrative like Bell Hooks's *Talking Back* (1989).

Why personal criticism now? Is it another form of 'anti-theory'? Is it a new stage of theory? Is it gendered? Only for women and gay men? Is it bourgeois? postmodern? post-feminist? Like the study of autobiography, the efflorescence of personal criticism in the United States in the 1980s has in part to do with the gradual, and perhaps inevitable waning of enthusiasm for a mode of theory whose authority – however variously – depended on the theoretical evacuation of the very social subjects producing it.

More specifically, the autobiographical mode in criticism joins and supports a renewed attention in contemporary cultural studies to the category of the SUBJECT: the pressure for more complex modulations of agency, capable of articulating the internal contradictions of subjectivity in a post-colonial and postmodern era. These new configurations have given rise in the United States both to 'identity politics' (collective movement-building based on the ground of a shared, often oppressed identity like the women's movement, the movement for civil rights, or gay and lesbian liberation) and its repudiation. For if 'identity politics' has challenged bourgeois universalist self-representation with all its unselfconscious exclusions, the micro-narratives of political self-consciousness have proved to be equally problematic self-identifications when they succumb to the lure of predictable positional discourses. Indeed, one of the reasons for the current proliferation of autobiographical criticism may well derive from a *crisis of representativity*: from a *positional* anxiety about speaking *as* and speaking *for* that doubles the postmodern crisis of REPRESENTATION.

To the extent that one of feminism's principal subjects has been an interrogation of the production of knowledge as a highly contextual activity, it is not surprising that the personalization of cultural analysis should emerge so massively out of its zones of inquiry. This of course does not mean either that only women, only feminist women, or all feminists do personal criticism; rather, that the material is there as well as a history of praxis. Feminist autobiographics (see Friedman, 1989) often entails the apparent paradox of self-representation (and ego formation) imbricated within a community: the figures of the female 'I' passed through a collective self-consciousness, like Gloria Anzaldúa's 'La Prieta' (1983) and Cherríe Moraga's 'La Guëra' (1983) which delineate a radicalized subjectivity linking women across cultural divides.

By the vulnerability of its self-location, personal criticism embodies a pact that what is at stake to one matters also to others: somewhere in the self-fiction of the personal voice is a belief that the writing is worth the risk. In this sense, by turning its authorial voice into spectacle, personal writing theorizes the stakes of its own performance: marking the cost of connection. The embarrassment this spectacle produces in readers is a sign that the performance is working. At the same time the embarrassment blows the cover of the impersonal as a masquerade of self-effacement, and points to the narcissistic FANTASY that inheres in the poses of self-sufficiency we identify with THEORY; notably, those of abstraction (*see* NARCISSISM).

To its detractors, the autobiographical act in criticism can seem to belong to the purview of privileged selves who get to call themselves and each other by their first names in print: an institutionally authorized exhibitionism. But this is to reduce a phenomenon of tremendous diversity in its aetiology, aims and practices to a specific symptomology (see Gallop's discussion, 1988, p. 4). At its best, the personal in these texts resists the seductive grandiosity of not only individual but collective self-display: group narcissism.

As a gesture of resistance these autobiographical acts may produce a new repertoire for feminist analysis and psychoanalysis in the decades to come. While doing research in the late 1960s about the persecution of the Jews in the Netherlands, the Dutch historian Jacques Presser coined the term 'egodocuments' to describe 'those documents in which a self intentionally reveals or conceals itself' (1979, p. 286). The term was subsequently adopted by feminists working with the research models of the International Women's Archives, and historian Mineke Bosch offers this definition of its range: 'all kinds of documents [diaries, autobiographies, memoirs, scrapbooks and personal letters] in which women present themselves as subjects, mostly in the first person' (1987, p. 166). In its movement towards self-representation, autobiographical criticism can be understood both as the 'egodocuments' of contemporary criticism's archives as well as more material for the history of feminist subjectivities.

See also LITERARY AND TEXTUAL CRITICISM; LITERATURE; MEN IN FEMINISM; OBJECT-RELATIONS THEORY; POSTMODERNISM.

PERSONAL/AUTOBIOGRAPHICAL CRITICISM

BIBLIOGRAPHY

Anzaldúa, Gloria, 1983: 'La Prieta', *This Bridge Called My Back: Writings by Radical Women of Color*, ed. Cherríe Moraga and Gloria Anzaldúa. New York: Kitchen Table: Women of Color Press, pp. 198–209.

Bosch, Mineke, 1987: 'A woman's life in a soapbox', *History Workshop: A Journal of Socialist and Feminist Historians*, 24, pp. 166–70.

Brownstein, Rachel M., 1982: *Becoming a Heroine: Reading about Women in Novels*. New York: Viking Press.

Caws, Mary Ann, 1990: *Women of Bloomsbury: Virginia, Vanessa, and Carrington*. New York and London: Routledge.

DuPlessis, Rachel Blau, 1990: 'For the Etruscans', *The Pink Guitar: Writing as Feminist Practice*. New York and London: Routledge, pp. 1–19.

Friedman, Susan Stanford, 1989: 'Women's autobiographical selves: theory and practice', *The Private Self: Theory and Practice of Women's Autobiographical Writings*, ed. Shari Benstock. Chapel Hill and London: University of North Carolina Press, pp. 34–62.

Gallop, Jane, 1988: *Thinking Through the Body*. New York: Columbia University Press.

Heilbrun, Carolyn, 1979: 'Woman as outsider', *Reinventing Womanhood*. New York: Norton, pp. 37–70.

Hirsch, Marianne, 1990: *The Mother/Daughter Plot: Narrative, Psychoanalysis, Feminism*. Bloomington: Indiana University Press.

Hooks, Bell, 1989: *Talking Back: Thinking Feminist, Thinking Black*. Boston: South End Press.

Johnson, Barbara, 1987: 'Gender theory and the Yale school', *A World of Difference*. Baltimore: Johns Hopkins University Press, pp. 32–41.

Miller, Nancy K., 1991: *Getting Personal: Feminist Occasions and Other Autobiographical Acts*. New York and London: Routledge.

Moraga, Cherríe, 1983: 'La Güera', *This Bridge Called My Back: Writings by Radical Women of Color*, ed. Cherríe Moraga and Gloria Anzaldúa. New York: Kitchen Table: Women of Color Press, pp. 27–34.

Presser, Jacques, 1979: *Uit het werk van dr. J. Presser*, ed. M. C. Brands (unpublished trans. Anneke Smelik). Amsterdam: Athenaeum Polak and van Gennep.

Rich, Adrienne, 1979: 'Vesuvius at home: the power of Emily Dickinson', *On Lies, Secrets, and Silence*. New York: Norton, 1979, pp. 157–84.

Schor, Naomi, 1987: *Reading in Detail: Aesthetics and the Feminine*. New York: Methuen.

Sedgwick, Eve Kosofsky, 1987: 'A poem is being written', *Representations*, 17, pp. 110–43.

Steedman, Carolyn Kay, 1987: *Landscape for a Good Woman: A Story of Two Lives*. New Brunswick: Rutgers University Press.

Tompkins, Jane, 1989: 'Me and my shadow', *Gender and Theory: Dialogues on Feminist Criticism*, ed. Linda Kauffman. New York and Oxford: Blackwell, pp. 121–39.

Walker, Alice, 1983: 'One child of one's own', *In Search of Our Mothers' Gardens*. San Diego: Harcourt Brace Jovanovich, pp. 361–83.

Williams, Patricia, 1989: 'On being the object of property', *Feminist Theory in Practice and Process*, ed. Micheline R. Malson, Jean F. O'Barr, Sarah Westphal-Wihl, and Mary Wyer. Chicago: University of Chicago Press, pp. 274–94.

NANCY K. MILLER

perversion   If, after Foucault's institutional deconstruction of the history of SEXUALITY, the whole late nineteenth-century epistemology of perversion has become suspect, then within feminist psychoanalysis it has become doubly so. Depending as it does on heterosexually prescriptive distinctions between 'normal' and 'deviant', the term itself may have become an anachronism, particularly in gay and lesbian studies. Though certain erotic practices traditionally coded as perverse (say, lesbian sadomasochism) may continue to be classified as such in so far as they constitute a transgressive counter-discourse to 'straight' sexuality or refer to mock gender performances (transvestism, strap-on dildos) that release the SUBJECT from the confines of repressive sex roles, it is none the less unclear whether gender-revisionist psychoanalysis really needs a clinical definition of perversion in its lexicon. Perhaps the term will endure most successfully as a synonym for sexual subversion, for that recuperation of the 'deviant' which positively re-inscribes the Latin root *pervertere*, meaning 'to twist', 'to turn the wrong way'. Certainly this recuperation would in its turn represent a deviation from the meaning originally operative in Freudian theory. 'Deviation from the instinct', understood in strangely temporal terms as 'lingering', extended fore-pleasure, or the deferral of coitus, emerges as the common denominator of perversion in the *Three Essays on the Theory of Sexuality* (Freud, 1905).

Within the early history of psychoanalysis the gendering of perversion helped to consolidate the type-casting of masculine and feminine identities already put into place by centuries of socially inculcated religious and domestic values. In conformity with class- and culture-bound norms women were habitually diagnosed as hysterical, maniacal, neurotic, frigid, sapphic, narcissistic, melancholic or psychotic – anything, it would seem, but perverse. Case histories of fetishism, masochism and sadism, from Richard von Krafft-Ebing's *Psychopathia sexualis* (1886) to Freud's essay 'Fetishism' (1927), typically featured male analysands. The protagonist of Sacher-Masoch's *Venus in Furs* was not Wanda, the dominatrix, but Leopold, the male masochist who, though whipped and trodden on by a woman, remained empowered in so far as it was he who authorized the conditions of his own bondage and enslavement.

311

And it is of course well known that Freud in his late essay 'Femininity' identified 'feminine traits' in the male with masochism, whereas the same behaviour in women – passivity, self-destruction – was construed as a woman's essential nature ('masochism, as people say, is truly feminine', wrote Freud: 1932, p. 102). Where evidence of female perversion was adduced – as when Lacan's teacher Gaëtan Gatian de Clérambault documented the masturbatory fantasies of lady silk fetishists in 1908 – there was a curious insistence on calling it something else. As if protecting some exclusive male prerogative, Clérambault maintained that his female fetishists, lacking the imagination of their male counterparts, were incapable of semanticizing the cloth so that it stood in for an imagined love-connection. Worshipped by women only for its instrumental value as a vehicle of orgasm, the piece of cloth failed, in Clérambault's terms, as a fetish. The exclusion of the female pervert in psychoanalytic history would hardly seem to be an issue worth quibbling over were it not for the fact that such omissions pandered to a tendentious depreciation of the feminine erotic Imaginary typical of the male medical establishment at the turn of the century. The reduction of female desire to the omnibus 'penis envy' serves as another example of this phallocentric bias (*see* FETISHISM; MASOCHISM; PENIS ENVY).

The issue at stake in Clérambault's case histories, namely, the GENDER of the perverse subject, itself rests on the larger problem of the interpretability of sexual objects, a problem lying at the heart of how the perversions have historically been defined and ordered in relation to each other. According to the Freudian classification, perversions such as paedophilia, autoerotism and necrophilia may be identified by the way in which the clinical subject manipulates another human being as object or instrument of JOUISSANCE. In the case of fetishism, transvestism and zoophilia, inanimate or non-human objects, living parts of the body treated as dead or partial objects substituted for the whole are 'surinvested' (overvalued) to the exclusion of all other targets of DESIRE (Freud, 1905, p. 16). The dismantled, dismembered body (Lacan's *corps morcelé*) is preferred to the integral or totalized corpus because it presents, as it were, a BODY composed of prosthetic parts (already split or symbolically castrated) rather than a body at risk of phallic loss. In each of these instances the choice of love-object is neither arbitrary nor convertible. Functioning as an ambient fetish or prosthesis, figured as an *idée fixe*, this object-type both motivates the fantasm and directs the questing path of the subject of perversion.

Within a Lacanian framework Freud's notion of the idealized surrogate PHALLUS ('Such substitutes are with some justice likened to the fetishes in which savages believe that their gods are embodied'; 1905, p. 18) is interpreted as an antidote to the *béance* or gaping wound (opening around the splitting of the ego) qualified by LACAN as LACK (*manque à être*). Like Clérambault's erotomaniac, who firmly believes that he *is* what is lacking in the Other (*objet a*), the perverse subject, in *being* lack, falls for the ontological illusion of his or her own 'lacklessness'. It is the credulity of the subject rather than his or her misguided sexual aim which qualifies as perverse. Though Lacan's model eschews gender restriction (both sexes can *be* lack), the definition of perverse object relations becomes more complicated in the matter of female fetishism *qua* maternal cathexis.

Idealization of object and instinct emerge as particularly significant processes in Freudian and post-Freudian theories of perversion. Claiming in 'Three essays' that the perversions were related through their 'idealization of the instinct', Freud identified as critical that juncture where 'the sexual instinct goes to astonishing lengths in successfully overcoming the resistance to shame, disgust, horror or pain' (1905, p. 27). This argument confirms what is held to be the *regressive* or archaizing impulse manifest in the (male) subject's putative harkening back to the last moment at which the mother could be regarded as phallic. The arresting of development at the anal erotic stage accounts, in Freud's scheme, for 'bestial' conduct: walking on all fours, coprophilia or the infantilism produced by masochistic rituals of humiliation and subjection. For feminism this concept of regression is particularly problematic since women, tenuously acculturated as subjects of history and typically assigned the PRE-OEDIPAL even within feminist psychoanalysis, have long been implicitly infantilized.

In addition to challenging fundamental tenets of phallocentric psychoanalysis, feminism may be shifting the parameters of what qualifies as perverse. Whereas traditionally attention has been devoted to determining the epistemological boundaries between, for example, sadism and masochism (is the sadist a masochist because he or she desires the slave's desire for pain?), scopophilia and sadism (producing the hybrid 'love of looking at cruelty') or fetishism and voyeurism (both depend on an aroused, fixating gaze), RAPE, abuse, incest and other forms of violence readily forked over to psychiatry and law may now increasingly come to be theorized psychoanalytically as forms of perversion.

See also SADOMASOCHISM; VOYEURISM/EXHIBITIONISM/THE GAZE.

BIBLIOGRAPHY

Adams, Parveen, 1989: 'Of female bondage', *Between Feminism and Psychoanalysis*, ed. Teresa Brennan. New York and London: Routledge, pp. 247–85.
Bonnet, Gérard, 1983: *Les perversions sexuelles*. Paris: Presses Universitaires de France.

313

PHALLIC MOTHER

Chasseguet-Smirgel, Janine, 1984: *Éthique et esthétique de la perversion.* Seyssel: Éditions du Champ Vallon.

Clavreul, Jean, 1980: 'The perverse couple', *Returning to Freud: Clinical Psychoanalysis in the School of Lacan*, ed. Stuart Schneiderman. New Haven: Yale University Press, pp. 215–33.

Ellis, Havelock, 1905–42: *Studies in the Psychology of Sex.* New York: Random House.

Freud, Sigmund, 1905: 'Three essays on the theory of sexuality', *SE*, 7, pp. 125–248.

Freud, Sigmund, 1927: 'Fetishism', *SE*, 21, pp. 147–58.

Freud, Sigmund, 1932: 'Femininity', *SE*, 22, pp. 112–35.

Kaplan, Louise J., 1991: *Female Perversions: The Temptations of Emma Bovary.* New York: Doubleday.

Krafft-Ebing, Richard von, 1965 [1886]: *Psychopathia sexualis*, trans. Harry E. Wedeck. New York: G. P. Putnam's Sons.

Lacan, Jacques, 1975: *Le Séminaire,* book 11. Paris: Seuil.

Lanteri Laura, Georges, 1979: *Lecture des perversions.* Paris: Masson.

McDougall, Joyce, 1980: *A Plea for a 'Measure of Abnormality.* New York: International Universities Press.

Masson, Jeffrey Mossaieff, 1986: *A Dark Science: Women, Sexuality and Psychiatry in the Nineteenth Century.* New York: Farrar, Straus and Giroux.

Rosolato, Guy, 1967: *Le Désir et la perversion.* Paris: Seuil.

SAMOIS, ed. 1982: *Coming to Power.* Boston, Mass.: Alyson.

Stekel, Wilhelm, 1971: *Sexual Aberrations.* New York: Liveright.

EMILY APTER

phallic mother   The PRE-OEDIPAL, phallic or archaic mother must be understood as a FANTASY – the child's fantasy of an omnipotent and absolutely powerful, sexually neutral figure. Freud argues that the child (presumably the boy) bestows on the mother what he attributes to himself. It is not simply that the boy accords the mother a genital organ similar to his own, although this is confirmed in the case study of Little Hans (Freud, 1909). Both sexes accord the mother a quasi-omnipotent position.

The pre-oedipal child's image of and relation to the mother is an extremely complex and constantly changing one. In the earliest neo-natal months, the child has no conception of its separation or distinctness from the mother. It is only at the time of the mirror stage (*see* IMAGINARY) that the child acquires an image of the mother as a total being, a coherent union of her composite parts, separate from the child. The figure of the mother remains the most frequent object of the child's narcissistic identifications and sexual desires, providing it with an image

314

of its own corporeal integrity and an object from whom it seeks sexual gratification (see Freud, 1905, p. 222).

For the pre-oedipal period, the mother remains the major figure dominating the child's psycho-sexual development, the object to whom the child's libido is directed, and prohibitor or inhibitor of the child's sexual wishes. Negatively and positively her own unconscious desire initiates and directs the child's SEXUALITY (see Laplanche and Pontalis, 1968).

The phallic mother is the fantasy of the mother who is able to grant the child everything, to be its object of desire, and in turn, to be the SUBJECT who desires the child as her object. As a result of the OEDIPUS COMPLEX, the mother's omnipotent status is transferred to the symbolic father; she is now construed as castrated or lacking. In disappointment and disgust, the child – of either sex – turns away from her.

In spite of the phallocentrism of Freud's account, in which the mother can never be represented simply as a female subject but only in male terms, as phallic or castrated, there is something psychically crippling about the unmediated pre-oedipal mother–child relation, where each offers the other a perfect satisfaction of desire. While constitutive of the child's emerging identity as a subject, this relation is stifling and, if unmediated, induces psychosis. It is only in so far as the woman remains submerged in her maternal role, with no other means of expression of her femininity, that the mother–child relation becomes invested with all significance the mother-as-a-woman might otherwise be able to express and have confirmed in the socio-economic world of work. The child may mean everything to her, and she remain everything for the child, leaving no room for growth and independence. This all-powerful mother figure can become the basis of the persecutory images of psychoses.

See also FETISHIZATION; MOTHER–DAUGHTER RELATIONSHIP; PHALLUS: FEMINIST PERSPECTIVES.

BIBLIOGRAPHY

Freud, Sigmund, 1905: *Three Essays on the Theory of Sexuality*, SE, 7, pp. 125–248.
Freud, Sigmund, 1909: 'Analysis of a phobia in a five-year-old boy', *SE*, 10, pp. 1–149.
Freud, Sigmund, 1925: 'Some psychical consequences of the anatomical distinction between the sexes', *SE*, 19, pp. 243–60.
Laplanche, Jean, and Pontalis, Jean-Baptiste, 1968: 'Fantasy and the origins of sexuality', *International Journal of Psycho-Analysis*, 49, pp. 1–26.

ELIZABETH GROSZ

315

phallogocentrism   Phallogocentrism is a conflation of 'phallocentrism' and 'logocentrism', and hence sometimes written as 'phallologocentrism'. Terry Eagleton 'roughly translates' this concept as 'cocksureness', the mechanism by which 'those who wield sexual and social power maintain their grip' (1983, p. 189). However, this masks the complex development of a term which brings together the feminist critique of PATRIARCHY and the deconstructionist critique of LANGUAGE.

The first attestation of 'phallocentric' in the *OED* is from 1927; but it is a word that gained currency in later feminist debates, where it sometimes seems to lack a specifically psychoanalytic context. Freud himself uses the word 'phallus' infrequently; but there is no doubt that it is central to his work. IRIGARAY (1985) gives an extended critique of Freud's phallocentrism. For Freud, man is *the* procreator and the little girl is (only) a little boy; individuals of both sexes go through the first libidinal stages in the same way and are thus subject to a phallic stage, but no vulvar or vaginal stage (Irigaray, 1985, pp. 24, 25, 28, 29). In this law of the self-same, women play the negative in the phallocentric dialectic: 'Finally in Freud sexual pleasure boils down to being plus or minus one sex organ: the penis, and "sexual otherness" comes down to "not having it"' (p. 52). 'Penis envy' serves as 'an essential factor in establishing the primacy of the male organ' and in making 'the phallus necessarily the archetype for sex' (p. 58). When the male is set up as the norm and the female as the deviation from that norm, then desire between women is 'incomprehensible to Freud . . . rarely encountered in phallocentric history in which value is the prerogative of the penis and its equivalents' (p. 101) (*see* PENIS ENVY).

In LACAN the centrality of the PHALLUS is as a linguistic, not a bodily, marker. Thus in the *Écrits* phallus and logos (word, truth) are sometimes juxtaposed: 'The phallus is the privileged signifier of that mark in which the role of the logos is joined with the advent of desire'; or again, 'the function of the phallic signifier touches here on its most profound relation: that in which the Ancients embodied the Noûs and the Logos' (1977, pp. 287, 291). It is to Lacan that Derrida turns for the exemplification of phallogocentrism. However, first we must examine logocentrism itself.

The *OED*'s first attestation of 'logocentric' is from 1934. At that time it denoted a theory which ascribed the central point of reference to reason, as opposed to 'biocentrism' which treated life as the central fact. The term is now overwhelmingly associated with the early work of Jacques Derrida. In *Of Grammatology* (1976) Derrida sought to show how a number of (male) writers (Rousseau, Saussure, Lévi-Strauss) have a bias towards the logos or word as metaphysical presence. For example, Rousseau praises the plenitude and authenticity of speech, even

316

though he admits that writing permits better communication with the beloved. In its habitual logocentrism, Western thought represses writing which, being subject to difference and deferral, is a threat to the speaking voice. Logocentrism thus gives us the illusion of immediate access to full truth and presence.

Hence both phallo- and logocentrism are monolithic systems: while the former privileges the phallus as universal arbiter of SEXUALITY, the latter privileges the Word as ultimate arbiter of truth. This equation finally becomes explicit in Derrida's critique of Lacan's seminar on Poe (Derrida, 1987). For Derrida, Lacan's reading sets out to show woman as 'the unveiled site of the lack of a penis' (p. 439). And this phallocentrism is also logocentric: the purloined letter reveals 'the contact of truth with itself in logos', a truth which has woman as its vehicle (p. 442). Lacan assigns truth to the (absent) place of female sexuality and makes the phallus the transcendental signifier (p. 465). Like Rousseau, he is biased in favour of the voice and against writing which, because of its inevitable tendency to fragmentation, would threaten the unity of both phallus and signifier. What this 'phallogocentric transcendentalism' cannot tolerate is the possibility that 'the phallus [is] divisible or reduced to the status of part object'. Then 'the entire edifice would collapse' (p. 478). But is Lacan reinforcing phallogocentrism or undermining it? Derrida speculates in a footnote: 'I might be tempted to say: Freud, like those who follow him here, is only describing the necessity of phallogocentrism, only explaining its effects, which are as obvious as they are massive. Phallogocentrism is neither an accident nor an error . . . It is an old and enormous root that must be accounted for.' However, 'the "description" is a "participation" when it induces a practice, an ethics, an institution, and therefore a poltiics that ensure the truth of the tradition' (p. 481n). For Derrida, Lacan thus reproduces without question an 'ethico-institutional discourse' based on patriarchal authority and full speech.

In Linda Kauffman's recent anthology (1989) a number of contributors extend phallogocentrism to new areas. Thus James J. Sosnoski claims that traditional (male) literary criticism is 'phallo/!logocentric', based on the notion 'that readings can be objective, impersonal, and detached', a notion which must (paradoxically) be defended by deadly competition between males (Kauffman, 1989, pp. 63, 64). Alice Parker, from a lesbian point of view, contrasts phallogocentrism with the feminine tropes of the semiotic, the chora and invagination (p. 212). And finally R. Radhakrishnan adds ethnicity and the 'Third World' to the debate with the coinage 'ethno-phallogocentrism' (p. 287). Phallogocentrism thus does not merely bear witness to a point of confluence between feminism, psychoanalysis and deconstruction; it also places feminism at the forefront of other political struggles.

PHALLUS: DEFINITIONS

See also BLACK FEMINIST CRITIQUE OF PSYCHOANALYSIS; LACK; RACE/ IMPERIALISM; THEORY.

BIBLIOGRAPHY

Derrida, Jacques, 1976: *Of Grammatology.* Baltimore and London: Johns Hopkins University Press.

Derrida, Jacques, 1987: *The Post Card: From Socrates to Freud and Beyond.* Chicago and London: University of Chicago Press.

Eagleton, Terry, 1983: *Literary Theory: An Introduction.* Oxford: Basil Blackwell.

Irigaray, Luce, 1985: *Speculum of the Other Woman,* trans. Gillian C. Gill. Ithaca, NY: Cornell University Press.

Kauffman, Linda, ed. 1989: *Feminism and Institutions.* Oxford: Basil Blackwell.

Lacan, Jacques, 1977: *Écrits: A Selection,* trans. Alan Sheridan. London: Tavistock.

PAUL JULIAN SMITH

phallus: definitions   In classical antiquity, the phallus was a representation of the erect male organ and a symbol of sovereign power. In Lacanian psychoanalysis, the term 'phallus' is used to emphasize the symbolic significance taken on by the penis in intersubjectivity and in the process of accession to the SYMBOLIC. In this sense, the phallus is said to be an abstract signifier which is not to be confused with the biological organ. It is claimed that, thanks to the theory of the phallus, Lacan can offer a non-biologistic theory of SEXUAL DIFFERENCE.

Although Freud makes frequent use of the adjective 'phallic', it is rare for him to employ the substantive 'phallus' and he usually does so with reference to the symbolic phallus of antiquity (1910, p. 125; 1918, p. 204). Elsewhere, (1923), 'phallus' and 'penis' are used almost interchangeably and it is difficult to argue that any conceptual distinction is indicated or intended. Nor does Freud's analysis of the phallic stage, in which sexual difference is predicated upon the phallic–castrated distinction, lead to the elaboration of the phallus concept.

It was in the 1950s that LACAN began to elaborate his own notion of the phallus. In the 1956 Seminar on the psychoses, the phallus is initially defined as the mediating element in the CASTRATION COMPLEX, as an imaginary object which the child comes to accept as being in the father's possession (Lacan, 1981, pp. 385–9). In the later paper on the meaning of the phallus (Lacan, 1982 [1958]), it becomes the privileged signifier marking the articulation of the logos with DESIRE. In this perspective, the object of the desire of the mother is the phallus, and the child wishes to

318

be the phallus in order to satisfy that desire. Desire is articulated with LACK. The transition to the possibility of *having* a phallus is effected thanks to the intervention of the law symbolized by the name of the father and to the reference to the SYMBOLIC. The sequence inaugurated by the child's realization that the mother does not have a phallus thus becomes a structural equivalent to Freud's castration complex.

The theory of the phallus is open to criticism on a number of grounds. Perhaps for euphemistic reasons, 'phallus' was used widely – and quite indiscriminately – as an alternative to 'penis' throughout the formative period of French psychoanalysis during the interwar period, and this was also Lacan's formative period. One of Lacan's theoretical inheritances is a certain terminological confusion compounded by translation problems. Lacanian references to 'the phallus – which as Freud makes clear is not the penis' (Safouan, 1982, p. 124) must be compared with the original German, as they are often based upon the inaccurate translations of Freud made in the 1930s. In other words, what appears to be a theoretical innovation on Lacan's part can be interpreted simply as a by-product of a faulty translation. Thus, Anne Berman's French version of Freud's 'Femininity' refers to '*le désir de posséder un phallus*'; the Standard Edition renders '*der Wunsch nach dem Penis*' much more accurately as 'wish for a penis' (Freud, 1933, p. 128). Berman's translation has been used to further the argument that the phallus–penis distinction can be traced back to Freud and has his theoretical authority. Similarly, when Lacan writes (1958, p. 83) of the Kleinian 'fact' of the child's apprehension that the mother 'contains' the phallus, he is substituting 'phallus' for Klein's 'penis in the mother's body'. In this context, it is interesting to note that, in the new translation of Freud currently being prepared under the direction of Jean Laplanche, the term 'phallus' does not appear (Bourguignon et al., 1989).

Definitional problems abound, particularly in the works of Lacan's followers, who frequently refer to the phallus both as a signifier and a symbol, even though most schools of linguistics make a strict distinction between the two. In terms of the Saussurean linguistics to which Lacan allegedly owes so much, the notion of a 'privileged signifier' or of 'the signifier of signifiers' is, moreover, distinctly unhappy in that a signifier has meaning only because it is different from other signifiers. Unlike the phallus, a signifier has no value in and of itself. No signifier can be privileged over any other signifier. If the function of the phallus is to put an end to the otherwise eternal sliding of the signifier and thereby to provide a minimal stability of meaning, it can only be, as Derrida (1975) has argued, a transcendental element, the non-determined element which determines other elements in the system, or even a metaphysical construct. The phallus's privileged relationship with LANGUAGE, and even the creative logos itself, means that it readily becomes an element in the conflation of language, metaphysics and phallocentrism known as PHAL-LOGOCENTRISM.

See also PENIS ENVY; PHALLUS: FEMINIST IMPLICATIONS.

BIBLIOGRAPHY

Bourguignon, Jean; Cotet, Pierre; Laplanche, Jean; and Robert, François, 1989: *Traduire Freud*. Paris: Presses Universitaires de France.
Derrida, Jacques, 1975: 'The purveyor of truth', *Yale French Studies*, 52, pp. 31–113.
Freud, Sigmund, 1910: *Leonardo da Vinci and a Memory of his Childhood*, SE, 11, pp. 59–138.
Freud, Sigmund, 1918: 'The taboo of virginity', *SE*, 11, pp. 191–208.
Freud, Sigmund, 1923: 'The infantile genital organization: an interpolation into the theory of sexuality', *SE*, 19, pp. 141–8.
Freud, Sigmund, 1933: 'Femininity', *SE*, 22, pp. 112–35.
Lacan, Jacques, 1982 [1958]: 'The meaning of the phallus', trans. Jacqueline Rose, *Feminine Sexuality: Jacques Lacan and the École Freudienne*, ed. Juliet Mitchell and Jacqueline Rose. London: Macmillan, pp. 74–85.
Lacan, Jacques, 1981 [1955–6]: *Le Séminaire*, book 3: *Les Psychoses*. Paris: Seuil.
Safouan, Moustafa, 1982: 'Feminine sexuality in psychoanalytic doctrine', *Feminine Sexuality: Jacques Lacan and the École Freudienne*, ed. Juliet Mitchell and Jacqueline Rose. London: Macmillan, pp. 123–36.

DAVID MACEY

phallus: feminist implications   Although Freud is frequently accused of biologism, and of privileging MASCULINITY and the phallus at the expense of FEMININITY and female SEXUALITY, his position is considerably more complicated than this. While it is true that on the one hand he wants to accord the penis a symmetrical role in the development of both masculinity and femininity (in this sense, feminist accusations of phallocentrism are well justified, for he accords no analogous role to female sexuality or sexual organs in the development of both sexes); on the other hand, Freud makes it clear that the phallic status of the penis is a shared, cultural FANTASY. He distinguishes between the penis, a biological organ which men have and women do not, and the phallus, a fantasized emblem of power and sexuality that the infant commonly attributes to the mother (*see* PHALLIC MOTHER). However, Freud cannot explain how and why the girl attributes to the mother a phallic status, if by phallic anything more than 'powerful' is implied, although this may seem plausible for the boy. Why describe the mother as phallic, rather than as simply powerful? There is clearly more at stake here than any simple attribution of power or powerlessness: the crucial political question is that of who defines female sexuality, in whose hands – and mouths – the power of definition lies.

Lacan's re-reading of the notion has helped to vindicate psychoanalysis against the charges of biologism and naturalism so commonly levelled at it by feminists. LACAN acknowledges that the phallus is a signifier, not an organ; to confuse them is to conflate a Real function with a Symbolic one. Yet it is on the basis of this conflation that women are construed as castrated.

By its presence or absence (for Freud) or through its relations of having or being (for Lacan), the phallus structures the relations between the two sexes. While Lacan concedes that this equation of penis and phallus is illusory, for him this illusion is constitutive of the structure of human DESIRE and the functioning of the SYMBOLIC order (see Lacan, 1977).

The phallus is the means by which the penis becomes the defining term for both sexes. Differences between two (or more) types of genitals become converted into the presence or absence of a single (i.e. male) term. If the penis assumes the function of the phallus, this is because female sexuality is considered a mutilation. Because it is a signifier, which can only be defined with reference to an entire field or network of other signifiers and signifieds, no one has a privileged access to or possession of the phallus. It exists only through the mediation of the other and the Symbolic order. It is for this reason that Lacan claims that the relations of the two sexes to the phallus are regulated by the two forms modifying the verb: being and having.

According to Lacan, the child must master the move away from being the phallus the mother desires – her phallus – to having it (if the child is a boy) or being it for someone else (if the child is a girl). To have or be the phallus, the child must enter the Symbolic order, acquiring a place as masculine or feminine. One can neither have nor be the phallus in oneself. It is not an attribute or property of a SUBJECT: only through an other's desire for the penis can a man have his possession of the phallus confirmed; and only through another desiring her body can a woman feel as if she is the phallus. This entails the symbolic equivalence of the man's penis and the woman's whole body: they are both objects of the other's desire.

As the imaginary or detachable penis, the penis the mother once had but lost, the phallus is an object that distinguishes the sexes and marks their oppositional status. the presence or absence of the phallus designates the positions of men and women respectively. On the other hand, as a signifier, it is a term that designates the possibility of the union of the two sexes, the copula of copulation. The phallus seems to 'fill' the 'LACK' (women's 'organic' lack, as well as a more ontological lack, a lack within desire itself). The phallus is thus both the sign of SEXUAL DIFFERENCE and the signifier of the object of the other's desire. The penis takes on the function of the phallus only because that organ can signify (in fact, in order to produce) the exclusion of women. In this process, the penis is displaced from being a real organ, to becoming an imaginary (detachable, present or absent) object, possessed by some, desired by others; after oedipalization, it functions as a symbolic term (an object of union and/or exchange) between the sexes.

The distinction between penis and phallus enables Lacan to problematize Freud's biologism and to replace it with a more social, linguistic and historical account. Yet feminists cannot afford to ignore the *a priori* privileging of the masculine within his account, nor can they too readily accept Lacan's claim that the phallus is a signifier like any other. It is clear from his account that the phallus is a master signifier, the 'signifier of signifiers', the term around which all other signifiers revolve. The phallus cannot be regarded simply as a neutral term which positions both sexes within the extra-familial social field, for the effects of such positioning are very different, and the narcissistic 'wound' to the woman's body depicted by the castration fantasy is the unspoken cost of men's positions of social and sexual primacy.

Freud and Lacan have been strongly defended by a number of feminists, most notably Juliet MITCHELL and Ellie Ragland-Sullivan, who claim that psychoanalysis merely describes rather than participates in the social subordination of women. For both, it is the anchoring term which 'saves' the subject from psychosis by granting it a social position outside the incestual web of desire in the nuclear family. However, the phallus cannot be a neutral signifier, as Ragland-Sullivan and Mitchell claim; the relation between the penis and the phallus is not arbitrary but is clearly socially and politically motivated.

See also BIOLOGY; LACK; PHALLUS: DEFINITIONS; PHALLOGOCENTRISM; PRIMARY CASTRATION.

BIBLIOGRAPHY

Adams, Parveen,1990: 'Representation and sexuality', *The Woman in Question*, ed. Parveen Adams and Elizabeth Cowie. London: Verso, pp. 233–52.
Freud, Sigmund, 1924: 'The dissolution of the oedipus complex', *SE*, 19, pp. 173–82.
Freud, Sigmund, 1925: 'Some psychical consequences of the anatomical distinction between the sexes', *SE*, 19, pp. 243–60.
Freud, Sigmund, 1931: 'Female sexuality', *SE*, 21, pp. 221–46.
Freud, Sigmund, 1933: 'Femininity', *SE*, 22, pp. 112–35.

Lacan, Jacques, 1977: 'The signification of the phallus', *Écrits: A Selection*, trans. Alan Sheridan. London: Tavistock, pp. 281–91.

Mitchell, Juliet, 1974: *Psychoanalysis and Feminism*. London: Allen Lane.

Mitchell, Juliet, and Rose, Jacqueline, eds 1982: *Jacques Lacan and the École Freudienne: Feminine Sexuality*, London: Macmillan.

Ragland-Sullivan, Ellie, 1986: *Jacques Lacan and the Philosophy of Psychoanalysis*. Urbana: University of Illinois Press.

ELIZABETH GROSZ

philosophy   Psychoanalysts and feminists pose profound challenges to the self-understanding of many philosophers. A dominant tendency among philosophers since Plato has been to claim a privileged relationship to truth: the task of philosophy (according to these philosophers) is to dis-cover reality, and truth was often understood as correspondence to it. Reality exists independently of our thought about it and truthful knowledge consists of re-presentations of bits of this reality. Without the philosopher's love of wisdom (*philosophia*), clarity of consciousness or power of reason, truth cannot be made present. Postmodernists call this set of beliefs the 'metaphysics of presence' (Derrida, 1978) or philosophy as the 'mirror of nature' (Rorty, 1979).

The plausibility of this set of beliefs, along with its supporting assumptions about the nature of reality, LANGUAGE and consciousness have been weakened by a number of challenges both within and outside philosophy. Modern SCIENCE appropriated the privileged relation to reality that philosophers had long claimed. Philosophers such as Descartes and Kant attempted to re-situate and rescue philosophy's privilege by locating it within the terrain of knowledge.

The task of philosophy was to give an account of *how* truthful knowledge is possible; philosophers were to construct 'metanarratives' (the term is that of Lyotard, 1984) in and through which individual bits of knowledge are integrated into a harmonious whole and legitimated. In such 'metanarratives' philosophers claimed to have privileged insight into the nature of the SUBJECT and the proper relationship between subject and OBJECT. This insight enabled them, they believed, to warrant and adjudicate between truth claims. Philosophy was to be the queen of the sciences, for only it could account for the possibility of truth and hence provide a secure ground for distinguishing between truth and error. Philosophers still reserved the right to pass judgement on the claims to truth and legitimacy of all other forms of knowledge.

This representation of philosophy depends upon and incorporates a prior set of assumptions about the nature of reality and reason. Reality

323

is homogeneous and harmonious, ruled by unitary laws we dis-cover but do not create. Reason is also lawful and unitary; it operates identically in every subject. To operate this way, reason must be free from and opposed to empirical contingency; it cannot be affected by the historical or bodily location of the subject. The subject must have privileged insight into the operation of reason; even its limits can be known and controlled. The language in and through which reason's representations about the subject or object are conveyed must be a neutral or transparent medium. It must convey information about but not constitute subjects, objects and the truth about them.

Each of these assumptions which support and justify philosophy's 'foundational' position has been called into question by psychoanalysts and feminists. These critiques overlap with, but also differ from, those of postmodernists such as Derrida, Lyotard and Foucault. Postmodernists discuss the philosopher's desire, the nature of language and reality and the relationships between the will to truth and the will to power. However, their deconstructions of what Rorty calls 'systematic' philosophy (Rorty, 1979, ch. 8) lack psychoanalysts' complex considerations of subjectivity and feminists' nuanced analyses of GENDER and its pervasive effects (Flax, 1990).

Freud and subsequent psychoanalysts have undermined our confidence in Kantian notions of an accessible, homogeneous, unitary and universal 'pure' reason and in Cartesian notions of a mind/body split. While there are many differences among psychoanalysts, similarities can be found in the philosophies of mind they present. The subject is de-centred and its reason is pervaded by conflict, DESIRE and disunity. Mind and consciousness are no longer equivalent; mind and body are not distinct; and reason loses its privileged position in and access to knowledge of our mental life.

In Freud's view, reason is a faculty of the ego, but the ego is affected by unconscious processes and material in ways that are in principle unknowable. Parts of the ego itself can be dynamically repressed, and it can be brought to serve either the id or the superego. Furthermore, since the ego is first a 'bodily' ego, mind and body are never dichotomous. Freud and later analysts such as KLEIN and LACAN suggest that our reason is far from 'pure'; desire has a powerful and constituting effect on the will to knowledge. Children's sexual curiosity or their will to appropriate the mother's body are initiating forces in constituting an 'epistemophilic instinct' (Klein, 1975). Lacan displaces the mastery and unity of reason by presenting the subject as constituted and necessarily split by its entrance into language and its desire for the Other (see OTHER/OTHER). As conceptualized by any of these analysts, reason cannot serve as a ground of certainty or reliable methods, an accurate recorder of empirical data, or a trustworthy adjudicator of truth claims.

Philosophy's position as the 'master discourse' of truth impelled the critiques of many academic feminists. As Foucault (1980) has argued, we always operate within discursive fields. These fields are constituted in part by rules which regulate what can be said, what must be excluded and what counts as a legitimate truth claim. In attempting to find a place for feminist discourses within academic institutions or intellectual life more generally, feminists have to confront the pre-existing regimes of truth. To the extent that philosophy has a special role in generating and sustaining these regimes, feminists have had to direct attention to its privilege, content and methods. However, feminists differ on the question of a successor project, that is, whether the problem is the inadequacy and gender bias of existing philosophic standards or the very idea of a relatively neutral regime of truth.

Writers such as Sandra Harding argue that feminists have an interest in and need for epistemological standards by which truth claims can be adjudicated. She believes that the production of 'less false' knowledge is a necessary aspect of the struggle for women's emancipation and that practices informed by such knowledge will result in a lessening of the sum total of domination (Harding, 1990). Psychoanalysis is useful for this project because it identifies dilemmas common to masculine identity formation, especially within existing sexual divisions of labour in which women have primary responsibility for the care of children. These masculine dilemmas affect both the content of and the methods favoured by male-dominated philosophy, and hence their discovery by feminists can lead to less false knowledge.

Other feminists, including Flax (1990), IRIGARAY, Cixous and Clément (1986) and Le Doeuff (1987) utilize psychoanalytic and postmodernist ideas to question women's will to or desire for truth. The psychoanalytic suspicion of the rationality of reason renders the very idea of a successor project problematic. Furthermore, the postmodernist stress on the conventional nature of order and of the violence required to impose it on the disorderly flux of things inspires a wish to foreground difference, to privilege disorder over order and the marginal over any singular regime. Feminists cannot be exempt from the will to power and its effects. In their efforts to highlight the consequences of gender-based domination they necessarily exclude their complicity in regimes of power and in the construction of narratives which displace other possible stories (Hooks, 1990; Gates, 1986).

On this view, feminists have a special interest in generating discourses of difference and in rescuing difference from its inscription within philosophy and elsewhere as always the other, the deficient form of the same. In fact, the very *appearance* of neutrality, homogeneity, unity or order, whether of reason, knowledge or reality, depends upon an interdependent and simultaneous set of moves: naming women as different in relation to the true measure of humanity (men), devaluing difference, and suppressing men's dependence on and complicity in this difference. Our understanding of reason, reality or knowledge depends on what they are not, on their difference from and superiority to other faculties or experiences such as passion, dreams, imagination or embodiment. Associating women with the BODY and the particular are two of the necessary conditions for the possibility of conceptualizing a disembodied and universal faculty (e.g. the Cartesian ego or Kant's pure reason) or form of knowledge. With the contaminating effects of difference located in women suppressed or denied, reason, reality or knowledge can acquire its unitary and universal appearance.

Some feminists have responded with a strategy of disrupting and disordering any attempt to re-construct unitary master narratives, even those with a 'feminist' content. Rather than insist that women's reason can be as 'pure' as men's, it is more productive to question the belief in (or wish for) the purity of reason, the relations of power and the forms of desire that necessarily underlie and generate any order. On this view, the pathology of systematic philosophy extends beyond its 'male-ordered' contents and methods to its intolerance of ambivalence, disorder and ambiguity and its dominating and relentless desire for closure, finality and certainty. What is needed is 'a form of philosophy that no longer considers its incompleteness a tragedy' (Le Doeuff, 1987, p. 207) as a counter to the forces of order (in ourselves and elsewhere) which always and necessarily constitute a lesser other to legitimate their will to power.

See also AUTONOMY; FEMINIST HISTORY; POSTMODERNISM; THEORY.

BIBLIOGRAPHY

Braidotti, Rosi, 1991: *Patterns of Dissonance: A Study of Women in Contemporary Philosophy*. Cambridge: Polity Press.

Cixous, Hélène, and Clément, Catherine, 1986: *The Newly Born Woman*. Minneapolis: University of Minnesota Press.

Derrida, Jacques, 1978: *Writing and Difference*. Chicago: University of Chicago Press.

Di Stefano, Christine, 1991: *Configurations of Masculinity: A Feminist Perspective on Modern Political Theory*. Ithaca, NY, and London: Cornell University Press.

Flax, Jane, 1990: *Thinking Fragments: Psychoanalysis, Feminism and Postmodernism in the Contemporary West*. Berkeley: University of California Press.

Foucault, Michel, 1980: *Power/Knowledge: Selected Interviews and Other Writings, 1972–1977*. New York: Pantheon.

Gates, Henry Louis, Jr, ed. 1986: *'Race', Writing and Difference*. Chicago: University of Chicago Press.

Harding, Sandra, 1990: 'Feminism, science and the anti-Enlightenment critiques', *Feminism/Postmodernism*, ed. L. J. Nicholson. New York: Routledge, pp. 83–106.

Hooks, Bell, 1990: *Yearning: Race, Gender, and Cultural Politics*. Boston: South End Press.

Jagger, Alison M., and Bordo, Susan R., eds 1989: *Gender/Body/Knowledge: Feminist Reconstructions of Being and Knowing*. New Brunswick: Rutgers University Press.

Klein, Melanie, 1975: 'Early stages of the Oedipus conflict', *Love, Guilt and Reparation and Other Works, 1921–1945*. New York: Delta, pp. 186–98.

Le Doeuff, Michèle, 1987: 'Women and philosophy', *French Feminist Thought: A Reader*, ed. Toril Moi. New York: Basil Blackwell.

Le Doeuff, Michèle, 1991: *Hipparchia's Choice: An Essay Concerning Women, Philosophy, etc.*, trans. Trista Selons. Oxford: Basil Blackwell.

Lyotard, Jean-François, 1984: *The Postmodern Condition: A Report on Knowledge*. Minneapolis: University of Minnesota Press.

Rorty, Richard, 1979: *Philosophy and the Mirror of Nature*. Princeton: Princeton University Press.

JANE FLAX

photography   The first fully mechanical form of image production, invented nearly simultaneously in England and France in 1839, photography has special claims to the attention of feminists. Inextricably linked to the emerging commodity culture of the nineteenth century, and popularly believed to operate as a direct transcription of the real, photography has been a significant cultural agent in the production, reproduction and dissemination of IDEOLOGY, including the ideology of GENDER. In semiotic terms, the photographic image is considered to be not only iconic – a status shared with any other picture – but indexical; that is to say, bearing a causal relation to its referent, as with footprints or X-rays. It is this property of photography that makes camera pictures admissible as evidence in court or for identity cards and passports, but perhaps even more profoundly, fosters the belief that photographs can be apprehended as transparent copies of the real. As a quintessentially realist form of image-making, photography has thus functioned to construct and confirm dominant conceptions of reality itself.

For the first two decades of its use, the most prevalent form of photography was the daguerreotype, developed by Nicéphore Niepce and Louis-Jacques Mandé Daguerre and presented to the French Academy of Science in 1839. A unique positive image produced on a polished, mirrored, metal support, the daguerreotype was principally employed for portraiture, produced either within photographic studios or, later, by itinerant photographers working outside urban centres. Fulfilling the social and cultural need for the self-representation of the ascendant bourgeoisie, the advent of the daguerreotype effectively liquidated such traditional forms of portraiture as the painted miniature and initiated, as well, a relative democratization of portraiture *as such* (Freund, 1980).

The scale of the daguerreotype portrait industry in Western Europe, Britain, and American was enormous, although by the early 1850s, it had largely been supplanted by positive/negative processes (e.g. wet collodion on glass, invented in 1851 by Scott Archer in England) which permitted for the unlimited production of positive prints from a single negative, thereby fully inaugurating what the German philosopher Walter Benjamin would dub the age of mechanical reproduction (Benjamin, 1969). But while portraiture was quantitatively the principal product of photography's first two decades, it was by no means its only application. Within this first period of its development and expansion, photography was applied to various documentary functions (e.g., topographic views, architecture and monuments, battlefields, and the depiction of those lands and peoples in the process of being colonized or otherwise exploited) within the framework of European triumphalist imperialism. In this respect, one should also note that photography was from relatively early on conscripted for the project of visually objectifying and classifying various categories of 'otherness' – criminals, deviants, hysterics, racial and ethnic others (Alloula, 1987; Gilman, 1976; Tagg, 1990). The camera was also employed for the propagandistic needs of the state, as, for example, in the dissemination of images of rulers and statesmen, and additionally functioned to support (if not construct) a recognizably modern conception of celebrity and fame (e.g., the widespread commerce in carte-de-visite photographs of performers, writers, politicians, criminals, etc.). Last, but hardly least, photography was almost immediately employed for erotic and pornographic production, in some ways continuing and in others inventing visual conventions of bodily display (overwhelmingly feminine) that had been developed in lithographic prototypes (Solomon-Godeau, 1986). Photography, moreover, emerges at a historical moment that witnesses simultaneously the birth of what the French Situationist Guy Debord (1983) termed 'the society of the spectacle' – an evolution of capitalism characterized by a commodity culture privileging IMAGE, display and visuality – and the institutionalization of modern (bourgeois) conceptions of gender in which the image of the feminine becomes itself the urspectacle. In this respect, the spectacle of the commodity and the spectacle of FEMININITY become themselves imbricated, and the camera has proved to be the technology *par excellence* to give them visual form.

By the end of the nineteenth century, various technological developments within the medium had further increased the camera's purview. Half-tone printing permitted the integration of photographs with type, thus enabling the production of photographically illustrated newspapers, magazines and advertising, the last itself of incalculable importance in eliciting and fuelling the mechanisms of consumer desire (Ewen and Ewen, 1982). In concert with other mass media, visual forms – pre-eminently film and television advertising – have functioned as an especially potent vehicle for the ideological construction of gender (Williamson, 1978; Coward, 1985). This power derives, at least in part, from photography's putative transparency, which Roland Barthes designated as 'the effect of the real' (Barthes, 1977), but also from its sheer ubiquity. In this respect, photography has come to comprise a virtual image environment, absorbed as much subliminally as consciously.

From a feminist perspective, the nature, terms and uses of the photographic medium therefore confront us with many of the same issues and problems in its historical context as in its contemporary uses, notwithstanding its subsequent technological developments and global assimilation. Numerous commentators have pointed out that the camera functions as an instrument of appropriation, possession and objectification (e.g. Sontag, 1977). Such attributes are signalled by the very vocabulary of photography: to take a picture, to aim the camera, to shoot a picture, to capture the SUBJECT. In its optical functioning, photography produces a fixed subject position, originally that of the photographer who is effaced at the instant of the exposure and whose position is visually occupied by that of the viewer. In so far as it was designed to parallel the organization of pictorial space derived from single-point Renaissance perspective (a single vanishing point, 'window' type construction and an ideal viewing point derived from the cone of vision model), the camera image has been theorized as in and of itself an ideological construct, producing an all-seeing spectator, illusionistically effacing the means of the image's production and creating the potent illusion that, in the words of Jean-Louis Baudry, 'the world appears to speak itself' (Baudry, 1980). If we factor into this analysis a sociological and historical consideration of photography's actual uses, including acknowledgement of who has possessed the means of REPRESENTATION and who has been represented, who has been the subject of photographic representation and who has been the OBJECT, it is evident that photographic use is profoundly implicated in issues of political, cultural and sexual domination. Furthermore, in its quotidian applications (family snaps, ritual commemoration – births, weddings, vacations, confirmations, etc.) photography may be seen to participate in the fully ideological project of confirming 'normative' bourgeois concepts of domesticity and family (Bordieu, 1965).

Psychoanalytically speaking, the photograph has prompted comparison with the structure of the fetish (Burgin, 1982; Metz, 1985) in so far as the camera image marks the conjunction of a look, an arrest, and an illusion of presence that belies the object's real absence. Burgin has additionally argued that analogies may be drawn between the structures of photographic meaning and psychic processes operative in the dreamwork, such as displacement and condensation (Burgin, 1982). In advertising and other mass-media imagery, as well as art photography, the fetishistic properties of the medium are frequently paralleled by the fetishistic terms of feminine representation itself. Accordingly, the interest of the photography/fetish homology for feminism resides in the social and cultural instrumentalities of photography; most specifically, in the medium's tendency to emblematize repetitively the status of women as objects of the photographic gaze, bearers of meaning rather than makers of it (Mulvey, 1984). In other words, the urgency of feminist interrogations of photography rests on the acknowledgement of the complicity of the camera in sustaining and perpetuating certain kinds of viewing relations that are themselves reflective of the unequal order of sexual and social relations.

See also FETISHISM; FETISHIZATION; FILM THEORY; VOYEURISM/EXHIBITIONISM/THE GAZE.

BIBLIOGRAPHY

Alloula, Mallek, 1987: *The Colonial Harem*. Minneapolis: University of Minnesota Press.
Barthes, Roland, 1977: *Image, Music, Text*, ed. and trans. Stephen Heath. New York: Hill and Wang.
Baudry, Jean-Louis, 1980: 'The ideological effects of the basic cinematographic apparatus', 'The cinematic apparatus', *Apparatus*, ed. Theresa Hak Kyung Cha. New York: Tanam Press, pp. 25–40 and 41–66.
Benjamin, Walter, 1969 [1936]: 'The work of art in the age of mechanical reproduction', *Illuminations*, ed. Hannah Arendt, trans. Harry Zohn. New York: Schocken Books and Harcourt, Brace and World, pp. 217–51.
Bourdieu, Pierre, 1965: *Un art moyen*. Paris: Minuit.
Burgin, Victor, 1982: 'Photography, phantasy, function', *Thinking Photography*, ed. Victor Burgin. London: Macmillan, pp. 177–216.
Coward, Rosalind, 1985: *Female Desires*. New York: Grove Press.
Debord, Guy, 1983: *The Society of the Spectacle*. Detroit: Black & Red.
Ewen, Stuart, and Ewen, Elizabeth, 1982: *Channels of Desire*. New York: McGraw-Hill.
Freund, Giselle, 1980: *Photography and Society*. Boston: David R. Godine.

Gilman, Sander L., 1976: *The Face of Madness: Hugh W. Diamond and the Origin of Psychiatric Photography*. Secaucus, NJ: Brunner-Mazel.

Metz, Christian, 1985: 'Photograph and fetish', *October*, 34, pp. 81–90.

Mulvey, Laura, 1984 [1975]: 'Visual pleasure and narrative cinema', *Art After Modernism: Rethinking Representation*, ed. Brian Wallis. New York and Boston: The New Museum of Contemporary Art and David R. Godine, pp. 361–73.

Solomon-Godeau, Abigail, 1986: 'The legs of the Countess', *October*, 39, pp. 65–108.

Sontag, Susan, 1977: *On Photography*. New York: Farrar, Straus and Giroux.

Tagg, John, 1990: *The Burden of Representation: Essays on Photographies and Histories*. Amherst, Mass: University of Massachusetts Press.

Williamson, Judith, 1978: *Decoding Advertisements*. London: Marion Boyars.

ABIGAIL SOLOMON-GODEAU

pleasure   Philosophical discussions of pleasure since antiquity have focused on three main issues: (1) how pleasure is to be defined and whether it is equivalent to happiness or DESIRE; (2) arguments for or against the doctrines of psychological or ethical hedonism (i.e. whether pleasure *should be* or *is in fact* the most desirable human goal); (3) theories about the nature of motivation and what impels us to strive towards different material and spiritual goals.

In this perspective, Freud's theory is basically a theory of motivation. His account of pleasure, or LIBIDO, presents it in terms of instinctual drives seeking satisfaction, indifferent to social or ethical restraints or to the requirements of self-preservation. (See Freud, 1930, for a discussion of the antagonism between the demands of instinct and the restrictions of civilization. A brief account of the problems raised by Freud's pleasure principle can be found in Laplanche and Pontalis, 1973, pp. 322–5.) However, the adequacy of this account was challenged by Freud himself in *Beyond the Pleasure Principle* (1920; see also 'Instincts and their vicissitudes', 1915); concluding that the pleasure principle could not account for the full range of psychic phenomena, he introduced a hypothetical death instinct to explain the consistent human pursuit of pleasure's opposite – pain, unpleasure, compulsive repetition of misery and so on (*see* DEATH DRIVE (FREUD)).

In contrast, feminist discussions place pleasure in a predominantly political context. The second-wave (post-1968) feminist response to Freud was initially hostile (*see* FEMINISM BEFORE PSYCHOANALYSIS), so paradoxically, the feminist defendants of women's right to pleasure often see psychoanalysis as an opponent, despite its stress on pleasure as a basic motivating principle (see Koedt, 1973 and the arguments of the sexual libertarians, below). This is only one of a number of tensions and paradoxes in the debates on the relationship between pleasure, psychoanalysis and politics.

In the 'sexual revolution' of the 1960s pleasure had translated relatively unproblematically into sexual liberation, which was seen as disruptive of capitalism, in that it provided the libidinal force underlying social revolution. The theory was provided by the Frankfurt school (Adorno, Horkheimer, Fromm, Marcuse) and by Wilhelm Reich who had been a pupil of Freud's. Whereas Freud had argued that sexual repression was a condition of civilization, the 1960s' euphoria had raised the possibility of a future revolutionary liberation from REPRESSION. Linking marxist and Freudian theory, sexual radicalism hypothesized that the triumph of Eros over Thanatos would end political and economic oppression as well as sexual alienation. But the feminism of the early 1970s, while vigorously claiming the right to sexual pleasure, and adopting the diagnosis of repression as 'false consciousness', was more likely to criticize the Frankfurt school approach for not addressing the link between PATRIARCHY and the institution of HETEROSEXUALITY (see Campbell, 1980). It was pointed out that sexual liberation is an illusory freedom, amounting mainly to the freedom of those already in a position of power (men) to exercise it still further. So while on the one hand women's pleasure was viewed as revolutionary, in that it threatened the traditional institutions of patriarchy – marriage, the family and normative heterosexuality – on the other hand it was seen as reactionary too. The mobilizing of pleasure, the counter-argument goes, makes women consumers, attaches them to domesticity and nurturance, and turns them into willing mannequins and sex objects. It is pointed out that their desires are mobile, that pleasure is constructed, and that the objects of pleasure are provided by advertising and commercial interests. Pleasure thus channelled distracts from the desire to effect social change (Coward, 1984).

The dilemma of pleasure is well illustrated by Laura Mulvey's celebrated 1973 essay 'Visual pleasure and narrative cinema' (reprinted in Mulvey, 1989), which initiated a still lively debate around the question of the pleasure of the female spectator (see FEMINIST CINEMA; FILM THEORY). Drawing on psychoanalytic theory, Mulvey argued that the pleasure women take in viewing films is dependent on identification with the male gaze which sets woman up as scopophilic object. The pleasure of the (voyeuristic) look is gained at women's expense: their pleasure lies in their own self-objectification. The pleasure afforded by classical cinema was to be scrupulously avoided by radical film-makers. This austere prescription readily lends itself to accusations of feminist puritanism; psychoanalytic theory here appears to provide the back-up for a kind of politico-moral prescriptivism. Some feminists have, therefore, attempted to go beyond the antitheses of feminism versus pleasure, moralism versus hedonism. There has been a reaction against the Frankfurt school idea of false consciousness and its modern avatars which seem in danger of producing authoritarianism and elitism in so far as they propose, implicitly or explicitly, a notion of 'truth' or 'authenticity' as the negation of false consciousness. Questions about where such authenticity is to be found, how it is to be truly expressed, who can claim possession of the truth, who is to define it and with what authority, have led to doubts about the very possibility of discovering an original sense of pleasure unmediated by oppressive social structures. Instead, the recognition of the human ability for playful dissimulation is given precedence over the impossible desire for authenticity (discussed in Wilson, 1985). It is suggested we playfully explore FANTASY in the name of pleasure, as though pleasure were somehow self-justifying. Ironically, this new swing towards pleasure sometimes draws on some of the same theorists (e.g. Barthes) who were used to support the *critique* of pleasure, and it seems less a solution to the dilemma than a reiteration of one of the two poles.

The bi-polar opposition of the 1970s still appears to be structuring the 1980s' debate between sexual libertarians and their opponents, even though both sides accept a version of constructionism (i.e. the view that the human being is socially constructed, and that there is no essential or original human nature predating society). Constructionism now straddles the poles of moralism versus pleasure. Libertarians claim the right to sexual pleasure, including the right to act out with consenting partners sadistic or masochistic scenarios (*see* SADOMASOCHISM). They refer to Foucault's theory of the construction of SEXUALITY in discourse and claim his support for the view that minority sexual preferences may constitute sites of resistance to power (see Rubin, 1984). For the opposition (see Jeffreys, 1990), consensual sadomasochistic activity seems uncomfortably close to non-consensual sexual violence – RAPE, sexual abuse, sexual exploitation. The anti-libertarians' main argument is that the libertarians *de-politicize* sexuality, thereby undercutting one of the most basic feminist insights. They tend to urge feminists – directly or by implication – to reconstruct their desires in line with their politics. As in the 1970s, both sides unite in their rejection of the psychoanalytic framework for understanding the libidinal drives and fantasies underlying sexuality; Jessica Benjamin's feminist psychoanalytic work on the relation between desire and domination stands out as a landmark in this otherwise hostile landscape (see BENJAMIN, 1988).

If we reject the notion of pleasure as a fundamental DRIVE, we lose its political value as a guide to the measurement of oppression and as a basic motivation for the development of a less oppressive and more pleasurable world. If *all* desire for pleasure is constructed, there is no reason to privilege some forms of pleasure over others, and (in theory anyway) such desires can be totally *re*constructed. The problem is that pleasure is recalcitrant; it may obstinately refuse to be 'politically correct' or politically reconstructed. Yet without retaining some concept of pleasure as libidinal energy, how are we to account for women's motivation to engage in feminist politics, to struggle and fight for a better world?

BIBLIOGRAPHY

Barthes, Roland 1973 [1957]: *Mythologies*, trans. Annette Lavers. London: Paladin.

Barthes, Roland, 1976 [1973]: *The Pleasure of the Text*, trans. Richard Miller. London: Cape.

Benjamin, Jessica, 1988: *The Bonds of Love: Psychoanalysis, Feminism and the Problem of Domination*. New York: Pantheon.

Campbell, Beatrix, 1980: 'A feminist sexual politics: now you see it, now you don't', *Feminist Review*, 5, pp. 1–18.

Coward, Rosalind, 1983: *Formations of Pleasure*. London: Routledge and Kegan Paul.

Coward, Rosalind, 1984: *Female Desire*. London: Paladin.

Foucault, Michel, 1979 [1976]: *The History of Sexuality*, vol. 1, trans. Robert Hurley. London: Allen Lane.

Freud, Sigmund, 1915: 'Instincts and their vicissitudes', *SE*, 14, pp. 109–40.

Freud, Sigmund, 1920: *Beyond the Pleasure Principle*, *SE*, 18, pp. 3–66.

Freud, Sigmund, 1930: *Civilization and its Discontents*, *SE*, 21, pp. 59–148.

Horkheimer, Max, and Adorno, Theodor, 1979 [1944]: *The Dialectic of Enlightenment*. London: Verso.

Jeffreys, Sheila, 1990: *Anticlimax: A Feminist Perspective on the Sexual Revolution*. London: The Women's Press.

Koedt, Anne, 1973: 'The myth of the vaginal orgasm', *Radical Feminism*, ed. Anne Koedt, Ellen Levine and Anita Rapone. New York: Quadrangle Books, pp. 198–207.

Laplanche, Jean, and Pontalis, Jean-Baptiste, 1973 [1967]: *The Language of Psychoanalysis*, trans. Donald Nicholson-Smith. London: Hogarth Press.

Marcuse, Herbert, 1955: *Eros and Civilization*. Boston: Beacon Press.

Mulvey, Laura, 1989: *Visual and Other Pleasures*. London: Macmillan.

Reich, Wilhelm, 1951: *The Sexual Revolution*. London: Vision Press.

Reich, Wilhelm, 1968: *The Function of the Orgasm*. London: Panther Books.

Rubin, Gayle, 1984: 'Thinking sex: notes for a radical theory of the politics of sexuality', Vance, 1984, pp. 267–319.

Vance, Carole S., ed. 1984: *Pleasure and Danger: Exploring Female Sexuality*. London: Routledge and Kegan Paul.

Wilson, Elizabeth, 1985: *Adorned in Dreams*. London: Virago.

MARGARET WHITFORD AND SADIE PLANT

pornography: definitions Definitions of 'pornography' are almost as many and as varied as is writing on the topic. They range from the liberal, for example, 'porn has a certain function or intention; to arouse its audience sexually, and also a certain content, explicit representation of sexual materials' (Williams, 1979, p. 103) to the radical feminist, for example, 'porn is the graphic depiction of women as vile whores' (Dworkin, 1981, p. 200). Following these definitions, there are broadly two critical perspectives on the subject: the liberal and the radical feminist. Liberals treat producers, consumers and critics of pornography alike as individuals with rights, for example, to liberty and AUTONOMY; rights whose exercise may be disallowed only when it 'harms' another. The liberal attaches great importance to the distinction between public and private domains. In so far as s/he advocates any restrictions at all on pornography (and liberals would prefer, on the whole, not to have to do this) these restrictions apply in the 'public' domain. People may do what they like, according to the liberal, in private. Liberals thus tend to be in favour of freedom of expression, and against censorship, stressing the freedom of 'pornographers' to produce, distribute and sell their materials. With a very few exceptions, the law tends to reflect a liberal position: in the UK, the law states that the criterion for censorship is whether the tendency of 'the matter charged' as obscene is to 'deprave and corrupt' those whose minds are open to such immoral influences.

Radical feminists (or 'cultural feminists' as some people in the US now call them) tend to criticize liberals on two counts. First of all, they say, the liberal's representation of anyone involved in the pornography industry as an 'individual' with rights obscures the fact that it is mainly women who are depicted in pornographic magazines and films, and mainly men who consume them. Live women models, and images of women in magazines and films, are presented as objects to be treated as the male consumer wishes. In a crucial sense, therefore, women models abrogate their freedom. They appear as flesh, as bodies, and not as fully rounded autonomous human beings. Secondly, radical feminists would wish to re-draw and sometimes question altogether the distinction drawn by the liberal between the 'public' and the 'private' domains. Many of the most horrible crimes against women involving pornography are in fact committed in the privacy of the home. To exempt this area from the operation of the law, radical feminists would argue, is to remove from its purview most crimes against women involving pornography.

The best known advocate of this radical or 'cultural' feminist position is Andrea Dworkin (1981). Dworkin believes that women's oppression is equivalent to male power; that this power is mainly expressed sexually; that heterosexual sex, is in a sense, violent; and that pornography is the main vehicle used by the male 'colonizers' to exercise their domination over their female territories. Pornography is violence against women.

Other radical feminists argue that pornography *causes* violence against women. The US radical feminist Robin Morgan, for example, adopted a slogan since taken up by European women's groups: 'Porn is the theory; rape is the practice' (Morgan, 1980, p. 139). Both groups of radical feminists advocate banning porn. Some suggest other forms of action. In the UK, groups that have advocated censorship include WAVAW (Women against Violence against Women), CAP (Campaign against Porn) and the 'Off the Shelf Campaign', a campaign directed against W. H. Smith, a major retail outlet for pornography in the UK.

The most widely read 'male' pornographic magazines, however – *Penthouse, Playboy, Men Only* and *Mayfair* – do not contain obviously violent images. Though there certainly is violent pornography around, and Andrea Dworkin gives some vivid examples, it is not typical. Moreover, the evidence on a link between pornography and violence against women is inconclusive. Some rapists may have 'used' pornography, but there is evidence that passages from the Bible (the Abraham/Isaac episode, for instance) or Greek tragedy (Agamemnon sending his daughter to death) have also had a powerful influence on violent behaviour. Banning pornography, therefore, would not do away with violent behaviour on the part of men towards women. Moreover, it is extremely difficult for those advocating censorship to come up with a definition that covers all and only the material they wish to have banned. History suggests that it is, in fact, far more likely that such legislation would be used against minority art forms, such as lesbian and gay literature, than against *Penthouse*.

Finally, the radical feminist perspective tends to downplay the role of class and race in the production and dissemination of pornography. Porn is multi-billion-dollar business. There are women who benefit from it. There is no doubt that much pornography objectifies women in that it violates their autonomy. Yet neither is it the paradigmatic expression of male power, as some radical feminists would have it (Rubens paintings, the images of women in *Cosmopolitan*, and much non-pornographic advertising also 'objectify' women), nor is it the case that it 'oppresses' all women in the same way.

It is possible, indeed, to be a feminist and to see something of value in some pornography. Some feminists have described Mills and Boon romantic fiction as pornography for women (see e.g. Modleski, 1980) and Freudian or Kleinian explanations have been offered for its popularity – the reader/heroine becomes like a child, desiring the powerful, absent father-figure. In other accounts, the hero becomes the mother, adored and adoring, for the child. Other feminists, indeed, would describe the radical feminist over-arching rejection of pornography as inappropriate, and as tending to obliterate sources of FANTASY, for lesbians as well as heterosexuals. Pornography, according to these 'anticensorship' feminists, cannot be abstracted from the context of its production and consumption. The isolated 'man in the long grey mackintosh' (if he exists at all) is not the only 'user' of pornographic magazines and films. To seek to repress all pornography, these feminists would argue, is to contribute to and help to sustain ideologies that devise hierarchies of acceptable/unacceptable SEXUALITY. These hierarchies range from the married, heterosexual couple, each fulfilling the other's desires, and neither requiring any further outlets for their fantasies, to the paedophiles (whom most would condemn). Somewhere along the way are lesbian and gay forms of sexuality, and various forms of PERVERSION. Pornography, the anti-censorship feminists would argue, is often a medium used in the production of erotic fantasy. To seek to ban all of it may be to advocate a prurient morality that is not far removed from the right-wing moralist perspective.

As will be apparent to the reader, psychoanalytic perspectives are notable for their absence in the vast majority of writing about pornography.

See also PORNOGRAPHY: FEMINIST PERSPECTIVES ON PSYCHOLOGICAL AND PSYCHOANALYTICAL THEORIES.

BIBLIOGRAPHY

Assiter, Alison, 1989: *Pornography, Feminism and the Individual*. London: Pluto Press.
Dworkin, Andrea, 1981: *Pornography: Men Possessing Women*. London: The Women's Press.
Griffin, Susan, 1981: *Pornography and Silence*. London: The Women's Press.
Kappeler, Susanne, 1986: *The Pornography of Representation*. Cambridge: Polity Press.
Lederer, Laura, ed. 1980: *Take Back the Night: Women on Porn*. New York: Bantam Books.
Modleski, Tania, 1980: 'The disappearing act: a study of harlequin romances', *Signs*, 5/1, pp. 435–48.
Morgan, Robin, 1980: 'Theory and practice, porn and rape', Lederer, ed., pp. 125–13.
Vance, Carol, ed. 1984: *Pleasure and Danger: Exploring Female Sexuality*. London: Routledge.
Williams, Bernard, 1979: *Report of the Committee on Obscenity and Film Censorship*. House of Commons Command Papers, no. 7772 (Williams Report). London: HMSO.

ALISON ASSITER

pornography: feminist perspectives on psychological and psychoanalytical theories   The area examined here is the ways in which feminist accounts of pornography have made use of psychological and psychoanalytical approaches. Mapping out this set of relations illustrates very clearly that one cannot deduce political or theoretical positions from broad foundational perspectives. On the one hand, the most radical of feminisms aligns itself with rather conservative psychological schools; on the other hand, feminists who ally themselves with psychoanalysis reject many of the prevailing psychoanalytical opinions on the subject as far too literal and narrow-minded. To understand the question of the interconnections between feminism, pornography and the 'psy' domain it is necessary to consider the political and cultural *contexts* of these appropriations.

The most dominant context of debate about pornography is the political framework provided by liberalism, in which questions are predefined in terms of a presumption in favour of liberty, especially freedom of speech, to be balanced against the curtailment of harms whose seriousness must weigh against the *prima facie* harm of interfering with freedom. In this context, all feminisms thus come to be defined by their relation to these liberal terms of reference (*see* PORNOGRAPHY: DEFINITIONS; for a different version of how feminism relates to liberalism, see Brown, 1981). Here the privileged sort of 'psy' approach has been positivist psychological studies seeking to examine whether or not pornography can be sufficiently demonstrated to be a causal factor in harms serious enough to warrant legal intervention, notably sexual crimes of violence. This debate has also had to address the 'Scandinavian' claim that pornography offers a functional alternative release for sexual tensions and therefore prevents harm. There is a vast literature on this subject. Early studies in the 1960s and 1970s concentrated directly on men's reactions to pornography. Yaffe (in Williams, 1979, p. 240) notes three models: (1) the arousal model (pornography intensifies already determined motivations to act in particular ways); (2) the imitation model (appealing actions will be imitated); and (3) the catharsis model (dissipation of the wish to act by vicarious participation). More recent studies have concentrated more on men's views about women, asking whether pornography promotes a total indifference to women's consent, or if it rather conveys the misleading message that all women are generally available for sex or actively enjoy aggressive sex despite protestations to the contrary (see Donnerstein et al., 1987). Over the years there have been two key shifts of emphasis for those who find the psychological evidence convincing. First, harm claims have been narrowed to the effects of pornography involving violence. Second, the search for unique causation has been challenged with the idea of 'probabilistic' (or 'multiple') causation (as adopted in the US Meese Report: Meese, 1986), according to which even if pornography is merely one of a bundle of causative factors, it should now be regarded as significant. None the less, such evidence has never been accepted by governments as justifying radical change in the law (i.e. sufficient to outweigh free speech considerations), a refusal that has led to radical feminist charges of political suppression of 'the facts'.

It is important to note that, while debates about this kind of research are often conducted within the terms of reference of positivist psychology, sometimes what is being attacked is the validity of positivist methods *tout court*. The British Williams Report (Williams, 1979), for instance, summarizes a number of important scepticisms about the use of official statistics and extrapolations from experimental situations; but these scepticisms are ultimately so wide-sweeping that they potentially undermine any positivist enterprise in the social sciences. Correspondingly, this raises questions about feminist use of empirical studies. Have radical feminists thus made themselves hostage to the fortunes of causal theories, subject to current judgements of what counts as proven or not? More widely, what is at stake in feminists choosing to conduct debate within an empiricist/positivist framework that is itself increasingly denounced in feminist epistemologies (see Harding, 1987)? Also, the categories emphasized in empirical studies are dubious – does the focus on the violent end of pornography distract attention from the element of insult involved in sexualizing representations and the overlap between soft-core pornography and advertising? To these objections the radical feminist reply has been, first, that to conventional psychology has been added the crucial evidence of women's experience, and second, that the eroticization of violence is itself a widespread cultural phenomenon of which pornography is merely the exemplary instance.

Among non-feminist anti-pornography writers Holbrook (1977) draws on Klein and Winnicott to condemn the 'masturbatory' aspects of pornography, meaning masturbation not so much as a physical practice but as a mode of FANTASY associated with pre-integrated states of infantile life where frustration is easily translated into forms of sadism. Despite an at least superficial resemblance to the feminist theme that pornography treats women as objects, this genre of argument has been taken up neither by radical feminists nor by those feminists who have sought to understand pornography by reference to psychoanalytical concepts, as opposed to behaviourist psychology.

If radical feminist involvement with positivist psychology may be defined by reference to the hegemony of liberalism and its routines for justifying legal intervention, then feminist uses of psychoanalysis must be associated with a quite different discursive context. Work here has sought distance from the whole issue of using law and, at the same time, declined to ally itself with what appears to be the apocalyptic moralism and directive normalization of the conventional psychoanalytically inspired writers. In this field the directive terms come from the context of film and media studies and the ways in which concepts such as voyeurism and FETISHISM have been deployed to conceptualize the representation of the female body in classic Hollywood narrative (*see* FEMINIST CINEMA; FILM THEORY; IMAGE; VOYEURISM/EXHIBITIONISM/THE GAZE). The starting point in this field was the argument that the sight of the female body always threatens to evoke castration anxiety and hence DISAVOWAL through the substitution of a fetish object – specifically the fetishizing of the woman's body itself (*see* FETISHIZATION), for instance in the giant screen close-up of a face that stops the narrative flow (which would otherwise lead to the discovery of castration (Mulvey, 1975)). Much analysis along these lines had developed before pornography suddenly came into prominence in the 1970s as a key issue. Hard-core visual pornography posed a *prima facie* counter-example, for here women's genitals were indeed on display, despite all the rules that seemed to say this was impossible in the presumed psychic economy of displacement. In the ensuing debate, Ellis (1980) sought to rescue the original analysis by arguing that fetishistic regimes were none the less upheld in pornographic film by the obsessive focus on women's PLEASURE as a new phallic substitute object, with a focus especially on aural signifiers as a compensation for the anxiety of castration. Willemen (1980), by contrast, emphasized the more culturally specific point that Mulvey's analysis had not initially claimed to be a universal or transhistorical account of all genres of REPRESENTATION but was, indeed, limited to classic Hollywood narratives. Pajaczkowska (1981) in turn rejected, as a misappropriation of metapsychology (and, moreover, a phallocentric one), the whole idea that women's naked bodies must provoke castration anxiety, given that the schema of fetishism centres on woman's LACK. Linda Williams's recent book (1990) thus generalizes from the concept of fetishism to argue that it points to the generally substitutive nature of all sexual desire as necessarily perverse (*see* PERVERSION). In these psychoanalytically informed debates pornography thus, ironically, achieves – as it does for radical feminism – an exemplary status as *the* site for displaying the truth of sex.

BIBLIOGRAPHY

Attorney General's Report, 1970: *Report of the Attorney General's Commission on Obscenity and Pornography*. Washington, DC: US Department of Justice.

Brown, Beverley, 1981: 'A feminist interest in pornography: some modest proposals', *m/f*, 5/6 (reprinted in *The Woman in Question*, ed. Parveen Adams and Elizabeth Cowie. Boston: MIT Press, pp. 134–48).

Donnerstein, Edward, Linz, Daniel, and Penrod, Steven, 1987: *The Question of Pornography: Research Findings and Policy Implications*. London: Macmillan.

Ellis, John, 1980: 'Photography/Pornography/Art/Pornography', *Screen* 21/1, pp. 81–108.

Harding, Sandra, ed. 1987: *Feminism and Methodology*. Bloomington: Indiana University Press; Milton Keynes: Open University Press.

Holbrook, David, 1977: 'The politics of pornography', *Political Quarterly*, 48/1, pp. 44–53.

Meese, 1986: Attorney General's Commission on Pornography, *Final Report of the Special Committee on Pornography and Prostitution* (Meese Report). Washington, DC: US Department of Justice.

Mulvey, Laura, 1975: 'Visual pleasure and narrative cinema', *Screen*, 16/3, pp. 6–18.

Pajaczkowska, Claire, 1981: 'The heterosexual presumption', *Screen*, 22/1, pp. 79–94.

Willemen, Paul, 1980: 'Letter to John', *Screen*, 21/2, pp. 53–66.

Williams, Linda, 1990: *Hard Core: Power, Pleasure and the 'Frenzy of the Visible'*. London, Sydney and Wellington: Pandora Press.

Williams, Bernard, 1979: *Report of the Committee on Obscenity and Film Censorship*, House of Commons Command Papers, no. 7772. (Williams Report). London: HMSO.

BEVERLEY BROWN

postmodernism   A highly unstable concept, used to designate either a particular mapping of contemporary experience, a movement in the arts and LITERATURE or a theoretical critique of the Western foundations of philosophical modernity. It has been defined as a new aesthetic characterized by pastiche, self-referentiality, fragmentation, hybridization of styles, linguistic multiplicity, and as a movement in PHILOSOPHY registering a crisis in the legitimation of Western knowledge through a breakdown of meta-narratives and the consequent end therefore of metaphysics and of all thought attempting to ground itself in first principles or final causes, such as God, Nature, Spirit. Similarly, 'postmodernity' has been variously defined as the Age of the Hyperreal, where all distinctions between truth and appearance, depth and surface, latent and manifest have broken down as REPRESENTATION gives way to simulacrum; as an era of capitalist expansion where spatial and temporal compression of the globe (through new information technologies, search for new markets, financial development) is producing a crisis in traditional conceptualizations of identity and history; as a new

341

political age of 'difference' where notions of democracy and consensus have failed under pressure from the emerging voices of those 'others' whose exclusion has facilitated the establishment of the dominants as part of an ostensible regime of truth, not one of power (*see* RACE/IMPERI-ALISM).

For some (Jameson, 1985) postmodernism is seen in largely negative terms as a symptom of late capitalism, whose ideas and artefacts are no more than further depthless surfaces of a commodified culture in which the possibility of opposition has collapsed with the loss of distinction between economic and cultural spheres. For others (Hutcheon, 1988), postmodern artefacts continue the modernist project of resisting the structures of capitalist society through strategies of defamiliarization, disruption and destabilization; however, they have recognized their own implication in consumer culture and, in parodically incorporating elements of this culture into their work, have relinquished the pursuit of the goal of aesthetic autonomy. In thus contributing to the breakdown of consensus about cultural values they have helped to produce a space for the emergence of ex-centricity and difference.

Until recently, definitions of and debates within postmodernism have had very little to say about feminism, and vice versa. However, an increasingly self-conscious hermeneutic perspectivism has arisen in much current feminist theory through the recognition of a basic dilemma in attempting to articulate a feminist epistemology: that women seek equality for and valorization of a gendered identity which has been constructed through the very cultural institutions and discourses which feminists have been challenging and dismantling. Because there can be no simple legitimation in throwing off a 'false consciousness' and revealing a 'true female identity', some feminist theorists have felt obliged to develop a self-reflexive questioning of their own legitimating procedures. The resulting discourses can be seen as both a reflection of and a contribution to that 'crisis of legitimation' which has been seen by its various theorists as a characteristic of postmodern culture. The slogan 'let us wage war on totality' is perhaps the postmodern equivalent of that earlier feminist announcement, 'the personal is the political'. But if the latter can be seen as a rallying cry, the former implies a hostile attitude towards implicit ideals of collectivism and community.

In fact, the feminist cry situated its politics firmly within what Lyotard wishes to denounce and what Jürgen Habermas calls the 'project of modernity' (see the relevant essays in Foster, 1985). For Habermas (as clearly for many feminists) this project is not exhausted, but it is incomplete. He defines the project as a political commitment which emerged during the Enlightenment, identifying itself via the concepts of truth, justice and subjectivity and founding itself on the belief that human beings are collectively engaged in a progressive movement towards moral and intellectual self-realization through the application of a universal rational faculty. Emancipation consists in the capacity of human beings to free themselves from irrational forces within and social determinants without. Freud's work has been seen as axiomatic for the former and the work of Marx for the latter, though the focus of much postmodernist theory has been to deconstruct or dismantle their writing, revealing its methodology and epistemology to be at one with an oppressive and authoritarian rationalism which has produced terror in place of emancipation and disguised its will to power as a disinterested desire for truth. Fragmentation, pastiche, parody, narrative disruption, specificity and the refusal to generalize are hailed as the only means of offering any resistance to capitalist structures of surveillance and control of the pleasure principle, and are seen as part of an assault on the bondage of thought to regulative ideals such as 'truth' and 'justice'.

It is apparent that both feminism and psychoanalysis arise as part of the project of modernity and yet both have been instrumental in exposing its contradictions and inadequacies. To this extent both can also be seen as discourses of postmodernity, and perhaps their great strengths lie precisely in this position of hesitation. As discourses arising out of modernity, each presents a version of continuous history which includes a founding 'myth of origins' with cross-cultural and trans-historical validity (male domination arising from economic inequality or exclusive mothering on the one hand, and primary maternal identification or REPRESSION through the intervention of the law of the father, on the other); each can be seen as what Foucault calls a 'technology of the self' (see Foucault, 1988), producing and maintaining an identity concept, which is then internalized so that it appears to arise from within the individual; and finally, each sees itself as an emancipatory project seeking to understand oppressive and irrational forces. Equally, however, each at times implies or articulates a critique of that same project: truth is revealed to be a fiction in the terms of a Nietzschean perspectivism which deflates the Pure Reason of the Cartesian view from nowhere and returns it to the limited and finite perspective of the situated historical body. Both have shown how 'woman' (or the UNCONSCIOUS, the BODY, DESIRE) is that Other whose exclusion was necessary to the very establishment of the rational, autonomous self and, in raising questions about the way in which claims to knowledge have been legitimated, both have finally turned their reflections upon themselves, foregrounding signification and problematizing their own forms of representation. Perhaps the most urgent question for feminists arising out of these theoretical developments is whether it is possible to embrace a position of hermeneutic perspectivism which continuously puts its own

343

epistemology under erasure without consequently relinquishing political efficacy and ethical conviction in an embrace of hermeneutic anarchism.

Discussions of feminism or of women writers have been singularly absent from most postmodern theory and criticism, despite a current obsession with what Alice Jardine (1985) has called 'gynesis': alterity as 'feminine', the attempt to name a space outside the logic of modernity which is not made possible by its structures and which is thus a sacred place. This space has been variously described as 'the body without organs' (the small boy's view of the mother?), 'becoming woman' (the male fantasy of plenitude?) or 'the hysterical body' (the object through which psychoanalysis arrived at its definition of the male subject?). Such theoretical developments can be viewed by feminists in a number of ways. As postmodernists register a sense of the collapse of the legitimacy of the grand meta-narratives of the West, are they not talking euphemistically of the loss of the legitimacy of patriarchal discourse? Is it simply a coincidence that at this precise moment they begin to intensify their interest in (and to master through the discourses of postmodernism) a space described as the feminine, but supposedly attached to neither male nor female bodies? Is it also simply a coincidence that at the precise historical moment when women, drawing on psychoanalysis as a narrative of coherence, have begun to establish their own sense of subjectivity, agency and history, postmodernists, drawing on psychoanalysis as a narrative of incoherence, have dismantled each of these categories as effects of power, desire, fictions which have become myths? Alternatively, of course, one can see in the postmodern reading of psychoanalysis a genuine potential for dismantling the fixity of GENDER and of gender in relation to SEXUALITY, and to begin dimly to imagine a subject beyond the epistemological and ontological categories of Western thought (one could argue that this is precisely the thrust of much recent feminist and postmodern fiction (*see* LITERATURE).

Central to Lyotard's work and to the whole postmodernist theoretical project is the belief that emancipatory discourses are no longer possible because there can no longer be a belief in privileged meta-discourses which transcend local and contingent conditions in order to ground the truths of all first-order discourses. GENDER can then no longer be stabilized by the law of the father, but equally it cannot be used cross-culturally to explain the practices of human societies, because in itself it becomes the repressive enactment of metaphysical authority. Similarly, the postmodern celebration of difference and its psycho-textual de-centring seem to open up spaces for the heterogeneous voices of women rather than the monolithic voice of Woman. Yet its concept of the feminine often says little to or for embodied women in the world of history who may feel that these voices from everywhere are simply the impersonal (male) voice from nowhere re-written in the theoretical discourse of postmodernism rather than that of modernism. Psychoanalytic feminist theory written from an object-relations position provides a further perspective on this in its analysis of the construction of gender identity and its view of masculinity as bound to structures of impersonality (Waugh, 1989; *and see* OBJECT-RELATIONS THEORY).

See also ART; AUTONOMY; FEMINISM OF DIFFERENCE; PHILOSOPHY; SCIENCE; SUBJECT; THEORY.

BIBLIOGRAPHY

Brennan, Teresa, ed. 1989: *Between Feminism and Psychoanalysis*. London and New York: Routledge.

Foster, Hal, ed. 1985: *Postmodern Culture*. London and Sydney: Pluto Press.

Foucault, Michel, 1988: 'Technologies of the self', *Technologies of the Self: A Seminar with Michel Foucault*, ed. Luther H. Martin, Huck Gutman and Patrick H. Hutton. London: Tavistock, pp. 16–49.

Hutcheon, Linda, 1988: *A Poetics of Postmodernism*. New York and London: Routledge.

Jameson, Fredric, 1985: 'Postmodernism and consumer society', Foster, 1985, pp. 111–26.

Jardine, Alice A., 1985: *Gynesis: Configurations of Women and Modernity*. Ithaca, NY, and London: Cornell University Press.

Lyotard, Jean-François, 1984: *The Postmodern Condition: A Report on Knowledge*. Manchester: Manchester University Press.

Waugh, Patricia, 1989: *Feminine Fictions: Revisiting the Postmodern*. London and New York: Routledge.

PATRICIA WAUGH

pre-oedipal As a term, this may refer to (a) the period of psycho-sexual *development* preceding the OEDIPUS COMPLEX in which the attachment to the mother is predominant, or (b) an unconscious psycho-sexual *structure*, in which the attachment to and fantasies about the mother are predominant. The structural account cannot be mapped, phase by phase, on to the developmental account. In practice, however, the two accounts are not always clearly differentiated, since the structure is enacted or exemplified within the developmental chronology of human biological existence, while development does not imply the complete abandonment of earlier psychic positions.

Freud had little to say about the girl's pre-oedipal stage. Significantly, he did not address it directly until 1931, in his essay on 'Female sexuality' (*see also* NEGATIVE OEDIPUS COMPLEX). Here he recognized that he had under-estimated the duration and intensity of the little girl's pre-oedipal attachment to her mother, and its significance for understanding her emotional ambivalence and later psycho-sexual life. Freud modifies his view of male and female oedipal symmetry in the light of work by a number of women analysts, whose gender, he thought, facilitated the pre-oedipal transference (see the work of Ruth Mack Brunswick and Jeanne Lampl-de Groot on the pre-oedipal in Fliess 1948; *see also* DEUTSCH; FREUD'S FEMALE PATIENTS/FEMALE ANALYSTS). He speculated that the woman's pre-oedipal relation with the mother is intimately related to the aetiology of HYSTERIA, and to female paranoia, which he links to pre-oedipal fears of being killed, perhaps devoured, by the mother, but these speculations remain undeveloped and, not surprisingly, the most significant work on the woman's pre-oedipal stage has been done by women.

One of the women who questioned Freud's theory of the oedipus complex, while continuing to assert her orthodoxy, was KLEIN. In her 1928 paper 'The early stages of the oedipus complex' (1988b), Klein summarized her view that the oedipus complex comes into operation much earlier than was hitherto supposed, and that oedipal tendencies make their appearance at the end of the first or beginning of the second year of life. However, since these primitive fantasies she describes relate to part-objects rather than whole objects, so that the parents are perceived in terms of individual organs and even as a 'combined parent figure' (see Klein, 1988a, c; 1989), they should properly be called pre-oedipal, since the mother and father are not yet clearly distinguished as whole and separate figures. The father exists, not as a prohibiting law, for example, but as a fantasied penis incorporated in the mother's body. Klein's work documents from clinical material the girl's ambivalence towards the mother, and the fear of being devoured, which Freud mentions in 'Female sexuality' (1931).

From the structural as opposed to the developmental perspective, the fantasies which Klein describes, rather than preceding a symbolic structuring process, are *effects* of it. According to LACAN, for example, the pre-oedipal is a retroactive construct which is effected after the oedipal stage. The pre-oedipal fantasies of fragmentation are not a primitive FANTASY but an IMAGINARY one, dependent on the emergence of the ego which is the precondition of having such fantasies at all. Whereas the developmental view assumes the innateness of the ego, the structural view assumes that the genesis of the ego is something to be explained. Both views can find some theoretical support in Freud, who puts forward differing and sometimes incompatible accounts of the ego. Lacan himself is less concerned with the pre-oedipal period than with its structural relation to the oedipal phase, and in his description of the emergence of the ego in the Imaginary stage accords a greater role to the father than the mother.

The feminist literature on women's relationship to the pre-oedipal mother has so far situated itself predominantly within a developmental perspective, while structural accounts do not appear to be centrally interested in the specificity of the woman's pre-oedipal phase. There are two principal accounts (both non-clinical) which have become reference points for the feminist developmental and structural currents respectively. The first is Chodorow's work (1978), which uses psychoanalytic theory to explain why women mother. In the process, she foregrounds the difference between boys and girls in the nature and quality of the pre-oedipal attachment to the mother, and her theory has been used to discuss the male as well as the female psyche. Although her work has given rise to considerable controversy (*see* CHODOROW; OBJECT-RELATIONS THEORY), it effectively focused feminist thought on the MOTHER–DAUGHTER RELATIONSHIP. The second is Kristeva's concept of the semiotic (1984). The semiotic is described in relation to the SYMBOLIC as pre-signifying energy: it is the space of the drives before they are organized by the symbolic. The semiotic does not correspond precisely to the pre-oedipal, since the pre-oedipal 'fragmented body' is said to be always already invested with semiosis. Thus the semiotic can be both oedipal and pre-oedipal; it is a condition of signifying, or a modality of the signifying process. As a space preceding the paternal Symbolic order, yet in relation with it, the semiotic is of potential interest to feminist explorations of ways in which the Symbolic order could be modified.

The proliferation of not quite synonymous theoretical categories – pre-oedipal/oedipal; Imaginary/Symbolic; semiotic/Symbolic – illustrates the problems in conceptualizing this elusive psychic phase or structure that until recently was of interest only to clinicians, and quite unavailable for analysis outside the clinical situation. Because of its elusiveness, perhaps, there has been a tendency to place undue hope in the possibilities of the pre-oedipal. Psychoanalytically oriented feminists (especially KRISTEVA, IRIGARAY and Cixous) have been, inaccurately, thought to be describing a pre-patriarchal space, a refuge in which women can find again that first closeness with the mother, so brutally curtailed by the paternal law, and perhaps even a site of resistance which could overturn the patriarchal order. Psychoanalytic readings, in contrast, emphasize the fantasy element in these idyllic and utopian accounts. Freudians and Lacanians argue for the necessity of the symbolic father, as third party, to break up the mother–child dyad and enable the child to enter the symbolic order.

However, Jessica BENJAMIN points out that psychoanalytic discussions tend to focus on the pre-oedipal mother and Symbolic father, while neglecting the pre-oedipal father and Symbolic mother. Benjamin (1988) is one of the few theorists to describe a pre-oedipal father. (See also

347

Kristeva's 'father of individual prehistory' in Kristeva, 1986.) She argues that a process of splitting takes place in psychoanalytic theory, in which the primitive, dangerous and regressive elements of the psyche are all assigned to the pre-oedipal mother, all the civilizing aspects to the oedipal father; a process which fails to recognize that both father and mother, at either stage, may be associated with both constructive and destructive aspects.

One of the most innovative of contemporary discussions is Silverman's (1988) critique of Kristeva, in which prominence is given to the notion of the negative oedipus complex. Silverman's uncompromising account rejects altogether the pre-oedipal domain either as an arena for feminist resistance to the Symbolic or as an erotic refuge. She argues that the pre-oedipal phase has improperly replaced the negative oedipus complex as an appropriate description of what, in the early history of the woman, precedes her desire for her father. In Freud's essay 'Femininity' (1933) there is an abrupt refusal to read the little girl's fantasy of maternal seduction as an unequivocal indication of the negative oedipus complex (although Freud discovered the positive oedipus complex through the fantasy of *paternal* seduction). Silverman situates the daughter's passion for the mother within the oedipus complex, making it an effect of symbolic castration. The implication of this is that the Symbolic father is not the only possible mediator between mother and child; this mediation could be effected instead by the Symbolic mother. This line of thought employs Lacanian theory without endorsing its patriarchal assumptions, and is certain to be both stimulating and controversial.

BIBLIOGRAPHY

Benjamin, Jessica, 1988: *The Bonds of Love: Psychoanalysis, Feminism and Domination*. New York: Pantheon.
Chodorow, Nancy, 1978: *The Reproduction of Mothering: Psychoanalysis and the Sociology of Gender*. Berkeley: University of California Press.
Fliess, Robert, ed. 1948: *The Psycho-Analytic Reader*. London: Hogarth Press.
Freud, Sigmund, 1931: 'Female sexuality', *SE*, 21, pp. 221–46.
Freud, Sigmund, 1933: 'Femininity', *SE*, 22, pp. 112–35.
Klein, Melanie, 1988a [1923]: 'The role of the school in the libidinal development of the child', *Love, Guilt and Reparation and Other Works, 1921–1945*. New York: Dell Publishing Company, pp. 59–76.
Klein, Melanie, 1988b [1928]: 'The early stages of the oedipus complex', *Love, Guilt and Reparation*, pp. 186–98.
Klein, Melanie, 1988c [1929]: 'Infantile anxiety situations reflected in a work of art and in the creative impulse', *Love, Guilt and Reparation*, pp. 210–18.
Klein, Melanie, 1989: *The Psycho-analysis of Children*. London: Virago.

Kristeva, Julia, 1984 [1974]: *Revolution in Poetic Language*. New York: Columbia University Press.

Kristeva, Julia, 1986: 'Freud and love: treatment and its discontents', *The Kristeva Reader*, ed. Toril Moi. Oxford: Basil Blackwell, pp. 238–71.

Silverman, Kaja, 1988: *The Acoustic Mirror: The Female Voice in Psychoanalysis and Cinema*. Bloomington, Indiana: Indiana University Press.

MARGARET WHITFORD

primary castration . In 1908, while analysing Little Hans, Freud arrived at the hypothesis that *all* children thought everyone had a penis (1909). He attributed this over-valuation of the organ to its erotic quality. From this hypothesis, Freud evolved a theory of primary castration which he called a 'complex', based on the FANTASY of castration or the absence of the penis. He saw this complex as a reaction to the enigma posed by the anatomical difference between the sexes: girls respond to the absence of a penis with 'penis envy', the sign of their feeling inferior to boys; boys respond with a complex arising from the fear of castration and showing up in an anxiety based on the belief that castration would be just punishment for sexual feelings.

Freud, not surprisingly, read the oedipal story as dramatizing male and female reactions to primary castration, a story about the tragic consequences of breaking the 'incest' taboo. As a psychoanalyst, Freud understood the oedipal tragedy as a socio-ethical imperative to normativize adult sexual relations along the lines of mother/father genital harmony and happy children. Other kinds of sexual relations are then interdicted because of the primordial power he imputed to castration anxiety: if the little girl feels envy of the little boy who has a penis, she can get rid of the envy when she grows up by acquiring her own 'substitute' penis in the form of a husband, a baby being further compensation; the boy likewise compensates for castration anxiety by normativizing his sexual relations in marriage, thereby eradicating castration guilt and anxiety: by giving his wife children, he gives her what she lacks.

In Freud's second topology, from 1923 on, the ego plays an increasingly primary role, gradually substituting for the instinctual drives of the first topology. He stresses the effects of castration anxiety on NARCISSISM in so far as an essential part of the ego's image is eminently vulnerable – for males – in relation to this organ (Freud, 1937, p. 250). Correlatively, classical analysts have argued that motherhood – baby = penis – is the state of ideal psychic health for women. One can therefore see why feminists have objected to Freud's biological account of the necessary and desired effects of the difference between the sexes.

PRIMARY CASTRATION

Lacan's view of primary castration has been described as a structural effect in the REAL where loss refers to a break in the infant/mother symbiosis (Ragland-Sullivan, 1986, pp. 55–7, 305–7); one can carry this further by focusing on the later Lacan's construction of a topological structuralism wherein the Real is first created as an order of trauma from the radical effects of loss itself, originary effects which return into LANGUAGE and human relations as JOUISSANCE effects. The infant is satisfied by food, a gaze, a voice, a touch, and so on, but when the object or effect is removed, the infant responds by wanting a repetition of the pleasure. At this moment of crisis, PLEASURE turns to reality, joy to pain, and *jouissance* is born as the paradoxical effects of a rapid oscillation between pleasure and pain, being and nothingness (Lacan, 1986; *and see* LACAN).

So whereas for Freud primary castration centres upon the significance of the penis, for Lacan it is the forming of an order of the Real for each body, where the contradictions that are present, but unassimilated in memory, are at issue. And this order is first and foremost established in reference to the mother, in so far as she is lost – unsayable, ungraspable – both in parts and as a whole primary object. Loss returns as Real effects that, although absent, are not empty or negative, but 'there' as contingent properties. To think that primary objects were ever possessed, or can be re-found, as object-relations feminists claim, is an Imaginary confusion of the visible with actual entities, and gives rise to the illusion of reparation or redemption via things or people (Miller, 1988, p. 130; Wright, 1984, pp. 81–4; *and see* IMAGINARY).

As early as *Family Complexes* and *The Four Fundamental Concepts*, Lacan was working with primary castration as a problematic concerning the structure of separation (Lacan, 1977c, pp. 213–14; 1984, pp. 25–35). Weaning, death, birth and many other experiences around which rituals are established are viewed as cultural ways to deal with literal separations. Lacan's innovation at this moment was to re-cast the idea of 'complexes' away from biological instincts and re-think them as imagos or visible images that make up matrices of meaning. The separation of infant from breast, of faeces from body, of voice from language, of eye from gaze, are generally thought to correspond either to the organ that produces the effect or to the product. Such Imaginary thinking interprets the relation of OBJECT to organ by either a theory of the object or a theory of the BODY. Lacan argued that certain partial features that emanate from a seemingly total object, the body, have in common the feature of no alterity, no specularity; they are not perceived in the mirror image (Lacan, 1977a, p. 4). Later the subject may learn to say something of Real effects inscribed in the body and covered over by fantasies. The separation itself leaves an inscription on the body, a Real aspect, that is therefore not fully conceptualized or assimilated as knowledge, although bits of it are decipherable in symptoms or in moments when *jouissance* effects appear (Lacan, 1977b, pp. 314–16; *and see* SYMPTOM). In Lacanian theory, primary castration points to the structuring power of separation: because 'object' consistencies are 'supposed' to fill a void, but cannot do so, they all bear the trace of death as the Real of loss.

In reading words like 'castration', post-structuralist feminists have interpreted Lacan to mean that women are castrated or lacking, while men are not. But Lacan's theory of primary castration corrects Freud's error in a way that is significant for feminism. Primordial anxiety does not concern an organ or the lack thereof, but the lack of a ratio by which to designate GENDER difference within an adequate libidinal economy (that is, without being autistic or psychotic). Lacan's formula for this is, 'There is no sexual relation': rather, there is opposition and impasse and the myriad relatings that seek to deny a culturally imposed divide between the sexes. For Lacan the fundamental *malaise* in society is the impasse between the sexes wherein one symbol – the PHALLUS – represents the constitution of LIBIDO around the masculine (Lacan, 1975, p. 90). Though feminists have taken issue with this seemingly phallocentric statement, the centrality of the phallus is linked to castration, not anatomically, but structurally. Since boys find themselves to be an exception to the rule of being like the mother, this discovery produces male castration anxiety, compensated for by identification with the group. The result is a major misunderstanding between the sexes which cannot be adequately explained by sociological or biological theories.

In Lacan's sexuation graphs in *Encore*, his point is not that males or females are castrated: primary castration is, rather, a matter of universals and particulars, the exception and the rule. Indeed, many males make the error of believing they are exceptions to the rule of castration – the LACK that is the SUBJECT – because they Imaginarize identity such that they lack nothing. Females who identify with this male fantasy make the same error. Identification with the exception is a refusal of primary castration, a certain clinging to a logic of the Whole which denies that anything has been subtracted from being (Millot, 1988; André, 1986).

But most important to Lacan's continued re-thinking of primary castration are the two directions it takes in his theory of the Real as the effect of words, images and events, subtracted from memory, but active in the body as *jouissance* effects. Herein the Real concerns history because it inscribes death in the body, around organs and words, joining Thanatos to Eros and burdening humans with the unresolved detritus of their lives. The kind of radical change that produces new freedoms concerns feminists, and such change only occurs in psychoanalytic separation of the ego from the symptom: the subject must learn in the clinic how to detach the fantasy from what emerges in the Real. Primary castration operates on the side of change in the Real, such that women could use it for their own cause, deriving from it an ethics wherein desire can be provisionally re-constituted.

See also CASTRATION COMPLEX; OEDIPUS COMPLEX; PENIS ENVY.

BIBLIOGRAPHY

André, Serge, 1986: Que veut une femme? Paris: Navarin.
Freud, Sigmund, 1909: 'Analysis of a phobia in a five-year-old boy', SE, 10, pp. 1–149.
Freud, Sigmund, 1937: 'Analysis terminable and interminable', SE, 23, pp. 209–54.
Lacan, Jacques, 1975 [1972–3]: Le Séminaire, book 20: Encore, ed. Jacques-Alain Miller. Paris: Seuil.
Lacan, Jacques, 1977a [1949]: 'The mirror stage as formative of the function of the I as revealed in the psychoanalytic experience', Écrits: A Selection, trans. Alan Sheridan. London: Tavistock, pp. 1–7.
Lacan, Jacques, 1977b [1960]: 'The subversion of the subject and the dialectic of desire in the Freudian unconscious', Écrits, pp. 293–325.
Lacan, Jacques, 1977c [1946]: 'The subject and the other: alienation', The Four Fundamental Concepts of Psycho-Analysis, trans. Alan Sheridan. London: Hogarth Press, pp. 203–15.
Lacan, Jacques, 1984 [1938]: Les Complexes familiaux. Paris: Navarin.
Lacan, Jacques, 1986 [1959–60]: Le Séminaire, book 7: L'Éthique de la psychanalyse, ed. Jacques-Alain Miller. Paris: Seuil.
Miller, Jacques-Alain, 1988: 'Extimité', Prose Studies, 11/3, pp. 121–31.
Millot, Catherine, 1988: Nobodaddy: L'Hystérie dans le siècle. Paris: Point Hors Ligne.
Ragland-Sullivan, Ellie, 1986: Jacques Lacan and the Philosophy of Psychoanalysis. Urbana and Chicago: University of Illinois Press.
Wright, Elizabeth, 1984: Psychoanalytic Criticism. London and New York: Methuen.

ELLIE RAGLAND-SULLIVAN

projection   As early as 1895 Freud wrote of projection, linking it with the state of paranoia. Projection is specifically viewed as a defence against homosexual impulses arising out of a narcissistic object choice (Freud, 1911; see NARCISSISM). In general, projection is considered a defence mechanism (see, for example, Freud, 1896). It describes a process whereby the subject's ego disowns unacceptable impulses by attributing them to someone else; the intolerable feelings are then perceived as coming from the other person who, from then on, appears to the subject as a persecutor.

Although LACAN does not make specific use of the term projection, he does locate the process in the IMAGINARY, thereby showing how parts of the subject can be transferred from the inside to the outside. For the subject derives its image from without, i.e., the mirror-other, and thereby is alienated from itself since the image is already outside (*see* OTHER/OTHER).

The concept of projection has been chiefly developed by the Kleinian School. KLEIN stresses the crucial role projection plays within the mother–infant relationship: emphasis is placed on the infant's fantasized experiences and innate aggressive impulses (death instinct) towards the maternal figure (*see* DEATH DRIVE (FREUD); PROJECTIVE IDENTIFICATION).

Following Klein, Wilfred Bion (1967) stresses the importance of the inter-personal interaction between mother and infant. He distinguishes between a pathological projection where the mother cannot tolerate the baby's projection so that the baby is forced to persist in its efforts to expel its negative feelings, and communicative projection where the mother returns to the baby its projection in a digestible form.

For feminism, the development of projection as a way of accounting for the specific mother–infant relationship has been important in a Freudian psychoanalysis dominated by the role of the father at the expense of the mother-figure. Orbach and Eichenbaum (1982) have employed projection to explore further the MOTHER–DAUGHTER RELATIONSHIP. They argue that the mother is prone to confuse her gender identity with that of the girl child, which can result in the mother's unacknowledged aggression and deprivation being projected on to the child, perceived as a narcissistic extension of mother.

Projection also describes the relationship to the IMAGE of the woman in sexual fantasy. For Lacan, woman becomes an object of FANTASY, the place where LACK is projected. The man thereby disowns his own experience and, as a result, produces both a denigrated and/or idealized image of the woman (*see* FETISHISM). IRIGARAY goes a step further, arguing that the notion of woman as the castrated male in psychoanalytic doctrine is produced by male imaginary projections; for woman can only be conceived in relation to a male model, the woman as simply the man-minus.

These various uses of projective mechanisms all illustrate the different ways in which fantasies are projected out into the social, constructing images of the other, in particular the feminine (as girl, woman and mother) with imaginary attributes. As psychic perceptions, projections do not reflect social realities (see PSYCHICAL REALITY). An increasing awareness of this disjuncture will help feminists disentangle the projections from the qualities of the woman as other, which have become so conflated in our culture.

BIBLIOGRAPHY

Bion, Wilfred, 1967: *Second Thoughts*. London: Heinemann, pp. 43–109.
Freud, Sigmund, 1895: 'Draft-H-Paranoia', *SE*, 1, pp. 206–12.
Freud, Sigmund, 1896: 'Further remarks on the neuro-psychoses of defence', *SE*, 3, pp. 157–68.
Freud, Sigmund, 1911: 'Psycho-analytic notes upon an autobiographical account of a case of paranoia (dementia paranoides)', *SE*, 12, pp. 1–84.
Freud, Sigmund, 1915: 'A case of paranoia running counter to the psychoanalytic theory of the disease', *SE*, 14, pp. 261–72.
Orbach, Susie, and Eichenbaum, Luise, 1982: *Outside In Inside Out: Women's Psychology, a Feminist Psychoanalytic Approach*. Harmondsworth: Penguin.

NICOLA DIAMOND

projective identification   The FANTASY of forceful, destructive and controlling intrusion of harmful excrements and split-off parts of the ego into the other, who is thereby felt to be the bad self.

The term was introduced by Melanie KLEIN (1980a, b) to describe a paranoid–schizoid defence against persecutory anxiety developmentally prior to the neurotic defence of REPRESSION, the latter being explained by some as first instituted in the name of the father. By contrast, projective identification initially involves defensive intrusion, in fantasy, into the mother's body, resulting in confusion of self and other. Analysis of paranoid–schizoid states of mind, Kleinians other than Klein argue, accordingly includes attending to the countertransference effect of being the object of the patient's projective identification (*see* TRANSFERENCE/COUNTERTRANSFERENCE). Increasingly this has involved extending the term to cover both psychotic and neurotic phenomena, projective identification now being understood as varying in the degree to which it involves intentional, violent, intrusive control of the OBJECT, or communication, via a benign process of instilling in the analyst the patient's state of mind. Implicitly or explicitly, analysts are often enjoined to be receptive to such PROJECTION, like the mother in containing her baby's otherwise sometimes intolerable anxiety (Bion, 1967).

Feminists might want to examine the good and ill effects of such idealization of women's mothering that Klein deconstructs in insisting on the hatred as well as love therein involved (Scott, 1990). Others have used the extension by post-Kleineans of the term projective identification to group psychology in order to explore the projection of disowned aspects of the self into the opposite sex (see Temperley, 1984). However, this does not necessarily involve the aggressive intrusion into others whereby Klein first implicitly distinguished projective identification from projection.

BIBLIOGRAPHY

Bion, Wilfred, 1967 [1962] 'A theory of thinking', *Second Thoughts*. London: Heinemann, pp. 110–19.

Hinshelwood, Robert D., 1989: *A Dictionary of Kleinian Thought*. London: Free Association Books.

Klein, Melanie, 1980a [1946]: 'Notes on some schizoid mechanisms', *Envy and Gratitude*. London: Hogarth Press, pp. 1–24.

Klein, Melanie, 1980b [1955]: 'On identification', *Envy and Gratitude*, pp. 141–75.

Scott, Ann, 1990: 'Melanie Klein and the questions of feminism', *Women: A Cultural Review*, 1/2, pp. 127–34.

Temperley, Jane, 1984: 'Our own worst enemies', *Free Associations*, pilot issue, pp. 23–38.

JANET SAYERS

psychical reality　The concept of psychical reality arose from a 'mistake'. In Freud's first attempt at formulating an aetiology for hysteria, he assumed that hysterical symptoms were based on a real trauma, paternal rape or seduction, and that accounts of paternal rape or seduction given by his hysterical patients were always descriptions of real events. In psychoanalytic discussions, the 'real event' is now the familiar term for seduction or RAPE as such. In revising his view that hysteria originated in real traumatic events, Freud arrived at his 'surprising discovery' (Freud, 1925, p. 24), the existence of psychical reality.

Psychical reality means that the fantasies a person had entertained but repressed (for instance, desire for a parent) and the reactions to those fantasies (for instance, guilt over the wish to dispose of the other parent) had the same effects on behaviour *as if* they had been real events: 'As if' becomes 'it is'. In psychical reality one feels as guilty as if the crime had occurred. Nor do the implications of psychical reality for real behaviour end there. Desire and guilt can be projected on to the parent; the parent, not the child, is made the point of origin for blame. Hamlet, for example, is a true male hysteric, marked by exaggerated scruples of conscience which were actually 'reaction-formations' to his own desires (Freud, 1900, p. 265).

355

In modifying his view that the paternal seductions his patient reported were real events, Freud was influenced by the self-analysis that was contemporaneous with, and conducted in the context of, his relationship with Wilhelm Fliess. This self-analysis revealed his own oedipal impulse, and this presumably influenced his re-evaluation of his hysterical patients' accounts. Just as he had found the oedipus complex in his psychical depths, so too (he assumed) the analogous impulse lay behind the women he analysed. Freud announced the OEDIPUS COMPLEX, meaning sexual love for the opposite-sex parent, and jealous hostility towards the other, on 15 October 1897, one month after the collapse of the SEDUCTION THEORY. He had gone as far as he could with himself; he assumed there was no hinterland in the women. In the published record he writes that in recognizing that the accounts of seduction were not all true, 'I had in fact stumbled for the first time upon the Oedipus Complex, which was later to assume such an overwhelming importance' (Freud, 1925, p. 34).

But the oedipus complex Freud discovered in his patients either assumed or led to another great mistake. The context for the momentous discovery of psychical reality and the simultaneous discovery of sexual impulses in children is also the clinical occasion for perpetuating the idea that a girl's father, not her mother, is her first love, a view Freud revised some twenty-five years later. The discovery and the oversight are two sides of the same picture. This leads to an obvious question. Is psychical reality, is the process whereby 'as if' becomes 'it is', the same in the masculine and the feminine case?

There is another point about psychical reality that should be noted. It is commonly supposed that, when Freud abandoned the seduction theory, he simultaneously assumed that all the accounts given him of seduction were false. This is not correct. What he abandoned was the idea that the *sole* cause of a psychoneurosis was an actual seduction. In his first published revision of the seduction theory he wrote that his case material at the time he formulated the seduction theory 'was still scanty, and it happened by chance to include a disproportionately large number of cases in which sexual seduction by an adult or by older children played the chief part in the patient's childhood. I thus over-estimated the frequency of such events (though in other respects they were not open to doubt). Moreover, I was at that point unable to distinguish with certainty beween falsifications made by hysterics in their memories of childhood and traces of real events' (Freud, 1906, p. 274).

The significance of the discovery of psychical reality was not so much that it discounted the accounts as 'real events', but more that it emphasized that fantasies of seduction had the same effect as real events: not only because they had the same effect, but also because, Freud argued, other people who had actually been seduced did not fall ill, the aetiological concern became the relative force of REPRESSION. The failure of repression, the splitting off of an idea or memory from consciousness, led to the formation of a SYMPTOM. The shift in emphasis from the real event to repression meant that 'it was no longer a question of what sexual experiences a particular individual had had in his childhood, but rather of his reactions to those experiences – of whether he had reacted to them by "repression" [*Verdrängung*] or not' (Freud, 1906, p. 277).

Before proceeding to the implications for feminism of this turning from real events to psychical reality, it should be recorded that Freud's first published recantation of the seduction theory is at odds, not only with the popular view, but with the famous letter to Fliess of 21 September 1897 in which Freud first retracted that theory (Freud, 1984). In that letter, he did not say that only some of his patients had not experienced real trauma. He said that he had had to abandon his *neurotica* (theory of the neurosis) and with it, the certain knowledge of the aetiology of HYSTERIA. There is no qualification here: Freud does not ask whether some of the accounts of sexual assault are true; he queries the idea that 'precisely the same conditions' prevail in each case, and he suggests that because there are so many cases of hysteria, there would have to be even more instances of seduction or assault, because seduction is not of itself enough to cause hysteria. Hysteria only occurs after an 'accumulation of events' and where another factor 'weakens the defence'. In fact, this passage is an early indicator of Freud's subsequent views on the formation of neuroses or psychoses, where the emphasis is 'multi-factoral': more than one incident or inclination is needed to determine an illness. But the letter itself says nothing about some of the accounts of seduction being true.

In addition, Freud exculpates the father to some degree in a report to the Vienna Psychoanalytic Society in January 1912, and, in his first history of the psychoanalytic movement, Freud wrote that the seduction 'aetiology broke down under the weight of its own improbability and contradiction in definitely ascertainable circumstances. Analysis had led back to these infantile sexual traumas by the right path, and yet they were not true' (Nunberg and Federn, 1962–75, 3, p. 7). At the same time, Freud's stress here is entirely on the idea that if the traumas were fictitious and the seduction scenes created in FANTASY, then psychical reality has to figure 'alongside practical reality' (pp. 17–18). Subsequently Freud wrote that the neurotic symptoms were 'not related directly to actual events but to wishful phantasies' (Freud, 1925, p. 34), and reiterated that psychical reality matters. Yet the earlier qualification on the renunciation of the seduction theory is echoed here. Freud recorded that his confidence in the seduction theory had been increased by cases where the sexual relations with the father or older brother persisted to a point 'at which memory was to be trusted' (1925, p. 34), and also that seduction still played a part, albeit a lesser one, in the aetiology of the neuroses. These qualifications also reflect Freud's doubts expressed in letters to Fliess, after the letter in which he first retracted his seduction theory. Freud's belief in the father aetiology was at one point strengthened (in other letters to Fliess of 12 and 22 December 1897), and his reluctance to reach a final view is entirely consistent with the measure of the emphasis throughout his work as a whole: namely, that sometimes the repression of real trauma was involved in the formation of symptoms; sometimes the symptoms originated in the repression of fantasy.

Because Jeffrey Masson's book *The Assault on Truth* (Masson, 1984) has had such unwarranted popularity, his argument that Freud suppressed the seduction theory as the result of a 'failure of courage' has to be mentioned here. When Masson first mentions Freud's public retraction of the seduction theory in 1905, he abstains from quotation. It would have been difficult to sustain an argument that Freud suppressed the seduction theory in the light of the relevant quotations from the initial retraction. In the 'Three essays on sexuality' of 1905 (and this is the only occasion in that year on which Freud refers to the seduction theory), Freud writes that he 'overrated the importance of seduction', which is different from discounting it; and he moreover goes on to list seduction as the most important of the accidental '*external* contingencies determining sexual activity and neurotic illness' (Freud, 1905, p. 190). Freud's detailed retraction of the seduction theory in the following year (Freud, 1906, p. 274) precisely does not say that his patients were lying; he says his patients' accounts were true. In fact, Masson does finally cite this passage in the latter part of his book: but he does so after arranging his early quotations in such a manner as to leave the reader with the impression that Freud entirely relegated the seduction theory to hysterical fantasy. Of course, had Masson made a case against the manner in which Freud's own views have been discounted in favour of the idea that all accounts of father–daughter incest were fantasies, he would have been on unimpeachable ground.

The notion that the memory of a real event, like a fantasy, could cause illness through its vicissitudes under repression survives in the later aetiology. What is of interest to us now is that this aetiology presents us with a persistent interplay between fantasy and material reality in Freud's model of health and pathology. It also shifts the focus of Freud's concerns to one of the foundation stones of psychoanalysis: the relative force of repression. It is because the psychical reality of a repressed fantasy can be as real in its effects as an actual traumatic event that Freud's discovery of psychical reality is the other foundation stone of psychoanalysis, and the beginning of psychoanalysis proper. Psychoanalysis is about the power of psychical reality and unconscious fantasy; about the magnitude of their effects. It is not, or not only, about how social relations are internalized (Brennan, 1991).

Psychical reality has become an issue in feminist discussions of psychoanalysis because it implies that there can be no automatic one-to-one correspondence between social events or expectations and the contents of the psyche. Thus CHODOROW has been criticized on the grounds that she assumes that familial relations, of themselves, will determine the content of sexual identity. The criticism is an over-simplification of Chodorow's complex analysis (she does in fact take account of fantasy), but the point remains: how much of masculinity and femininity is determined by psychical realities that are beyond the reach of, or prior to, socialization? Lacanians would answer, a great deal. So would Kleinians. For instance, in KLEIN's theory, an infant will have a fantasy about a 'bad mother' that deprives it of satisfaction or causes it pain *no matter what* the actual behaviour of the parent in reality happens to be. On the one hand, this emphasis on psychical reality relieves actual parents of responsibility (mothers, as usual, being the main target: *see* MOTHERHOOD). On the other hand, it raises the problem of whether there is something intractably patriarchal in psychical reality, if certain patriarchal unconscious fantasies exist prior to or beyond the reach of social influence, and hence of social change (*see* PATRIARCHY). The psychoanalytic, feminist state of the art on this question is a *non liquet*, meaning a verdict of 'not proven'. Probably the most productive approach to the question lies with Freud himself, in that he emphasized the interplay of psychical and material/social realities, an interplay developed by Klein, who believed that an unconscious fantasy could be either reinforced or negated by actual social experience. So even in the unlikely event that there are pre-existent psychical realities that incline the sexes to a framework of masculinist domination, social reality could cancel out their effects. Given that some Lacanians would say that the formation of psychical reality makes patriarchy inevitable, it should be noted that the Lacanian emphasis on the (unconscious) 'desire of the Other' suggests a way in which the unconscious patriarchal fantasies of one generation could be transmitted to the next. The very idea of transmission entails that if these unconscious fantasies change, then the dead patriarchal weight of previous generations will lie less heavy on the shoulders of the living.

See also ESSENTIALISM.

PSYCHICAL REALITY

BIBLIOGRAPHY

Adams, Parveen, Brown, Beverley, and Cowie, Elizabeth, 1981: 'Editorial', *m/f*, 5/6, pp. 2–4.

Brennan, Teresa, 1988: 'Controversial discussions and feminist debate', *Freud in Exile: Psychoanalysis and its Vicissitudes*, ed. Edward Timms and Naomi Segal. New Haven: Yale University Press, pp. 254–74.

Brennan, Teresa, 1991: 'An impasse in psychoanalysis and feminism', *A Reader in Feminist Knowledge*, ed. Sneja Gunew. London: Routledge, pp. 114–38.

Freud, Sigmund, 1900: *The Interpretation of Dreams*, SE, 4, 5.

Freud, Sigmund, 1905: *Three Essays on the Theory of Sexuality*, SE, 7, pp. 125–248.

Freud, Sigmund, 1906: 'My views on the part played by sexuality in the aetiology of the neuroses', *SE*, 7, pp. 269–80.

Freud, Sigmund, 1914: 'On the history of the psycho-analytic movement', *SE*, 14, pp. 1–66.

Freud, Sigmund, 1925: 'An autobiographical study', *SE* 20, pp. 7–70.

Freud, Sigmund, 1984: *The Complete Letters of Sigmund Freud to Wilhelm Fliess: 1887–1904*, ed. Jeffrey M. Masson. Cambridge, Mass.: Harvard University Press.

Laplanche, Jean, and Pontalis, Jean-Baptiste, 1986: 'Fantasy and the origins of sexuality', *Formations of Fantasy*, ed. Victor Burgin, James Donald and Cora Kaplan. London: Methuen, pp. 3–34.

Masson, Jeffrey, 1984: *The Assault on Truth: Freud's Suppression of the Seduction Theory*. London: Faber.

Nunberg, Hermann and Federn, Ernst, 1962–75: *Minutes of the Vienna Psycho-Analytic Society*. 3 vols. Trans. M. Nunberg with N. Collins. New York: International Universities Press.

Rose, Jacqueline, 1986: *Sexuality in the Field of Vision*. London: Verso.

TERESA BRENNAN

R

race/imperialism   Race and imperialism are not equivalent, but related topics. While *race* is the marker of distinct groups of human population by genetically transmitted physical traits, or by geographic, national or historical distribution, *imperialism* refers to the acts by which one nation extends its sovereignty over another by means of territorial, economic or political aggrandizement. In the recent histories of imperialism, such as those of the aggression of European nations (notably Spain, Portugal, France and England; also Belgium and Holland) against the native peoples of the Americas, Africa and Asia in the past few hundred years, the issue of race often becomes that of *racism* – the use of race to justify imperialism by discriminating against those who are non-white. This interlocking relationship between race or racism and imperialism continues today, most visibly in countries (such as France, Germany, the USA and Japan) where the lowest stratum of the labour fource is composed of foreign workers from Third World countries, or where racial differences have historically determined one group's cultural hegemony over another (such as apartheid in South Africa, and the conflicts between groups of Anglo origin and groups of black, Hispanic, native American and Asian origins in the USA). Questions of race and imperialism pertain to issues of personal and cultural identity, and play an increasingly important role in cultural and discursive politics.

One of the first writers to address the relationships between race, imperialism and psychoanalysis was the black psychiatrist Frantz Fanon (1925–61). Fanon's works represent an early attempt to mark the relation between the native and the colonizer with a critical analytical structure. He perceives that relation in oedipal terms, portraying the native as an angry son who wishes to kill the father (the white man) and put himself in the father's place. Fanon argues that the native's identity is necessarily a violent one. He posits violence as a cleansing force that would free the native from his inferiority complex and despair, and restore his self-respect.

Fanon's works were published in English during the 1960s, while former colonies around the world were establishing their political independence. During the same period, interest in psychoanalysis was intensifying in the West, especially in France. The 1960s and early 1970s also saw the publication of what are now known as first-generation feminist works, such as Betty Friedan's *The Feminine Mystique* (1963), Kate Millett's *Sexual Politics* (1970), and *The Second Sex* (1972), the English translation of Simone de Beauvoir's *Le Deuxième Sexe* (1949), which collectively protested against a particular kind of violence: the patriarchal violence experienced by women in a male-dominated society. What these three fields of interest – de-colonization, psychoanalysis, feminism – have in common is a continual interrogation of identity. Whether conducted in political, psychoanalytic or sexual terms, this interrogation often assumes an antagonistic (or oedipal) relation between the self and its other(s)/oppressors.

However, when the 'self' and its 'other' are constructed primarily as victim and oppressor, the violence that underlies such a construction remains subservient to the idea of a unified human subject. This subject is presumed to have its own free will – and thus its capacity for resistance – outside the mediation of LANGUAGE. 'Self' and 'other' thus remain reified, and the relation between them remains mechanical. In all three of these fields, the question that ultimately surfaces is: how might identification be conceived beyond the presupposition of a unified human subject? How might 'the other' be conceived beyond the paradigm of violence?

The intersection between feminism and anti-imperialism is a particularly difficult one because both discourses have claims to what might be called their preferred victims – woman in one case and native in the other – and both insist on the analytical primacy of that victim's identity. While anti-imperialists may argue that women's issues must wait until the 'larger' process of de-colonization has been completed, feminists reject the way much anti-imperialist discourse replicates the aggressive power structures it criticizes. For instance, how far does the violent position of the native as described by Fanon have relevance for women in their relation to men? When one of the major tasks set by feminists is the undoing of sexual violence, it is difficult, perhaps impossible, to adopt unproblematically the emphasis placed on violence as such. On the other hand, anti-imperialists tend to dispute the exclusive promotion of women's rights as a perpetuation of the privileges of the white middle class. For both feminism and anti-imperialism, the relation between 'self' and 'other' – a relation that involves GENDER, race and class – constitutes the core of the problem. If the self can no longer be presumed to be a unified centre of decision, how might a feminist *and* anti-colonialist discourse be constructed?

Post-structuralism plays a crucial, though not entirely adequate, role in responding to these questions. Post-structuralism is frequently associated with the writers Jacques Derrida, Michel Foucault, Roland Barthes and Jacques LACAN. It can briefly be described as the way of thinking that recognizes the mediation of language in all human undertakings and that contests the notion of a human SUBJECT with its own free will, consciousness or agency outside language. Lacan's most significant contribution lies in the way he introduces language in re-interpreting Freud's works. In Lacanian psychoanalysis, the intervention of post-structuralism means the restoration of a split, rather than unified, subjectivity, in which 'self' and 'other' are intertwined through signification. Post-structuralist psychoanalysis displaces the oedipal structurations of envy, violence and so forth on to the play of language and discourse, which are now the chief loci for investigating questions of identification.

The dimension of language opened up by post-structuralism and post-structuralist psychoanalysis means that feminists and anti-imperialists are confronted with a fundamental problem of methodology. Either they can continue to re-invoke oedipal structures and perpetuate the reified relation between 'self' and 'other' by uniformly attacking man and/or the white man as the universal oppressor; or they can broaden the concern for their preferred victim's identity to one for other oppressed groups as well. The latter is possible only if attention is paid not to one universalist notion of 'woman' or 'native' but to the processes of identification-construction that take place in language, psychic processes and institutions, so that the 'other' is no longer simply regarded as a Manichean opposite to the self, but always already a part of it. It is along these lines – of women and natives no longer as rebellious daughters and sons who keep fighting the father and the father alone, but as socially situated persons who join others' struggles – that feminism and anti-imperialism work best together in a way that is informed by psychoanalysis.

Works devoting equal attention to race, imperialism, feminism and psychoanalysis are rare. This has much to do, historically, with the socially and economically privileged status enjoyed by the practice of psychoanalysis in the West. Because of this, even feminist anti-imperialist critics tend to dismiss psychoanalysis as no more than an ideologically suspect Western institution which participates in the imperialism they are criticizing. These critics prefer to view the problems of identification non-psychoanalytically, accounting for the relations between self and other by way of institutions of political and ideological control, unequal divisions of labour and other types of collective social structures that ultimately rely, once again, on the notion of a unified human subject. Psychoanalytic categories such as REPRESSION and DESIRE, which challenge such a notion and which have been applied by literary critics with highly significant nuances to the texts about men and women in the First World, remain largely unexplored in writings by and about formerly colonized peoples. In this area much work needs to be done.

See also BLACK FEMINIST CRITIQUE OF PSYCHOANALYSIS; BLACK FEMINIST PSY-CHOTHERAPY; IDENTIFICATION; OTHER/OTHER; SUBJECT.

BIBLIOGRAPHY

Fanon, Frantz, 1968 [1961]: *The Wretched of the Earth*. Trans. Constance Farringdon. New York: Grove Press.
Fanon, Frantz, 1967 [1952]: *Black Skin, White Masks*. Trans. Charles Lam Markmann. New York: Grove Press.
Gates, Henry Louis, Jr, ed. 1986: *'Race', Writing, and Difference*. Chicago and London: University of Chicago Press.
Minh-ha, Trinh, T., 1989: *Woman, Native, Other: Writing, Postcoloniality and Feminism*. Bloomington, Indiana: Indiana University Press.
Spivak, Gayatri Chakravorty, 1987: *In Other Worlds: Essays in Cultural Politics*. New York and London: Methuen.

REY CHOW

rape: political perspectives　In English law, rape is narrowly defined as 'unlawful sexual intercourse with a woman who at the time of inter-course does not consent to it' (quoted in Tomaselli and Porter, 1986, p. 10). But as Sylvana Tomaselli points out, it is a term which has been 'extended in its use to cover all heterosexual acts, or all advances initi-ated by men, as well as the latter's treatment of nature' (ibid.).

On the question of rape, psychoanalysis and feminism do not seem to meet on any common ground. John Forrester succinctly summarizes the disjunction as follows. Whereas for feminism, rape is an issue of social conflict *between* individuals, psychoanalysis confines itself to conflict *within* individuals, and is exclusively interested in the domain of the UNCONSCIOUS where the legal question of consent is irrelevant (1986, p. 67; *see also* PSYCHICAL REALITY).

For psychoanalysis, rape as an external reality is bracketed; the ques-tion becomes that of FANTASY, and is linked to MASOCHISM and feminine passivity (*see* SEDUCTION THEORY). Both Karen HORNEY and Helene DEUTSCH see women's rape fantasies in these terms. For example, Horney suggests that they may be compulsive repetitions of a fantasy of sexual relations with the father, in which the woman is wounded and 'castrated'. There is an unfortunate convergence between the clinical discussion of rape fantasies and popular cultural myths which assume the complicity of the woman ('she asked for it'). Feminists argue that psychoanalysis is not immune from cultural influence (see Irigaray, 1991). It was not really until feminism challenged the 'normalizing' tendencies of psychoanalysis that the question of a link between violence and male sexuality was addressed, and 'normal' masculinity problematized.

From a feminist perspective, the psychoanalysts Nadelson and Notman (1979) have argued for the definition of trauma to be extended to rape. Psychoanalysis has long recognized that, where a traumatic external force (war, torture, community disasters) breaks the balance between the internal adaptive capacity and the environment, reactions may not necessarily indicate neurosis, but rather the attempts of the functioning individual to cope in situations of catastrophe. Such a redefinition affects the nature of the clinical intervention (*see* CLINICAL PERSPECTIVES).

Thus, although the feminist rejection of Freud (see Brownmiller, 1976) and of psychoanalysis as an instrument of male domination can be attributed partially to a misunderstanding of the specificity of psychoanalysis and its distinction between conscious and unconscious mental life, at the same time the feminist critique of psychoanalysis forces the consideration that psychoanalytic theorization may be seriously inadequate here, and that psychoanalysis may not have taken into account its own complicity with the cultural construction of MASCULINITY and FEMININITY. For feminism, rape is not a question of fantasy, but one of domination. It is more likely to be seen as both systemic and systematic: 'nothing more or less than a conscious process of intimidation by which *all* men keep *all* women in a state of fear' (Brownmiller, p. 15; *see also* PATRIARCHY). Although most feminist analyses do not accept Brownmiller's view that rape or the threat of rape is the single most important instrument whereby a patriarchal system maintains its supremacy, they tend to converge in their agreement that rape is an aspect of a system of power-relations characterized by violence against women, in which other phenomena, such as incest, domestic violence, pornography and prostitution perform the same function, regardless of the contingent intentions of the male client or perpetrator (Wilson, 1983). These accounts of systemic violence have generated in their turn intense debates about the links between violence and sexuality (*see* PLEASURE, SADOMASOCHISM).

Both feminists and psychoanalysts have analysed men's unconscious fear and hatred of women; many feminists go on to argue that the rapist is not usually abnormal or pathological, and that there is no sharp dividing line between ordinary 'masculinity' as it is constructed in our culture and the actions of the rapist: he may be 'the boy next door' (Dworkin, 1982). The emphasis of feminist action, therefore, has been towards social change, both to check manifestations of male violence and also to tackle the construction of masculinity and femininity. Feminists have focused their efforts in two domains in particular, neither of which has been of particular concern to psychoanalysis. The first is that of legal reform (see Temkin, 1986); the second is that of support systems for women, in the form of rape crisis centres (see London Rape Crisis Centre, 1984; and Roberts, 1989). Feminism has also provided considerable sociological analysis, unpacking 'rape' or sexual violence into a range of often quite dissimilar categories – sexual harassment at work, father–daughter incest, inter-racial rape – with quite different practical, legal and political implications. The psychoanalytic account of violence or aggression is not thought to be adequate to deal with the many different forms which violence may take, nor to tackle the specificity of rape as a social and cultural phenomenon.

See also RAPE: PROBLEMS OF INTENTION.

BIBLIOGRAPHY

Brownmiller, Susan, 1976: Against Our Will. Harmondsworth: Penguin.
Deutsch, Helene, 1948: 'The significance of masochism in the mental life of women', The Psycho-Analytic Reader, ed. Robert Fliess. London: Hogarth Press, pp. 195–207.
Dworkin, Andrea, 1982: 'The rape atrocity and the boy next door', Our Blood. London: The Women's Press, pp. 22–49.
Forrester, John, 1986: 'Rape, seduction and psychoanalysis', Tomaselli and Porter, 1986, pp. 57–83.
Griffin, Susan, 1982 [1971]: 'The politics of rape', Made from this Earth. London: The Women's Press, pp. 39–58.
Horney, Karen, 1967: Feminine Psychology, ed. Harold Kelman. New York: Norton.
Irigaray, Luce, 1991 [1985]: 'The poverty of psychoanalysis', The Irigaray Reader, ed. Margaret Whitford. Oxford: Basil Blackwell, pp. 79–104.
London Rape Crisis Centre, 1984: Sexual Violence: The Reality for Women. London: The Women's Press.
Nadelson, Carol C., and Notman, Malkah T., 1979: 'Psychoanalytic considerations of the response to rape', International Review of Psycho-Analysis, 6, pp. 97–103.
Roberts, Catherine, 1989: Women and Rape. Hemel Hempstead: Harvester Wheatsheaf.
Temkin, Jennifer, 1986: 'Women, rape and law reform', Tomaselli and Porter, 1986, pp. 16–40.
Tomaselli, Sylvana, and Porter, Roy, eds 1986: Rape. Oxford: Basil Blackwell.
Wilson, Elizabeth, 1983: What is to be done about Violence against Women? Harmondsworth: Penguin.

MARGARET WHITFORD

rape: problems of intention   Rape, or violently enforced sexual intercourse without consent, is a crime. Hard to prove before the courts, and
for feminism the central token of patriarchal domination, rape is barely
touched upon by Freud; yet views of rape have been deeply if mistakenly
influenced by psychoanalysis. The issue of rape therefore sits particularly uneasily between psychoanalysis, law and feminism.

The difficulty of proving a crime that depends for its definition on the
testimony of a witness who experiences her position as that of the primary victim has made legal practice turn to psychoanalytically inspired
ideas concerning intention. Intentionality is at odds with psychoanalysis,
which theorizes the conflicts and countercurrents within the SUBJECT that
make intention ambiguous. Moreover, given the centrality of consent in
the definition of rape, it is remarkable that the intention to commit rape
depends on the intention of the victim not to be raped. For this reason
legal practice has too often shifted from examination of the defendant's
intention to examination of the victim's. Any sign of ambivalence in the
latter then tends to cast doubt on the intention of the former. Such
doubts have often sprung from the vulgarization of psychoanalytic ideas
about female MASOCHISM (Freud, 1924; but cf. Silverman, 1992), rape
fantasies (DEUTSCH) and Freud's withdrawal of the seduction theory put
forward in 'The aetiology of hysteria' (Freud, 1896). More generally,
the discovery of the UNCONSCIOUS complicated the very notion of intention.

Freud may not have written on rape, and may in various matters have
taken a position partial to men, but he always emphasized the radical
nature of the difference between the unconscious and the conscious.
Psychoanalysis is in fact alien to law: whereas the law focuses on
conflict between subjects, psychoanalysis is only interested in conflicts
within them. The principled and indispensable ethical indifference of
psychoanalysis may give offence to those who expect help, but such
offence rests on a deep misunderstanding of the theory. There is an
inherent reason within both psychoanalysis and law why no appeal to
psychoanalysis to mitigate a rape charge makes sense. Since there is no
negation in the unconscious, there is neither yes nor no; hence, no consent can be located in the unconscious. Regardless of the question
whether particular desires of a masochistic nature have been influenced
by social inequities, desire is not consent. Only by acknowledging this is
it possible to convict individual men of rape. The feminist argument that
rape fantasies emerge from social pressures (Brownmiller, 1976) has a
dangerous other side to it. For the resulting claim that society makes
men into rapists (Dworkin, 1982) relieves individuals of their responsibility and thus makes legal indictment impossible. Legally speaking,
consent requires the ability to assent, and a subject paralysed by

ambivalence, hampered in her ability to resist, is equally hampered in her ability to assent. This holds obviously also for children who are legally unable to consent under any circumstance. Feminists have much to gain from a focus on the legal aspects of rape (MacKinnon, 1983), and one of their first tasks here should be to make a strict separation between those legal aspects and psychoanalytically based arguments.

Another major legal issue is that of evidence. Legal discourse sometimes measures evidence in terms of demonstrated resistance, thus tying it again to consent (Edwards, 1981). This line of argument has a long history. According to Williams (1953), if in these circumstances the woman failed to use all means open to her to repel the man, including shouting for help, the jury may well think it unsafe to convict him. The age-old law of Deuteronomy 22 stipulates exactly the same thing (Tanner, 1979): evidence that the woman screamed for help is the only evidence that the man raped her. Although there are surely other means of establishing a lack of consent, this form of proof, echoing the old law, sounds more convincing than it really is. Screams can be staged, while the capacity to scream can be eliminated practically (in an isolated location) or psychically (by paralysis).

For a second aspect of the evidence problem, psychoanalysis does have relevance. The rape victim stands in court as a witness, a situation which evacuates her sense of self; as such, it is an uncanny repetition of the experience of rape itself. Testimonies of rape survivors (Griffin, 1979) show that the most central element of the experience is the sense of being deprived of the self; being physically penetrated without her consent, the subject feels evacuated from within. One defence against this assault on one's subjectivity is to evacuate the place of one's own initiative; paradoxically, endorsing the evacuation of subjectivity is the only way in which the victim can hold on to some sense of self. Hence the feeling that the woman was 'not really there'; was witnessing the event as if from the outside; felt her limbs turn to jelly, or counted to a hundred in order to stay away from the psychic scene. The incapacity actively and maximally to resist the rape, explained either as the consequence of fright or as caused by ambivalence – and it needs to be stressed that in neither case does it point to consent – is also caused by this evacuation of subjectivity. This position of the woman 'beside herself' can produce serious mental disturbance, especially if it confirms an older experience whose memory trace is reactivitated. The very situation in the courtroom, where again her 'no' is not believed and the displacement of her subjectivity is repeated, makes it extremely difficult to hold up a convincing testimony. Instead of casting doubt upon her reliability as a witness, this difficulty should be understood in terms of the similarity between the two situations, and therefore as confirmation of the rape rather than the opposite. In other words, whereas the workings of the unconscious are irrelevant for the existence of consent, they are relevant for an understanding of the behaviour of the woman as witness likely to establish the lack of it.

The bone of contention between feminism and psychoanalysis regarding rape is the SEDUCTION THEORY and its withdrawal. The term 'seduction' is arguably a euphemism for rape, in spite of reasons that may partly justify it. Forrester (1990) claims that Freud called the imposition of sexual experience on a young child 'seduction' because, according to clinical evidence, the event was not, at the moment of its traumatic memory, remembered as rape. The memory indicated feelings of guilt, shame, helplessness, even DESIRE and love: the subject felt somehow implicated, but this is not a convincing reason to call the event seduction. Given that the perpetrator is most often a parent or another person close to the young child, this sense of implicatedness is not surprising: the child's love for the person makes the abuse worse, the betrayal and hence the trauma more severe. Arguably, guilt, also arising in cases where the rape victim is older (Smart and Smart, 1978), is a secondary defence mechanism against the threat to the subject's sense of self. By implicating herself she can at least hold up a token of subjectivity: I am guilty (or desiring), hence, I am.

It is clear that any appeal to psychoanalysis to minimize either the criminal fact of rape or the need for effective treatment is a highly suspect political misuse of psychoanalysis. The political question for feminism of how to theorize and counter rape (Russell, 1982; Woodhull, 1988) has been made acute by Foucault's attempt to de-criminalize it (Diamond and Quinby, 1988; for a critique of Foucault see Plaza, 1981). But there is another political aspect to the use and abuse of psychoanalysis in this regard. More pervasively, the tendency to allegorize rape needs to be analysed within a psychoanalytically oriented literary criticism, as a defence for the reader, who is implicated in the ambivalences suggested by, or projected upon, cultural accounts of rape. On one level, the tendency to explain rape allegorically is an escape from the horror that any view of rape forces the reader to face (e.g. Judges 19). On another level, the allegorical myths of rape suggest wrong answers to the juridical dilemma disturbingly close to those given by the misusers of psychoanalysis. Thus the story of the rape of Lucretia, allegorically interpreted as representing the wrongs of dictatorship, was taken from the victim by Brutus who used her experience – and her body, in another, symbolic, rape – to initiate the revolution leading to the Roman republic. But the interpretation of the rape attributed to Lucretia by Livy and Ovid was that of a wrong for which she was not responsible yet for which she punished herself with death. 'Somehow' she had to suffer, since she was the subject violated, hence, the subject of violation. Rape can, however, be used allegorically in a reversed perspective: not to escape the horror of the experience but to sharpen focus on the horror in the event with which it is being compared. This is how Buchi Emecheta (1983) uses the motif of rape in *The Rape of Shavi*.

Finally, the one issue in rape where psychoanalysis is both relevant and liable to misuse, and which is too little addressed, is that of the rapist. Just as in court, where the evidence is so easily shifted from rapist's to victim's intention, so in psychoanalytical studies of rapists the tendency is to shift from the rapist to the woman, and via her to his mother (West et al., 1978). The tendency to typecast rapists – to claim that there is one particular type of man raping women – hampers the understanding of the ways in which patriarchal society fosters hostility to women and thus encourages *different* kinds of men, with different psychoanalytical problems, to act their problems out in rape.

But the primary question is why men rape; in this sense, rape is not a women's issue but a men's issue.

See also PATRIARCHY; PSYCHICAL REALITY; RAPE: FEMINIST PERSPECTIVES.

BIBLIOGRAPHY

Bal, Mieke, 1991: 'The semiotics of rape', *Reading 'Rembrandt': Beyond the Word–Image Opposition*. Cambridge: Cambridge University Press.

Brownmiller, Susan, 1976: *Against Our Will: Men, Women, and Rape*. New York: Simon and Schuster.

Diamond, Irene, and Quinby, Lee, eds 1988: *Feminism and Foucault: Reflections on Resistance*. Boston: Northeastern University Press.

Dworkin, Andrea, 1987: *Intercourse*. London: Arrow Books.

Edwards, Susan, 1981: *Female Sexuality and the Law*. Oxford: Martin Robertson.

Emecheta, Buchi, 1983: *The Rape of Shavi*. London: Fontana.

Estrich, Susan, 1987: *Real Rape: How the Legal System Victimizes Women Who Say No*. Cambridge, Mass.: Harvard University Press.

Forrester, John, 1990: 'Rape, seduction, psychoanalysis', *The Seductions of Psychoanalysis: Freud, Lacan and Derrida*. Cambridge: Cambridge University Press, pp. 62–82.

Freud, Sigmund, 1896: 'The aetiology of hysteria', *SE*, 3, pp. 191–221.

Freud, Sigmund, 1924: 'The economic problem of masochism', *SE*, 19, pp. 159–70.

Griffin, Susan, 1979: *Rape: The Power of Consciousness*. New York: Harper and Row.

MacKinnon, Catherine, 1983: 'Feminism, marxism, method and the state: toward feminist jurisprudence', *Signs*, 8/4, pp. 635–58.

Plaza, Monique, 1981: 'Our damages and their compensation; Rape: the will not to know of Michel Foucault', *Feminist Issues*, 1, pp. 25–35.

Russell, Diana, 1982: *The Politics of Rape*. New York: Stein and Day.

Silverman, Kaja, 1992: *Male Subjectivity at the Margins*. London: Routledge.

Smart, Carol, and Smart, Barry, 1978: 'Accounting for rape: reality and myth in press reporting', *Women, Sexuality and Social Control*, ed. Carol Smart and Barry Smart. London: Routledge and Kegan Paul, pp. 89–103.

Tanner, Tony, 1979: *Adultery in the Novel: Contract and Transgression*. Baltimore: Johns Hopkins University Press.

West, D. J., Roy, C., and Nichols, Florence, 1978: *Understanding Sexual Attacks: A Study Based upon a Group of Rapists Undergoing Psychotherapy*. London: Heinemann.

Williams, Glanville L., 1953: *Criminal Law: The General Part*. London: Stevens and Sons.

Woodhull, Winifred, 1988: 'Sexuality, power and the question of rape', Diamond and Quinby, 1988, pp. 167–76.

MIEKE BAL

reading as/like a woman 'Reading as a woman' and 'reading like a woman' refer to two different projects within feminist literary criticism.

Ever since the late 1960s, women have been (re-)reading LITERATURE – especially literary texts written by men – from a feminist perspective. Convinced that female experience is often (fatally) misrepresented there, these critics have sought to expose the misogyny inherent in large parts of our cultural heritage. At the same time, neglected works and genres by women authors have been re-read with a view as to how such works depict female experience, and to reveal why these texts were excluded from the canon.

Such criticism is basically thematic, focusing either on the plot structure of a literary text, or on the psychological make-up of its protagonists. It often takes the form of 'images of women criticism', analysing the female characters in the works of an author, a genre, a period. Studying the images of women in fiction almost always means studying 'false' images of women in fiction (as opposed to some 'real' image that literature somehow never quite manages to convey). Because it is based on the content of a literary text rather than on its formal structures or on the intricacies of the reading process itself, 'reading as a woman' often ignores the theories and methods developed by reader-response criticism.

'Reading as a woman' rests on the (tacit) assumption that GENDER is the decisive factor in all human activity: women *are* different from men, therefore they *read* differently – reading is seen to be grounded in BIOLOGY. Its second assumption is that there must be an obvious and *viable*

371

continuity between all female experience (be it literary or non-literary) as well as between the experiences of all women. Literature is linked to life. For this mode of criticism, the highest possible literary value is 'authenticity', a value that is frequently invoked and hardly ever defined.

Kate Millett's *Sexual Politics* (1970) is the pioneering (and still inspiring) study of this mode of criticism in its discussion of works by D. H. Lawrence, Henry Miller, Norman Mailer and (as a counter-example) Jean Genet. Judith Fetterly's *The Resisting Reader* (1978) is a more sophisticated version of the same critical venture, 'a self-defense survival manual for the woman reader lost in "the masculine wilderness of the . . . novel"' (p. viii). Up to today, 'reading as a woman' constitutes a lively and controversial field that covers a vast area of the total landscape within feminist literary criticism. It continues to produce illuminating and exciting studies.

In a subsequent phase of feminist criticism (or rather in 'another' phase, since the two co-exist), the gender-based assumptions of this specific feminist venture have been problematized: is it possible to 'read as a woman'? Isn't the (culturally conditioned) male gaze so encompassing that women cannot possibly evade it? Isn't the SYMBOLIC order so dictatorial that women have to succumb to it if they want to function in society? If so, reading *as* a woman could hardly be possible. If the misogyny of male writing was to be exposed, an alternative, a 'reading like a woman', would have to be posited as a hypothesis. (It follows that once the woman who reads is a hypothesis, a mere philosophical construct, men, too, can read 'like a woman'.)

The implicit assumption in this alternative position is that reading is a socially acquired and culturally conditioned act, shared by both men and women – moreover, that women have always been forced to read 'as men'. For women to read 'like a woman' requires an intentional and voluntary act of 'unlearning', an act of 'defamiliarization' with their gender roles. (Similarly, if men want to read 'like a woman', they must try to overcome the gender-based habits and assumptions imposed on them by a patriarchal culture.)

Shoshana Felman (1975) addresses these problems by asking the following questions: 'How can one speak from the place of the Other? How can the woman be thought about outside of the Masculine/ Feminine framework, *other* than as opposed to man, without being subordinated to a primordial masculine model?' (p. 4). What is implied by these questions is that it might indeed be possible for critics (male or female) consciously to devise strategies of thought which, when employed, will enable them to slip through the grasp that culturally acquired gender roles have on them. Should they succeed, literary theory and criticism will (again) become a quasi gender-neutral ground, even if one from which the gender bias of the literature discussed can be exposed and deconstructed.

Not only the point of view, but also the subject matter of the critical enterprise shifts in this second phase. The question is no longer an imaginary IDENTIFICATION with 'authentic' female experience (literary or non-literary). Rather, attention is paid to the male-engendered stereotypes and strategies that underlie notions like 'female experience', or to the phallocentric vision (the sexual politics) that informs literary works. Not the meanings of a text (its semantic levels), but the linguistic procedures through which meaning is brought about (its semiotic levels), are analysed.

Psychoanalytically speaking, what is at stake in both feminist reading projects is the question of female subject formation, the definition of FEMININITY. Both 'reading as' and 'reading like' a woman are to a large extent based on static (and essentialist) concepts of FEMININITY, seeing it either as biologically determined or as socially and/or culturally constructed (and conditioned). These are problematic stances to take: ever since the advent of post-structuralism, *all* human subjectivity has been conceived of as open, de-centred, and essentially *in flux*. (Post-structuralist theory, however, has its own, specific problems with accounting for femininity.) What is called for is a more 'dynamic' concept of femininity, one that allows for both the cultural and the unconscious forces that act upon subject formation and that sees femininity as neither simply achieved nor ever complete.

Another problem that needs to be considered is that of methodology. The question here is how to integrate the theories and methods developed by reader-response criticism into a reading project with a feminist impetus. Reader-response criticism, itself a highly diverse and controversial field (see Freund 1987), rests on the assumptions that our relationship to a literary text is inevitably a hermeneutic construct (with its own blind spots), that all perception necessarily involves interpretation and that there is no automatic or even viable relation between fiction and life. In Stanley Fish's words, the issue 'is simply the rigorous and disinterested asking of the question, what does this word, phrase, sentence, paragraph, chapter, novel, play, poem, *do*' (1980, pp. 26–7), as opposed to the (more conventional) question, what does a literary text *mean*?

For reader-response criticism, what reading *does* is more important than what a literary work might mean (how it depicts female experience, or how it negotiates the male stereotypes underlying it). In and by itself, reader-response criticism occupies interesting theoretical ground. But, then again, it cannot in itself solve the methodological dilemmas of every feminist reading project. One major shortcoming of reader-response criticism is that although it has supplied us with a wide variety

373

of different and colourful reader constructs (for instance, the mock reader, the super-reader, the informed reader, the implied reader, the competent reader, and many more), it does not allow for a *gendered* reader: most reader-response theories see reading as a hermeneutic act, and thus as gender-neutral.

To sum up: what has to be analysed by a feminist reading project are the intricacies of female subject formation as well as those of the reading process. The central issue is how to account for the effects the structures in a literary text have on the dynamic activities a gendered reader engages in when processing a text. In other words: any literary text contains rhetorical devices, layers, linguistic strategies, points of view; these structures guide the hermeneutic and *conscious* acts of making sense of literature, as well as the *unconscious* acts of transference and counter-transference that take place between text and reader. What we need is indeed a viable and continuous relation – not, however, one in and among the 'authentic' experiences of all women, but a viable relation between these linguistic structures on the one hand and, on the other, the various cultural, social, biological and unconscious levels of female subjectivity, itself a basically fragile and incomplete entity. This will not be an easy theoretical venture to undertake.

See also LITERARY AND TEXTUAL CRITICISM; SUBJECT; TRANSFERENCE/COUNTERTRANSFERENCE.

BIBLIOGRAPHY

Culler, Jonathan, 1982: 'Reading as a woman', *On Deconstruction: Theory and Criticism after Structuralism*. London: Routledge and Kegan Paul, pp. 43–64.
Felman, Shoshana, 1975: 'Women and madness: the critical phallacy', *Diacritics*, 5, pp. 2–10.
Fetterly, Judith, 1978: *The Resisting Reader: A Feminist Approach to American Fiction*. Bloomington and London: Indiana University Press.
Fish, Stanley, 1980: *Is There a Text in This Class?* Cambridge, Mass. and London: Harvard University Press.
Freund, Elizabeth, 1987: *The Return of the Reader: Reader-Response Criticism*. London and New York: Methuen.
Millett, Kate, 1970: *Sexual Politics*. Garden City, NY: Doubleday.

EVELYNE KEITEL

Real, the The concept of the Real appears in various guises in the development of Lacan's thought, but it is never a re-formulation of Freud's reality principle. The reality principle is a regulatory principle, reflecting the necessity for any organism to pursue protracted and indirect courses in order to achieve satisfaction of instinct, complicated in the case of human beings by the need to conform to social constraints. Although it has the recalcitrance of nature as a component, the principle itself is in no way definitive of that nature. Lacan's concept, on the other hand, is much nearer to an ir-regulatory principle, having its origin in that recalcitrance.

In his first period, in the 1950s, Lacan described the Real as a brute, pre-Symbolic reality which returns in the form of need, such as hunger: one can think of the 'object' of hunger as the breast, bottle or the mother. Such images or symbols are considered to be IMAGINARY objects, both more and less than the Real object which in and out of itself, is nothing, unconceptualized, but none the less an absolute. Indeed, if the first Real object is the attempt to satisfy hunger, from its inception the Real bespeaks its own impossibility: of necessity each experience of hunger, because it can never be finally quelled, alternates pleasure with displeasure in acts of repetition (Lacan, 1986).

In the 1960s and early 1970s Lacan attributed a series of properties to the Real in addition to a structural causality. A conflict comes from our seeking the OBJECT of satisfaction in things or in others, despite the fact that the aim always misses its goal; the 'object' is really the satisfaction of Oneness. We seek satisfaction because we always lose what we think we had in a prior moment. The Real appears as a blockage when we seek to re-possess an object that has disappeared. Freud describes the OBJECT as always 're-found' (Freud, 1905, p. 222), whereas Lacan stresses that, if it is re-found, then it must have already been lost. If one conceives the object as Freud did (the 'breast'), then it is not real, but IMAGINARY or phantasmatic. But although the *object* we seek does not exist as such, it operates effects all the same; that is, the very failure of the attempt to objectify shows that the Real remains. Brute reality resists the imposition of the FANTASY.

Whatever one hopes will compensate for the loss of the object is called by Lacan the *objet a*, a semblance which fills up the hole that keeps us from being one with ourselves. The Real appears in whatever concerns the radical nature of loss at the centre of words and being. As such, it is the *agency* of the letter and *l'être*. We are not 'beings' except under the sign of SEXUALITY, where we are constituted in a Real moment of which no 'being' has memory, but to which each tries to give voice in words, images and symptoms.

Lacan thus has moved away in the second period from any correlation of the Real with BIOLOGY and need, by elaborating a theory of the Real body – a kind of meta-body – imposed on the biological organism. It is constituted *a priori* in primordially repressed, pre-specular objects that cause the DESIRE that gives rise to fantasies of satisfaction. The Real always re-appears at the place where an excess of JOUISSANCE indicates loss, on the body, around certain objects, situations, names, persons, making things other than what they seem: a part of the *objet a* remains as an inert presence in every act, an irreducible residuum that will not dissolve. Both males and females fetishize 'objects' of satisfaction as a result of the Real of anxiety and the breakdown of idealization (*see* FETISHIZATION; HYSTERIA).

In the 1970s, in Lacan's third period, it is not the object *per se* that is at issue, but the impossible goal of maintaining consistency. The illusion of consistency rests on inert myths or fantasies which insist and persist, despite being subverted by the discontinuities that intervene in our efforts at Oneness. The mythic effects of this inertia have implications for feminism. Conflict – binding/unbinding – between the sexes comes from the *structure* of the Real, where each person's partner is the Other (Lacan, 1975, p. 38; *see* OTHER/other). This unbridgeable gap between the sexes is marked by 'castration anxiety'. There is no signifier which will adequately define GENDER because we have to lose the primary object (through separation) if we are to become speaking animals: we learn our identities as alienations because gender is defined in terms of what one must lose to be either this or that (Lacan, 1977b, chs 12, 16). In this third theory, Lacan argues that our failures to align anatomy and sexuality in terms of myth and gender produce symptoms. However diverse one's libidinal preferences, every person – except a psychotic – identifies as principally male or female (Lacan, 1970, p. 240).

When Lacan claims that 'there is no sexual relation', he is saying that there is no signifier adequate to support a harmony between the sexes. Love and sexual relations try to bridge the gap of a lacking signifier in the Real. Feminist theories that extol the literal breast (KLEIN, Segal, Winnicott) or the female genitalia (Cixous, IRIGARAY) challenge Lacan's supposed rejection of the 'real' female body, without taking account of those texts of his where Woman is the centre of his theories, as that part of the Real which people can only think 'imaginarily' since it is beyond or outside grammatical language and visible artefact.

Feminist theories in the 1980s and 1990s are beginning to account for Lacan's Real, where woman dwells beyond LANGUAGE and gender identity in a closer proximity to sexuality and pain than man does. It is because women identify with the female body – unlike men, who identify with the group – that Real effects make themselves felt more palpably in women. The confusion of Woman with mother, the first lost object, taunts humans with a structural burden that only makes sense if one understands the incest taboo as a myth, elaborated to explain a child's desire to know what the mother wants of him or her (Lacan, 1977a, pp. 200, 218). Woman is the object *par excellence* because she holds out the promise of reparation in the sense that the first order – the Real – is constituted in terms of losses linked to woman *qua* primary other. The basic structure of the oedipal myth is a taboo against Oneness. Thus, the incest taboo forbids what is impossible, the Oneness of two. Sexual incest is possible, but psychic incest – where two identify as one – produces the structure of psychosis where the Real appears in the undifferentiation of an unborn subject, in the 'lack of lack' (Ragland-Sullivan, 1986, pp. 156–7). The incest taboo against identificatory fusion with the mother is a structural taboo of the Real, a forbidding of what fails to create a proper name, a Symbolic identity, a social link.

See also CASTRATION COMPLEX; FEMININITY; LACAN; LACK; OEDIPUS COMPLEX; SYMPTOM.

BIBLIOGRAPHY

Freud, Sigmund, 1905: *Three Essays on the Theory of Sexuality*, SE, 7, pp. 125–248.
Lacan, Jacques, 1970: 'Pour une logique du fantasme', *Scilicet*, 23, pp. 223–73.
Lacan, Jacques, 1975: *Le Séminaire*, book 20: *Encore*, ed. Jacques-Alain Miller. Paris: Seuil.
Lacan, Jacques, 1977a: 'On a question preliminary to any possible treatment of psychosis', *Écrits: A Selection*, trans. Alan Sheridan. London: Tavistock, pp. 179–225.
Lacan, Jacques, 1977b: *The Four Fundamental Concepts of Psychoanalysis*, trans. Alan Sheridan. London: Hogarth Press.
Lacan, Jacques, 1986: *Le Séminaire*, book 7: *L'Éthique de la psychanalyse*. Paris: Seuil.
Ragland-Sullivan, Ellie, 1986: *Jacques Lacan and the Philosophy of Psychoanalysis*. Urbana, Illinois: University of Illinois Press.

ELLIE RAGLAND-SULLIVAN

representation A term which can be used to describe either a mental image or an exterior image such as in a painting or in a book. It also has a political or juridical meaning, for example when MPs represent their constituencies. In the political sense it is clear that the representative is not identical to the represented, that it is a legal fiction of equivalence which permits the substitution, and that it is the absence or silence of the represented which necessitates or permits the representation. Representation in the artistic sense also seems to suppose the absence of the represented object. Some political theories and some aesthetic theories would argue, however, that representations are valued according to their proximity to the represented. In the case of mental representations there is even greater ambiguity: some would argue that a mental representation is really a presentation to the mind, and others that the term should only be employed when a perception or an image previously formed is recalled to mind. In either case, the relationship between the represented object and the representation has troubled thinkers for many centuries; the possibility of false representations, not only because our senses deceive us (as on seeing a stick in water), but also because 'men' deceive women, is a longstanding philosophical and political problem. Men's deception may of course be (comfortingly) assumed to be an individual or aleatory phenomenon, but has often been perceived more radically as an ideological structure.

Representation concerns feminists in two different ways: on the one hand, the general process by which people are brought to make representations and the role of SEXUAL DIFFERENCE in that process or, at least, in the theorization of that process; on the other hand, the content and structure of gendered representations. Psychoanalysis, like feminism, is deeply concerned with the first question, yet psychoanalytic theories of representation have frequently not given any more succour to feminists than mimetic theories. The second question has greatly exercised feminists: women have been challenging the way in which they (and men) have been represented, and the gendering of other representations, since long before the term feminism was available to them. Over recent decades some feminists have borrowed from psychoanalysis in order to sharpen their analysis of various representations (film, literature, advertising and so on). But other feminists would argue that psychoanalysis is a double-edged tool.

Mimetic theories of representation claim that a representation is no more than a reflection of reality, be that reality a historically specific one or a natural and eternal one. Whether the reality of sexual difference is determined by economic and political forces or is a biological given is no more significant here than the nature of the theory of representation, since if representations do nothing to affect what they represent, then a critique of representations achieves no more than (perhaps) increasing information about existing social conditions. Thus some socialist feminists, such as the sociologist Christine Delphy (1984), argue that it is less important to analyse representations of women and ask whether these are positively or negatively valorized, than it is to analyse and change the underlying material conditions of women's lives. Other thinkers, such as Annie Leclerc (1974), present certain aspects of women's existence (such as childbirth or menstruation) as relatively unchanging, and argue that our experience of these has changed largely because of the (negative) way in which they have been represented by PATRIARCHY. This presupposes quite a different theory of representation, that is, that representations are constructed, do not reflect an underlying reality, but shape our 'experiences' of reality. A third kind of feminist theory of representation would claim that there is no hidden bedrock of reality; rather, that any reality to which one has access is shaped by the representations of it which one encounters. This third kind of theory has a problem with the question of determination: what shapes the representations which construct our lives? That question is most easily answered by a position which claims that representations and the material condition of our social existence mutually influence each other, whether or not we claim, with Louis Althusser, that the economic is determinant in the final instance (*see* IDEOLOGY).

Many feminists (Simone de Beauvoir, Kate Millett, Juliet MITCHELL, Luce IRIGARAY) have indeed tackled the representation of women within psychoanalysis. The first feminists to attack Freud (Beauvoir and Millett, for example) for representing women as inadequate men suffering from PENIS ENVY have themselves been much criticized for paying insufficient attention to the detail of Freud's texts – the complexities, contradictions and admissions of ignorance. Freud's 'Some psychical consequences of the anatomical distinction between the sexes' (1925) and 'Female sexuality' (1931) have been particular targets for feminists, as has his analysis of Dora, which has been the subject of a film, a play by Hélène Cixous and numerous articles (see Bernheimer and Kahane, 1985). Lacan's representation of women, for example his description of Bernini's statue of the ecstatic St Theresa as an obvious example of female JOUISSANCE, has also been much criticized by feminists.

The feminist critique of gendered representations has focused above all on the representation of women as OBJECT of male desire, whether goddess or whore, and the concomitant REPRESSION of female desire. Historically women have frequently been represented as visions of beauty; the female body has been made the primary locus of SEXUALITY and of visual PLEASURE. While attention has been paid to a wide variety of forms of representation, it is the critique of cinema where stakes now seem particularly high, both because (for those who believe that representations affect perception) of the mass audience reached and because the representations of female and male GENDER roles seem peculiarly conservative. Feminist critique of other forms of popular culture (for example Rosalind Coward's *Female Desire*, 1984) has engaged less explicitly with psychoanalysis than feminist critique of the cinema has, although there often seems to be a reference to psychoanalysis without the use of its technical vocabulary, perhaps owing to a wish to be accessible to a wider audience. For example, Judith Williamson writes without mentioning castration: 'The threat posed to a value system based on possession of the penis, by the very possibility of its absence, is enormous' (1985, p. 49), although she does refer explicitly to LACAN in her work on decoding advertisements. On the side of high culture, one example of a feminist literary critic who systematically uses psychoanalysis to tackle the question of the representation of women is Naomi Schor, who argues for 'clitoral criticism', a female paranoid attention to detail (Schor, 1985). She claims that textual details overlooked by male critics often refer fetishistically to the female body, and that re-fetishizing the fetish may help in understanding the relationship between woman and representation (*see* CLITORAL HERMENEUTICS).

The feminist engagement with cinema – as the pages of *Screen* bear witness – has persistently drawn on Lacanian theory, particularly the theory of the SUBJECT, in order to discuss primary and secondary processes at work in the cinema spectator. The Lacanian split and castrated subject is allowed an imaginary self-coherence by representational art. Some feminists insist that the identity of the spectator (particularly of Hollywood cinema) is necessarily inscribed as masculine whatever the biological composition of any given audience (Doane, 1988; Mulvey, 1975). Mainstream cinema, Mulvey argues, codes the erotic into the language of the dominant patriarchal order where pleasure is either that of the voyeur gazing on the (female) object of DESIRE (*see* VOYEURISM/FETISHISM/THE GAZE) or that of narcissistic IDENTIFICATION with male movie stars as ego ideals. Since the female form is, by virtue of its lack of a penis, a reminder of castration, anxiety is generated which, Mulvey claims, is resolved either sadistically in narratives where women are investigated, made guilty, punished, saved and so on, or by a fetishistic cult of the female star immobilized in a fixed IMAGE. The only escape for the feminist is via a new language of desire in alternative cinema, which can 'free the look of the camera into its materiality in time and space and the look of the audience into dialectics, passionate detachment' (Mulvey, 1975), rather than subordinating both of these to illusion, to the look of characters in narrative film. However, the destruction of visual pleasure as we know it can be seen as elitist, quite apart from the fact that much alternative cinema (and writing) may be formally iconoclastic and yet on the level of content include much which is familiarly sadistic, fetishistic, voyeuristic and so on. Ruby Rich and others argue that the spectator can subvert structures and produce her own reading even of mainstream filmic texts (see Rich, 1980). De Lauretis (1984) raises the question of the process, in which both unconscious and historical factors play their part, in the way images on the screen articulate meaning and desire for spectators. Narrative and visual pleasure need not always serve the purpose of 'oppression': what matters is the position of the (female) spectator in relation to these pleasures. She argues that we need not accept the psychoanalytic perspective which assumes a male subject and the PHALLUS as the signifier and standard of visibility (*see* FEMINIST CINEMA; FILM THEORY).

Griselda Pollock (1988) uses similar strategies to those of feminist film theory in her analyses of art history. Art historical questions include those of women as producers and consumers of ART, that is to say, as representers and as readers of representations who necessarily bring a framework of intelligibility to their readings and also add to their ideological baggage with each new reading; and include those of art historians who represent 'creativity' as the province of the masculine individual 'genius', and the typical art object as the passive woman. Pollock combines a materialist feminism which insists on the social construction of SEXUAL DIFFERENCE and a psychoanalytic approach which recognizes the role of the UNCONSCIOUS in the scopic field and in the specificities of (sexualized) pleasure.

It seems that a great deal could be at stake for feminists, and that much work remains to be done, in and on the question of representation. Almost any text can be analysed in terms of its reference to sexual difference; this is true not only of poems or paintings but also of, say, the texts of PHILOSOPHY or SCIENCE (where, relatively speaking, less psychoanalytical feminist work has been done). Feminists' attention to rhetorical details as well as to larger structures insistently produces readings in terms of sexualized representations, no doubt the product of material circumstances but, equally, shaped by unconscious processes. The imbibing of these varied representations, sometimes contradictory but nevertheless patterned in ways which reinforce inequality, must surely become a labour, a fruitful struggle to produce readings against the grain and revealing the grain, and to produce new representations, however much these are still caught in ideological and metaphysical webs and still need to be analysed and re-produced.

See also ART; FEMINIST CINEMA; FILM THEORY; IMAGE; LITERARY AND TEXTUAL CRITICISM; LITERATURE; PHOTOGRAPHY.

BIBLIOGRAPHY

Adams, Parveen, ed. (1991): *Rendering the Real: A Special Issue*, October, 58.

Bernheimer, Charles, and Kahane, Claire, eds 1985: *In Dora's Case*. New York: Columbia University Press.

Coward, Rosalind, 1984: *Female Desire: Women's Sexuality Today*. London: Paladin.

de Lauretis, Teresa, 1984: *Alice Doesn't: Feminism, Semiotics, Cinema*. Bloomington: Indiana University Press.

Delphy, Christine, 1984: *Close to Home. A Materialist Analysis of Women's Oppression*. London: Hutchinson.

Doane, Mary Ann, 1988: *The Desire to Desire: The Woman's Film of the 1940s*. London: Macmillan.

REPRESSION

Freud, Sigmund, 1925: 'Some psychical consequences of the anatomical distinction between the sexes', *SE*, 19, pp. 243–60.

Freud, Sigmund, 1931: 'Female sexuality', *SE*, 21, pp. 223–46.

Leclerc, Annie, 1974: *Parole de femme*. Paris: Grasset.

Mulvey, Laura, 1975: 'Visual pleasure and narrative cinema', *Screen*, 16/3, pp. 6–18.

Pollock, Griselda, 1988: *Vision and Difference*. London and New York: Routledge.

Rich, Ruby, 1980: 'In the name of feminist film criticism', *Heresies*, 9, pp. 74–81.

Schor, Naomi, 1985: *Breaking the Chain: Women, Theory, and French Realist Fiction*. New York: Columbia University Press.

Williamson, Judith, 1985: *Consuming Passions*. London: Marion Boyars.

JUDITH STILL

repression   A major mechanism of psychical defence. Of all the vicissitudes that a drive can undergo this is the one producing the most radical effects. However, it is not available from birth but is inaugurated when there is a sharp cleavage between the conscious and the UNCONSCIOUS with the advent of the OEDIPUS COMPLEX. Until then, the PRE-OEDIPAL child may have access to a number of other defences, such as reversal, DIS-AVOWAL, or turning the SUBJECT into the OBJECT; but only repression is a permanent form of defence, for it alone implies the activities of a timeless, unchanging unconscious. Indeed, repression both presupposes and establishes the unconscious. It ensures that the satisfaction of a sexual drive no longer brings PLEASURE, but instead yields unpleasure.

Freud suggests that repression must operate in two distinct stages or forms. First, there is a primal or founding repression, which has the role of constituting and organizing the UNCONSCIOUS. Then there is a further series of repressions, all in some form based on the images and wishes repressed by primal repression: these Freud calls 'after-pressure' or repression proper. It is the latter which constitute the vast bulk of unconscious contents. Primal repression founds the unconscious as a barrier. It involves a fixation of the ideational or mental component of the DRIVE with the energetic component, which are subsequently severed from each other and are subject to separate fates: the ideational component is banished into the unconscious, while the energetic component is transformed into another affect (see Freud, 1914, p. 148).The second stage of repression affects all the relevant derivatives of the primal event; that is, it represses anything that reminds one of, or is related to, what is primally repressed. This makes the oedipus complex, which is the object of primal repression, the organizing nucleus of the unconscious. Freud argues that these derivative repressions are the product both of a repulsion by consciousness and of a simultaneous attraction or 'after-pressure' by the primally repressed. They are all structured by their relations to this infantile (mythic) event, which explains the largely infantile nature of the unconscious. All later repressions, including adult ones, are based on and anchored to these key infantile events, which are permanently stored in an unchanging fashion in the unconscious.

Freud argues that repression cannot be a momentary action, a singular event, for if this were the case, the repressed would reappear as soon as the action ceased. Repression demands a persistent expenditure of energy to keep the repressed in its place. The force that the repressed exerts towards consciousness is counteracted by an opposing force which Freud describes as an 'anti-cathexis'.

Repression relegates the ideational representative of the drive, that is, an idea which is cathected with a quota of libidinal energy coming from an instinct, to the unconscious. The repressed is thus an idea which is charged with an amount of energy. The act of repression severs the energy from the idea. The ideational representative is then banished from consciousness to the unconscious. The energy may undergo one of three fates: the drive may be suppressed without trace; or it may be transformed from one kind of affect into another (e.g. desire transformed into fear); or it may be converted into anxiety. Repression is successful if *both* the idea and the affect disappear entirely, or else are transformed into emotions that avoid unpleasure. When repression is not entirely successful, a SYMPTOM may emerge. This symptom is a result, however, not of repression itself but of the return of the repressed.

Repression, and the lifting of repression, which allows the repressed material to return, paradoxically occur simultaneously. This is difficult to understand only if we retain a temporal or hydraulic model of repression. If repression entails the (prior) fixation of an ideational representative, it is this fixation or coding that enables the repressed to return as a symptom. The symptom (dreams, slips, jokes) all exhibit a lowering of the unconscious barrier and a temporary or relatively permanent return of the repressed, encoded with a specific (unconscious) signification. The return of the repressed is made possible by the cathexis of the unconscious idea breaking through the barrier of anti-cathexis. It utilizes the techniques of the unconscious (the primary processes) to disguise itself and form a substitute, which is the basis of the symptom.

In Freud's account of the oedipus complex repression is the central means by which the boy resolves the castration threat: he represses his desire for the mother through the establishment of the superego which is based on his IDENTIFICATION with the father-figure. This repression definitively ends his sexual attachment to the mother, and he thus enters the latency period. Although Freud presumes that repression must operate in the case of the girl as well, he remains obscure about what it is that she represses. For example, he claims that the girl's superego is weaker than the boy's (see Freud, 1924); yet he also implies that in some senses at least, the girl is more repressed, and less sexual, than the boy. The girl does not repress her DESIRE for the mother, for instead, she turns away from the mother for not protecting her against castration. Nor is it clear how she has access to the establishment of a superego, given that an identification with the father's authority is precluded precisely because of her castrated status. If the girl does not resolve her oedipus complex through repression but, as Freud claims, gradually accepts her castrated position and may remain in an oedipal attachment to her father for many years, then Freud leaves entirely obscure how her unconscious is formed. It may be for this reason that IRIGARAY asks whether women have an unconscious, or rather, whether women *are* the unconscious, the repressed, for men.

See also MOTHER–DAUGHTER RELATIONSHIP; WOMEN'S PSYCHOLOGICAL DEVELOPMENT.

BIBLIOGRAPHY

Brennan, Teresa, 1992: *The Interpretation of the Flesh*. London: Routledge.
Freud, Sigmund, 1914: 'Repression', *SE*, 14, pp. 141–58.
Freud, Sigmund, 1915: 'Instincts and their vicissitudes', *SE*, 14, pp. 109–40.
Freud, Sigmund, 1924: 'The dissolution of the oedipus complex', *SE*, 19, pp. 173–82.
Irigaray, Luce, 1977: 'Women's exile', *Ideology and Consciousness*, 1; also available in *The Feminist Critique of Language: A Reader*, ed. Deborah Cameron. London: Routledge, 1990, pp. 62–76.

ELIZABETH GROSZ

S

sadomasochism

Freud

Following Krafft-Ebing's coinage and classification of 'sadism' and 'masochism' as sexual perversions in 1886 (Krafft-Ebing, 1965), Freud refers to sadism and masochism as 'sexual aberrations' in the first of his *Three Essays on the Theory of Sexuality* (1905). He emphasizes, however, that unlike other terms for pleasure in pain or cruelty (such as 'algolagnia') 'the names chosen by Krafft-Ebing bring into prominence the pleasure in any form of humiliation or subjection' (1905, p. 157). Pain, then, may not be the motivating factor or desired result of sadism or MASOCHISM; rather, sadism or masochism may deliver other satisfactions deriving from mastery (sadism) or the fantasy of being childlike or helpless (masochism).

Although sadism and masochism are consistently listed among the PERVERSIONS in his writings, from the very first Freud is at some pains to include them under the rubric of more or less 'normal' sexuality. Thus he suggests that 'sadism and masochism occupy a special position among the perversions, since the contrast between activity and passivity which lies behind them is among the universal characteristics of sexual life' (1905, p. 159).

'Sadomasochism' is not a term which Freud tends to use; he prefers to discuss 'sadism' and 'masochism' separately, although he does repeatedly suggest that the two terms are linked, that a sadist is always in some measure also a masochist, and a masochist always engaged in encouraging and perpetrating sadistic acts against him- or herself. Sadistic and masochistic scenarios, however, in most psychoanalytic accounts, seem to be quite different and independent of one another.

For the most part, Freud's work on sadism and masochism may be divided into two distinct phases. The first, comprising 'Instincts and their vicissitudes' (1915) and 'A child is being beaten' (1919), considers the sexual instinct or LIBIDO to be, in its first appearance, coincident with

385

the ego- or self-preservative instincts. In this view sadism, as *activity*, an initial life-preserving instinct or aggressivity in relation to external stimuli, appears as the first erotogenic stage, and masochism, or passivity, emerges as a secondary development. According to this earlier theory, masochism only emerges when the activity which characterizes sadism undergoes one of two vicissitudes or changes: either it turns into its opposite, passivity; or rather than becoming focused on others or the world, it 'turns round' against the subject's own ego. Four years later, focusing on the FANTASY, frequent among his patients, that 'a child is being beaten', Freud demonstrates that what initially looks like, indeed, what began as a sadistic wish – 'a child is being beaten' – is, in the final analysis, a disguised masochistic wish; namely, that 'I am being beaten.' Appearing in female patients at the point of a transferral of affections from the mother to the father, the fantasy 'a child is being beaten'/'I am being beaten' operates as the convergence between the sexual attachment to the father and a doubled sense of guilt for that attachment, both for desiring the father and for abandoning the mother. This convergence of guilt and sexuality into fantasies of punishment is what Freud calls 'the essence of masochism' (1919, p. 189), a secondary reaction to primary aggressive sexual impulses (*see* KLEIN).

Beyond the Pleasure Principle (1920) and 'The economic problem in masochism' (1924) are generally taken as expressions of Freud's second phase of work on sadism and masochism, and a reversal of his earlier opinion that sadism is a component of the primary sexual impulses. In this second phase, the introduction of the notion of the 'death drive', or the basic entropic tendency of any organism to return to stable, inorganic compounds, engages in competition with the life-preservative and sexual instincts (*see* DEATH DRIVE (FREUD)). The ruling principle of psychic life, then, is no longer understood to be PLEASURE, but rather, 'reality', a principle which allows for the negotiation of some displeasure in the service of the life instincts. To survive the originary conflict between the libido and the death instincts, the libido must defuse the threat of death in two ways, both internally and externally. With the help of the development of the musculature, the libido disposes of much of the destructiveness of the death instinct by directing it towards external objects. (In time, this activity, if sexualized, may come to characterize sadism.) Some of this destructiveness remains internal to the organism, however, and must be 'bound' there; this is accomplished by means of a 'libidinal sympathetic excitation accompanying the tension of physical pain and feelings of distress' (1924, p. 163). The excitation of the libido 'converts' the destructive impulses arising from the death instinct into life-preserving or libidinal forces; this, Freud says, 'we must recognize as the original erotogenic masochism' (1924, p. 164). Masochism, then, as a manifestation of the death drive, rather than the result of a guilty sadism, is, in Freud's later view, a primary, quietistic strategy of survival, an orchestrating passivity, a masquerade of inactivity. Its aetiology is earlier than, and separate from, that of sadism.

In sum, as far as Freud is concerned, neither masochism nor sadism is initially destructive in intent; rather, they are both complex means of survival, modes of negotiating the hostility of the external world or the destructiveness of the death instinct.

After Freud, the term sadomasochism is frequently taken up to describe the intra-subjective violence which characterized the masochism of Freud's first phase – the situation in which one produces and exercises violence against oneself. Following this more specifically analytic usage, the term 'sadomasochism' has also come to describe inter-subjective relations in which one person, often female, plays a predominantly 'passive' role, the other, often male, a predominantly 'active' one. Freud repeatedly suggests that the masochistic or passive is 'feminine', and the sadistic or active is 'masculine'. Although most of the masochistic patients whom he (as well as Krafft-Ebing, Havelock Ellis and Theodor Reik) discusses are male, masochism is all too frequently, by analytic as well as other literature, taken to be a characteristic most applicable to women. A number of feminists have criticized this conflation of the masochistic with the female, some simply condemning it, some arguing that the cultural options available to women are such that women more frequently adopt strategies of apparent passivity than strategies of apparent activity; but in either case, one 'acts' in order to get what one wants. This latter argument corresponds with Freud's later notion of masochism: the masochist is not entirely passive, but only wishes to seem so in order to avoid the destructiveness of the death instinct. To this end, then, he or she seeks another person as an object, but this other person, rather than being figured as the acted-upon object, 'has to take over the original role of the subject', taking an active role and inflicting his or her desires on the masochist. In a similar although not perfectly symmetrical dynamic, the sadist must orchestrate the survival of his or her victim, acting out not a suspension of life but a suspension of death. To this end, except in extreme cases, the sadist is, no matter how active, subordinated and bound to the life and wishes of the victim. A pure sadism or a pure masochism cannot really function.

Feminist perspectives

A debate about sadomasochism within feminist circles in the US, Australia and Britain has been one of the outcomes of the political insistence upon a woman's right to control her own sexuality. 'Why should this apparently sectarian issue monopolize feminists' attention to such a degree? . . . [T]he S/M debate is a focus for a number of more basic conflicts that go to the heart of what the women's movement means' (Hunt, 1987, p. 81). For example, what are the inter-relations and over-determinations among SEXUALITY, violence, power and GENDER? Are the inequalities of power which women experience and the violence from which many women suffer historical, political or psychological in origin? Can they be changed? How? How are the linkages between power, violence and sexuality manifest in psychological relations and accounts, sociological relations and accounts? What, indeed, is the best way to analyse and describe these relations, and what sort of analysis will afford women the greatest power? Do relationships between women differ fundamentally from relationships between men and women?

Throughout the 1980s, the feminist debate over sadomasochism has been loosely organized around two different and often opposed uses of the term: first, sadomasochism as one among many possible lesbian sexual practices; and secondly, sadomasochism as a social and psychological metaphor for inter-personal relations between a dominant, most often understood to be male, and a submissive, most often understood to be female (see Benjamin, 1988; Dworkin, 1989; and MacKinnon, 1987). At the heart of both uses of the term, however, is an analysis that links sexuality with power and violence: in the first case, in order to assert control over violence and power by using it; in the second case, in order to identify and thus control mechanisms of violence at both the psychological and the social level. It may be argued that neither of these projects is bound to be completely successful, and that, especially from a psychoanalytic perspective, violence is never quite so manageable. While this may be so, many feminists, actively seeking to address and negotiate questions of violence, power and sexuality, tend to understand sadomasochism as either a potentially liberatory practice or an abusive constraint, a SYMPTOM of all that is wrong with our culture, and a dynamic which must be eradicated at all levels.

As a practice, lesbian sadomasochism claims that, regardless of the origin of the linkage between sexuality, power and violence – even if it is a result of a history of patriarchal social and psychological oppression – rather than being suppressed, the power and violence linked to sexuality may be harnessed and theatricalized for greater sexual pleasure and greater understanding of that pleasure. This is not to say that one may always do as one likes, but that there is no sexuality at the present time that is not riddled with complexity, contradiction and 'patriarchal' etc. constraints; LESBIANISM is certainly no safe haven from the violence of the world.

The 'coming out' of lesbian feminist sadomasochists countered, in the late 1970s and early 1980s, a radical feminist analysis which linked male sexuality under PATRIARCHY with violence and the commodification and objectification of female bodies. At a point when the differentiation of concerns among women of different race and class backgrounds seemed, to some radical feminists, to threaten the cohesiveness of the women's movement, the growing consciousness that violence against women permeated almost every woman's experience and consciousness seemed to promise a more or less universal issue over which all women could be united. The undeniable and continuing importance of RAPE crisis centres, shelters for battered women and incest survivors' groups has led many feminists, concerned to eradicate abuse, to link male domination with violence, and to criticize and disavow any activity which might link eroticism with violence, objectification or FETISHISM. Extremes of this position have been reached with claims that, under patriarchy, any REPRESENTATION of a woman or of female sexuality, whether in painting or story, film or photograph, whether explicitly pornographic or not, is violence against women (see Dworkin, 1989; MacKinnon, 1987; Linden et al., 1982). Indeed, by some accounts, all forms of sexual activity except for (but possibly including) non-penetrating, non-genitally organized, non-hierarchical sex between two women is bound to be tainted by patriarchy and therefore, in one way or another, a form of violence against women. At its most extreme, such an analysis returns female sexuality to a purely nurturant ideal, one in which pleasure, taken for oneself, is unhealthy or contaminated. At its most general, such an analysis insists that female sexuality is fundamentally different from male sexuality, and that the social and psychological aspects of sexuality may be changed by political and politically correct activity. Public expressions of sex, even of desire, between women have often been considered unacceptable because 'women have been terrorized by sexuality and [are] sick of it' (English et al., 1987, p. 68). Such analyses have culminated in the banning of the expression of 'deviant sexualities' – for example, lesbian sadomasochism – from meeting spaces in women's centres (for an example of this, see Feminist Review, 1987, pp. 277–304); in 1980 in the US, the passage of a resolution by the National Organization of Women in favour of lesbian and gay rights but against sadomasochism, PORNOGRAPHY, pederasty and public sex (see Aldefer et al., 1981, pp. 92–3); and the public excoriation and denunciation of various 'deviant' feminists (see Vance, 1984, pp. 431–9). This wave of universally-minded feminist counter-repression in the face of patriarchal oppression has been characterized by Gayle Rubin, an outspoken proponent of lesbian sadomasochism, as 'the missionary position of the women's movement' (English et al., 1987, p. 70). In effect, Rubin argues, the attempt to 'save' women from male sexual domination and control has, paradoxically, itself become a form of the domination and control of women's sexuality.

Within a political sphere, then, lesbian sadomasochism is not only a contested form of feminist sexual expression, but a polemical rejoinder to the contention that all violence is the same, and unavoidably in the service of patriarchy. All sexual relationships involve negotiations of power, and lesbian sadomasochists maintain that acknowledging that power and putting it to work is the most direct route towards understanding it and re-routing it away from abuse. To this end, then, sadomasochism as a *practice* involves a theatricalization of or play with power, dominance and submission. Within a controlled and consensual scenario, sadomasochism may engage fears and difficulties with power; for some, it seems to be cathartic and healing.

Within a psychoanalytic context, lesbian sadomasochism re-engages the complexity and range of erotic wishes and activities; lesbian S/M is important because it refuses a simple and one-sided conflation of violence, men, male-identification, rape, pornography and perversity. Rather, lesbian sadomasochism, as both practice and polemic, re-opens the question of female sexuality and agency. Women are not, nor need they remain, merely victims. To remain passive to one's own victimization is a way of collaborating with it. But one may fight back by appropriating the signs of that victimization and putting them to new uses. Thus, in some way, this debate about power and sexuality is also a debate about LANGUAGE, and the symbolic, political status of particular signs (see Stewart, 1989–90; Williams, 1989). How can and do women take up and re-deploy the signs of masculinity and femininity? What are the many and varied ways in which women may negotiate power, violence and sexuality? Certainly not by merely saying no – that would be merely to leave the power to signify in the hands where it already lies.

See also HETEROSEXISM; WOMAN-IDENTIFIED WOMAN/RADICAL LESBIANISM.

BIBLIOGRAPHY

Adams, Parveen, 1989, 'Of female bondage', *Between Feminism and Psychoanalysis*, ed. Teresa Brennan. London and New York: Routledge, pp. 247–65.
Aldefer, Hannah, et al., eds 1981: *Heresies*, 12: 'The Sex Issue'.
Benjamin, Jessica, 1986: 'The alienation of desire: women's masochism and ideal love', *Psychoanalysis and Women: Contemporary Reappraisals*, ed. Judith Alpert. Hillsdale, NJ: Analytic Press, pp. 113–38.
Benjamin, Jessica, 1988: *The Bonds of Love*. New York: Pantheon.
Butler, Judith, 1990: 'The pleasures of reception', *The Role of Affect in Motivation, Development and Adaptation*, vol. 1: *Pleasure Beyond the Pleasure Principle*, ed. Robert Glick and Stanley Bone. New Haven: Yale University Press, pp. 259–75.

Deleuze, Gilles, 1989 [1967]: 'Coldness and cruelty', in *Masochism*. New York: Zone, pp. 7–138.

Dworkin, Andrea, 1989: *Pornography: Men Possessing Women*. New York; E. P. Dutton.

English, Deirdre; Hollibaugh, Amber; and Rubin, Gayle, 1987: 'Talking sex: a conversation on sexuality and feminism', *Sexuality: A Reader*, ed. Feminist Review. London: Virago, pp. 63–81.

Feminist Review, ed. 1987: *Sexuality: A Reader*. London: Virago.

Freud, Sigmund, 1905: *Three Eessays on the Theory of Sexuality'*, *SE*, 7, pp. 123–245.

Freud, Sigmund, 1915: 'Instincts and their vicissitudes', *SE*, 14, pp. 111–40.

Freud, Sigmund, 1919: '"A child is being beaten": A contribution to the study of sexual perversions', *SE*, 17, pp. 175–204.

Freud, Sigmund, 1920: *Beyond the Pleasure Principle*, *SE*, 18, pp. 1–64.

Freud, Sigmund, 1924: 'The economic problem in masochism', *SE*, 19, pp. 155–72.

Hunt, Margaret, 1987: 'Report of a conference on feminism, sexuality and power: the elect clash with the perverse', *Coming to Power: Writings and Graphics on Lesbian SM*, ed. SAMOIS. Boston: Alyson Publications, pp. 81–9.

Kaplan, Louise J., 1991: *Female Perversions: The Temptations of Emma Bovary*. New York: Bantam Doubleday Dell.

Krafft-Ebing, Richard von, 1965 [1886]: *Psychopathia sexualis*, trans. Harry E. Weddeck. New York: G. P. Putnam's Sons.

Linden, Robin Ruth et al., eds 1982: *Against Sadomasochism: A Radical Feminist Analysis*. East Palo Alto, California: Frog in the Well.

MacKinnon, Catherine, 1987: *Feminism Unmodified: Discourses on Life and Law*. Cambridge, Mass.: Harvard University Press.

Reik, Theodore, 1957: 'Masochism in modern man', *Of Love and Lust*. New York: Farrar, Straus & Giroux, pp. 195–366.

Silverman, Kaja, 1988: 'Masochism and male subjectivity', *Camera Obscura*, 17, pp. 31–66.

Stewart, Susan, 1989–90: 'The Marquis de Meese', *Critical Inquiry*, 15/1, pp. 162–92.

Vance, Carole, ed. 1984: *Pleasure and Danger*. Boston: Routledge and Kegan Paul.

Williams, Linda, 1990: *Hard Core: Power, Pleasure and the Frenzy of the Visible*. Berkeley: University of California Press.

KARIN M. COPE

science   Science is an important contested zone in the world today. Its definition, legitimate purposes, functions, social meanings, politics and value are hotly debated in non-feminist as well as feminist circles.

391

Disputants over the scientific status of psychoanalysis have frequently talked past each other because of commitments to conflicting notions of science. This account will focus on some central feminist concerns about science, the contributions of psychoanalysis to these discussions, and whether there could be (or already are) specifically feminist sciences.

Feminist critiques of the sciences can be divided into five main focuses: sexism in the social structure of the sciences and in the science education that recruits young people to science careers; sexist and androcentric misuse and abuse of the sciences, their technologies and applications; sexist and androcentric bias in the problematics, concepts, research designs, interpretation of data, sorting of evidence, presentation of results of research, purposes and functions of research in biology and the social sciences; androcentric meanings and metaphors for nature, the scientist and research processes; and androcentric theories about science and, more generally, knowledge-seeking.

It is to the last two of these critiques that explicit and implicit psychoanalytic tendencies have made the greatest contributions. Dorothy Dinnerstein's (1976) re-reading of Freud and Norman Brown persistently pointed to the damaging consequences of linking women with nature and men with culture: science was complicitous in keeping women as men's 'other' (*see* OTHER/OTHER). Historian Carolyn Merchant (1980) identified the tendency of early modern scientists to try to accumulate approval for their otherwise morally repulsive scientific projects by claiming that science would restore men's control over women/nature/fate. Evelyn Fox Keller (1985) pointed to the gendered meanings of hierarchy in models of nature in various areas of BIOLOGY that are apparently far removed from human interests (e.g. development in slime mould). She used insights from OBJECT-RELATIONS THEORY to challenge such key metatheoretical and epistemological notions as the control of nature, the distortion of objectivity in 'objectivism' and the search for the 'laws of nature'.

Luce IRIGARAY (1985) argued that the very LANGUAGE of science is defensive in a peculiarly masculine way, limiting the possibilities for processes of reciprocity, exchange, permeability, fluidity and appreciation of difference. Jane Flax (1990) analysed the history of 'the problems of philosophy' in the West from Plato to Rousseau – including epistemological problems – as reflections of the preoccupations of cultures that were locked into the frozen social relations characteristic of the developmental concerns of male two-year-olds. Susan Bordo (1987) analysed the psychological drama and imagery of Descartes's *Meditations* to reveal the 'masculine' nature of modern science, the birth of the mind as mirror of nature, and the 'death of nature' (*see* PHILOSOPHY).

392

All women bear race as well as GENDER. The construction of the Other in racial as well as gender form by the sciences has been the topic of several striking analyses (*see* RACE/IMPERIALISM). For example, historian of psychiatry Sander Gilman (1985) analysed the development and growth of stereotypes of marginalized groups in medieval travel writings, scientific studies of the physiognomy of prostitutes, depictions of the SEXUALITY of women and children of European and 'Other' descent in Viennese art, and the writings of Mark Twain, Freud and Nietzsche. Historian of primatology Donna Haraway (1989) argues that for Westerners, primates occupy the taboo border not only of the social and natural worlds, but also of racial and sexual 'difference'. Moreover, there are significant national differences in the agendas of Japanese, Indian, and US primatologists and in what they 'discover' about primate nature, and, thus, about 'human' sexual and racial 'nature' (*see* SEXUAL DIFFERENCE).

Feminists have not only criticized the sciences; they have also generated systematic knowledge. Without less partial and distorted descriptions and explanations of nature and social life, how can we improve women's nutrition, health, legal status, work conditions, economic and political opportunities, our 'natural' environment, family relations or relations with men and each other? Feminism requires science as well as political struggles: the two must guide each other. Thus the question arises whether there can be sciences *for women*, rather than primarily for men in the dominant social groups – and sciences that do not replicate the sins for which feminists have criticized mainstream science.

Practising scientists, including many feminist activists, are tempted to answer that there can be good science or bad science, but not such a thing as feminist science. The practices that some want to refer to as feminist science are really just plain good science, they say. This response certainly can be strategically useful for feminists, but it fails to recognize the important role of political and social change in the advance of knowledge. Feminism has *forced* re-evaluations of inadequate models of biology and social relations, as have other liberatory social movements today and in the past. In this important sense, feminism is *inside* the processes of scientific inquiry no less than sexism, class struggle and imperialism have been.

A second response has been to define feminist science as *feminine* science. Feminist science is then the kinds of systematic knowledge-seeking that have historically been women's work, such as healing, midwifery, child-care, or emotional work and/or sciences incorporating rather than avoiding and devaluing such 'feminine' concerns as the emotions, relationship and reciprocity, an ethic of responsibility rather than of rights, and participatory rather than hierarchical relations. This 'gynocentric'

393

stance forces critical re-evaluation of the political processes through which fields of systematic knowledge-seeking get legitimated and de-legitimated, and of the distorted understanding of science, nature and social relations generated by scientific enthusiasm for misogyny. However, its excessively narrow definition of what can count as feminist science appears to mire women and feminism in the realm of the Other and to accept gender ideology about the reasonable division of the world into feminine and masculine practices and qualities. It appears irrelevant (at best) to attempts to create systematic descriptions and explanations of *everything* in the natural and social worlds that advance the contradictory but nevertheless necessary project of empowering women while simultaneously undermining the restriction of females to the feminine.

Perhaps the most widespread answer to the question 'Can there be feminist sciences?' among the feminist metatheorists of science has been 'Yes, but only after the revolution.' Significant advances towards feminist sciences can be made now primarily through critiques of existing sciences; but large-scale social changes would have to occur in order to see anything that could reasonably be thought of as feminist science. Agendas for the extraordinarily expensive research in physics, chemistry and much of biology that are so central to the political economy are set in international councils and are heavily dependent on state and industrial funding. This position leads us to recognize the roles of women and science in the global political economy.

However, this position also inadvertently adopts the view of science as a necessarily monolithic and totalitarian enterprise that is characteristic of mainstream and especially positivist natural science ideology. It assumes that, until feminist science provides the dominant paradigm for systematic knowledge-seeking in general, and thus presumably is no longer in debate with other science tendencies about the fundamental principles of scientific research, feminist science is only a partially developed field and not yet a true science. It fails to see that theories about science are *inside* the institutions and practices of the sciences, not just a pre- or metascientific activity. However, in the social sciences, with their history of plural research traditions, one finds feminist sociologies, psychologies, anthropologies, economics, linguistics and the like co-existing in partially overlapping and partially conflictual relations with marxist, empiricist, humanistic, functionalist, phenomenological, hermeneutical and other theoretical and research traditions. The various metatheories continue to shape scientific method in each research tradition while themselves developing and changing over time. Why not insist that the social sciences should provide the model for the natural sciences, rather than vice versa as positivists have argued? If we extract the notion of scientific knowledge-seeking out of its Eurocentric, natural science and positivist paradigms we can continue to pay close attention to the concerns of the 'after the revolution' analysis while finding good reasons to conceptualize feminist science as already existing now.

There are yet more reasons to find such a proposal controversial. Some feminists have argued that the very idea of feminist sciences is misguided. It is important, they say, only to disrupt the dominant discussions and practices and to refuse to provide positive accounts of 'what we should do' or 'this is how the world is'. The move to alternative agendas and accounts prematurely truncates critical discussion, reflects an arrogant delusion that one individual or some particular group of them can answer such questions, and makes feminism liable to easy incorporation into dominant institutions in a kind of bohemianized status. Women's mocking laugh is more effective at disrupting patriarchal projects than any positive programme could be. This response, like the others, should not be dismissed, for it raises important issues about feminist politics and strategies. Nevertheless, it does not help feminist policy-makers who need to know what the best assessments today are of 'how the world is' and 'what we should do about it' as they attempt to remedy and forestall damage done to women's lives by sexual violence, the health-care and court systems, dangerous technologies and a profit-driven world economy. The restriction of feminist science tendencies only to protest and to mocking laughs, important as such strategies are, also accepts a kind of bohemian containment of feminism.

One way to think about feminist science projects is that they have constructed stronger, more competent criteria for objectivity, rationality and, indeed, science itself than the mainstream has been willing to accept. A science that has no systematic way to detect and eliminate such distorting culture-wide assumptions as the rightness of male supremacy and white supremacy, whatever the sentiments of its practitioners may be, is simply not maximally objective. Rather than reject such notions as obstacles to feminist agendas, they can be prised out of their sexist, racist and bourgeois containers and appropriated and transformed to serve feminist ends.

Feminism needs sciences that distinguish between 'how the world is' and 'how we want it to be' more effectively than the sciences of androcentric, bourgeois groups in the West that have no principled means of separating legitimated knowledge from their 'folk sciences'. Modern science has been neither modern enough nor scientific enough in this respect, exactly because its gaze is forever firmly fixed only outwards. It cannot systematically turn its powerful explanatory lenses on itself or the culture-wide assumptions that shape its problematics. This is an issue internal to feminism also, as feminism struggles to construct global agendas that defeat rather than advance cultural imperialism. To engage in these appropriative projects is not to assume that the feminist mind can be a glassy mirror of nature, capable of reflecting a world that is ready made and out there for the reflecting. On the contrary, it is to insist on socially situated knowledge – with equal weight on both parts of the term. However, progress toward such a goal requires, also, that people of European descent develop understandings of gender and feminism that do not simply continue to advance the West at the expense of the 'rest'. Obtaining knowledge requires that I grasp what I look and sound like from the standpoint of others' lives, not just from my own perspective.

These discussions leave many issues unresolved. Are there any theories of the UNCONSCIOUS that permit the positive evaluation of knowledge-seeking agendas that feminisms seem to need? After all, as indicated above, women need to know how to increase their economic viability (*all* women's economic viability), decrease violence against women, etc., etc., and these are projects that require scientific answers – that is, empirically adequate, systematic and causal ones. If psychoanalytic tendencies cannot develop theories that empower women in these necessary projects, psychoanalysis will be the loser for it will seem increasingly irrelevant – perhaps even obstructionist – to the concerns of the majority of the world's women. There are other issues, too. Are feminist science tendencies still too loyal to the Enlightenment? What kinds of international links can advance the decentring of Eurocentric preoccupations from Western feminist science critiques and replace them with the issues central to the vast majority of the world's women – health, economic viability, ecological balance? What are the central science questions in the global feminisms that are forming?

See also AUTONOMY; PATRIARCHY; PHALLOGOCENTRISM; POSTMODERNISM; THEORY.

BIBLIOGRAPHY

Bordo, Susan, 1987: *The Flight to Objectivity: Essays on Cartesianism and Culture*. Albany: State University of New York Press.

Dinnerstein, Dorothy, 1976: *The Mermaid and the Minotaur: Sexual Arrangements and Human Malaise*. New York: Harper and Row.

Flax, Jane, 1990: *Thinking Fragments: Psychoanalysis, Feminism and Postmodernism in the Contemporary West*. Berkeley: Univesity of California Press.

Gilman, Sander L., 1985: *Difference and Pathology: Stereotypes of Sexuality, Race, and Madness*. Ithaca, NY: Cornell University Press.

Haraway, Donna, 1989: *Primate Visions: Gender, Race and Nature in the World of Modern Science*. New York: Routledge.

Harding, Sandra, 1991: *Whose Science? Whose Knowledge? Thinking from Women's Lives*. Ithaca, NY: Cornell University Press.

Harding, Sandra, and Hintikka, Merrill, eds 1983: *Discovering Reality: Feminist Perspectives on Epistemology, Metaphysics, Methodology and Philosophy of Science.* Dordrecht: Reidel.

Irigaray, Luce, 1985: 'Is the subject of science sexed?', trans. Carol Mastrangelo Bove, *Cultural Critique*, 1, pp. 73–88.

Keller, Evelyn Fox, 1985: *Reflections on Gender and Science.* New Haven: Yale University Press.

Merchant, Carolyn, 1980: *The Death of Nature: Women, Ecology and the Scientific Revolution.* New York: Harper and Row.

Nelson, Lynn Hankinson, 1990: *Who Knows: From Quine to a Feminist Empiricism.* Philadelphia: Temple University Press.

SANDRA HARDING

seduction theory   The 'seduction theory' was named by Freud's disciple and biographer Ernest JONES in reference to Freud's early hypothesis (*c*.1893–7), later abandoned, that HYSTERIA results from the affective pressure of a repressed memory of sexual trauma in the hysteric's childhood. Freud hypothesized that whenever there was hysteria, it could be traced back to an experience of sexual abuse directed against the hysteric in childhood, and that the repressed trauma associated with that abuse was the necessary and sufficient cause of hysteria. Freud extended this theory of hysteria to all psychoneuroses, which he interpreted as neuroses of failed psychic defences attempting to ward off repugnant ideas. The seduction theory was Freud's initial approach to the origin of REPRESSION and the enigma of the onset of childhood sexuality.

At this early stage of his thinking, Freud believed that normal childhood was a pre-sexual phase of life; and so he thought that, if there was a memory of childhood sexual experience, that experience must have come to the child from outside and would have been unpleasant, bewildering, physically unexciting and psychically unintegrated. It would require the intervention of dawning sexual knowledge at puberty to achieve its full distressing effect, and then would be bound up with memories and fantasies associated with masturbation and with imagined, overheard, or witnessed acts of sex between other people or between animals. Freud believed at this time that, unless one's childhood had been free of substantial sexual irritation, the awakening of SEXUALITY in adolescence would trigger childhood memories of overwhelming affect which damaged the ego in its attempts to keep them from consciousness. Though his letters to Fliess between 1896 and 1897 continue to puzzle over the relation between imaginary and real childhood sexual scenes, Freud took a strong public stand in favour of tracing mental illness to actual childhood sexual abuse, in 'Further remarks on the neuro-psy-choses of defence' (1896a) and 'The aetiology of hysteria' (1896b), papers cited with approval by seduction theory revivalists during the 1970s and 1980s, including the French feminist group *Psychanalyse et politique* and Florence Rush, Judith Lewis Herman and Jeffrey Moussaieff Masson, all of whom regard Freud's renunciation of the seduction theory as a sign of his complicity with patriarchal silencing of women and children.

In these early papers Freud revealed and theorized reports of infant victimage. In the former, Freud wrote of the specific cause of hysteria: 'It is not enough that there should occur at some period of the subject's life an event which touches his sexual existence and becomes pathogenic through the release and suppression of distressing affect. On the con-trary, *these sexual traumas must have occurred in early childhood (before puberty), and their content must consist of an actual irritation of the genitals (of processes resembling copulation)* (1896a, p. 163, Freud's italics).

The clarity and insistence with which Freud claimed in 1896 to have discovered in actually experienced sexual traumas in childhood the source of pathogenic memories are blurred by his frequent use of the ambiguous term 'scene' in relation to seduction and by the complicated role of FANTASY, which, he discovered, makes PSYCHICAL REALITY more decisive than material reality in the world of neurosis (1916, p. 370). This issue remains problematic in Freud's early and late writings. For example, in his letter to Fliess of 2 May 1897, Freud writes that hysteria 'goes back to the reproduction of scenes. Some can be obtained directly, others always by way of fantasies set up in front of them. The fantasies stem from things that have been *heard* but understood *subsequently*, and all their material is of course genuine' (1892–9, p. 247, Freud's ital-ics). However we interpret the 'scene' which the hysteric's symptoms are supposed to reproduce, it is a *psychic* scene, for Freud's 'seduction the-ory' specifies that it is what the mind does with the scene – not any orig-inal experience *per se* – that determines symptoms (*see* SYMPTOM). The element of pathogenic unconscious memory – a *psychic* element – is often ignored in the controversy surrounding Freud's views on seduc-tion. It needs to be emphasized in order to keep the discussion from pos-ing the issue simply as a debate over whether or not childhood sexual molestation frequently occurs and causes psychological damage to its victims, the reality and prevalence of which Freud continued to assert until the end of his life (see 1931, p. 231 and 1940, p. 187).

Since Freud himself initially suspected that most actual seductions were by fathers, a high incidence of psychoneuroses pointed to numer-ous incestuous fathers. Freud's uneasiness with this frequency which his original theory implied may have been partly determined by the death of his own father in October 1896, and was influenced by the self-analysis Freud conducted between 1895 and 1897, culminating in the discovery of his own OEDIPUS COMPLEX within three weeks of his abandonment of the seduction theory (1892–9, pp. 263–6). In 'The Freudian cover-up' (1977), Rush argues that Freud's complex personal motivation for disbelieving the seduction theory included his need to idealize fathers as part of the process of mourning his own (see also Balmary, 1982). Masson (1984), on the other hand, attempts to show that Freud dropped the seduction theory out of intellectual cowardice, a desire to exonerate Fliess from malpractice and a wish to improve his own professional ties to the medical estabishment of his day. Whatever Freud's personal motives were and however wrong he may have been about the improbability of a high incidence of incest among his patients, a crucial theoretical issue for him was that it is psychoanalytically undecidable whether or not a traumatic memory is traceable to a real event (p. 260).

Freud's initial presentation of the oedipus complex brought to light erotic wishes of children as fixed upon the parent of the opposite sex. But whereas this turn-of-the-century theorization of oedipal wishes presented them as deriving from the child's biological maturation, Laplanche and Pontalis (1973) suggest that the oedipus complex may be read as a response on the part of the child to the parents' construction of the child's sexuality.

At the time when Freud proposed the seduction hypothesis of neuroses, he also employed the words 'abuse', 'rape', 'attack' and 'fright'; after he dropped it, he tended to refer to it by 'seduction' alone. As opposed to 'attack', 'seduction' implies mutuality, or ambiguity about the passive and active roles of the participants, thus perhaps tending to conflate Freud's earlier narrative of child molestation with his superseding oedipal narrative.

Alice Miller (1984) holds that Freud's oedipal theory of spontaneous childhood sexual development is a fraud serving to place guilt on children for what audults do to them. In similar spirit, Catherine Clément (Clément and Cixous, 1986) examines how the history of Freud's changing views on the relation between seduction and hysteria makes the guilt of fathers ultimately fictional. Freud's first narrative had blamed the father as the guilty one: hysterics are victims of sexual aggression. In this theory, the father's love is over-possessive, violating the cycle of generations and making it impossible for the hysteric to marry and move away from the family bond: his Law is perverse, '"Thou shalt love no other than me"'. In the second narrative, which Clément calls 'The lying daughters', Freud proposes that the hysteric's traumatic scenes were not real but based on something *heard*, bits of

399

family legend perhaps. There is still guilt in this model, but the guilt is now the daughter's: the hysteric, projecting her own desire, fantasizes a seduction. In the next theory of seduction, according to Clément, the mother is guilty. Here Clément interprets the passage from Freud's 1933 essay on 'Femininity', where he suggests that the fantasy of seduction by the father is an effect of the oedipus complex, whereas it is through the mother's pre-oedipal bodily ministrations that 'the phantasy touches the ground of reality' (1933, p. 120). The guilt associated with the enigma of the onset of the hysteric's sexuality has wandered from father to daughter to mother, where it touches ground. The issue of the child's cleanliness and dirt makes the maid, or the mother doing the maid's work, the seductress in this scenario. An epilogue to this story analyses maid and governess figures in Freud's case histories as seducers who may finally break the vicious circle enclosing women in family roles (Clément, in Clément and Cixous, 1986, pp. 41–54).

The scene of seduction is displaced to the sphere of discourse by Jane Gallop (1982). Like Clément, Gallop seeks women's liberation in seduction away from family roles. Emphasizing the undecidability between passivity and activity in a seduction, Gallop sees feminist psychoanalysis as 'seduction' of 'daughters' out of their resistance to psychoanalysis, which she metaphorizes as 'the father'. Writing herself into the history of psychoanalytic accounts of seduction, Gallop finds in feminist interrogations of psychoanalytic master texts a written 'seduction of the father', who is made to show his desire and thus undermine his 'impassive mastery' (1982, p. xv). For Freud 'seduction' was a euphemism for incest (1914, p. 17). Gallop's metaphorical use of 'seduction' to mean rhetorical persuasion and exposure of DESIRE in language transforms the grim story Freud first told of traumatic abuses of power within families.

Like Gallop, Jean Baudrillard (1990) valorizes seduction as an anti-patriarchal strategy, though his discourse is metaphysical, not psychoanalytic. A recanting marxist and a trickster, Baudrillard, in *Seduction*, flirts with what he sees as the feminist essentialism of Luce IRIGARAY. Attacking Irigaray for biologism in her equation of women's linguistic difference with women's anatomy, Baudrillard opposes power in the domain of the symbolic to power in the domain of the real, claiming that seduction represents mastery over the symbolic, where actual power resides, not in nature. Though he wishes to subvert binary oppositions, equating them with masculinity, Baudrillard himself opposes seduction to production, and theorizes the seductive power of artifice over materiality, and thus the power of 'the feminine' (i.e. pleasing appearances) over 'the masculine' (the exigencies of production). Baudrillard has nothing to say about the power exerted by the seductive father in the patriarchal family, but claims that seduction is transsexual. Seduction can reverse the power differences between men and women because it *plays* on those differences while undermining the difference between activity and passivity, seducer and seducee. He invokes Joan Riviere on femininity as MASQUERADE and points to such feminine wiles as make-up and posing, to argue that femininity is the model for the power of images to seduce consumers in postmodernist mass culture. In this model, woman as sign and her image as simulacrum are read not as symptoms of patriarchal exploitation, but as examples of the power of appearances to fascinate. In place of Freud's initial theory of abusive sexual intercourse between adult and child, and Gallop's view of mastery through discursive intercourse, Baudrillard theorizes the politics of visual domination. The metaphorizing away of child abuse is problematic in both Gallop and Baudrillard.

BIBLIOGRAPHY

Balmary, Mary, 1982 [1979]: *Psychoanalyzing Psychoanalysis: Freud and the Hidden Fault of the Father*, trans. Ned Lukacher. Baltimore and London: Johns Hopkins University Press.

Baudrillard, Jean, 1990 [1979]: *Seduction*, trans. Brian Singer. London: Macmillan.

Clément, Catherine and Cixous, Hélène, 1986 [1975]: *The Newly Born Woman*, trans. Betsy Wing. Minneapolis: University of Minnesota Press.

Freud, Sigmund, 1892–9: 'Extracts from the Fliess Papers', *SE*, 1, pp. 173–280.

Freud, Sigmund, 1896a: 'Further remarks on the neuro-psychoses of defense', *SE*, 3, pp. 162–88.

Freud, Sigmund, 1896b: 'The aetiology of hysteria', *SE*, 3, pp. 119–221.

Freud, Sigmund, 1905: *Three Essays on the Theory of Sexuality*, *SE*, 7, pp. 135–245.

Freud, Sigmund, 1910: 'Five lectures on psycho-analysis', *SE*, 11, pp. 5–47.

Freud, Sigmund, 1914: 'On the history of the psycho-analytic movement', *SE*, 14, pp. 3–66.

Freud, Sigmund, 1916: *Introductory Lectures on Psycho-analysis*, *SE*, 16.

Freud, Sigmund, 1931: 'Female sexuality', *SE*, 21, pp. 223–46.

Freud, Sigmund, 1933: 'Femininity', *SE*, 22, pp. 112–37.

Freud, Sigmund, 1940: *An Outline of Psycho-analysis*, *SE*, 23, pp. 139–208.

Gallop, Jane, 1982: *Feminism and Psychoanalysis: The Daughter's Seduction*. London: Macmillan.

Herman, Judith Lewis, 1981: *Father–Daughter Incest*. Cambridge, Mass. and London: Harvard University Press.

Hunter, Dianne, ed. 1989: *Seduction and Theory: Readings of Gender, Representation, and Rhetoric*. Urbana and Chicago: University of Illinois Press.

Laplanche, Jean, 1989 [1987]: *New Foundations for Psychoanalysis*, trans. David Macey. Oxford: Basil Blackwell; 1st edition Paris: Presses Universitaires de France, 1987.

SEXUAL DIFFERENCE

Laplanche, Jean and Pontalis, Jean-Baptiste, 1973 [1967]: *The Language of Psycho-Analysis*, trans. Donald Nicholson-Smith. New York: Norton.

Masson, Jeffrey Moussaieff, 1984: *The Assault on Truth: Freud's Suppression of the Seduction Theory*. New York: Farrar, Straus and Giroux.

Masson, Jeffrey Moussaieff, ed. 1985: *The Complete Letters of Sigmund Freud to Wilhelm Fliess, 1887–1905*. Cambridge, Mass. and London: Harvard University Press.

Miller, Alice, 1984 [1981]: *Thou Shalt Not Be Aware: Society's Betrayal of the Child*, trans. Hildegarde and Hunter Hannum. New York: Farrar, Straus and Giroux.

Rush, Florence, 1977: 'The Freudian cover-up: the sexual abuse of children', *Chrysalis: A Magazine of Women's Culture*, 1, pp. 31–45.

DIANNE HUNTER

sexual difference   It is impossible for the speaking SUBJECT not to take up a position as a man or a woman (Mitchell, 1982, p. 6). This point is Lacan's: the assumption of LANGUAGE by the subject is, in our culture, inflected by sexual difference. The interests of psychoanalysis and feminism explicitly intersect on the question of the way in which the morphological terms 'male' and 'female' (the so-called data of biology) have been welded to definitions of cultural roles (the becoming masculine or feminine of the subject) such that these are 'naturalized' and so give a justification.

Feminism's response to psychoanalysis on this issue has been mixed. Early discussions focused on the 'roles' or 'character traits' as differential and proper modes of being. The negative tendency of this work was to generate new but still normative descriptions. In response to this, some feminists refuse to accept the psychoanalytic explanation of the way a 'woman' is induced into 'femininity' by patriarchal culture. Recent work, because it sees psychoanalysis as the study of the resistance to culturally prescribed identity lying at the heart of psychic life, has looked again to the theories of sexual difference occurring in Freud's work. It has become the occasion for a double-edged critique of how positions which construct identity come to be fixed, naturalized or instantiated, and of how such fixations are not only unstable, but come to disturb the fixating regulation itself. By returning analytic technique to the study of cultural definitions as themselves symptomatic, and in showing how morphology is not only shaped by but itself shapes linguistic definitions, the process of grounding through which such definitions become 'facts' is exposed. Such a critique allows feminism to account for the facticity which has been so effective in articulating social roles, while at the same time demonstrating the contingency of this unstable reification of the masculine and feminine which is never achieved by the subject in any neat, successful way. Freud's structure of sexual difference as the founding moment of sexual identity – in which psychic structures come to be articulated through biological categories – thus deserves a closer look, as it suggests the paradigm for such an argument.

A preliminary note: while it is useful to look at the psychoanalytic elaboration of the concept, 'sexual difference' is not a psychoanalytic term. Freud concentrated on the 'distinction' (*Entscheidung*) between the sexes, and Lacan on the 'relation' (*rapport*) between the sexes. 'Sexual difference' as a term in feminism derives from work that is influenced by deconstruction: see Abel (1980), or Eisenstein and Jardine (1980). Its history is closely tied to the concept of feminine sexuality (*see* CASTRATION COMPLEX; ESSENTIALISM; FEMININITY).

In the fourth preface to his *Three Essays on the Theory of Sexuality* (1905), Freud states that his work on SEXUALITY had a different status from the more purely 'psychological theses' of his theory. It lies between two equally difficult regions: on the one side is 'the frontier of biology'; on the other, after the introduction of the OEDIPUS COMPLEX, it prepares the ground of metapsychology – the introduction of cultural laws. 'Sexuality' is thus a knot between biological givens, psychic structures and social structures expressed as myths and laws; this knot must be instantiated as the subject, the place as well as the product of this articulation.

In these essays, the first, provisional definition of sexual difference is that between the various sexual aberrations, understood as deviating from the purpose of biological reproduction. Freud proposes a displacement of 'sexuality' from the realm of the biological – where its characteristics are manifest as sexed genitals – to that of the normative: different sexualities make up the component sexual instinct and are distinguished by their aim, their object and their somatic sources. All instincts are tied to excitations occurring on a bodily surface: sexual instincts originate in the so-called erotogenic zones – the mouth, the anus and the genitals. The normative aim of the instinct is then the achievement or release of tension that the instinct represents, which often – when autosatisfaction is not possible – involves attaching the possibility of such a release to an external stimulus capable of producing satisfaction. While it is easy to see how the originating erotogenic zones can be said to give the shape to the sexualities (the so-called sexual phases), how this leads to the sexing of the OBJECT – the external stimulus – and the subject will prove to be more difficult.

The sexual marking of these objects, which motivates the translation of analytically understood (zonal) sexuality back into the biological pairing of male and female, only occurs at the moment of the genital phase, in which Freud subordinates the component sexual drives to their reproductive end. But this is a two-step process: the first aim of the genital phase is autoerotic satisfaction. Until this point, the penis and the clitoris are given a morphological equality (the clitoris is called a little penis); indeed, children are said to come into an undifferentiated awareness of their erotogenic zones and the achievement of PLEASURE through them. These zones are marked not by masculine and feminine terms, but by an active or passive relation taken towards the process of obtaining their satisfaction. While the active–passive polarity will come to be allied with the masculine–feminine polarity, Freud is very clear here that this attribution must be suspended until after the moment of unifying subordination. When this occurs is something of a conundrum, for the genitals must be already morphologically sexed if they are to be experienced as such by the child, whose psyche can only be 'sexed' after a recognition of their difference occurs. During the subsequent latency period, the SUBLIMATION of the sexual instincts leads to the creation of masculine and feminine characters which re-emerge in relation to a bodily sexual drive only in puberty. At the nexus of this exchange, in which the biological characteristics come to mark both the subject and the object of the (zonal) sexual aim, are the oedipus and castration complexes.

This suture is crucially related to the sexual researches of children, which for Freud are the prototype for oedipal sublimation, a mastery deemed necessary to the development of a properly adult, and sexed, character. Such mastery is tied to the child's gaining independence as a psychic individual and to its achieving its own pleasures. This independence is related to the genital phase in that it seems the first closed system of completely satisfying autoerotism. The anxiety produced by this autonomy precipitates the threat of castration, provoking the memory of a difference between genitals in which the meaning of the female genitals now represents the loss of the male. Because this meaning is resonant with the loss of other satisfactions – chiefly the potential loss of the human object – the mark of difference also resonates beyond the immediate physical context, and results in a self-identification of the entire subject with his or her own narcissistically satisfying organ which is now tailored to the masculine–feminine polarity exemplified by ego ideals. This IDENTIFICATION is the first step towards the social order and is an intellectual apprehension of the demands of what Freud terms 'social respectability'.

Freud's discussion of sexuality occurs in the context of his 'discovery' of the meaning that neurotic symptoms express: PERVERSIONS are defined as expressions of a previous state of the sexual drive, the analyst's first access to primordial sexuality, whose structure is provided by the narrative of infantile sexuality. Freud derives this structure not from the empirical data of children's sexuality but from the adult neuroses: the supposedly primordial experiences appear to provide the interpretation of the later symptoms. A similar inversion can be found in the relation of psychic structures and biological organs. Freud insists that the only trace of unconscious or conscious processes reside in the phenomena of psychic or somatic manifestations. The sexual instinct, which measures the sexual excitation occurring in the endosomatic source, is a psychic representative structuring the ego. But we have access to this organization only through its psychosomatic displacements – the neurotic symptoms. Analysis constructs (normative) sexuality as the matrix within which these symptoms are to be interpreted.

Recent debates on sexual difference have taken as their point of departure Lacan's substitution of linguistics in the place of biology. The relation of the subject to the PHALLUS – the signifier of the desire of the Other – and the access to the SYMBOLIC it implies, take the place of the genital phase as the subordinating mechanism which will thereafter regulate the (non-)relation of the sexes. This emphasis on symbolization risks ignoring the role played by morphology in psychic structuring, and so has difficulty accounting for why the phallus comes to be the privileged signifier which organizes sexuality, and for why the wedding of *psyche* and *morphe* has had the powerful effect that it has. However, its focus remains the difficulty involved in the assumption of the subject position.

See also BIOLOGY; BODY; GENDER.

BIBLIOGRAPHY

Abel, Elizabeth, ed. 1980: *Writing and Sexual Difference*. Chicago: University of Chicago Press.

Brennan, Teresa, ed. 1989: *Between Feminism and Psychoanalysis*. London and New York: Routledge.

Eisenstein, Hester, and Jardine, Alice, eds 1980: *The Future of Difference*. Boston: G. K. Hall.

Freud, Sigmund, 1905: *Three Essays on the Theory of Sexuality*, SE, 7, pp. 125–248.

Heath, Stephen, 1978: 'Difference', *Screen*, 19/3, pp. 51–112.

Irigaray, Luce, 1985 [1977]: *This Sex Which Is Not One*, trans. C. Porter. Ithaca, NY: Cornell University Press.

Mitchell, Juliet, 1982: 'Introduction I', *Feminine Sexuality: Jacques Lacan and the École Freudienne*, ed. Juliet Mitchell and Jacqueline Rose. London: Macmillan, pp. 1–26.

Ragland-Sullivan, Ellie, 1987: '"Beyond the phallus?"; the question of gender identity', *Jacques Lacan and the Philosophy of Psychoanalysis*. Urbana and Chicago: University of Illinois Press, pp. 267–308.

DEBRA KEATES

sexuality Since Freud, the definition of sexuality has become radically modified. After some hesitations, sexuality has been evicted from the realm of biology and now belongs to the realm of psychoanalysis, that of the psyche (Freud, 1925). However, it is not enough to make the distinction between the biological and the psychic: the importance of social representations of sexuality, varying from one social group to another, was always well known inasmuch as they were conscious. What is specific to psychoanalysis is the articulation of sexuality with the UNCONSCIOUS; in other words, for psychoanalysis, human sexuality is the sexuality of the subject of the unconscious, to which it is the key, as Freud's early works on HYSTERIA made clear. The specificity of the psychoanalytic definition of sexuality is also visible in Freud's choice of the terms 'LIBIDO' and 'DRIVE' which cannot be assimilated to instinct. In psychoanalysis, clinical experience demonstrates that sexuality is not a question of instinct; if it were, relations between men and women would be no more complex than the encounter between male and female animals or between sperm and egg. Clinical evidence shows that in the human subject, because of the existence of the unconscious, the natural order defined by the reproduction of the species is disturbed. Thus, from 'The three essays on sexuality' (1905) onwards, human sexuality as drive is linked to PERVERSION and then to FANTASY.

The term 'subject' (of the unconscious), which LACAN re-deploys and then subverts by giving it the meaning of 'subjected', enables us to clarify the Freudian theory which problematizes the use of the terms 'man' and 'woman'. Freud correctly claims that, as far as the unconscious is concerned, sexuality is neither masculine nor feminine according to a biological or sociological definition of this duality, but rather that there is only one kind of sexuality, which is phallic. This claim has given rise to much misinterpretation, and it immediately provoked a feminist revolt, based on a misunderstanding. In order to avoid a sterile dispute, it is necessary, first, to define the PHALLUS, and second, to posit that, when we are speaking of the unconscious, subjective truth is not equivalent to, or reducible to, the domain of the factual. Lacan's reading of Freud enables us to avoid certain aporias. The two Freudian theses which have given rise to so much confusion are the CASTRATION COMPLEX and the privilege of the phallus, two theses central to psychoanalysis which define the route taken by sexuality. Lacan's return to Freud has therefore centred on the assertions which follow from these theses: 'the libido is phallic' and 'access to subjectivity, that is to say, to sexuality, must for the human subject pass through the defile of the castration complex.'

The first Freudian impasse was the biological one; it arose out of the definition of penis, clitoris and vagina as organs, and out of the failure to differentiate clearly between penis and phallus. The other stumbling block was the mother. In 'Female sexuality' (1931), Freud points to the necessity of re-thinking the OEDIPUS COMPLEX of the little girl in the light of the under-estimation – including his own – of the role of the mother in the girl's sexual development. However, these two impasses did not prevent him from retaining the oedipus complex, which should be seen rather as a logical structure than as a developmental moment. The oedipus complex refers to the process which transforms a phallic sexuality, one and the same in both sexes, into two different subject-positions, masculine and feminine, none the less organized by an identical libido. The consequences of the 'rock of castration' (Freud, 1937, p. 209) for the human subject are formulated by Freud in the following way: what organizes male sexuality is the fear of castration, which produces the relation between men and women in the form of 'horror' and 'disgust'; for women, sexuality is organized around PENIS ENVY, and their relation to men revolves around protest and hatred.

Although Lacan retains the equation of sexuality with phallic libido, and the thesis that human unconscious sexuality is one and the same in both sexes, his revision of Freudian theory clarifies the concept of phallus and distinguishes between an IMAGINARY and a SYMBOLIC order. The symbolic function of the phallus is defined by Lacan as the castration function, i.e. 'sacrifice of *jouissance*' (*see* JOUISSANCE): this function of LACK, of which the phallus is the symbol, arises not from the anatomical difference between the sexes, but from the fact that human beings, whether male or female, are required to inscribe themselves in what is their only natural milieu: LANGUAGE. As far as the imaginary phallus is concerned, it inscribes the sacrifice of *jouissance* on the body, i.e. the body image, and can sometimes be fantasized in relation to the penis, or the clitoris, or even the vagina, as Freud showed. The phallus is therefore at the same time a signifier and an image; in both cases it is correlated with symbolic or imaginary lack. This formulation of the oedipal myth allows Lacan a way out of the Freudian biological impasse and enables the articulation of DESIRE with SEXUAL DIFFERENCE.

In terms of drive and desire, there is no human sexuality outside the *castration complex*, and the phallic function which effects castration at a symbolic level. However, it must be noted that while sexuality and castration are linked axiomatically by psychoanalysis as a science of the unconscious, this fact does not enable us to differentiate between male and female sexuality. For this reason, Lacan considers that there is no PRE-OEDIPAL sexuality, although there may be pre-genital sexuality. Further, as a general point, human sexuality, that is desire, is always pre-genital, or more precisely, always partial. There is no whole sexual object; fantasy shows that human desire always revolves around a part without a whole. The missing part, belonging to the body of the other, is invested phallically, and derives from this its value as a desirable object.

But in that case, how should we approach the question of male and female sexual desire? Lacan offers two solutions. The first could be formulated in this way. On the masculine side, one has it (the phallus) without being it; on the feminine side, one is it, without having it (see Riviere, 1929, often referred to by Lacan). This first formulation maintains a symmetry between the two sexes in relation to sexuality, founded on a universal castration function; but since this does not necessarily imply complementarity, the relation between the sexes becomes problematic. Lacan's second solution (1975) goes further: although he continues to defend the primacy of castration, he puts forward formulas defining a masculine and a feminine sexuation where there is neither symmetry nor complementarity. As Freud had already suggested when he placed the oedipus complex at the centre of his theory, human sexuality can only be understood as the result of a process of sexuation; it does not spring either from anatomy or from social role. It is sexuation which produces a sexed subject-position in the unconscious. That is why Lacan can now speak not of pre-defined men and women, but of speaking beings who inscribe themselves in one place or the other. For subjects with an unconscious, sexuality does not function in such a way that we can isolate and distinguish two distinct groups; the 'man' part includes everyone who inhabits language, and from this point of view, everyone's sexuality is phallic, or masculine; the 'woman' part includes those subjects 'not all' of whose sexuality is phallic. 'Not all' does not mean 'not at all'; as a result, the two groups neither complete each other nor find themselves in opposition. Rather, the woman part 'supplements' the man part, in such a way that it implies a different, non-phallic *jouissance*.

If sexuality is defined in terms of both castration and sexuation, we can conceive of two types of sexual *jouissance*, distinct, but not opposed. On the one hand, there is the sexuality which is shared by all speaking beings, men or women, a phallic sexuality in which the formula of *jouissance* is provided by fantasy, i.e. the mode of relation between the 'lacking' subject produced by inscription in language, and the object which fills the lack. Freud (1919) gives a vivid illustration of the role of this fundamental fantasy in his famous text 'A child is being beaten' (see MASOCHISM; SADOMASOCHISM). Sexual satisfaction depends on the fantasy, to such an extent that the sexual relation is reduced to a relation between SUBJECT and OBJECT. On the other hand, to a certain extent the feminine part of sexuality evades the logic of castration: part of it remains outside language. Lacan has given two examples, taken from mysticism, of this supplementary feminine sexuality: St Teresa and St John of the Cross, biologically speaking a male and a female, socially speaking, a man and a woman. In this way he demonstrates that, for Freudian psychoanalysis, sexuality, situated between phallic desire and feminine *jouissance,* knows no other law than the logic of the unconscious.

BIBLIOGRAPHY

Brousse, Marie-Hélène, 1987: 'La Formule du fantasme', *Lacan,* ed. G. Miller. Paris: Éditions Bordas, pp. 105–24.
Freud, Sigmund, 1905: *Three Essays on the Theory of Sexuality, SE,* 7, pp. 123–246.
Freud, Sigmund, 1919: '"A child is being beaten": a contribution to the study of the origin of sexual perversions', *SE,* 17, pp. 175–204.
Freud, Sigmund, 1925: 'Some psychical consequences of the anatomical distinction between the sexes', *SE,* 19, pp. 241–60.
Freud, Sigmund, 1931: 'Female sexuality', *SE,* 21, pp. 221–46.
Freud, Sigmund, 1937: 'Analysis terminable and interminable', *SE,* 23, pp. 209–54.
Lacan, Jacques, 1975: *Le Séminaire,* book 20: *Encore.* Paris: Seuil.
Lacan, Jacques, 1977a: 'Subversion of the subject and dialectic of desire', *Écrits: A Selection,* trans. Alan Sheridan. London: Tavistock, pp. 292–325.
Lacan, Jacques, 1977b: *The Four Fundamental Concepts of Psychoanalysis.* London: Hogarth Press (see especially chapters 12 and 13).
Riviere, Joan, 1929: 'Womanliness as a masquerade', *International Journal of Psycho-analysis,* 10, pp. 303–13.

MARIE HÉLÈNE BROUSSE
(*trans. Margaret Whitford*)

subject, the   The term 'the subject' has become increasingly popular both in contemporary feminist theory and within the social sciences and humanities. Its origins as a term are difficult to pin down: it could be said that Aristotle theorized a unitary, singular, self-reflective being which provided an early anticipation of the current use of the term; but it could be equally plausibly suggested that, as a term designating a self-conscious being, it can be dated back to Abelard. Most commonly, however, its origins are attributed to Descartes, who regarded the subject as a unified being of disparate parts, mind and body, each with their own attributes. However, it is in reaction to this Cartesian inflection that many feminists have turned to theorists of the nineteenth century, especially Marx, Freud and Nietzsche, to provide a displacement of Cartesian dualism.

The notion of the subject is differentiated from a number of cognate terms that appear to have a similar range of references: human being, self, person, agent. Its increasing popularity is to a large extent the result of its being the preferred term in what might be called 'anti-humanist' conceptions of the human being. Humanism has been a prevailing commitment of philosophical and political theories since the Renaissance. On the one hand, it opposes religious dogmatism that places the human subject in a secondary position relative to a divine cosmological order. On the other hand, it opposes the tendency in the natural sciences to privilege objective facts and scientific laws, stressing instead experience and any affirmation of subjectivity. Humanism is committed to the primacy of what is immediately given to consciousness, of lived experience. It is allied to liberalism and individualism, and is opposed to mechanistic reductionism. It criticizes de-personalization of experience or consciousness in behaviourism, relying on metaphors of alienation, self-estrangement, reification and objectification in social and political theory. It is committed to privileging

1 the human over the divine and/or the natural;
2 the individual over the social and its structures;
3 consciousness over the UNCONSCIOUS;
4 freedom and agency over determinism and causality;
5 knowledge of self over knowledge of others or the world;
6 what is experienced over what is objectively known.

Nietzsche, Freud, Marx and Saussure, in their different ways, all problematized the self-transparency, mastery and givenness of subjectivity, and can thus be regarded as precursors of contemporary anti-humanism. Since Nietzsche's assault on PHILOSOPHY as a discipline that misconstrues the power and force of the BODY, anti-humanism has criticized the self-evidence and transparency of consciousness and the aspirations of human agency to the ideals of self-creation and unmediated access to the world and knowledge of it, focusing instead on the social and historical *production* of consciousness.

There are today two major lines of assault on humanism, both of which are of direct relevance to feminists, even if one remains, as yet, rather undeveloped: theories, primarily marxist, of *ideology* – i.e. belief systems, representations and practices that are false, distorted or misleading representations of reality: and accounts of *corporeality* – such as those developed by Nietzsche, Foucault and Deleuze – which tend to oppose the psychoanalytic emphasis on the interior of subjectivity by focusing mainly on the subject as an object of social inscription (e.g. Gatens, 1991).

While the roots of anti-humanism lie in the nineteenth century, since its resurgence in and after 1968 two names in particular have been associated with anti-humanism and with the re-introduction of the category of the subject – the French marxist, Louis Althusser, and the French psychoanalyst, Jacques Lacan. Both see their work as the reading and restoration of the principles of the discourses within which they work, those of Marx and Freud respectively. Concentrating on Freud for the moment, it can be said that for Freud the subject is not the centre (of consciousness or of discourse) but merely the cipher through which the unconscious manifests itself. The desiring subject is the effect, the end-product of processes of which it is not aware, let alone able to change (Freud, 1900). To invert one of Lacan's formulations, the subject is *constituted* not *constituent*, an effect of structures rather than their cause. This may help to explain Lacan's rather unsettling definition of the signifier: the signifier represents a subject for another signifier, inverting its humanist counterpart, a model of communication, in which the self represents a sign for another self.

This encapsulates the differences between humanist and anti-humanist notions of LANGUAGE: the humanist privileges the self as the origin and destination of discourse. Discourse, ART, REPRESENTATION are forms of communication, messages representing one self (the author, the first person) to another (the listener, the second person). By contrast, Lacan takes the signifier (the material component of discourses) as primary, the signifying chain as the medium of exchange, and the subject, not as the source of discourse, but as the locus through which the discourse is spoken. By submitting to the laws of the signifier, the subject takes up a place in language and is thus, unknown to itself, submitted to social law (the Symbolic). It is not the subject who speaks; rather, the subject is, as it were, spoken through by discourse, law and culture. Lacan, following Freud, has displaced the subject from its central position as constitutive agent to reposition it as the SYMPTOM of a broader underlying (psychical/linguistic/economic/libidinal) system (Lacan, 1977a).

Althusser aimed to problematize the reliance of humanism, especially humanist marxism (of which the Frankfurt school is today the leading proponent), on the centrality of consciousness and self-consciousness in notions of the political community and political change. Rather than relying on the individual's access to reason as the basis of communal existence and socio-political action, Althusser postulates the existence, prior to that of the individual or reason, of an unrecognized process of production, an ideological process generating individuality and reason according to its (historical) requirements. For him, ideology must be understood as a distorted reflection of 'men's' (his word) real, i.e. material, relations. It is a system that distorts and obscures the real operations of power leading individuals to accept values and practices not necessarily in their own interest. It is a belief system as well as a system of everyday practices, institutions and social structures which function to rationalize and justify prevailing social values and conventions (Althusser, 1971b).

Humanism takes experience as its starting-point, and thus unwittingly becomes complicit in the propagation of IDEOLOGY. Instead of being an index to what is universal, natural or unmediated, experience is an effect, a product of unrecognized class (and, feminists have added, sex and race) interests (see RACE/IMPERIALISM). What is given to the subject as raw experience is always already invested with political values. For Althusser, it is not subjects who produce ideology but ideology which produces, or interpellates (biological) individuals as subjects of a particular kind. Thus although the general category of subject, subject with a capital S, is universal and external, particular forms of subjectivity are always historically and culturally specific (Foucault, 1976).

Althusser's notion of ideology and his reliance on the category of subject is strongly influenced by Lacan's notion of the split subject. In turn, Althusser has served to provide Lacan's work with political credibility and a set of historical credentials that have vindicated psychoanalysis in the face of the hostility and suspicion many marxists and feminists felt towards it over the problematic notions of class and sexual equality (see MATERIALIST CRITIQUE OF PSYCHOANALYSIS). It is largely through Althusser's advocacy of Freud and Lacan that marxist feminists, and most particularly, MITCHELL (1974), turned to psychoanalysis in order to seek terms by which marxist analyses of class may be integrated with feminist analyses of personal and sexual relations. By providing the bases of an account of the social production of subjectivity, psychoanalysis as it were 'officiated' at the union of marxism and feminism. It provided the intermediary links between the social and the individual that both marxism and feminism needed to explain. Althusser, mediating Lacan, and in turn mediated by Mitchell, showed that central categories of feminist thought, concepts like 'the personal sphere', 'experience', 'the self', needed to be contextualized in order to see the contributions that ideological and power relations have invested in them – that is, that they cannot be uncritically accepted at face value.

Lacan's account of subjectivity is located at the conjunction of his notion of the ego, the mirror stage and the IMAGINARY order on the one hand: and, on the other, his notion of the unconscious and the SYMBOLIC order. Much of Lacan's polemics on the notion of the subject takes the form of his attempts to defend Freud's notion of the narcissistic ego from the humanist encroachments of ego-psychology and Freudian revisionism (Lacan, 1977b). American analysis, and to a lesser extent, British psychoanalysis, have tended to be dominated by an ego-psychology that aims to strengthen the ego by reinforcing the values of the superego, securing the analysand's identifications with the analyst as a form of ego-ideal (as a role model of sorts). This is, for Lacan, a problematic gesture which secures, at most, social conformity but no understanding of subjectivity. Ego-psychologists aim to return conscious, rational control and decision capacities to a functional, realistically oriented ego. Ego-psychology thus falls into a fundamentally conservative ideology. Taking social contexts for granted, it functions to adjust and re-integrate individuals back into these social contexts, questioning and modifying the individual but leaving the social order entirely unexamined and uncriticized. The ego, in this sense, can be read as a pure effect of ideology, the subject of misrecognition.

The mirror stage introduces a sense of identity and of separateness from the maternal body and the world of others. It provides a border or boundary defined by the child's skin. But the identity and unity offered by the mirror stage and Imaginary identifications (in which the self is defined through its identification with the image of others) are precarious: the identity of the subject is always modelled on an other with whom it confuses itself, the ego being set up as an alter ego. The identity posed for the subject through its identification with its own image in a mirror has no stability or internal cohesion. The ego is thus, Lacan claims, always produced as constitutively alienated. It is not as if there is a self outside or before this alienation (as humanism presumes); the subject is produced by and as this alienation. The self is modelled on an other. The self is thus inherently intersubjective, a paranoid and alienated construct: the ego is always an other, always split between an illusory stability and a unity and recognition of its (potential) autonomy (see OBJECT; OTHER/OTHER).

The subject is, then, from its outset, divided between an IMAGE of itself as a unity (an image provided by its mirror reflection or its identification with the totalized image of another) and the perception of itself as a site of fragmentation and disorganized experience. This rupture, at the very heart of the ego or sense of self, is irremediable. The split is augmented and transformed with the child's entry into and resolution of the OEDIPUS COMPLEX. The oedipus complex is responsible for the child's first repressions. In order to resolve the complex, the child must abandon its DESIRE for the mother as a love-object and transfer at least part of its attachment to the father-figure. The boy does this through identification with the father's authority; the girl, through taking on the father as a substitute love-object for the mother, although in her case, this separation is much more tenuous and protracted (Lacan, 1977c).

Like Freud, Lacan concentrates mainly on the boy's symbolic development. In accepting the father's law, exemplified in the castration threat, the boy identifies with paternal authority and represses his desire for his mother. In identifying with his father, he establishes a superego which carries out the first repressions. With the creation of the superego and the primal REPRESSION of the desire for the mother, the unconscious is formed. The boy thus becomes a subject, an 'I' able to function within a (patriarchal) Symbolic order. The corresponding processes in the case of the girl are considerably more obscure: for one thing, it is never clear that she becomes a subject and attains an identity in the same way the boy does.

The processes of oedipalization create a second-order rupture within subjectivity, this time not between the image of fragmentation and the image of unity that structures the ego, but between the subject's consciousness and the unconscious. The subject's most intimate infantile wishes and desires are relegated to the unconscious, leaving little if any trace of what is repressed in consciousness. In other words, consciousness is not even aware that those thoughts, wishes and impulses to which it has access have already undergone careful selection and censorship, that consciousness is necessarily incomplete and unrepresentative of psychical life in general.

Perhaps even more strongly than Freud, Lacan insists on the radical heterogeneity of the unconscious and its recalcitrance and opacity to conscious scrutiny, the ways in which the 'language of the unconscious' disturbs and intervenes into the language of consciousness, undermining the subject's self-certainty and capacity to know. This insight is central to Lacan's challenge to the humanist presupposition – a dominant one since at least the time of Descartes – that the conscious subject is the locus of truth and knowledge. Lacan, drawing out the implications of Freud's analysis of the unconscious, 'de-centres' dominant notions of human subjectivity unquestioningly assumed in philosophy, sociology, psychology and linguistics. He challenges the presumption of an autonomous, ready-made subject by elaborating his notion of the socio-linguistic (Symbolic) constitution of subjectivity. Lacan claims that the subject, instead of being self-given and self-transparent, a subject radically incapable of not knowing itself, as Descartes assumed, is the end-result, a product, of processes that constitute it as an ego or unified self (the Imaginary) and as a social and speaking subject (the Symbolic). The subject is constructed through its necessary relations to others and the Other.

This broad anti-humanist project, in which psychoanalytic theory plays a decisive role, has implications and effects for feminist theory as well. Above all, it indicates that the notion of some intrinsic or essential identity, an inalienable 'self', is an ideological construct and not a pre-given fact. It challenges the liberal and humanist conception of a core or essence of humanity, to stress instead the historically, politically, culturally, sexually and racially specific ways in which subjects are constructed. It means too that feminists need to be wary of claims that base their validity on an uncritical notion of lived experience, for lived experience is itself a complex product of unrecognized social forces. Lived experience must be accounted for but it can no longer be understood simply on its own terms. It is now understood as symptomatic, and something to be interpreted; as 'raw data' rather than as self-evident and unquestionable truth. The implications of anti-humanism for feminist conceptions of subjectivity are not entirely negative: a whole new range of feminist projects, projects around the various processes of subject formation, were engendered.

It is in this broad anti-humanist conception of the subject that the work of most contemporary French feminists, particularly KRISTEVA and IRIGARAY, must be positioned. These theorists do not rely on a notion of reason or enlightenment, as many liberal feminists tend to, in their attempts to de-stabilize the patriarchal containment of women (see Gatens, 1991). Kristeva focuses on what might be understood as the subject-in-crisis, subjects at the moments of their most tenuous integration and functioning, within poetic, transgressive texts and representational practices, subjects on the verge of psychotic collapse or fetishistic introjection, borderline cases, melancholia and other psychical extremes (see Kristeva, 1984, 1989). Irigaray, by contrast, analyses the possibilities of the sexually specific subject, the possibilities for the articulation of a female subjectivity, thus far submerged under the universality or 'humanity' of masculine models. Her project involves providing a conceptual, linguistic and erotic space in which feminine subjectivity may begin to articulate itself (IRIGARAY, 1985).

BIBLIOGRAPHY

Althusser, Louis, 1971a: 'Freud and Lacan', Lenin and Philosophy and Other Essays, trans. B. Brewster. London: New Left Books, pp. 123–70.

Althusser, Louis, 1971b: 'Ideology and ideological state apparatuses', Lenin and Philosophy and Other Essays, pp. 171–86.

Foucault, Michel, 1976: Discipline and Punish: The Birth of the Prison. New York: Pantheon.

Freud, Sigmund, 1900: The Interpretation of Dreams, SE, 4, 5.

Gatens, Moira, 1991: Feminism and Philosophy: Perspectives on Difference and Equality. Cambridge: Polity Press.

Irigaray, Luce, 1985 [1977]: This Sex Which Is Not One, trans. Catherine Porter. Ithaca, NY: Cornell University Press.

Kristeva, Julia, 1984 [1974]: The Revolution in Poetic Language, trans. Margaret Waller. New York: Columbia University Press.

Kristeva, Julia, 1989 [1987]: Black Sun: Depression and Melancholia, trans. Leon Roudiez. New York: Columbia University Press.

Lacan, Jacques, 1977a: 'The agency of the letter in the unconscious or reason since Freud', *Écrits: A Selection*, trans. Alan Sheridan. London: Tavistock, pp. 146–78.

Lacan, Jacques, 1977b: 'Aggressivity in psychoanalysis', *Écrits*, pp. 8–29.

Lacan, Jacques, 1977c: 'The signification of the phallus', *Écrits*, pp. 281–91.

Lacan, Jacques, 1977d [1973]: *The Four Fundamental Concepts of Psychoanalysis*, trans. Alan Sheridan. London: Hogarth Press.

Mitchell, Juliet, 1974: *Psychoanalysis and Feminism*. London: Allen Lane.

Silverman, Kaja, 1983: *The Subject of Semiotics*. New York: Oxford University Press.

Smith, Paul, 1988: *Discerning the Subject*. Minneapolis: University of Minnesota Press.

ELIZABETH GROSZ

sublimation   The transformation or diversion of sexual drives into other 'cultural' or 'moral' activities. Freud's fullest account appears in 'The ego and the id' (1923): an original erotic object-cathexis is withdrawn and de-sexualized – sublimated – through narcissistic identification, which founds the superego as the internalized moral agency of the parents. LACAN writes that sublimation 'elevates an object to the dignity of the Thing': sublimation dislodges the object from the system of exchange and representation, 'subliming' it to a fixed, intransigent, opaque position. Lacan's example is the woman of courtly love literature, who becomes, in Slavoj Žižek's phrase, 'the sublime object of ideology', the absent point around which a cultural system turns (Lacan, 1986, pp. 133–4; Žižek, 1989). Julia KRISTEVA defines sublimation as 'the possibility of naming the pre-nominal, the pre-objectal'; taking up the role of the mother in KLEIN, Kristeva defines sublimation as the initial infantile symbolization of the PRE-OEDIPAL maternal other at the margins of LANGUAGE and oedipalization (Kristeva, 1982, p. 11; Klein, 1986, p. 97).

For GENDER studies, then, sublimation is a crucial concept, since it traces the vicissitudes of SEXUALITY in cultural production. In addition, the connection drawn by Freud between sublimation and HOMOSEXUALITY has implications for gay and feminist theories of object-choice, social formation and cultural activity. In 'Leonardo da Vinci and a memory of his childhood' (1910), Freud inter-implicates artistic sublimation and male homosexuality via the mechanism of NARCISSISM. In this scheme, narcissism accounts for both homosexual object-choice (liking the like) and for the de-sexualization and diversion of LIBIDO, since narcissism is a function of the ego rather than sexual drives (Laplanche, 1980, pp. 38–45, 104–9). This triangulation of HOMOSEXUALITY, sublimated sexuality and narcissism has influenced 'homosocial' accounts of society as founded on structures of male bonding which repress SEXUAL DIFFERENCE (IRIGARAY, 1985; Sedgwick, 1985). Finally, from the 'Three essays on sexuality' (1905), Freud presents sublimation as an operation on the 'component' or non-genital drives, a scheme which suggests the 'perverse' and non-phallic dimensions of social formations: creativity, intellectual research and economic exchange as anal, oral, sado-masochistic, voyeuristic or homosexual rather than strictly oedipal.

See also SADOMASOCHISM; VOYEURISM/EXHIBITIONISM/THE GAZE.

BIBLIOGRAPHY

Freud, Sigmund, 1905: *Three Essays on the Theory of Sexuality*, SE, 7, pp. 125–245.
Freud, Sigmund, 1910: *Leonardo da Vinci and a Memory of his Childhood*, SE, 11, pp. 59–138.
Freud, Sigmund, 1923: 'The ego and the id', *SE*, 19, pp. 12–59.
Irigaray, Luce, 1985 [1974]: *Speculum of the Other Woman*, trans. Gillian Gill. Ithaca, NY: Cornell University Press.
Klein, Melanie, 1986: 'The importance of symbol-formation in the development of the ego', *The Selected Melanie Klein*, ed. Juliet Mitchell. New York: Free Press, pp. 96–111.
Kristeva, Julia, 1982: *The Powers of Horror: An Essay on Abjection*. New York: Columbia University Press.
Lacan, Jacques, 1986: *L'Éthique de la psychanalyse*, text established by Jacques-Alain Miller. Paris: Seuil.
Laplanche, Jean, 1989: *La Sublimation*. Paris: Presses Universitaires de France.
Sedgwick, Eve, 1985: *Between Men: English Literature and Male Homosocial Desire*. New York: Columbia University Press.
Žižek, Slavoj, 1989: *The Sublime Object of Ideology*. London: Verso.

JULIA REINHARD LUPTON

surrealism   Of the various avant-garde movements that flourished in Europe in the first part of this century (Futurism, Dada, Expressionism, Constructivism, among others), the one most closely linked to psychoanalysis in its theoretical interests and artistic practices was Surrealism. Founded in 1924 in Paris by a group of young poets under the leadership of André Breton, Surrealism became an international movement with a revolutionary programme in both art and politics; whereas most marxists in the 1930s (and later) disdained Freud, the Surrealists sought to combine Freud and Marx. Central to Surrealist aesthetics was the 'revolutionary' exploration of dreams, SEXUALITY and the UNCONSCIOUS, primarily by a method that Breton (in the first Surrealist Manifesto,

1924; 1969, p. 26), called 'psychic automatism'. Comparable to the psychoanalytic method of free association, automatism was thought to correspond to the 'actual functioning of thought . . . in the absence of any control exercised by reason' (p. 26).

In 1929, when the Spanish painter Salvador Dali joined the movement, automatism was complemented by a new psychoanalytically inspired concept, 'paranoia-criticism'. Dali's ideas about the possible parallels between paranoia and avant-garde artistic practice, although elaborated independently, were strikingly confirmed by Jacques Lacan's 1932 doctoral dissertation on paranoia (Lacan, 1932). In the first issue of the surrealist-dominated art journal *Minotaure* (1933), Dali's essay on paranoia-criticism (citing Lacan as an authority) was followed by an essay by 'le Docteur' himself, in which LACAN drew a positive parallel between the symbolic expressions of paranoid patients and individual artistic style. For Dali, paranoia-criticism was not only a method of interpretation but a means of artistic creation, imposing the artist's 'delirious' constructions on reality.

Although the Surrealists paid frequent homage to Freud, some critics have claimed that they did not really understand the Freudian concept of the unconscious (Houdebine, 1971). Freud himself found the Surrealists' interest in his work puzzling, and was totally unresponsive to their art (he considered it 'crazy'). Nevertheless, Surrealism must be credited with being the first artistic movement to recognize the radical implications of psychoanalysis and to attempt a systematic exploration of dreams and fantasies – with sexuality playing a preponderant role – in the production of artistic works. Their achievements in poetry, prose narrative, painting, PHOTOGRAPHY and film have exerted an enormous influence, right down to the present day.

The links among Surrealism, psychoanalysis and feminism are complicated and can be presented here only in the most summary fashion. A feminist analysis will note, as a start, that just as Freud and Lacan elaborated some of their most important concepts on the basis of work with women patients, so the Surrealists often found embodiments of their ideas about the irrational, dreams and the unconscious in female figures. Perhaps the most memorable of these is the title character of what is probably the best known work of Surrealist writing, Breton's *Nadja* (1928). In Breton's story, Nadja appears alternately as a Surrealist visionary and as a destitute, mentally unbalanced young woman. The fascination she exercises on Breton seems to be due precisely to her closeness to the edge of madness – and, in the end, to her unfortunate fall over the edge. (Nadja was not a fictional creation, but a real person, who spent the last thirteen years of her life in a psychiatric hospital.)

It was the same year as he published *Nadja* that Breton co-authored, with Louis Aragon, an article 'The fiftieth anniversary of hysteria'. The article referred to the French psychiatrist Jean Martin Charcot's famous lessons on HYSTERIA (Freud studied with Charcot in 1885–6), and emphasized the amorous relations between female hysterics and their male doctors; it was illustrated by photographs from the archives of the Salpêtrière hospital, showing Charcot's 'star' female hysterics in various *'attitudes passionnelles'*, as he called them. In 1933, Dali published a photomontage titled *The Phenomenon of Ecstasy*, consisting of close-ups of women's faces, including the smiling face of a statue. Many years later, Lacan – remembering, perhaps, his early association with Dali and Surrealism – made his commentary on Bernini's statue of Saint Teresa in ecstasy the centrepiece of his discussion of female JOUISSANCE (Lacan, 1975).

Starting in the late 1960s, with the rise of a new wave of avant-garde activity in France, Surrealism elicited a great many new commentaries and criticisms – notably from writers associated with the journal *Tel Quel*, whose revolutionary aspirations and interest in Freud and Marx was highly reminiscent of Surrealism. Julia KRISTEVA, a major theorist of the *Tel Quel* group, elaborated a psychoanalytic model of avant-garde writing which placed primary emphasis on the subject's relation to the maternal body (Kristeva, 1984). Among her exemplary avant-garde writers was Antonin Artaud, who had been an active member of the Surrealist group in its early years (Kristeva, 1977).

Kristeva's approach was not explicitly feminist, however. The feminist critique of Surrealism, which has produced a great deal of uneven work over the past twenty years, was inaugurated by Xavière Gauthier's psychoanalytically oriented study (1971). Gauthier focused on the role of the woman as OBJECT in Surrealist poetry and art, and concluded that whether they idealized the female body or attacked and dismembered it, the male Surrealists were using the woman to work out their rebellion against the father. More recently, psychoanalytically oriented feminist critics have speculated on the difficulties as well as the inspiration that women artists encountered as they sought to pass from 'object' to 'subject' in the practice of Surrealist art (Chadwick, 1985). Some feminist theorists have suggested that contemporary avant-garde writing by women can be read as being both inspired by and critical of earlier work by male Surrealists (Suleiman, 1990). These approaches, which recognize not only the misogynistic aspects of Surrealism but also its positive appeal to women artists (notably in its invitation to explore the inner world of FANTASY without abandoning an actively critical attitude toward reality) promise to yield a more balanced account – one that will emphasize the positive links between contemporary feminist ART and the innovative, critical energy of the avant-garde.

See also FEMINIST CINEMA; LITERATURE; REPRESENTATION; UNCANNY.

SYMBOLIC, THE

BIBLIOGRAPHY

Breton, André, 1964: *Nadja*. Paris: Gallimard.

Breton, André, 1969 [1924]: 'Manifesto of Surrealism', *Manifestos of Surrealism*, trans. Richard Seaver and Helen R. Lane. Ann Arbor: University of Michigan Press, pp. 3–47.

Breton, André, and Aragon, Louis, 1928: 'Le Cinquantenaire de l'hystérie', *La Révolution surréaliste*, 11, pp. 20–2.

Caws, Mary Ann; Kuentzli, Rudolf; and Raaberg, Gwen, eds. 1991: *Surrealism and Women*. Cambridge, Mass.: MIT Press.

Chadwick, Whitney, 1985: *Women Artists and the Surrealist Movement*. Boston: Little, Brown.

Dali, Salvador, 1933: 'Interprétation paranoïaque-critique de l'image obsédante "L'Angélus" de Millet', *Minotaure*, 1, pp. 65–7.

Gauthier, Xavière, 1971: *Surréalisme et sexualité*. Paris: Gallimard.

Houdebine, Jean-Louis, 1971: 'Méconnaissance de la psychanalyse dans le discours surréaliste', *Tel Quel*, 46, pp. 67–82.

Kristeva, Julia, 1984 [1974]: *Revolution in Poetic Language*, trans. Margaret Waller. New York: Columbia University Press.

Kristeva, Julia, 1977: 'Le Sujet en procès', *Polylogue*. Paris: Seuil, pp. 55–106.

Lacan, Jacques, 1932: *De la psychose paranoïaque dans ses rapports avec la personnalité*. Paris: Le François.

Lacan, Jacques, 1933: 'Le Problème du style et les formes paranoïaques de l'expérience', *Minotaure*, 1, pp. 68–9.

Lacan, Jacques, 1975: *Le Séminaire*, book 20: *Encore*. Paris: Seuil.

Suleiman, Susan Rubin, 1990: *Subversive Intent: Gender, Politics, and the Avant-Garde*. Cambridge, Mass.: Harvard University Press.

SUSAN RUBIN SULEIMAN

Symbolic, the   In developing his theory of the Symbolic order, LACAN is indebted to Saussure and Jakobson, as well as to C. S. Peirce's notion that 'symbol means pact' (Lacan, 1977, pp. 61–2). While Peirce (1955, pp. 113–15) contended that a symbol was a *convention* founded on a social pact – that is, a symbol has a fixed meaning arising out of the consensus of social groups about some particular equivalence – Lacan argues that human law and LANGUAGE developed *pari passu* and sees in the example of gift-giving and the community ties of Bronze Age Greek commerce a contiguity of speech with the gift as act, object or, finally, sign, conveying that trust which binds groups and expresses itself in passwords, sometimes nonsensical words, or in the two broken halves of a pledge token (Greek *sumbolon*, Latin *tessera*). But, at the level of *symbol*, a gift is already a signifier (not a sign) of any pact.

Lacan was more particularly indebted to Lévi-Strauss's theory of a 'symbolic' exchange of goods and persons as the basis for a cultural law.

420

Moreover, Lacan's notion contests Lévi-Strauss's literalist ideal of the symbolic: he renews the meaning of 'symbol' away from the traditional notion of something standing for something else. He shows Lévi-Strauss's concept of binary exchange as itself a problem: if gifts or words are *symbols* of an exchange between people or animals, the pact made by an exchange is already a third thing, a sign that exchange is itself the structure of the social act. That is, the symbol does not refer to content or value – goods or women – but to the human potential for acquiring language. But for symbols or things to become language – to be verbally re-presented – they must first disappear as object or image. The effect of such a loss is the creation of an empty place in the wake of a given symbol. Symbols only enter the field of language, making the *infans* (without speech) a speaking creature, when loss is added, when a symbol – such as a breast or a bottle – disappears as a fullness, when an infant loses the primary OBJECT, the mother as a presence.

In Lacan's first theory of the Symbolic, words are not, as Freud thought, opposed to things; words create the world of things (Lacan, 1977, p. 65). The Symbolic arises out of the naming of things. A word functions to block an identificatory sense of a thing once it is named. Naming the body alienates it, castrates its momentary pleasure of an illusionary wholeness and any Imaginary fusion it maintains with an 'object'. In linking names to things, the word kills the thing as immediate presence. Language as a system imposes rules upon the human organism's chaotic identifications with objects and gives rise to the desire for the linkage of body, IMAGE and word; it gives rise, that is, to the social order (the Other; *see* OTHER/OTHER).

Lacan's second theory of the Symbolic locates the pleasure principle at the heart of the Symbolic order, making of language a senseless autonomous death mechanism, and turning it into a repetitious reality principle made up of imposed words and fictions which we then take as the basis of our views of self and world and call reality or perception (Lacan, 1986). There is nothing innate that gives rise to language: no innate ideas (Descartes), no biological stages or agencies (Freud), no *a priori* unconscious (Laplanche), no biological givens (Chomsky). Language itself serves as the signified that tells the particular story of the knotting (or not) of the three orders (IMAGINARY, Symbolic, REAL) in an individual's life in terms of acquisition of gender as an identity. The master or key signifiers (S_1) in any life elaborate a belief or knowledge system (S_2) which re-presents a SUBJECT that lacks, but makes the field of language function all the same. The subject not findable in grammar *per se* is the unconscious subject of DESIRE. This signifier ($\emptyset$) is the indeterminate in language, that is, the unconscious subject is supported by the *objet a*, which gives rise to the quest for JOUISSANCE. Nevertheless, the signifier is pre-determined in the sense that what is said is touched by the *objet a* as a stopper or limit on signification. Any effort to fill up the hole in the Other reveals an impossible core – the Real which blocks the smooth flow of communication – that the Symbolic strives to pacify, balance or circumvent. In so far as a signifier cannot signify itself, but can re-present subjects for another signifier, a sense of 'self' is born at the same time as language becomes memory, covering over the subject as response of the Real in the Imaginarized–Symbolic material of subjective FANTASY. The very conviction of selfhood disguises its origin in the Real, which cannot be symbolized.

In his third theory of the Symbolic, the Real that lies beyond language appears in an excess of *jouissance* at a moment of enigmatic 'truth' that subverts expected behaviour or response (Lacan, 1975). Time functions to create an interval between signifiers, making possible a materialization of the *objet a* combined with the indeterminacy of language to reveal the body – *jouissance* effects – as the cause of mind. The person *qua* subject is not a content or essence, then, but a discontinuity in the apparent continuity of world, language and relations. In so far as language seems complete within itself, it can take itself to be the essence of the human as reason or mind, dismissing whatever goes against its grain as irrational, dysfunctional, contradictory, and so on. Although Lacan overturned Saussure's linguistic sign, Saussure's sign was itself a critique of phenomenological theories of meaning and quasi-substantialist theories of language. This critique has been adopted by post-structuralist feminists who take the male/female divide as an intertextual play of infinite language differences, subject positions that one can disseminate infinitely.

Feminists have rejected Lacan's notion that culture itself arises from the imposed differentiation of masculine and feminine, especially via language (Lacan, 1975). Reading Freud on IDENTIFICATION Lacan was the first to realize that no seemingly coherent identification with language and culture could occur without a turning away from Imaginary objects of plenitude (usually the mother) in the name of a Symbolic differential. At this juncture the 'no' of the Symbolic delimits the world of reality by the split or castration between language and *jouissance*. In this logical space, the mother introduces the signifier for difference, the *name* of the father. Loss of the mother as immovable identificatory object creates a lack-in-being (*manque-à-être*). Lacan subverts Freud's phallocentric and biological biases to show that a structuration of SEXUAL DIFFERENCE sets up individual limits of pleasure and pain, rather than a privileging of one sex over the other (André, 1986; Millot, 1988). Lacan calls this identificatory turn the 'phallic signifier', the signifier that has no signified except the LACK that makes desire possible for both sexes.

Feminists have thought that Lacanian *lack* – denoted by the phallic signifier – meant that women do not have a penis. But Lacan's 'lack' is a 'lack-in-being', common to both sexes. Although many feminists still think of the Symbolic order as masculinist, synonymous with the father's name or some phallic law, the crucial point for contemporary feminism is an ethical one. It needs to address the clinical issue of a mediative function of the Symbolic as that which separates the Imaginary from the Real, creates loss and forms the necessary distance from the other's *jouissance*. If the mother desires that her child be one with her, her desired object, that child, whether male or female, will lack the basis for exchange out of the family plot that makes society possible as the alterity of the Other, opening up the potential for learning, creating, and changing the order of things as they are.

See also PHALLUS.

BIBLIOGRAPHY

André, Serge, 1986: *Que veut une femme?* Paris: Navarin.

Baas, Bernard, and Zaloszyc, Armand, 1988: *Descartes et les fondements de la psychanalyse*. Paris: Navarin–Osiris.

Lacan, Jacques, 1975 [1972–3]: *Le Séminaire*, book 20: *Encore*, ed. Jacques-Alain Miller. Paris: Seuil.

Lacan, Jacques, 1977 [1953]: 'The function and field of speech and language in psychoanalysis', *Écrits: A Selection*, trans. Alan Sheridan. London: Tavistock, pp. 30–113.

Lacan, Jacques, 1986 [1959–60]: *Le Séminaire*, book 7: *L'Éthique de la psychanalyse*. Paris: Seuil.

MacCannell, Juliet Flower, 1986: *Figuring Lacan: Criticism and the Cultural Unconscious*. London: Croom Helm.

Miller, Jacques-Alain, 1991: 'Language: much ado about what?', *Lacan and the Subject of Language*, ed. Ellie Ragland-Sullivan and Mark Bracher. New York: Routledge, pp. 21–35.

Millot, Catherine, 1988: *Nobodaddy: L'Hystérie dans le siècle*. Paris: Point Hors Ligne.

Peirce, Charles Sanders, 1955: *Philosophical Writings of Peirce*, ed. Justus Buchler. New York: Dover.

ELLIE RAGLAND-SULLIVAN

symptom 'Woman is a symptom of man' seems to be one of Jacques Lacan's most notoriously 'anti-feminist' theses (Lacan, 1975b, pp. 107–8). There is, however, a fundamental ambiguity about it which reflects the shift in the notion of the symptom within Lacanian theory.

SYMPTOM

At the beginning of Lacan's teaching, in the early 1950s (Lacan, 1977; 1988b, p. 159), symptom was conceived as a Symbolic, signifying formation, a coded message addressed to the big Other (the synchronous Symbolic order) which later, retroactively, was supposed to confer on it its true meaning (*see* OTHER/OTHER). The symptom arises where the word fails, where the circuit of the Symbolic communication is broken; it is a kind of prolongation of the communication by other means; the failed, repressed word articulates itself in a coded, ciphered form. The implication of this is that the symptom can not only be interpreted but is, so to speak, already formed with an eye to its interpretation: it is addressed to the big Other presumed to contain its meaning. In other words, there is no symptom without its addressee: in the psychoanalytic cure the symptom is always addressed to the analyst, an appeal to him to deliver its hidden meaning. Hence, there is no symptom without transference, without the position of some subject presumed to know its meaning. Precisely as an enigma, the symptom, so to speak, announces its dissolution through interpretation: the aim of psychoanalysis is to re-establish the broken network of communication by allowing the patient to verbalize the meaning of his/her symptom; through this verbalization, the symptom is automatically dissolved (*see* TRANSFERENCE/COUNTER-TRANSFERENCE).

So, in its very constitution, the symptom implies the field of the big Other as consistent, complete, because its very formation is an appeal to the Other which contains its meaning. Here, however, the problems begin: why, in spite of its interpretation, does the symptom not dissolve itself? Why does it persist? The Lacanian answer is, of course, *enjoyment* (JOUISSANCE). The symptom is not only a ciphered message, but also a way for the subject to organize his/her enjoyment. That is why, even after the completed interpretation, the subject is not prepared to renounce his/her symptom; that is why s/he loves his/her symptom more than him/herself. In locating this dimension of enjoyment in the symptom, Lacan proceeded in two stages.

First, he tried to isolate this dimension of enjoyment as that of FANTASY, and to oppose symptom and fantasy through a whole set of distinctive features: symptom is a signifying formation which 'overtakes itself' towards its interpretation – that is, which can be analysed; fantasy is an inert construction which cannot be analysed, which resists interpretation. Symptom implies and addresses some non-barred, consistent big Other which will retroactively confer on it its meaning; fantasy implies a crossed-out, blocked, barred, non-whole, inconsistent Other. Symptom (for example, a slip of the tongue) causes discomfort and displeasure; yet we gladly explain to others the meaning of our slips; their inter-subjective recognition is usually a source of intellectual satisfaction. In contradistinction, when we abandon ourselves to fantasy (for example, in day-dreaming) we feel immense pleasure, yet it causes us great shame and discomfort to confess our fantasies to others. When confronted with the patient's symptoms, we must first interpret them and penetrate through them to the fundamental fantasy as the kernel of enjoyment which is blocking the further movement of interpretation; then we must accomplish the crucial step of going through the fantasy, of obtaining distance from it, of experiencing how the fantasy formation masks and fills out a certain void, an empty place in the Other.

But here again another problem arises: how do we account for patients who have, beyond any doubt, gone through their fantasy, but whose key symptom still persists? What do we do with a symptom, this pathological formation which persists not only beyond its interpretation but even beyond fantasy? Lacan tried to answer this challenge with the concept of *sinthome*, a neologism containing a set of associations (synthetic–artificial man, synthesis between symptoms and fantasy, Saint Thomas, the saint . . .: Lacan, 1988a). Symptom as *sinthome* is a certain signifying formation penetrated with enjoyment: it is a signifier as a bearer of *jouissance*, enjoyment-in-sense (enjoy-meant).

Symptom thus has a radical ontological status: conceived as *sinthome*, it is literally our only substance, the only positive support of our being, the only point that gives consistency to the SUBJECT. In other words, symptom is the way subjects 'avoid madness', the way they choose something (the symptom-formation) instead of nothing (radical psychotic autism, the destruction of the Symbolic universe) through the binding of enjoyment to a certain Symbolic formation which assures a minimum of consistency to being-in-the-world. If the symptom in this radical dimension is unbound, it means 'the end of the world'. The only alternative to the symptom is nothing: pure autism, a psychic suicide, surrender to the DEATH DRIVE up to the total destruction of the Symbolic universe. That is why the final Lacanian definition of the end of the psychoanalytic process is *identification with the symptom*. The analysis achieves its end when the patient is able to recognize, in the REAL of his/her symptom, the only support of his/her being. That is how Freud's *wo es war, soll ich werden* must be read: you, the subject, must identify yourself with the place where your symptom already was; in its pathological particularity you must recognize the element which gives consistency to your being.

This shift in the notion of the symptom allows us to locate precisely the thesis 'woman is a symptom of man'. Conceiving the symptom as articulated by Lacan in the 1950s, as a *ciphered message*, makes woman–symptom appear as the sign, the embodiment of man's fall, which attests to the fact that man 'gave way as to his desire' (Lacan,

1986, p. 368). We thus have the male world of pure spirituality and unbroken communication, the universe of ideal intersubjectivity; woman is *not* an external, active cause which lures man into fall but a *consequence*, a materialization of man's fall. So, when man purifies his desire of the pathological remainders, woman disintegrates in precisely the same way as a symptom dissolves itself after a successful interpretation, after we have symbolized its repressed meaning. Does not Lacan's other notorious thesis – the one claiming that 'woman doesn't exist' – point in the same direction? Woman does not exist in herself, as a positive entity with full ontological consistency, but only as a symptom of man.

If, however, we conceive the symptom as it was articulated in the late Lacan – namely, as a particular signifying formation which confers on the subject its very ontological consistency, enabling it to structure its basic, constitutive relationship towards *jouissance* – then the entire relationship is reversed: if the symptom is dissolved, the subject itself loses the ground under its feet, disintegrates. 'Woman is the symptom of man' thus comes to mean that *man himself exists only through woman* qua *his symptom*: all his ontological consistency is suspended from his symptom, is 'externalized' in his symptom. In other words, man literally *ex-sists*: his entire being lies 'out there', in woman. Woman, on the other hand, does *not* exist, she *insists*, which is why she does not come to be through man only. There is something in her that escapes the relation to man, the reference to the phallic signifier, and Lacan attempted to capture this excess by the notion of a *'not-all'* *feminine jouissance* (Lacan, 1975a). The relationship towards the death drive is also reversed: woman, taken 'in herself', outside the relation to man, embodies the death drive, apprehended as a radical, most elementary ethical attitude of uncompromising insistence, of 'not giving way to . . . '. She is therefore no longer conceived as fundamentally 'passive' in contrast to male activity: the act as such, in its most fundamental dimension, is 'feminine'. Is not the act *par excellence* Antigone's act, her act of defiance, of resistance (Lacan, 1986)? The suicidal dimension of this act is self-evident. When Lacan says that the only act which is not a failure, the only act *stricto sensu*, is suicide, he thereby re-confirms the 'feminine' nature of act as such: inasmuch as men are 'active', they take refuge in relentless activity in order to escape the proper dimension of the act. The retreat of man from woman (the retreat of the hard-boiled detective from the *femme fatale* in *film noir*, for example), is thus effectively a retreat from the radical ethical stance of the death drive: we are now at the exact opposite of the image of woman as one incapable of a proper ethical attitude.

See also FEMININITY; LACAN; SYMBOLIC.

426

BIBLIOGRAPHY

Lacan, Jacques, 1975a: *Le Séminaire*, book 20: *Encore*. Paris: Seuil.

Lacan, Jacques, 1975b: 'Seminar of 21 January 1975', *Ornicar?* No. 3, pp. 104–10; see also Juliet Mitchell and Jacqueline Rose, eds, (1982), *Feminine Sexuality: Jacques Lacan and the École Freudienne*. Trans. Jacqueline Rose. London: Macmillan, pp. 162–71.

Lacan, Jacques, 1977 [1966]: 'The function and field of speech and language in psychoanalysis', *Écrits: A Selection*, trans. Alan Sheridan. London: Tavistock, pp. 30–113.

Lacan, Jacques, 1986: *Le Séminaire*, book 7: *L'Éthique de la psychanalyse*. Paris: Seuil.

Lacan, Jacques, 1988a: 'Joyce le symptôme', *Joyce avec Lacan*. Paris: Navarin, pp. 21–9.

Lacan, Jacques, 1988b [1975]: *The Seminar of Jacques Lacan*, book 1: *Freud's Papers on Technique*. Cambridge: Cambridge University Press.

SLAVOJ ŽIŽEK

T

theory 'Theory is good, but it doesn't prevent things from existing'. This dictum from the celebrated French neurologist Jean-Martin Charcot made an indelible impression on Freud, and a tension between the claims of theory on the one hand and those of empirical observation on the other is visible throughout his scientific career. 'The foundation of science, upon which everything rests . . . is observation alone', Freud wrote in 'On narcissism: an introduction' (1914, p. 77), and numerous stern warnings were to follow: 'The intellect and the mind are objects for scientific research in exactly the same way as any non-human things' (1933, p. 159). Psychoanalysis had brought illusions, emotional demands and wishful impulses within the purview of SCIENCE, but this was not a reason for it to depart from the scientific outlook; and observation, provided always that the analyst knew what to observe, was the key to an understanding of unconscious as well as conscious mental activity. 'Theory' in this view was a necessary ally for the empirical researcher, providing him with provisional vantage points from which to survey and organize his material; but in the end, when his data were complete and true inferences had been drawn from them, theory could and should be discarded.

Yet Freud, while granting little dignity to hypotheses and theories in his official philosophy of science, was a hypothesizer of the most fertile and resourceful kind. Not only were his theories numerous, but certain of them were proclaimed with vehemence long after his attempts to corroborate them had been abandoned. At the end of *The Interpretation of Dreams* Freud used the term 'theoretical fiction' to describe a state of affairs that a given theory seemed to require or predict but for which no supporting evidence could as yet be found (1900, p. 603), and much of the continuing interest of his scientific writings lies in the multifarious uses that he found for working fictions of this kind. Just as the analyst could punctuate the clinical encounter by placing 'constructions' or *ad hoc* part-interpretations upon the analysand's material, so the analytic theorist could give a positive role to merely speculative writing in the working out of his irreproachably 'scientific' views. Both as a clinician and as a theorist, Freud was prepared to acknowledge that arriving at the truth took time, and that certain journeys were so beset by difficulty that they were likely to prove interminable.

The fact that Freud himself hesitated between widely different valuations of theory does not necessarily create a problem for anyone wishing to pursue a single gendered reading of his work. Indeed, a case can be made for seeing his anti-theoretical and his pro-theoretical views as equally caught up in a phallocentric mythology of exploration and conquest. If we confine ourselves to his two favourite self-images – those of archaeologist and *conquistador* – and bring these into alignment with his own definitions of MASCULINITY in *Three Essays on the Theory of Sexuality* and elsewhere, then such a case seems secure. For the Freudian archaeologist, who is an empiricist *par excellence*, and the Freudian conqueror, who moves in glory from one speculative exploit to the next, are both presented as masterful and heroic, as enthusiasts for hardness, activity, audacity and penetration. Besides, so many of Freud's early patients were female, and he so readily thought of women as having a 'greater proneness to neurosis and especially to hysteria, (1905, p. 221), that a pattern of unexamined associations soon established itself: if women were the problem then men were the solution; if female sexuality was a 'dark continent' then it fell to a pioneering male to explore it; if unknowing was a form of feminine weakness and passivity, then knowledge, pursued or achieved, must be a masculine prerogative.

Seen against a European philosophical background in which reason itself has often been figured as male, this masculinist strain in Freudian theory may seem to have a dispiriting inevitability about it. Scientific rationality as Freud understands it proceeds not by excluding or overcoming the feminine but by treating it as a particularly challenging and recalcitrant piece of subject matter. To get FEMININITY right at last, and to grasp it as a mental attribute of men and women alike, would be to unlock one of the last great enigmas that the human scientist faces, but the rational theory-building manoeuvres leading up to this triumph cannot themselves usefully be thought of as feminine. For Freud, it would be as preposterous to think in these terms as to suggest that when science attended to wishes or superstitions it should become wishful and superstitious in the process.

Those studying the gender status of the notion 'theory' in psychoanalysis cannot do better than consult certain of the outstanding works recently produced by feminist philosophers: Genevieve Lloyd's *The Man of Reason* (1984), Michèle Le Doeuff's 'Women and philosophy' (1980) or Morwenna Griffiths and Margaret Whitford's collection *Feminist*

Perspectives in Philosophy (1988). These works all display an exemplary self-awareness in their unravelling of misogynistic sub-texts in European thought. Genevieve Lloyd speaks for an entire generation of innovative feminist philosophers when she warns that attempts to define the feminine court the danger of being distorted by the unanalysed structure of male norms and female complementation that underlies them (1984, p. 105). In the case of psychoanalysis as practised by Freud, attention paid to the 'structural features' of his gender concepts and to his gendering of theory itself is likely to produce surprising results, for while there is much misogyny on the surface of his writings their sub-text is often, from the viewpoint of feminism, of a potentially emancipatory kind.

One of the prime responsibilities of 'theory' for Freud is that of allowing conventional notions of SEXUAL DIFFERENCE to be called into question, for those notions simply cannot cope with the heterogeneous sexual wishes and dispositions that clinical observation reveals within the individual. Freud does this by maintaining dialectical tension at a variety of theoretical levels: between biological and psychological modes of explanation, between the separate logics of unconscious and preconscious–conscious mental processes, between gendered and gender-neutral models of the human drives, between developmental and synchronic models of the individual subject. Freud developed a theoretical style in which heterogeneity was the order of the day. The house of human SEXUALITY as theorized by Freud contains many mansions, and more than a few hovels and punishment cells too. Besides, during a long literary career he changed his mind dramatically on a number of major topics.

All this means that Freudian 'theory' has proved a mobile and multiform stimulus to feminist debate. It has been worked with, worked against, ironically subverted, satirized; it has been found good in certain parts, and outrageously deficient in others. But even Freud's most uncompromising detractors use his diction as an indispensable lingua franca for the discussion of gender issues. In the work of feminists such as Hélène Cixous and Luce IRIGARAY crucial aspects of the psychoanalytic project have moved into a new phase of creativity. Indeed, it could be argued that feminist theory, propelled by psychoanalysis or by reservations about it, is the only arena in which serious work on sexual difference is currently being conducted. The new 'theory' that feminism is bringing into view is neither male nor female, neither feminine nor masculine: it is, rather, a theory that keeps on asking itself about the ways in which gender notions – including those that govern 'theory' itself – are constructed and perpetuated in society. The centrality that psychoanalytically informed feminist theory now gives to this question allows it to maintain a robust set of connections with the world of feminist political struggle.

See also GENDER; IDEOLOGY; PHILOSOPHY; THE UNCONSCIOUS.

BIBLIOGRAPHY

Brennan, Teresa, ed. 1989: *Between Feminism and Psychoanalysis*. London and New York: Routledge.

Freud, Sigmund, 1900: *The Interpretation of Dreams*, SE, 4, 5.

Freud, Sigmund, 1905: *Three Essays on the Theory of Sexuality*, SE, 7, pp. 123–245.

Freud, Sigmund, 1914: 'On narcissism: an introduction', *SE*, 14, pp. 67–102.

Freud, Sigmund, 1933: 'New introductory lectures', *SE*, 22, pp. 1–182.

Griffiths, Morwenna, and Whitford, Margaret, eds 1988: *Feminist Perspectives in Philosophy*. London: Macmillan.

Irigaray, Luce, 1984: *Éthique de la différence sexuelle*. Paris: Minuit.

Le Doeuff, Michèle, 1987: 'Women and philosophy', *Feminist Thought: a Reader*, ed. Toril Moi. Oxford: Blackwell, pp. 181–209.

Lloyd, Genevieve, 1984: *The Man of Reason: 'Male' and 'Female' in Western Philosophy*. London: Methuen.

Mitchell, Juliet, 1974: *Psychoanalysis and Feminism*. London: Allen Lane.

Moi, Toril, 1985: *Sexual/Textual Politics: Feminist Literary Theory*. London: Methuen.

MALCOLM BOWIE

transference/countertransference Laplanche and Pontalis (1973) define transference as a 'process of actualization of unconscious wishes', a process in which 'infantile prototypes re-emerge and are experienced with a strong sensation of immediacy' (p. 455). Transference primarily takes place in the analytic situation, and may therefore be said to consist in the analysand's unconscious PROJECTION of infantile wishes on to the figure of the analyst. This process is normally accomplished through the IDENTIFICATION of the analyst with an important childhood figure. Countertransference is broadly defined as the 'whole of the analyst's unconscious reactions to the individual analysand – especially to the analysand's own transference' (Laplanche and Pontalis, 1973, p. 92). In Freud's own writings, the concept of transference is notoriously slippery and difficult to grasp. The reason for this elusiveness is that Freud's analytical *practice* came up against the phenomenon long before he had developed an adequate understanding of transference as a theoretical *concept*. Freud's major statements about transference can be found in three papers on the technique of psychoanalysis written within the space of half a decade: 'The dynamics of transference' (1912);

431

'Remembering, repeating and working through' (1914); and 'Observations on transference love' (1915). Towards the end of his life he added some further, crucial observations on transference in the paper entitled 'Constructions in analysis' (1937).

Yet it has often been argued, by feminists and non-feminists alike, that the very first recorded case in the history of psychoanalysis, Josef Breuer's account of his treatment of 'Anna O.' in 1881 and 1882, encountered serious difficulties precisely because of the analyst's ignorance of the phenomenon of transference (Freud and Breuer 1895). In the same way, Freud concludes his account of his failed 1901 attempt to analyse the recalcitrant patient known as 'Dora' by claiming that the major reason for the failure of Dora's analysis was his own lack of understanding of the transference (1905). In both cases, the analyst failed to understand the way in which his own persona figured in the patient's fantasies, or – even more disturbingly – failed to see that he himself was compounding the error by projecting his own unconscious wish for gratification on to the patient. From a feminist perspective these case histories are instructive because they demonstrate how transference may become an explosive but hidden factor in the interaction between a woman and a male figure of authority. A series of important feminist readings of the relationship between Freud and Dora are collected in Bernheimer and Kahane (1990).

In a significant revision of Freud's views, LACAN focuses on the problem of authority in the analytic situation, and links it to the question of knowledge. For him, 'transference is unthinkable unless one sets out from the subject who is supposed to know' (Lacan, 1977, p. 253). From a feminist perspective the most suggestive work on transference and countertransference has been done precisely on questions of authority and knowledge. Drawing on Lacan's understanding of transference as a demand for love directed towards a 'subject supposed to know', Shoshana Felman (1987) has brilliantly demonstrated how the teaching situation may be theorized through these concepts. For Felman, psychoanalysis itself is a pedagogical process where the analysand arrives with the expectation that the analyst *be* the 'subject supposed to know', the imaginary container of total and totalizable knowledge about the analysand's own suffering. Far from shoring up such a belief, however, the analytic process requires an interaction in which the analyst 'must be taught by the analysand's unconscious'; in this way, the analyst becomes a 'student of the patient's knowledge' (Felman, 1987, p. 83). The analytic process can only come to its paradoxical end when the student – and now this term encompasses both of the participants in analysis – realizes that it is impossible to embody or embalm knowledge in an authoritarian display of mastery. In this sense, the aim of analysis is to reach the point of ignorance, where both parties acknowledge that *nobody* knows, that *nobody* can fulfil the demand for completion and plenitude implied in the imaginary FANTASY of the 'subject supposed to know'.

Applied to teaching situations outside psychoanalysis, Felman's analysis has far-reaching consequences. Reading student–teacher relationships in terms of transference (the students' unconscious demands on the teacher) and countertransference (the teacher's reactions to the tranference), Felman enables us to produce a critical analysis not only of the teacher who attempts to set herself up as a 'subject supposed to know' – as the bearer of phallic plenitude – but also of her students' demand that she do so. For the implications of Felman's analysis are not only that the 'subject supposed to know' is an imaginary illusion, but that students and teachers alike may be more than tempted to collude in its construction, since, at least initially, it would seem to grant narcissistic satisfaction to both parties. The consequences of encouraging such a fantasy, however, are dire. As all imaginary constructs, this one too is bound to founder in the encounter with reality. The result is frustration, disappointment and feelings of betrayal and grief. Needless to say, these are precisely the tensions traditionally observed between male masters and disciples. In case we become too sanguine about the chances of avoiding such mishaps, it is instructive to observe that the relations between Freud and Lacan and their respective disciples exhibit all the hallmarks of such highly charged transferential conflicts. The feminist interest of Felman's analysis is that it enables us to deconstruct a phallocentric and authoritarian view of teaching as well as of knowledge. It also serves to warn against the temptation to counter patriarchal models of learning by setting up *women* in the traditional role of subject supposed to know.

This is not to say that we can do *without* the illusion of a subject supposed to know. Just like the analytical process, the teaching process is paradoxical. Without transference there can be no analysis: without the motivating illusion of a subject supposed to know, teaching will not take off. Teaching as well as analysis, then, would seem to require its participants at one and the same time to construct *and* deconstruct the illusion of the subject supposed to know. To emphasize only one of these aspects to the detriment of the other would precisely be to remain in the grip of the love–hate relationships of unanalysed transference. No wonder Freud thought teaching was an impossible profession.

Felman's text does not explicitly cast itself as feminist. Already in 1976, however, the French philosopher Michèle Le Doeuff elaborated a strikingly acute feminist reading of the situation of female students in a prestigious, male-dominated subject. Focusing on the teaching of philosophy in

TRANSFERENCE/COUNTERTRANSFERENCE

France, Le Doeuff's essay 'Long hair and short ideas' (Le Doeuff, 1989) demonstrates how, in relation to female students, not only teachers, but male philosophy students as well, often 'attempt to adopt the stance of "the one who knows": knows which books to read, what to think about this commentator on that philosopher, what lectures are worth going to, etc.' (Le Doeuff, 1989, p. 119). Revealing their inability to imagine a woman capable of relating directly to PHILOSOPHY, such young male intellectuals reproduce their own relationship with their favourite masters; it is an 'attempt to become masters in their turn,' Le Doeuff caustically comments, 'as if becoming the object of a transference were the only way of resolving one's own transference.' In this way, she continues, 'many young women definitively abdicate all conceptual self-determination in the course of their studies and allow themselves to be guided by a male fellow-student who is supposed to be more brilliant than they are' (p. 119). The problem with such female transference on to a male subject supposed to know is that it blocks the woman's direct access to philosophy, and thus prevents her from making her own experiences of frustration and achievement in relation to her chosen subject. However brilliant she may be, Le Doeuff writes, such a process will inexorably cast her as subordinate, as an eternal disciple. In this sense, the philosophical relationship between Simone de Beauvoir and Jean-Paul Sartre, Le Doeuff argues, is an instructive example of the negative effects on the woman of what I will now venture to call an erotico-theoretical transference relation. For whatever de Beauvoir's own achievements may have been, after meeting Sartre she never dared to imagine herself as a philosopher in her own right. *He* related to philosophy, *she* related to him. Le Doeuff further develops her analysis of women's relationship to education in *Hipparchia's Choice* (Le Doeuff, 1991).

Drawing on Le Doeuff and Felman's pioneering work, feminists may now go on to develop more precise analyses of the position of female teachers and other female authority figures. In this way psychoanalytic theory and practice may help feminists to become aware of – and thus to influence and transform – the transference situations of everyday life. For after all, for Freud as for feminists, the aim of analysis is to produce change.

See also NARCISSISM; PATRIARCHY; PHALLOGOCENTRISM; UNCONSCIOUS.

BIBLIOGRAPHY

Eernheimer, Charles, and Kahane, Claire, eds 1990: *In Dora's Case: Freud–Hysteria–Feminism*, 2nd edn. New York: Columbia University Press.
Felman, Shoshana, 1987: *Jacques Lacan and the Adventure of Insight: Psychoanalysis in Contemporary Culture*. Cambridge, Mass. and London: Harvard University Press.

Freud, Sigmund, 1905: 'Fragment of an analysis of a case of hysteria', *SE*, 7, pp. 1–122.

Freud, Sigmund, 1912: 'The dynamics of transference', *SE*, 12, pp. 97–108.

Freud, Sigmund, 1914: 'Remembering, repeating and working through', *SE*, 12, pp. 145–56.

Freud, Sigmund, 1915: 'Observations on transference love', *SE*, 12, pp. 157–74.

Freud, Sigmund, 1937: 'Constructions in analysis', *SE*, 23, pp. 255–69.

Freud, Sigmund, and Breuer, Otto, 1895: *Studies on Hysteria, SE*, 2.

Lacan, Jacques, 1977 [1973]: *The Four Fundamental Concepts of Psychoanalysis*, trans. Alan Sheridan. London: Hogarth Press.

Laplanche, Jean, and Pontalis, Jean-Baptiste, 1973 [1967]: *The Language of Psychoanalysis*, trans. Donald Nicholson-Smith. New York: Norton.

Le Doeuff, Michèle, 1989: 'Long hair and short ideas', *The Philosophical Imaginary*. London: Athlone; Palo Alto, Calif.: Stanford University Press, pp. 100–28.

Le Doeuff, Michèle, 1991: *Hipparchia's Choice: An Essay Concerning Women, Philosophy, etc.*, trans. Trista Selous. Oxford and Cambridge, Mass.: Blackwell.

TORIL MOI

U

---

uncanny, the In his essay 'The uncanny' (1919), Freud takes a rare step outside his usual domain to consider a neglected category of aesthetics, the emotional nature of which he believes to be especially disposed to psychoanalytic illumination. He begins his inquiry phenomenologically by recalling 'that state of feeling' and by preparing himself for such an 'experience' so that, even as he attempts to demystify the illusory power of this aesthetic, he remains susceptible to its effects. Freud regards the uncanny as that class of the frightening which 'arouses dread and horror' in the old and long familiar; the problem for psychoanalysis is to reveal how this comes about, how it is possible that the familiar can become unfamiliar and terrifying.

Further etymological research informs Freud that the term 'uncanny', *unheimlich*, implies the term *heimlich*, thus having the double semantic capacity to mean its opposite, signifying at once the homely, familiar, friendly, comfortable, intimate and the unfamiliar, uncomfortable, alien and unknown. Besides having the power to signfy antithetical meaning, the uncanny also has the power to signify the development of meaning in the direction of ambivalence, from that which was familiar and homely to that which has become unfamiliar, estranging. Moreover, Freud uses Schelling's gloss of the term – that which ought to have remained secret and hidden but has come to light – to orient uncanny semantics in the direction of psychoanalytic theory, implying that the uncanny is what ought to have remained repressed and unconscious but which has frighteningly surfaced into (pre-)conscious perception. The rest of his essay is devoted to a discussion of exemplary figures or expressions of uncanniness, including a reading of E. T. A. Hoffmann's *The Sandman*, a review of Otto Rank's interpretation of demonology and the double, and a theoretical elaboration of his 'conclusion' that the uncanny is the return of an earlier state of mind, a primitive animism or infantile NARCISSISM that should have been repressed or surmounted in the course of racial or individual evolution. Once flourishing in cultures dominated by mythology and religion, in modern scientific culture this

436

archaic mind makes literature its province where it persistently resists the norms of realism and confounds any distinction between FANTASY and reality.

'The uncanny' has received greatest attention from post-structuralists, literary theorists and feminists who read it as a formula for a genre of subversion and as a disclosure of the irrepressible literariness of psycho-analysis, with literature being the uncanny double of THEORY and dis-course. Seeking out the most radical implications of Freud's essay, critics subject his interpretation of *The Sandman* to further reading, informed by Freud's own discussion of the play of uncanny ambivalence. Noting his attempt to reduce narrative ambivalence in Hoffmann's story to one possible motif of castration anxiety, they focus on what is omitted from his reading, discerning uncanny motifs whose uncanniness Freud finds intolerable and which he covers over even as he would have them dis-covered.

Hélène Cixous notes Freud's overlooking of the figure of the doll, whose animation uncannily subverts the familiar border which divides life and death, exposing a gap in the unity of reality where death enters into the picture as what cannot be directly represented, as what life is not – its repressed Other, the latent condition of our being: becoming inanimate, *unheimlich*. Such non-representable absence points to the undoing of structures of difference on which social order depends (Cixous, 1976).

Jane Marie Todd points out Freud's neglect of the female figure and its connection to the motif of the gaze (through which the hero (un)veils his castration anxiety) as especially conspicuous, given his earlier claim that woman's genitalia are a primary source of uncanny feeling. Todd links castration anxiety to femininity, based on what Freud says in 'Some psychical consequences of the anatomical distinction between the sexes' (1925) and in 'Fetishism' (1927) about the power of the female body to provoke horror in the eye of the beholding male (*see* FETISHISM). She notes furthermore that he overlooks the uncanny connection between the motif of castration and the motif of seeing the animate become inanimate (and vice versa), though this connection is implied in the larger context of his writing. Thus, for Todd, 'the uncanny' poses as yet unasked questions concerning the psychoanalytic structuring of the gaze: (1) is it the female body which is uncanny because it exposes a mutilation from which the man averts his gaze so as not to be reminded of the horrifying threat of castration; or (2) is it the female gaze which is uncanny because it exposes the male gaze which is focused on seeing what is not there, thus recalling the repressed vision of castration; or (3) is it the desire to be female that re-surfaces as a fear of death which is uncannily castrating? Where is the power of horror to be located and why does Freud insist on privileging only the male gaze, its animistic or narcissistic projections? What are the social implications of Freud's 'conclusive' reading of *The Sandman*: is it the norm that male desire should find its most satisfying focus on a woman whose gaze is unilluminating, powerless, merely reflective? (Jane Marie Todd, 1986; *and see* VOYEURISM/EXHIBITIONISM/THE GAZE).

How does the sight of woman condition the phantasmatic connection between the uncanny and castration anxiety? Terry E. Apter notes that Freud views only the specular arena of male narcissism, reducing the focus of Hoffmann's narrative to the hero's identification with the doll, with the inanimate–passive–feminine object of paternal DESIRE, thus limiting interaction to father and son. Apter points out that Freud omits mention of the existence of the other, living woman in the story whose philosophical speculations cast the hero's animistic world-view in a demystifying light, thereby de-animating/castrating him and prompting his regressive flight to the female automaton who, seemingly, comes to life in his potent, animating gaze. But while the vision of the castrating woman is as horrifying as the sight of the castrated female, the source of horror cannot be said to lie in the discovery of SEXUAL DIFFERENCE (Apter, 1982, pp. 38–9).

Kaja Silverman affirms that the uncanniness of castration does not essentially hinge on woman's difference. The 'horror' the boy is said to experience upon first seeing the female body must originate from some earlier knowledge of 'castration', of division and splitting, before he is made to fear the loss of an organ – or else how could this horror be uncanny, strangely familiar? The uncanniness of woman can be explained as the effect of PROJECTION on to the female body from a source within, from the boy's own psychological history (Silverman, 1988, pp. 17–18) (*see* CASTRATION COMPLEX).

Shoshana Felman derives a model of reading for uncanny effects in literature based on the play of projected fear and desire as disclosed in Freud's structural description of the castrating/castrated gaze. Reading for the uncanny opens the text to the problematization of sexual identity and to the generation of uncanny ambivalence as opposed to the reductive literalization of sexual meaning. The compelling enigma of Henry James's *Turn of the Screw* depends on the power of literary rhetoric to locate the source of the uncanny in two places at once, in madness and in ghosts, turning and re-turning the key to interpretation around its double (Felman, 1982). Like the phallic screw of James's story, the golden girl in Balzac's story, 'The girl with the golden eyes', merely serves as a prop in casting the illusion of the sexual identity of desire. Here the uncanny is the effect produced when, instead of serving as a mirror image of masculine sovereignty and reflecting precisely what the male gaze intends to see – masculine self-identity – the mirror of FEMI-NINITY reflects the desire of another, of a woman; to be precise, of his sister, his castrated counterpart. Here the uncanny signifies a radical duplicity, a potential for subverting the code of MASCULINITY which is built into the structure of representation itself (Felman, 1981) (see FETISHIZATION).

Rosemary Jackson claims that Freud recognized the counter-cultural effects of the uncanny when he associated the uncanny with taboo, in particular with the taboos of incest and death. Since the uncanny articulates fantasies of taboo-transgression, it may be regarded as a literature of subversion. Conversely, it could also serve to reinforce order by supplying a vicarious fulfilment of transgression, neutralizing the subversive impulse (Jackson, 1981, pp. 70–2).

In her theory of abjection, KRISTEVA elaborates Freud's notion of the uncanny as taboo. Abjection is the horror of not knowing the boundaries distinguishing 'me' from 'not-me', a primary uncanny which precedes and conditions the horror of castration, and which is generated by the repulsive fecundity and generative power of the maternal body as sensed by the embryonic superego. Fear and dread of being overwhelmed by that body give rise to feelings of abjection which find expression in rituals of purification; these rituals, in turn, lay the foundations for instituting sexual difference and for establishing hierarchical social order. Kristeva re-reads Freud's account of the taboos organizing the avoidance and/or purification of the maternal body as the expression, not of men's generalized dread of woman but as women's power of horror; it is this power which both founds the most primitive culture and mobilizes the most sophisticated creative writer. The writer of abjection is, as she sees it, the greatest safeguard against collective narcissistic fantasies, such as those entertained by feminism in its power-seeking identification with an imaginary PHALLIC MOTHER (Kristeva, 1982). Though Kristeva's 'abjection' is conceptualized from a position within patriarchal society, it prompts feminists to ask how a women's culture might define abjection without self-abasement, or how it might be instituted through taboos of masculinity, a taboo of RAPE, for instance.

Formations of the uncanny have been historically as well as structurally and phenomenologically defined. Tzvetan Todorov outlines the transformation of the uncanny since the gothic, from forms of the marvellous (the supernatural) to those of the purely fantastic (the inexplicable) to the uncanny (the fantasmatic unconscious) (Jackson, 1981, pp. 24–5). In chronicling the history of horror motifs this century, John Grixti observes that the late 1970s and early 1980s were dominated by images of sadistic misogyny, possibly in reaction to the women's movement (Grixti, 1989, p. 23). Against reactionary theories and histories of the uncanny, feminist theorists might consider Jackson's critique of the limits of thematic subversion and the potential for subversive articulation of the uncanny at the level of syntax and structure. Wright's exploration of the uncanny and SURREALISM outlines a positive aesthetic for feminist appropriation (Wright, 1989), an appropriation which may be seen in the early work of British women surrealists.

BIBLIOGRAPHY

Apter, Terry E., 1982: 'The uncanny', *Fantasy Literature: An Approach to Reality*. London: Macmillan, pp. 32–47.

Cixous, Hélène, 1976: 'Fiction and its phantoms: a reading of Freud's *Das Unheimliche* (the "uncanny")', *New Literary History*, 7, pp. 525–48.

Dolar, Mladen, 1991: '"I shall be with you on your wedding-night": Lacan and the uncanny', *Rendering the Real: A Special Issue*, ed. Parveen Adams. *October*, 58, 5–23.

Felman, Shoshana, 1981: 'Turning the screw of interpretation', *Literature and Psychoanalysis, the Question of Reading: Otherwise*, ed. Shoshana Felman. Baltimore: Johns Hopkins University Press, pp. 94–207.

Felman, Shoshana, 1982: 'Rereading femininity', *Yale French Studies*, 62, pp. 19–44.

Freud, Sigmund, 1919: 'The uncanny', *SE*, 17, pp. 217–56.

Freud, Sigmund, 1925: 'Some psychical consequences of the anatomical distinction between the sexes', *SE*, 19, pp. 241–60.

Freud, Sigmund, 1927: 'Fetishism', *SE*, 21, pp. 147–58.

Grixti, Joseph, 1989: *Terrors of Uncertainty: The Cultural Contexts of Horror Fiction*. London: Routledge.

Jackson, Rosemary, 1981: *Fantasy: The Literature of Subversion*. London: Methuen.

Kofman, Sarah, 1991 [1974]: *Freud and Fiction*, trans. Sarah Wykes. Cambridge: Polity Press.

Kristeva, Julia, 1982: *The Powers of Horror: An Essay on Abjection*. New York: Columbia University Press.

Silverman, Kaja, 1988: *The Acoustic Mirror: The Female Voice in Psychoanalysis and Cinema*. Bloomington: Indiana University Press.

Todd, Jane Marie, 1986: 'The veiled woman in Freud's *Das Unheimliche*', *Signs*, 2/3, pp. 519–28.

Wright, Elizabeth, 1989: 'The uncanny and surrealism', *Modernism and the European Unconscious*, ed. Peter Collier and Judith Davies. Cambridge: Polity Press.

DIANNE CHISHOLM

unconscious, the Elaborating the concept of an unconscious, which differs radically from conscious awareness and from pre-conscious states as well, was decisive in distinguishing Freudian psychoanalysis from other psychologies, as well as from the philosophical and poetical versions of it up to Freud's time. Adumbrations of the Freudian unconscious can be found in Schopenhauer, Fichte, and Nietzsche (see Levine, 1923), but neither the romantic theory of a creative unconscious nor that of a mythic substratum persisting transindividually (the two major pre-Freudian forms) comprises the ground of the Freudian unconscious (Lacan, 1977a). Even less does the philosophical thought of William James, Freud's contemporary, wherein the unconscious is seen as 'shortcuts in the brain' or hidden forms of a rationality simply operating without our awareness, so rapidly that no memory remains. Carl Jung's transindividual Collective or Impersonal Unconscious, containing primordial images or archetypes (e.g. 'the feminine') found in recurring dream symbols, resembles James's *Varieties of Religious Experience*, and has occasionally resonated with women but rarely with feminists (*see* JUNG).

For Freud, these are still forms of latent thought which do not differ in kind from conscious thought; unconscious thought is something different from its manifestations (see Žižek, 1989, pp. 13–14). It is rather a parallel thing which speaks and functions in ways homologous to those of the conscious subject, but without its knowledge and according to an entirely different logic, a different set of linguistic operations and a different imagery from those characterizing the conscious mind, even in its pre-conscious states. This is because the conscious mind is primarily and originally constituted around the root form of negation, variously figured as prohibition, taboo, denial; even the rhetorical form, metaphor, is a structure founded on a primordial exclusion – 'this (like) this' implies 'and (not like) that'. The unconscious 'knows no negation'. These negatives and 'cuts' which, according to all modern theories of thought at least since Hegel were seen as primordial, are, for Freud, entirely absent from the unconscious.

The Freudian unconscious has an energy, logic and ethics of its own, radically incompatible with and heterogeneous to the contents of consciousness and the pre-conscious because it consists of subsets or fragments of conscious systems joined differently than they would be in conscious orders, in which they must obey the laws of reason and rational logic. Nevertheless, Freud's theory posits the existence of a relationship among the three (Cs, Pcs, Ucs), though it is one to be inferred only by the analyst, never directly observed. This is primarily because the unconscious is rooted in unavowable and unavowed wishes or desires which have undergone REPRESSION such that their content remains foreign to, forbidden by the consciousness, which expends considerable energy in barring knowledge of and/or memory of such desires from itself. The unconscious does, however, find indirect expression – through nuances, gestures, mistakes, dreams, where these forms take place as lapses, faults or mistakes. Through these parapraxes the analyst can discover the particular energy charge attached to the latent and/or manifest content of the (failed) expression.

Freud's first topology had a 'mechanical' quality, linked to physics, but it was early interfered with by economic, archaeological and transcriptive vocabularies opening the way to understanding the working of the unconscious in systematic, rhetorical and linguistico-literary terms (Freud, 1900, 1925). In all cases, however, the crucial distinction is of a gap or discontinuity between the conscious and the unconscious. Yet despite this radical split, the unconscious is, for Freud, the site of *causality*: the affect associated with the event, wish, thought whose representation has been barred from consciousness retains its power to charge the conscious representation in often wildly inappropriate ways. In 'The unconscious' Freud makes clear that if 'desire did not attach itself to a representation or manifest itself in an affective state, we could know nothing about it' (1915, p. 177). Thus, though its representative or signifier is buried, the desire is not, but is ever ready to surge forth and be born in the gap separating conscious from unconscious. Every structure that 'sutures' or stitches up the gap is a way of offering an unconscious drive a means of expression, realizing an articulation to DESIRE: the dream, the neurosis, the parapraxis, the work of art.

Thus any popular notion of a 'hydraulic' version of the unconscious, of a reservoir of repressed wishes, yields to a 'topological' or mapping system of site locations, where what is being played on stage is prompted by 'another scene', the fantasies and wishes of which are reconfigured in the consciousness, but which remain the constant, if unknown, referent or OBJECT of the second scene. In positing a 'primal scene', as in 'The Wolfman', Freud tended to insist (some say overinsist) on the installation of oedipus in the first fantasy production (1918, p. 29). The oedipal character of the first unconscious scene marks his translation of the primal scene into social and cultural terms. In the topology of the personal pronominal triangle of ego/id/superego Freud begins to focus on the intimate linkage between the individual 'primal scenes' and the cultural ones where the unconscious as such, rather than a generalized superego, insinuates itself fully as cause of cultural formations.

This is where feminism takes issue with the Freudian unconscious. Irigaray (1985, pp. 218–23) writes of an alternative female unconscious rooted in a different primal scene of relation not to the paternal phallus but to the body of the mother as origin. For many, the cultural unconscious inscribed as 'that other scene' remains oedipal in character: it is a set-up of sexual positions taken in relation to the PHALLUS in ways that 'reproduce the social and familial order, the order in which the phallus coincides with the father' (Adams, 1989, p. 250). Adams defines the strongest challenge to Freud's unconscious as the feminist power to question whether the unconscious representations of 'the other scene' which articulate it to the social order can be altered in response to changing material conditions of women in ways that preclude the (by now) utter predictability of the oedipal formula.

Lacan also understands the unconscious as an other scene: 'Since Freud the unconscious has been a chain of signifiers that somewhere (on another stage, in another scene, he wrote) is repeated, and insists on interfering in the breaks offered it by the effective discourse and the cogitation that it informs' (1977c, p. 297). This unconscious relates if anything more tightly to the laws governing civil and rational life, but as a lapse or break in the (circular) chain of signifiers, where meaning circulates backwards and forwards. When the chain loses a signifier $ needed to keep the chain of meaning unified, in the gap, some thing (e.g. an *objet a*) appears in its place, making the link in a different way and to a different fantasy scene in the unconscious. This 'thing' is the unconscious cause of the drives (for Lacan *cause* and *chose* are one word), which turn on it – an *objet a*. Through it desire strays from 'the field of the Other' or oedipus (Lacan 1977b, p. 142) and gains access to the (phallic) 'One'. Although the *objet a* might be thought similar to Winnicott's 'transitional object' through which the child emerges from primary narcissism into mature object 'relations', there is only minimal attention to the unconscious in Winnicott. It is virtually eradicated in the kind of object-relations feminism (Chodorow, 1989, pp. 114–53; see also Brennan, 1988, pp. 258–9) which followed Michael Balint's effort to drive the *drives* out of post-Kleinian analysis. After Klein, those who attend to the unconscious see it through rather Heideggerian eyes, as the (maternal) 'reserve' of signifiers or metonyms, linked to a mother rather than to a father. These include Torok and Abraham's (1976) unconscious 'crypt' in the ego, which harbours foregone JOUISSANCE; and Julia Kristeva's *chora* (1980) as figure of the unconscious, and her depiction of an unconscious, threatening 'uterine space' (1987).

BIBLIOGRAPHY

Adams, Parveen, 1989: 'Of female bondage', *Between Feminism and Psychoanalysis*, ed. Teresa Brennan. London and New York: Routledge, pp. 247–65.
Brennan, Teresa, 1988: 'Controversial discussions and feminist debate', *Freud in Exile: Psychoanalysis and its Vicissitudes*, ed. Edward Timms and Naomi Segal. New Haven and London: Yale University Press, pp. 254–74.

UNCONSCIOUS, THE

Chodorow, Nancy, 1989: *Feminism and Psychoanalytic Theory*. London and New Haven: Yale University Press.

Freud, Sigmund, 1900: *The Interpretation of Dreams*, SE, 4, 5.

Freud, Sigmund, 1915: 'The unconscious', SE, 14, pp. 159–218.

Freud, Sigmund, 1918: 'From the history of an infantile neurosis' ('The Wolfman'), SE, 17, pp. 1–122.

Freud, Sigmund, 1925: 'The mystic writing pad', SE, 19, pp. 227–32.

Irigaray, Luce, 1985 [1974]: *Speculum of the Other Woman*, trans. Gillian Gill. Ithaca, NY: Cornell University Press.

Kristeva, Julia, 1980: *Desire in Language*. New York: Columbia University Press.

Lacan, Jacques, 1977a: 'The Freudian unconscious and ours', *The Four Fundamental Concepts of Psychoanalysis*, trans. Alan Sheridan. London: Hogarth Press, pp. 17–28.

Lacan, Jacques, 1977b: 'The Freudian thing', *Écrits: A Selection*, trans. Alan Sheridan. London: Tavistock, pp. 114–45.

Lacan, Jacques, 1977c: 'The subversion of the subject and the dialectic of desire in the Freudian unconscious', *Écrits: A Selection*, pp. 292–325.

Levine, Israel, 1923: *The Unconscious: An Introduction to Freudian Psychology*. London: Leonard Parsons.

Torok, Maria, and Abraham, Nicholas, 1986: *The Wolf Man's Magic Word: A Cryptonomy*. Minneapolis: University of Minnesota Press.

Wilden, Anthony, 1980: *System and Structure*. London: Tavistock.

Žižek, Slavoj, 1989: *The Sublime Object of Ideology*. London: Verso.

JULIET FLOWER MACCANNELL

V

virginity   Feminist psychoanalytic interest in the concept of virginity
has been notably less extensive than in the cases of PENIS ENVY and the
CASTRATION COMPLEX, to which virginity is related in Freud's discussion,
although the concept occupies considerably more importance in Jungian
thought. Yet in their discussions of a feminine JOUISSANCE, feminist studies influenced by LACAN have focused surprisingly often on specific
(albeit putative) virginal bodies.

During his early work with Breuer, Freud had often noted what he
termed 'virginal anxiety' (a combination of anxiety neurosis and HYSTE-
RIA) aroused in young women by the possibility of sexual relations (see
Freud, 1893–5, p. 134). Later (1905), he noted Dora's fascination with
the Sistine Madonna of Raphael. In 'The taboo of virginity' (1918)
Freud drew on anthropological accounts of the attitudes of primitive
tribes to the defloration of a virgin, and argued that it was 'a generalized
dread of women' which was the real source of the elaborate taboo surrounding virginity in such cultures. Freud asserted that the defloration
of virgins by someone other than the future husband – a practice followed in many primitive societies – was intended to spare the future
husband from the unconscious hostility which such an act is liable to
provoke, due to the wound to the woman's NARCISSISM which it effects.
According to Freud, defloration activates the woman's penis envy, in 'an
archaic reaction of hostility' which can lead to frigidity (1918, p. 208).

Lou Andreas-Salomé commented in a letter to Freud that this taboo
might be a trace of an earlier, matriarchal, social order in which
woman had been autonomous (1972, p. 89). Her suggestion has been
partially echoed in several Jungian interpretations of virginity (e.g.
Harding, 1971; Hall, 1980). Yet recent feminist writers influenced by
psychoanalysis have also questioned Freud's attribution of the taboo
on virginity to penis envy. Kofman (1973), for example, has criticized
Freud's use of a literary text – Hebbel's drama *Judith* – to justify his
thesis. Jacobus (1986) and Ramas (1985) have also discussed Dora's
fantasy of the Madonna and consequent phantom pregnancy as 'an

immaculate conception' which denies the power of the phallus. This feminine *self-conception*, Jacobus suggests, can be compared to 'Freud's own attempted theoretical self-conception, his abjection of the mother, and his installation of the oedipal perspective as the only angle on the pre-oedipal' (p. 193). In fact, Lacan (1977) had already associated a more destructive virginal figure, that of Diana, Roman goddess of chastity, with the role of the UNCONSCIOUS in Freudian theory.

It was in a response to feminist criticism of his work that Lacan mentioned Bernini's sculpture of St Theresa as an example of female JOUIS-SANCE, (1982). IRIGARAY too (1985a) focused on the (implicitly virginal) body of the female Christian mystic for her exploration of *jouissance* in a chapter entitled 'La Mystérique'. She also refers (1985b) to the disruption of a virginal feminine autoerotism by masculine penetration and defloration, and argues that women should keep themselves apart from men long enough to learn to defend their desire. More recently (1989), Irigaray has suggested that virginity should be made a civic concept. KRISTEVA (1986), in a parallel but somewhat different exploration of woman's bodily *jouissance*, has explored the mythology of the Virgin Mary. Initially she associated virginity with a homosexual economy which none the less reinforced the patriarchal bias of the symbolic order (1977). Later (1986), she interpreted Christianity's privileging of the 'virginal maternal' as a means of according a position within the symbolic order to a discourse of MOTHERHOOD. She also suggested that the cult of the Virgin was a defence against female paranoia, since thereby woman could repudiate the other woman (i.e. the personal mother). In spite of her criticisms of the often conservative role of the Christian cult, Kristeva associated the Virgin Mother and her attributes with a return of the repressed (that is, of primary processes) in patriarchal culture. Thus, whether as metaphor or as physical reality, the figure of the virgin continues to occupy a position of importance within feminist debate.

BIBLIOGRAPHY

Andreas-Salomé, Lou, 1972: *Sigmund Freud and Lou Andreas-Salomé: Letters*, ed. E. Pfeiffer. New York: Harcourt Brace Jovanovich.
Freud, Sigmund, 1893–5: *Studies on Hysteria*, SE, 2.
Freud, Sigmund, 1905: 'Fragment of an analysis of a case of hysteria', SE, 7, pp. 1–122.
Freud, Sigmund, 1918: 'The taboo of virginity', SE, 11, pp. 193–208.
Hall, Nor, 1980: *The Moon and the Virgin: Reflections on the Archetypal Feminine*. London: The Women's Press.
Harding, Esther, 1971: *Woman's Mysteries*. New York: G. P. Putnam's Sons.
Irigaray, Luce, 1985a [1974]: *Speculum of the Other Woman*, trans. Gillian C. Gill. Ithaca, NY: Cornell University Press.

Irigaray, Luce, 1985b [1977]: *This Sex Which Is Not One*, trans. Catherine Porter. Ithaca, NY: Cornell University Press.

Irigaray, Luce, 1989: *Le Temps de la différence: pour une révolution pacifique*. Paris: Librairie française d'éditions.

Jacobus, Mary, 1986: *Reading Woman: Essays in Feminist Criticism*. London: Methuen.

Kofman, Sarah, 1973: *Quatres romans analytiques*. Paris: Éditions Galilée.

Kristeva, Julia, 1977 [1974]: *About Chinese Women*. London: Marion Boyars.

Kristeva, Julia, 1986: 'Stabat mater', *The Kristeva Reader*, ed. Toril Moi. Oxford: Basil Blackwell, pp. 160–86.

Lacan, Jacques, 1977: 'The Freudian thing', *Écrits: A Selection*, trans. Alan Sheridan. London: Tavistock, pp. 114–45.

Lacan, Jacques, 1982: 'God and the *jouissance* of the woman', *Feminine Sexuality: Jacques Lacan and the École Freudienne*, ed. Juliet Mitchell and Jacqueline Rose. London: Macmillan, pp. 137–48.

Ramas, Maria, 1985: 'Freud's Dora, Dora's hysteria', *In Dora's Case: Freud–Hysteria–Feminism*, ed. Charles Bernheimer and Claire Kahane. London: Virago, pp. 149–80.

PHILIPPA BERRY

voyeurism/exhibitionism/the gaze Voyeurism and exhibitionism are the active and passive forms of scopophilia, the DRIVE to look. Although Freud suggests that scopophilia is simply one of the many drives whose source resides in infantile sexual development, it is clear that even for him, it occupies an especially significant place, through its direct links to the desire for mastery (i.e. the conversion of the position of passivity in activity) and the desire to know (epistemophilia). Scopophilic impulses play a key role in the quest for knowledge and mastery of the world. Phylogenetically, he suggests, the increasing prominence of sight among all the senses, and the increasing place of scopophilia in the accumulation of knowledges, is the consequence of 'man's' upright posture (Freud, 1927).

Although scopophilia can be divided into an active form in which the SUBJECT looks at an OBJECT, and a passive form in which the subject desires to be looked at by some other subject, Freud claims that both find their origins in a more primitive narcissistic phase in which the subject takes a part of its own body as its (exhibitionistic) object. In this autoerotic scopophilia, active and passive, subject and object, remain blurred, undecidably one and the other. The active and passive forms emerge only gradually from this prior stage, which provides the preconditions for both active and passive positions. Freud claims that this

447

primitive scopophilic bedrock always leaves its contours on the later overlays (Freud, 1914, p. 131).

Because the earlier 'layers' are inaccessible except retrospectively, i.e. through the influences and effects of the later layers, voyeurism and exhibitionism are always necessarily bound up with each other. The effects of the retrospective re-transcription of the earlier phase provides it with new meanings and a new impetus, and this occurs most decisively and with the greatest impact as a result of the oedipal re-writing of the PRE-OEDIPAL drives. In the case of scopophilia, the active and passive positions become coded as masculine and feminine respectively (following the oedipal correlation of activity with MASCULINITY and the phallic, and passivity with FEMININITY and castration). Voyeurism has become associated with masculinity, and exhibitionism with femininity. This is not without its clinical ironies in so far as clinically speaking exhibitionism is, along with fetishism, almost exclusive to men. The female equivalent to male exhibitionism is kleptomania.

Much of feminist FILM THEORY, in particular, has relied on Freud's notion of scopophilia to describe and analyse the effects of film on spectators. Laura Mulvey's landmark article 'Visual pleasure and narrative cinema' (1989; originally published 1975) identified the position of the female filmic protagonist as exhibitionistic object of the male gaze, and argued that, whether the audience was male or female, their spectatorial roles remain voyeuristic and function in complicity with the gaze of the male protagonist or hero. Her initial insights have led to a number of different feminist responses regarding the role of vision in film and its degrees of implication in phallocentrism, contesting and modifying Mulvey's one-to-one correlation between masculinity and voyeurism, and femininity and exhibitionism (see especially Silverman, 1988; and Rose, 1987; *and see* FEMINIST CINEMA).

Many feminists who have utilized the concepts of voyeurism and exhibitionism have, sometimes in an unrecognized fashion, conflated Freud's notion of scopophilia with Sartre's notion of 'the look' and Lacan's account of the gaze, three closely related but nevertheless significantly different conceptions of looking. It is in contrast to Sartre's notion, and in consolidation of Freud's, that Lacan's account of the gaze is developed. For Sartre, the look is fundamentally objectifying: by means of the look the subject is capable of being transformed into an object, reduced from a self-conscious subject, a being-for-itself, to a being in-itself and for-others. The look can induce in the subject a sense of unmitigated shame at his/her being. Sartre illustrates this with the example of the voyeur who is caught with his eye to the keyhole by a third party who induces in him shame and humiliation. But for Sartre, even though the subject always has an ontological primacy over the other, none the less the look is necessarily capable of reciprocation. The objectifying, gazing subject recognizes in the gazed-upon objectified object that there is always the possibility that he too will be looked at, he too may be objectified in the very same way that his gaze has objectified the other. At the root of this power struggle between the looker and the looked-upon object is a recognition that the object of the look is also a subject, and thus capable of being at the centre of perspective, capable of looking as well as being looked at.

LACAN carefully distinguishes the gaze from the phenomenology of seeing that Sartre outlines. As a drive, the gaze is always an excess over mere seeing: as in the case of all drives, the gaze is fundamentally oriented towards a LACK (Lacan, 1977, pp. 182–3).

For Lacan, seeing is a function of both the subject looking from a singular perspectival point, where what it sees is outside of itself (Lacan, 1977, p. 80), and the possibility of being seen. The subject is defined as that which is seeable, capable of being shown, being seen without necessarily being able to see either the observer or itself. Lacan strongly disagrees with Sartre's reciprocal gaze: for Lacan the possibility of being observed is always primary (see Rose, 1987, chs 7 and 10).

The gaze is not an internal attribute, like a bodily perception; it is situated outside. By this Lacan means that, like the PHALLUS, like DESIRE itself, the gaze emanates from the field of the Other. Sartre's account of the objectifying nature of the look is possible, not because of the power of the other, but because the other's look is justified, legitimized, by the Other. It is the result of being placed in the field of the Other.

Many feminists, particularly those working on film and visual representation, have conflated the look with the gaze, mistaking a perceptual mode with a mode of desire. When they state baldly that 'vision' is male, the look is masculine, or the visual is a phallocentric mode of perception, these feminists confuse a perceptual facility open to both sexes to use as they are able with sexually coded positions of desire within visual (or any other perceptual) functions as a means to an end. Vision is not, cannot be, masculine (nor the tactile or the auditory, feminine); rather, certain ways of using vision (for example, to objectify) may confirm and help produce patriarchal power relations. With some exceptions (notably Rose), feminists have rarely utilized Lacan's notion of the gaze, although they have borrowed the word and used it to theorize in terms of the Sartrean look.

See also OTHER/OTHER.

BIBLIOGRAPHY

Freud, Sigmund, 1914: 'Instincts and their vicissitudes', *SE*, 14, pp. 109–140.
Freud, Sigmund, 1927: 'Civilisation and its discontents', *SE*, 21, pp. 57–146.

VOYEURISM/EXHIBITIONISM/THE GAZE

Lacan, Jacques, 1977 [1973]: *The Four Fundamental Concepts of Psychoanalysis*, trans. Alan Sheridan. London: Hogarth Press.

Mulvey, Laura, 1989: 'Visual pleasure and narrative cinema', *Visual and Other Pleasures*. London: Macmillan, pp. 14–26.

Rose, Jacqueline, 1987: *Sexuality and the Field of Vision*. London: Verso.

Sartre, Jean-Paul, 1974: *Being and Nothingness*. Harmondsworth: Penguin.

Silverman, Kaja, 1988: *The Acoustic Mirror: The Female Voice in Psychoanalysis and Cinema*. Bloomington: Indiana University Press.

ELIZABETH GROSZ

W

woman-identified woman/radical lesbianism   The woman-centred perspective derives from the theoretical writings of lesbian feminism in the early 1970s. It specifies a political commitment to putting women first and to establishing women's autonomy (Eisenstein, 1984). New York Radicalesbians first coined the term in a broadsheet published under the title *Woman-Identified Woman* (Radicalesbians, 1970), making probably the first and most widely acknowledged statement of the political lesbian 'movement' (Allen, 1982). Radicalesbians use the term to distinguish the revolutionary, self-defining woman who finds sexual and emotional satisfaction with other women from the 'real woman', who identifies with patriarchal femininity and who is dependent on her relations with men for her sense of legitimacy and authenticity. The critique of the patriarchal 'woman' draws upon existentialist and marxist rather than psychoanalytic thinking, elaborating notions of false consciousness and bad faith to describe women who continue to play out the roles of domestic servitude impressed upon them by masculinist IDEOLOGY. Revolutionary woman-identified women advocate the voluntary withdrawal of women from the traditional family and the formation of separatist collectives for the purpose of engendering a new woman-centred self-consciousness. Such a revolutionary call to action seems conspicuously naïve in the absence of a theory of DESIRE, but by the mid-1970s the woman-centred perspective had become the most powerful mobilizing force of the women's movement. After that time, it lost impetus, possibly as a result of its extremist splinterings (Allen, 1982) and its failure to re-define SEXUALITY. One of the most radical formulations of this position, eloquently represented by Monique Wittig, claims that women should seek to abolish the category and class of 'woman', since it is structurally bound to the dominant category and class of 'man' and cannot be rehabilitated (Allen, 1982). An opposite totalizing position, formulated by Adrienne Rich, proposes to expand the term 'lesbian' to include all woman-identified women, thereby undermining attempts by PATRIARCHY to reduce LESBIANISM to sex and, at the same time, centring

451

women's historical and existential sense in themselves, as women, and not as men's dependants and subordinates (Allen, 1982; Eisenstein, 1984). All positions agree, however, that until lesbianism is made an explicit part of history and a common discourse, women will not have sufficient sense of sexual choice to amass the collective power to negotiate and determine the meaning and value of their sex/sexuality.

Recent developments in lesbian feminist intellectual circles suggest that the polarized extremes of political lesbianism which emerged in the 1980s are being replaced by collective projects designed to articulate a specific lesbian sexuality/subjectivity and to constitute a lesbian body politic. For instance, contributions to the new anthology *Lesbian Philosophies and Cultures* (Allen, 1990) are decidedly separatist: in place of a metaphysical concern with totalizing categories – defining 'lesbian' as inclusive of all woman-identified women, or conversely, as a whole new category exclusive of woman-identified women – there is an epistemological concern with LANGUAGE, meaning, and knowledge of the BODY. This work looks forward to the collective engendering of the lesbian subject through extensive consciousness-raising, talking and writing, through representing and communicating desire and sexuality among lesbian poets and theorists. Marilyn Frye speaks of the need for a linguistic community to materialize, generate and circulate meaning that arises from bodily self-knowledge, of a lesbian 'sex' that needs symbolic representation to take hold in memory and history. Words imported from the vocabulary of HETEROSEXUALITY are not adequate, merely imposing their phallocentrism on inarticulate yet radically other experience, leaving lesbian desire speechless, meaningless and, ironically, less sexual. Michèle Causse frames her observations on emerging lesbian epistemologies in Hegelian terms. Accordingly, French-speaking theorists have risked 'death' by writing the passing of the woman-object, by explicitly mortifying representations of FEMININITY and by mourning a lost complementarity they knew as mirrors for men's self-reflecting half-world. Risking death, they enter history as ex-objects, subjects who know their own bodies through a writing practice that is at once separatism, re-appropriation and self-legitimation.

None of these contributors turns to psychoanalysis as a fruitful source of theoretical appropriation. At most, they refer to psychoanalysis to identify the terms of the masochistic triad (castration–RAPE–childbirth) in terms of which the lesbian feminist woman refuses to constitute herself any longer. Perhaps they have been persuaded by Wittig's rejection of (Lacanian) psychoanalysis because of its irremediable conceptualization of sexuality as essentially heterosexual and its representation of difference as absolutely phallic (Wittig, 1980).

See also BISEXUALITY; HETEROSEXISM; HOMOPHOBIA; HOMOSEXUALITY.

BIBLIOGRAPHY

Allen, Hilary, 1982: 'Political lesbianism and feminism – space for a sexual politics?', *m/f*, 7, pp. 15–34.
Allen, Jeffner, ed. 1990: *Lesbian Philosophies and Cultures*. New York: State University of New York Press.
Eisenstein, Hester, 1984: 'Lesbianism and the woman-identified woman', *Contemporary Feminist Thought*. London: George Allen and Unwin, pp. 48–57.
Radicalesbians, 1970: *Woman-Identified Woman*. New York: New England Free Press.
Radicalesbians, 1973: 'The woman-identified woman', *Radical Feminism*, ed. Ann Koedt, Ellen Levine and Anita Rapone. New York: Quadrangle Books, pp. 240–5.
Rich, Adrienne, 1980: 'Compulsory heterosexuality and lesbian existence', *Signs*, 5, pp. 631–60.
Wittig, Monique, 1980: 'The straight mind', *Feminist Issues*, 1/1 (Spring), pp. 103–10.

DIANNE CHISHOLM

women's psychological development   Women's psychological development refers to a process of change and growth involving experiences and capabilities which affect psychological vitality and sense of self. A key question of psychoanalysts and feminists is whether changes in women's experiences of self and their relationships over time lead to a greater vitality or higher levels of psychological functioning (however defined), or to psychological diminution and/or neurotic symptoms.

Women's psychological development within a world which is male-dominated is essentially problematic and contains a central and paradoxical problem of relationship: since women's voices disrupt a societal and cultural world which men have largely created and govern, women are pressed to take themselves out of relationship for the sake of 'relationships' and thus bring themselves into line with the world around them. Psychological development then centres around women's struggle for relationships in a world where their desires for genuine connection with others and their curiosity about the world are bound to make trouble. Hence, women's development involves societal and cultural change and becomes inescapably political.

This connection between women's psychological health and societal and cultural transformation became evident at the beginning of psychoanalysis, since psychoanalysis began with women's voices, specifically the voices of late adolescent and young adult women, speaking about

453

their experiences of relationships. The early discoveries of psychoanalysis, including the invention of 'the talking cure' as a method of treatment, centred on the realization that hysterical women were 'suffer[ing] from reminiscences', that women's 'love had become separated from [their] knowledge', and that these disconnections or dissociations were being sustained by hysterical blindness, by paralysis, and most commonly by 'a loss of voice' (Freud and Breuer, 1895). In the early days of psychoanalysis, women's voices were freed by hypnosis or free association in the context of relationships where psychiatrists were listening to and learning from women (*see* FREUD).

From women, Freud learned about the prevalence of incest and other forms of child abuse within seemingly respectable families. Listening to women thus brought psychoanalysis into tension with a society and culture which depended on their silence and their not knowing. Women's voices, or more precisely the voices of women patients, essentially disappeared from psychoanalytic writings, yielding to the voices of psychoanalysts speaking about women within the framework of psychoanalytic theory (*see* FREUD'S FEMALE PATIENTS/FEMALE ANALYSTS).

In the 1970s, with the revival of the women's movement, women's voices were heard again. The differences between these women's voices and those of psychological theory were strikingly audible, re-opening to basic re-formulation both the tenets of psychoanalytic theory and the description of human development. Women's sense of self differed from psychologists' descriptions of 'the self' and women's approaches to conflicts reflected a different experience of relationship and a different understanding of reality (see Gilligan, 1977, 1982; and also Miller, 1976, 1984). If women know themselves by listening to themselves and differentiating their voices from the voices of others around them, then in the course of their development they will hear the dissonances between their own voices and the voices of others, including those who have the power to construct and enforce societal and cultural realities.

Women's ability to speak from experience and listen to themselves is complicated by the voices which they take in, especially those which trivialize their experiences and label women's responsiveness to themselves 'selfish'. Within a male-dominated society and culture, women are encouraged to make and maintain relationships by becoming 'selfless' and 'good', to care only for others, and to rely on others to care for them. This essentially confusing move to take oneself out of relationship for the sake of 'relationships' creates a major obstacle to women's psychological development (see Gilligan, 1982, 1990; and also Miller, 1984, 1988).

Feminist psychologists in the 1970s and 1980s have begun to create a feminist psychology by listening to women and then staying with them

454

in the face of dissonances between women's voices and accepted psychological truths or cultural verities (see especially Belenky et al., 1986; Chodorow, 1974; Gilligan, 1977, 1982, 1990b; Jack, 1991; Miller, 1976, 1984, 1988; Steiner-Adair, 1991). This approach is radical in that it involves re-thinking the most basic psychological concepts such as the concepts of 'self' and 'relationships', learning from women about the centrality of connections and the effects of disconnections on psychic life, paying attention to the value which psychologists have placed on detachment and separation, and re-considering the language of psychological writing. Four questions about voice thus become central to a feminist psychology: who is speaking? in what body? telling what story about relationships, from whose perspective or from what vantage-point? and in what societal and cultural framework?

The integration of this voice-centred approach to psychological inquiry with research on women's psychological development has yielded knowledge which speaks to some of its central riddles and to the differences observed between the development of women and men. Girls in general seem to flourish psychologically during childhood and then experience a kind of psychological narrowing as they reach adolescence – a time which marks a sudden drop in girls' resilience and a marked increase in depressive symptoms, dissociative phenomena, eating disorders, suicidal thoughts and gestures, as well as behaviour which leads them into trouble with society and renders them economically and politically powerless. Furthermore, the girls who suffer psychologically in adolescence often have not experienced psychological difficulties in childhood, but instead had seemed to be among the most psychologically vital.

Recent studies of women's development have documented a relational crisis which girls face as they approach adolescence and a struggle or moment of resistance (Gilligan, 1990b, 1991; Brown and Gilligan, in preparation; Brown, 1991; Rogers, 1991). This resistance arises in response to pressures to secure connections with others by silencing themselves (Jack, 1991). What begins as girls' healthy resistance to disconnections which are psychologically wounding tends, however, to turn into a political resistance or struggle, since their insistence on knowing what they know through experience and their willingness to be outspoken or to stay in authentic or genuine connection with others brings them into conflict with the prevailing order of relationships. In short, they will discover through experience the realities which feminists write about: the prevalence of men's voices in societal and cultural institutions, and the disparities in economic and political power between women and men. Consequently, that very political resistance involving clarity of knowing and a seemingly straightforward courage which women subsequently struggle to regain (see Jordan, 1988) tends to turn back into a psychological resistance.

This understanding of women's psychological development provides the basis for a theory which is at once psychoanalytic and feminist. The classical description of psychological development turns out to be a description of that of boys and men. Living within a patriarchal society, boys tend to face a relational crisis in early childhood when they are pressured to give up relationship for the sake of 'relationships' and also to claim their manhood. Girls face a similar relational crisis at the time of their adolescence, and adolescence correspondingly becomes the turning-point in their development. However, this asymmetry between men and women within a patriarchal society creates a potential for resistance. Girls' desires for relationship and their curiosity about relationships are less inchoate, more articulate, more elaborated through experience and less laced with early loss and terror; at adolescence they question the necessity of losses and renunciations which are psychologically damaging but which have been seen as inevitable.

From findings such as these emerges a hope of societal and cultural transformation. Current evidence suggests that women's psychological resilience depends on the strength and authenticity of women's relationships, and that relationships between girls and women at the time when girls reach adolescence can strengthen healthy resistance in girls and help women to regain lost voices.

See also AUTONOMY; CHODOROW; MOTHER–DAUGHTER RELATIONSHIP; NEGATIVE OEDIPUS COMPLEX; OEDIPUS COMPLEX.

BIBLIOGRAPHY

Belenky, Mary; Clinchy, Blythe; Goldberger, Nancy; and Tarule, Jill, 1986: *Women's Ways of Knowing: The Development of Self, Voice and Mind*. New York: Basic Books.

Brown, Lyn Mikel, forthcoming: 'Telling a girl's life', *Women and Therapy*, 11/3, 4, pp. 71–87.

Brown, Lyn Mikel, and Gilligan, Carol, in preparation: *Meeting at the Crossroads: Women's Psychology and Girls' Development*. Cambridge, Mass.: Harvard University Press.

Chodorow, Nancy, 1978: *The Reproduction of Mothering: Psychoanalysis and the Sociology of Gender*. Berkeley: University of California Press.

Freud, Sigmund, and Breuer, Josef, 1895: *Studies in Hysteria*, SE, 2, pp. 135–83.

Gilligan, Carol, 1977: 'In a different voice: women's conceptions of the self and of morality', *Harvard Educational Review*, 47/4, pp. 481–517.

Gilligan, Carol, 1982: *In a Different Voice: Psychological Theory and Women's Development*. Cambridge, Mass.: Harvard University Press.

Gilligan, Carol, 1990a: 'Prologue' and 'Teaching Shakespeare's sister: notes from the underground of female adolescence', *Making Connections: The*

Relational Worlds of Adolescent Girls at Emma Willard School, ed. Carol Gilligan, Nona P. Lyons and Trudy Hanmer. Cambridge, Mass.: Harvard University Press.

Gilligan, Carol, 1990b: 'Joining the resistance: psychology, politics, girls and women', *Michigan Quarterly Review*, 29/4, pp. 501–36.

Gilligan, Carol, 1991: 'Women's psychological development: implications for psychotherapy', *Women and Therapy*, 2/3, 4 (also in press as Carol Gilligan, Annie Rogers, and Deborah Tolman, eds, *Women, Girls and Psychotherapy: Reframing Resistance*. New York: Haworth Press).

Jack, Dana Crowley, 1991: *Silencing the Self: Depression and Women*. Cambridge, Mass.: Harvard University Press.

Jordan, Judith V., 1988: 'Clarity in connection', *Work in Progress*, 29. Wellesley: Stone Center Working Paper Series.

Miller, Jean Baker, 1976: *Toward a New Psychology of Women*. Boston: Beacon Press.

Miller, Jean Baker, 1984: 'The development of women's sense of self', *Work in Progress*, 12. Wellesley: Stone Center Working Paper Series.

Miller, Jean Baker, 1988: 'Connections, disconnections and violations', *Work in Progress*, 33. Wellesley: Stone Center Working Paper Series.

Morrison, Toni (1970). *The Bluest Eye*. New York: Pocket Books.

Rich, Adrienne (1979). *On Lies, Secrets, and Silence: Selected Prose 1966–1978*. New York: Norton.

Rogers, Annie, 1991: 'A feminist poetics of psychotherapy', *Women and Therapy*, 2/3, 4, pp. 33–55.

Steiner-Adair, Catherine, 1990: 'New maps of development, new models of psychotherapy: the psychology of women and the treatment of eating disorders', *Psychodynamic Treatment of Anorexia Nervosa and Bulimia*, ed. C. Johnson. New York: Guildford Press.

CAROL GILLIGAN

Women's Therapy Centre, The   The centre started in 1976 to test out the viability of providing a feminist psychotherapy service in Britain run by women for women. Its founders, Luise Eichenbaum and Susie Orbach, aimed to influence other mental health services for women and to develop a feminist psychoanalytic theory of women's psychological development. From the beginning, the demand for the psychoanalytically oriented psychotherapy for individual women was overwhelming. The development of a programme of workshops or theme-centred groups (see Krzowski and Land, 1988), training courses for professionals, and an advice and information service on psychotherapy and counselling resources for women, have all been responses to this demand. There are now Women's Therapy services in several British cities and a Women's Therapy Centre training institute in New York.

The centre was the outcome of a particular convergence of ideas and developments from within the women's movement, from psychoanalysis and from the broader field of mental health. By the mid-1970s the earlier feminist critiques of Freud (particularly from the US, whose psychiatric establishment was overtly dominated by Freudian ideas, see e.g. Millett, 1969) had given way among some feminists to a desire to study the UNCONSCIOUS from a feminist perspective in order to grapple with the question of how women had internalized their position in society. Thus feminist theoreticians such as Juliet MITCHELL (1974) and the French group *Psychanalyse et politique* converged with feminists who, through their experience in consciousness-raising groups and a wide range of feminist political organizing, came to ask similar questions.

Eichenbaum and Orbach came from the latter group; they became professional psychotherapists in the US. The concept of the unconscious could help them to understand the vicissitudes of a psychic life as a powerful determinant in the politics of everyday experience; and to theorize the psychological development of the girl (Eichenbaum and Orbach, 1985, p. 13). Others came to work with Eichenbaum and Orbach from the anti-psychiatry movement, from the Reichian and humanistic self-help therapy group, Red Therapy (with its critique of power-relations), and from the more traditional psychotherapeutic and psychiatric social work trainings. The work of the 'anti-psychiatry' movement built on a connection between madness and social experience and a belief in the possibility of making sense of psychotic experience through psychotherapy. Drawn to the centre by the feminist perspective lacking in their own establishments, they strengthened the ethos of the centre, that all women should be offered psychotherapy which did not reproduce old forms of pathologizing women.

Thus, at the Women's Therapy Centre a mixture of influences was to be found: the growth movement, existential psychotherapy, Mitchell's work with its interest in LACAN, and most of the different strands of contemporary British psychoanalytic thought. Given this mixture, why is it that the British school of object-relations has had such an influence on the centre's work?

KLEIN and subsequent object-relations theorists had taken the psychoanalytic focus away from the centrality of the oedipal conflict to the earlier relationship between mother and infant, which paved the way for the feminist interest in the MOTHER–DAUGHTER RELATIONSHIP and their shared gender as central to the understanding of women's psychology. But it was the work of Fairbairn, Guntrip and Winnicott which attracted Eichenbaum and Orbach in two ways: first, their clinical observations 'echoed our own experience of women clients. Second, the construction of personality was based within a relational context.'

458

(Eichenbaum and Orbach, 1985, pp. 13–14). Eichenbaum and Orbach, and subsequent writers from the centre, were clear about the limitations of these psychoanalysts' work used within a feminist context: none of them understood women's position in society, nor did they recognize the mother as a person in her own right. It followed that they offered no critique of the family and its role in perpetuating a patriarchal society. Lastly, they did not recognize the salience of gender from the start of the infant's life.

Eichenbaum and Orbach's starting-point was that 'the oppressed mother must negotiate her relationship with her daughter around and within the fact of her own subordination' (Eichenbaum and Orbach, 1987, p. 59). The mother has repressed her dependency needs to become a carer for others; faced with her needy and helpless baby daughter she both wants to give her daughter what she has not had and withdraws from the intimacy which threatens to arouse her own repressed longings. The 'push–pull' dynamic of the early mother–daughter relationship leads the baby girl to split off that part of her which arouses so much anxiety in the mother (in the way that Fairbairn describes the schizoid split) and to develop her capacity to tune into the mother's needs: this capacity enables her to mother others in the future. The authors relate this to Winnicott's concept of the 'false self'. The daughter is becoming a carer for others in compliance with society's demands; she will become a woman who wants to complete herself by catching a man (*see* MOTHERHOOD).

Eichenbaum and Orbach argued that the social understanding of the unconscious relationship between mother and daughter had profound implications for the therapy relationship. They suggested that traditional psychotherapists would continue to deny the importance of unconscious social attitudes towards women and would collude with seeing women's dependency as something to be denied and pathologized. A feminist perspective on the other hand, allows the psychotherapist to become aware of this fear of women's dependency and to address other painful consequences of PATRIARCHY such as anorexia, bulimia and sexual abuse. It is the possibility of intimacy with the psychotherapist, and the client's defences against intimacy, which become the focus, rather than the more traditional emphasis on the woman's difficulty in separating and not being able to accept her deprivation.

This work involved a constant and close examination of the transference and countertransference feelings of client and psychotherapist (*see* TRANSFERENCE/COUNTERTRANSFERENCE), which had implications for the power relationship between psychotherapist and client, in that the feminist critique of psychoanalysis saw it as a male-dominated form of treatment used as a way of controlling women (see Chesler, 1972). It was considered inappropriate for the psychotherapist to share her feelings in the consulting room. Instead, women should know as much as they wanted about the process of psychotherapy (Eichenbaum and Orbach's books are written to be accessible to the lay reader). The crucial check on the psychotherapist's abuse of power lay in her commitment to a constant examining and re-examining of her countertransference to see how and where she might be internalizing oppressive and patriarchal attitudes to women. Later this approach has been extended to look at countertransference issues in work with lesbians, women with disabilities and black women (*see* BLACK FEMINIST PSYCHOTHERAPY; LESBIANISM: CLINICAL PERSPECTIVES).

As the Women's Therapy Centre developed, the commitment to offering a psychotherapy service for women which recognizes the salience of GENDER has remained and been developed to include the awareness of differences between women. Important work has been done on women's themes such as abortion, eating problems and sexual abuse. However, there has been a growing debate which first emerged in writing in *Living with the Sphinx* (Ernst and Maguire, 1987) about whether there was one specific form of 'feminist' psychotherapy, within the mainstream object-relations psychotherapists at the centre, and between them and a Lacanian viewpoint. While that volume contains papers which continue and develop previous work, it also emphasizes the continuities between the centre and mainstream object-relations work (see papers by Ernst and Maguire, 1987). These authors also suggest that Eichenbaum and Orbach's emphasis on the provision of a psychotherapy relationship in which dependency can be explored can lead to an avoidance of the negative transference. They both develop more detailed accounts of the way in which the outer world (social reality) is incorporated into the girl's psychological development. Maguire suggests that both boys and girls have to deal with their feelings in relation to an all-powerful mother, but, as against Klein, argues that the envy in the mother–daughter relationship is exacerbated by women's internalized low sense of social value. Ernst sees the potential of Winnicott's concepts of transitional space and transitional objects as points where external and internal worlds meet, enabling us to conceptualize the effects of social issues on psychological development. While the object-relations view has been on the importance of gender in the very earliest stages of the infant's life, the Lacanian view (expounded in Bar's paper in Ernst and Maguire, 1987), is that gender identity is forged through the girl discovering her lack of the PHALLUS and the painful relinquishing of the FANTASY of being the centre of her mother's universe. Here the father is seen as a key figure in the girl's psychological development, while most other writers from the centre (with the exception of Maguire) focus on the father's absence.

While the centre was developing its clinical and theoretical work, its own changes as a women's institution have reflected both current issues for feminists and current struggles of voluntary agencies to survive the attack on local government and public sector services. Its history, similar to other innovative projects in the 1970s, was of transition from a charismatic leadership to a collectively run organization which was seen as reflecting feminist principles. Political and theoretical debates and the demands of the service itself have moved the centre on from its tacit assumption that one can generalize about women to acknowledging the differences between women.

The recognition that psychoanalytic psychotherapy will have a particular meaning for a lesbian because of the psychoanalytic establishment's pathologizing of HOMOSEXUALITY, and the need to understand a black woman's experience in its own terms rather than in comparison to white experience seen as the norm, have led the centre away from universalizable theory towards a postmodernist framework. As feminists and psychotherapists, the centre's staff have a variety of ways of addressing these issues. At the theoretical and clinical levels it can return to some of the methods developed for exploring gender: first, recognizing the reality of external oppression and the need for the psychotherapist to make herself knowledgeable about it; second, addressing the psychotherapist's countertransference to see where she may be reinforcing social oppression through her own internalization of society's values.

See also CLINICAL PERSPECTIVES; MICHIGAN PSYCHOANALYTIC COUNCIL.

BIBLIOGRAPHY

Chesler, Phyllis, 1972: *Women and Madness*. New York: Doubleday.

Dana, Mira, and Lawrence, Marilyn, 1990: *Fighting Food*. London: Penguin.

Eichenbaum, Luise, and Orbach, Susie, 1985: *Understanding Women*. Harmondsworth: Penguin.

Eichenbaum, Luise, and Orbach, Susie, 1987: 'Separation and intimacy', *Living with the Sphinx*, ed. Sheila Ernst and Marie Maguire. London: The Women's Press, pp. 49–67.

Ernst, Sheila, and Goodison, Lucy, 1981: *In Our Own Hands*. London: The Women's Press.

Ernst, Sheila, and Maguire, Marie, eds 1987: *Living with the Sphinx*. London: The Women's Press.

Hogget, Paul, and Holland, Sue, 1977: 'People's Aid and Action Centre', *Humpty Dumpty*, 8, pp. 18–23.

Krzowski, Sue, and Land, Pat, eds 1988: *In Our Experience*. London: The Women's Press.

Millett, Kate, 1969: *Sexual Politics*. New York: Rupert Hart Davies.

Mitchell, Juliet, 1974: *Psychoanalysis and Feminism*. Harmondsworth: Penguin.

Orbach, Susie, 1978: *Fat is a Feminist Issue*. London: Hamlyn.

SHEILA ERNST

Index

INDEX

INDEX

Lacan, Jacques, *cont.*
  on 'The Purloined Letter', 317
  psychic development, 23–4
  psychosis, 201–2
  and the Real, 374–7
  no sexual relation, 206, 351, 376
  on the *sinthome*, 425
  refusing specificity to female subject,
    80
  split subject, 298, 363, 380, 412–3
  and surrealism, 418
  and the Symbolic, 420–3
  symptom, 203
  and transference, 432–3
  and the unconscious, 66, 109, 207, 443
  woman as man's symptom, 59, 175,
    206, 423, 425–6
Lacanian psychotherapy, 460
lack, xv, 43, 45, 53, 72, 89, 130, 164, 175,
    203, 205–6, 207–9, 312, 313, 423,
    449
  feminine as l., 80, 119, 120, 322, 340
  l. in the Other, 298, 313
  phallic l., 281
  phallus a representative of l., 93
  projection of, 353
  pronoun 'I' as bearer of l., 214
Laing, R. D., 259, 260
Laius, 291, 293
  L. complex, 238–9
  and homosexual paedophilia, 293
Lakoff, Robin, 208, 215b
Lampl-de Groot, Jeanne, 136, 275, 276b,
    346
Land, Pat, 457, 461b
language, xvii, xviii, 8, 24, 43, 57, 109,
    122, 163, **209–15**, 252–3
  female relation to, 282
  as fiction, 421
  Kristeva on l., 194–6
  and phallic law, 93
  pre–verbal infantile experience, 284
  Real barred from perceptual l., 210
  sexual difference constituted in l., 104,
    179
  interpellating the subject, 250
  word as arbiter of truth, 317
Lantini Laura, Georges, 314b
Laplanche, Jean, 22–23, 24, 26b, 57b,
    73b, 85, 86, 87, 88b, 160b, 171,
    173b, 271, 278, 280b, 294, 295,
    296b, 315b, 320b, 331, 334b, 360b,

399, 401b, 402b, 417b, 421, 431,
    435b
laughter, 75
Lauter, Estella, 189, 190b
Lautréamont, Comte de (Isidore Ducasse),
    75
Lawrence, D. H., 372
Lawrence, Marilyn, 461
Lazarre, Jane, 268, 270b
Lechte, John, 200b
Leclerc, Annie, 378, 382b
Lederer, Laura, 337b
Le Doeuff, Michèle, 325, 327b, 429, 431b
  on women students, 433–4, 435b
Lee, Jonathan Scott, 207b
Leeks, Wendy, 14, 15b
Leland, Dorothy, 33b
Leonard, Linda, 189, 190b
Leonardo da Vinci, 9, 158, 171, 416
Lerner, Harriet Goldhor, 48, 49b
Lerner, Leila, 239b
lesbianism, xv, 30, 81, 158, 215–20
  clinical perspectives, **220–2**
  rejection of male complementarity, 452
  counter-transference issues, 220
  Freud and l., 220–1
  pathologization of l., 220
  polarization v. collectivity in lesbian
    politics, 452
  in relation to pre–oedipal love, 221
  radical l., 451–3
  and sadomasochism, 388, 389, 390
  in Wittig's novels, 233–4
Lessing, Doris, 281
Levinas, Emmanuel, 182
Levine, Israel, 441, 444b
Levine, Robert, 4, 9b
Levine, Sherrie, 13
Lévi-Strauss, Claude, 141, 142, 144b, 293,
    296b, 316, 420–1
Lewes, Kenneth, 151b, 158, 159, 160b
Lewin, Bertram D., 118b
Lewis, Jane, 113b
liberalism, 410
  liberal notion of essence of humanity,
    414–5
libido, 36, 38, 60–1, 154, 158, 167,
    222–3, 386, 407
  seen as masculine by Freud, 77–8, 406
Liddington, Jill, 103b
Lidoff, Joan, 282, 285b
Lidz, Ruth W., 7, 8b

474

INDEX

INDEX

INDEX

INDEX

INDEX

Printed in the United States
740200001B